JOB

EVALUATION

A Basis for Sound Wage Administration

JAY L. OTIS *Professor of Psychology and Director of the Psychological Research Services, Western Reserve University*

RICHARD H. LEUKART *Assistant Secretary The National Screw & Manufacturing Company*

Second Edition

Englewood Cliffs, N. J.
PRENTICE-HALL, INC.

PRENTICE-HALL INDUSTRIAL RELATIONS AND PERSONNEL SERIES

DALE YODER, *Editor*

BELCHER   *Wage and Salary Administration*
BELLOWS   *Psychology of Personnel in Business and Industry, 2nd ed.*
CARPENTER   *Case Studies in Collective Bargaining*
DANKERT   *Contemporary Unionism in the United States*
DANKERT   *Introduction to Labor*
DAVEY   *Contemporary Collective Bargaining*
DUBIN   *Human Relations in Administration*
GALENSON   *Comparative Labor Movements*
GOMBERG   *A Trade Union Analysis of Time Study, 2nd ed.*
HABER AND COHEN   *Readings in Social Security*
HARDMAN AND NEUFELD   *The House of Labor*
HENEMAN AND TURNBULL   *Personnel Administration and Labor Relations:*
A Book of Readings
LINDBERG   *Cases in Personnel Administration*
MILLER   *American Labor and The Government*
OTIS AND LEUKART   *Job Evaluation, 2nd ed.*
PFIFFNER   *Supervision of Personnel*
SHARTLE   *Occupational Information, 2nd ed.*
SMITH   *Collective Bargaining*
TAYLOR   *Government Regulation of Industrial Relations*
THOMPSON   *Personnel Management for Supervisors*
YODER   *Personnel Management and Industrial Relations, 3rd ed.*
YODER   *Personnel Principles and Policies*

To

Elodie and Marjorie

for their encouragement

Preface to the Second Edition

THE ATTEMPT OF THE FIRST EDITION TO construct an organized presentation of the field of job evaluation has met with gratifying acceptance. Accordingly, in this revision, we have retained the plan of the first edition. We have presented the principles and meaning of various systems of job evaluation and pointed out the individual steps necessary in establishing wage and salary administration procedures based on job evaluation. The emphasis on practical, tested, "how-to-do-it" examples has been retained and, we trust, improved; for it has become apparent that those who use this book desire suitable attention to mechanical details, as well as to general principles.

In order to stimulate the application of the principles and procedures of job evaluation to practical situations, case problems at the end of each chapter have been added in this edition. Any similarity of the facts in any case problem to those in any given company is purely coincidental.

The technique of job evaluation is now widely accepted as sound and effective business procedure. The administration of the pay systems thus established is a recognized function in a large segment of modern industrial management. It has seemed logical, therefore, to resist any impulse to include in the scope of this work associated material in other very closely related activities in industrial relations, personnel, and general management. We have attempted to limit references to merit rating, collective bargaining, incentive pay systems, and so on, to the material necessary to describe the liaison between job evaluation and these other fields. Many of these related fields are covered in books devoted solely to the subject or as major sections of more general treatises.

In preparing this edition of *Job Evaluation*, the authors have received invaluable suggestions and criticisms from readers of the first edition and practitioners of wage and salary administration. For this friendly assistance, the authors are most grateful.

In addition to expressing sincere gratitude to the many colleagues, friends, and other interested persons who so conscientiously offered helpful criticism, the authors wish to acknowledge again the outstanding services of Mrs. Jean D. Clyde, who efficiently and carefully guided the detailed operations essential to completing successfully a revision of this kind.

The authors were guided in their revision by the many helpful suggestions made by Professor Dale Yoder and Professor Edgar Williams, who read the revision in manuscript.

Cleveland, Ohio   THE AUTHORS

Preface to the First Edition

FOR SOME TIME THE AUTHORS HAVE FELT
the need, in their respective fields of education and industry, for
an organized presentation of the essentials of wage and salary
administration based on job evaluation. With a book of this type
it is possible to conduct a college course on the subject without
depending on reading material of limited scope and point of view.
Likewise, such a book makes it unnecessary for business executives,
their employees, and union representatives to rely on their individual abilities to distill out of the many separate sources an understanding of the essence of sound wage and salary administration and
its techniques.

The development of methods to secure a sound wage administration policy is similar to the growth found in other categories of
science and business. Isolated pioneering and experimentation with
individual techniques in the teens of this century when modern
scientific management was developing, followed by refinement and
combination of these techniques, have led to a more or less well-
defined field which can be designated by the term "Wage and Salary
Administration." As an integrated business function, however, the
latter is rarely found in a highly developed state. Some companies
analyze and describe jobs before establishing pay rates and incentive
payment plans; others have arbitrary, symmetrical pay structures,
and still other have elaborate wage control systems without a
standard pay structure.

In the literature of wage and salary administration, the *meaning*
of the individual job evaluation operations in relation to the objectives of the entire job evaluation and wage determination process
has seldom been explored. Rogers' characterization of the field of
counseling is rather applicable in this connection: ". . . a field
where good intentions and a desire to be of assistance have been
accepted as substitutes for the careful formulation of the principles
involved."* The authors have attempted to delineate the principles of sound wage and salary administration based upon job
evaluation and to present them, together with illustrations of tech-

*Rogers, Carl R., *Counseling and Psychotherapy* (Boston: Houghton Mifflin Company, 1942), p. 16.

niques, in a single volume. The executive, the union leader, and the student can concentrate on the basic essentials and achieve an understanding of each aspect of wage and salary administration. The readers then may study critically the various individual systems and adapt one or more to their own particular uses.

No informed person believes that job evaluation will eliminate completely the strife and conflict caused by basic wage demands. However, organizations whose wage and salary structure is based upon sound job evaluation procedures have the facts and methods for dealing fairly with the numerous wage grievances which arise. Thus, the strife and conflict in the cases of individual employees is reduced; such a decrease in friction tends to promote more stable working relationships among management, employees, and unions.

ACKNOWLEDGEMENTS

We wish to thank the many authors, editors, and publishers who granted permission to quote original material. In these cases full credit has been given to both author and publisher; any omission which may be discovered is not due to intent. Special thanks are due the American Management Association, the National Industrial Conference Board, the Ohio Bell Telephone Company, and the American Institute of Bolt, Nut and Rivet Manufacturers for permission to quote extensively from their records. A debt of gratitude is due the members of the staff of the Personnel Research Institute of Western Reserve University for their many contributions, and to the National Screw and Manufacturing Company, which not only granted permission to quote from their records, but also permitted the authors access to their files of job evaluation data.

We are also indebted to H. P. Ladds, George R. Kloppman, Herman H. Lind, H. J. McMahon, C. C. Lane, E. A. Mentges, W. C. Treuhaft, Hazel K. Allen, C. Forest Bookman, Jr., and A. H. Laning for the opportunity to work on a wide variety of problems in the field of wage administration and to draw upon the experiences thus gained for much of the material presented in this book.

We sincerely appreciate the constructive advice and assistance furnished by friends and colleagues. To Marjorie Leukart, David J. Chesler, and Irene Salmi who spent many hours in editing and criticising the manuscript, to Howard R. White who is primarily responsible for the bibliography, to Marjorie Mitchell Parks for statistical assistance, and to Jean D. Clyde, Anne Polzer, and Bertha Petschauer who typed the manuscript, our many, many thanks.

THE AUTHORS

Contents

ix

Part Three

ANALYZING JOBS

Part Four

EVALUATING JOBS

Part Five

ESTABLISHING THE PAY SYSTEM

Part Six

WAGE AND SALARY ADMINISTRATION

Part One

Introduction to Job Evaluation

1

An Introduction

THE PAY ENVELOPE RECEIVED BY THE FAC-
tory employee, the weekly check received by the clerk, and the
monthly check received by the executive represent their standard
of living and mode of life.

Wages and salaries must reach an acceptable level before work
can be enjoyable and interesting. But in addition to receiving good
wages, workers must be able to attach certain values to their jobs
before they can feel that they are obtaining a maximum personal
return. Individuals will often accept jobs that offer such desirable
features as security, prestige, good hours, good working conditions,
interest, and opportunity for advancement at a lower wage than
comparable jobs less well endowed with such non-monetary values.
The wage paid is not only a function of the work performed; it is
in part a function of the conditions under which it is performed.
For example, Cabot[1] has emphasized such factors as: sufficient
difficulty and crudeness to call out latent desire for mastery; monotony so balanced by variety as to suit the individual's needs; a
good boss; a chance to achieve something; a title; connection with
some institution, firm or cause that can be loyally served; and
honorable and pleasant relations with comrades in work. The work
of Chant[2] revealed that such factors as opportunity for advance-

[1] Richard C. Cabot, *What Men Live By* (Boston: Houghton Mifflin Co., 1914),
pp. 27–28.
[2] S. N. F. Chant, "Measuring the Factors that Make a Job Interesting," *The
Personnel Journal*, XI, No. 1 (June 1932), p. 3.

3

ment, steady work, opportunity to use one's own ideas, opportunity to learn various skills, and a good boss were judged by 100 department store employees and 150 Y.M.C.A. members to be more important than high pay.

There is no doubt that these intangible factors are important, but the wage and salary structure must be adequate and fair before they assume major importance. Such personnel issues as grievance procedures, vacations with pay, and seniority become major problems only after the wage rates have been settled.

The attitude toward earnings is based upon the way in which the wage dollar is divided among *all* workers. A particular wage or salary is considered large or small only when it is compared with others. This means that in wage administration we are dealing not only with an absolute amount but also with a relative amount. If the wage dollar is divided in such a manner that a person receives a wage somewhat below that of workers on comparable jobs, he feels that his salary is low and that an inequity exists. Unless there is a formalized wage structure, such inequities may occur without the knowledge of management, and sometimes without the knowledge of workers.

Many factors combine to make it essential to pay some workers more than others. The individual needs of a worker are sometimes taken into consideration in the determination of his wage; in other instances his personal qualifications and characteristics are the important factors. In general, however, employers apparently attempt to pay the same basic wage for jobs which are similar in duties and difficulty.

One of the major differences among jobs is wages. Jobs at the same level of difficulty should pay approximately the same wage, and those of greater difficulty or worth should pay a higher wage. Some sound basis for classifying jobs in terms of worth or difficulty must be established. If jobs are classified according to factors judged to be important by both management and workers, and are then given a wage value in proper relationship to the factors chosen, an acceptable wage structure should result. This wage structure will have the function of placing a monetary value on each job as it is related to other jobs, but not necessarily of placing an absolute monetary value on each job. The absolute value is usually determined by such considerations as prevailing rates in the community for comparable jobs, the economic conditions of the industry, government regulation, and the results of collective bargaining.

CLASSIFICATION OF JOBS

Employees tend to classify their own jobs. They compare the jobs they now have with the ones in which they were formerly employed. They compare the work now assigned to them with work assigned to others. Jobs are classified as desirable or undesirable in many different ways. Some jobs are difficult, others are easy; some jobs require a great deal of physical strength, others require little or none; some jobs can be learned in a few minutes, others take several years; some jobs are a source of pleasure and satisfaction, others are routine and dull.

Management also classifies jobs. At times the classification depends upon the scarcity of suitable employees to perform a particular series of tasks. At other times, the classification depends upon such factors as learning time, responsibility, and the amount of administrative ability required. Since management and workers each have their own ways of classifying jobs, both joints of view must be considered in arriving at a classification system for purposes of wage administration.

What do we mean by job classification? So far, the *differences* among jobs have been emphasized. If we are to classify, however, it is essential that the *similarities* among jobs be determined. Job classification is an orderly arrangement of similar jobs into classes or grades which are recognizably different. "The essence of a classification consists in the fact that certain things are thought of as related in certain ways to one another." [3] The individual assigned to the task of job classification is not expected to invent or create; his task is to discover the sameness or similarity in the jobs that he classes together.

There are many methods of classifying jobs, each depending on the purpose of the classification. The classification system used by the Bureau of the Census and the one presented in the *Dictionary of Occupational Titles* are examples of systems in current use. According to Wolf, classifications made for special, practical purposes are usually called *artificial classifications*.[4] Grouping similar jobs into classes for the purpose of wage administration is perhaps an artificial classification, since only those factors that are related to the monetary worth of the jobs are considered. This does not necessarily mean that job classification for wage administration is

[3] A. Wolf, *Essentials of Scientific Method* (New York: The Macmillan Company, 1925), p. 30.
[4] *Ibid.*, p. 33.

inaccurate or incomplete, but simply that it is designed to serve a specific, important purpose. Errors, therefore, will be avoided if the purpose of the classification is kept in mind at all times.

Job analysts, industrial engineers, and industrial psychologists have attempted to reduce to some sort of order the chaos which has existed in the field of job classification. To date, no system of classification has been constructed that has universal application. It is questionable whether the field of occupations will ever be classified as satisfactorily as the physical and biological sciences. Some form or method of classification will probably rise above others as being most desirable, but at the present time no single system can claim this honor.

WAGE INEQUITY PROBLEMS

In October, 1942, under Executive Order 9250, a wage freeze, known as the Economic Stabilization Act, went into effect. The Executive Order revealed weaknesses in the wage structures of many plants where employers were unable to make the necessary adjustments and to remove the inequities that were discovered. Most attempts at sound wage administration based upon some form of job classification usually show the relationship between the classification and the present wage structure to be quite high, an indication that most wage structures are basically sound, but the presence of inequities makes both workers and employers question the wage structure itself.

On the other hand, inequities will be found in practically every wage system. An inequitable wage can best be defined as a wage which is either higher or lower than the accepted range for the job. If not properly understood, such inequities cause friction among employees, between management and employees, and even within the ranks of management itself. For example, when one worker in a group obtains a wage advantage over his fellow workers, he soon discovers that he has lost popularity and that his advantage is resented. When an employee or a group of employees is paid a wage below the standard for a job, each bears a resentment against management. When the workers in one department are favored over the workers in other departments, the supervisors of the less favored departments resent the discrimination against their workers.

Many wage structures are based upon tradition and have never been formalized. Whether or not any specific wage is fair is difficult to determine because there is usually no accepted, clear-cut wage structure available for comparison. It is difficult to guard against an inequity in a situation like this, because when a wage is adjusted it is usually done on an individual job basis without regard to other jobs. Until such time as a formal wage structure is created, inequities will arise to cause trouble and internal dissension.

Wage levels and the supply of employees

A scarcity of employees tends to raise the general wage level, and an oversupply tends to lower it. When either condition exists in a particular occupational group, wage inequities can easily occur. The occupational group, realizing that the skills it represents are in demand, is apt to obtain a wage advantage over other groups normally found on the same wage level. The employers who need such workers to maintain production may resort to pirating labor from other employers by offering high wages and other inducements. These conditions create wage inequities and an upward spiral of wages for all workers, as demonstrated by the rapid rise of wages during the early days of the defense program.

An oversupply of workers in a particular occupation endangers the established wage structure because during the period of oversupply these workers are often willing to accept a lower wage in order to obtain employment. When a wage structure is based upon the supply and demand in workers rather than upon work performed, inequities in the structure are bound to occur.

Systematic wage administration—the basis of employer-employee understanding

A majority of the companies in the United States have no definite program for administering the wages and salaries paid to their workers. It is surprising to find that a nation that has installed production systems, inspection systems, and work simplification procedures which have enabled it to outproduce almost the entire world has done little to bring the same thorough research to wage and salary administration. In organizations that pride themselves on precision workmanship, one often finds that workers performing the same tasks are paid at widely differing wage rates, and that there are no logical reasons for the existing relationships among the rates for different occupations.

However, increasing numbers of companies are turning to systematic and orderly methods of classifying jobs and determining wage rates. The technique most frequently used to correct these wage conditions and install more systematic methods of pricing jobs is *job evaluation*. Job evaluation is based upon job facts obtained through job analysis.

Tead and Metcalf [5] have described job analysis as "an organized statement or record of all the facts descriptive of the content of and the modifying factors surrounding a job or position." Job analysis is therefore the process or technique of determining facts about jobs. The record of these facts is found in the *job description* and *job specification*. The job description is usually a written description of the operations, duties, methods, working conditions, equipment and material used, lines of authority, and other essential facts about a job or position. The job specification is a statement of the qualities or abilities that a worker must possess to perform the job in a satisfactory manner.

Whenever management decides to establish or to correct a wage structure, and uses job analysis to obtain the necessary facts to classify jobs properly, it finds that it not only must record the facts of a job description and a job specification but also must evaluate these facts. The technique of job evaluation has been defined by Gray [6] as follows:

Job Evaluation: The complete operation of determining the value of an individual job in relation to the other jobs in the organization. It begins with job analysis to obtain job descriptions and job specifications and includes the process of relating the descriptions by some system designed to determine the relative value of the jobs or groups of jobs.

The decision to administer a wage and salary program upon the basis of observed facts should be made by management and employees together, since both are concerned. Employees who overvalue their services, either as individual craftsmen or as an industrial group, endanger the welfare of their own organization and the organization which employs them. Employers who undervalue the services of their employees also endanger the welfare of their enterprises and their employees.

Riegel points out that the satisfaction men can enjoy as participants in creative effort is reduced and offset when they feel they are being exploited. He goes on to say, "In so far as reasonable procedures and standards are found for the adjustment of pay questions, those areas of controversy are narrowed. Moreover, when the 'full values' of services thus determined are paid and re-

---

[5] Ordway Tead and Henry C. Metcalf, *Personnel Administration* (New York: McGraw-Hill Book Company, Inc., 1933), p. 235.

[6] Robert D. Gray, *Systematic Wage Administration in the Southern California Aircraft Industry,* Industrial Relations Counselors, Inc., New York, 1943, p. 89.

ceived, and there is an appreciation of the supporting reasons for those values, the satisfaction of the parties to the employment relationship is greatly enhanced." [7]

It is important that the bases on which wages and salaries are determined be understood. Naturally not all workers will have a clear understanding of the many details necessary for the establishment of a sound job classification, but it is desirable that certain individuals who have the confidence of the workers understand and accept the basic principles involved.

The use of the word "scientific" with respect to wage and salary administration has met with some opposition from those whose definition of science limits the use of the term to areas of knowledge and investigation which can be studied with some degree of demonstrable exactness. If a science is thought of as accumulated knowledge systematized and formulated with reference to the discovery of general truths, or if it is thought of as a branch of study concerned with observation and classification of facts, no one would deny the desirability of approaching the problem of wage and salary administration from a scientific viewpoint. It has been the observation of the authors that when a basic disagreement concerning the relative worth of a particular job occurs, it is usually based upon error—or incomplete facts—about the job in question. A reanalysis of the job with respect to other jobs usually clarifies the situation.

Job analysis and job evaluation do not replace judgment in the administration of a pay structure. They merely provide facts—insofar as facts can be obtained through observation—on which management and employees may base their decisions. Decisions thus made should be far sounder than those based upon general impressions. Whether or not the collection of facts through job analysis is a management function, a union function, or a joint responsibility is not nearly so important as whether management and employees are willing to abide by the facts once they have been determined. All too often job analysis has been used to substantiate a point of view rather than to secure facts upon which a point of view can be established. If orderly procedures in wage administration are to be developed, the discovery and use of job facts are essential.

An excellent statement of the principles involved in the collec-

---

[7] John W. Riegel, *Salary Determination,* Report No. 2, Bureau of Industrial Relations (Ann Arbor: University of Michigan Press, 1940), pp. 1–2. The authors are deeply indebted for permission to quote extensively from this report.

tion and use of job data obtained by job analysis is found in a union chairman's manual dealing with the principles of job evaluation. The excerpt shows not only how the data are collected, but how they are to be used.[8]

The union and the company have jointly completed a program of job evaluation of shop occupations. The purpose of job evaluation is to make an analytical study of the contents and functions of all jobs in order to develop a description of their characteristics, to appraise these characteristics according to their relative importance and value, and to establish a sound basis for setting equitable rates and rate ranges. To this end a joint committee of union representatives and management representatives collaborated to conduct a job-evaluation study of all occupations at Lockheed and Vega. The program works as follows:

1. An occupational analyst studies each occupation. He contacts workers, foremen, group leaders and leadmen and watches the job as it is being performed.

2. He prepares a description on a form sheet.

3. He submits the description to the industrial relations research department for review, and then to the job-evaluation committee.

4. The job-evaluation committee calls in the foreman in each department in which a job appears and the group chairman whose names are suggested by the union business representative for the purpose of reviewing the job-description sheet.

5. When the job-description sheet has been checked, each job will be "evaluated" by assigning to it a certain number of points, indicating the degree to which various characteristics are present in the job.

6. When all the jobs have been evaluated a revision of the rate structure will be undertaken. Management will propose certain new rates which will be subject to negotiation. Rates will not be fixed automatically according to the job-evaluation scale. The purpose of the plan is to obtain a better relation of rate to job: the rate should reflect the skill, responsibility, danger involved, mental equipment and training needed to perform it. The purpose is not to lower rates of certain employees. Those who are now being paid rates that are out of line because they are too high can be transferred to work which has a higher value. Those who are now underpaid will be classified upwards. In an industry that is growing like aircraft, constantly improving its methods of production in order to turn out more planes for national defense, job evaluation is never completed. The agreement provides that as changes in manufacturing processes bring about changes in the content of jobs, or cause new jobs to be created, the company shall develop and establish an appropriate rate, shall inform the union in advance and negotiate with the union on request.

[8] Robert D. Gray, *Systematic Wage Administration in the Southern California Aircraft Industry* (New York: Industrial Relations Counselors, Inc., 1943), pp. 75, 76.

The procedure has so many advantages for both the management of an industrial enterprise and the officers of the union that there should be little objection to its installation. It gives the employer an opportunity to make orderly wage adjustments for necessary job changes in such a manner that the friction caused by these changes should be reduced to a minimum; it gives the union officers an opportunity to explain to the membership the reasons for their acceptance of certain wage decisions; and it gives the union an orderly method for the policing of the entire pay structure. If an inequity occurs, the machinery exists to correct it.

Implications

There probably will always be a difference of opinion as to the percentage of the earnings that a company should pay to employees and to investors. Employees and employers will each try to obtain a larger share of the money earned by the industrial enterprise. If employees are classified on the basis of type of work, such as supervisory, administrative, professional, clerical, factory, and executive, there will be differences of opinion among each one of these groups as to the relative amount each group should obtain. Since the problem is complicated, arbitrary decisions are often required and compromises are sometimes necessary, but recognition of the right of each group to a fair share of the total income is essential for the continuation of the industrial enterprise.

The employer should recognize that his pay structure is effective only insofar as it is accepted by all members of his organization. It should be so constructed that modifications are possible whenever new inequities are created through changes in jobs or working conditions. The employer should understand also that he must be able to prove to every worker that the wage structure is fair and that its administration is without favoritism or bias.

Employees must realize that the internal consistency of a wage structure is of utmost importance and that it is possible to deal with an employer only when the system is basically sound and basically fair to every employee. The feelings of individual employees who believe that they are unfairly paid in comparison with their fellow workers will not be assuaged by a general increase in wages.

The use of job analysis in building and maintaining a pay structure is at the present time an accepted procedure. As refinements in the job-analysis process are made, the accuracy of wage and salary payments will increase.

OBJECTIVES OF JOB EVALUATION

The decision to measure or rate jobs should only be made with the intent to reach certain objectives which are important to both management and the worker. Although there are many by-products of job evaluation, the purpose of a job evaluation installation is to work toward a solution of the many wage and salary administrative problems which confront those responsible for this aspect of business and industrial activity. These may be considered the most important objectives of a job-evaluation program:

1. The establishment of sound wage differentials between jobs.
2. The discovery and elimination of wage inequities.
3. The establishment of a sound wage foundation for incentive and bonus programs.
4. The maintenance of a consistent wage policy.
5. The creation of a method of job classification so that management and union officials may deal with major and fundamental wage issues during negotiations and grievance meetings.
6. The installation of an effective means of wage control.
7. The collection of job facts to aid in the following:
    a. Selection of employees
    b. Promotion and transfer of employees
    c. Training of new workers
    d. Assignment of tasks to jobs
    e. Accident prevention
    f. Improving working conditions
    g. Administrative organization
    h. Work simplification

In order to accomplish these objectives jobs must be measured by a job-evaluation system. However, before a description of the different systems is given, it might be wise to study what we mean by "jobs," "positions," and job analysis.

What is a job?

The term "job" is often used without precise definition. In order to avoid any possible confusion of terms and to emphasize the importance of determining the precise limits of each job being analyzed, it is advisable to consider this definition in some detail. A job and a position in the technical sense are now customarily defined somewhat as follows:

Position: a collection of tasks, duties, and responsibilities regularly assigned to and performed by a single individual.

Job: (1) a position; or

(2) a group of positions involving substantially the same duties, skills, knowledge, and responsibilities; or

(3) a number of positions, or groups of tasks, which are somewhat similar in nature and worker requirements, and which are performed by a number of workers who customarily change about from one position to another.

In job evaluation, we are concerned with the job, rather than the position as such, since we evaluate the job, not the individual. By way of illustration we may note that the *position* of Heat Treat Foreman is the same as the *job* of Heat Treat Foreman since there is only one person who occupies the job.

As an example of the second meaning of *job,* the one most commonly found in industry and business, we may take the positions of three Cyanide Furnace Operators who use identical furnaces to harden similar products of the same kinds of metals. These three positions would be considered one job, provided there were no specialization or other essential difference between them which would make it impossible or even difficult to interchange workers among the positions. Thus, interchangeability of workers among positions of *similar content* may assist the analyst in determining the precise limits of the jobs with which he is dealing.

The third type of job which may be encountered is sometimes called a "group" or "gang" job. An example of this variation is the Furnace Feeder who loads material into the furance and removes it at the proper time. A group of five or six of these workers may load and unload a number of furnaces of various types, each furnace requiring a somewhat different routine, which varies with the type of article being treated. While the operations performed at any one furnace do not vary greatly from time to time, no one worker is assigned to it constantly; this furnace may require for a short time the attention of one or two or three workers, who move to other furnaces when they are through with it and temporarily join other small groups of Furance Feeders in various combinations as the work demands. A somewhat different example of this type of job is found sometimes in assembly operations involving, for instance, a punch press where four workers fit the parts loosely into a jig and a fifth completes the assembly by feeding it under the ram of the press and removing the assembled part from the jig. If each worker takes his turn at the punch press regularly once or twice a shift, this becomes a group job including the duties of both assembly and punch press operation.

Job analysis and job evaluation

Job analysis is the basis not only for job rating but also for selection, training, transfer, and promotion. The primary function of this volume, however, is to study the use of job analysis in wage and salary determination and administration, and only secondary emphasis will be placed on its use in these other personnel activities.

Job evaluation is an important application of job analysis. As Yoder [9] points out, "In many firms and throughout the various divisions of the federal and state governments, job analysis has frequently been made the basis for job rating and job classification. Jobs have been compared and organized to provide a classified service or system of job classification. The classification is then utilized as a basis for salary and wage control throughout the entire organization. It provides, at the same time, a basis for determining appropriate promotions and transfers."

Since there are many modifications in each of the various job-evaluation systems, it is obvious that care should be exercised in selecting a system which serves such an important function as wage administration. The main criteria for selecting an appropriate job-evaluation system are ease of use, suitability to the types of jobs being evaluated, acceptability to management and workers, and technical excellence. The job-evaluation system is a means to an end. It is good or bad only insofar as its application results in a sound or unsound job classification.

Kinds of job-evaluation systems

Job-evaluation systems tend to fall into certain major classifications: quantitative and nonquantitative; rating of the total job and rating of attributes of the job; and point values in terms of money and point values in terms of job difficulty. Moore divides the commonly used methods of job evaluation into three classes: [10]

1. The departmental order-of-importance method
2. The grade-description method
3. The job-rating method

There is some question, however, as to whether Moore's classes cover all of the possible types.

The War Manpower Commission used a fourfold system of classi-

---

[9] Dale Yoder, *Personnel Management and Industrial Relations,* 3rd ed. (New York: Prentice-Hall, Inc., 1948), p. 147.

[10] Herbert Moore, *Psychology for Business and Industry* (New York: McGraw-Hill Book Company, Inc., 1942), pp. 295–304.

fying evaluation systems.[11] Two are described as non-quantitative and two as quantitative. The War Manpower Commission scheme is as follows:

1. Nonquantitative evaluation measures
   a. The ranking system
   b. The job-classification system
2. Quantitative evaluation measures
   a. The point system
   b. The factor-comparison system

Table 1-1, taken from the *Informational Manual on Industrial Job Evaluation Systems,* presents a comparison of the four systems.

TABLE 1—1.   Comparison of the four basic systems of job evaluation •

Ranking system	Classification system	Point system	Factor comparison system
The Job Analysis: A narrative description of the job with the duties, responsibilities, degree of difficulty, and required qualifications clearly brought out.		*The Job Analysis:* A narrative statement of duties and qualifications. In addition, the job is broken down into the important compensable factors, such as required experience and training, mental effort, and physical effort. The amount to which each factor is present in the job is indicated by a short narrative statement.	
Methods of relating jobs	*Methods of relating jobs*	*Methods of relating jobs*	*Methods of relating jobs*
Jobs are ranked in their order of relative difficulty or value to the company, and grade levels are sometimes defined after the jobs have been ranked.	Jobs are allocated to grade levels which are defined arbitrarily prior to evaluating jobs.	Jobs are related by factorial analysis. A restricted number of fairly specific factors are selected for application to a limited number of types of work. The point values are predetermined before analysis of jobs and are decided arbitrarily, and the degree of each factor is expressed by a definition.	Jobs are related by factorial comparison. The factors used are assumed to be fundamental to all jobs and of universal application, the point values are set after analysis of jobs from existing rates of "key" jobs, and the degrees of each factor are expressed by sample jobs.

An interesting classification of job-evaluation systems is advanced by Lytle.[12] His classification lists five major groups:

[11] *Informational Manual on Industrial Job Evaluation Systems,* War Manpower Commission, Bureau of Manpower Utilization, Division of Occupational Analysis and Manning Tables, August, 1943.

[12] Charles W. Lytle, *Job Evaluation Methods* (New York: The Ronald Press Company, 1946), p. 32.

1. The ranking or grading method, sometimes called labor classification.
2. The straight-point method.
3. The weighted-in-money method, advertised as "the factor comparison plan."
4. The weighted-in-points method without separate treatment of universal requirements.
5. The weighted-in-points method with separate treatment of universal requirements.

Under the classification system advanced by Lytle the ranking and grading methods are grouped into a single class, whereas they were accorded separate classification in the two arrangements described previously. It should also be noticed that the point method is broken down into four methods, according to whether or not the points are weighted and how they are weighted. Both the Lytle and the War Manpower Commission schemes list the factor-comparison plan as a separate method. The classification of evaluation systems used in this book follows the one advanced by the War Manpower Commission because the authors feel that the quantitative and nonquantitative breakdown has wider application.

Job-evaluation rating scales

A measuring scale designed to evaluate jobs must recognize the fact that jobs do not fall to a zero level of difficulty or worth or rise to a set maximum of difficulty or worth. Therefore, jobs must be measured on a scale that has an indefinite minimum and an indefinite maximum.

The rating scale is a method of recording estimates. The scale is not a tool of exact measurement, like a ruler or a stop-watch, but a record of subjective impressions that have neither the reliability nor the objectivity of more exact measuring devices. However, in spite of the fact that rating scales serve as a method of obtaining estimates only, they are a distinct improvement over uncontrolled judgment and mere opinion. Until such a time as more objective and exact methods are available, the best approach to job evaluation is some type of rating scale. The four systems of job evaluation classified above and now in current use are examples of different types of rating scales.

A poor job-evaluation rating scale is not without value if the scale is used by individuals who possess the ability to make objective, consistent, and accurate judgments. In fact, a good job-evaluation system in the hands of individuals who are attempting to adapt that system to their own ends or who are, through lack of knowledge or job information, unable to record consistent and accurate judgments, might result in a poorer job classification than a poor scale in the hands of competent people.

The more objective and exact the rating scale, the better the final job classification. The ideal would be to perfect a method of rating jobs so that the same results would be obtained by informed union officials and by similarly able management representatives. Job rating scales are not designed to be a tool either of management or of labor. They are designed to enable people interested in the welfare of the employees and the organization to determine the relative difficulty and worth of the jobs being performed. Since there is always danger that an evaluation system will be misused, the objective should be to construct a system so clear and so easy to use that misuse will be difficult.

The greatest use of rating scales has been in the evaluation of personnel. Rating methods have been successfully used in schools, in large industrial, mercantile, and financial institutions, and in research organizations devoted to the study of personality problems. Rating scales have been used to measure conduct, to evaluate personnel, to study children and child development, to judge works of art, and, of course, to classify and evaluate jobs.

Before discussing the various types of rating scales it is perhaps wise to illustrate the necessity for using such aids when making judgments. There are instruments for measuring the exact weight of individuals. If, however, scales for weighing people did not exist, only estimates of weight could be made. If a group of individuals were assembled and asked to judge a person's weight, we might find that their various estimates were in terms of pounds, kilograms, stone, or other units. These estimates would not be comparable, and would have to be reduced to the same standard. When the judgments were finally compared, it might be that some of the raters judged the weight of the individual with his clothes on, and some judged his weight when stripped. If, however, a rating scale were constructed, it would be possible to ask the judges for their judgments under standard conditions and in terms of a unit of measurement which was known to all. Ratings made under the conditions described above would certainly fall far short of the accuracy of a value obtained by using a well-calibrated instrument for measuring weight in terms of pounds and fractions of pounds. In job evaluation, however, where such accuracy is not possible, a device for recording subjective judgment is necessary so that a judgment about one job can be directly compared with those of other jobs. These rating scales are discussed in Chapters 4, 5, and 6.

SUGGESTIONS FOR STUDY AND RESEARCH

1. Ask at least ten people the following question: "What do you believe is most important in determining the wage which should be paid to workers?" Try to get them to list the factors which they believe should be taken into consideration in determining wage differentials.

2. Write a brief essay on "Why I believe a sweeper should earn less than a toolmaker."

CASE PROBLEM

You are a young assistant in the personnel department of a small company. Your supervisor has asked you to prepare a statement for line management on the desirability of installing a job evaluation system in the factory and one in the office. Your management knows little about job evaluation and systematic wage administration. It has been setting wage rates in an arbitrary manner for some time. There is a possibility that the plant will be organized, and the personnel department believes it would be wise to prepare for this by setting up a workable classification of jobs and a consistent wage structure.

Prepare a statement for top management which will show the advantages of a sound wage structure and the benefits which will accrue to the organization. Confine your statement to two typewritten pages so that this statement will serve as a basis for discussion at the management committee meeting.

2

Planning a Job-Evaluation Program

IN ORDER TO CARRY OUT SUCCESSFULLY THE evaluation of jobs in a company, thorough preparation for all steps is absolutely essential from the very beginning. From the original discussions of the objectives, advantages, and need for systematic evaluation of the jobs in the company, to the final steps that put the established system into effect, a clear understanding of the objective and of the orderly sequence of steps necessary to reach that objective must be retained by the person in control of the work. This requires careful planning of each major portion of the task.

THE MANAGEMENT DECISION

The first step, and probably the most important one, is the decision of the management of the company to undertake the job. The decision must be arrived at by the topmost operating head of the company, without undue pressure or "selling" by others, and with full knowledge of all that is involved. This decision is an extremely important one, because it affects all phases of the operation of the business, and sets the course of personnel operations in the company for years to come.

The decision to install systematic job evaluation is a decision in favor of sound management. The decision to analyze, describe, title, and evaluate jobs is the decision to clarify the prime unit of personnel administration—the job performed by the worker. This decision commits the company to the discovery and systematic tabulation of facts about its jobs. The orderly accumulation of job information encourages and facilitates analysis of the job structure. This decision also commits the company to self-discipline with respect to pricing jobs and paying men. This means abandoning the practice of making rate adjustments based on expediency, pressure, favoritism, caprice, incomplete information, or indeed on any basis other than agreed-upon observations and facts interpreted in terms of established standards. Self-discipline is imposed in the interests of controlling payroll cost, establishing equitable distribution of wages and salaries, eliminating sources of employee dissatisfaction, establishing systematic wage administration, and fostering good employee relations.

Obviously, then, the decision to establish wage and salary rates on the foundation of the evaluation of jobs is not based primarily on such considerations as initial cost, availability of personnel, and interference with operating routine. Rather, this decision is considered in relation to the basic management philosophy of the company.

The importance of this free, unhampered decision by the top executive to undertake job evaluation, and to follow through with the steps necessary to operate successfully on the basis of the resulting structure, cannot be overemphasized. One reason, of course, is the importance of the decision itself in inaugurating a far-reaching management policy in the company. Another vital reason is the fact that the company must support the work of job evaluation from the initial stages of getting the project under way to the final establishment of wage and salary administration on the basis of the resulting classification structure. Management support, technical competency, and intellectual honesty are prerequisites to a successful and useful evaluation.

One illustration of the importance of management support is in the announcement and explanation usually sent out to all employees when the work begins. This announcement ordinarily is most effective when signed by the president after discussion and consultation with the executive staff of the company. It is then understood by all employees that this step has the full support and backing of the management, which intends to profit from it in terms of increased efficiency and lowered unit production costs through controlled wage and salary administration and improved human relations. The announcement also should outline the direct employee benefits and advantages that this program will provide.

On the other hand, if this work is announced by the Standards Department or the Industrial Relations Department as a staff program, it is possible, even likely, that it will fall into the classification of a "pet project" of the staff department. The result might well be unnecessary resistance, lack of cooperation, and misinterpretation, all due to poor comprehension of the purpose and scope of the program. Such difficulties can be particularly damaging in their effect on the final result. Collection of the job information necessary to accurate evaluation requires the assistance of workers, foremen, and supervisors in furnishing complete, pertinent, and accurate facts. Workers or supervisors who try to beat the system will cause unnecessary difficulty and delay in arriving at the true facts.

Strong, active management support is equally important in all the subsequent steps of job evaluation. The full cooperation of supervisors in giving the necessary time to the job analysts, and in making all the important, detailed arrangements to facilitate their work in the department, can greatly expedite the work. Such seemingly minor details as adequate working space, supplies and materials, and stenographic assistance must be readily available to the analysts if they are to be in a position to organize the work most effectively and carry it on without unnecessary difficulties.

The final test of management's acceptance and support is in the willingness to accept the facts as determined and organized in the job evaluation. Since almost no wage structure can be expected to be internally consistent throughout unless it has been established on some type of job evaluation, it is inevitable that many shifts in the relationships of the jobs to each other will be indicated by the results of the job evaluation. For example, some jobs historically classified in a group as "common labor" may fall into several separate job classifications, each with different job content and different requirements, and each with a different evaluation, resulting in different rates of pay. Furthermore, these "common labor" jobs may have higher ratings and correspondingly higher pay rates than some jobs for which it has been the practice to pay the same or higher rates.

This necessity for the readiness of management to discount or disregard the traditional or "sacred cow" features of the wage structure is illustrated further by problems arising from titling of jobs. A company which has operated without written definitions of titles has of necessity developed a *more or less* accepted understanding of the meanings of these titles as related to groups of tasks—i.e., jobs. When these jobs are analyzed and described, and the titles are thus defined, it may be discovered that many titles are inappropriate in that the general meaning of the title gives a false impression of the job as it actually exists in the company. Such discrepancies in job titling may be responsible for some of the inequities in the rate structure of the company.

When descriptions and definitions have been established for job titles, the titles themselves lose significance except as convenient "handles" in referring to jobs. In other words, when job content is described, it is then neither necessary nor advisable to depend on the title to carry all the meaning of the job.

The experience of one company illustrates these two points. The job of Toolmaker A had always been paid on a higher range of rates than the job of Machinist A. This apparently was in line with common practice in the community and in industry in general. When the jobs in the company were evaluated it was found that the job of Toolmaker A was rated at a lower level than the job of Machinist A in the centralized machinery and equipment repair shop, but at a higher level than the job of Machinist A in some of the production departments, where maintenance and repair were confined to one or two types of machines. When this situation was thoroughly rechecked, it was found that the evaluation had resulted in a correct relative rating of these jobs. The explanation lay in the fact that the machinists in the production departments and toolmakers in the tool department were performing duties customarily associated with these titles, but the machinists in the centralized shop were required to diagnose machine troubles, rebuild machines, and sometimes redesign certain features of the machines. Thus, by separating these two machinist jobs which had been previously grouped under the same title, and describing and evaluating accurately the duties performed in each, it was possible to eliminate a troublesome pay inequity.

After management is satisfied that a thorough and honest job evaluation has been done, the final step is to adopt this method of pricing jobs and to adhere faithfully to the spirit of the system in wage and salary administration. This aspect of management acceptance is discussed more fully in later chapters.

WHO WILL DO THE JOB?

The installation of systematic wage and salary administration based on a thorough-going job evaluation is an important undertaking which involves a major management decision and careful planning. As in the case of other major projects carried out by a company, it is necessary to determine what people are going to do the job and what their training, experience, education, and other qualifications should be.

In general, there are three ways this part of the plan can be arranged. One possibility is for the company to engage a management engineering firm with a staff that specializes in job evaluation. Following a second method, a number of companies have successfully established job evaluation themselves by assigning the task to a qualified employee, or by hiring a man with the necessary experience or qualifications as a full-time employee to do the job and to carry on the necessary maintenance. The third possibility is to engage a management engineering firm on a consulting basis to supervise and advise company personnel in accumulating the necessary information and evaluating the jobs.

Management engineers

Advantages. Probably the easiest method, so far as the company is concerned, is to employ a firm of management engineers to come into the company to do the job. This method, which is not uncommon, has a number of advantages, provided of course that the firm selected knows how to do a successful job evaluation installation. One advantage is that this method has been used by a great many plants in the installation of incentive systems, revision of plant layout, and establishment of production planning, scheduling, and control. Consulting firms themselves are accustomed to operating in this fashion, and the companies they serve also are familiar with this method of operation. Thus the presence of strangers in the company, delving into details of its operation, would not necessarily be new and startling. It is a common observation that individuals from outside the company are usually judged to be fair and impartial, since they do not have a continuing close operating relationship or position to defend, augment, or maintain within the company. Such persons are assumed to be concerned entirely with doing the best job possible on the basis of the facts as they find them, and with arriving at a system that will be practical and workable.

Additional advantages of such an arrangement stem from the fact that the process of job evaluation may take a considerable period of time, and thus may not be completed before some of the initial interest and drive resulting from the management's decision to install job evaluation has lagged a little. The primary job of the management engineer in such a situation is to carry the job evaluation through to completion; his devotion to the continuation and completion of the job does not depend on the personal interest of the management of the company, but on his contract with the company to do the whole job. Furthermore, the company which has committed itself to the job by engaging specialists to carry it out would hesitate to permit the delays or interruptions which might occur if the work were being done by employees of the company.

Finally, the training and experience of professional consultants specializing in job evaluation can rarely be duplicated by an employee or several employees of the company. The professional management engineer does not have to rely on books or manuals on the subject, or on consultation with other companies which have been through the process. He has his own experience, possibly in many different types of companies and industries, as well as his knowledge of the technical aspects of job evaluation itself. His approach to methods, procedures, and problems is based on previous encounters with identical or similar situations in other companies.

Disadvantages. An evaluation carried out completely by staff members of a management engineering firm has some definite disadvantages also. One of the principal difficulties of this method is that, when the job is turned over in its entirety to persons outside the company, the management and staff of the company need not assume any responsibility for the progress of the work or for the results.

Another important factor is the attitude of company personnel to a job which has been done by others—one in which they have not played a responsible part. In discussing this point, Coley says: "Since no amount of advertising or sales promotion, however clever, will achieve this end, the real focal point of our discussion is how the supervisors and the workers can *participate* in wage administration. Their participation is essential to their understanding of the process; this understanding in turn is essential to their acceptance of its results." [1] When employees of the company participate in the actual process of job evaluation, they tend to feel that they have played an important part in its establishment. As a result, they are much better acquainted with the whole proceeding, and much more active in backing it than they otherwise would be. By excluding company personnel from the development phase, an excellent oppor-

[1] W. R. Coley, "Selling Job Rating to the Supervisory and Working Force," Personnel Series No. 39, American Management Association. 1939, pp. 17–22.

tunity to acquaint these people with the details of job evaluation is lost.

Consultants from outside the company are also at a disadvantage in that they can operate most effectively only when they have a rather sound grasp of the traditions, mores, organizational structure, and social structure of the company. Such factors are more important in job evaluation than in some other services which such firms perform, because job evaluation deals with the relationships between the workers and their jobs. Thus the very structure of the jobs in a company will usually reflect, to some extent at least, the influence of workers in the jobs, and perhaps will reflect that of individuals in management positions. Such considerations will not necessarily affect the evaluation of the jobs, since it is the job that is rated, not the worker; nevertheless, the understanding of the effect of such factors on the job structure can greatly facilitate the job evaluation.

The most serious objection to carrying out the job evaluation without active company participation is the extreme likelihood that it will be considered, upon completion, to be a perfected system that should stand as *the job* structure from now on. It is true that the job evaluation will provide the basis for a sound wage structure for many years to come, but it will do so only if it is operated as a dynamic structure that must be kept up to date at all times. It is essential that all changes in jobs in the company be recognized by corresponding changes in the job evaluation material—both descriptions and ratings. Otherwise, the ratings on various jobs will become the target for criticism from supervisors, workers, management, and the union within a very short time. Thus the completed evaluation is not a finished product in any sense, except that it is an established method of administering wages and salaries, a method which can be adjusted to take into account changes in jobs, creation of new jobs, and changes in the wage and salary structure.

Company employees

Advantages. The second general method of carrying out a job evaluation—entirely by employees of the company—overcomes many of the drawbacks just cited under the first method. For example, if it is done properly, so that the necessary clearances, explanations, management backing, and proper organization are provided for, it becomes a company project; a great many persons feel they have made a personal contribution to it and are therefore prepared to support it vigorously. This method provides an opportunity for training the personnel in the company who are going to be responsible for operating the wage structure on a continuing basis. If employees from various departments are borrowed to analyze jobs and write job descriptions and specifications, they carry back to their departments a first-hand knowledge of the basis of job evaluation and are in a position to explain some of the basic principles to their co-workers. Most important of all, it is to be expected that a company which undertakes job evaluation on its own, with the solid backing of top management, will assume full responsibility for the results and thus be sure that a satisfactory job is done. Furthermore, employees of the company who are directly, or even indirectly, associated with the evolution of the job evaluation are in a position to develop an understanding of the necessity for keeping the evaluation accurate and up to date.

Disadvantages. As in the case of the first method, however, certain difficulties are likely to be encountered. An activity of this sort frequently starts out with considerable momentum, only to be overtaken by inertia after the original active interest is dampened by time-consuming, tedious detail and plugging effort. Also, emergency situations or other new projects may be allowed to interfere with and sidetrack the job evaluation unless it has strong leadership and strong management support. Moreover, serious problems are to be anticipated in the technical phases of the work if the personnel responsible for it have not had actual experience with job evaluation. In such circumstances the company should be prepared to devote a considerable amount of time to the job, and to pay for a great deal of experimentation and trial and error, in order to overcome the many individual problem situations which inevitably will be encountered in the course of the project. Job evaluation is a technical operation which requires professional competence, a thorough understanding of the principles and consequences involved, and experience with the techniques.

Consulting service

The third method—the use of a consulting service—involves both outside assistance and the use of company personnel. As a result this method tends to combine most of the advantages of the other two methods and eliminate most of their shortcomings. For example, the consultants bring with them the prestige of technicians who have specialized in this field. Their primary interest is in doing the best job evaluation possible, and carrying it through to completion as expeditiously as possible. The experience of the consultant in the planning and organization of job evaluation work, and in the techniques and operations involved in different types of companies presenting different types of problems, is provided by this method.

By providing for the maximum degree of participation by company personnel in the job evaluation, under the guidance of consultants, the company can realize the advantages of employee participation and, at the same time, utilize the skill and experience of the management engineering firm. The combination of these two methods, to realize the full benefits of each, and to neutralize the disadvantages of each, seems to be the practical approach to this phase of the work.

In its advisory letter to businessmen, Labor Relations Advisors makes the following statements based on contacts with many companies who have had experience with job evaluation:

We believe that unless a company has an extensive experience in job-evaluation work and a tested technique, it would be wise to utilize the services of an industrial engineering organization. Such organizations have an accumulated experience and technique which is invaluable. We hasten to add, however, that we are not among those who believe a company can call in an engineering firm and simply turn the job over to it. A company which does that makes almost as serious a mistake, in our judgment, as the company which, lacking experience and a technique, tries to do the job itself.[2]

SELECTING AND TRAINING THE STAFF

It should be emphasized at this point, however, that whenever persons without experience in job evaluation are used in such work, they must be thoroughly trained in the techniques of job evaluation and must be very carefully supervised. This applies to employees who are skilled in time study, production methods engineering, and personnel work, as well as to those in less closely related fields. The reason for this is that the analysis and description of jobs for evaluation purposes is different in some very important respects from the collection and organization of job information intended for other uses. Therefore, it is important to avoid making the assumption that workers in these fields know how to analyze jobs for job-evalu-

[2] *Labor Relations Advisory Letter,* June 15, 1945, Labor Relations Advisors, 10 East 43rd Street, New York.

ation purposes. Regardless of which one of the above three general methods of installing job evaluation is selected, the designation of the persons who are going to do this work is very important. In discussing this point, the Industrial Management Society makes the following statement:

> If possible, it would be well to hire an engineer familiar with the techniques of job evaluation. If this is not possible, some individual having a high degree of analytical ability and balanced judgment should be given the responsibility for occupational rating. To assure that a good job will be done by such an individual, there are several attributes which must be dominant: (1) good general knowledge of manufacturing practices; (2) high degree of analytical ability; (3) well-balanced judgment; (4) absolute honesty; (5) ability to write clear job descriptions; and (6) ability to secure co-operation of foremen and personnel.[3]

These six attributes should be considered in the selection of a management engineering or consulting firm as well as in the selection of personnel within the company to participate in the job rating.

In addition to the six attributes listed above, it is especially important that persons working in this field should have a thorough understanding of wage and salary administration as it affects industrial relations and personnel administration. In the development of a job-evaluation system for a company, it is essential that the ramifications and consequences of the installation of a system of this sort be thoroughly understood before the work begins, and be kept in mind throughout the undertaking. The person in charge of the job-rating must understand that rates on individual jobs and the relationship between rates on all jobs in the structure are a fundamental condition of employment in the company and a fundamental factor in personnel administration and industrial relations. The establishment of a systematic wage and salary payment plan on the basis of job evaluation is a basic step which sets the pattern for all personnel operations that have anything at all to do with job rates. Failure to understand and appreciate the importance of job evaluation in this respect can lead to errors in the final result, and can lay the groundwork for many future difficulties. In other words, in evaluating a job for purposes of establishing a rate of pay, it must be remembered at all times that we are not establishing the

---

[3] *Occupational Rating Plan*, Industrial Management Society, 205 West Wacker Drive, Chicago, 1943, pp. 20–21.

money value of the output of that job to the enterprise as a whole; rather we are deciding, in the final analysis, how much money we should pay to a human being who will perform the duties that are required by the job in question. We are pricing jobs from the human point of view, not from the mechanical standpoint.

The appreciation of the importance of job evaluation in industrial relations is particularly significant in the selection of a consulting firm to be responsible for this work in the company. Many former mechanical and industrial engineers have been placed in key positions in industrial relations, either through necessity or through lack of understanding of the proper functions of industrial relations. Similarly, engineering firms, specialists in the mechanical aspects of engineering, have assumed themselves competent to install job-evaluation systems using staff members trained and qualified only in the mechanical aspects of industrial management. There are, of course, many instances in both types of cases where the individual has made good. Such success, however, is not due to the mechanical training of these individuals, but rather to their understanding and appreciation of the human relations factors inherent in workers-on-jobs. Considerable care should be exercised, therefore, to select engineering, personnel, or psychological consulting firms that have had experience in dealing with human relations problems in industry and can assign staff members who are thoroughly cognizant of the fact that in job evaluation they are dealing with fundamental factors in industrial relations.

One other important factor regarding the selection of persons to do this job should be pointed out. In order to complete a successful system of job evaluation, it is necessary that a great mass of accurate detail regarding individual jobs be collected by job analysis, and recorded as fully as possible in job descriptions and job specifications. As a practical matter, this is virtually impossible; it is not necessary to record *all* detail, but rather *all significant* detail. In many completed job descriptions and specifications it will be found that some items of information that are necessary to arrive at the best possible rating of the job are not recorded in written form. As a practical solution to this difficulty, it has been found advisable to include in the group of persons actively working with job evaluation, at least one person with long years of experience in the company and a large amount of accurate, detailed information about individual jobs throughout the organization. In one company, where such an employee spent full time advising the job analysts, the employee's intimate knowledge of the company's jobs saved much time in organizing meaningful detail and establishing the significance of various details about the jobs. He was able to review the facts which had been collected on each job and indicate to the analyst the significance and importance of these details. This fund of knowledge greatly facilitated the process of actually rating the jobs, and resulted in a much more accurate evaluation than otherwise would have been possible.

In summarizing what it believes to be a sound approach to job evaluation, the *Labor Relations Advisory Letter* gives the following outline:

1. A company should first define its OBJECTIVES in undertaking job evaluation. Those objectives should be fair to the employees as well as the company. They should be defined with sufficient clarity to make it possible to transmit them to those who will do the work.

2. An industrial engineering organization should be given the job of planning the job evaluation, supplying the experience and technique, directing the work, and doing much of the work. *But,* the company should be sure that the engineers' thinking is in harmony with company objectives . . . should be sure it understands the technique and evaluating factors the engineers propose to apply . . . should be sure those evaluating factors are applicable to company jobs and operations.

3. The company should supplement the engineers' experience and technique with the company's own detailed and peculiar knowledge of its operations and jobs. One or more appropriate company men should be assigned *full time* to work with the engineers through all stages of the job evaluation and bring to the work an intimate knowledge of operations and jobs. There is more than meets the eye in job evaluation. There is a considerable element of judgment. The company's own men should participate in forming these judgments. There are those who object to this extensive company participation. We regard it as indispensable.[4]

SYSTEMATIC PREPARATION

When the management of the company has decided that job evaluation is to be installed and has further decided who is going to be responsible for carrying it to a successful conclusion, the next step is to determine, in advance and in some detail, how this job is to be done. Here again, top management must enter into major decisions regarding policies and methods of operation. There are four major policy decisions that must be made by top management at this point. These are:

[4] *Labor Relations Advisory Letter,* June 15, 1945, Labor Relations Advisors, 10 East 43rd Street, New York.

1. Which jobs in the company are going to be evaluated and which are to be considered as outside the scope of job evaluation.

2. What information and explanations are to be given to supervisors, foremen, and workers regarding the job evaluation, and how this shall be done.

3. What role, if any, the union or other worker representatives or individual workers will play in the job evaluation.

4. What arrangements are to be made for administering the wage structure based on job evaluation after it is completed.

Which jobs are to be evaluated?

The jobs in any company are likely to fall into a number of different major groupings as far as philosophy of payment is concerned. In a manufacturing concern, some workers are paid an hourly rate, while others are paid a salary—weekly, monthly, or annual. It is likely that these two groups of workers should be paid on the basis of the somewhat different characteristics or requirements of their jobs. Certainly, the wage structure for workers paid by the hour is somewhat different from that for the salaried workers. In plants where a single labor organization has been designated as the sole bargaining agent for the production workers, it is probable that this group of hourly-paid workers is further divided into those who are eligible to belong to the bargaining unit and those who are not. Those workers not included in the bargaining unit are probably those in clerical and supervisory jobs.

Various groups of workers which constitute units for collective bargaining purposes are defined in individual cases by the National Labor Relations Board. In cases where there are several different bargaining agents for different groups of production workers in the company, it must be decided whether one job-evaluation system will be applied to all of these various groups or whether more than one is required. In either case it also must be determined whether one wage structure will serve for all of these groups or whether separate ones are needed.

With regard to the supervisory jobs, some may be paid on an hourly basis but be excluded from the bargaining unit, while others, such as foremen and production department managers, may be paid on a salary basis. Within the group of workers who receive salaries, there will be a number of different subgroups. First of all, those in the higher salary brackets, say those receiving more than $12,000 a year, may be excluded entirely from the job-evaluation plan because of the difficulty of evaluating jobs at this level. Such jobs do not readily fit into any salary structure in the company which would include other jobs because, in this category, the salary often is based upon the individual rather than upon the particular duties and responsibilities involved in the job itself.

Of those salaried workers who remain, there is then a further breakdown into those who are on jobs which are considered "exempt" from the provisions of the Fair Labor Standards Act and those who are classified as "nonexempt." Some companies pay nonexempt office workers on a straight hourly basis, although even in this case they are distinguished from factory or production workers who are also paid on an hourly basis. In any case, nonexempt office workers, who must be paid at the rate of time and one-half for all hours over forty in one week, must be paid on a wage structure different from that of exempt employees, who are not paid in terms of the hours they work.

Thus the salaried nonexempt pay structure must be set up in terms of both salary rates and equivalent hourly rates for the purpose of computing overtime pay. The important distinction between these two groups of office workers with respect to salary structure is that the base salaries for workers who are exempt from payment for overtime should generally be great enough so that the company may expect such workers to work whatever hours are necessary to perform the duties which they are assigned. Thus the base salary rate structure for exempt workers is generally quite a bit higher than that for nonexempt workers. The distinction between exempt and nonexempt workers in terms of the requirements of the Fair Labor Standards Act, therefore, is a particularly important one and must be determined very carefully. When these groupings of workers for job-evaluation purposes have been completed, the work can then proceed on the basis of these various groups. As an example, the breakdown in a manufacturing concern is shown in Table 2–1. By way of contrast, the breakdown for a department store is shown in Table 2–2.

The order in which each of these groups is covered will depend on conditions in the company itself. In one instance, it may be advisable to complete the groups of hourly-paid workers before the salaried groups. The order which is worked out here may be used as a "selling" device for the whole job-evaluation program. In some instances, the group, preferably a small one, which is most out of line, and in which it is most urgent to increase pay in order to eliminate inequities, may be taken first as an example to other groups of workers in the company.

TABLE 2—1.   Job evaluation groups in a manufacturing concern •

Employee group	Job evaluation manual	Pay structure
Salaried workers:		
Officers and Executives (above $12,000)	Not evaluated	
Supervisory, Administrative, and Professional (exempt)	Office	{ Supervisory, administrative, and professional
Office clerical (nonexempt)	Office	Office clerical
Foremen (exempt)	Office	Foreman
Hourly paid workers:		
Assistant foremen (nonexempt)	Office	Assistant foreman
Factory workers (in bargaining unit)	Factory	Factory
Factory workers (not in bargaining unit)	Factory	Factory

"Selling" supervisors and workers

The task of analyzing jobs in the organization for the purpose of collecting and recording job information must be carried out with the cooperation and active support and participation of employees, particularly of supervisors. Consequently, it is essential that these employees have at least a general understanding of what is being done, what is expected of them, and what the objectives of this work are. If this understanding is not developed carefully before the analysts start to collect job information, misunderstandings, false information, and considerable suspicion and antagonism may be experienced.

TABLE 2—2.   Job evaluation groups in a department store •

Employee group	Job evaluation manual	Pay structure
Salaried workers:		
Officers and executives	Not evaluated	
Sales supervisory	Sales	Sales supervisory
Sales	Sales	Sales
Non-sales		
Supervisory and administrative	Clerical	Supervisory and administrative
Clerical	Clerical	Clerical
Hourly paid workers (workroom):		
Maintenance	Workroom	Workroom
Manufacturing	Workroom	Workroom

More than explanation and information are necessary, however, if enthusiastic cooperation is to be expected. Each supervisor should be shown how job evaluation will benefit him, personally, make his job easier, and make him a better supervisor. In other words, he should be told what he wants to hear about job evaluation. The same approach should apply in selling job evaluation to the employees whose jobs and pay may be affected by its results. The worker should be told how job evaluation will benefit him and his fellow workers. He should be shown how it will assure him that on his job, and on any other job he may hold in the future, he will be paid in proper relation to the pay of workers on all other jobs in the evaluation, and on the basis of factual job requirements. The worker, too, will develop a desirable positive attitude if he is told what he wants to hear about job evaluation.

To be successful, this sales appeal, like all others, must be directed to the wants, hopes, desires, and possible fears of the people whose opinions are to be molded. The strictly logical approach may not be the easiest or most effective in selling job evaluation. The appeal must gain the attention and interest of supervisor and worker alike, and must be aimed to elicit appropriate cooperation on the basis of an aroused desire to see the job evaluation properly installed and working effectively.

The concept of controlled participation is advanced in an article by Daniels [5] in which he describes the process of winning acceptance for the job evaluation plan by making it possible for foremen, supervisors, and workers to participate in the installation of a wage structure based on job evaluation. It is generally accepted that understanding and acceptance are closely related. Through working together constructively and following a plan with definite objectives, management can participate by setting the goals to be reached and the general methods to follow, and then obtain participation in the actual study itself.

As pointed out earlier, the initial step in developing among key employees an understanding of their role in job evaluation is actually taken at the time when the company is discussing the advisability of installing a job-evaluation system. At this time, the top executives of the company should be fully exposed to all of the advantages and implications of job evaluation, so that they may comprehend thoroughly what is involved. It is extremely important that this phase of the work be carried out very carefully. This same process of indoctrination may be used with the other executives and supervisors on down the line at the time when the actual work of collecting job information is about to begin. In order that there may be no misconceptions, information and explanation to super-

[5] Harry W. Daniels, "Winning Acceptance for the Job Evaluation Plan," *Personnel,* American Management Association, Vol. 30, No. 1 (July 1953), pp. 30–33.

visors should be in writing. Employees, of course, should also receive written information about the job evaluation. Moreover, in order that there may be full opportunity for supervisors to discuss and ask questions about job evaluation, it is advisable to hold meetings on the subject, at least with the supervisors. The supervisors then will be in a position to discuss some of the details of job evaluation with their employees, who may have some questions after studying the written information on the subject released to all employees. Such meetings provide top management, the supervisors, and those directly concerned with carrying out the evaluation an opportunity to discover and correct misunderstandings and misinterpretations regarding the objectives of job evaluation and the operations which are necessary to carry it out.

The essential information regarding job evaluation may be passed on to employees by a letter from a top line executive of the organization. Such a letter should (1) announce that the job evaluation is going to be carried out, (2) explain briefly what job evaluation is, (3) state specifically and clearly what the objectives of the company are in undertaking job evaluation, and (4) include some information on how the work is to be done. A sample letter of this type which was used quite successfully in the job-evaluation program undertaken by a department store is shown in Figure 2–1.

Such a letter can also be used as the basis for discussion with groups of supervisors since it covers the major fields in which these supervisors might have questions regarding the project. The discussion can follow the letter step by step, with full opportunity for questions on each phase of the project.

Many other methods of explaining and selling job evaluation have been used, some involving considerable ingenuity and showmanship. Sound slidefilms and cartoons, sound or silent movies, posters, and charts have been prepared and used successfully, particularly by larger companies where the investment is justified by the number of people to be reached. Certainly a majority of companies that publish house organs have taken advantage of this medium for explaining and selling job evaluation, building confidence in the fairness and impartiality of the men and the methods employed, and perhaps informing employees of the progress and completion of the various steps in the process. Booklets on job evaluation, paragraphs in the employee handbook, and individual explanations to employees who have questions or are affected specifically by changes resulting from the evaluation are examples of the many different types of methods which have been used success-fully. The media and techniques used vary widely, and usually are based on employee communication practices and techniques suit-able to the character of the individual company.

NOTICE

From Office of General Superintendent

JOB-EVALUATION

The _____ Co. is undertaking a project known as Job Evaluation. This is one of the suggestions made by employees in the Inventory of Ideas, directed by Mr. _____ last fall.

Job Evaluation is a process of establishing a sound relationship between all of the jobs in the store, according to skill, effort, responsibility, customer contacts, and working conditions. Through this process we hope to accomplish the following:

1. Provide a record of all job requirements in order that we may have a sound basis for selection, placement, and training.

2. Reclassify, subject to War Labor Board approval, part or all of our salary rate ranges according to skill, effort, and responsibility. These salary ranges will recognize the differences between jobs so that those having similar or identical requirements are paid alike and those having different requirements are paid accordingly.

3. Help to eliminate pay inequities in the future.

4. Provide a plan of progression and promotion within departments and between departments.

5. Provide the framework for a periodic review and fair appraisal by Management of the work of each individual.

6. Increase job satisfaction and reduce possible causes of dissatis-faction.

Individuals' salaries will not be reduced by this project. Warranted adjustments will be made, subject to War Labor Board approval.

Between now and Fall all employees representing each different job will be interviewed by a job analyst (employed and trained by _____ who will direct the project), to make a record of what the job requirements are. Where two or more people hold identical jobs, a limited number will be interviewed. All analyses made will be reviewed by the department head and a committee of _____ Co. employees. The first to be interviewed will be non-selling employees.

Based upon the experience of other organizations like ours, we feel confident that the above objectives will be accomplished.

July 18, 1945

(Signed) _____
General Superintendent

Fig. 2—1. Letter to employees.

Role of worker representatives

It is extremely important at this point to discuss and to decide what part the union officers, committeemen, stewards, or other individuals who represent the workers will play in setting up the job evaluation. While the establishment, classification, and evaluation of jobs is generally considered to be a management responsibility and function, nevertheless the establishment of wage rates, which is a direct and primary consequence of job evaluation, is subject to collective bargaining with respect to any group represented by a union. Therefore, in order to be in a position to negotiate wage rates established on the basis of job evaluation, worker representatives must be acquainted with the method by which the relative values of jobs have been established in the evaluation process.

The simplest, most effective way to bring this about is to arrange for representatives of the workers to participate in the evaluation. Since the collection and recording of information about jobs as a basis for evaluation or rating is a matter of obtaining and recording complete and accurate facts, there can be little objection to union participation and little chance for disagreement in these phases of the work. Since the rating of jobs is also a matter of dealing with facts and interpretation of facts, the same applies in this case. Incidentally, this same reasoning applies to the foremen and department supervisors as well, and their participation in these processes provides an excellent opportunity for educating them in the details of job evaluation.

In order for them to participate it is not necessary that the union officers and the foremen actually analyze jobs, record information about them, and rate them. It is quite sufficient for the supervisors and union representatives to be consulted in the analysis of jobs, to provide information for the job analysts, and to review the information recorded by the job analyst to satisfy themselves that this information is complete and accurate.

It is evident, then, that if the worker representatives and department foremen and supervisors are to participate in this way in the job evaluation, it is necessary to plan for such participation at this point in the process. Subsequently, when the job analyst goes into a department to analyze the jobs there, he contacts the foreman and the union officer. He explains to them how he will collect the job information, asks for their cooperation, and consults them from time to time as he is working in the department. Finally, he has them initial the first draft of the written information on the job to indicate their approval. While there are many possible variations in the details, this general procedure has been found quite satisfactory.

The same general approach may be taken with respect to the rating of jobs. The actual initial rating may be done by individuals or committees of analysts, consultants, foremen, supervisors, and company executives. This does not preclude, however, the advisability of establishing agreement between management and worker representatives on the evaluation of every job. This phase of the work, too, might well be planned at this point. These considerations are discussed in more detail in later chapters.

Arrangements for administration

It was pointed out earlier that job evaluation is the basis for systematic wage administration, not a standard that can be established for all time. In other words, the unit of job evaluation—the job—is not by any means static or fixed in any organization, and consequently the job structure will change continuously. As a matter of fact, it will be found that some jobs analyzed at the beginning of the project will have disappeared or changed materially before all of the jobs have been analyzed. It is necessary at the very outset, therefore, to recognize that the job evaluation must be kept up to date at all times, and it is wise to make definite arrangements to provide for this.

The simplest approach is to select the person who is going to be responsible for administering the job-evaluation system and keeping it up to date, and then see that he occupies a key position in the establishment of the job evaluation. In this way, he will become thoroughly grounded in the technique itself, will be familiar with problems which arise during the process of evaluating jobs, and, when the work is done, will be in a position to take over the administration. The selection of the individual and the establishment of his position in the organization must be done with as full an understanding as possible of the requirements of this job and its place in the company and should be done on the basis of sound organization and management principles.

If arrangements for the administration of the wage structure established upon the framework of the job evaluation are not made adequately or are not made soon enough, the system very quickly will get out of hand and give rise to dissatisfaction and grievances. A job-evaluation system which is inaccurate and not up to date may be worse than no system at all. A job evaluation that includes written detailed information about jobs brings to light discrepancies that might be overlooked in a system where wage rates are established on the basis of undefined titles. In either case, however, the sources of dissatisfaction are there; it is just that with job evaluation they are identified and can be corrected, while without such information the real cause of the difficulty may be very hard to find.

Establishing procedures

The next major step in getting ready for the job evaluation is the setting up of the tools and procedures that are to be used in actually doing the job.

Job Evaluation Manual. This is a most important tool because it forms the basis and sets the pattern for the work to be done. The manual will define in detail the job factors or elements which are to be analyzed and described to form the factual basis for the rating of jobs. This is discussed in detail in Chapters 4, 5, and 6.

It is the basic measuring stick that will be applied to the jobs in determining relative values for wage or salary payment purposes. The development of this measuring stick is an extremely important step; all of the key personnel in the company should thoroughly understand the manual and should play an active part in its preparation. It is probable that more than one such manual will be required for any company, since all jobs in the company are not compensated according to the same payment plan. As a minimum in industrial plants, one manual is required for office types of jobs and one for production jobs.

Job Analysis Procedure. Establishment of the analysis procedure is next. The system by which job information is collected should be similar to the organization of the rating manual. Reason: the facts collected by the job analysis will be used as the basis for describing the job and for establishing facts which will be used to arrive at the proper rating for each element to be considered in the job ratings. For example, if Education is to be one of the elements on which the jobs are to be rated, the job-analysis procedure must provide for obtaining and recording the necessary facts about the educational requirements of each job so that these facts can be used as the means for arriving at the rating for this factor on every job.

Job-Information Forms. Description and specification forms also should be set up at this point. The job-description form should provide the necessary space for the identifying information in the heading and appropriate space for recording the definition and description of the job. The style of writing job descriptions and the amount of detail which will be included will also be decided at this time. The job-specification form must also have provision for the necessary identifying information in the heading. The body of this form will provide for recording the facts about the job which pertain to each of the elements on which the jobs are to be rated, and also for recording the point value or other indication of rating on each of these factors. Thus, the job-description form and the job-specification form, prepared on the basis of the information collected and recorded in the process of the job analysis, carry the basic facts about the job that are necessary and pertinent to the evaluation. These two forms become the permanent record of the job evaluation on each job until such time as the job is eliminated or changed. When a change occurs in the job, it is reanalyzed and a new description and new specification are prepared so that a new evaluation can be made.

Control Procedures. It will be found advisable also to set up a schedule to be followed in collecting the job information. This form can be utilized in taking notes on each job so that it will furnish the source data from which both descriptions and specifications can be written.

It is important to establish at this time a common understanding with key executives of the company as to the standard concept of what constitutes a "job." (See pages 12-13.) The concept agreed upon must be followed consistently in the process of setting up the job-evaluation system. This is principally a matter of deciding how fine or how broad are to be the groupings of workers under a single job title. For example, in a production machine shop, there might conceivably be only four major jobs to cover all production workers —Toolmaker, Complicated Machine Operator, Simple Machine Operator, and Laborer. In such a case, the descriptions and specifications for each of these four jobs would necessarily be very broad and in very general terms. It would also follow that although individuals classified under a single title would be performing very different duties requiring different skills, abilities, and responsibilities, yet the rating of this broad job would apply to all of these individuals and they would all receive the same rate. This would, of course, actually establish inequities rather than eliminate them.

The rating for the job of Laborer, for example, would have to be established on the basis of the maximum degree of each factor which was present in the duties of any one individual in the group. As a result, this broad job might have to be assigned a very high rating on Physical Effort because a few of the workers within the job performed duties requiring a great amount of physical effort. The remainder, possibly the great majority, of the workers in that job would not be required to expend the same amount of physical effort. The resulting evaluation of the job of Laborer would be quite high with a correspondingly high wage rate in comparison to other jobs in the company. The workers performing duties requiring a lot of physical effort would demand to be transferred to lighter Laborer duties since there would be no difference in pay. It is obvious, then, that the workers should be divided into small enough groups so that all the workers classified under a single job title are performing essentially identical duties, requiring identical degrees of skill, responsibility, effort, and tolerance of working conditions.

Since the job evaluation is to be accomplished by analyzing all of the jobs in each department, it is only logical to attempt to establish in the beginning a list of all the jobs which are to be analyzed and evaluated. This may not be as easy at it sounds, particularly if no standard titling procedure has heretofore existed in the company. Some very broad job titles, such as Laborer, for example, may have been in common use in the company. In such cases, it may be necessary to break down these broad classifications into individual jobs and assign new titles to the jobs which are delineated in this manner. In other cases, it may be found that several different job titles are applied to workers all of whom are doing essentially identical jobs. For example, the titles Gridley Screw Machine Operator and Davenport Screw Machine Operator may be in use where the title Screw Machine Operator, covering both groups of workers, is quite sufficient and accurate. Where there is any doubt, however, it is much better to follow the finer breakdown since combinations of jobs can be made quite easily later on.

The simplest and most effective method for establishing the lists of job titles which are to be followed in analyzing and describing jobs is to arrange for the foremen and supervisors to set up these lists of job titles for their respective departments. If this is not feasible, this work can be done by the job analyst from information supplied by the foremen. So far as possible, the listing of jobs to be covered should be worked out and decided on before analyzing the jobs in order to avoid much confusion, recombining, and redividing of job titles later on. It is probable that the decisions made at this point will not be final since a quick review of job titles in each department cannot take into account all the details which will be discovered at the time of the analysis of the individual jobs and even subsequently at the time of rating the jobs. However, when the job analyst enters a department with a substantially accurate and complete list of the jobs which he is to analyze in the department, his work can be planned and carried out much more smoothly and quickly than would otherwise be possible.

This discussion of listing job titles to be covered by the job evaluation has been predicated on the assumption that the work will be carried out by departments because there are very few jobs which cross departmental lines, i.e., very few cases in which identical jobs are found in two or more departments. Of course, this is not a true assumption for all companies. If most jobs do not cross departmental lines, then the simplest way to proceed is by departments. If, however, in a great many cases the same job is found in more than one department, then this procedure should be modified so that the list of jobs to be covered is plantwide, without regard to department, and the process of job analysis should be carried out on that basis. In any event, the listing of jobs to be covered provides the basis for an operating control of the analysis of jobs and the subsequent steps in completion of the job evaluation. When the complete listing of plant job titles is established, a plantwide control for the carrying out of the job evaluation can be set up.

A Job Evaluation Control form shown in Figure 2–2 was used very successfully in one company as an operating control of the entire process from the analysis of the jobs to the final establishment of the point values. In the use of such a form, the current plant job titles, as listed by the foremen or by the job analyst, are entered in the first column. Where it is anticipated that one of these job titles is to be broken down into two or more specific job titles for evaluation purposes, blank lines should be left so that these new job titles can be entered on the form in the column "Suggested Job Title." Thus, after this form has been reviewed and discussed with the foreman, the present plant job titles will appear in the first column and the job titles to be followed in the job evaluation will appear in the column "Suggested Job Title." These latter job titles may be revised again after the job descriptions are completed and the accepted titles entered in the last column, "Final Job Title."

As a check on the listing of the plant job titles, the number of workers employed—male, female, and total—should be entered in the columns indicated. Thus, the count of workers as tallied by plant job title can be checked against the total number of workers to discover any omitted titles or similar discrepancies. As a more

JOB EVALUATION CONTROL

DEPARTMENT NAME _____ NUMBER

| PLANT JOB TITLE | NUMBER EMPLOYED | | | PROGRESS CONTROL | | | | | | | | | | | | | JOB CODE | SUGGESTED JOB TITLE | FINAL JOB TITLE |
	MALE	FEMALE	TOTAL	JOB ANAL.	DESCR. WR.	DESCR. ED.	SPEC. WR.	SPEC. ED.	DESCR. & SPECIF'N CLEARED STD.	DESCR. & SPECIF'N CLEARED FMN.	PTS. ASSND.	RATING CLEARED STD.	RATING CLEARED FMN.	TYPED				

Fig. 2—2.

positive check on the listing of titles by departments, the names of the workers actually employed in each department can be set up in a card file and the plant job title for each can be entered on the card. The Job Evaluation Control form can then be made up from this card file, thus insuring complete coverage of all workers employed in the department at that time. It should be noted also that some jobs may at the moment be vacant and provision should be made to include these jobs at the time or to include them later on as they may be filled.

When the Job Evaluation Control is established and checked, it is then necessary to arrange with the personnel department or with the foremen to receive notice of any new jobs which are established or of any changes which are made in the jobs as listed on the control form. While this job-evaluation control procedure may appear to be an unnecessary refinement, it has been found to work quite successfully, particularly in large companies, where it has served as a very effective up-to-the-minute control of the job evaluation as it proceeds.

The section headed "Progress Control" is particularly valuable when a large number of jobs is involved and when several job analysts are working at the same time. In such cases, very close supervision and thorough training are essential, particularly if these job analysts are borrowed from various departments within the company and thus are trained for this job. The "Progress Control" suggests a procedure to be followed in a situation of this kind. The person assigned to the control of the project should maintain the Job Evaluation Control, keeping it up to date with new and changed job titles and checking progress of the work, job by job, as indicated on the form. When a job or group of jobs is assigned to a particular job analyst, his initials and the date can be entered in the column headed "Job Anal." As the description and the specification are written and edited, check marks can be entered in the appropriate columns to show the progress and to serve as a schedule for the work.

Similar entries for clearance of descriptions and specifications, and of point ratings with the worker representatives and the foremen, also can be shown in the columns provided. The actual point value, or other indication of evaluation, can be entered in the "Points Assigned" column, to be changed subsequently if necessary. This provides a rough check, on the Job-Evaluation Control, of the evaluation of all of the jobs in each department or other grouping of the jobs on the basis of which the control is set up. The sample Job-Evaluation Control form shown in Figure 2–2 provides for step-by-step control of the evaluation process, by jobs, from the original analysis to the first typing.

The card file of employees may be used as suggested above as a further check on the completeness of the coverage of jobs. If kept up to date throughout the process of the evaluation, including such information as is shown in the sample in Figure 12–1 (page 366), this file may be used at the completion of the job evaluation to provide the basic data for computing the wage curve. It will prove useful in making all other necessary calculations which might be considered advisable in analyzing the results of the job evaluation in terms of costs. Also, in carrying out changes in rates or rate ranges in converting from the current wage structure to the new wage structure based on the job evaluation, this record is basic.

GETTING THE JOB ANALYSTS STARTED

In going to work on the actual first step in the job evaluation— the analysis of the jobs—it is important that the job analysts be grounded as thoroughly as possible in the procedures and techniques which they are to follow, as well as in the broad policies within which these procedures and techniques have been established. If employees are being used who are without experience in job analysis for the purpose of job evaluation, it is essential that they receive very close supervision and training on the job, and that their work be carefully edited, especially in the first stages; it is just as important that they understand the policies under which they are operating and the reasons why these particular policies have been adopted. Their contacts with department supervisors, foremen, and representatives of the workers are particularly important in the smooth operation of the whole job. They must make these contacts carefully and thoroughly with a full appreciation of the importance of the part they are playing in the company's industrial relations. It is essential, for example, in obtaining information about jobs from workers and their representatives, and from foremen, that analysts confine the discussion to questions of fact and arrive at an analysis of the job which is accurate and as complete as is necessary. Statements of workers, union representatives, and foremen should be verified wherever possible by observation of the worker on the job. Judgments should be checked against objective information where such is available.

CONCLUSION

In conclusion, it should be re-emphasized that the various points discussed or illustrated in this chapter are principles which must be followed and adapted to the particular situation if the installation of job evaluation is to go along with a minimum amount of difficulty and with the sound backing of all concerned, from the workers on the jobs to top management. The application of these principles has been described in many individual articles by technicians who have had experience in this field. Careful attention to important details in the planning stage of a job-evaluation project will greatly facilitate the work involved in carrying it through and will eliminate many of the difficulties which might arise without such careful preparation.

SUGGESTIONS FOR STUDY AND RESEARCH

1. Write a letter to the employees in a small, friendly office telling them that a job analyst will visit them in the near future to evaluate their jobs.
2. Write a letter to the foremen of a factory, asking them to cooperate with the job analysts who will be analyzing the jobs in their departments.

CASE PROBLEM

Upon the recommendation of the director of industrial relations, the president of a large cast iron foundry has given his approval to the installation of job evaluation to cover all jobs except those of the officers of the company. The 300 office employees include a personnel staff of 18 people and an industrial engineering staff of 7 people, 4 of whom are time study engineers engaged in maintaining the standard hour incentive system. There are formal apprenticeship programs for patternmakers and coremakers. There are 900 hourly employees engaged in the highly mechanized foundry operations.

PROBLEM: Give a complete outline of the plan to be followed in installing the job evaluation in the various job groups in the company, including (1) What to do, (2) Who will do it, and (3) How it is to be accomplished. Outline, for the director of industrial relations, the explanation of this plan to the officers of the union, as the plan affects employees in the bargaining unit.

3

Job Evaluation and Collective Bargaining

THE APPROACH TO JOB EVALUATION IN A company where employees are organized will be different from the approach in a company where they are not. A company that deals with its employees directly should so organize its job-evaluation study that it will gain maximum employee acceptance. The presence of an independent union or of a local union affiliated with an international union makes it desirable for the company to conduct its job-evaluation study in such a manner that prior acceptance can be obtained, if possible, from the union representatives.

A company or union that wishes to pay jobs on the basis of their relative difficulty should use an evaluation method which is suited to the needs of the organization where the jobs are found. A company or a union desiring to maintain a wage advantage for certain jobs at the expense of other jobs cannot subscribe to a job classification based upon sound job-evaluation procedures, because the attempt to maintain the advantage would be apparent. Some form of job evaluation is desirable if jobs of equal worth and difficulty are to be assigned the same base wage. The internal consistency of the wage structure is an important consideration in the creation and maintenance of good industrial relations, and a sound job-classification structure is an important basis for a sound wage structure.

In a pamphlet entitled, "Men and Unions," an unusual but sound observation was made concerning the attitude of employees toward wages. This observation is important because it highlights the point that employees are very conscious of inequities in the wage structure. That part of the pamphlet which applies to this problem is quoted in full.[1]

To sum up in one sentence why employees want to belong to unions: It is because of the benefits they get or hope to get. Most of the benefits they name can be measured in dollars, and the rest have intangible, but none the less real, values.

"The union puts money in our pockets," or some variation of that theme, is by far the most frequently given reason. Of the thousands of ways in which employees chose to express their reasons for union membership, more than 18 per cent added up to more money, and countless others were at least indirect pocketbook reasons.

What a union can do to lift the level of wages is no longer as important to employees as union activities to correct inequities in the wage structure. Most employees seem quite willing to credit management with sincere intention that wages in the company shall not lag behind the cost of living, behind wages of other companies in the area, or behind wages of competitors in the same industry. The union gets a good deal of credit when an across-the-board wage increase is negotiated, but most employees now recognize that the company should get at least part of the credit.

Wage inequities are a different matter. There the employee does not compare his own income with prices in the grocery store, nor with strangers who work in other plants in the area or in some remote plant in another part of the country. Instead, he compares his own wages with what he thinks other people in his own plant, doing much the same kind of job, are making. If his own personal job evaluation system leads him to the conclusion that somebody else is getting paid more for the same kind of work than he is, a wage inequity has developed. Parenthetically it may be stated that few management policies seem to be as much a mystery to men as the system for establishing wage rates. This has led to a great deal of suspicion and distrust.

Employees of many companies say that they have found that the union can do much more to correct wage inequities than they as individuals can. In consequence, more employees gave the correction of wage inequities as a reason for wanting to belong to a union rather than such other reasons as greater security, seniority protection, and the improvement of working conditions.

UNION SHOP OR OPEN SHOP

Unorganized plant or office

In those plants or offices where the employees are unorganized, the complete responsibility for the creation and maintenance of a

---

[1] John G. Mapes, "Men and Unions" (New York: Group Attitudes Corporation, 500 Fifth Ave.), pp. 6–7

sound wage structure falls upon management. This does not mean that the employer should not take the employees into his confidence; it merely means that the responsibility for the creation of the wage structure must be assumed by management. In an unorganized plant or office, management thus has a great deal of freedom in the selection of the job-evaluation plan, and in determining the resulting wage structure. In such a situation the company should select a job-evaluation system which will give the most accurate results. Chapters 4, and 5, and 6 are devoted to the description of various systems and to the criteria which should be followed in selecting a particular system. The system selected should be one that can be explained easily to workers.

It is undesirable to be secretive about the job-evaluation study. If management decides to conduct a job-evaluation study, it should proceed to do so forthrightly and openly. When an individual employee is interviewed or observed to obtain job-description data, he should be informed about the purpose of the interview or observation. For informing the entire employee group, the usual channels of communication—plant magazines, letters, meetings— are recommended. Since it is sometimes difficult to demonstrate job evaluation, great care should be exercised in presenting the information so that it will be understood.

Organized plant or office

In those situations where the employees have elected to be represented by unions, the company has the responsibility of bringing the representatives as well as the individual employees into the job-evaluation picture in a suitable manner. As pointed out above, there is less freedom of action in a company where the employees are organized. This does not mean that the resulting value of the study is lessened; it means only that a procedure designed to aid in the construction of a sound wage structure should be selected which is acceptable to all concerned: management, employees, and union representatives.

In those places where the local union is independent or is unhampered by national policy there will be a greater opportunity for cooperation. Again, this does not mean that the limitations placed upon locals by international or national organizations will limit the value of the job-evaluation study. There is no reason why the lack of complete freedom of action on the part of either the company or the local union organization should affect the final wage structure.

If both the company and the union wish to pay on the basis of proper job differentials, the establishment of proper checks and balances should not affect the derivation of fair job differentials.

The procedures which will be described in the following chapters of this book can and should be used in the establishment of a wage structure. However, an examination of these procedures as they should be used in working with organized labor in the establishment of a wage structure is desirable, since many organizations are hesitant to proceed in the use of a new method until the attitude of organized labor is known.

JOB EVALUATION—A FACTUAL BASIS FOR BARGAINING ON WAGES

Agreement on a procedure specifically designed to establish equitable wages for employees, as a substitute for hit-or-miss methods, is a desirable point of departure in wage negotiations. Job-evaluation methods lend themselves either to company use or to joint participation. These methods provide a picture of the relative difficulty of the jobs under consideration and, at the same time, through the job descriptions, specifications, and point values, show the relationship of these jobs to comparable jobs in the community. Some form of job evaluation is essential if jobs of equal worth and difficulty are to be assigned the same base wage. It is believed that the internal consistency of the wage structure (see Chapter 1) is as important for good industrial relations as are the absolute wage values of jobs. In other words, a sound job-classification structure is an important basis for a sound wage structure. If it is desired that collective bargaining proceed on the basis of facts, then job evaluation should be utilized so that the bargaining will be on a factual rather than an emotional basis.

To refuse to accept fully the findings of a particular job-evaluation study is entirely within the rights of either party to a collective bargaining conference, but to refuse to accept job-evaluation methods as a means of determining relative job difficulties is a refusal to proceed on the basis of one of the best methods available of obtaining job facts.

UNION ATTITUDES TOWARD JOB EVALUATION

According to the *U.E. Guide to Wage Payment Plans, Time Study, and Job Evaluation,*[2]

[2] *U. E. Guide to Wage Payment Plans, Time Study, and Job Evaluation,* United Electrical, Radio and Machine Workers of America, New York, 1943, pp. 77–80.

The local union should refuse to become a party to or be bound by any point-rating systems which management may use to establish job evaluations. It should not appear in the contract. As with time study, the U.E. lets the company use whatever method it pleases but under close union surveillance. . . . The union should always reserve the right to challenge any job values which it finds unsatisfactory and to utilize any and all factors bearing on the case.

This attitude can be contrasted with that of unions insisting that job evaluation be a joint undertaking.

The statement of policy of the United Electrical, Radio and Machine Workers of America certainly in no way limits the freedom of a company in using job evaluation to determine proper job differentials. It merely states that the union can either accept or reject the findings of the job evaluation. If the evaluation is sound and the union wishes to price the jobs on the basis of job differentials, the policy will allow a local to accept the findings of job evaluation. On the other hand, if the job evaluation is not sound, or if the union wishes to gain an advantage amounting to an inequity for certain jobs, then it may challenge the evaluation. The implications of this policy insofar as conducting the job-evaluation study is concerned are discussed below.

In cases where unions are not informed about job evaluation, it is difficult for them to subscribe to job-evaluation findings. It is important, therefore, to make sure that unions understand job evaluation and its application. Smyth and Murphy [3] believe that,

As a general rule, union participation in job evaluation has the advantage that greater understanding and acceptance of the plan will be achieved thereby. After experiencing the administration of job-evaluation plans with and without participation of employees and representatives, the authors feel that if the plan used is sound and is fairly administered both labor and management will be satisfied with and will benefit from joint participation.

Some unions believe that the evaluation should be carried out by management, but other unions believe that some form of joint participation is desirable. On the other hand, certain managements feel that their relationship with their employees is benefited by participation in job evaluation, and other managements feel quite strongly that job evaluation is a management function and that unions should not participate in the evaluation study. The reasons for these opposite points of view are probably many and the history of employee-management relationships is probably the best guide

[3] By permission from *Job Evaluation and Employee Rating,* by Richard C. Smyth and Matthew J. Murphy, p. 78. Copyrighted 1946 by McGraw-Hill Book Co., Inc

in deciding whether the job evaluation should be carried out by joint participation or whether the study should be conducted on a unilateral basis. Furthermore, joint participation can vary from the general approval of the plans by the union to actually working with management in the collection and evaluation of the job data.

Two of the major issues confronting unions and management when negotiating wage clauses are (1) the relative rates to be assigned to jobs, and (2) the absolute wage rates. There should be little major disagreement about the relative rates for jobs, provided a sound and fair evaluation study has been made. The removal of this problem from the wage discussion should clear the air for the determination of the absolute amount to be paid each classification.

A point of union interest in job evaluation

The company establishes jobs. The creation of a job and the collection of a series of tasks to form a job is a management function, because the organization can function only when individuals are assigned tasks which contribute to production. Jobs, as they are currently performed by workers, are the basis for most aspects of collective bargaining. Whenever management changes job content, however, the change is important to unions, because it affects such things as wage structure, seniority, and other matters that are of interest in collective bargaining. From this point of view it is desirable for the union to keep informed about job content, because the latter is the basic ingredient in the whole wage picture. When job evaluation is employed to group the individual jobs into a series of job classes, it becomes easier for both the union and the company to police the wage structure.

Job evaluation as part of the contract

There are some companies which believe that job evaluation as a technique should be included in the union contract itself, and there are others which believe that the inclusion of a job-evaluation clause in the contract is undesirable. There are problems which both parties should consider seriously before agreeing to the inclusion of such a clause in the contract. If, for example, management feels that job evaluation is a definite management function, the clause should probably be omitted from the contract. If the union feels that it might endanger its member-officer relationship, it probably should be omitted from the contract. However, when the wage structure is based on job evaluation, and both parties agree that it should be the basis for the wage agreement, then its inclusion in the contract might aid in wage negotiations.

A schedule of jobs and the salary rates determined by collective bargaining may be incorporated in the contract, or, if too detailed, may be put in a separate classification book and referred to by an appropriate notation in the contract. There are disadvantages of identifying jobs by titles only; to avoid confusion, job descriptions should be prepared so that rates may be referred to job duties.

The labor contract may also contain such statements as: "the job title and job definition describe the duties the employee is expected to perform;" and, "the employer will analyze and describe new jobs, and the analysis and evaluation shall be accepted by both parties as the basis for the determination of the proper job classification for such new jobs." Any organization is expected to grow and change, so proper provision for changes in the job classification should be made in the agreement.

In a recent volume, Smith [4] gives in outline form the various questions which should be answered if a clause concerning job evaluation is to be included in the labor contract:

1. Who shall determine the method of job evaluation to be used?
   a. The company?
   b. The union?
   c. Both parties through a joint committee or by mutual consent?
   d. An outside organization or individual?
      (1) Selected by the company?
      (2) Selected by the company and the union?
2. Shall reference be made to the method adopted or in use?
3. Who shall make the job evaluation and the classification?
   a. The company?
   b. The union?
   c. Both parties through a joint committee or by mutual consent?
   d. An outside organization or individual?
4. Shall the plan be publicized and explained?
   a. To all union internal and external representatives?
   b. To all employees?
5. How shall wage rates or rate ranges be assigned to the evaluated jobs? Shall they be listed in the agreement?
   a. Individually to each job?
   b. By job-classification grades?

[4] Leonard J. Smith, *Collective Bargaining* (New York: Prentice-Hall, Inc., 1946), pp. 93-95.

6. Who shall determine the wage rates or rate ranges for the jobs or labor grades?
   a. The company?
   b. The company and the union through a joint committee or by mutual consent?
   c. An outside organization or individual?

7. How shall the wage rates or rate ranges be determined?
   a. Arbitrarily?
   b. By mutual agreement?
   c. In relation to existing company rates?
   d. In relation to prevailing area rates?

8. Shall the union be permitted to review and approve the evaluations and classifications of all jobs before they become final?

9. Shall the classification and description of all jobs be included as part of the agreement?

10. Shall the listing of all employees into the job classifications be included as part of the agreement?

11. Shall provision be made for periodic reviews of all job classifications?
    a. How often shall they be made?
    b. Who shall be a party to the review?
       (1) The original parties to the job evaluation?
       (2) Company and union representatives?
       (3) Company representatives only?
       (4) An outside organization or individual?

12. Shall the reclassification of any jobs be subject to union approval or consent?

13. When shall the reclassifications of jobs and the employees involved on these jobs become effective?

14. Shall the review procedure be used when changes occur in jobs?
    a. Elimination of jobs?
    b. Modification of jobs?
    c. Addition of new jobs?

15. Shall provision be made for an appeal of any job evaluation or classification decision?
    a. Level of the grievance procedure applicable?
    b. Shall it be arbitrable?
    c. Shall the union be required to submit its reasons for the appeal?

16. Shall the relationship between job evaluation and basic wages be set forth?

These questions listed by Smith make an excellent check list for many of the aspects of conducting a job evaluation. They contain areas for discussion concerning the matter of union participation discussed above. These questions should be studied carefully before making a decision concerning the inclusion of job evaluation in the labor contract.

EXTENT OF UNION PARTICIPATION

There are three levels or degrees of union participation in a job evaluation study and in the maintenance of a wage structure on the basis of job evaluation. These three degrees are: (1) no participation; (2) a review of the job-evaluation findings; and (3) actual participation in obtaining the job-evaluation information.

No participation

There are situations in which the company must proceed alone in a job-evaluation study without any participation on the part of employees or their representatives. This may be due simply to the fact that the company feels that job evaluation is strictly a management function, and in such instances it neither invites the union to participate nor solicits any help whatever from the union. In other instances, the company may desire union participation, but the union may refuse to participate or simply not be particularly interested. In any event, situations occur where the complete burden of job evaluation is on management, and under these circumstances management uses the findings as *its* basis for wage negotiations and in so doing may not even mention how it obtained the findings.

Review of findings

Perhaps the most common method of union participation is for the union to review the findings of the job-evaluation study, then accept these findings if they are sound and to the best interests of the employee, or reject the findings if they are discovered to be otherwise. Although the statement of policy of the United Electrical, Radio and Machine Workers of America seems to preclude any participation in job evaluation, it evidently permits a local union to review the findings of an evaluation and challenge any findings which it considers unsatisfactory, and to utilize any and all factors bearing on the jobs which are considered satisfactory. When a review of the job-evaluation study by the employees or their representatives is considered the most desirable procedure, the selection of the job-evaluation method and the collection and organization of the job-evaluation data are the responsibility of management. An understanding of the plan on the part of the employees is one of the first steps in the review procedure. If there is a question about the validity of the job-rating method, the question should be raised early, and the method should be examined and checked to make sure that it is doing the job that it was designed to do. Some unions have experts on their staff who review these plans to make sure that the application of the plans will not result in any injustice. In any event, the plan itself should be understood by the employees or their representatives before any acceptance of the final classification is made.

Most job-evaluation studies result in three major sets of data: the job descriptions, the job specifications, and the job values. The purpose and the function of the description have already been described. It is essential, however, that the employees or their representatives study the job descriptions to make sure that the descriptions and their accompanying titles truly represent the jobs as they are now being performed. In the administration of the wage structure, job changes must be taken into consideration, and it is essential that acceptable job descriptions be prepared so that, when job changes occur, a comparison of the duties of the job before and after it changed can be made. The review of these descriptions requires less in the way of technical knowledge than does the review of the other two sets of job-evaluation data. Employees and union officials can be found who are well acquainted with the jobs, and they can check the job descriptions against the jobs as they are now being performed. Since a great deal of confusion can arise through the misuse of job titles and through the lack of proper job identification, it is essential that the review of the job description data result in an acceptance of the job facts and the job identities.

The job specifications are designed to specify the amounts of ratable or compensable factors which are involved in a job. In other words, the job rater has been called upon to make a judgment concerning the amount of experience, education, and responsibility which is demanded by the job. This is in the field of judgment rather than in the field of exact or observable facts and it requires ability to compare one job with another on each one of these compensable factors. It is recommended that the individuals charged with reviewing the job data, whether they be union or management representatives, be given thorough training in the writing and reviewing of job specifications. A great deal of consistency of thought is required to review a large set of job-specification data and to make sure that each job receives its fair allotment of each factor involved in the evaluation.

The third set of data to be reviewed is the job ratings, or the results of the application of the job-evaluation system to each job. These job values are designed to show the difficulty of each job in relation to the others. The type of system used will determine in part the method of review required. Chapters 10 and 11 of this book show the way in which jobs are evaluated. These chapters will be of value in setting up the necessary procedures for reviewing the job ratings. The use of job-rating scales and methods for checking the ratings are described in detail. The reviewing of these ratings for accuracy should be done in such a way that the best rating and rerating procedures are employed.

The review of the descriptions, specifications, and ratings can be carried out by individual employees or employee representatives, or it can be carried out by a joint committee. There is no reason why the job-evaluation data should not be given to the union for complete review, but since there are some possibilities for misunderstanding which can be avoided during a joint review, it is perhaps desirable to carry out the review by a committee of both management and union representatives. Since the purpose of this review is to improve, to check, and to verify the accuracy of the job-evaluation data, every method possible should be used to reach these objectives. The final job classification, and, in fact, the final wage structure, is no more accurate than the accuracy of the basic information, so careful review is extremely desirable.

Joint participation

If the third method, joint participation, is to be used in the entire wage study, it then becomes necessary to have each step carried out by representatives of both management and employees. This joint participation does not necessarily mean that each job fact must be obtained by both parties, but it does mean that the methods and procedures and the general conduct of the job-evaluation study be carried out as a cooperative enterprise. It has been pointed out above that a job evaluation is a technical matter, and since it is technical, it is not always desirable to use individuals who lack training in this field to collect the data and to make the original validation ratings. For each step of the job-evaluation study to be a joint undertaking, the various parts of the study should be conducted in such a way that there is either joint participation or a feeling of cooperation on the part of both parties concerned.

It is perhaps desirable in such a study that the job-evaluation system be selected jointly by the cooperating groups. Such studies as the *Sperry Gyroscope Study,* in which the job-evaluation system was constructed by a joint committee in cooperation with a consulting organization, illustrates one method of joint participation. The same committee could well have examined a series of plans and selected another which it believed would suit the needs of the company and the employees. In any event, the first step is to select a job-evaluation system which is satisfactory to both management and union representatives.

The next step is to decide who is going to conduct the study. There are three sources of persons to conduct the study: (1) Company job analysts, (2) Company and union job analysts, (3) Outside consultants.

If it is decided that the company job analyst will collect the data, then joint participation takes the form of a complete review of these data by a union-management committee. In fact, several union-management committees can be used so that more persons who are acquainted with the details of the jobs being reviewed can be used as committee members. The use of company and union job analysts to describe and to evaluate jobs has much in its favor from the point of view of joint participation or the feeling of joint participation, but it tends to create a somewhat awkward situation because two individuals perform a job which can often be performed better by a single person. It is therefore preferable for the company and the union to agree upon acceptable job analysts than to use representatives from both groups to analyze each individual job.

There are at the present time individual consultants and consulting organizations which have acquired considerable skill and experience in job evaluation. Some consulting organizations specialize in one type of industry. Most of these consultants are hired by management, but their professional reputation depends upon the fairness and accuracy demonstrated in their work. Their data are usually well organized and presented in a meaningful manner. The job-evaluation material obtained by such people can be reviewed by a joint union-management committee. This approach tends to be as unbiased as can be obtained, and when a neutral consultant is employed by both parties the findings usually are not questioned seriously.

As pointed out above, it is quite difficult to use joint participation in the collection of job description and job specification data. However, it is possible to use a joint committee in rating each job. Under the review procedure, the ratings are prepared by management and reviewed either by the union or by a union-management committee. Under the joint committee the ratings are made by a committee composed of representatives of both the company and the employees. The way in which this committee functions is described in Chapter 10 of this book.

The three degrees of union participation just mentioned open up the question of the desirability of complete understanding of job-evaluation procedures by all individuals concerned. It has already been pointed out that the company has a responsibility to its own supervisors and to employee representatives in keeping both groups fully informed concerning the basis on which wages are determined. Union members must have three conditions in mind at all times in dealing with matters pertaining to wages. First, in those situations where job evaluation is in use they find it extremely desirable to have a knowledge of the basis for the wage structure so that in collective bargaining they will not be at a disadvantage because of lack of information. Second, it is necessary for the union representatives to justify the various wage decisions to union members. Without a complete and accurate knowledge of the basis of the wage determination, it would be difficult for these representatives to keep their membership fully informed concerning the wage structure. Third, a union representative must have a complete knowledge of the system and its operation in order to police the wage structure once it has been installed. Whether or not the union participated in the job evaluation, it is quite essential that the members understand all aspects of the evaluation.

The degree of union participation should be specified in the contract. Some unions may wish to participate while others may wish to check management findings. However, the way the wages are to be determined for new jobs should be understood. Of greater importance is the procedure for setting the rates for jobs which have been changed. The nature of the relationship between the company and the union should be studied carefully so that sound working relationships can be maintained on all aspects of job evaluation.

Illustrative clauses are found below: [5]

A.   Job Evaluation—General

A job-evaluation committee consisting of two permanent members of the union and two permanent members from the management shall point-

[5] C. Wilson Randle, *Collective Bargaining Principles and Practices* (Chicago: Houghton Mifflin Company, 1951), pp. 232–33.

rate all jobs held by production and maintenance workers. This committee, having point-rated all present jobs and mutually agreed as to the proper evaluation of each job, shall similarly evaluate new jobs or shall reevaluate present jobs when there is a change in job content, thereby determining proper wage level within the wage structure. Further, on the basis of job evaluations, this committee will determine the various job classifications by department.

B. Job Evaluation by Reference Including a General Increase

It is mutually agreed that all hourly rates will be determined by job evaluation. The evaluation plan, its use and application, together with all intermediate calculations, is described in the "Job-Evaluation Manual" attached hereto. It is further agreed that after the hourly rates of the jobs are calculated by evaluation, they shall be increased in such amount as to result in an over-all average increase of 2¢ an hour over present rates.

The methods of making the wage changes sanctioned by the bargaining agreement are many and variable. In general, they conform to the techniques just described. Some, however, may utilize a combination of these techniques and others may adopt a wage-change methodology unique in itself but suited to the particular firm's wage structure and requirements.

A BASIS FOR MUTUAL TRUST

Any system which approaches some objectivity in wage administration and is not weighted in favor of the company in any way carries with it a basic fairness that union representatives can demonstrate to union members. The system itself is such that full information concerning it can be given to the membership, and for the first time a wage structure can be demonstrated in its entirety. Not only can the structure be presented but the procedures which were used in building that structure can be explained to the membership.

Under a good job-evaluation system, the wage structure is subject to corrective modification without disrupting the entire system. For example, in a job change a worker can have his job reevaluated and reclassified without disturbing the basic classification itself. In fact, any employee whose job has changed sufficiently to be upgraded can be upgraded without the necessity of a complete wage review. The company can police its own system and in turn be policed by the union. The responsibility for making the necessary wage adjustment when job changes occur should be placed on the company, but the union should make sure that the necessary changes are made. This type of system makes it easier, then, for unions to watch the administration of wages.

In the industrial type of union, a proper wage relationship between the jobs requiring little skill and those requiring a high degree of skill should be maintained. If it is accepted that the relative difficulty of jobs should be taken into consideration in pricing them, then an industrial type of union, in order to maintain a proper balance between jobs in varying skill levels, needs a method of maintaining that balance. These unions have found that job evaluation is valuable to them in maintaining such balances. The craft unions have in the past been somewhat less interested in job evaluation than the industrial unions. However, this type of job measurement can also be of value to these unions in maintaining proper differentials between the various crafts.

It was mentioned at the beginning of this chapter that any company or any union that wishes to pay jobs on the basis of difficulty and in the fairest known manner should attempt to base its wage structure upon some form of job evaluation. The willingness to abide by job facts, carefully collected and properly evaluated, is a step toward mutual confidence and trust. In the field of wage administration there is much emotional thinking, and it is desirable to substitute "fact-finding" techniques for emotional opinions. Job evaluation has reached the *useful* stage and is worthy of the combined acceptance of the parties to a collective bargaining contract.

SUGGESTIONS FOR STUDY AND RESEARCH

1. Develop a clause which you believe should be included in a collective bargaining contract, to show how you would want the "Review of Findings" method of participation to operate.

CASE PROBLEM

A new management has just taken over a small manufacturing plant. It finds that wage inequities have crept into the wage system. The union is aware of this and would like to have them corrected. The union is insisting on "joint participation." Draw up an agreement which would permit "joint participation" in a job evaluation study, showing the responsibilities which should be assigned to management and those which should be assigned to the union.

Part Two

Job Evaluation Systems

4

Nonquantitative Systems

SELECTION OF A SUITABLE JOB-EVALUATION
system is the main problem which confronts an organization when
it plans a job-classification study. Systems are available which
can be used either in their present form or in modified forms to suit
the particular needs of the individual organization. There are four
major systems from which a choice may be made: Ranking, grade
description, point rating, and factor comparison. Ranking and grade
description represent systems which are relatively simple and easy
to explain. The point-rating and factor-comparison methods are
more complex.

CHOOSING A SYSTEM

The first decision to make is whether to use a quantitative or
nonquantitative method of evaluation. For those who do not wish
a quantitative system the first two evaluation systems mentioned
are preferable. For those who feel that the quantitative approach
to classification is better, either the point-rating or the factor-comparison method should be used.

Every person with some experience in the field of job evaluation
tends to be a strong advocate for that system with which he is most
familiar. Once an analyst has used a system successfully, he builds
up a background of understanding which allows him to be more
consistent in making judgments than he would be if he were required to become familiar with a new system each time he evaluates

the jobs in an organization. This may explain why there is resistance to the modification of a system already in use or to the selection of a new evaluation system in preference to one which has been used before. Since management and labor acceptance of a job-evaluation system is necessary before it will be of maximum value, both should realize that with careful study and application any sound system can be applied without too much difficulty.

Selecting a system already in use in other organizations

Many personnel procedures must be confined to the organization which installs them if they are to have maximum value. The same selection technique when used by many firms in the same community loses its value. Training procedures, for example, when well conceived, give the organization which develops them a competitive advantage over another which is deficient in the training of employees. In the field of job evaluation, however, an organization gains when its system is adopted by others, especially when arrangements are made for the exchange of job evaluation and wage information. The use of a single evaluation system in several plants makes it possible to compare jobs in one plant with jobs in other plants to discover whether or not wage discrepancies exist. It is believed to be desirable to keep the wages paid for jobs in one organization in line with the wages paid for the same jobs in other organizations.

The work of Kress for the National Electrical Manufacturers' Association and for the National Metal Trades Association is an excellent illustration of an attempt to evaluate jobs throughout an entire industry by using the same evaluation system. More recently, the American Institute of Bolt, Nut and Rivet Manufacturers, now the Industrial Fasteners Institute, devised a job-evaluation system which is so constructed that an industry-wide application of the system can be made.[1] At the same time the system can be modified to suit the needs of an individual plant. In this industry, as in the two industries served by Kress, there is a reasonable degree of assurance that wages for jobs similar in difficulty are being compared directly. All too often wages are compared by industry and by labor on the basis of job titles, but such titles do not

---

[1] *Handbook of Job Evaluation for Factory Jobs,* Personnel Research Institute of Western Reserve University, American Institute of Bolt, Nut and Rivet Manufacturers (Cleveland, 1946), now Industrial Fasteners Institute. The authors appreciate the permission granted by Mr. Herman Lind, President of the American Institute of Bolt, Nut and Rivet Manufacturers, to quote freely from this work.

always represent the same levels of difficulty. Standardization of job titles, and perhaps labor grades, will probably result through job evaluation, so that wage-reporting will attain an accuracy which it does not now possess.

There is much to be gained from using a job-evaluation system which has already been used successfully in other organizations. In instances where an existing system does not meet the particular needs of an organization, a new one must be developed.

Modification of an existing system

If permission can be obtained from the authors of an appropriate system, it is worth while to consider borrowing and modifying it to meet the needs of the organization. For example, in a modern plant, where the best working conditions have been provided, the factor of working conditions might be unimportant, but in an old plant this factor might be very important in the minds of the workers. When a system already in use is modified, the advantages of building a new system and of using a tested system are combined. The reputation of the borrowed system aids in gaining the acceptance of the modified system by management and employees.

In the procedure followed by the Industrial Fasteners Institute [2] a plan was submitted which could be used without modification by its members, but at the same time procedures were described which could be followed by member companies who desired to modify the system to suit their individual needs. Such a procedure is valuable because it allows a company to construct a system with a minimum of effort. Many plans have been described in detail by trade associations and individual companies, and in publications of such organizations as the American Management Association, the American Psychological Association, the Society for the Advancement of Management, and the Industrial Management Society. Permission to modify these plans can usually be obtained.

It is often possible to take one idea from one plan and another from a second plan and combine them into an evaluation system which serves the needs of the organization far better than the modification of a single system.

Construction of a new system

It is desirable that everyone involved in job classification be thoroughly acquainted with the system and its application. When

[2] *Ibid.*

individuals join together in the construction of something new, they seem to understand and use it more intelligently than when a system is handed to them ready made. Since many people who are not expert in the field will be involved in a job-evaluation study, their participation in the construction of the system, either as actual workers or in the capacity of reviewers, will aid in gaining helpful cooperation.

The problems involved in the construction of a new system depend upon the type of system chosen for use. The job-ranking or departmental order-of-importance method does not as a rule require much more than the construction of various forms and a definite formulation of procedures.

In using the grade-description method a careful analysis of each job is necessary, and carefully predetermined classes must be established. Each grade in the structure must be so well defined that placing an analyzed job into the proper grade is relatively easy. A considerable amount of group effort is required in building a grade-description classification structure. Since there is the possibility that certain jobs will have tasks which extend beyond a particular grade, a great deal of thoroughness and ingenuity is required in describing each grade. The construction of the grade-description method can be based upon a job evaluation made by one of the other types of evaluation systems. For example, if the point-rating method is used to set up a series of labor grades, it is then possible to write a grade description for each labor grade and to use this grade description as a rating scale for the analysis of new jobs. The same results can be obtained, of course, when either the factor-comparison method or the job-ranking method is used.

The most popular method today is the point-rating method. If a company decides to construct a new point-rating system, it should be careful in selecting the factors which are important in the evaluation of its jobs. As soon as each factor has been defined, a series of degrees for each factor is determined and the definitions for the degrees are written. A choice must be made between the straight-point method, in which the factors are not weighted, and the weighted-in-points method, in which each factor is weighted according to the way it contributes to the worth of the jobs. In the straight-point method accepted factor differences are not taken into consideration, so the job analyst must be prepared to weight each selected factor as it contributes to the total worth of the job. The procedure for doing this is described in Chapter 5.

An excellent description of the construction of a job-comparison sheet, the heart of the factor-comparison method, is given by Benge, Burk, and Hay.[3] Any company intending to use their method must, however, construct its own factor-comparison scale. Lytle [4] has called this method the "weighted-in-money method."

THE JOB-RANKING METHOD

Ranking system—departmental order-of-importance

One of the easiest methods of classifying jobs is to rank them from the most important to the least important. This is usually referred to as the *departmental order-of-importance method* because the general practice is to have department heads and supervisors arrange the jobs in their departments in order of importance. A central committee is usually given the responsibility of coordinating these rankings and grouping the jobs into grades or classes.

Dr. Marion A. Bills, in a report on job rating as applied to clerical workers, states, "Several types of classifying jobs have arisen where the classification was in fact a ranking rather than a classification; that is, each supervisor ranked his jobs in the order that he considered them of importance, and the personnel director then shuffled the jobs of other departments into these jobs. To the best of my knowledge this type of handling the classification of jobs has not stood the test of time. . . ." [5]

The departmental order-of-importance method has many shortcomings, but it does utilize a basic rating method which is better than no system of classification. The *Informational Manual on Industrial Job Evaluation Systems* [6] classifies the ranking system as a nonquantitative method of listing jobs in order of difficulty. According to the manual this system is sometimes referred to as the "card-sorting system," because it arranges jobs from high to low like the cards of a playing-card deck. In fact, the names of jobs are often placed on separate cards and then arranged in the order of their difficulty.

[3] Eugene J. Benge, Samuel L. H. Burk, and Edward N. Hay, *Manual of Job Evaluation* (New York: Harper & Brothers, 1941).

[4] Charles W. Lytle, *Job Evaluation Methods* (New York: The Ronald Press Company, 1946).

[5] M. A. Bills, *Origin of Job Classification and Its Early History*, Life Office Management Association, Annual Proceedings (1934).

[6] *Informational Manual on Industrial Job Evaluation Systems*, War Manpower Commission, Bureau of Manpower Utilization, Division of Occupational Analysis and Manning Tables (August 1943).

The rankings for the jobs in each department require a considerable amount of checking and verifying to eliminate disagreements among raters, since each job is evaluated not in terms of wage rates but in terms of other jobs. The ranking must be done without reference to such factors as present wage rates, efficiency of the employee, and traditional level of the job in the organization. If a large number of jobs are being ranked, the ranking method makes finer distinctions in job difficulty and importance than are necessary or even possible. The pure job-ranking method gives the rater no framework on which to hang his judgments. As a rating method, however, the ranking technique is one of the best known. It gets at the heart of the problem because the basic technique is to compare each job with the other jobs in the particular group under consideration.

The ranking method of rating is sometimes referred to as the *order-of-merit method*. It is easy to use and, what is quite important, easy to understand. Its simplicity, however, is no guarantee of accuracy, and it should be used with caution.

It was pointed out above that the ranking method is one of the easiest techniques to explain to persons who are unskilled in job evaluation. With the use of certain safeguards, which are explained below, it is probably as accurate a method of classifying jobs as any other system. It is usually difficult for rankers to explain the process whereby they made their final ratings. However, certain procedures used in ranking jobs can also serve as a basis for explaining the reasons for the rankings.

Because of its simplicity, job ranking takes less time and has a smaller amount of paper detail than the other methods. If it is preceded by careful job analysis, it can result in a practical job classification that is superior to arbitrary rate-setting. Where a job classification in a minimum amount of time is the major objective, the ranking method is the way to achieve it.

There are, however, disadvantages to the ranking method. Among these is the difficulty of securing raters who are familiar with all the jobs in the work unit being ranked. It is possible to use a simple statistical technique, as described below, to combine rankings which are incomplete so that this disadvantage can be overcome in part. A major fault lies in the type of judgment which the rater is called upon to make. Since he is asked to keep the "whole job" in mind when sorting the jobs according to worth, he is apt to be influenced by such factors as present rate, quality of persons on the job, and prestige value. It is very difficult in judging the "whole job" to keep a consistent point of view. Different raters use different bases for their judgments, thus invalidating some of the ratings. Of course, these same criticisms can to some degree be applied to the other systems.

When the same care is exercised in using the ranking method as in applying the more elaborate systems, the final classification of jobs should be approximately the same. Another serious error is ranking job titles only. Job titles used alone are often misleading and unless the rater is intimately acquainted with all of the jobs, grave rating errors will occur. Job facts should not be taken for granted. All data must be verified before they are used; job titles should be followed by job definitions, and these in turn should be based upon complete job descriptions.

In preparing a job-ranking procedure for use, it is recognized that few persons in an organization are well enough acquainted with the jobs to rank them all. If such a person does exist, he is likely to have definite prejudices for or against those jobs which he knows well and be neutral toward those jobs with which he is not so well acquainted.

The five steps

Step 1. Job Analysis, Job Descriptions, Job Titles. Job descriptions should be prepared for each job. In addition, job specifications, or statements about the qualities the workers should possess in order to adjust to the job demands, must also be prepared. Figure 4–1 shows a job description which was written for the job of Payroll Clerk. It should be noted that the job description contains a "sentence description" or summary statement of the job. This should be used, along with the job title, not only to identify the job but also to aid the raters in making accurate judgments. The work of the Kimberly-Clark Corporation is an excellent illustration of the job-ranking method. As reported by W. F. Cook,[7]

The first step was to reach an agreement on the duties and the requirements of each occupation. The payroll, of course, showed the title for each occupation but the titles were never very descriptive, and were sometimes misleading. A written analysis—a word picture of each occupation —was necessary. . . . I think that such analyses [job analyses] are an absolute necessity to any wage negotiation which is more than mere political maneuvering. Even when you have previously agreed on just

[7] W. F. Cook, *The Technique of Wage Negotiation and Adjustment,* Personnel Series No. 30 (New York: American Management Association, 1937), pp. 8–16.

what the occupation is, it is difficult to reach an agreement on how much the occupation is worth; but when you are side-tracked into arguments about whether the job is this or that, agreement on the worth of an occupation is hopeless.

NAME:	INTERVIEW DATE: 12–10–42
LOCATION: Comptroller's Office	APPROVAL DATES:
SECTION: Comptroller's Office	Worker: 12–12–42
	Dir. Supervisor: 12–14–42
PRES. TITLE: Payroll Clerk	Department Head: 12–16–42
DIR. SUPERVISOR: Asst. Comptroller	DESCRIPTION WRITTEN: 12–11–42
DEPARTMENT HEAD: Comptroller	JOB ANALYST:

SENTENCE DESCRIPTION: Under general supervision maintains records of employee classification and prepares payrolls from time cards, including preparing classification card, checking, verifying, listing, typing and running tapes.

DETAILED DESCRIPTION OF JOB:
Machine Equipment used includes typewriter.
Perform the following operations in connection with the preparation of payroll:

60% Typing	1. Receive approved Personnel Action or letter of Appointment.
5% Filing	2. Prepare index card from Personnel Action or letter of Appointment; file index cards in classification file; file Personnel Action or letter of Appointment alphabetically.
Computation	3. Verify employee's reporting date by phone with section supervisor of worker.
Calculation	4. At close of payroll period receive two copies time card from official supervisor of worker and check same against classification file.
20% Posting	5. Transcribe time card data to time-sheet spread separating normal and overtime and extending to total earned for period.
Checking	6. Run tape on time card and check against time-sheet spread.
15% Misc. Clerical	7. Check time card and time-sheet spread for correctness of daily entries, rates paid and total hours worked.
100% Total	8. Run tape on yellow copy and check against individual items copied.

9. Prepare one typed original and three carbon copies of time-sheet spread; run tape of typed copy; and check against time-sheet spread.
10. Following examination of typed copy by business office, type salary check from white copy with exception of portion to be completed by Check Writer.
11. Balance total of checks against typed copy.
12. Transmit checks to business office for signatures and distribution.

Perform sundry clerical tasks during slack periods where needed in assigned or other section such as checking, typing, filing, etc.

From Robert D. Gray, *Classification of Jobs in Small Companies*, Bulletin No. 5, Industrial Relations Section (Pasadena: California Institute of Technology, 1944), p. 11.

Fig. 4—1.   Job description, payroll clerk.

All who have worked in the field soon come to realize that clear and accurate occupational or job descriptions are the basis for the real work of job evaluation.

One technique which has been used successfully to rank jobs is to write on a small card the job title and a brief description telling the significant facts about the job. With this method the rater has a description in front of him at all times.

Step 2. Choosing the Raters—Selecting the Jobs. The job-ranking method has been called the *departmental order-of-importance* method because the usual procedure is to rank jobs by departments and to follow this by integrating the separate ranks so obtained into a single over-all ranking. The reason for this procedure is that in most organizations it is difficult to find persons who know all the jobs to be rated, but fairly easy to find persons who know all the jobs in one department. Such individuals as the foremen, assistant foremen, shop stewards, and department supervisors usually know the jobs in their departments. In addition to these, personnel workers, production managers, job analysts, and plant superintendents can also be chosen as raters. They should be instructed to rank only those jobs which they know well enough to judge. If office jobs are to be evaluated, the office manager, department supervisors, and union representatives may be chosen as raters. It is almost impossible to rank factory jobs with clerical jobs. Cook [8] asks,

Is it feasible to make a direct comparison between any occupation and any other occupation, for the purpose of determining which of the two deserves the more pay? A comparison of the duties and requirements of the occupation of piccolo player with the duties and requirements of the occupation of prize fighter does not indicate which occupation deserves the more pay, because the two occupations have so little in common; but what about the comparison between the maintenance millwright and the paper machine tender? . . . comparison should be made between occupations in related types or fields of work—occupations which have something in common and which tend to fall in the same group so far as "outside market" values are concerned.

The best procedure therefore is to evaluate jobs within natural divisions.

The qualifications of the raters are quite simple. First, they must know the jobs they are being called upon to rank; second, they must be capable of giving unbiased judgments; third, if they do

[8] W. F. Cook, *The Technique of Wage Negotiation and Adjustment,* Personnel Series No. 30 (New York: American Management Association, 1937), pp. 8–16.

know the earnings of each job, they must make a sincere attempt to disregard present wages in making their judgments.

More accurate ratings can be obtained by combining the judgments of several raters than by using a single set of ratings. If there are ten departments in the factory there probably will be ten sets of final rankings, one for each department. Occasionally one man knows jobs in more than one department so that a set of rankings for more than one department can be obtained. A set of ratings of this type is helpful in combining the ten sets into a single set. The method of integrating such department rankings is described in detail below.

Step 3. Ranking.

1. USING CARDS. It was stated above that job descriptions can be abbreviated and placed on small cards which are sorted into the rank order desired. The most difficult job or the job having the most worth is given the rank of 1, the next most difficult, the rank of 2, and so on. If two jobs tie for a rank, each is given the average of that rank and the one following. For example, if two jobs tie for rank 8, they are both given the rank 8.5.

One of the authors of this volume once had the problem of ranking the finished garments made by a group of 80 student workers. The following procedure was used:

a. Raters were required to examine the workmanship of each garment carefully so that some idea of the quality of workmanship could be obtained.

b. Raters were required to place each garment into one of two piles, labeled, "Best" and "Poorest." The piles were then re-examined to make sure that 50 per cent of the garments were in one and 50 per cent in the other.

c. Four new labels were prepared: "Best of the Best"; "Poorest of the Best"; "Best of the Poorest"; and "Poorest of the Poorest." The garments in the pile labeled "Best" were then equally distributed into the two piles labeled "Best of the Best" and "Poorest of the Best." The garments in the pile labeled "Poorest" were distributed equally into the two remaining piles. Again the raters were required to re-examine the garments to check their distributions.

d. Starting with those in the "Best of the Best" pile, the raters ranked the garments, 1 for the very best, 2 for the next best, and so on. The same procedure was followed for each of the other piles. The result was that all of the garments were finally ranked from 1 to 80.

If the job titles and a job summary are placed on cards, the above procedure can be followed. When there are only a few jobs in a department, such an elaborate ranking procedure is not necessary. For larger departments, however, dividing the jobs into successively smaller groups makes it possible to secure more accurate rankings than can be obtained when the raters attempt to make their judgments without such an aid.

2. RANKING BY THE METHOD OF PAIRED COMPARISON. Considerable research has been undertaken to increase the reliability and accuracy of ratings, and one technique in particular has tended to improve the ranking method. In this method the rater compares each job being rated with every other job being rated. To do this the jobs to be ranked are paired (as described in the following paragraphs), so that it is possible to make a judgment between two jobs without having to keep the remaining jobs in mind.

The number of comparisons to be made for a given number of jobs is $\frac{N(N-1)}{2}$, where N equals the number of jobs to be ranked. For example, if there are six jobs in a department, the number of comparisons equals $\frac{6(6-1)}{2}$ or 15. If there are 28 jobs in a department, the number of comparisons to be made equals $\frac{28(28-1)}{2}$ or 378. The task of making the judgments is reduced because the rater is required to make only one decision at a time, namely, which of the two jobs is the more difficult. By limiting the problem of ranking to a single pair at a time, the rater can study the comparison to the exclusion of all others. This method has resulted in more reliable judgments than have been obtained by any other ranking method. Suppose, for example, the jobs in a small clerical department were the following:

Information Clerk	Transfer Clerk
Mail Order Clerk	Adjuster
Refund Clerk	Collection Clerk

The first step is to pair each job with every other job as illustrated in Figure 4–2 which shows not only how the jobs should be arranged, but also how the judgments were recorded.

The comparisons are randomized (arranged so that the order is not in a definite job sequence). Care has been taken to place each job in the second position of the pair as frequently as in the first. The rater underlines the job in each pair which he considers the more difficult of the two. Figure 4–3 presents the results of one rater's comparisons of the data in Figure 4–2.

INSTRUCTIONS: In each of the pairs of jobs listed below, underline the job which you believe is more difficult and should receive the higher wage. Please be sure to make a choice for each pair even though it may be hard to distinguish between the difficulty level of the two jobs.

Information Clerk	Mail Order Clerk
Mail Order Clerk	Adjuster
Collection Clerk	Transfer Clerk
Refund Clerk	Information Clerk
Collection Clerk	Mail Order Clerk
Adjuster	Collection Clerk
Information Clerk	Collection Clerk
Transfer Clerk	Adjuster
Information Clerk	Transfer Clerk
Refund Clerk	Transfer Clerk
Mail Order Clerk	Refund Clerk
Refund Clerk	Collection Clerk
Transfer Clerk	Mail Order Clerk
Adjuster	Refund Clerk
Adjuster	Information Clerk

Fig. 4—2. An example of the paired comparison rating.

Job	Number of times judged more difficult	Rank
Information Clerk	0	6
Mail Order Clerk	2	4
Refund Clerk	3	3
Transfer Clerk	1	5
Adjuster	5	1
Collection Clerk	4	2

Fig. 4—3. Summary of ratings made by job comparisons.

A second method of arranging jobs for the purpose of making paired-comparison ratings has been used which is not so accurate as the one just described, but which is somewhat easier to construct and use. This method is illustrated in Figure 4–4. In the second row, for example, Information Clerk and Transfer Clerk are judged to be less difficult than the job of Mail Order Clerk. This method is accurate because each paired comparison is made twice, and care must be taken to eliminate inconsistent judgments. If, for example, in row 2 Mail Order Clerk is judged to be more difficult than Transfer Clerk, and in row 4 Transfer Clerk is judged to be more difficult than Mail Order Clerk, then an inconsistent judgment has been made and it is necessary for the rater to review his work to correct the inconsistency. The number of times one job has been judged to be more difficult than the others is obtained by summing the

	Infor- mation clerk	Mail order clerk	Refund clerk	Transfer clerk	Adjuster	Collec- tion clerk	Totals
Information Clerk							0
Mail Order Clerk	x			x			2
Refund Clerk	x	x		x			3
Transfer Clerk	x						1
Adjuster	x	x	x	x		x	5
Collection Clerk	x	x	x	x			4

The x indicates that the job in the horizontal row is more difficult than the job in the vertical column in which the x is placed.

Fig. 4—4. Comparison of six jobs by means of paired comparison table.

crosses in the row and recording the number in the "Totals" column. These totals can then be used to determine the job ranks.

The paired-comparison method of job ranking is especially well adapted to the industrial or office job evaluation situation. It is often difficult for a supervisor or worker to find the time to rank jobs by the card method. With the paired-comparison method, the jobs can be judged at odd moments during the day.

Step 4. Statistical Treatment of Rankings. For those individuals who are interested in a thorough statistical analysis of paired-comparison results, the studies of Thurstone [9] and of Symonds [10] are recommended. It is questionable how far the statistical refinement of ranking data should be carried. If the analysis becomes too complicated, much of the desired simplicity of the ranking method is lost.

Symonds points out that ranks yield a peculiar kind of distribution, in that every individual or job is one step away from the next. In dealing with other types of data, however, the differences between adjacent scores are rarely the same. When, for example, men are ranked according to height, it will be found that the actual differences in height between adjacent men are not the same. When jobs are ranked, the differences between adjacent jobs are not actually the same either, and the differences between some of the adjacent jobs may be far greater than between others.

The problem of combining incomplete rankings, caused by the

[9] L. L. Thurstone, "An Experimental Study of Nationality Preferences," *Journal of General Psychology* (1928), pp. 405–425; "The Method of Paired Comparisons for Social Values," *Journal of Abnormal and Social Psychology* (January–March 1927), pp. 384–400.

[10] Percival M. Symonds, *Diagnosing Personality and Conduct* (New York: D. Appleton–Century Co., 1931), pp. 86–93.

lack of familiarity of some of the raters with the job being rated, is quite easy to solve. Since series of ranks do not constitute a scale of equal units, it is necessary to exercise caution in combining the ranks when some of the judges have been unable to rank all the jobs. Suppose for example, that there are 20 jobs in a department, and one rater is able to rank 20, a second rater 15, and a third rater 12, and that it is desired to combine the three sets of ratings into a single one. Before combining them, it is advisable to reduce each set of ratings to the same scale. Hull [11] points out that ranks should never be averaged except where the roughest approximations are desired, and he recommends transmuting ranks into equivalent linear scores by using a 10-point scale. His method assumes that the things being ranked follow the normal curve of distribution. Although it is doubtful whether jobs in all companies follow the normal curve of distribution, a normal distribution in the case of incomplete rankings may be assumed. Following Hull's procedure, the transmutation is brought about by the use of a simple formula and the table shown in Table 4–1. With these, any series of ranks can be translated into corresponding linear scores. To take an illustrative problem, let us transmute to linear scores the six jobs previously ranked by means of paired comparison, Figure 4–4.

In the formula (Table 4–2), R is the rank of a particular job and N is the total number of jobs being ranked. The present position of the job of Adjuster would be $\frac{100(1 - .5)}{6} = 8.33$. The per cent position of the remaining jobs is computed in the same manner. The per cent position is transmuted into linear scores by using Table 4–1. These linear scores appear in the last column of Table 4–2. It should be noted that Hull has included a table compiled by Mr. Selmar C. Larson, from which the scale equivalents may be read off directly for all ranked scores or jobs from 10 to 50 ranks.

A second illustration is given in Table 4–3 to show how incomplete job ranks can be combined. If, for example, there are twenty jobs in a department and as mentioned above, one rater ranks 20, a second 15, and a third 12, the ranks are transmuted to units of amounts, which are totaled and averaged. The final averages are then reranked. It seems like a great deal of work to combine the judgments of selected raters, but the sole alternative is to use only those raters who are intimately acquainted with all the jobs in the department. Since such individuals are hard to find, it is usually

---

[11] Clark L. Hull, *Aptitude Testing* (Yonkers-on-Hudson, New York: World Book Co., 1928), pp. 386–390.

TABLE 4—1.   Table for transmuting "per cent position" in ranked series into scores or units of amount on an ordinary scale of ten points •

Per cent position	Scale score	Per cent position	Scale score	Per cent position	Scale score
.09	9.9	22.32	6.5	83.31	3.1
.20	9.8	23.88	6.4	84.56	3.0
.32	9.7	25.48	6.3	85.75	2.9
.45	9.6	27.15	6.2	86.89	2.8
.61	9.5	28.86	6.1	87.96	2.7
.78	9.4	30.61	6.0	88.97	2.6
.97	9.3	32.42	5.9	89.94	2.5
1.18	9.2	34.25	5.8	90.83	2.4
1.42	9.1	36.15	5.7	91.67	2.3
1.68	9.0	38.06	5.6	92.45	2.2
1.96	8.9	40.01	5.5	93.19	2.1
2.28	8.8	41.97	5.4	93.86	2.0
2.63	8.7	43.97	5.3	94.49	1.9
3.01	8.6	45.97	5.2	95.08	1.8
3.43	8.5	47.98	5.1	95.62	1.7
3.89	8.4	50.00	5.0	96.11	1.6
4.38	8.3	52.02	4.9	96.57	1.5
4.92	8.2	54.03	4.8	96.99	1.4
5.51	8.1	56.03	4.7	97.37	1.3
6.14	8.0	58.03	4.6	97.72	1.2
6.81	7.9	59.99	4.5	98.04	1.1
7.55	7.8	61.94	4.4	98.32	1.0
8.33	7.7	63.85	4.3	98.58	.9
9.17	7.6	65.75	4.2	98.82	.8
10.06	7.5	67.48	4.1	99.03	.7
11.03	7.4	69.39	4.0	99.22	.6
12.04	7.3	71.14	3.9	99.39	.5
13.11	7.2	72.85	3.8	99.55	.4
14.25	7.1	74.52	3.7	99.68	.3
15.44	7.0	76.12	3.6	99.80	.2
16.69	6.9	77.68	3.5	99.91	.1
18.01	6.8	79.17	3.4	100.00	.0
19.39	6.7	80.61	3.3		
20.83	6.6	81.99	3.2		

TABLE 4—2.   Illustration of transmuting ranks to linear scores •

Job title	Rank	Per cent position	Scale or linear score
Adjuster	1	8.33	7.7
Collection Clerk	2	25.00	6.3
Refund Clerk	3	41.66	5.4
Mail Order Clerk	4	58.33	4.6
Transfer Clerk	5	75.00	3.7
Information Clerk	6	91.66	2.3

$$\text{Per cent position} = \frac{100\ (R - .5)}{N}$$

necessary to use raters who know some of the jobs thoroughly and who will not rank the jobs with which they are not familiar.

Garrett [12] believes that merely averaging the ranks assigned to a job by several raters is the best technique from the point of view of simplicity and time required and that it is as accurate as the one illustrated. The last column in Table 4–3 shows the ranks which were obtained when the ranks assigned to each job by the three raters were averaged and reranked. The next to the last column in

TABLE 4—3.   Ranks transmuted into units of amount •

Job *	Ranks Rater 1	2	3	Units of amount 1	2	3	Total	Avg.	Comb'd Rank Units of amt.	Avg. of ranks
A	1		1	8.7		8.3	17.0	8.5	1	1
B	2	4		7.8	6.4		14.2	7.1	3	3.5
C	3	2	3	7.3	7.5	6.6	21.4	7.1	3	2
D	4		2	6.9		7.3	14.2	7.1	3	3.5
E	5	1	7	6.5	8.5	4.8	19.8	6.6	5	5
F	6	3	5	6.2	6.9	5.6	18.7	6.2	6	6
G	7	5		5.9	6.0		11.9	5.9	7	7.5
H	8		4	5.6		6.1	11.7	5.8	8	7.5
I	9	6	6	5.4	5.7	5.2	16.3	5.4	9	9
J	10	9	10	5.1	4.7	3.4	13.2	4.4	12.5	11
K	11	7	8	4.9	5.3	4.4	14.6	4.9	10	10
L	12	10		4.6	4.3		8.9	4.5	11	13
M	13	8	9	4.4	5.0	3.9	13.3	4.4	12.5	12
N	14	11		4.1	4.0		8.1	4.0	14	14
O	15	13		3.8	3.1		6.9	3.5	16	16
P	16	12		3.5	3.6		7.1	3.6	15	16
Q	17		11	3.1		2.7	5.8	2.9	17	16
R	18	14		2.7	2.5		5.2	2.6	18	19
S	19		12	2.2		1.7	3.9	1.6	19	18
T	20	15		1.3	1.5		2.8	1.4	20	20

* Letters are used rather than job titles because the ranks are the important part and the listing of job titles would cause unnecessary confusion.

[12] H. E. Garrett, "An Empirical Study of Various Methods of Combining Incomplete Order of Merit Ratings," *Journal of Educational Psychology*, XV (1924), pp. 157–172.

the same figure shows the ranks based upon the average of the units of amount. Naturally, there is a high degree of agreement between the two sets of ranks, since both are based upon the same data. A good rule to follow is to transmute ranks to units of amount whenever the raters give rather incomplete data. When only one or two jobs are missing from the submitted rankings, little harm can result from averaging the ranks.

Step 5. Integrating Department Rankings. When the jobs in each department have been ranked, the next step is to combine the department rankings into a single set of ranks. It would obviously be impossible to rank several hundred jobs from ten to fifteen departments into a single set of ranks without some overlapping of ranks. Since the objective of such a procedure is to arrive at a series of labor grades, one technique would be to make job comparisons across department lines in an attempt to key the jobs to each other. Figure 4–5 shows a chart which can be used in making such comparisons.

The Bookkeeping Department jobs have been tentatively ranked, but the distance between adjacent jobs can be changed as the jobs in the remaining departments are ranked. Suppose, for example, that the top ranking job in the Cost Department is Senior Cost Accountant. When comparing this job with the position of Senior Accountant in the Bookkeeping Department, it could fall at a higher level, at the same level, or at a lower level. By placing this job where it ought to fall, the remaining jobs in the Cost Department can be assigned levels comparable to the jobs in the Bookkeeping Department. After this has been accomplished, the positions of the jobs in the Bookkeeping Department can be reviewed. The positions in the Factory Payroll Department can then be compared with those in the first two departments. This procedure is followed for the remaining departments so that the final classification resembles that made by Hopwood and illustrated on page 86.

The use of independent raters for this step is recommended, but since few can be found who know all of the jobs in all of the departments, a committee to integrate the various jobs must sometimes be substituted.

The *Informational Manual on Industrial Job Evaluation Systems* [13] describes this step as follows:

[13] *Informational Manual on Industrial Job Evaluation Systems,* War Manpower Commission, Bureau of Manpower Utilization, Division of Occupational Analysis and Manning Tables (August, 1943), pp. 6–7.

When all the departmental rankings have been made, it is necessary to combine them into one organizational ranking. This combining necessitates agreement between department heads and their supervisors on interdepartmental relationships, which at times may be quite difficult to establish, because consideration of the present job holder and his salary may color the determination of the interdepartmental relations. This is best done by the use of an organization chart which lists each department on a separate line with its ranking of the individual jobs extended horizontally. Individual jobs and also departments can then be compared vertically and the relationships among them determined.

BOOKKEEPING	COST DEPARTMENT	FACTORY PAYROLL	OFFICE PAYROLL	SECRETARIAL	PERSONNEL	PRODUCTION CONTROL
Senior Accountant						
Bookkeeper						
Cashier						
Accounting Clerk						
Bookkeeping Machine Operator						
Comptometer Operator						
War Bond Record Clerk						
Clerk Stenographer						

Fig. 4—5.   Departmental job comparison chart.

From the organizational ranking obtained by collating the departmental rankings, it is possible to determine the number of groups or grades of jobs that are present in the organization. These groups or grades may then be carefully defined to insure the proper future allocation of new or revised jobs.

THE GRADE-DESCRIPTION METHOD

This system, sometimes called the classification system, consists in sorting all the jobs being evaluated into grades or classes which have been predetermined and arranged in order of importance. These grades are usually established in advance by a committee composed of persons in the organization who have a clear picture of all the jobs in the organization.

In order to set up a series of grades or classes, some analysis of the positions to be classified must be made. One of the clearest statements of the meaning of grade classification is found in the work of the Committee on Position-Classification and Pay Plans in the Public Service.[14]

Reduced to its simplest terms, classification of positions means the process of finding out, by obtaining the facts and analyzing them, what different kinds or "classes" of positions, calling for different treatment in personnel processes, there are in the service; it further includes making a systematic record of the classes found and of the particular positions found to be of each class. The duties and responsibilities of the positions are the basis upon which classes are determined and the individual positions assigned or "allocated" to their appropriate classes.

This method assumes that the classes will be established on the basis of duties and responsibilities. The committee report goes on to say that the allocation of positions to classes is based upon the essential characteristics of the work performed and not upon the education, experience, background, or ability that the incumbent employees happen to possess or lack.

A threefold classification, Unskilled, Semiskilled, and Skilled, can be used to classify certain types of jobs. When these three grades are properly defined in terms of job duties and responsibilities, the job analyst can place jobs in the appropriate grade without too much difficulty. A more elaborate system of grades is illustrated by the classification of office positions made by E. H. Little for

[14] *Position-Classification in the Public Service,* Civil Service Assembly of the United States and Canada (Chicago: 1942), p. 3.

the United States Rubber Company. This is based on prior work of Dr. Marian Bills. The groupings are as follows: [15]

A. Work of office-boy or messenger-boy character.

B. Simple operations. Use of a few definite rules. Routine operations performed under close supervision.

    1. Simple clerical work requiring no experience; or training, but no experience, on simple machines, such as sorting, key punch, ditto and adding machines.

    2. Simple clerical work but requiring some experience to perform job satisfactorily.

    3. Outside training but little experience on more difficult machines, such as, typewriter, non-listing calculators, multigraph, etc.

C. Requiring recognized clerical ability. Application of a large number of rules though definite and specific; or considerable experience on machines listed under B-3.

    1. Requiring recognized clerical ability, but the exercise of no definite responsibility, either because of the character of the work, or the closeness of supervision.

    2. Experienced operators on following machines: typewriter, non-listing calculators, bookkeeping and tabulating machines.

    3. Work of C-1 character but of a more responsible nature.

D. Requiring complete and intensive knowledge of a restricted field.

    1. As above.

    2. Work of D Grade plus supervisory responsibility of a minor character.

E. Requiring knowledge of general policies; command of general rules and principles with application to cases not previously covered and may require long experience with the Company.

    1. Work of the above character where experience is not necessarily long but must have been gained within the Company.

    2. Work of a more technical or more difficult character, but experience not necessarily within the Company.

    3. Work of E-1 Grade plus supervisory responsibility.

    4. Work of E-2 Grade with long experience with the Company. Or work of D Grade which is not subject to check and therefore where the promotion of the employee on the job is generally undesirable.

F. Work of a highly technical confidential nature or of semi-executive supervisory character.

    1. Highly technical or confidential work.

    2. Semi-executive and supervisory in character.

Little's grading scheme is actually a rating scale. Any criticism of such a system is a criticism of it as a method of rating or grading

[15] E. H. Little, *Some Considerations in Installing a Salary Administration Plan,* Office Executives' Series No. 27 (New York: American Management Association, 1927), p. 10.

jobs. The grade-description method may lack specificity among the different grades and it may be difficult to explain to the workers, but as a method it can be made specific and it is useful.

J. O. Hopwood [16] constructed a classification scheme for grading positions for the Philadelphia Electric Company. Figure 4–6 outlines the gradation of all the positions in the organization by a scale of service grades. Numbers are used to indicate the grades, and letters are used to indicate further division within the grades. It should be kept in mind that Figure 4–6 presents material in outline form, and that an evaluation method such as this should be based upon more detailed statements of characteristics and responsibilities.

Additional material given by Hopwood to illustrate the two dimensions of job classification is shown in Figure 4–7. Levels and grades are indicated vertically in this chart, and functions are shown horizontally. According to Hopwood, "There is no basis for ranking one class of functions higher than another, except as the jobs which it includes may be graded higher. Accounting, for example, may outrank designing because it contains jobs of a higher level or the reverse may be true in some organizations."

Figure 4–7 contains not only service grades and functional classes, but also rate ranges and minimum intelligence levels. Rate ranges can be determined at the same time that the grade-description method is constructed, but it is probably better to establish the classification scheme first, and to determine wages after all of the jobs have been classified.

Many organizations have established rough job classes on which they attempted to set descriptive limits. A rough classification is the beginning of an evaluation method. Since one of the objectives of job evaluation is to establish labor grades or position classifications, this might serve as a rating scale for a complete review of all jobs in the organizational unit being studied. The grade-description method is definitely a nonquantitative approach to setting values on each job in an organization. In spite of the many faults it is reported to have, the method is worthy of consideration for companies that do not find feasible or necessary the use of a more elaborate system. Before discussing the construction of a grade-description scale, some of the advantages and disadvantages of this method of job evaluation should be examined.

[16] J. O. Hopwood, "Administration of Wages and Salaries," *Personnel*, American Management Association, Vol. 11, No. 4 (May 1935), pp. 103–106.

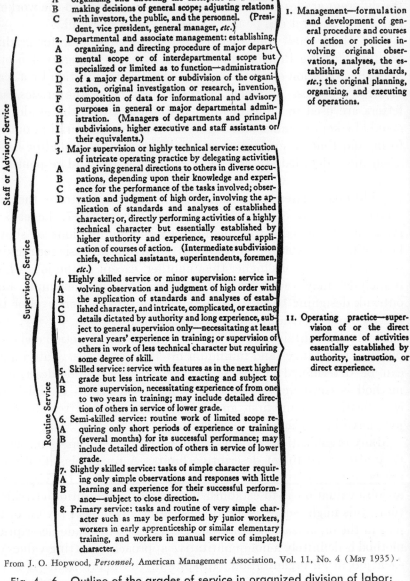

1. General management: establishing general procedure,
   A organizing and directing the enterprise as a whole;
   B making decisions of general scope; adjusting relations
   C with investors, the public, and the personnel. (President, vice president, general manager, *etc.*)

2. Departmental and associate management: establishing,
   A organizing, and directing procedure of major depart-
   B mental scope or of interdepartmental scope but
   C specialized or limited as to function—administration
   D of a major department or subdivision of the organi-
   E zation, original investigation or research, invention,
   F composition of data for informational and advisory
   G purposes in general or major departmental admin-
   H istration. (Managers of departments and principal
   I subdivisions, higher executive and staff assistants or
   J their equivalents.)

3. Major supervision or highly technical service: execution
   of intricate operating practice by delegating activities
   A and giving general directions to others in diverse occu-
   B pations, depending upon their knowledge and experi-
   C ence for the performance of the tasks involved; obser-
   D vation and judgment of high order, involving the application of standards and analyses of established
   character; or, directly performing activities of a highly
   technical character but essentially established by
   higher authority and experience, resourceful application of courses of action. (Intermediate subdivision
   chiefs, technical assistants, superintendents, foremen,
   etc.)

4. Highly skilled service or minor supervision: service in-
   A volving observation and judgment of high order with
   B the application of standards and analyses of estab-
   C lished character, and intricate, complicated, or exacting
   D details dictated by authority and long experience, subject to general supervision only—necessitating at least
   several years' experience in training; or supervision of
   others in work of less technical character but requiring
   some degree of skill.

5. Skilled service: service with features as in the next higher
   A grade but less intricate and exacting and subject to
   B more supervision, necessitating experience of from one
   to two years in training; may include detailed direction of others in service of lower grade.

6. Semi-skilled service: routine work of limited scope re-
   A quiring only short periods of experience or training
   B (several months) for its successful performance; may
   include detailed direction of others in service of lower
   grade.

7. Slightly skilled service: tasks of simple character requir-
   A ing only simple observations and responses with little
   B learning and experience for their successful perform-
   ance—subject to close direction.

8. Primary service: tasks and routine of very simple character such as may be performed by junior workers,
   workers in early apprenticeship or similar elementary
   training, and workers in manual service of simplest
   character.

Executive Service

Staff or Advisory Service

Supervisory Service

Routine Service

I. Management—formulation and development of general procedure and courses of action or policies involving original observations, analyses, the establishing of standards, *etc.*; the original planning, organizing, and executing of operations.

II. Operating practice—supervision of or the direct performance of activities essentially established by authority, instruction, or direct experience.

From J. O. Hopwood, *Personnel,* American Management Association, Vol. 11, No. 4 (May 1935).

Fig. 4—6. Outline of the grades of service in organized division of labor; classification scheme for grading positions, grades, and sub-grades.

Advantages and disadvantages

The major disadvantage of the grade-description method is the extreme care required in writing the grade descriptions. It is difficult to write a single general statement which describes such factors as complexity of duties, nonsupervisory and supervisory responsi-

Service Grades		Accounting	Boiler Operating	Clerical Service	Designing	Gen'l Administration	Machine Construction	Selling	Rate Ranges Monthly Basis	Minimum Intelligence Grades
I. Management: 1. General management	A					President			1600–2250	A
	B					Vice-President			1400–2000	A
	C								1250–1750	A
	D					General Manager			1125–1500	A
	E								1000–1325	A
2. Departmental and associate management	A	Controller							890–1175	B
	B								810–1075	B
	C								725–975	B
	D								650–875	B
	E	General Auditor							575–785	B
	F								510–700	B
	G				Mechan. Engineer			Sales Manager	450–625	B
	H								400–560	B
	I	Auditor				Executive Assistant	Plant Supt.		350–500	B
	J								315–450	B
II. Operating practice: 3. Supervision or highly technical service	A	Senior Account.			Chief Designer		General Foreman	Jobbing Salesman	280–400	B
	B								250–360	B
	C	Accountant			Senior Designer		Shop Foreman		225–325	C+
	D			Chief Clerk A					200–295	C+
4. Highly skilled or minor supervision	A	Junior Account.	Boiler Engineer	Chief Clerk B	Designer		Machinist 1st Class	Senior Salesman	180–265	C+
	B			Senior Clerk A					160–235	C+
	C	Book-keeper	Asst. Blr. Engineer	Senior Clerk B	Asst. Designer		Machinist 2nd Class	Salesman	140–210	C
	D								125–185	C
5. Skilled service	A	Assist. Bookkpr.	Boiler Operator	Clerk A	Junior Designer		Bench Hand	Junior Salesman	110–165	C
	B				Senior Draftsman				95–145	C
6. Semi-skilled service	A		Stoker Operator	Clerk B	Draftsman		Machinist Helper		80–130	C–
	B		Head Ashman		Junior Draftsman		Special Laborer		70–115	C–
7. Slightly skilled service	A		Ashman	Asst. Clerk	Tracer		Laborer		60–100	D
	B								50–85	D
8. Primary service				Junior Clerk	Junior Tracer		Shop Boy		40–75	D–

From J. O. Hopwood, *Personnel*, American Management Association, Vol. 11, No. 4 (May 1935).

Fig. 4—7. Table of classification (titles, placements, and rate ranges are illustratıve only).

bilities, and necessary qualifications. Each grade must be described in fairly general terms, but these general terms must be such that a job with specific duties and sometimes unique responsibilities and qualifications can be compared with them. If they are too general, the assignment of jobs to the grades will be unreliable. If they are too specific, they probably will not cover all of the jobs being classified.

It often happens that a job has tasks which fall at several grade-description levels. When this occurs it is difficult to determine the grade-description level for the job. Some responsible positions have a certain amount of routine work which must be performed; some routine jobs include a few tasks that fall at a high level of difficulty. Confusion results when the grade-description scale is applied to jobs like these. Someone must decide whether to classify the job on the basis of the highest skill demanded or at the level where a majority of the duties fall. If the former policy is followed, some routine jobs with a single difficult task could be given an unwarranted rating. If the second alternative is followed, the job analyst must not only secure a job description but determine the amount of time spent performing each task, and since jobs are not static, the establishment of a set time for each task is difficult if not impossible.

The major advantage of the grade-description type of job-evaluation scale is that most firms and workers have some rough conception of the general classification structure into which various jobs fall. Starting with these general conceptions, it is relatively easy to arrive at a job-classification structure which fits the immediate needs of the organization. Sometimes this rough classification is based upon present salaries; sometimes it is based upon the importance or difficulty of the jobs. The procedure makes it relatively easy to secure general agreement about the classification of a majority of the jobs.

In describing the classification structure of Bills and Little, reported on page 84, Moore [17] writes as follows:

The difficulty with such a classification is its lack of specificity among the different grades, and the consequent lack of meaning it has for the different workers whose promotional possibilities are determined by it. To tell a worker that his position involves the "application of a large number of definite and specific rules," and that the position of a fellow worker involves "command of general rules and principles with application to cases not previously covered," gives him no idea of the relation between the two positions, or of the qualities necessary for the second position, or of the kind of training through which he must go in order to get to his desired goal.

It should be pointed out that this statement is not exactly fair to the system proposed by Bills and Little. In the first place, the

[17] Herbert Moore, *Psychology for Business and Industry* (New York: McGraw-Hill Book Company, Inc., 1942), pp. 295–304.

grade descriptions were probably intended primarily for management use and were designed for a unilateral job evaluation. In the second place, such terms as "definite rules," "specific rules," "general rules and principles," "command of," and "cases not previously covered" are either defined or take on meaning which permit consistent application of the scale to job classification. In the third place, it is the job descriptions which should contain the "qualities necessary for the second position" and the "kind of training through which he must go to get to his desired goal." Including the qualifications and training requirements for each job in the grade-description scale itself would make it so detailed that no one could possibly use it for job classification. The grades as described by Bills and Little are probably not as specific as might be desired, but making them too specific would make it more difficult to classify a job than to use a general definition for each grade.

The grade-description scale should be used to describe the level of the job to the worker. The job descriptions should be designed to show him why that level was selected and also to show him the duties, training requirements, responsibilities, and the qualifications necessary to perform his job satisfactorily.

After a firm has completed a job evaluation by means of some method other than grade description and has set up a series of classes or labor grades, it is relatively easy to build a grade-description scale. In fact, many firms do have a verbal description for each labor grade and in time tend to think of jobs in these terms. For example, referring to a job as "grade 5 level" or as a "class 2 job" is a method of conveying the meaning of job difficulty and job worth to others. When an organization begins to think of its jobs in terms of grade-description levels it is beginning to use job evaluation in a way which aids salary and wage administration. For those who have had machine-shop experience and who are acquainted with skilled-trade classifications, the terms Machinist A, Machinist B, and Toolmaker A have real meaning and convey an idea of job difficulty, job content, and job worth which would be desirable for all positions in the organization. The grade-description method tends to integrate this type of meaning into the job-classification structure more quickly than the other job-evaluation methods.

Preparing the grade-description scale

It was stated above that jobs must be classified according to type and to level. The grade-description method is an evaluation technique designed to classify jobs of a single type according to level.

The first step, therefore, is to decide upon the type of position which is to be classified by the grade-description scale. The usual breakdown of jobs according to type is shown below.

1. Factory	3. Supervisory
2. Clerical	4. Sales

If the organization is very large, a finer breakdown can be constructed. For example, the factory jobs could have the following breakdown:

1. Factory
    a. Machine Operations
    b. Manual Operations
    c. Skilled (Crafts)
    d. Inspection

A grade-description scale could then be constructed for each type of factory job. Since such a fine breakdown is not needed in most organizations, the grade-description scales to be illustrated will cover only the main types of jobs. The original and most frequent breakdown of factory, clerical, supervisory, and sales could be changed to: factory, including supervision; clerical, including supervision; and sales.

The purpose of pointing out these different major types of jobs is to emphasize the fact that the first step in constructing a scale according to the grade-description method is to determine the types of jobs to be evaluated. The task of constructing a usable grade-description scale is thus made much easier than it would be if the types of jobs to be evaluated were not limited beforehand.

Determining the number of grades or classes

The number of grades or classes partially depends upon the history of the company, that is, the traditional number of job classes which have been used in the payment of workers. One other consideration is the range of jobs or positions to be covered by the scale. If the scale is to be applied only to jobs below the supervisory level, there would obviously be fewer grades than there would be if supervisory level jobs were included. In the Westinghouse classification, for example, the jobs covered ranged from unskilled to those at the policy-making level. By the use of broad classes the wide variety of positions were assigned to relatively few grades. As one examines the broad classifications used by Westinghouse,[18] Un-

---

[18] *Salaried Employment Policy, Position Analysis and Classification*, Industrial Relations Manual, Westinghouse Electric and Manufacturing Co. (1936).

skilled, Skilled, Interpretative, Creative, Executive, Administrative, and Policy-Making, it can be seen that levels within these classes are required.

A minimum of six or seven grades and a maximum of seventeen or twenty will cover most of the systems in use today. There seems to be a trend toward fewer classes of jobs within a wage structure. Lytle [19] believes that ten to twelve classes are optimum. The determination of the number of grades to be used in the grade-description method depends upon such factors as:

1. Type of job included
2. Range of salary or wage
3. Range of job skills
4. Company upgrading policy
5. Policy of promotion within a grade
6. Collective bargaining considerations
7. Tradition in the industry

In general, from six to twelve classes should meet the needs of most organizations. If the salary range of the jobs being evaluated is great the number of grades selected will probably be greater than when the range is small. Similarly, the greater the range of skills, the greater the number of grades required. In a plant studied by one of the authors, the range of skills in the factory where 100 workers were employed was very narrow because the jobs covered simple assembly tasks only. In another organization employing approximately 150 workers the range of skills was very broad. In the first instance, 6 labor grades were required and in the second, the jobs were classified into 11 grades. Some organizations prefer to advance employees by upgrading; others promote by increasing salaries within a grade. In the former instance it is desirable to have a large number of labor grades. Some organizations use as many as 22 grades, and in these instances upgrading is fairly common. When an organization uses only a few labor grades, there is a tendency to have a relatively wide wage range so that increasing salary within the grade is used as a reward for merit. An example of the former technique would be an employee reclassified from Assembly Worker Class D to Assembly Worker Class C and given an increase in salary at the same time. Whenever a bilateral study is made, the question of number of labor grades is a matter of joint decision: the wishes of both management and the worker are considered. It is difficult to violate tradition when industry or local plants have been using

[19] Charles W. Lytle, *Job Evaluation Methods* (New York: The Ronald Press Company, 1946), p. 136.

a set number of labor grades, so the selection of number of grades should depend in part upon previous experience in the organization making the job evaluation study.

Writing the grade descriptions

An examination of most grade-description scales shows some lack of consistency and uniformity in the descriptions for each grade. The worker, when required to describe his own job, or the job analyst is asked to cover such points as duties, contacts with others, responsibilities, and supervision given and received. In judging the total worth of a job the persons making the judgments are asked to cover such factors as difficulty of work, volume of work, responsibility, supervision received, supervision given, experience required, special knowledge necessary, and special training required either on the job or before being assigned to it. As pointed out in *Job Evaluation Systems*,[20]

It is first necessary to set up certain job levels or grades and define these job levels in terms of the elements of the jobs in the organization, in which the duties and responsibilities are clearly defined for each level. Such a system must be based on the principles of variation in difficulty, as represented by the number and kind of rules which regulate the work done, and the degrees of responsibility, as indicated by whether or not the operations are subject to check.

If the jobs are described and analyzed in a set manner, each grade level must be defined in terms of the major areas covered in the job analysis. What these major areas are depends upon what the persons evaluating the jobs have decided is important. The areas may also vary with the type of job being evaluated. Most grade descriptions mention these general areas:

1. Type of work and complexity of duties
2. Education necessary for performing the job
3. Experience necessary for performing the job
4. Supervision given and received
5. Responsibilities
6. Effort demanded

Riegel [21] gives an illustration of an occupational grading procedure that contains valuable information. The employer and employee

---

[20] *Informational Manual on Job Evaluation Systems*, War Manpower Commission Bureau of Manpower Utilization, Division of Occupational Analysis and Manning Tables (August 1943), p. 7.

[21] John W. Riegel, *Wage Determination*, Bureau of Industrial Relations (Ann Arbor: University of Michigan Press, 1937), pp. 63–64.

representatives in the company were asked to remember these factors when comparing one occupation with another:

a. Supervision and leadership of subordinates; organizing, training, and directing them; welding them into a loyal and effective working unit.

b. Cooperation with associates who are not in the line of authority and with non-employees of the Corporation; exchange of opinions on controversial matters involving tact, diplomacy, appreciation of the other persons' problems and point of view, etc.; necessity for and degree of teamwork; exchange of information, etc.

c. Probability and consequence of errors, assuming that the occupation is filled by an experienced, conscientious employee. Graders should consider typical errors that are apt to be made and the consequences of each in terms of waste, damage to equipment, delays, complaints, confusion, spoilage of product, discrepancies, etc.

d. Initiative and resourcefulness; requirements concerning originality, creativeness, exercising judgment, analyzing conditions and independently reaching decisions, planning, estimating, dealing with variables, etc.; extent to which supervision is received.

e. Minimum experience requirements, including both preliminary experience and experience on the occupation; estimated time required for inexperienced but otherwise qualified person to reach a satisfactory degree of proficiency.

f. Minimum education requirements; amount of schooling or study absolutely necessary to successfully fill the occupation.

If the original grade descriptions are defined in the terms used in making occupational comparisons, the use of the grade-description method will be relatively easy. Jobs differ so much in content that a classification based on value or worth of content alone is impossible. Since classification depends first of all upon similarities, such factors as the above, that are common to most jobs, are important in writing grade descriptions. Few of the existing systems, however, describe the grades in terms like those used by Riegel. Including all factors in the description for each grade is perhaps not necessary, but if a job is to be described in a certain manner and later is to be compared with the description of each grade, the grade descriptions should be in terms of the job descriptions. Coordinating the material of the job descriptions with the grade descriptions is the first step in constructing a grade-description scale.

Riegel [22] gives an illustration of a classification plan for evaluating clerical positions. It is somewhat similar to the one proposed by Hopwood (see page 87). It gives both the class level and

[22] John W. Riegel, *Salary Determination*, Report No. 2, Bureau of Industrial Relations (Ann Arbor: University of Michigan Press, 1940), p. 112.

class description. There is a classification for each set of closely related services; one classification for routine clerical services, a second for operators of office machines, a third for clerical supervisors, and a fourth for maintenance employees. Figure 4–8 gives the plan for clerical employees in detail. In assigning a clerical job to one of these grades, the job analyst is also assigning a salary to the job. An examination of Figure 4–8 shows that two grades, D and F, are missing. Although Riegel gives no reason for this omission, it does provide an opportunity to observe the effect when two class levels are omitted.

CLASS   DESCRIPTION OF WORK

A. Messenger service jobs. Frequently combined with sorting and the operation of simple machines, to fill in time; but the messenger service is the chief duty, characteristic of the class.

B. Manual clerical operations requiring knowledge of a limited number of well-defined rules. This class of positions includes some of the filing jobs, some of the identification work, some of the posting and computing jobs, and, in general, those jobs where only a definite and specific change is made in the material handled.
    Doing the work, subject to check.
    Checking the work, or doing the work without subsequent check, or having charge of a small unit of the work.

C. Positions in which the operations require knowledge of a large number of rules which are, however, precise and explicit. Any points not clearly covered by these rules are referred to the supervisor.
    Doing the work, subject to check.
    Checking the work, or doing it without subsequent check, or handling the more difficult C details, or having charge of a small unit of C work.

E. Positions in which the operations require complete and intensive knowledge of a restricted field and action on questions not previously raised, calling for application of a general rule to a particular transaction.
    Doing the work, subject to check.
    Checking the work, handling doubtful papers, requiring adjustments of difficulties, making special calculations or doing the more complicated E work.

G. Positions calling for technical training, professional background, or knowledge of the general principles of the business.
    Doing the usual work on this level.
    Handling the more complicated problems.

Fig. 4—8. Clerical positions—grade description.

A second illustration, given by Gray,[23] shows a grade-description scale for both clerical employees and shop and service employees. His descriptions of job classes were based upon the ranking of the jobs: the definitions of each grade were written after the jobs were assigned to classes. The definitions are presented in Figure 4–9.

Although these grade descriptions are rather rough classifications,

[23] Robert D. Gray, *Classification of Jobs in Small Companies*, Bulletin No. 5, Industrial Relations Section (Pasadena: California Institute of Technology, 1944), p. 21.

they serve the purpose of bringing together jobs similar in worth or difficulty. The classification of all clerical jobs into three groups and all factory jobs into five groups, including some supervisory jobs, is somewhat unusual. Other grade-description scales usually have a finer breakdown of jobs.

CLERICAL EMPLOYEES

Class

C-1 Routine clerical work such as typing; simple repetitive calculations; work under close supervision following definite rules.

C-2 Secretarial and advanced clerical work in which substantial judgment, discretion, and initiative are involved.

C-3 Supervision of three or more persons doing C-1 or C-2 work; substantial knowledge of some specialized field such as accounting; complicated calculations.

SHOP AND SERVICE EMPLOYEES

S-1 Repetitive work under immediate supervision and involving no unusual hazard or extra effort; requires no previous training.
Example: watchman; janitor.

S-2 Repetitive work under general supervision; repetitive work under immediate supervision, but involving unusual hazard or extra physical or mental application; no special training before employment, and very short training on the job.
Example: guard; routine inspection or assembly; box maker.

S-3 Semi-skilled work requiring exercise of judgment by employee in making decisions; specialized training or experience in operating tools required.
Example: difficult assembly and inspection; rough carpentry; operation of machine tools to moderate tolerances.

S-4 Skilled work involving broad knowledge of a recognized trade; read and interpret difficult blueprints; responsibility for materials and equipment; set up and operation of a variety of machine tools to close tolerances.
Example: machinist; plumber; carpenter; steamfitter; electrician; supervision of S-2 or S-3 work.

S-5 Supervision of S-3 or S-4 work; precision work; highest degree of skill and experience; requires knowledge of two or more skilled trades.
Example: tool and die maker; instrument maker; pattern maker; lens grinder.

Fig. 4—9. Description of job classes.

Two general methods can be followed in writing grade descriptions for use in job evaluation. The first method is illustrated in Figure 4–9. The jobs are classified before grade descriptions are written. Gray points out that in smaller companies the over-all classification of the job can be made immediately without resorting to a complicated system such as point rating. "Whenever it appears, therefore, that there are a small number of jobs to to be appraised and when it is not necessary to determine minute differences among them, it is possible to develop a job-classification plan by grading each job as a whole in accordance with its difficulty and importance." [24] Since a committee rather than a single person should be assigned the task of grading jobs, uniform instructions should be issued to all members of the committee. The instructions given by Gray are reproduced in Figure 4–10.

The Job Classification Committee has been established to make recommendations on the specific grade or class to which jobs should be assigned.

It is important that each member of the Committee study the job descriptions carefully and develop his own classification or grading of these jobs before the Committee meets. Differences in classification made by various members will be ironed out in the meetings.

As a member of the Committee it is important that you perform the following operations before the next meeting:

A. Read the job descriptions.

B. Group them into appropriate grades or classes.

This step can be made as follows:

1. Read one job description carefully.

2. Read another job description carefully and then make a decision as to whether the second job should be put in the same classification as the first one or should be placed in a higher or lower classification.

3. Read a third job description and decide how this job compares with the first two jobs classified.

4. Repeat this operation until all other jobs have been classified. You may have arranged the jobs in rank order or you may have decided that several jobs are of the same rank order. *Notice that it is the job or job description that is classified—not the man on the job.*

In ranking these jobs it may be of value to pay particular attention to the general "difficulty" of the job. In measuring this you can consider such factors as: (a) length of training or experience required for the job, (b) the number and variety of duties performed, and (c) "responsibility" of the job as measured in terms of effect on cost, supervision of others, and safety of others. In appraising responsibility for supervision it may be desirable to consider the number of people supervised, the number of functions supervised, and the "difficulty" or "importance" of work supervised.

Minor differences among jobs, especially those arising from poor working conditions, unusual hours, or accident hazards, may be indicated by using a + mark. Thus in the lowest job classification there may be some jobs rated as 1 and others as 1+. No consideration should be given to characteristics such as honesty or dependability because these characteristics are required of all personnel.

Be prepared to bring to the Committee meeting a summary of your recommendations. This summary should indicate the names of jobs assigned to each of the classes you were able to distinguish. The number "1" should be given to the lowest-rated class. It is probable that the minimum class can be readily discovered at present whereas the top class may not become apparent for some time.

At the meeting of the Committee the ratings or classifications given by each member will be summarized and tabulated in order that we may readily see how much uniformity of opinion exists. In your classification you may bear in mind the possibility of having a minimum number of classifications with a substantial range in rates.

Fig. 4—10.   Instructions to members of the job classification committee.

[24] *Ibid*, pp. 15–18.

After the committee members have finished the classification, they will discover that the number of grades is limited. Once the jobs have been classified, the descriptions of the jobs assigned to each class are used as the basis for writing each grade definition. Gray's technique makes it possible to use jobs as illustrations for each grade shown.

The same method of securing grade descriptions can be used when either a factor-comparison or a point-rating system is used. Whenever a number of jobs are sorted into "pay groups" these can be called grades or classes. The jobs and their descriptions in each pay group can be used as the basis for writing the grade descriptions. All systems of job evaluation can be used to serve as the basis for writing grade descriptions if the similar jobs are placed into a reasonable number of groups. Grade-description scales can then serve as the basis for the classification of new jobs and for the re-evaluation of old ones which have changed in difficulty or content. It is not necessary, of course, to use these grade descriptions to evaluate jobs, but the possibility of doing so is present in all job evaluation methods.

In a study of factory jobs made by the authors for The National Screw and Manufacturing Company, approximately 550 jobs were placed in eight classes or labor grades, and grade descriptions written for presentation to the War Labor Board.[25] These class descriptions were not prepared to serve as grade descriptions, but with a little editing and rewriting they could serve that purpose. Figure 4–11 gives the preliminary class descriptions for these factory jobs.

The second method of constructing a grade-description scale is to establish a number of predetermined grades in advance of the job classification. A committee describes the grades, and after the scale has been constructed the jobs are then assigned to these grades. If job descriptions are available for reference, it will be easier for individuals to construct appropriate grade-description scales. In fact, it is absolutely necessary for the individuals either to have job descriptions available for study or to have a thorough knowledge of the duties and requirements for all of the jobs in the unit being evaluated. The definitions are usually written first for the two extreme grades. Describing the lowest grade level is relatively easy.

---

[25] This study was made under the direct supervision of Dr. Franklin G. Moore, Consultant for the Personnel Research Institute at Western Reserve University, Cleveland, Ohio.

Class 1

Jobs included in Class 1 are very simple. None requires over one month of experience and most can be learned satisfactorily in one week. Light laboring jobs such as janitor or sweeper and other light unskilled jobs are in this class. Many jobs having to do with packing the product come in this category. Often the most difficult part of the job is that the worker must be on his feet nearly all of the time.

Class 2

This class includes more jobs and more employees than any other. Most of these are concentrated on the numerous semi-automatic machine feeding, sorting and inspecting jobs. Most of the laboring jobs in the plant also fall within this bracket. Helpers and service men as well as learners on machine jobs are for the most part included here too. So also are operators of relatively simple equipment. As a rule the experience requirements for jobs in Class 2 run between one week and three months. Responsibility on these jobs are usually very small although they often rate high on effort.

Class 3

Almost as many jobs are included in Class 3 as in Class 2. Operators of machines of medium difficulty are included here. Inspection jobs involving responsibility and discretion are in this class. Most of the jobs involving learning or helping to set up and operate complex machines are Class 3 jobs, as are some maintenance jobs of semi-skilled variety. This class is definitely one covering semi-skilled jobs.

Class 4

The setting up and operating of most of the plant machines are included in this class. Class 4 also covers many maintenance jobs and a variety of individual jobs involving considerable skill. Few of these jobs can be learned in less than one year and most require from one to three years of experience. Responsibilities on these jobs are usually substantial.

Class 5

Jobs in this class are all of a high degree of skill and as a rule take up to five years to learn. Most of them also involve substantial responsibilities for products and materials and frequently considerable responsibility for the work of others. Skilled maintenance jobs, setting up complex machines, and some floorman's jobs are included. These latter jobs include certain minor supervisory activities.

Class 6

Only jobs requiring a high degree of skill are in this class. Most of the small number of jobs included are floormen. On all of these, both the experience and responsibility demands of the jobs are high. The most highly skilled maintenance department jobs are also in Class 6, as are several machinist, toolmaker, and die-maker jobs. As a general rule, from five to eight years of experience is required on these jobs. An ability to work independently with only a small amount of supervision is characteristic of most of these jobs.

Class 7

This class covers jobs similar to those in Class 6 except that these are a little more exacting. There are only three jobs in this class. These are the Patternmaker, Toolmaker, Grade B, and the most difficult Floorman's job in the plant. Eight to ten years of experience is required.

Courtesy of The National Screw & Manufacturing Company, Cleveland, Ohio.

Fig. 4—11.   Classification of factory jobs—explanation of classes.

Class 8

Jobs in this class are the most difficult, and require the most skill of any jobs in the plant. The men on these jobs are expected to be able to plan and carry out their work with little supervision. Only the top toolmaker and machinist jobs merit inclusion in this bracket, and these rank here largely because the men on this work must almost be machine designers to carry out their work. Much of the equipment in the plant is especially built, or is very old, and parts must be designed and made by these men. These jobs, calling for from eight to ten years of experience, are the top jobs in the plant.

Fig. 4—11. (cont.)

Such a grade description as the following fits a simple clerical job:

Class 1. Simple routine jobs requiring no previous experience or special training; may involve routine checking or simple alphabetical and numerical filing.

At the top level we find:

Class 9. Highly responsible positions involving a considerable amount of experience and training, both general and specific. Usually responsible for a group of operations of the company. Included are some jobs of more authority and responsibility than similar jobs in Class 8.[26]

The above grade descriptions set the limits of a group of clerical jobs found in a fairly large company.

Once these two extreme classifications have been written, one desirable technique is to check the accuracy and completeness of the grade descriptions by using them to classify some of the jobs falling at the extremes. Try to grade a group of extreme jobs to make sure that the descriptions as written will serve the purpose of classification. After grading jobs that fall at the two extremes, the remaining jobs have two extreme classes: the next higher grade at the low end and the next lower grade at the high end. In the above case these are Classes 2 and 8 which are described as follows:

Class 2. Routine clerical positions requiring little experience and training, except for some high school. May include general filing, typing, simple machine operation and ordinary clerical work.

Class 8. Jobs which are highly technical in nature with responsibility for accuracy and initiative in carrying out these technical duties. Most of these include responsibility for a group of operations with some considerable latitude for individual action.

When these two grade descriptions are written, there remains the middle group, Classes 3, 4, 5, 6, and 7, to define and classify. Classes 3 and 7 are defined, then Classes 4 and 6, and finally Class 5. Some people find it easier to start at the top or the bottom and define the

---

[26] The National Screw & Manufacturing Company, Cleveland, Ohio.

grades in order. This is a good method to follow when the jobs have been ranked.

Remember that the grade-description method involves the construction of a *single rating scale* designed for the evaluation of all the jobs in the work unit for which the scale was constructed. All rules applicable to rating-scale construction should be followed in devising a grade-description method for use in job evaluation.

SUGGESTIONS FOR STUDY AND RESEARCH

1. Develop a new method of job classification which might be applied to teachers in colleges. This is a substitute for the instructor through professor classification.

2. Review the United States Civil Service Classification plan and compare it with the industrial plans outlined in this chapter.

CASE PROBLEM

Select twenty factory jobs from the Dictionary of Occupational Titles (U. S. Department of Labor). Copy the job definitions on cards, one for each job, so that each set will contain all twenty jobs. Prepare a set of cards for each student in the class. The jobs should be selected so that there will be some relatively unskilled and some highly skilled jobs. There should also be some jobs in the average range of difficulty.

PROBLEM: Follow the recommendations for using the job-ranking method as outlined in this chapter. Have half of the class use the simple ranking technique and have the other half rank the jobs by using the paired comparison method. Which method resulted in greater rater agreement? Which method was easier to use? Why were some jobs ranked high? Why were others given a low rank?

PROBLEM: Use the set of cards prepared for the problem above. Ask the students to assign the jobs to the Classification System for Factory Jobs (Table 4-11). Discuss the similarities and differences found in the ratings. Compare this method with the ranking method.

Note: Keep in mind that this is an exercise and that in actual practice complete job descriptions should be used.

5

Quantitative Systems—the Point Method

IN THE PRECEDING CHAPTER TWO TECH-
niques were outlined which are primarily nonquantitative. In the
hands of individuals skilled in their use, these techniques become
valuable tools in job classification. Some workers in the field of
job evaluation, however, prefer a classification system that assigns
numerical values to job characteristics. The attempt to quantify
in order to reduce jobs to a common denominator so that they can
be compared directly is one of the most successful methods of determining the relative difficulty of jobs. Both the factor-comparison
method and the point-rating method accomplish this.

SIMILARITY OF QUANTITATIVE SYSTEMS

There is a belief that any evaluation system, when correctly applied to a series of jobs, will result in approximately the same classification. There is need, however, for careful research to substantiate this belief. Such research should not only compare the two
quantitative systems; it should also compare the many modifications of these systems so that their differences and similarities when
applied will be made known.

The quantitative method of job evaluation makes it possible to
subject each job to thorough analysis and to divide all jobs into
finer classifications than can be obtained through the nonquanti-

tative methods of ranking and grade description. To date there has not been enough research on the application of different methods of job evaluation to the same jobs. Such comparisons should be made to determine if approximately the same classifications would be obtained when the same jobs are evaluated by different methods.

The Personnel Research Institute of Western Reserve University has made one study in this area. A large national organization with divisions in the major commercial centers of the United States instructed each division to establish a wage structure based on job-evaluation and to key its wages to the "going rates" in the local area. Each division was instructed to retain a local job-evaluation consultant to help in accomplishing this objective. The Personnel Research Institute was engaged to work with the division located in Cleveland, Ohio. There were twelve different plans based upon twelve different job-evaluation systems. A modified ranking system, point plans, and factor comparison plans were used, so most of the current job-classification plans were employed in this study. After each division had set up its own wage structure based on its own job-evaluation system, the central authority decided that it wanted a single wage plan for all of the divisions. This study was an attempt to convert these twelve systems to a common one.

The following is from the Personnel Research Institute study.[1]

Job evaluation as a technique for determining what each job in an organization is really worth has long been accepted as a fundamental activity in personnel management. Research in this field has advanced to the point where job evaluation no longer requires strenuous effort to be "sold" to management. On the contrary, management is to an ever-increasing degree seeking out the expert for help in solving its wage administration problems.

With respect to methodology, there are four basic systems of job evaluation in use today. These are: (1) the ranking system; (2) the job classification system; (3) the point system; and (4) the factor comparison system. With few exceptions, all evaluation systems are variations of these four basic systems. Personnel literature abounds with reports of results obtained with all of these systems, with the proponents of a particular system citing the advantages of their particular system and the disadvantages of other systems. To the best knowledge of the writers, however, there have been few, if any, direct comparisons of two or more systems. In spite of the dearth of research in this particular aspect of job evaluation, however, it is practically accepted as a truism among the experts that the particular system used is not nearly so important as

[1] D. J. Chesler, Jay L. Otis, and M. R. Lohmann, "The Personal Research Institute Study of the Commonality of Job Evaluation Systems: A Common Conversion Scale for Different Job Evaluation Systems." (Unpublished. Clients did not desire publication at the time the study was made.)

the integrity and accuracy with which it is installed, policed, and maintained. If most systems yield the same results, obviously the problem of deciding upon a system to adopt boils down to questions of time, ease of understanding on the part of neophytes in this type of work, and ease of installation and maintenance.

Most organizations are accustomed to and satisfied with their present systems. In spite of certain (often debatable) inadequacies and weaknesses of a particular system, nevertheless it is usually an acceptable procedure in operation, with little inclination on the part of management to make any but minor revisions, and a strong disinclination to switch to an entirely different system. This consideration is the key to the difficulties that are encountered in making direct comparisons of jobs in different organizations. In the last analysis, the problem boils down to the fact that the *unit of job worth* differs from system to system.

As may be inferred from the foregoing, one purpose of the present study was to make a direct comparison of different job evaluation systems in different organizations. The second, and primary, purpose was to develop an over-all plan, which would classify jobs of equal difficulty, organization to organization, in such a way that these jobs would fall in the same labor grade. It was not the purpose of the study to develop a common plan to replace the plans already in use in the different organizations. Rather the purpose of the over-all plan was to serve as a common measuring stick for comparisons among different systems.

Participating Organizations and Types of Job Evaluation Systems in Use

The organizations participating in the study were the **12** divisions of a large (unnamed) organization. Precise information as to the type of job evaluation system used by each of the divisions was not available to the writers. However, it is known that among the **12** divisions, variations of the four basic systems were in use. Each of the divisions had developed its own system independently of any other division. Differences among the **12** systems are apparent in the range of the unit of job worth. These ranges in terms of highest evaluated job and lowest evaluated job in each division were as follows:

Division	
A	81– 785
B	90– 671
C	15– 151
D	108– 423
E	112– 543
F	115– 540
G	121– 324
H	106–1437
I	114– 685
J	80– 790
K	169–1617
L	85– 350

In comparing the ranges listed above, it should be remembered that the 12 divisions, being members of one large organization, are very similar in organization and operations, so that jobs evaluated high or low in one are the same or very similar to jobs evaluated high or low in another.

The Jobs Selected for Study

Twenty-seven jobs, common to all 12 divisions, and ranging from very simple to very difficult, were selected for study. Twenty-two of these were clerical or professional jobs and five were non-clerical jobs. These non-clerical jobs were ultimately eliminated from the study when it was discovered that several of the divisions used two different job evaluation manuals—one for clerical and professional jobs, and the other for non-clerical (or maintenance) jobs. Since this would in effect increase the number of systems to be included in the study, and since only five jobs would be common to these extra systems, it was decided, after a preliminary survey of the data, to base the results only upon the 22 clerical jobs.

Methods and Results

Job descriptions and job specifications for the jobs were prepared and sent to each of the divisions. Each division was instructed to rate each of the job specifications with its own job evaluation manual. These ratings comprise the raw data for the study. Differences in the unit of job worth used by the various divisions are very apparent. For example, the job of addressograph operator receives 20 points on the Division C scale and 481 points on the Division J scale. This, of course, is caused by the use of a different job evaluation system.

As the first step in the statistical treatment of the data, correlation coefficients among the 12 divisions were computed. These are presented in Table 5–1, Intercorrelations: Individual Division Ratings. The correlation coefficients range from .86 to .98 with an average of .95. This indicates unusually high agreement among the 12 divisions in assigning point values to the 22 clerical jobs.

In other words, the high value of these correlation coefficients indicates that within each of the 12 systems, the 22 jobs were rated very much alike, in spite of the fact that the unit of job worth differed from system to system and in spite of the fact that the systems differed in methodology. Here was conclusive proof that the 12 systems had a great deal in common although each system used different units and different methods of arriving at the difficulty value of a job. If these correlation coefficients had been of a lower order, say .50 or .60, proceeding with the study would have been a debatable issue since the evidence would have indicated too little commonality among the 12 systems to make it possible to combine them into a single system. However, the evidence indicates a great deal of commonality among the systems, and justifies the attempt to find a common scale which will express that commonality. To the knowledge of the writers no other study has shown such high relationships between job difficulty ratings as are presented in Table 5–1.

The averages of the correlations of each division with every other division range from .92 (Division H) to .95 (Division I). These average

TABLE 5—1. Intercorrelations: individual division ratings •

Division	A 1	B 2	C 3	D 4	E 5	F 6	G 7	H 8	I 9	J 10	K 11	L 12	Total 13
1. A		.96	.93	.95	.93	.91	.93	.90	.94	.97	.92	.98	.96
2. B	.96		.86	.94	.94	.92	.92	.95	.97	.93	.96	.94	.95
3. C	.93	.86		.94	.97	.98	.94	.96	.98	.91	.96	.95	.96
4. D	.95	.94	.94		.90	.92	.92	.88	.94	.96	.91	.96	.92
5. E	.93	.94	.97	.90		.97	.92	.97	.95	.92	.96	.93	.97
6. F	.91	.92	.98	.92	.97		.93	.95	.97	.90	.95	.92	.94
7. G	.93	.92	.94	.92	.92	.93		.90	.94	.91	.92	.92	.94
8. H	.90	.95	.96	.88	.97	.95	.90		.95	.86	.95	.89	.96
9. I	.94	.97	.98	.94	.95	.96	.94	.95		.93	.98	.94	.95
10. J	.97	.93	.91	.96	.92	.90	.91	.86	.93		.92	.98	.93
11. K	.92	.96	.96	.91	.96	.95	.92	.95	.98	.92		.93	.94
12. L	.98	.94	.95	.96	.93	.92	.92	.89	.95	.98	.93		.95
13. TOTAL	.96	.95	.96	.92	.97	.94	.94	.96	.95	.93	.94	.95	
Mean (1–12)	.94	.94	.94	.93	.94	.94	.92	.92	.95	.92	.94	.94	M = .95

correlations are measures of commonality between one division and all the others, and indicate that all of the systems have a great deal in common with each other.

Since it was discovered that raw point ratings when added to form a composite score for each job failed to yield a unit of job worth which would show more commonality with all 12 systems than did any individual system with the remaining 11 systems, it was decided to reduce all the original point ratings to a common basis first and then to combine the values so derived into a new set of 22 job values for each of the 12 divisions. In summing the 12 division values for any job, each division would thus contribute equally to the common scale rating for that job. Such a procedure gives us a control over the relative importance or weight of the units of job worth in the composite score for each job, which is lacking when raw ratings are summed.

The raw ratings of each of the 12 different systems, were, therefore, converted to a common distribution in which the mean and standard deviation were assigned specified values—in this case, the mean being 50 and the standard deviation, 15. In simpler terms, this means that the 22 ratings of each division were converted to a new set of values in which the average rated job was 50, the lowest rated job was approximately 5, and the highest rated job was approximately 95. Such converted ratings are actually "z-scores," but will be referred to hereafter as "standard ratings." In effect we have at the outset eradicated the differences in the unit of job worth among the 12 systems, and we are free to add these units, subtract them, or manipulate them in any other way, since we are dealing with only one kind of unit—the standard rating unit.

The sums of the 12 standard ratings for each job were computed. Correlation coefficients between raw ratings for each division and total standard ratings were as follows:

Division	
A	.97
B	.98
C	.98
D	.96
E	.97
F	.97
G	.96
H	.96
I	.99
J	.95
K	.97
L	.97

The average of the above coefficients is .97. This is decidedly higher than the average correlation of any individual division against all other divisions. As a matter of fact, with the exception of Division J, all of the coefficients in the above list are higher than the highest average coefficient obtained by any individual division when raw ratings were correlated against each other, and in the case of Division J the coefficient is equal to the highest average coefficient of any individual division.

It is questionable whether any other statistical procedure would yield an average correlation coefficient greater than .97 since we are approaching the limits of almost perfect agreement between individual systems and a common system. From the point of view of the practical problem to be solved by this study, the coefficients presented above are highly significant and justify accepting as the common scale one in which the unit of job worth is based upon standard rating values. This standard rating system was accepted as the common plan.

For the sake of greater accuracy and greater consistency, it was decided, therefore, to compute second degree curves and trend equations for each division. There was little doubt that this procedure was warranted and that it would yield results that would ultimately make for much more accurate conversions on the part of individual divisions. The final results justified the decision. It must be remembered that in attempting to convert individual division values to the common plan scale values we are converting not only 12 individual division plans, which may or may not possess inadequacies within themselves, but also the human judgments which have gone into the application of these plans to 22 selected clerical jobs.

The findings of this study indicate that there is a great deal in common among the various job-evaluation systems. It is the authors' belief that the primary consideration in the selection of a job-evaluation system is its acceptability to those involved. Advantages and disadvantages are found more in the work required in installing and administering a system than in the final accuracy of a system which is judged to be appropriate for the kind of job being rated. Most workers in the field will agree that systems which intercorrelate .95 on the average are sufficiently similar to be substituted for each other without changing the final classification of jobs. In the case of the study just described, all divisions were able to use the common evaluation system after converting their point values to common scale point values without appreciably changing the classification of their jobs.

The two major job-evaluation systems using numerical values as the basis of job classification are the point-rating method and the factor-comparison method. Lytle [2] divides these two types of systems into four: (1) the straight-point method; (2) the weighted-in-points method without separate treatment of universal requirements; (3) the weighted-in-points method with separate treatment of universal requirements; and (4) the weighted-in-money method, sometimes called the factor-comparison method.

The point-rating method is similar to the grade-description

[2] Charles W. Lytle, *Job Evaluation Methods* (New York: The Ronald Press Company, 1946), p. 32.

method in that each job is measured by being compared with a rating scale. However, the point-rating method, instead of using one rating scale, employs a rating scale for each factor.

THE POINT SYSTEM

The point system of job evaluation is sometimes referred to as point rating. As Moore says, "[This] method of job evaluation has no well established name and there are countless variations of it in use. We can call all the variations 'Point' plans and they will be sufficiently identified . . ." [3] In this volume the terms *job rating*, *point rating* and *point system* are used interchangeably. Practically every frequency study made shows that the point system is the most commonly used. Publicity given to certain specific point systems and their successful use has created acceptance of this type of job evaluation.

The point system or point-rating method is a procedure for evaluating jobs by separately appraising each of the factors or compensatory characteristics, such as skill, effort, responsibility, and working conditions, and combining the separate evaluations into a single point score for each job. In this method a series of rating scales is constructed, one for each of the factors which have been selected as important in the work of the position. A certain number of points are allowed for each scale. According to the *Informational Manual*,[4] the most common of the compensable factors which have been used in factory wage-evaluation studies are: [5]

1. Education
2. Experience
3. Initiative and ingenuity
4. Physical demand
5. Mental or visual demand
6. Responsibility for equipment or process
7. Responsibility for material or product
8. Responsibility for safety of others
9. Responsibility for work of others
10. Working conditions
11. Unavoidable hazards

Figure 5–1 is a complete point-rating plan developed by Asa Knowles.[6] It shows the job factors, the degree to which each factor is required, and the number of points accorded each degree. Knowles

[3] Franklin G. Moore, "Statistical Problems of Job Evaluation," an address delivered to the American Statistical Association (January 1946).

[4] *Informational Manual on Industrial Job Evaluation Systems*, War Manpower Commission, Bureau of Manpower Utilization, Division of Occupational Analysis and Manning Tables (August 1943), p. 32.

[5] This group of factors is used by the National Electrical Manufacturers' Association in one of the most widely known job-evaluation programs. It should be pointed out that these factors were designed to be used with factory jobs.

[6] Asa S. Knowles, *Job Evaluation for Hourly and Salaried Workers* (New York: Supervision Publishing Co., Inc., 1943), p. 17.

uses job factors, classified under four major headings: Skill, Responsibility, Effort, and Working Conditions. Skill is subdivided into mental, manual or motor, and social skills. Responsibility is subdivided into responsibility for determining company policy, for work of others, for good will and public relations, and for company cash. Effort is subdivided into mental effort and manual effort. Working Conditions has no subdivision. For every job factor there is a rating scale with five degrees. Each degree has been assigned a certain number of points based upon the judged relative importance of the factor.

Figure 5–1 illustrates the more common type of point-rating method. The Industrial Management Society [7] has developed an occupational rating plan for manual or shop occupations which in parts uses a two-dimensional rating system. Figure 5–2 shows the breakdown of Attribute 1, Physical Effort, into amount of strength required and endurance or length of time it is applied. Strength is rated in the horizontal row, and Endurance in the vertical column. In addition to such descriptive phrases as "Exertion Not Sustained" and "Heavy (100–200 lbs.)," illustrative jobs are given for the ratings to indicate the possible point values. Illustrative jobs are frequently used in the construction of rating scales for the point method.

The point-rating method is essentially a series of rating scales for the factors selected. Points are assigned depending upon the relative importance of the factors. The differences among jobs are therefore reflected in the different values which are assigned to the factors. By the use of the point system, each job is reduced to a numerical value so that similarities and differences in work and difficulty are discovered.

Early point-rating plans

Although some evaluation studies were made as early as 1910, they were more representative of the grading method than the point system. Some of the first examples of the use of the point-rating method are found in the work of Kingsbury [8] and Lott [9] but this method received its greatest popularity through the work of Kress

[7] *Occupational Rating Plan,* Industrial Management Society, 205 West Wacker Drive (Chicago, 1943).

[8] Forrest A. Kingsbury, "Grading the Office Job," *Administration* (1923), pp. 267–275; 393–401; 537–548; 669–680; and *Management and Administration* (1923), pp. 73–78.

[9] M. R. Lott, *Wage Scales and Job Evaluation* (New York: The Ronald Press Company, 1926).

JOB FACTORS	FIRST DEGREE	Max. Pts.	SECOND DEGREE	Max. Pts.
I. SKILL A. *Mental* 1. *Resourcefulness* (Demand for meeting situations; expediency required in formulating and doing.)	Must work under supervision. No particular need for expediency or aggressiveness. No stringent demands for resourcefulness in quality and quantity of work.	20	Aggressiveness desirable. Occasional need for formulating a method for own work.	40
2. *Analytical ability* (Discrimination; breaking down problems into parts.)	Analytical ability required in isolated instances. Usually handles part of one operation.	35	Analysis needed in few instances. Most analysis in own or related work.	70
3. *Ability to make decisions* (Need for establishing a point of view decisively.)	No requisite of making decisions other than those connected with own closely supervised work.	15	Makes decisions which affect small group, such as small department or section of small one.	30
4. *Ability to do detail work* (Accuracy and efficiency.)	Must do job well, but detail work and confidence are not essentials of the work.	20	Small amount of detail work. Must do work efficiently, but errors are closely watched.	40
B. *Manual or Motor* (Speed, accuracy, and experience needed to perform mechanical operations.)	Does simple routine tasks which do not require special mechanical skill in operations. Accuracy and reaction time not of great importance.	10	Must do simple arithmetic operations on few office machines, at reasonable speed. Normal reaction time.	20
C. *Social* 1. *Capacity for getting along with others* (Includes cooperation, personality and appearance.)	Does not come in contact with associates to a great degree. Appearance and personality desirable, but not of great importance.	30	Neatness, affability, and good personality advisable. Must get along well with associates within a small section.	60
2. *Capacity for self-expression* (Necessity for transmitting ideas, conveying opinions.)	Work of mostly mechanical nature, with not much opportunity for self-expression.	10	Few changes for self-expression. Must determine salient points of things on occasional instances.	20
II. RESPONSIBILITY A. *For Determining Company Policy* (Necessity for determining company's course of action.)	Carries out company policy and may make suggestions to superior as to changes. Minor changes are the greatest part of such.	20	Often suggests changes in procedure because of frequent office contacts. Applies mostly to affairs within departments.	40
B. *For Work of Others* (Ability needed in leading and supervising others.)	Responsible only for own work. Includes individual work, or work of "flow" nature.	30	Small amount of supervision. Performs mechanical operations, and may control some work.	60
C. *For Goodwill and Public Relations* (Development and maintenance of goodwill with customers, public.)	Very little contact with customers or public in any way. Direct contact negligible.	20	Only contact with customers and public, checked communications or occasional telephone calls.	40
D. *For Company Cash* (Judgment needed in expenditure of company funds.)	Authorizes spending or spends not more than $25 monthly. Petty cash fund in few instances.	10	Cash expenditures amount to from $25 to $100 monthly.	20
III. EFFORT A. *Mental* (Mental-visual demands, concentration, mental prowess, coordination of senses.)	Work necessitates minimum of mental attention. Concentration and hand-eye coordination to a small degree.	40	Occasional mental and visual attention required, but not exacting or highly concentrating in nature.	80
B. *Manual* (Physical position requirements, including standing, sitting positions.)	Comfortable position; minimum of lifting and physical work. May do work easily in prescribed time.	20	Some physical exertion resulting in fatigue. Physical exertion needed on occasion.	40
IV. WORKING CONDITIONS (Disagreeableness of working environment, including noise, hazards, monotony, and clothes spoilage.)	Tasks pleasant; little noise and confusion; small chance of injury; little clothes spoilage; air and light very good.	20	Slight noise of office machines; slight tiring of monotony of work; tasks pleasant and agreeable.	40

From *Job Evaluation for Hourly and Salaried Workers*, by Asa S. Knowles. Copyrighted 1943 by The

Fig. 5—1.   Chart for evaluating jobs paid on a salary basis.

THIRD DEGREE	Max. Pts.	FOURTH DEGREE	Max. Pts.	FIFTH DEGREE	Max. Pts.
oes mostly own work; occasionly consults supervisor for information. Must plan work in relation to others. Aggressiveness quired.	60	Must review and approve work of associates. Aggressiveness imperative. Must have ability to plan and make others carry out plans of work.	80	Responsible for many functions which require coordination. High degree of imagination and aggressiveness essential.	100
nalysis of much material within nall unit, such as a small department or operation within it.	105	Analysis covers wide scope. Affects two or more departments or sections simultaneously.	140	Great analytical ability needed in appraising statements, sales records, economic situation, etc.	175
ust make decisions as to how epartment is to be run. Coordinates units, establishes ideas.	45	Decisions important in branch or section of departments. Must know how to carry through action.	60	Must make decisions carefully and rapidly. Formulate ideas instantaneously.	75
osition requires detail work of erage degree. Errors not easily ctified.	60	Errors are costly. Must do detail work within department. Confidence of position needed.	80	Work requires intricate detail in various tasks. Must know job well and do it expertly.	100
ust have knowledge of use of veral machines. Use machines fairly complex nature; fast action time.	30	Knowledge of many office machines needed. Very fast reaction time. Requires knowledge of how machines function.	40	Use of intricate office equipment. Must do complex operations in a very accurate manner.	50
ust get along with large group associates. Friction with fellow workers may result in unfavorable work. Appearance must e good.	90	Must possess affable and tactful qualities. Comes in contact with fellow workers frequently and must impress them.	120	Excellent appearance necessary. Personality important in getting best quantity and quality of work from associates.	150
eas are given, but they must e transmitted to customers, ablic or superiors in adaptable anner.	30	Must convey ideas to customers and public with basis for presentation. Must know significant facts.	40	Must convey ideas to large groups through writing, speaking, or graphic presentation.	50
ay determine minor policies of mpany with close control of pervisors; may make company olicy seem different to others.	60	Determines company policy for large group of workers. Bad execution would result in considerable loss. Departmental authority mostly.	80	Responsible for determining policy on large scale. Determines policy for positions in lower degrees.	100
upervises large number of orkers or department. Organizes d coordinates with supervisors.	90	Responsible for coordination of group of departments. Supervises associated operations.	120	Supervision of policies; control of training and coordinating work of departments.	150
ossible loss of goodwill by close ontact with customers through tters or personal interview.	60	Considerable contact with customers, other businesses, and public. Tact and diplomacy needed.	80	Builds and maintains goodwill of company. Directly responsible for public relations — choice of salesmen, etc.	100
pproves cash expenditures of 100 to $500 monthly.	30	Authorizes cash expense of from $500 to $1000 as a monthly average.	40	Authorizes and approves of cash expenditures of over $1000 monthly.	50
lose mental attention, but not ontinuous.	120	Continuous attention required. Close and exacting attention to tasks necessary.	160	High degree of concentration imperative. Close and continuous mental application.	200
onstant repetitive work of mehanical nature. Small amount f lifting and carrying.	60	Considerable work of strenuous physical nature. Sustained manual effort due to physical position.	80	Strain from continuous application to tasks. Work is constant and tedious on body, tiring.	100
ome dirt and discomfort and oise caused by office machines. verage clothing spoilage. Chance f injury small, i.e., addressing achines, presses.	60	Continuous work of monotonous nature. Considerable discomfort and noise. Relatively high clothes spoilage.	80	Noisy, monotonous repetitive work. High clothes spoilage. Chance of bodily injury relatively great.	100

Supervision Publishing Company, New York.

Fig. 5—1 (cont.).

ENDURANCE	STRENGTH (Measured in pounds of force applied without mechanical aid)			
	Column A (0–1) *Very Light* Up to 5 Lbs.	Column B (2–3) *Light* 5 to 30 Lbs.	Column C (4–7) *Medium* 30 to 100 Lbs.	Col. D (8—) *Heavy* 100–200 Lbs.

ROW 1 (0–2)
 	
EXERTION
NOT
SUSTAINED
	0 Gateman
	
	0 Watchman
	
	3 Gager
		2 Pattern Maker Wood
		2 Surface Grinder,
		  Tool Room
		3 Punch Press No. 1
		  Setter
		4 Hand Screw Machine
		
		4 Engine Lathe,
		  Tool Room
			4 Inspector, Casting
			5 Janitor, Industrial
			
			5 Tool Crib Attendant
			
			5 Auto Scr Mach
			  Setter
			5 Plater
			
			7 Electrician
				8
				
				9
				
				10 Millwright
				
				10 Mover,
				   Piano

ROW 2 (3–5)
 	
ORDINARY
SUSTAINED
EXERTION
	3 Elevator
	  Operator
	3 Counter &
	  Packer
	3 Assembly
	  Work
	  (Light, simple)
	5 Light Spot
	  Welder
	
	5
		5 Shop Patrolman
		5 Bench Core Maker
		
		5 Band Saw,
		  Tool Room
		5 Milling Machine,
		  Tool Room
		6 Crane Operator,
		  Bridge Type
		
		6 Milling Machine,
		  Repetitive
		6 Punch Press, Nos.
		  3—4—5
		7 Shaper, Wood
		8 Punch Press, Nos.
		  6–7
			7 Crater
			7 Gas Brazer, Job Shop
			7 Electric Truck Oper.
			
			7 Finish Sprayer, Prod.
			
			7 Rivet Squeezer
			
			8 Single Sp. Drill
			  Press
			8 Power Shear
			  Metal Sh.
			8 Power Shear,
			  Print Sh.
			8 Trucker, Metal Parts
			8 Arc Welder
			9 Common Laborer,
			  Aver.
			9 Casting Chipper
			10 Blacksmith
			
			11 Common Laborer,
			   Hvy.
				10 Carpenter
				
				12
				13 Iceman
				
				15 Stevedore

ROW 3 (6—)
 	
CONSTANTLY
SUSTAINED
EXERTION
	6 Typist
	7 Print Press
	  Feeder
	8 Very Light
	  Conveyorized
	  Assembly
		9
		
		10
		
		12 Light Conveyorized
		   Assembly Work
			12
			
			13 Scrap Baler
			
			14 Beef Skinner
				10 Stoker
				   (Ship)

From *Occupational Rating Plan* of the Industrial Management Society.

Fig. 5—2.   Physical Effort—Attribute No. 1 (measured by the amount of strength required, and by the length of time it is applied).

for the National Electrical Manufacturers' Association and the National Metal Trades Association.

An attempt to rate the abilities necessary for successful job performance was made in 1922 by Viteles, who was at that time primarily interested in determining occupational qualifications for the jobs being analyzed. As Viteles points out,[10]

The scientific study of occupational qualifications requires (1) a simplified classification of specific mental traits; (2) a standard rating technique; and (3) a direct examination of work activities by trained observers. These criteria have been applied . . . in the development of a job *psychographic method* in job analysis

[10] Morris S. Viteles, *Industrial Psychology* (New York: W. W. Norton and Co., Inc., 1932), p. 150.

Thirty-two mental traits were selected and carefully defined by Viteles. Each trait was rated on a five-point scale to designate the extent to which it was necessary for satisfactory performance on the job. The scale values were as follows:

1. Negligible
2. Barely significant
3. Significant
4. Of great importance
5. Of utmost importance

An illustration of the job psychograph in Figure 5–3 is based upon a careful job analysis of the occupation of Power Sewing Machine Operator.[11] Viteles was interested primarily in the relative differences among the traits being rated, rather than in the differences among jobs. For example, the job of Power Sewing Machine Operator calls for a high degree of Coordination A (fine finger coordination), Coordination B (eye-hand coordination), Visual Discrimination, and Space Perception. Whether these abilities are greater or less than those required for a job receiving similar ratings cannot be determined from this type of rating scale. The technique is extremely valuable in discovering qualifications necessary for successful job performance and, indirectly, in selecting tests to predict job performance. The psychograph is useful in the hands of an industrial psychologist who is acquainted with the meaning of the terms used in the psychograph, but it has limitations when employed by an untrained individual.

To overcome objections to the job psychograph, and to develop a similar system that would show differences in degree between jobs, the Occupational Characteristics Check List was developed. This was later called the Worker Characteristics Form.[12] Figure 5–4 is an illustration of this method of occupational analysis. The terms employed are more easily understood by the untrained worker than are the technical terms used in the job psychograph. In addition, each job is measured in terms of the amount of each characteristic demanded of the worker to perform the job satisfactorily. The job analyst checks column A, B, or C to indicate the degree to which each characteristic is demanded.

The job analyst is instructed to compare the worker on the job with persons in general in estimating the amount of the character-

[11] Jay L. Otis, "The Prediction of Success in Power Sewing Machine Operating," *Journal of Applied Psychology*, XXII, No. 4 (1939), p. 355.

[12] William H. Stead, Carroll L. Shartle, and Associates, *Occupational Counseling Techniques* (New York: American Book Co., 1940), pp. 176–177.

istics required. This type of rating form is not a job-rating, but a worker-rating, device. It is an attempt to rate the job in terms of the human qualifications required to perform it. Users of the scale state that periodic comparisons of ratings of the same job made at

JOB PSYCHOGRAPH

Job: Power Sewing Machine Operator

	1	2	3	4	5	REMARKS
1. Energy			X			
2. Rate of Discharge			X			
3. Endurance		X				
4. Control		X				
5. Coordination A				X		
6. Coordination B					X	
7. Initiative		X				
8. Concentration			X			
9. Distribution (of attention)			X			
10. Persistence			X			
11. Alertness		X				
12. Associability		X				
13. Visual Discrimination				X		
14. Auditory Discrimination	X					
15. Tactual Discrimination	X					
16. Kinaesthetic Discrimination			X			
17. Space Perception				X		
18. Form Perception		X				
19. Accuracy			X			
20. Visual Memory		X				
21. Auditory Memory	X					
22. Kinaesthetic Memory			X			
23. Understanding		X				
24. Understanding Q	X					
25. Observation			X			
26. Planfulness		X				
27. Intelligence	X					
28. Intellect	X					
29. Judgment	X					
30. Logical Analysis	X					
31. Language Ability	X					
32. Executive	X					

Fig. 5—3.

different research centers have shown sufficient agreement to warrant its use.

These two rating techniques, the Job Psychograph and the Occupational Characteristics Check List, have demonstrated that it is

1. Job Title _____ 2. Date _____ 3. Code _____
4. Establishment No. _____ 5. Industry _____
6. Branch _____ 7. Dept. _____

Indicate the MINIMUM amount of each characteristic demanded of the worker in order to do the job satisfactorily by putting an X in Column A, B, or C.

The amounts designated by A, B, and C are as follows:

A. A very great amount of the characteristic, such as would be possessed by not more than two out of a hundred persons.

B. A distinctly above average amount of the trait, such as would be possessed by the highest thirty per cent of the population but less than the amount designated by A.

C. An amount of the trait less than that possessed by the highest thirty per cent of the population.

In checking these items, think of people in general, not just persons on the job.

If some characteristic is demanded which does not appear in this list, write it in and check as described above.

Amount of characteristics			*Characteristics required of worker*
C	B	A	
			1. Work rapidly for long periods.
			2. Strength of hands.
			3. Strength of arms.
			4. Strength of back.
			5. Strength of legs.
			6. Dexterity of fingers.
			7. Dexterity of hands and arms.
			8. Dexterity of foot and leg.
			9. Eye-hand coordination.
			10. Foot-hand-eye coordination.
			11. Coordination of independent movements of both hands.
			12. Estimate size of objects.
			13. Estimate quantity of objects.
			14. Perceive form of objects.
			15. Estimate speed of moving objects.
			16. Keenness of vision.
			17. Keenness of hearing.
			18. Sense of smell.
			19. Sense of taste.
			20. Touch discrimination.
			21. "Muscular" discrimination.
			22. Memory for details. (Things)
			23. Memory for ideas. (Abstract)
			24. Memory for oral directions.
			25. Memory for written directions.

U. S. Dept. of Labor, U. S. Employment Service.

Fig. 5—4.   Occupational characteristics check list.

| Amount of characteristics | | | Characteristics required of worker |
C	B	A	
			26. Intelligence.
			27. Adaptability.
			28. Ability to make decisions.
			29. Ability to plan.
			30. Initiative.
			31. Understanding of mechanical devices.
			32. Attention to many items.
			33. Oral expression.
			34. Skill in written expression.
			35. Teamwork—cooperation on the job.
			36. Tact in dealing with people.
			37. Memory of names and persons.
			38. Personal appearance.
			39. Concentration amidst distractions.
			40. Emotional stability.
			41. Work under hazardous conditions.
			42. _____
			43. _____
			44. _____
			45. _____
			46. _____
			47. _____
			48. _____
			49. _____
			50. _____

Definitions for Added Characteristics:

Fig. 5—4 (cont.).

possible to rate a job in terms of the qualifications necessary to perform it. Scales of this type have certain weaknesses in that they are too long and utilize units which are not accurately defined. Terms such as "barely significant," "of great significance," and "of utmost significance" in the Job Psychograph are apt to mean different things to different raters. It is true also that the use of the "general population" as a rating standard in the Occupational Characteristics Check List implies that each rater will have the same concept of the general population.

Commonly used job factors

Job factors chosen to measure the monetary or difficulty value of a job are somewhat different from those selected to measure worker characteristics. Seventeen point systems for the evaluation of factory jobs and twelve systems for clerical and supervisory jobs were studied by the authors to determine what factors were used most frequently to point-rate jobs. The results of this study are found in Figures 5–5 and 5–6. Figure 5–5 shows the factors most commonly used in point-rating systems for factory jobs. These have been classified under the major headings of skill, effort, responsibility, and working conditions. Under skill, most of the systems included education, experience, and motor or manual dexterity. The remaining factors were used less frequently.

Under the heading of effort, mental effort and physical effort were used most frequently. Such factors as visual demand, fatigue, and monotony were less frequent.

Under the heading of responsibility most of the systems emphasized responsibility for the work of others, responsibility for the safety of others, and responsibility for machinery and equipment.

Working conditions as a major heading was used in nearly half of the systems studied. Such factors as hazards, occupational disease, dirtiness, and disagreeableness were most frequent.

Some of the systems studied used the major factors—skill, effort, responsibility, and working conditions—without further subdivision. This is in line with a recent trend to limit the number of factors in the point-rating systems.

Figure 5–6 shows the factors listed for the clerical job evaluation systems. Education, training, mental requirements, resourcefulness, and social skills appeared most frequently under the heading of skill. Effort was limited to mental effort for the most part, with physical effort appearing only a few times. Considerable emphasis was placed on the responsibility factors. Effect of errors, confidential data, personal contact work, dependability, and supervision of others were the major responsibilities. Working conditions played a far less important role in clerical evaluation plans than in factory plans.

Figures 5–5 and 5–6 illustrate the factors used in a few of the systems in existence today. However, a more complete analysis would probably reveal somewhat the same findings. The lists are designed to be helpful in selecting factors to be used when constructing a new point system or when modifying an existing one.

Factor degrees

In practically all point systems each factor is divided into several degrees, ranging from a very little to a great deal. For example, the

SKILL

Education
Education or Mental Development
Education or Trade Knowledge
Schooling
Experience
Previous Experience
Experience and Training
Training Time
Time Required to Become 80% Efficient
Training Required
Time Required to Learn Trade
Time Required to Adapt Skill
Job Knowledge
Knowledge of Machinery and Dexterity with Tools
Knowledge of Materials and Processes
Knowledge

Mentality
Accuracy
Ingenuity
Initiative and Ingenuity
Judgment and Initiative
Mental Capability
Intelligence
Resourcefulness
Versatility
Job Skill
Manual Dexterity
Dexterity
Degree of Skill and Accuracy
Manual Accuracy and Quickness
Physical Skill
Details
Aptitude Required
Difficulty of Operation
Ability to do Detailed Work
Social Skill

EFFORT

Mental Effort
Mental Application
Mental or Visual Demand
Concentration
Visual Application
Physical Effort
Physical Application

Physical Demand
Physical or Mental Fatigue
Muscular or Nerve Strain
Fatigue Due to Eye Strain
Fatigue
Honesty of Effort
Monotony of Work
Monotony and Comfort

RESPONSIBILITY (FOR)

Safety of Others
Material or Product
Equipment or Process
Machinery and Equipment
Material and Equipment
Work of Others
Supervision of Others
Supervision Exercised
Cost of Errors
Effect on Other Operations
Necessary Accuracy in Checking, Counting and Weighing

Spoilage of Materials
Protection of Materials
Equipment
Product
Physical Property
Plant and Services
Cooperation and Personality
Dependability
Adjustability
Coordination
Details to Master
Quality

WORKING CONDITIONS

Unavoidable Hazards
Hazards Involved
Exposure to Health Hazard
Exposure to Accident Hazard
Occupational Hazard Disease
Danger—Accident from Machinery or Equipment
Danger—from Lifting

Surroundings
Dirtiness of Working Conditions
Environment
Job Conditions
Difficulty in Locating Work Elsewhere
Attendance
Disagreeableness

Fig. 5—5. Factors selected for factory point-rating systems.

SKILL

Mental Requirement
Mentality
Mental Application
Creative Ability
Judgment
Analytical Ability
Initiative
Resourcefulness
Versatility
Skill Requirement
Complexity of Duties
Personal Qualifications Needed for
  the Job
Personal Requirements
Ability to Make Decisions
Managerial Techniques
Character of Supervision Given
Difficulty of Work

Education
Preparation for the Job
Essential Education and
  Knowledge
Basic Knowledge and Experience
Experience, Knowledge and
  Training Necessary
Previous Experience
Training Time
Experience and Training
Capacity for Getting Along with
  Others
Capacity for Self Expression
Social Skill
Ability to do Detailed Work
Ability to do Routine Work
Manual or Motor Skill
Office Machine Operation
Manual Dexterity

EFFORT

Physical Requirement
Physical Application
Physical Effort
Physical Demand
Physical or Mental Fatigue

Manual Effort
Pressure of Work
Mental Effort
Volume of Work
Attention Demand

RESPONSIBILITY (FOR)

Executive Responsibility
Personnel
Supervision of Others
Work of Others
Monetary Responsibility
Commitments, Property, Money or
  Records
Company Cash
Dependability and Accuracy
Accuracy
Details
Quality
Effect of Errors

Material
Equipment
Records
Confidential Data
Methods
Determining Company Policy
Market
Contact with Others
Contact with Public, Customers,
  and Personnel
Goodwill and Public Relations
Cooperation and Personality

WORKING CONDITIONS

Job Conditions
Tangible Surroundings
Intangible Conditions
Working Conditions

Personal Hazard
Monotony
Attention to Details
Out-of-Town Travel

Fig. 5—6. Factors selected for clerical point-rating systems.

scale for the factor of education or trade information as found in a
job-evaluation manual for factory jobs,[13] shown in Figure 5–7,

[13] Jay L. Otis, *Job Evaluation Manual for Factory Jobs,* Personnel Research
Institute, Western Reserve University, Cleveland. Ohio.

illustrates the manner in which a factor is set up in rating-scale form. The use of both formal education levels and comparable trade-information and shop-knowledge levels in a single scale is quite common. This does not penalize the job which is rich in knowledge and low in formal education requirements.

SCHOOLING

Refers to formal school training or equivalent. This factor appraises the requirements for the use of spoken English, shop mathematics, drawings, measuring instruments, and general background.

Degree	Educational and knowledge requirements	Points
1	Requires the ability to speak English, to read, write, or add and subtract. Equal to or equivalent of six-grade education.	10
2	Requires the ability to understand mill orders and order sets or to be able to read micrometers or read measuring gages other than fixed gages. Eighth-grade or equivalent education required.	30
3	Must understand simple drawings such as drawings of the product, to understand all written instructions or to be able to make up production reports. Tenth-grade or equivalent education required.	60
4	Must be able to understand complicated drawings such as drawings for machine design, layout, placement of line shafting or for new construction, etc., or be able to make up lengthy complicated reports. High school education or equivalent required.	90
5	Must be able to understand complicated physical or technical relationships such as the operation of electric motors, magnetism, steam pressures, etc. Two years of college or equivalent required.	120

Fig. 5—7. Factor of education or trade information.

Weighting of Factors. It is obvious that not all of the factors chosen are of equal importance. In order to arrive at the proper value of a job, the differences in the relative importance of the various factors must be determined. Some point systems utilize the straight-point method, that is, each factor is weighted equally. In general, however, factors are weighted according to their judged importance.

Assignment of Points to Degrees. After the relative importance of each factor has been determined, it is possible to assign points to the degrees. Table 5–2 shows the allocation of points to degrees and the relative weights given to the major job factors. Some systems assign points to degrees on the basis of an arithmetical progression. For example, in Table 5–2 the total points for Degree 1 are 100, and for Degree 5, 500. Some systems, however, use a geometric progression to allocate points to degrees. If such a progression were used in Table 5–2, the point values for Experience might be 20, 40, 80, 160, 320 for degrees 1, 2, 3, 4, and 5 respectively.

TABLE 5–2.   Points assigned to job factors •

| Factor | | Degree | | | |
	1st	2nd	3rd	4th	5th
1. Education	14	28	42	56	70
2. Experience	20	40	60	80	100
3. Initative	22	44	66	88	110
4. Physical Demand	8	16	24	32	40
5. Mental Demand	8	16	24	32	40
6. Responsibility for Equipment or Process	5	10	15	20	25
7. Responsibility for Material or Product	5	10	15	20	25
8. Responsibility for Safety of Others	2	4	6	8	10
9. Responsibility for Work of Others	4	8	12	16	20
10. Working Conditions	7	14	21	28	35
11. Hazards	5	10	15	20	25

ADVANTAGES AND DISADVANTAGES OF POINT SYSTEM

A system has advantages and disadvantages which vary from situation to situation. The characteristics discussed below are presented so that some prior knowledge of the problems which may be encountered will be available.

Advantages

The point system makes use of the graphic and descriptive types of rating scales that most students in the field accept as being relatively reliable and valid. The scale lends itself to the evaluation of jobs because the degree definitions (see Figure 5–7) are usually written in job terms applicable to the type of job being evaluated. The agreement among raters is usually quite close. In a recent evaluation study of approximately 400 jobs [14] a joint company and union committee agreed with 94 per cent of the ratings made by personnel consultants. Of the remaining 6 per cent, about half of the ratings were increased and half decreased. In all, approximately 4,800 judgments were reviewed.

As pointed out in Chapter 1, employee and employer acceptance

[14] Jay L. Otis, and Franklin G. Moore, *Comparison of Independent Job Ratings With Union-Management Job Ratings,* an unpublished study.

of an evaluation system is necessary if full advantage is to be secured from the application of job evaluation to wage administrations. The wish of either management or labor to include a certain factor or even to eliminate a factor can be granted without changing the final job classification appreciably.

The aim of all job-evaluation systems is the determination of job classes. The total point values given the jobs make it easy to divide them into labor grades or job classes. The number of classes can be determined by the arbitrary selection of point ranges; or the number of classes desired may be predetermined and the point ranges varied accordingly.

The fact that point values obtained for each job show the relative differences among the jobs in numerical terms makes it possible to assign monetary values to the numerical values in a consistent manner. The method for so doing is described in detail in Chapter 13.

Human judgment cannot be completely eliminated from determining job values, but it can be exercised so that errors are reduced to a minimum. The point values and resulting job classification are designed to be basically fair to all workers; a standard for determining these point values has been used which can be applied by employees as well as by management.

Trained workers are able to use the point system with a consistency and validity which matches that of management representatives. This type of job evaluation is more difficult to "manipulate" than are the other types of systems. Intentional bias is easy to detect and is, therefore, less apt to occur. An evaluation plan of this type increases in accuracy and consistency with use. The employment of such a system in obtaining the original classification of jobs usually results in modifications and interpretations of degree definitions which make it easier to apply in new situations. In keeping a job classification up to date a job analyst is required to rate new jobs and to rerate jobs which have changed in content. It is desirable that the system of classification be of value both in the original classification and in the task of maintaining a sound classification and wage structure.

Disadvantages

The point system is difficult to construct. Writing degree definitions, as well as factor definitions which have the same meaning for each job analyst who uses the system, demands a considerable amount of skill. Allocating the proper weights to each factor and then assigning point values to each degree, without being unfair to either the easy or the difficult jobs, requires careful study and research.

The point system is difficult to explain. The concepts of factors, degrees, relative weights, point values, and pricing the point values are not easy to demonstrate to workers or supervisors. Patient instruction and clear illustrations are necessary. If workers fail to gain a clear understanding of the system used to determine their rates of pay they will be suspicious of it and antagonistic to it.

The evaluation of jobs by means of the point system is a time-consuming process. An intensive study of each job, during which it is rated on each factor, is usually made by at least two or three persons. These independent ratings are combined into a final point value for each job. There is considerable clerical detail in recording, combining, checking, and adding ratings.

CONSTRUCTING A POINT-RATING PLAN

The six steps

Step 1. *Types of Jobs.* In constructing a point-rating plan the first question concerns the range of the jobs which are to be evaluated. For example, is the plan for factory jobs only? Should a plan be constructed which can be used for both factory jobs and factory supervisory positions? Are the executive positions included in the classification? Experience indicates that a plan designed for jobs of a relatively narrow type, such as factory, clerical, or supervisory, will result in a more accurate classification of these jobs than can be obtained by a plan designed to cover a wide range. The first step, therefore, is the classification of jobs by "type" so that appropriate factors can be selected which will determine the value of the jobs.

Step 2. *Selections of Factors.* The factors contributing to the value of factory jobs are not the same as those for clerical jobs. The list of job factors in Figures 5–5 and 5–6 shows that there are differences as well as similarities. They may be used as a starting point for the selection of factors, but it should be kept in mind that the lists are by no means complete. The selection is not too difficult if it is based upon certain criteria or rules. Although consideration should be given to certain statistical findings discussed later, certain rules should be followed:

a. The factors chosen must be ratable. The amount of each factor required must vary from small to large among the different jobs. For example, a factor such as Supervision should vary from the supervision of no workers to responsibility for the supervision of all the employees in a work group. If the jobs selected for evaluation are *all* below the supervisory level, there is only one category applying to these jobs: "supervises no one"; therefore, the factor is of no use in evaluating the jobs.

b. The factors chosen must be ones which are judged to be important. In general, there has been agreement about the major characteristics which are common to all jobs. The most important of these are skill, responsibility, effort, and working conditions; such additional factors as education, mentality, resourcefulness, and accuracy occur less frequently. The factors of beauty and age are found in some job-evaluation systems, but they are primarily worker characteristics rather than job values and have, or should have, little importance in determining the values of jobs. Only those factors should be included which, when evaluated, will determine accurately the rate of pay or the relative worth of the job.

c. The factors must not overlap in meaning. Each one should be a measure of one and only one aspect of the job. For example, such a factor as "accuracy" is somewhat the same as "effect of errors." If the definitions show that they do overlap in meaning, then one factor is receiving a double weight. If this is recognized and taken into consideration, no harm is done; however, it is better to have a single factor for each job characteristic or job value.

d. The factors must meet both employer and worker standards. In the discussion above of the applicability of a job-evaluation scale, acceptance by both management and workers was emphasized. The same principle holds in the selection of job factors. Although the factor of working conditions is quite common in job-evaluation systems, in one organization both management and workers believed it should be eliminated because the management had gone to considerable expense to improve working conditions throughout the plant. However, they finally agreed to include the factor on the ground that it would tend to force management to maintain good working conditions.

e. The factors must be universal in application or be applicable to the type of jobs for which the system was constructed. The factor-comparison method uses job factors with broad general meanings which make them universal in application. These same factors can also be used in the point systems. However, the point system can make use of specific factors—for example, when the scale is to be used for factory jobs only, those which apply to office jobs need not be included.

Those factors should not be included on which practically all the jobs are given the lowest ratings. They only arouse suspicion and add little to the evaluation of a majority of the jobs.

f. A Simplified Scale. Recently a series of studies was conducted which was designed to indicate the fallacy of using many factors to rate a job. As Viteles has pointed out, "The general tendency seems to favor [the use of] many rather than few factors, in direct violation of the 'law of parsimony' which should find a place in this as it does in other fields of analysis." [15] In the same article Viteles states, "The findings of the psychological laboratory support the judgment of the practical job analyst who insists upon reducing the number of factors to be appraised to a minimum consistent with the adequate differentiation of jobs." The number of factors, according to Viteles, should probably never be greater than ten and can in most instances be limited to five.

This point of view is supported by Lawshe and Satter, who subjected the job rating data from three plants to Thurstone's factor-analysis technique.[16] Although eleven factors were used in the job-evaluation scale, the factor analysis revealed that two, Skill Demands and Job Characteristics, accounted for most of the relative differences between the jobs as measured by the entire scale. In other words, this study showed that a classification based upon these two factors would closely resemble a classification based upon eleven factors. In a second plant the factor analysis showed Skill Demands and Job Characteristics—Non-Hazardous could be used in place of the eleven factors. Four factors, Skill Demands, Job Characteristics—Hazardous, Job Characteristics—Non-Hazardous, and Attention Demand were the most representative of the eleven factors used in a third plant.

In a second attempt to demonstrate the feasibility of reducing the number of factors Lawshe [17] found by using the Wherry-Doo-

[15] Morris S. Viteles, "A Psychologist Looks at Job Evaluation," *Personnel*, Vol. 17, No. 3 (February 1941), p. 166.

[16] C. H. Lawshe, Jr., and G. A. Satter, "Studies in Job Evaluation: I. Factor Analyses of Point Ratings for Hourly-Paid Jobs in Three Industrial Plants," *Journal of Applied Psychology*, Vol. 28, No. 3 (June 1944), pp. 189–198.

[17] C. H. Lawshe, Jr., "Studies in Job Evaluation: II. The Adequacy of Abbreviated Point Ratings for Hourly-Paid Jobs in Three Industrial Plants," *Journal of Applied Psychology*, Vol. 29, No. 3 (June 1945), pp. 177–184.

little selection method,[18] that Experience, or learning time, plus Hazards plus Education for plant A, Experience plus Initiative plus Responsibility for the Safety of Others for plant B, and Experience plus Hazards plus Initiative for plant C, resulted in a fairly high relationship with the total point values for the original eleven factors. Lawshe concludes, "If the three-item abbreviated scale were employed in plant A, 62% of the jobs would remain in the same labor grade, 37.2% would be displaced one labor grade, and 0.8% would be displaced two labor grades." In spite of the rather large number of jobs which would be increased or decreased one labor grade, Lawshe concludes that a simplified scale consisting of three or four items would probably yield results that are practically identical with those obtained by a more complex system. Two studies conducted by Lawshe and Satter [19] in which factor analysis was used resulted in different abbreviated scales for each plant, and three entirely different abbreviated scales were obtained when the Wherry-Doolittle Shrinkage Selection method was used.

How would one go about building an abbreviated scale? There is no way of knowing which one of the shorter scales obtained by Lawshe would best apply to a given plant. Constructing a shorter scale would necessitate a complete job evaluation using a longer scale. Either factor analysis or the Wherry-Doolittle technique would have to be applied to the data, and a shorter scale so derived would be used to keep the system up to date. These savings are not very great.

Lawshe concludes [20] that the differences between point ratings assigned by a longer, original scale and those assigned by the abbreviated scale are unimportant, partly because of the probable unreliability of the point ratings. It must be kept in mind that management and employees might not wish to accept an abbreviated scale as a substitute for a longer one when only 62 per cent of the jobs rated by the shorter scale remain in the same labor grade.

These studies are very useful in selecting *the most important* factors for use in the scale. They also help in determining the rela-

[18] William H. Stead, Carroll L. Shartle, and Associates, *Occupational Counseling Techniques* (New York: The American Book Co., 1940), pp. 245–252.

[19] C. H. Lawshe, Jr., and G. A. Satter, "Studies in Job Evaluation: I. Factor Analyses of Point Ratings for Hourly-Paid Jobs in Three Industrial Plants," *Journal of Applied Psychology*, Vol. 28, No. 3 (June 1944), pp. 189–198.

[20] C. H. Lawshe, Jr., "Studies in Job Evaluation: II. The Adequacy of Abbreviated Point Ratings for Hourly-Paid Jobs in Three Industrial Plants," *Journal of Applied Psychology*, Vol. 29, No. 3 (June 1945), p. 183.

tive value of each factor if an abbreviated scale is to be derived from a longer one.

As few factors as possible should be selected in determining the relative value of the jobs being evaluated. As long as an adequate differentiation, which meets worker and management standards, is obtained, the factors selected are doing the job they are expected to do. It is extremely difficult to define a few complex factors so that the definitions have the same meaning for all job analysts. At the same time it is very difficult to select numerous factors without having some which overlap in meaning. The application of statistical or quantitative methods to the selection of factors is desirable, but qualitative considerations are equally important. For example, when an unskilled worker on a dangerous job is told that the value of jobs in his plant as statistically determined gives 99 per cent to "skill demands" and the remaining 1 per cent to "job characteristics —non-hazardous," neither he nor the union can be blamed for vigorously opposing the determination of his wage by this kind of job evaluation. It is possible to obtain worker and management acceptance and still keep the number of factors selected at a desirable minimum.

Step 3. Definition of Factors. The meaning of the job factors must be clear to those who use them. In order to make sure that each job analyst has the same interpretation of a factor, a definition is necessary. The definition is usually a formal statement of the meaning or significance of the title word or phrase. Definitions attempt to limit or to outline the exact meaning we wish to attach to a word. There is a human tendency to read our own ideas or concepts into a word or phrase. Since everyone's background of experience and training is not the same, it is reasonable to expect that words and phrases will be interpreted differently unless they are defined.

Each factor selected for the point-rating system should represent one aspect of the total job value. In order to measure job values accurately the rater must have an understanding of each factor and must constantly check his understanding or it will tend to change as the evaluation is carried out. For example, if the factor of education is defined as "formal education or school training" only, and a rater adds a new meaning to this factor, such as "job knowledge," after he is part way through his ratings, the factor has a meaning in the ratings of the later jobs which it does not have in the early ratings. This, of course, results in a rating error. The same thing happens when two raters assign different meanings to the same factor in rating the same jobs. Each factor must be clearly defined and carefully explained to the raters so that each factor will truly measure one and the same aspect of the total job value. Examples of definitions of job factors are given below. It should be observed that definitions of general factors are much broader than those for specific factors.

DEFINITION OF GENERAL FACTORS

Example 1.[21] Mental Requirements—either the possession of and/or the active application of the following:

A. (inherent) Mental traits, such as intelligence, memory, reasoning, facility in verbal expression, ability to get along with people, and imagination.
B. (acquired) General education, such as grammar and arithmetic; or general information as to sports, world events, etc.
C. (acquired) Specialized knowledge, such as chemistry, engineering, accounting, advertising, etc.

Example 2.[22] Skill—that which must be (with whatever composes it) already possessed by the worker, what he must bring.

DEFINITION OF SPECIFIC FACTORS

Example 1.[23] Education—schooling or its equivalent.

Definition: This characteristic is a measure of the general knowledge required for successful performance on any particular job.

Discussion: Actual formal education is not necessarily essential in developing knowledge; hence the Committee has avoided measuring knowledge required for a given occupation in terms of years of schooling. Instead, knowledge has been measured in terms of what the job required in terms of what the employee has to know in such matters as shop mathematics, blueprint reading, chemical and physical principles, etc. It is obvious that it requires a greater degree of knowledge (education or its equivalent) for a person to meet the requirements of a Toolmaker than it does for a person to meet the requirements of Sweeper.

Example 2.[24] Experience—The time it takes to attain full manual and mental proficiency on the job under ordinary work conditions without the specific course training for the job. If organized training is available on this job, rate this factor as it would be if these people had not received the training.

[21] E. J. Benge, *Job Evaluation and Merit Rating, A Manual of Procedures,* National Foremen's Institute (New York: 1944), Figure 6.

[22] Charles W. Lytle, *Job Evaluation Methods* (New York: The Ronald Press Company, 1946), p. 55.

[23] *Joint Job Evaluation Manual,* Sperry Gyroscope Co., Inc., in conjunction with Local 450, United Electrical Radio and Machine Workers, C.I.O. (Brooklyn, 1943), p. 12.

[24] *Job Evaluation Manual for Factory Jobs,* The National Screw and Manufacturing Co., Cleveland, p. 3.

When a general factor, such as mental requirements or skill, is defined as above, it can be seen that an extremely wide range of job requirements is covered. Definitions for specific factors of education and experience are much more precise, limited in scope, and consequently much clearer. In setting a value for mental requirements it is almost impossible to determine the exact basis for each judgment, because jobs can be high in mental requirements for several different reasons.

The selection of pertinent factors, each one of which is a measure for a particular job value, makes it relatively easy to write definitions of exact meaning and significance.

Step 4. Defining Degrees for Each Factor. Evaluation of the job on each of the selected factors is achieved by means of a series of "degrees" or categories, each having a different point value. For example, the experience factor is sometimes composed of the following degrees:

Degree	Amount of Experience
1	Up to one month
2	Over one month to three months
3	Over three months up to one year
4	Over one year up to three years
5	Over three years

The factors selected are usually divided into degrees before the relative values of the factors are determined, because the importance of each factor is somewhat easier to determine if the degree categories have been established than it is with just the factor definition alone. The establishment of degrees for each factor is similar to the process of defining the various levels of a grade-description scale. (See Chapter 4.)

The major difficulty in determining degrees is to make each degree either equidistant (in amount required) from the two adjacent degrees, or to make the distance a known amount. Suppose the following point values were assigned to the degree levels in the example immediately above: degree 1, 20 points; degree 2, 40 points; degree 3, 60 points; degree 4, 80 points; degree 5, 100 points. On the basis of point values the intervals between adjacent degrees are the same. However, the range of experience which each degree represents is not the same

What was the basis for the allocation of points? Perhaps it was the judgment of the individuals on the committee chosen to adapt an existing system to plant needs. Edward N. Hay recently stated that the point-method scales are based on the assumption that successive levels of difficulty for each factor represent uniform increments from level to level. "No advocate of the point methods has presented evidence to substantiate the assumption that the successive levels on a scale of this kind are in fact equidistant. On the contrary, there is every reason to believe, by examination of the scales, that the intervals are quite irregular." [25] Hay points out that in the factor-comparison method the intervals are always equal because they were judged so by a group of trained evaluators, and because of the further fact that the weights on the scale are derived directly from salaries already proved to be sound. Intervals on the factor-comparison scale are usually geometrically related and reflect the existing salary structure which, for most organizations, tends to increase on a geometric progression from the lower to the higher jobs.

M. R. Lohmann, Vice Dean of the Oklahoma Institute of Technology, Oklahoma Agricultural and Mechanical College, in a private communication to the author, agrees with Hay that it is difficult to substantiate the assumption that successive levels on a scale are in fact equidistant. Lohmann would go further and state that the differences between degrees must be equidistant either in an absolute (that is, arithmetic) or geometric progression. For example, when the degree definitions are written, it may be the intention of the writer to divide the total span of difficulty into five equal parts, and to have the difference between degree one and degree two of the same magnitude as the difference between degree two and degree three, and so forth. According to Lohmann, it may also be the writer's intent to make the differences in a geometric progression; that is, to make degree two ten per cent more difficult than degree one, and degree three ten per cent more difficult than degree two, and so forth. Lohmann believes that the degree definitions can divide the range of difficulty for each factor in either an arithmetic or geometric pattern. It can be quite conclusively demonstrated mathematically that errors may be introduced in a point system of job evaluation when arithmetic and geometric progression of points are not used with the appropriate arithmetic and geometric progressions of degree definitions. This is illustrated in step six below.

Hay makes a new contribution to job-evaluation rating scale construction when he applies "Weber's Law" to the establishment of degrees. The law as expressed by Fechner [26] is stated in two ways:

[25] Edward N. Hay, "Characteristics of Factor Comparison Job Evaluation," *Personnel*, American Management Association (May, 1946).

[26] George T. Ladd and Robert S. Woodworth, *Elements of Physiological Psychology* (New York: Charles Scribner's Sons, 1911), pp. 360–379.

(1) The addition of equal units of sensation is accomplished by the successive multiplication of the stimulus by a constant fraction; or (2) to make sensation increase in arithmetical progression, the stimulus must increase in geometrical progression.

In job-evaluation terms, Fechner's expression of "Weber's Law" means that in order for the differences between two degrees to be perceptible, the degrees must be increased in value or difficulty as required by the job by the successive multiplication by a constant. For example, it would be easier to make accurate ratings on experience required if the degrees were 1 month, 3 months, 9 months, 27 months, and 81 months than if they were 1 month, 2 months, 3 months, 4 months, 5 months, and so on. This means that each factor must be divided into degrees which are sufficiently different so that a job-rater can readily perceive the differences in jobs when rating them.

Figures 5–8 and 5–9 show what is meant by "just noticeable differences" in job evaluation. In Figure 5–8 it may be difficult to rate a job for the amount of experience required with a high degree of consistency because the differences between adjacent levels are small. In Figure 5–9, however, it is much easier to judge the amount of experience required because the "differences between levels" have been increased. The amount of agreement between job analysts will be increased if care is taken to keep the differences between degrees sufficiently great to permit sound and consistent judgment in comparing jobs. The following rules are designed to aid job analysts in defining degrees for each factor in a rating scale:

Rule 1. The number of degrees selected should be no more than are needed to differentiate adequately and fairly between all the jobs being rated. If, for example, working conditions are the same for all but a few jobs, and for these few jobs the conditions are approximately the same, two degrees or levels of working conditions are sufficient. On the other hand, if the experience required varies from a single day to a maximum of ten years, it is obvious that several degrees are required.

Rule 2. Degrees should be selected so that jobs fall at each level. It is unwise to have a minimum level at which no jobs fall, and it is also unwise to have a degree at such a high level that no job can reach it, because greater employee acceptance can be obtained when all degrees are used. The scales should be so constructed that they fully apply to the jobs being rated.

Rule 3. Each degree should be clearly defined in terms which the workers can understand. The use of difficult and unusual

The time it takes to attain full manual and mental proficiency on the job under ordinary work conditions without the specific course training for the job. If organized training is available on this job, rate this factor as it would be if these people had not received the training. It should be remembered that under ordinary work conditions it will take some time for a worker to have the opportunity to get acquainted with all aspects of the work. The time considered should be that needed for persons with no experience.

Time	Points
Less than one week	10
More than one week to one month	20
More than one month to three months	40
More than three months to six months	60
More than six months to one year	80
One year and over: 80 plus 16 points per additional year	
One year	80
Two years	96
Three years	112
Four years	128
Five years	144
Six years	160
Seven years	176
Eight years	192
Nine years	208
Ten years	224

Fig. 5—8.   Experience.

What is the length of time usually required by a worker to obtain sufficient work experience to perform the job duties effectively?

Does the job require one or both of the following: previous experience on related work, or lesser positions, within or outside the organization and/or a period of adjustment or "breaking in" on the job itself?

The "Rating" is the total required experience before being placed on the job plus the period of adjustment or "breaking in" on the job itself.

Level	Points
I	200
(Over 6 years)	
II	138
(4 years to 6 years)	
III	92
(2 years to 4 years)	
IV	60
(1 year to 2 years)	
V	40
(6 months to 1 year)	
VI	28
(3 months to 6 months)	
VII	22
(1 month to 3 months)	
VIII	20
(Up to 1 month)	

Fig. 5—9.   Experience.

words, even though they are highly descriptive, should be avoided. The language of the shop and office is preferred. To gain worker acceptance, worker understanding is essential.

Rule 4.   Avoid the use of ambiguous terms. Such terms as *intelligence, character, sociability* should be defined to eliminate any chance of misinterpretation. It will also be found that such terms as *average, fairly, exceedingly, extremely, poor, small, large* do not convey the same meaning to each job analyst.

Rule 5.   Definitions of degrees should be written in objective terms. A subjective definition uses such general terms as *self-reliance, tact,* and *loyalty.* An objective definition describes degrees in terms of what the worker must do on the job or in terms which do not depend upon judgment. "Must lift a heavy load" is a subjective description, whereas "must lift 75 lbs." is an objective description.

Rule 6.   In writing degree definitions use examples as much as possible. These are helpful in clarifying points and in making the degree definitions more objective. Figure 5–10 presents a series of degree definitions in job terms and also illustrates the use of job examples which make each degree level more meaningful. This is Attribute No. 8 in the *Occupational Rating Plan* of the Industrial Management Society. Figure 5–11 illustrates an elaborate and effective approach to degree definition. This factor was devised by a joint union-management committee as part of the job-evaluation study at the Sperry Gyroscope Company.

Preparation of degree definitions and determination of the number of degrees for each factor are difficult and important parts of job rating scale construction. This stage of the study is crucial. A poorly constructed rating scale will result in unreliable and inaccurate ratings. No individual should be wedded to a particular type of scale or to a particular system. The scale should be so constructed that the degrees and their definitions can be constantly improved and that ease of use, understanding, and accurate evaluation will result.

Step 5.   Determining the Relative Values of Job Factors. The job factors should not all have the same weight or be considered equally important in measuring the value of a job. The relative values are usually assigned on a percentage basis according to the proportionate amount each factor contributes to the total worth of the job. Table 5–3, which shows the findings of four major plans, gives some idea of how others have judged the relative value of these factors. Skill receives the highest weight on all four plans,

	POINTS	
1. Unable to speak, read or write English	0	Ditch Digger, Section Hand
2. Able to speak English	1	Factory Sweeper, Common Laborer, Casting Chipper, Punch Press Nos. 1, 2, 3
3. Able to read and write very simply	2	Janitor, Punch Press Nos. 4–5, Light Simple Assembly, Single Spindle Drill Press, Elevator Operator, Crane Operator (Bridge Type)
4. Able to read with ease, do simple arithmetical calculations. Equivalent to 6th grade	3	Elevator Operator, Bench Core Maker, Trucker Metal Parts, Counter and Packer, Polisher and Buffer, Jolt and Squeeze Molder, Electric Truck Operator
	4	Chauffeur, Tool Room Band Saw, Wood Shaper, Gas Brazer, Power Shear Metal Parts, Crater, Gager, Finish Sprayer
5. Able to read and write with ease, do average calculations, read blue prints. Equivalent to 8th grade	5	Arc Welder (Job Shop), Casting Inspector, Main Gate Watchman, Repetitive Mill Hand, Steel Shop Fabricator, Punch Press Nos. 6–7, Plater
	6	Wood Shop Carpenter, Metal Planer, Printshop Power Shear, Tool Room Lathe, Bench Molder, Shop Patrolman
6. Able to compile reports, write letters, keep records, use fair to good grammar. Equivalent to 2 years' high school	7	Mail Carrier, Wood Pattern Maker, Millwright
	8	Retail Clerk, Layer-out, Castings and Details, Tool Room Milling Machine, Tool Crib Attendant, Casting Inspector
	9	Jig Borer, Shop Production Clerk, Toolmaker
7. Fair knowledge of several subjects, able to write average letters, use good grammar, make difficult calculations. High school, or equivalent	10	General Lineman, Structural Sheet Layerout, Precision Surface Grinder
	11	Stenographer, Auto Screw Machine Set-up
8. Elementary technical training, as acquired in 1st year college, or in 4-year technical high school.	12	Die Maker
	12	Maintenance Electrician
	13	Melter of Alloys to Specifications, Detail Draftsman or Tracer
	14	
	15	Draftsman on Complicated Test Equipment
	16	Maintenance of Complicated Test Equipment
	17	Instrument Man, Surveying
	18	Maintenance of Very Complicated Electrical Equipment
	19	Tool Designer
	.	
	.	
	.	
	.	

(From *Occupational Rating Plan* of the Industrial Management Society.)

Fig. 5—10. Schooling, Attribute No. 8.

(Mental training received in school, or by any other means of education, to develop characteristics not readily acquired by actual work or experience on any job.)

TABLE 5—3.   Summary of relative point values of four point-rating plans •

NEMA and NMTA	GENERAL ELECTRIC	WESTINGHOUSE	U. S. STEEL
Skill	*Skill*	*Skill*	*Skill*
Education 70 (14%)	Mentality 100 (12½%)	Education 100 (18½%)	Skill 100 (10%)
Experience 110 (22%)	Skill 400 (50%)	Experience 100 (18½%)	Dexterity 50 (50%)
Initiative & ingenuity 70 (14%)	Total permitted—500 (62½%)	Aptitude 125 (28½%)	Accuracy 80 (8%)
Total permitted—250 (50%)		Total permitted—325 (60½%)	Education or mental development 100 (10%)
			Experience & training 120 (12%)
			Total permitted—450 (45%)
Effort	*Effort*	*Effort*	*Effort*
Physical 50 (10%)	Mental 50 (6¼%)	Physical 40 (7½%)	Mental 100 (10%)
Mental—visual 25 (5%)	Physical 50 (6¼%)	Mental 40 (7½%)	Physical 60 (6%)
Total permitted—75 (15%)	Total permitted—100 (12½%)	Visual 40 (7½%)	Total permitted—160 (16%)
		Total permitted—120 (22½%)	
Responsibility	*Responsibility*	*Responsibility*	*Responsibility*
Equipment 25 (5%)	Responsibility 100 (12½%)	Safety of others 25 (4½%)	Safety of others 50 (5%)
Material or product 25 (5%)		For product 25 (4½%)	Supervision 50 (50%)
Safety of others 25 (5%)		For equipment 25 (4½%)	Materials 90 (9%)
Total permitted—100 (20%)		Total permitted—75 (13½%)	Machinery and equipment 50 (5%)
			Total permitted—240 (24%)
Job Conditions	*Job Conditions*	*Job Conditions*	*Job Conditions*
Working conditions 50 (10%)	Working conditions 100 (12½%)	Unusual features 20 (3½%)	Hazards 50 (5%)
Hazards 25 (5%)			Surroundings 40 (4%)
Total permitted—75 (15%)			Connecting expense 10 (1%)
			Fatigue 50 (5%)
			Total permitted—150 (15%)
ALL	ALL	ALL	ALL
500 (100%)	800 (100%)	540 (100%)	1,000 (100%)

From *U. E. Guide to Wage Payment Plans, Time Study, and Job Evaluation.*

and the job-conditions factor either receives the lowest weight or ties for the lowest weight.

In judging the relative value of each factor it must be kept in mind that these factors are common to all jobs, and that their relative values are to be judged as they contribute to the difficulty and

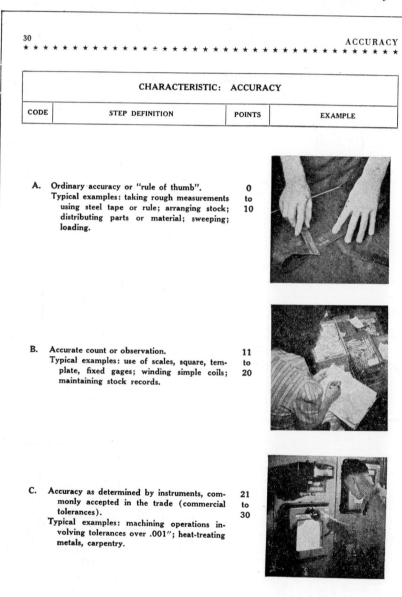

Fig. 5—11. Degree definitions.

worth of all jobs. The sum total of the amounts assigned to a job rated on each factor determines the difficulty or worth of that job.

How are the relative values determined? Usually in somewhat the same manner as money values are prorated among the factors on the factor-comparison method. The following method of as-signing relative values to the factors has been used successfully in several studies:

1. One or more juries are selected to judge the relative values of the factors.

2. These juries are instructed to study the job-evaluation manual care-fully, especially the factor definitions and degree definitions.

ACCURACY   31
★ ★

CHARACTERISTIC: ACCURACY (Continued)			
CODE	STEP DEFINITION	POINTS	EXAMPLE

D. Precision accuracy. Tolerances below .001″ achieved by machine manipulation. Typical examples: operation of bench lathe, precision grinder, engine lathe, jig borer.   31 to 40

E. Hight precision accuracy achieved manually. Typical examples: precision fitting of gears, bearings, shafts, punch and die sets.   41 to 50

Fig. 5—11 (cont.).

3. Each member of the jury is asked to rank the factors in order from the one which contributes most to the total value of the jobs to the one which contributes least.

4. Instructions are then issued to members of the jury: "Assuming that the relative values when totaled should equal 100 per cent, distribute this 100 per cent among the factors according to your judgment of their relative values. Make sure that the values assigned total 100 per cent."

5. The relative values so obtained are averaged.

In a recent study made by the Personnel Research Institute of Western Reserve University, the relative values listed in Table 5–4 were obtained by staff members of the Institute and two independent juries. The findings of these two juries were presented to a committee and a committee average was obtained. The final relative values were based on the jury results and an examination of the assignment of relative values in other job evaluation systems. Table 5–4 shows the averages and final relative values.

TABLE 5—4.   Comparison of averages and relative values for factors used to evaluate factory jobs •

Factor	PRI average	Committee average	Final value
1. Experience	16%	19%	20%
2. Education	10	11	12
3. Responsibility for Product and Materials...	11	8	8
4. Responsibility for Machinery, Tools and Equipment	9	8	8
5. Responsibility for Work of Others	8	5	6
6. Responsibility for Safety of Others	4	5	4
7. Resourcefulness	11	11	12
8. Monotony	6	3	4
9. Mental and Visual Effort	7	8	7
10. Physical Effort	7	10	9
11. Surroundings	5	6	5
12. Hazards	6	6	5
	100%	100%	100%

From *Handbook of Job Evaluation for Factory Jobs,* Personnel Research Institute of Western Reserve University, Industrial Fasteners Institute [formerly American Institute of Bolt, Nut and Rivet Manufacturers] (Cleveland: 1946), p. 46.

The assignment of values on the basis of subjective judgment is necessary, since there is no known method and no criteria for determining the relative values in an objective manner; until some accepted standard is found, the values must be based upon subjective judgment. Fortunately there is a high degree of agreement among workers, managers, and consultants.

Step 6. Assigning Point Values to Degrees. Once the relative value of each job factor has been obtained the next step is to assign points to the degrees in each factor. When assigned to jobs and totaled, these points become the job values used in determining the correct relative wage. There are two ways of assigning these point values: (1) by arithmetic progression, and (2) by geometric progression. It is difficult to say which method is better, since no specific study of the problem has come to our attention.

Lohmann again comments in a private communication to point out that three things are always related: the kind of degree definitions, the kind of point progression, and the earning curve that expresses the relationship between points and dollars. This relationship must be understood if one is to design a good point system, for it is here that errors can be built into the system. For example, if arithmetic points are used on arithmetic definitions, a curved or second degree wage curve will result. If the point progression is changed to a geometric progression, it will produce a straight-line wage curve. The error occurs, as pointed out above, when a geometric progression of points is used on degree definitions that are designed to be arithmetically equidistant, or an arithmetic progression is used on a geometrically designed series of degree definitions. In actual practice, the errors tend to compensate for each other, and the result is adequate. For certain jobs which have an unusual combination of requirements, the errors accumulate and the result is totally unacceptable.

Arithmetic progression

One way to assign point values is to keep the difference between each degree the same. For example, Table 5–5 below shows how points are assigned to a few of the factors in a scale on the basis of an arithmetic progression.

TABLE 5—5.   Points assigned to factors •

| Factor | Degree | | | | |
	1st	2nd	3rd	4th	5th
Skill					
1. Education	15	30	45	60	75
2. Experience	20	40	60	80	100
3. Initiative	22	44	66	88	110
Effort					
4. Physical	8	16	24	32	40
5. Mental	9	18	27	36	45

On a scale of this type a single point value is assigned to the degree. If the job analyst places a job in Degree 3 on Experience, he automatically assigns 60 points to the job.

Table 5–6 shows how points are assigned to a factor using an arithmetic progression and also a range of point values for each

TABLE 5—6.   Educational requirements •

DEFINITION: This factor is rated according to the minimum education necessary to allow an understanding of the position.

Degree	Point Value
1. Grammar school or equivalent	0
2. Up to 2 years High School or equivalent	2–4
3. Up to 4 years High School or equivalent	6–8
4. Up to 2 years Special Training above a High School education or its equivalent	10–12
5. Up to 4 years Special Training above a High School education or its equivalent	14–16

From *Clerical Position Evaluation Plan,* Revere Copper and Brass, Inc., 230 Park Avenue, New York.

degree. The selection of Degree 3 for a job would be followed by a second judgment as to whether 6, 7, or 8 points would be allotted to the job.

Geometric-type progression

The use of a geometric progression in assigning point values to degrees is based upon the premise that each degree increases a given percentage above the preceding one. Examples of systems using a geometric progression, or one that approximates such a progression, are shown in Tables 5–7 and 5–8.

TABLE 5—7.   Assignment of point values according to geometric-type progression •

Factors	Levels						
	I	II	III	IV	V	VI	VII
1. Complexity of duties	70	44	28	18	11	7	
2. Character of supervision given	50	32	20	13	8	5	
3. Scope of supervision	40	25	16	10	6	4	
4. Supervision received	50	28	16	9	5		
5. Experience	100	68	46	32	22	15	10
6. Essential education and knowledge	90	50	28	16	9		
7. Confidential data	40	22	13	7	4		
8. Effect of errors	50	28	16	9	5		
9. Contacts with others	120	67	38	21	12		
10. Pressure of work	50	23	11	5			
11. Working conditions	40	13	4				
12. Sales techniques required	160	74	34	16			
13. Knowledge of merchandise	140	79	44	25	14		

Assignment of points when different numbers of degrees are used

It is a mistake to assume that each factor must have the same number of degrees. Only those degrees should be used which are necessary to define the observable levels. A problem arises when a varying number of degrees is used. This problem is caused by the fact that it is desirable to have both the lowest- and the highest-degree point values assigned in proportion to the relative importance of each factor. In assigning point values for a varying num-

TABLE 5—8.   Assignment of point values according to geometric progression—
responsibility for safety of others •

The responsibility of the employee for the safety of others, or the extent of injury to others which he can prevent. Accidents to the employee himself are to be rated under Hazards and are not to be considered here.

DEGREE	AMOUNT OF RESPONSIBILITY	POINTS
1	Almost no responsibility for safety of others	5
2	Only reasonable care to own work is required to insure safety of others, and accidents, if they should occur, would be minor in nature	10
3	Care must be exercised to avoid possibility of danger to others. Care by others, however, usually can efface much of the hazard that carelessness on this job can create	20
4	Carelessness by employee would occasionally cause lost time, accidents to other workers. Serious accidents unlikely	40
5	Safety of others depends almost entirely on correct action of employee. Dangerous situations likely to result in serious injury to others if person performing this job is careless	80

(From *Occupational Rating Plan* of the Industrial Management Society.)

ber of degrees, when using an arithmetic progression, the procedure outlined below is helpful.

1. Set up a table similar to Table 5–9 and list the degrees or levels from high to low, Degree I being the highest. In this case the relative values assigned to the factors on a percentage basis were multiplied by 10, so the total for the values of Degree I is 1000. The percentage values were assigned to the lowest degree levels for each factor. These when totaled equal 100.

2. Subtract the lowest degree point value from the highest. For example, the highest degree for Experience, Degree I, was assigned 200 points and the lowest, Degree VIII, was assigned 20 points. The difference is 180.

3. Divide the difference by 7, since there are seven spaces to receive values: the interval between I & II, II & III, III & IV, and so on. The dividend or common difference is 25.7 or 26. In all cases divide the difference by one less than the number of degrees.

4. Add the common difference obtained in Step 3 to the value

TABLE 5—9.   Assignment of point values based upon the relative importance of each factor—arithmetic progression •

Factor	Degrees							
	I	II	III	IV	V	VI	VII	VIII
1. Experience	200	174	148	122	97	71	46	20
2. Education	120	93	66	39	12			
3. Responsibility for product and materials	80	62	44	26	8			
4. Responsibility for machinery, tools, and equipment	80	62	44	26	8			
5. Responsibility for work of others	60	42	24	6				
6. Responsibility for safety of others	40	31	22	13	4			
7. Resourcefulness	120	93	66	39	12			
8. Monotony	40	28	16	4				
9. Mental and visual effort	70	49	28	7				
10. Physical effort	90	70	50	29	9			
11. Surroundings	50	35	20	5				
12. Hazards	50	39	27	16	5			

for the lowest degree to obtain the point value for the next higher degree. Add twice the common difference to the lowest value to obtain the point value of the next higher degree. Add three times the common difference to the lowest value to obtain the point value for the next higher degree, and so on, rounding off the decimal at each step.

Geometric progressions for job evaluation manuals can be computed relatively easily by the use of logarithms. It is not necessary fully to understand logarithmic theory and calculations to follow the method about to be described.[27]

Before computing a geometric progression for a job-evaluation manual by logarithms, the following information must be available. (See Table 5–10.)

1. The number of levels (degrees) assigned to each factor in the job evaluation manual.

2. The relative weights assigned to each factor in the job evaluation manual.

3. The ratio of the progression desired, that is, the relationship of the highest level in any one factor to the lowest level in the same factor. For computational convenience, both of these levels should be divided by the lowest level so that the ratio is in an x to 1 form. For example: highest level = 100, lowest level = 20; ratio = 100/20 or 5 to 1.

[27] Prepared by Norman G. Halpern, Research Associate, Psychological Research Services, Western Reserve University.

A job analysis of the assignment of geometric point values is found below:

TABLE 5—10.   A job evaluation manual—levels, assigned weights, and ratio of progression •

Factor	Levels	Assigned weight
1. Essential knowledge	I II III IV V VI VII	18
2. Experience	I II III IV V VI VII	20
3. Supervision received	I II III IV V	10
4. Supervision given	I II III IV V	10
5. Number supervised	I II III IV V VI	6
6. Responsibility for production	I II III IV V	14
7. Responsibility for confidential matters	I II III	3
8. Responsibility for getting along with others	I II III IV	10
9. Pressure of work	I II III IV	6
10. Working conditions	I II III	3

Ratio of Progression: 5 to 1

1. Look up the log of the ratio of the progression desired in any standard logarithm table. Example: Ratio is 5 to 1; look up the log of 5 which is found to be .698970.

2. Divide the logarithm by the number of levels minus one $(n-1)$ for each factor. Example: Factor 2, Experience, has been assigned 7 levels. Divide: .698970 by $7-1$; $\dfrac{.698970}{7-1} = \dfrac{.698970}{6} = .116495$.

3. Look up the antilog (or the actual number) corresponding to the log obtained in Step 2 in any standard logarithm table. Example: Antilog .116495 = 1.308.

4. For any one factor, the antilog obtained in Step 3 is a constant (K). The lowest level in the progression is always the assigned relative weight. (Level VII in Factor 2, Experience, has been assigned the weight of 20. This automatically is the point value for the lowest level.) Multiply the constant (K) by the lowest level to get the next higher level: $20 \times 1.308 = 26.2$.

5. Keep multiplying each computed level by K to obtain the next higher level. Round point value figures to the nearest whole number only after all calculations have been executed. Example:

	Rounded point value
Level VII has been assigned the value of	20
Level VI = 20 × 1.308 = 26.2	26
Level V = 26.2 × 1.308 = 34.2	34
Level IV = 34.2 × 1.308 = 44.8	45
Level III = 44.8 × 1.308 = 58.5	59
Level II = 58.5 × 1.308 = 76.6	77
Level I = 76.6 × 1.308 = 100.1	100

Check: The highest point value divided by the lowest should equal the desired ratio—100/20 = 5.

The point values which have been assigned to the ten factors, using this method, are found in Table 5–11.

TABLE 5—11. Assignment of point values based upon the relative importance of each factor—geometric-type progression ●

Factor	Levels						
	I	II	III	IV	V	VI	VII
1. Essential knowledge	90	69	53	40	31	24	18
2. Experience	100	77	59	45	34	26	20
3. Supervision received	50	33	22	15	10		
4. Supervision given	50	33	22	15	10		
5. Number supervised	30	22	16	11	8	6	
6. Responsibility for production	70	47	31	21	14		
7. Responsibility for confidential matters	15	7	3				
8. Responsibility for getting along with others	50	29	17	10			
9. Pressure of work	30	18	10	6			
10. Working conditions	15	7	3				

Checking relative value of factors and degrees

It has been demonstrated above that the range of value for any factor is from some minimum amount to some maximum, with all jobs having some degree of the factor. It is believed that some jobs should include the minimum and maximum amounts, but occasionally changes in skill requirements may result in degrees of a factor that apply to no jobs in the unit being evaluated. It has also been demonstrated that the maximum and minimum value of any factor is usually different from other factors. The maximum of points allowed for effort, for example, is generally not as high as the maximum for skill, while the minimum for effort is lower than the minimum for skill. The exact value placed on each factor is not necessarily a logical and precise process. However, some process, as indicated above, is usually involved in determining the value to be placed on each factor.

M. R. Lohmann has given permission to use material from an article entitled "Job Evaluation," to be published in the *Journal of the American Institute of Industrial Engineers*. This is taken from a paper given before the Fifth Annual Industrial Engineering Conference on the campus of the University of California, both at Berkeley and Los Angeles. Lohmann writes as follows:

In chairs, the relative value of strength, weight, padding, and proportion is not determined by the manufacturer or seller, but by the buyer or customer. In the long run, it is the customer not the seller who determines the price. It is true, of course, that the seller initially establishes a price for chairs, but if in the judgment of the customers the price is out of line with other chairs of comparable quality, the chairs won't sell until either the quality is increased or the price lowered. Thus, it is the combined judgment of many consumers that determines the relative weight of the elements of quality. The process is unsystematic and probably something like the example that follows: The customer attempts to determine the degree of each element of quality possessed by the two different chairs. One chair may be stronger but heavier, with more padding but poorly proportioned. The customer then attempts to weigh the different degrees of each factor to arrive at some total or sum, which is the total quality to which he compares price. For example, he tries to determine if the extra strength is off-set by the greater weight or whether the value of the extra padding is off-set by the loss in proportion. The chair he purchases will be the one which in his evaluation has the most quality per dollar of price.

The evaluation of jobs is essentially a similar process but more systematic for greater consistency. There is no scientific method of determining the relative value of effort as compared to skill. There is also no scientific method of determining the relative value of different degrees of skill. The only values that are pertinent to this problem are the customers of jobs, the employees, for it is they who judge the salary and determine if it is fair and equitable.

All job evaluation plans determine the relative value of the degrees of the factors by either breaking down by ranking and rating some key or bench-mark jobs (factor comparison system) or by testing empirically determined values on a group of bench-mark jobs (point systems).

The principal criterion in the selection of these bench-mark jobs is that the relative wage or salary currently paid should be considered by employees to be fair and equitable. The employees may be unsatisfied about the absolute amount, but should not be dissatisfied with the relationships of the wage rate of one bench-mark job to another.

The system of weighting the degrees of the factors is satisfactory when, after the bench-mark jobs are evaluated and the total difficulty points determined, the points made by plotting the difficulty points against the present salary or wage of the jobs is in some continuous line, either straight or curved. It is important to note that the value or the number of difficulty points assigned to any degree of any factor is determined from jobs whose relative pay is already satisfactory. The expectation is, of course, that other jobs measured by the same system of values that were satisfactory for the bench-mark jobs will be measured equally as satisfactory.

If in rating the bench-mark jobs with the points established in the manner described in Steps 1–6 the curve is neither straight nor an acceptable second-degree curve, then some part of the process of determining both the relative values of the factors and the points assigned to the degrees of the factors is not producing a point system which agrees with the relative values of the bench-mark jobs. One can assume that the error is either in the selection of the bench-mark jobs or in the point system. Since this "validation" step of the construction of the point system assumes that the employees and the employer would accept the bench-mark jobs and the relative difference in value between them, a correction in the point system is probably the best correction to make. This is done by examining first the relative importance assigned to the factors to make sure that this is not causing the bench-mark jobs to fall out of line when plotting their point values against their wages. If the relative value of these factors seems to be acceptable, the next step is to determine the influence of the degree levels on the curve. It may be that the jobs which are out of line are those falling at a degree level for a certain factor or factors which should have fewer or more points assigned to bring the out-of-line bench-mark jobs in line. In most instances, if steps 1 through 6 are followed carefully, the bench-mark jobs will fall in line on the wage curve. This step is a "validation" step, and should result in a system which is not only acceptable as a system, but one which has survived a preliminary trial on carefully selected bench-mark jobs.

JOB-EVALUATION MANUALS

The final job-evaluation system is usually in manual form and is referred to as the rating manual. This manual becomes the measuring stick for the determination of the relative value of the jobs being classified. It is important to note that the manual consists of a series of rating scales, one for each factor, and each scale is part of the total measuring stick. The final job value depends on both the excellence of the rating scales and the skill of the analyst who uses them. The illustrative manuals which follow are included so that the reader will be able to visualize a complete point-rating job-evaluation plan. The authors are indebted to the Personnel Research Institute of Western Reserve University, to Revere Copper and Brass, Incorporated of New York, and to the Industrial Fasteners Institute for permission to reproduce the complete manuals.

ILLUSTRATIVE MANUALS—POINT-RATING JOB EVALUATION PLANS

JOB EVALUATION MANUAL FOR
CLERICAL AND SUPERVISORY POSITIONS
Prepared by
Personnel Research Institute of Western Reserve University
Cleveland, Ohio

Summary of Factors

1. Character of supervision received
2. Character of supervision given
3. Number supervised
4. Work experience
5. Essential knowledge and training
6. Dexterity
7. Responsibility for money, securities and funds (to be used only in rating clerical, specialist and supervisory personnel)
8. Responsibility for machinery and equipment (to be used only in rating maintenance personnel and foremen)
9. Responsibility for getting along with others
10. Responsibility for confidential matters
11. Responsibility for accuracy—effect of errors
12. Pressure of work
13. Monotony
14. Unusual working conditions

1. CHARACTER OF SUPERVISION RECEIVED

To what degree does the immediate supervisor (a) outline methods to be followed, (b) outline results being accomplished, (c) check progress of the work, (d) check tasks completed, (e) handle exceptional work items and (f) correct errors made?

Level   *Points*

1. *General Direction*—The employee here establishes work procedures and performance standards in conformance with administrative policies and completes assigned duties with virtually no reference of detail to higher supervision; determines the structure and function of a work unit composed of employees of various skills and responsibilities; arbitrates questionable items within the limits of general company policies 45

Level   *Points*

2. *Direction*—A definite work objective is set by higher supervision and the employee is permitted to perform assigned duties in conformance with work procedures and performance standards with which he has a limited recommendatory connection; sets up the standards of performance, adapts a time schedule for work to be completed and devises work practices and procedures for himself and others in conformance to general policies of the company **36**

3. *General Supervision*—The employee here assumes responsibility; he is presumed to know the routine work details and performance standards of his job and to perform assigned tasks without appreciable advice or spur from the immediate superior; plans and arranges own work schedule under specified standard practices; refers questionable items to the immediate supervisors when in doubt as to procedure **27**

4. *Supervision*—A close check over the specific details of the employee's work is not necessary, but out of the ordinary phases of the work are referred by him to the immediate superior for advice and direction; proceeds alone on routine tasks following standard practice instructions; refers all questionable items to the immediate supervisor **18**

5. *Immediate Supervision*—The employee performs assigned tasks in accordance with specific and detailed instructions; how the work is done and progress made are checked periodically by the immediate supervisor; works on short assignments with a regular check of performance at frequent intervals **9**

2. Character of Supervision Given

To what degree does the employee (a) assign tasks to others, (b) outline the methods others are to follow, (c) outline the work they are to accomplish, (d) check the progress and production of other employees, (e) handle exceptional cases referred to him by others, and (f) correct the errors others have made? What place does the job occupy on the organization chart?

Level   *Points*

1 *Direction* of the work of employees and may direct work of several departments. Establishes standards of performance and policies of a general nature. Makes work assignments to employees possessing a variety of skills. Assigns objectives to be accomplished rather than setting specific methods for doing the job **55**

2. *General supervision* in which the employees being supervised assume responsibility. Employees know the routine work details and performance standards of the jobs and do not require spur from superior. Subordinate employees may make work assignments to others **44**

3. *Supervises* without maintaining a close check over the specific details of the employees' work, but out of the ordinary phases of the work are referred to person on job being rated for advice and

Level	Points

direction. Responsible for maintaining satisfactory performance of employees **33**

4. *Close supervision* over a group of employees involving assigning of duties, giving frequent instructions, checking work, and handling ordinary difficulties **22**

5. *None,* but might occasionally show another employee how to perform a task **11**

3. Number Supervised

What is the "size' of the supervisory responsibility of this job in terms of the number of persons supervised? (Both direct and indirect supervision are to be considered.)

Level	Points

1. Supervises more than 60 other employees **35**
2. Supervises from 25 to 59 other employees **29**
3. Supervises from ten to 24 other employees **24**
4. Supervises from four to nine other employees **18**
5. Supervises one to three other employees **13**
6. Supervises no one, but might occasionally show another employee how to perform a task **7**

4. Work Experience

How much work experience must an average employee have to perform the job duties satisfactorily? Does the job require either (a) previous experience on other jobs in the company or in other industrial concerns, or (b) a period of adjustment on the job itself, or both (a) and (b)? (The specification that will be considered is the total experience required— previous work experience plus "breaking in" time. Special attention should be given to knowledge of company policies, practices, procedures and personnel required on the job.)

Level	Points

1. Requires more than eight years' experience on this job and progressively important jobs in the company or in an outside organization **100**
2. Requires up to eight years' experience on this or related jobs in the company and elsewhere **84**
3. Requires up to three years' experience on this and related jobs in the company and elsewhere **68**
4. Requires up to one year's experience on this and related jobs in the company or in an outside organization **52**
5. Requires up to three months' experience on this job or others of a similar character **36**
6. Requires up to one week's experience on this job with no previous experience in work of this type **20**

5. Essential Knowledge and Training

What is the basic knowledge, specified education and specialized training required to learn or perform this job? (These requisites may be the result of formal education or independent study.)

Level   *Points*

1. *Knowledge:* Intensive and thorough knowledge of a specialized field requiring independent research and creative work is required.
   Education: Equivalent to a Master's degree or above 85
2. *Knowledge:* Thorough knowledge of a technical field such as accounting, finance, business administration, economics, statistics.
   Education: The equivalent to four years of college, business or technical school ....: 71
3. *Knowledge:* Broad knowledge involving advanced mathematics, accounting, statistics, responsible secretarial work, purchasing, economics, labor laws, commercial law, tabulating methods.
   Education: The equivalent to four years of high school, plus two years of college composed of applicable courses. Night or extension or correspondence school credits can be accumulated to equal two years of college 58
4. *Knowledge:* Stenography, use of office equipment such as a bookkeeping machine, calculating machine or tabulating equipment is required.
   Education: Four years of high school plus specific course requirements as indicated in part in "Knowledge" above 44
5. *Knowledge:* Knowledge of arithmetic, spelling, grammar or general high school subject matter is required.
   Education: High school graduation 31
6. *Knowledge:* No specific knowledge is required to perform the assigned job tasks. Ability to read, write, and perform simple mathematical computations can be a requirement.
   Education: Less than high school graduation 17

6. Dexterity

Does the job require the ability to move the fingers, hands, arms, feet or legs nimbly and accurately, to judge accurately through the sense of touch and the sense of hearing, or to control accurately the movements of the hands from what the eyes see?

Level   *Points*

1. Requires a high degree of coordination of repetitive manual operations and may involve a high degree of sensory discrimination, such as operating a telephone switchboard or an IBM proof machine 20
2. Requires a moderate degree of repetitive manual operations, such as operating an adding machine or typewriter 12
3. The type of tasks performed requires little or no motor ability 4

7. Responsibility for Money and Securities

(To be used only in rating clerical, specialist and supervisory personnel.)

How much money, securities and funds might be charged to the employee at any one time? What authority does the employee on this job have to initiate or approve the release of valuables?

Level   *Points*

1. Responsible at any one time for more than $1,000 worth of money and negotiable securities or has the authority to initiate or approve the release of a similar amount of funds   30
2. Responsible at any one time for $500 to $1,000 worth of money and negotiable securities or has the authority to initiate or approve the release of a similar amount of funds   25
3. Responsible at any one time for $100 to $500 worth of money and negotiable securities or has the authority to initiate or approve the release of a similar amount of valuables   20
4. Responsible at any one time for $25 to $100 worth of money and negotiable securities or has the authority to initiate or approve the release of a similar amount of valuables   16
5. Responsible at any one time for up to $25 worth of money or negotiable securities or non-negotiable securities in any amount ..   11
6. Has no responsibility for money, securities or funds; may act as as a witness or checker   6

8. Responsibility for Machinery and Equipment

(To be used in rating maintenance personnel and foremen only.)

How much damage or loss to machinery and equipment vital to company operation could be caused by neglect, carelessness or willfulness? (The loss of service, inconvenience and confusion caused and cost of repairs should be considered.)

Level   *Points*

1. Responsible for the use or operation of equipment or machinery where considerable and continual care is needed to avoid substantial damage or great loss of operating time and efficiency through breakdown and/or responsible for the general maintenance and repair program. Probable loss—$1,000   30
2. Responsible for the use or operation of equipment or machinery where more than routine care is required to prevent damage or loss of operating time and efficiency through breakdown and/or responsible for the maintenance and repair of complex mechanical devices or for major building repairs. Probable loss—$500.00   24
3. Responsible for the use or operation of equipment or machinery where failure on the part of the worker or the employee to exercise due care or to report maintenance needs to the immediate superior could cause loss of efficiency through breakdown, and/or respon-

Level *Points*

    sible for the maintenance and repair of simple mechanical devices
or for routine or minor building repairs. Probable loss—$100.00   18
4. Responsible for use or operation of equipment or machinery that is
not easily damaged to any serious extent; failure to keep equipment or machinery in condition would result in some loss of effi-
ciency. Probable loss—$10.00   12
5. Responsible only for maintenance supplies of little value that are
expected to be consumed in the course of ordinary operations   6

9. Responsibility for Getting Along with Others

Is the employee on this job required to meet and deal with people outside the department in which he works? Are they employees of the
company or others? How are the contacts made? How frequently? What
is the purpose of the contacts?

Level *Points*

1. Regularly represents the company and interprets its policies and
practices to all types of people within the organization and outside   25
2. Has contacts by telephone, correspondence or personal meeting
with persons in other departments or outside the company to obtain or supply factual information; tact is required in these contacts and the employee assumes the responsibility for harmonious
relationships   18
3. Has regular contacts with other departments in the furnishing or
obtaining of information or reports; requires tact to avoid misunderstanding in contact where improper handling could affect
results; however, the primary responsibility for harmonious relationships is assumed by the immediate superior   12
4. Personal contacts limited to routine dealings (furnishing and obtaining information upon request) with other individuals in the
same department   5

10. Responsibility for Confidential Matters

Is integrity and discretion in safeguarding confidential and restricted
information required on this job? What is the nature of the information?
To what degree is its meaning understood? Would disclosure affect internal relationships only or would external and customer relationships
be affected? (Only such confidential and restricted information as the
employee handles in his regular work routine is to be considered. It is
recognized that every person might obtain confidential and restricted
information by accident or subterfuge.)

Level *Points*

1. Has access to information relating to company policy and practices which is restricted to specified persons and knows its full
meaning. The utmost discretion and integrity are recognized re-
quirements for the job   30

Level   *Points*

2. Works regularly with some information which is restricted to specified persons; discretion and integrity are recognized requirements for the job 18
3. Works with no information which is restricted to specified persons   6

11. Responsibility for Accuracy—Effect of Errors

What is the seriousness of a mistake or error in judgment on this job? Who would discover it? How long might be taken to correct it? Would it affect the work of the individual making the error, others in the same department, other departments or persons outside the company? Might the company suffer embarrassment, financial loss, injury to good will or loss of time required to correct the mistake or error in judgment? What might be the extent of such a loss?

Level   *Points*

1. Mistakes made might cause considerable financial loss; errors in judgment might result in loss of prestige by the company in its dealings with others 20
2. Mistakes made are difficult to detect prior to audit; an error in judgment would cause confusion in the work routine but would have little or no effect upon the company's relationships with others 16
3. Mistakes detected in succeeding steps of the work operation; up to three man-hours' time might be required to correct the mistake   12
4. Mistakes detected upon the completion of the work cycle; up to one man-hour's time might be required to correct the mistake 8
5. Little or no opportunity to make an error is present in the job 4

12. Pressure of Work

What degree of concentration on either minute job details or many tasks of the job is required? At what pace must the employee work? Must a large volume of work be processed within a specified, limited time? Must attention be shifted frequently from one to another job detail? Are there interruptions, distractions or confusing influences? (Energy output is not necessarily involved in these considerations, but simply the required rate of performance.)

Level   *Points*

1. Requires constant concentration on a very large volume of work which must be completed within a limited period of time 24
2. Requires close concentration with occasional periods of average pressure 18
3. Flow of work and character of duties involves uniform mental attention 12
4. Flow of work or character of duties is intermittent and requires close attention only at intervals 6

13. Monotony

How frequently are the same tasks repeated during the working day? Do they require repetition of muscularly tiring movements? What individual factors might create a feeling of monotony?

Level   *Points*

1. Performs extremely repetitive and confining tasks requiring constant concentration on the work and the necessity for completion; monotony is a definite factor of the job 15
2. Has to be at work place for considerable periods of time with little or no opportunity to vary the tasks performed; monotony is recognized as a factor of the job 11
3. Has a limited variety of tasks to perform, but has some opportunity to alter the work routine 7
4. Has a variety of tasks to perform; routine tasks are not an essential part of the job; the variety is considered to be such as to arouse interest 3

14. Unusual Working Conditions

(Not to be confused with rotating shift work or night work for which a premium is paid.)

Level   *Points*

1. Works under unusual conditions, perhaps at the sacrifice of personal safety, comfort and convenience (such as continuous travel out of the city or in the heat and noise of a boiler room) 10
2. Works regularly under poorer than average conditions; illumination and ventilation are considered only adequate (as in an enclosed vault or workroom space) 6
3. Works regularly under desirable conditions; illumination and ventilation are good; distractions are held to a minimum considering the type of work performed 2

REVERE CLERICAL POSITION
EVALUATION PLAN

DEFINITIONS OF VARIOUS FACTORS USED AND EXPLANATION
OF THE VARIOUS DEGREES COMPRISING EACH FACTOR

Used on All Clerical Positions

———

REVERE COPPER AND BRASS INCORPORATED

230 Park Avenue   New York, N. Y.

Factor No. 1 — Elemental Factor Value

As a basis for employment, the company demands certain characteristics which are considered essential for all positions, such as willingness to work, a certain ambition, neatness, personality, honesty, dependability, certain physical specifications, etc., and, therefore, when considering wage differentials between jobs, we do not attempt to rate these common factors but instead base all rating differentials on the prime position factors above these common ones. Lack of these characteristics is obvious and will destroy all chances of promotion.

To grant a value for these characteristics and to value them similarly for all jobs, we are inserting a constant factor which we will call "Elemental" and assigning it 45 points   45

Factor No. 2 — Educational Requirements

This factor is rated according to the minimum education necessary to allow an understanding of the position. It should be remembered here that it is the desire to concentrate on the requirements of the position and not the value of the education acquired by the man employed in the position.

Point Value

1. Grammar School or equivalent   0
2. Up to 2 years High School or equivalent   2–4
3. Up to 4 years High School or equivalent   6–8
4. Up to 2 years Special Training above a High School Education or its equivalent   10–12
5. Up to 4 years Special Training above a High School Education or its equivalent   14–16

Factor No. 3 — Practical Experience Required

The degree of this factor is determined by the amount of experience judged necessary to fulfill minimum position requirements.

Point Value

1. Where no experience is necessary   0
2. Where some experience is preferable, but can be accumulated during 3 to 4 months' employment with the company   1–3
3. Where sufficient experience would necessitate approximately one year of employment with the company in related positions   4–6
4. Where the necessary experience would require approximately three years' employment with the company in related positions   7–9
5. Where considerable experience is necessary in related positions so as to acquire a thorough overall knowledge; this experience to absorb approximately five years   10–12
6. Where extensive experience is imperative in order to fulfill the position requirements. This would be considered as requiring over five years' company experience in related positions   13–15

FACTOR No. 4—ANALYTICAL REQUIREMENT AND
COMPLEXITY OF WORK

This factor recognizes the difficulties and complications of the assigned task and measures the extent to which the work involved requires analytical ability, exercise of judgment, initiative and ingenuity.

Point Value

1. Where the assigned task is of a simple nature and obvious conditions can be readily recognized 0
2. Where the assigned tasks consist of routine or standard matter, but demand recognition of a deviation from the accepted routine 1–3
3. Where the assigned tasks necessitate a weighing of facts and the exercise of a limited amount of judgment in decisions. It also involves performance of several different kinds of clerical or manual operations 4–6
4. Where the assigned tasks make it necessary to devise data, requiring certain initiative and ingenuity, solve special problems, and make reliable decisions 7–9
5. Where it is necessary to ascertain certain facts, weigh them and present important or costly decisions to management without the benefit of guidance 10–12
6. Where unusual and important facts must be weighed and analyzed, calling for an extreme exercise of good judgment and where independent action is essential and will have a bearing on quality or cost 13–15

FACTOR No. 5—ACCURACY

This factor considers the importance of the work as regards its opportunity for errors and the relative magnitude of the consequences. It also recognizes the availability of supervision to detect errors promptly and the amount of dependence placed on the accuracy with which the task is performed.

Point Value

1. Where possibility of error is negligible. All jobs require a certain degree of accuracy 1–2
2. Where the preliminary routine work is assigned and where errors are possible, but easily detected and corrected 3–4
3. Where the cost of correction will be considerable due to the difficult nature of the work and the degree of dependence placed on the performances 5–6
4. Where work is of a very complicated nature and where cost of correction will be great in either time or money 7–8

FACTOR No. 6—MEMORY

This factor values the necessity for retaining a variety of facts which may be associated with others, and will have a bearing on the efficient performance of the position.

Point Value

1. Where this element is relatively unimportant 0
2. Where it is desirable to retain simple facts about current orders and standard practices 1–2
3. Where a retention of a variety of facts adds greatly to the efficiency of the task 3–4
4. When the retention of a variety of repetitive facts or figures is necessary for constant use and where the memorized facts are difficult to retain because they are not associated with others 5–6
5. Where the efficiency of the task depends largely upon the retention of non-repetitive complicated facts, which would be extremely costly if time were taken to consult written data 7–8

Factor No. 7 — Manual Dexterity

This factor is intended to attribute a value to those tasks which require a degree of dexterity, but which involve only a few of the other factors because of the nature of the work.

Point Value

1. Ordinary Clerical Work 0
2. Adding Machine and Calculator Operators 1–2
3. Typists, Tabulator Key Punchers, Filing, Telephone Operators, Waitresses 3
4. Dictaphone Operators, Stenographers, Elliott Fisher Operators, Comptometer Operators 4
5. Bookkeeping Machine Operators 5

Factor No. 8 — Supervisional Requirements

This factor values the degree of supervision exercised over the work of others, and takes into consideration the nature of the work as well as the number of employees.

Point Value

1. Where no supervision is exercised 0
2. Where a group of employees must be supervised, but where the nature of the work calls for little directing, instructing, training or planning 1–3
3. Where a small group of not more than five in number must be supervised, but where it is frequently necessary to train and instruct, direct and plan the work involved 4–6
4. Where a group of more than five is involved, and where the nature of the work calls for frequent instructions, training, planning and directing 7–9
5. Where a small group is involved, but where the nature of the work involves the direction of highly skilled, specialized tasks or work of a complicated nature 10–12
6. Where a large group is involved and where the nature of the work requires a co-ordination of varied phases of highly skilled technical or complicated work 13–15

Factor No. 9—Conditions of Work

This factor takes into consideration the physical effort expended and the place of work.

Point Value

1. Sound-proof office or where only slight noises are apparent   0
2. Noisy office or room   1
3. Where much walking or standing is necessary to the efficient performance   2–3
4. Where the position consists almost entirely of standing or walking and where work must be done under extremely noisy conditions   4–5

Factor No. 10—Continuity of Work

This factor refers to the degree of continuous performance without benefit of interruptions or breathing spells due to necessary conversations with others, etc.

Point Value

1. Where ample time for stoppage of work is possible due to any causes   0
2. Where work is varied and necessitates some stops for discussion or advice   1
3. Where the work is routine and planned for long periods with little opportunity for interruption   2–3
4. Where it is imperative to stay at the task constantly with rare opportunities afforded for breathing spells   4–5

Factor No. 11—Physical Strain on Senses

This factor recognizes the nervous or eye-strain connected with certain tasks or positions.

Point Value

1. Where there are few involuntary interruptions or very little close figure work which demands concentrated vision   0
2. Where part of the work involves eye-strain   1
3. Where the major portion of the work involves constant eye-strain or close figure work   2–3
4. Where numerous involuntary interruptions are part of the day's work, requiring much concentration and nervous strain to again pick up the trend of thought or stoppage point   4–5

Factor No. 12—Relations or Contacts

This factor measures the extent and relative difficulty and importance of the work handled with and through other departments or other companies in connection with the effect these contacts may have on plant or public relations.

Point Value

1. Where this factor is negligible   0
2. Usual contacts with other departments within the company on matters involving flow of work which has been standardized to a large extent and requires no decisions   1-2
3. Contacts with other departments within the company on matters involving decisions or disposal of certain activities which may lead into many discussions as to the best disposal or decision   3-4
4. Contacts within the company or with the public or both which involve the making of substantial adjustments which involve money or company policy   5-6
5. Contacts within the company or with the public or both which involve important agreements or disposal of serious matters which could greatly affect future relations   7-8

JOB EVALUATION MANUAL
FOR FACTORY JOBS

from the

HANDBOOK OF JOB EVALUATION

INDUSTRIAL FASTENERS INSTITUTE

Cleveland, Ohio

(Formerly American Institute of Bolt, Nut and Rivet Manufacturers)

Copyright 1946

INTRODUCTION

This evaluation plan is designed for use by the members of the American Fasteners Institute. A sound wage structure is fundamental to good industrial relations. Job Evaluation is a method of classifying jobs in terms of their general characteristics and requirements, and this classification serves as a factual basis for determining a fair wage policy.

The Job Evaluation Manual consists of a series of rating scales designed to aid in the assignment of point ratings. There are twelve rating scales, one for each selected factor.

1. EXPERIENCE

What is the length of time usually required by a worker to obtain sufficient work experience to perform the job duties effectively? Does the job require one or both of the following:

> Previous experience on related work, or lesser
> positions, within or outside the organization
> and/or
> a period of adjustment or "breaking in" on the
> job itself?

The "Rating" is the total required experience before being placed on the job plus the period of adjustment or "breaking in" on the job itself.

Level I. Over 6 years	200 Points
Level II. 4 years to 6 years	138 Points
Level III. 2 years to 4 years	92 Points
Level IV. 1 year to 2 years	60 Points
Level V. 6 months to 1 year	40 Points
Level VI. 3 months to 6 months	28 Points
Level VII. 1 month to 3 months	22 Points
Level VIII. Up to 1 month	20 Points

2. EDUCATION

Refers to formal school training or its equivalent in general knowledge which requires some instruction. This factor measures the requirements for the use of shop mathematics, drawings, measuring instruments, and general educational background.

Level I .... 120 Points

Must be able to understand complicated drawings such as drawings for machine design. Broad shop or trade knowledge involving complicated specifications and advanced shop mathematics. High school education or equivalent required.

Level II .... 66 Points

Must be able to understand simple drawings such as drawings of the product, to understand all written instructions, or to be able to make up simple production reports. Tenth grade or junior high school education or its equivalent required.

Level III .... 35 Points

Requires the ability to understand production orders. Must be able to read micrometer or read measuring gauges other than fixed gauges. Eighth grade or equivalent education required.

Level IV .... 19 Points

Requires the ability to speak, read and write English or simple addition and subtraction. Equal to or equivalent to sixth grade education.

Level V .... 12 Points

Does not require the ability to read or write.

3. RESPONSIBILITY FOR PRODUCT AND MATERIALS

The responsibility for preventing waste or loss of raw material, partly finished products, or finished products through carelessness or poor workmanship. Consider the probable number of pieces which may be spoiled in any lot before detection and correction, the value of the material and labor and the possibility of salvage.

Level I .... 80 Points
  Precision work on expensive material using machines that need exacting setting and adjustment. Machine adjustments all made by operator and not by set-up man, and not built into the machine. Single loss could run over $1,000.00, but is usually between $200.00 and $1,000.00.

Level II .... 44 Points
  Considerable care on part of worker necessary to avoid losses. Machine or process requires careful setting on precision work and attention from worker. Scrap or rework might occasionally run up to $200.00, but is usually between $50.00 and $200.00.

Level III .... 23 Points
  Substantial loss from poor tooling, machine setting or poor workmanship could occur occasionally before ordinary checks would detect the poor work, or repeated small losses could occur. Worker must exercise care to avoid losses. Large losses possible but losses per week should rarely go over $50.00.

Level IV .... 13 Points
  Small losses might occur. Poor workmanship or mistakes might cause occasional losses in serap, rework, or returned goods up to $25.00 in a week. Poor work usually caught quickly by inspectors or others before damage is great.

Level V .... 8 Points
  Nominal. Little or no possibility of causing poor work or material waste due to poor workmanship or mistakes.

4. RESPONSIBILITY FOR MACHINERY, TOOLS, AND EQUIPMENT

The responsibility for preventing damage that could be caused by lack of ordinary care for the machinery, tools, and equipment used in the performance of the job. Consider the cost of repairs and the loss of production due to machine down-time. (Note: Do not consider the extreme amount of damage that it would be possible to do intentionally or that a beginner under little or no supervision could cause.)

Level I .... 80 Points

> Considerable and continual care needed to avoid sub-
> stantial damage to machinery, tools, and equipment.
> Losses could run over $1,000.00. Usual loss between
> $500.00 and $1,000.00.

Level II .... 44 Points

> More than routine care needed to prevent damage to
> machines, tools, or equipment. Loss resulting from not
> being careful could run as high as $500.00. Serious pro-
> duction losses could result from failure to keep machines
> in running order.

Level III .... 23 Points

> Failure on the part of the worker to exercise due care,
> to report maintenance needs to Foreman could cause
> repeated small losses or occasional damage of as much
> as $100.00.

Level IV .... 13 Points

> Equipment used has only nominal value or is not easily
> damaged seriously. Few possibilities of causing loss
> of over $10.00. Failure to keep machine running would
> cause loss in output.

Level V .... 8 Points

> No responsibility in any way for machinery, tools, and
> equipment other than simple tools, locker room facili-
> ties, workbench, etc.

5. RESPONSIBILITY FOR WORK OF OTHERS

The responsibility of the employees for assisting and instructing other
employees in the performance of their work. It includes also the responsibility of one employee toward a group of employees in a department if his
work bears directly on their work, either because he performs a service or
because of sequential or group work.

Level I .... 60 Points

> Exercises direction over the jobs done by from ten to
> fifty employees of various skills. Work assignments
> frequent and often complex. May set up equipment for
> other workers for complicated jobs on complex ma-
> chines.

Level II .... 29 Points

> Directs the work of a small group of workers (up to 10)
> of medium skills. Work assignments relatively simple.
> Analytical inspection. May classify defects by cause,
> make up records, recommend corrective measures. May
> make tools or set up machines for other workers, jobs
> of medium or simple complexity.

Level III .... 14 Points

> Close sequential relationships to other jobs. Failure to

keep up will affect many other workers very quickly. Discretionary inspection work of others. Must exercise judgment as to seriousness of defects without pre-set measuring devices. Separates defects by kind. Exercises direction over two or more workers, or advisory or occasional direction over several.

Level IV .... 6 Points

Work related to others in a sequential way. Work on which others depend. Failure to keep up may affect other workers. No direct supervision of others.

6. RESPONSIBILITY FOR SAFETY OF OTHERS

The responsibility of the employee for the safety of others, or the extent of injury to others which he can prevent. Accidents to the employee himself are to be rated under Hazards and are not to be considered here.

Level I .... 40 Points

Safety of others depends almost entirely on correct action of employee. Dangerous situations likely to result in serious injury to others if person performing this job is careless.

Level II .... 22 Points

Carelessness by employee would cause lost time accidents to other workers. Serious accidents unlikely.

Level III .... 12 Points

Care must be exercised to avoid possibility of danger to others. Care by others, however, usually can offset much of the hazard that carelessness on this job can create.

Level IV .... 6 Points

Only reasonable care to own work is required to insure safety of others, and accidents, if they should occur, would be minor in nature.

Level V .... 4 Points

Almost no responsibility for safety of others.

7. RESOURCEFULNESS

Requirements for determining and formulating methods for doing work. Demand for meeting situations and carrying out difficult assignments not covered by usual standards or precedents.

Level I .... 120 Points

Requires outstanding ability to work independently toward general results. Often no precedent for and little help in carrying out assigned tasks. Must originate, plan, adapt, invent, and contrive to accomplish tasks. Supervisor may work with rather than direct operator in solution of problems.

Level II .... 66 Points

Requires exercise of a great deal of ingenuity to do unusual and difficult work. Standard methods usually inadequate to cover the situation. General supervision available on call at most times but operator is expected to work out his own problems as a rule.

Level III .... 35 Points

Some originating and planning of work called for. Tasks are varied and standard procedures do not always cover the situation. Supervision available if needed but operator expected to work out problems of medium difficulty without much direction.

Level IV .... 19 Points

Some variety in jobs. Operator expected to exercise some discretion in applying variations of standard methods to the work. Supervision available at all times.

Level V .... 12 Points

Little resourcefulness required. Procedures simple and repetitive. Ample supervision on any variations from standard.

8. MONOTONY

Relates to the degree of monotony or variability of the work.

Level I .... 40 Points

Extremely monotonous and confining jobs. Constant repetition of task with short cycle. Highly repetitive routine task.

Level II .... 20 Points

Worker at workplace for long periods with little opportunity to vary the work. Routine recognized as definite part of job.

Level III .... 9 Points

Jobs having some variety with opportunity to vary monotony by doing other tasks occasionally. Worker may leave workplace or works at several places.

Level IV .... 4 Points

Has variable tasks to perform; may be away from workplace frequently. Routine work not an essential part of the job.

9. MENTAL AND VISUAL EFFORT

Requirements of using the eyes to observe or discover certain conditions. Consider the closeness of detail being observed, duration, and pressure of periods of work. Consider the degree of concentration required, keep the volume and pressure of work in mind as this work demands mental and visual effort and attention.

Level I .... 70 Points

> High degree of concentration due to heavy volume and
> pressure of work. Very close, exacting use of eyes on
> jobs where exacting coordination or observation is re-
> quired. Usually a job where tension is found.

Level II .... 34 Points

> Close visual attention to operation required at all times.
> Must be aware of job details and may be required to
> distribute attention over several details in order to co-
> ordinate work properly. Continuous feeding of semi-
> automatic machines where eye-hand coordination re-
> quired.

Level III .... 16 Points

> Flow of work and character of duties involves normal
> mental and visual attention. Operation may call for
> frequent but not continuous observation. Inspection
> work where flaw or error is easily detected.

Level IV .... 7 Points

> Flow of work and character of duties is intermittent
> and requires attention only at intervals. No pressure of
> work or only occasional work pressure. Operation in-
> volves nothing beyond casual watching and occasional
> action.

10. PHYSICAL EFFORT

Physical effort relates to the amount and continuity of effort required.
Consider the availability or lack of availability of materials handling
devices.

Level I .... 90 Points

> Continuous or highly repetitive physical exertion work-
> ing with heavy weight material. Hard work with con-
> stant physical strain or intermittent severe strain. Lift-
> ing over 75 pounds required. May be called upon to pull
> or push equivalent to the lifting requirement.

Level II .... 50 Points

> Considerable physical effort, usually handling average
> weight material or frequently working with heavy
> weight material. May be called upon to lift up to 75
> pounds and to pull or push the equivalent of the lifting
> requirement.

Level III .... 26 Points

> Repetitive or sustained physical effort; usually han-
> dling light or average weight material, or occasionally
> works with heavy weight material. Lifting not over 35
> pounds. May be called upon to pull or push equivalent
> to the lifting requirement.

Level IV .... 14 Points

Physical effort required for frequent handling of light weight material or occasionally works with average weight material. Lifting not over 25 pounds. May be called upon to pull or push equivalent to the lifting requirement.

Level V .... 9 Points

Light work requiring little physical exertion.

11. SURROUNDINGS

Consider the surroundings or conditions under which the job must be done and to what extent these conditions are disagreeable. Keep in mind the presence of such conditions as exposure to dust, dirt, oil, heat, fumes, extreme cold, noise, vibration, and wetness.

Level I .... 50 Points

Continuous and intensive exposure to several very disagreeable elements.

Level II .... 25 Points

Disagreeable working conditions due to several disagreeable elements or to one very disagreeable element. These conditions would be present to the extent where they would noticeably affect the work of those present. They would no longer be considered merely a nuisance factor.

Level III .... 12 Points

Worker may get dirty or have exposure, occasional or constant, to some of the elements listed above, but only in a very minor degree.

Level IV .... 5 Points

Good working conditions. Practically no disagreeable elements. Clean surroundings.

12. HAZARDS

The hazards, both health and accident, that are connected with or surround the job, even though all usual safety measures have been taken.

HAZARDS ON THE JOB

Level I .... 50 Points

Exposure to occupational disease or accidents that might result in serious permanent disability. Accidents happen frequently in spite of precautions.

Level II .... 28 Points

Exposure to accident or health hazards that might cause incapacitation. Possibility of eye injuries, loss of fingers or serious burns. Frequent minor injuries likely but more serious accidents are very rare.

Level III .... 15 Points

> Exposure to lost time accidents, involving more serious cuts, bruises, muscle strain, allergies or some exposure to occupational disease, which would not be permanently incapacitating in nature. Rare exposure to more serious hazards.

Level IV .... 8 Points

> Work having minor health hazards, accidents outside of minor injuries such as abrasions, cuts, and burns are improbable.

Level V .... 5 Points

> Work having almost no accident or health hazards.

SUGGESTIONS FOR STUDY AND RESEARCH

1. Obtain the relative importance of each factor for each of the point-rating systems found at the end of this chapter. Follow the instructions on pages 133–137.

2. Distribute the points on a geometric progression for the *Job Evaluation Manual for Clerical and Supervisory Positions* found on pages 142–144.

CASE PROBLEM

CONSTRUCTING THE JOB EVALUATION MANUAL: As a group project, construct a point-rating manual for an industry or jobs familiar to the group, or to which there is access for observing the jobs actually in operation, interviewing supervisors, executives, and perhaps those employed on the jobs, also.

PROBLEM: Select a jury from the faculty and from local industry to establish the weights reflecting the relative importance of the factors included in the system. Get approval of the manual from at least one company to which it would apply. Try to get the comments of foremen, workers on the jobs, worker representatives, personnel director, and superintendent of the company. Put this manual in finished form and supply a copy to each one in the group for later use in evaluating jobs.

6

Quantitative Systems—the Factor-Comparison Method

THE FACTOR-COMPARISON METHOD HAS BEEN associated with Eugene J. Benge, and much of its contribution to the field of job evaluation is a result of his work in perfecting this method. He was one of a group of job analysts employed by the Philadelphia Rapid Transit Company to study all jobs and rates in order to establish proper rate bases and rate relationships. These analysts found that the point system had definite limitations and worked out another job evaluation plan which ultimately was called the factor-comparison method of job evaluation. [1] The plan is described as one which will yield approximately the same rates whether used by an employer, by representatives of employees, or by outside consultants.

More recently Edward N. Hay has written extensively about the factor-comparison method, and has perhaps contributed most to its present acceptance. As described below, there has been a tendency to modify this method so that the relative values assigned to jobs are based upon numerical values other than the present wage structure of the company applying the method to its jobs. The factor-comparison and point-rating methods have been compared in such a manner that their proponents have attempted to prove the superiority of one over the other. Actually, as has been mentioned elsewhere, both systems have advantages and disadvantages which vary depending on the conditions under which they are used.

[1] Eugene J. Benge, Samuel L. H. Burk, and Edward N. Hay, *Manual of Job Evaluation* (New York: Harper & Brothers, 1941) pp. 14–15.

Since both the factor-comparison and point-rating methods of evaluation are discussed in this book, a review of Benge's objections to the point-rating method will clarify the relative value of these two methods. All evaluation systems have some weaknesses, but the important consideration is that all systems must be examined from the point of view of their applicability to a particular evaluation situation. The weaknesses of one system might be found in whole or in part in all other evaluation systems.

Benge discusses the weaknesses of the point-rating systems in *Job Evaluation and Merit Rating*.[2] These weaknesses are summarized as follows:

1. A fixed number of factors, such as a dozen or two dozen, for which points will be assigned, must be established. Hence, the point system assumes that all jobs are composed of those factors and only those factors. . . .

2. The assignment of point values for varying degrees of each factor is arbitrarily done. . . .

3. Upper limits of the points to be assigned to the several factors must be arbitrarily established. . . .

4. The point system sets up seeming refinements which are not inherent in the judgments made by use of them. . . .

5. A unit is created which is undefined. This unit is a point. . . .

6. Factors are frequently undefined. . . .

7. Under the point system the job analysis itself tends to set the value of the job rather than the job comparison. . . .

The weaknesses emphasized by Benge apply to most of the point-rating methods in use, but to attribute these weaknesses to the basic concept of point systems is somewhat unfair. The point-rating method is based upon the selection of factors which vary in number according to the needs of the organization making the study, but it is not necessary for these factors to cover all jobs. The factor-comparison method compares jobs on the factors of mental requirements, skill, physical requirements, responsibilities, and working conditions. These same factors, or combinations of them, form the basis for point-rating evaluation systems.[3] There is no doubt that some jobs have a high value because of unusual circumstances. As illustrated by Benge, the job of department store model would receive a low rating on the point-rating system because the method would not take poise and pulchritude into consideration. It must

[2] Eugene J. Benge, *Job Evaluation and Merit Rating*, National Foremen's Institute (New York: 1943), pp. 18–21.

[3] *Job Evaluation*, Studies in Personnel Policy, No. 25 (1940), National Industrial Conference Board, Inc., 247 Park Avenue, New York, pp. 5–30.

be remembered, however, that jobs should first be classified according to type, and a point-rating scale designed for either clerical or factory workers would not be suitable for the job of dress model. There is no reason why a system which works very well for practically 100 per cent of the jobs should be abandoned because it cannot be applied to one or two unusual jobs. In answer to Benge, it may be argued that a factor-comparison scale constructed for clerical jobs would be of little use in classifying the job of dress model. In a recent department store job-evaluation study [4] the job of dress model was rated on a point-rating scale designed for sales personnel. The modeling job involved so much in the way of knowledge of merchandise and sales ability that no injustice followed from the application of a point-rating scale. So long as the factors are carefully chosen for the type of job being rated, the use of factors should in no way be considered a fatal weakness of the point systems.

The assignment of point values in an arbitrary manner is also mentioned as a weakness of the point systems. The use of the word "arbitrary" implies that point values are assigned in a manner independent of rule or standard procedure. However, the method of assigning point values to show the relative worth of each factor is not very different from assigning cents per hour to the various jobs in the job-comparison scale. In both cases a great deal of judgment must be used and the end result is the assignment of relative values to the factors which were selected to evaluate the jobs being classified. It is surprising to note the agreement that is obtained by independent investigators in assigning relative weights to job factors. Variations from 45 to 62½ per cent [5] in relative weight in four systems are not great when it is considered that these systems vary in number of job factors from 6 to 11. Since these four systems were used in four different situations, greater variation should be expected than if they were devised for the same situation.

Many point systems set upper limits for the points to be assigned to the several factors, but it is not true that they must be established. The *Occupational Rating Plan* of the Industrial Management Society,[6] a point system, does not set an upper limit to the

[4] Jay L. Otis, "Study of Job Classification Methods for Jobs in a Large Department Store," unpublished study.

[5] *Job Evaluation*, Studies in Personnel Policy, No. 25, National Industrial Conference Board (247 Park Avenue, New York: 1940), p. 130.

[6] *Occupational Rating Plan*, Industrial Management Society (205 West Wacker Drive, Chicago: 1943).

assigned points. In most systems the range of points is so established that few if any jobs reach the minimum and no jobs reach the maximum number of possible points. If the range of point values is too narrow to measure the jobs, the range can be increased without invalidating the point system.

No job-rating scale should be so constructed that the judgments are inaccurate because of too fine gradations for each factor. Some point systems are so elaborate in this respect that no person could be consistent in making judgments. This is a good criticism of some point-rating systems, but the fault is due to poor construction of the scale rather than to any inherent weakness of the point system itself. The factor-comparison system overcomes this weakness by choosing widely spaced jobs for the job comparison scale. However, it would be difficult to judge the relative positions of Punch Card Operator and File Clerk for the factor of mental requirements,[7] if these two jobs were selected for a factor-comparison scale.

Whenever the units are in terms of cents per hour or dollars per week or month, they are defined in monetary terms. The point systems use points which are not defined in monetary terms until the jobs have been classified and priced. The purpose of using points is to express qualitative and quantitative differences in jobs in terms of some scale. The use of a point scale with undefined units is permissible because these units are usually assigned to meaningful descriptive phrases for the degrees of each factor. The assumption and establishment of relative weights for each factor and a consistent breakdown of these weights into degrees make it possible to evaluate jobs. Since the units of the point-system scale will ultimately be given a monetary value and since this scale will be used to set rates for new jobs and for old jobs which have changed in content, the undefined point value takes on a monetary definition *after* the jobs have been classified. The early application of the factor-comparison method, on the other hand, weighted the factors in terms of money units *before* the jobs had been classified. As mentioned above, per cent values, or 100-point allocations, have now been substituted for money values. This is described on page 190.

Whenever a factor is selected for use in job evaluation it should be defined in such a manner that it has the same meaning for all who use the system. A point-rating system which does not have a good definition of each factor will be difficult, if not impossible, to

---

[7] Eugene J. Benge, Samuel L. H. Burk, and Edward N. Hay, *Manual of Job Evaluation* (New York: Harper & Brothers, 1941), p. 47.

apply. However, this statement applies no more to the point-rating method than it does to the factor-comparison method. Any point-system scale should define its factors completely and accurately, but the failure of one job analyst to do so does not mean that all point systems are weak.

One of the fundamental differences between the point system and other systems lies in the fact that the job facts, rather than the job comparison, tend to set the value of the job. It is first necessary to analyze each job thoroughly; then, on the basis of the facts so obtained, the job is measured by comparing the job facts with the gradations on the scale. The point-rating method uses the scale to set the job value. The ranking method and the factor-comparison method measure jobs by comparing one job with other jobs.

Advantages and disadvantages of the factor-comparison method

The factor-comparison method has advantages which are not found in the other methods of job evaluation. First, excellent descriptions of how to construct a job-comparison scale are available. This means that any person who has some knowledge of job evaluation can follow the procedures which have been outlined and can construct a usable scale.

A second advantage lies in the fact that a scale is constructed for each type of job and for each new application. It is difficult to take a scale constructed for one company and apply it to other companies. Since the essence of the method is the comparison of jobs to be rated with key jobs which have been "scaled," the key jobs should be exactly the same for each company using the same scale; key jobs are rarely identical, however, and new scales are usually constructed. This means that each application of this method is tailor-made for the organization.

As mentioned above, the factor-comparison method usually has but five factors. This constitutes a third advantage of the system, since there is very little "overlap" among these factors. Whenever many factors are used there is the possibility that two of the factors will receive the same or approximately the same interpretation, and that one aspect of the system will receive a double weight. Although in using a few factors there is the danger that some of the important attributes will be omitted, the factor-comparison method has included the important ones. Since this tends to simplify and shorten the task of evaluation, it can be considered an advantage.

A fourth advantage lies in the fact that the evaluation scale is expressed in cents per hour or the monetary unit customarily followed in pricing the jobs.[8] This means that once the cents per hour have been assigned to the "key" jobs for each factor, the use of the scale shows not only the relative differences among jobs, but also the value of the job in monetary terms. There is no necessity for converting points into cents after the values have been obtained, because the original construction of the scale takes care of this conversion. If the scale is constructed accurately, and if the key jobs are correctly priced in the first place, the resulting job-comparison scale serves as a tool for pricing all other comparable jobs. The factor-comparison method was first presented during a period when wages were relatively stable and the resulting job-comparison scale could serve as a tool for pricing all other comparable jobs. Actually the evaluation scale is not expressed in "cents per hour" except at the original installation of the job-evaluation plan, and it does not have to be expressed in those terms even then. The salaries or wages of the key jobs represent index numbers or points. The relationship between points and dollars varies with time, whether the points are expressed in the point system or in the monetary units used in the factor-comparison system. That is, the value of a point may be adjusted in accordance with inflation or deflation. The use of money values rather than arbitrarily selected points usually tends to result in a straight line curve when the evaluated job values are compared with the actual wages. This is an advantage because many believe that it is easier to explain a straight line curve to employees than a second degree curve. Chapter 13 illustrates the construction of the wage curve.

A fifth advantage lies in the form of the scale itself. It is patterned after the man-to-man comparison scale devised for rating officers in World War I. Whenever a judgment is made, it is made in terms of a comparison. The rater can say to himself that the job of stenographer has more responsibility than the job of file clerk and less responsibility than the job of teller; that it most nearly resembles the job of ediphone operator, but has perhaps just slightly more responsibility than that position. In this respect the factor-comparison method has an advantage over methods not employing the man-to-man rating principle.

That the job-comparison scale is relatively easy to use is a sixth advantage. Employees, union representatives, and supervisors can

[8] See discussion of this point on pages 180–183.

quickly be taught to use the scale. If the original values are assumed to be correct, there should be considerable agreement between raters. Since the same type of evaluation scale can be used for all jobs, the person trained on one scale can easily transfer to other scales.

In building a job-comparison scale the job analyst is instructed to select about 15 or 20 key jobs, varying in salary from the lowest to nearly the highest, whose duties are clearly defined and whose rates are not subject to controversy. The first major disadvantage of the system is found in these prerequisites. In a plant where the entire wage structure is under dispute management officials would find it extremely difficult to locate a single job which was not alleged to be underpaid or overpaid. This, however, is not always the case, and in most instances no difficulty is incurred. This is true because in the selection of key jobs, one is not concerned whether the jobs are underpaid or overpaid in comparison with the rates paid in comparable jobs elsewhere, since the primary concern is in the relationships between the rates paid in this particular company or industry. It is not difficult today to find a considerable number of jobs where management and labor can agree that the job relationships are equitable without agreeing on whether the whole wage scale should go either up or down. This possible disadvantage has also been eliminated by the use of per cents. The use of wages to set new wages has some psychological disadvantages. The selection of key jobs can now be made on the basis of established skill levels, available job knowledge, and job importance, rather than on wage rates not subject to controversy.

Although the exact factors recommended by the persons who developed the factor-comparison method may be used for any study, they probably should be modified and redefined to suit the needs of job-comparison scales for other types of jobs. One of the advantages of selecting factors which both the employer and the employees judge to be important is lost when one set of factors is used for all types of evaluations.

It may seem to be a real disadvantage when there is a change in the duties or an increase in the responsibility of one or more of the key jobs. This is not necessarily true, because once the key jobs have served their purpose as comparison jobs during the original installation, they lose their designation as key jobs and become just another job in the organization. Therefore, any change in duties or responsibilities of the key jobs has no effect on the entire plan and the changed key job is re-evaluated in the same manner as any other job which changes in duties and responsibilities. The comparison scale, once constructed, consists of all the jobs in the organization, because the strength of the factor-comparison system lies in the fact that one job can be compared with *all* other jobs in the organization, not just with the key jobs.

Several complicated steps in the construction of the job-comparison scale make it difficult to explain to employees. Complexity is not necessarily a reason for rejection, but there are situations where management does not have the complete confidence of the workers, and a complicated system might result in a rejection of the entire classification structure.

The advantages and disadvantages of the factor-comparison method tend to balance one another, just as those of the other types of evaluation systems do. Benge, Hay, and others have used this method in many situations with excellent results. Its introduction into the field of job evaluation has aided in the development of the cross-comparison method,[9] which can be applied to jobs evaluated by any system. The job-comparison idea has been applied to the point-rating method with excellent results. As a method of job evaluation, the factor-comparison method is definitely worth considering, either in its original or in some modified form.

CONSTRUCTING A JOB-COMPARISON SCALE

The eight steps—original method

Two excellent descriptions of the steps involved in the construction of a job-comparison scale have been prepared.[10, 11] The description below is based mostly upon the work of Benge, Burk and Hay, with some slight modification. The outline is given in sufficient detail so that any person who desires to construct his own job-comparison scale can do so. For those desiring more detailed instructions, the references cited would be helpful.

In any job-evaluation study there is considerable planning to be done before starting the study itself. The planning of the job evaluation study is discussed in Chapter 2. The following ma-

---

[9] See Chapter 11.

[10] Eugene J. Benge, *Job Evaluation and Merit Rating*, National Foremen's Institute (New York: 1943).

[11] Eugene J. Benge, Samuel L. H. Burk, and Edward N. Hay, *Manual of Job Evaluation* (New York: Harper & Brothers, 1941).

terial gives a step-by-step procedure for the planning of the study and the analysis of the jobs.

Step 1. Preparation of the Job Descriptions. Job descriptions must be prepared before the job-comparison scale is constructed. It is absolutely essential that they be written for the selected key jobs (see Step 4). The recommendation that each employee as well as each supervisor should fill in job forms provides a useful method of securing necessary information, because the employees feel that they are participating in the job evaluation. Remember, however, that the employee or supervisor is rarely a trained job analyst. Descriptions obtained from them should be checked carefully by a trained job analyst. (See Chapter 8.)

Step 2. Preparation of Job Specifications. Job specifications should be written for each position being evaluated. The job specifications should be written in terms of the factors used in the job-comparison scale. If the factors recommended by Benge are used, the specifications would include mental requirements, skill, physical requirements, responsibilities, and working conditions. Benge has listed the items appearing on certain job specifications to show the type of descriptive material which is useful both in constructing and in using a job comparison scale.[12] His suggestions are reproduced in Table 6–1. Figure 6–1 shows a job specification for Electric Welder.[13] The suggestions of items to be incorporated into the job specifications found in Table 5–11 and the sample job specification, Figure 6–1, show the type of information which is usually found in a job specification. The job specifications are extremely useful additions to the job descriptions and are valuable in increasing the accuracy of job ratings. A detailed description of writing job specifications is found in Chapter 9.

Step 3. Assumptions. According to Benge, "the factor comparison method utilizes certain assumptions" which should be mentioned before the actual construction of a job-comparison scale is described. These assumptions are:

1. The evaluation scale should be expressed in cents per hour—not in points. For salaried employees dollars per week or per month would be used as the unit. . . . When a job has been evaluated according to the five major factors normally used as bases of comparison, it is merely necessary to total the cents per hour, or dollars per week or month, in order to arrive at the actual rate. . . .

---

[12] Eugene J. Benge, *Job Evaluation and Merit Rating,* National Foremen's Institute (New York: 1943), Figure 8.
[13] *Ibid.,* Figure 9.

TABLE 6—1.   Items appearing on job specifications •

(Classified according to major factors)

Mental Requirements	Skill	Physical Requirements	Responsibility	Working Conditions	Heading and Closing
Years formal education	Kind of muscular co-ordination	Nature of physical effort	For tools	*Place*	Title of form
Kind and amount of special education	Degree of proficiency	Steady or intermittent	materials	outdoor	Title of position
Kind of technical knowledge	Precision required	Semi-automatic	equipment	indoor	Alternate titles
Kind of work instruction provided:	Repetitive	Rest periods	methods	platform	Dept. and location (or division)
Written	Varied	Good voice	records	overhead	Normal force
Oral	Time experienced person to acquire acceptable proficiency	Minimum height	property	underground	Name of immediate superior
Intelligence	Dexterity	Minimum weight	money	scaffold	Duties
Mathematics used	fingers	Minimum age	savings	pit	Remarks
Prepare reports	hands	Maximum age	employee contacts	unlocalized	Date
Fluency in speech	legs	Sex	public contacts	*Type*	Prepared by
Monotony	Precision required	Color	for work of others	desk	Approved by
Distractions	Layout	Unusual strength	Other	bench	
Meet emergencies	Set up	hands		machine	
Read blue-prints	Templates	arms		counter	
Personal qualities	Jobs which train for this one	legs		*Surroundings*	
Instructs others	Jobs to which this leads	back		clean	
Memory for ——	Good handwriting	Endurance		dirty	
Other	Kind of sensory training:	Neat appearance		greasy	
	Sight	Keen hearing		orderly	
	Hearing	Eyesight rating		*Illumination*	
	Smell	Color discrimination		natural	
	Touch	% standing		artificial	
	Taste	% sitting		glare	
	Muscular	% walking		*Atmosphere*	
	Other	% other		natural	
		Other		ventilated	
				draughty	
		Working conditions (cont'd.)		noxious gas	
		Hazards (cont'd.)		fumes, odors	
		hearing		dust	
		lungs		dry	
		violence		humid	
		hands		moist	
		feet		*Hazards*	
		Gangwork		fire	
		Type of co-worker		electricity	
		Crowded		muscular strain	
		Regular working hours from—— to——		sight	
		Other			

Courtesy of the National Foremen's Institute.

2. The number of factors on which comparative judgment should be made should not exceed seven. In actual practice five are normally used—these five are:

Mental Requirements   Physical Requirements
Skill   Responsibilities
            Working Conditions

3. Job specifications should be subdivided into the same categories as the evaluation scale. . . .

JOB SPECIFICATION

JOB TITLE Electric Welder-Shop **DEPT.** Maintenance **DIV'N.** Salvage **NORMAL FORCE** 1

DUTIES: Welds cracked and broken bases, rods, support brackets, etc. Repairs salvaged parts. Re-builds worn surfaces. Does the necessary welding in making safety guards. Some spot welding of miscellaneous nature.

Mental Effort	Skill	Physical Effort	Responsibility	Working Conditions
–6 years gen'l educ'n. Kind of special educ'n. Kind of work knowledge: Effect of heat and electricity on various metals-- correct welding heat in order not to burn metal. Mathematics used Reads ~~some~~ blueprints Prepares records: Instructs others Rec. constant sup'v'n. X Monotony X Distractions Per. Qualities Needed: _ High Intelligence _ Patience	Kind: Fixing metal parts in position for welding. Connecting one electrode to work, and holding other electrode in hand. Striking arc by momentarily touching work. Joining metal by moving arc along edges to be joined. X Dexterity Inexper. time to learn: 2 years Desirable prior exper.: Acetylene welder or welder's helper. Precision or work limits Seldom closer than 1/16". Co. jobs which train for Apprentice welder.	Kinds: Lifting parts, mostly weighing under 20 pounds. Holding electrode 60% standing 20% bending 20% sitting Operation: X Varied X Repetitive Semi-auto. X Intermitt ___ Semi-auto. Age limits 25 to 50 Minimum height ___ Minimum weight 150 lbs. Sex—M X or F Color—W X or B _ Much fatigue _ Very active work _ Great strength X Good eyesight _ Color discrimination Other physical factors: Strong lungs.	Kind of equipment: Welding machine, electrodes, table. Kind of tools: Shield, goggles, hood, heavy gloves, files, hammer. Kinds of materials: Iron and steel parts. Kind of property: Machine parts. For savings—how: Salvaging old parts For work of others: For employee contact: Other responsibility:	Place: Indoor. Type: Shop and bench work. Surroundings: Noisy; dirty; crowded. Atmosphere: Dusty; draughty. Illumination: Poor. Hazards: Burns, shock, eyestrain Other:

REMARKS:

PREPARED BY EJB   **APPROVED** LBR

4. There should be no upper limit to the amount allowable for a given factor. . . .

5. Each main factor of a job should be compared against that factor in other jobs, rather than some pre-determined scale for that factor. . . .

6. Repeated judgments of competent persons, based on job specification data, should be averaged to yield the final figures.[14]

The acceptance of these assumptions is quite important if the job analyst is to use the factor-comparison method as it was originally conceived. In actual practice the first assumption is sometimes changed so that the "total cents per hour, or dollars per week or month" becomes a measure of the relative value of the job rather than an "actual rate." This is the only assumption which is modified appreciably.

Step 4. Selection of Key Jobs. In any organization certain jobs stand out because they are well known, easy to recognize, and common to many other organizations. The jobs used in the job-comparison scale of the factor-comparison method are usually these more common jobs. In conducting community wage surveys jobs are selected for wage-comparison purposes which are common to a wide variety of industrial, business, and civic organizations. These well-known jobs are usually referred to as key jobs.

The key jobs are the heart of the factor-comparison method. Selecting them is difficult because the criteria for their selection (see page 174) will eliminate many jobs from consideration. The evaluation committee or the job analysts are instructed to select about twenty-four jobs whose varying rates in salary, from the lowest to approximately the highest, seem to be in line with community rates. The duties of these jobs must be clearly defined. It can be seen that for organizations with few jobs, the comparison scale is practically the job classification itself. For a larger organization, the key jobs should be representative of the type of job to be included in the evaluation survey.

The assignment of a wage rate to a key job is sometimes difficult because different employees on this key job may be paid at varying rates. For single-rate jobs the single rate should be used; for jobs with a wage range the average wage rate may be used in the key-job computations, provided the average is truly representative. In any event a fair and acceptable rate must be assigned to each key job.

The job descriptions and job specifications will be helpful in

14 *Ibid.*, pp. 22–23.

selecting the key jobs. If a committee constructs the job-comparison scale, discussions of jobs to be included will be helpful. Any job which causes controversy in the committee should not be used as a key job. Probably fifteen to twenty-five jobs can be found which the committee can rank without too much difficulty.

Step 5. Ranking of Key Jobs by Factors. When the key jobs have been selected, copies of the job descriptions and job specifications should be distributed to members of the ranking committee, who should study them to make sure that they understand the details and difficulties of each job. Committee members should have a definition of each factor, and, if necessary, the definitions should be edited and altered so that they mean the same thing to each member of the committee. For those individuals who may wish to construct a job-comparison scale, the definitions of the factors used by Benge are found in Figure 6–2.

As soon as the committee is trained in ranking, the jobs should be ranked from easy to difficult for each of the five factors. The same procedures for ranking as described in Chapter 4 can be used for this step. It is recommended that a form be used to record the rankings so that the ranks assigned to each job for each factor can be averaged. If one job is given ranks which are widely separated, it is usually a sign that the job is not clearly understood by the committee and probably should not be used as a key job. A form useful in recording ranks is presented in Figure 6–3.

Step 6. Averaging Ranks of Key Jobs. The ranking of the key jobs by several people is followed by some method of combining the ranks into a single rank. One method is to average the ranks assigned to each key job and to rank the averages. It sometimes happens that the rankings of one or two persons are so atypical that the average rank obtained for the group is not representative of the job-analysis committee. Such atypical ratings are caused by lack of knowledge of the jobs, lack of ability to rank, intentional bias, carelessness, or some other factor. If the reasons for the uncommon judgments are known, it is permissible to drop those judgments, but if no justification for the atypical ratings can be discovered, it is best to include them in obtaining the average. When the average ranking of the key jobs has been obtained for each factor, the data are ready for the next step. Table 6–2 shows the average ranks of 15 tentative key jobs assigned by a job-evaluation committee. This illustrates the kind of rankings obtained as the first committee action in the preparation of a job-comparison scale.

Step 7. Distribution of Rates. For each key job the rate per

1. MENTAL REQUIREMENTS

Either the possession of and/or the active application of the following:

A. (inherent) Mental traits, such as intelligence, memory, reasoning, facility in verbal expression, ability to get along with people and imagination.

B. (acquired) General education, such as grammar and arithmetic; or general information as to sports, world events, etc.

C. (acquired) Specialized knowledge such as chemistry, engineering, accounting, advertising, etc.

2. SKILL

A. (acquired) Facility in muscular coordination, as in operating machines, repetitive movements, careful coordinations, dexterity, assembling, sorting, etc.

B. (acquired) Specific job knowledge necessary to the muscular coordination only; acquired by performance of the work and not to be confused with general education or specialized knowledge. It is very largely training in the interpretation of sensory impressions.

Examples

(1) In operating an adding machine, the knowledge of *which key* to depress for a sub-total would be skill.

(2) In automobile repair, the ability to determine the significance of a certain knock in the motor would be skill.

(3) In hand-firing a boiler, the ability to determine from the appearance of the firebed how coal should be shoveled over the surface would be skill.

3. PHYSICAL REQUIREMENTS

A. Physical effort, as sitting, standing, walking, climbing, pulling, lifting, etc.; both the amount exercised and the degree of the continuity should be taken into account.

B. Physical status, as age, height, weight, sex, strength and eyesight.

4. RESPONSIBILITIES

A. For raw materials, processed materials, tools, equipment and property.

B. For money or negotiable securities.

C. For profits or loss, savings or methods' improvement.

D. For public contact.

E. For records.

F. For supervision.

(1) Primarily the complexity of supervision *given* to subordinates; the number of subordinates is a secondary feature. Planning, direction, coordination, instruction, control and approval characterize this kind of supervision.

(2) Also, the degree of supervision *received.* If Jobs A and B gave no supervision to subordinates, but A received much closer immediate supervision than B, then B would be entitled to a higher rating than A in the supervision factor.

To summarize the four degrees of supervision:

Highest degree — gives much — gets little
High degree — gives much — gets much
Low degree — gives none — gets little
Lowest degree — gives none — gets much

5. WORKING CONDITIONS

A. Environmental influences such as atmosphere, ventilation, illumination, noise, congestion, fellow workers, etc.

B. Hazards—from the work or its surroundings.

C. Hours.

From Benge, *Job Evaluation and Merit Rating,* Figure 8.

Fig. 6—2. Definitions of factors used in job comparison scale.

RANK	REQUIREMENTS			RESPON-SIBILITY	WORKING CONDITIONS
	Mental	Skill	Physical		
1......................					
2......................					
3......................					
4......................					
5......................					
6......................					

From Eugene J. Benge, Samuel L. H. Burk, and Edward N. Hay, *Manual of Job Evaluation* (New York: Harper & Brothers, 1941), p. 107.

Fig. 6—3. Key job ranking data sheet.

hour, week, or month is distributed over the five factors by each member of the committee. Average ranks are useful in dividing the money rate for each job into five parts and assigning each part to one of the five factors in accordance with its estimated importance. This procedure is followed for each key job, and the rankings of the distribution of rates according to the relative importance of each factor are checked with the job-rankings for each factor to make sure there is no discrepancy.

Usually rates and ranks are not alike the first time the rates are distributed. These differences can, for the most part, be adjusted.

TABLE 6—2. Average ranks of 15 tentative key jobs assigned by job evaluation committee •

Job	Average rank assigned in				
	Mental require-ments	Skill	Physical require-ments	Respon-sibility	Working conditions
Toolmaker	1.4	1.1	13.5	3.3	12.5
Patternmaker	2.7	2.1	12.4	4.4	11.8
Machinist No. 1	3.3	2.8	7.2	4.2	10.4
Car electrician	4.2	3.5	4.8	5.7	8.3
Substation operator	1.9	3.6	14.3	1.2	14.2
Pipefitter No. 2	5.4	5.3	4.1	6.2	5.9
Painter	6.2	6.2	7.9	7.9	7.1
Concrete form maker	11.3	9.3	5.3	9.2	5.7
Poleman	10.0	10.2	2.3	11.0	2.3
Drill press operator	8.1	7.4	10.3	7.1	10.2
Motorman	6.9	4.5	11.2	2.4	9.2
Rammer	14.1	11.4	1.0	13.4	1.1
Carpenter's helper	9.1	8.6	9.2	10.1	11.3
Porter	12.2	12.7	6.7	12.2	3.9
Laborer	13.1	14.1	3.1	13.9	3.4

Courtesy of National Foremen's Institute, Inc.

In certain cases, however, a key job which cannot be brought in line is either overpriced or underpriced and should be eliminated from the scale. Table 6–3 illustrates the problem involved in ranking and distributing rates so that ranks are not violated. The table shows how the hourly rates were distributed according to the relative value of the factors and according to the ranks of fifteen jobs.

TABLE 6—3. Average distribution of present hourly rates according to ranks •

	Present rate	Mental re- quire- ments	Rank	Skill	Rank	Phys- ical re- quire- ments	Rank	Re- spon- sibility	Rank	Work- ing con- ditions	Rank
Toolmaker	2.12	56.3	3	75.4	2	29.0	7	33.1	4	17.7	12
Patternmaker	2.12	61.6	1	76.8	1	23.5	10	36.3	3	13.3	14
Machinist No. 1	2.02	49.9	5	73.8	3	28.1	8	31.7	5	18.9	11
Car electrician	2.04	53.4	4	62.3	4	33.3	4	29.2	6	26.4	4
Substation operator	1.89	57.3	2	48.5	5	9.4	15	63.7	2	9.7	15
Pipefitter No. 2	1.56	25.5	6	46.2	6	32.2	5	28.1	7	24.4	5
Painter	1.38	23.2	8	43.2	7	24.8	9	24.4	8	22.3	7
Concrete form maker	.92	11.7	13	19.3	11	21.6	12	16.6	11	22.8	6
Poleman	1.20	12.9	11	16.6	12	44.2	2	15.9	12	30.1	2
Drill press operator	1.15	20.2	9	32.7	9	18.9	14	24.2	9	19.1	10
Motorman	1.77	25.3	7	42.1	8	23.2	11	64.9	1	21.6	9
Rammer	1.10	7.4	15	9.7	13	50.4	1	11.5	13	31.5	1
Carptener's helper	1.06	17.9	10	30.4	10	20.7	13	20.5	10	16.3	13
Porter	.80	11.3	14	7.0	14	29.9	6	9.2	15	22.1	8
Laborer	.97	12.7	12	6.9	15	40.7	3	9.4	14	26.9	3

Courtesy of National Foremen's Institute, Inc.
Dollar-value increase 230% by the author.

The procedure just described is performed by each committee member, and the rates assigned to each job are averaged to obtain the rate which is to be used on the job-comparison scale. It has been recommended that the rankings be repeated weekly until each member of the committee has ranked the jobs three times. It is also important to have each person assign the rates to the jobs several times to obtain an average of his own assignment of rates.

Step 8. The Job-Comparison Scale. An illustration of job-comparison scales for key positions is found in Table 6–4. The scale is the result of a great deal of work and thinking on the part of a group of individuals who know the jobs in the unit being studied. It represents the man-to-man type of rating scale where men being rated are compared with men on the scale who have been chosen as representative of degrees of difference in the trait being rated. In this case, jobs to be rated are compared with other jobs which vary in degree according to job factors. It is of interest to note that the money figures in Table 6–3 are 230% higher than the ones in the scale published by Benge in 1941. His figures were probably based upon data prior to 1941.

TABLE 6—4.   Job comparison scale, factor-comparison method •
(money values increased 230% by author)

Cents	Mental effort	Skill	Physical effort	Responsibility	Working conditions
80					
79					
78					
77					
76		Pattern maker			
75					
74		Machinist No. 1			
73					
72					
71					
70					
69					
68					
67					
66					
65					
64				Substation operator	
63					
62	Pattern maker				
61					
60					
59					
58	Substation operator				
57					
56					
55					
54					
53					
52					
51	Machinist No. 1		Rammer		
50					
49		Substation operator			
48					
47					
46		Pipefitter No. 2			
45					
44		Painter	Poleman		
43					
42					
41			Laborer		

TABLE 6—4.   Job comparison scale, factor-comparison method (continued)

Cents	Mental effort	Skill	Physical effort	Responsibility	Working conditions
40					
39					
38					
37				Pattern maker	
36					
35					
34					
33					
32		Drill press operator	Pipefitter No. 2	Machinist No. 1	Rammer
31					
30		Carpenter's helper			Poleman
29					
28			Machinist No. 1	Pipefitter No. 2	Laborer
27					
26					
25	Pipefitter No. 2		Painter	Drill press operator	Pipefitter No. 2
24					
23	Painter		Pattern maker	Painter	Painter
22					
21	Drill press operator		Carpenter's helper	Carpenter's helper	
20					
19					
18	Carpenter's helper		Drill press operator		Machinist No. 1
17					Drill press operator
16		Poleman		Poleman	Carpenter's helper
15					
14	Poleman				Pattern maker
13					
12	Laborer			Rammer	
11					
10					
9		Rammer	Substation operator	Laborer	Substation operator
8					
7	Rammer	Laborer			
6					
5					
4					

If the evaluation committee discovers that the agreed-upon rankings do not correspond with the average monetary evaluation—the assignment of rates to jobs as shown in Step 7—they must attempt to eliminate the discrepancies by slight changes in the average rates assigned to those jobs. If an agreement cannot be reached on the proper adjustments to be made in bringing the rankings and monetary valuations in line, the jobs should be discarded as key positions. These discrepancies are caused by such circumstances as errors in the original rankings, an inequity in the wage paid to the job, an error in ranking, or a wage inequity in one or more of the other key jobs which throws the remaining key jobs out of line.

Although loss of key jobs may seriously affect the usefulness of the job-comparison scale, the remaining key jobs will as a rule furnish the committee with five separate measuring sticks, one for each factor.

Each measuring stick will have a number of points from lowest to highest, distributed at varying intervals along the scale. Each point on each scale will be characterized or defined by a key job. Examination of these measuring sticks will indicate a number of points at which there is a wide spread between some one job and the key job immediately above or below it. Moreover, the selection of key jobs must be further validated.[15]

The inclusion of supplementary key jobs on the job-comparison scale overcomes two problems: loss of key jobs, and the wide spread between key jobs on the scales. If a list of additional jobs is chosen, preferably ones over which there is no controversy as to the rates being paid, these supplementary jobs can be rated by using the key jobs on the job-comparison scale. When this has been completed, the individual ratings of the new jobs can be averaged and discussed. Those which vary considerably can be rerated, if the raters so desire, and averaged again. If the ratings continue to deviate more than 10 per cent from the lowest to the highest estimate, they should, according to Benge, Burk, and Hay, be discarded. At the same time that the supplementary jobs are being rated, the original key jobs can be re-examined and tested against the new jobs and in this manner receive further validation.

Supplementary jobs serve the purpose of checking the key jobs. They can now be added to or "slotted" into the job-comparison scale, where they will make up for key jobs discarded in earlier stages of development of the job-comparison scale, and close the gaps between the key jobs in the original scale. The final job-comparison scale, therefore, consists of the original key jobs and the supplementary jobs that have met the criterion of rating agreement.

[15] Eugene J. Benge, Samuel L. H. Burk, and Edward N. Hay, *Manual of Job Evaluation* (New York: Harper & Brothers, 1941), p. 113.

Use of the job-comparison scale

Five rating scales or measuring sticks, one for each of the five factors, are the basis for the factor-comparison method. When completed, these rating scales should consist of the retained key jobs and about fifty supplementary key jobs. Fewer jobs can be used in the scale for small companies; more supplementary key jobs can be included for companies with 500 or more jobs. The next task is to evaluate all other jobs. Independent judges, a rating committee, or, for larger organizations, several committees can perform the work. If speed is necessary, evaluation of one job in all five scales at once is preferable to comparing all jobs to one scale at the same time.

The process followed in valuing jobs is illustrated by the following instructions given to analysts in one company.[16]

1. Re-read descriptions of key and auxiliary jobs and become thoroughly familiar with them.

2. Each analyst will select from the descriptions of all the remaining jobs those which he himself has prepared and rate them first, rating the others afterwards. This will produce more accurate results because his greater familiarity with the jobs he has described will permit more accurate ratings of those jobs than of others. This has the effect of enlarging each analyst's measuring stick before he starts valuing the jobs less familiar to him.

3. Begin the rating by making a rough ranking of the job descriptions, placing those of lowest probable value on top.

4. Take one job description at a time and read it carefully. Then compare its mental requirements with those of the key or auxiliary jobs that seem closest to it. In making this comparison take account not only of the requirements themselves but of the "intensity" with which they must be used. By intensity is meant the proportion of the total time during which the quality must be used on that job.

5. After completing the comparison, select the Mental Requirement step rate which seems correct for the job being valued and write this value on the job description sheet in the space summarizing Mental Requirements.

6. Each analyst will then write the number of the job on a "Cross Index Form" [shown as Figure 6–4] adding any remarks that will help recall the job when other jobs are later compared with this one. This gives an ever-increasing number of jobs for comparison.

7. Proceed in the same manner, by comparing this same job with the key jobs in the Skill Requirements scale; then for Physical Requirements, for Responsibility, and finally for Working Conditions.

The job raters using this job-rating method have the opportunity

16 *Ibid.*, pp. 119–121.

```
MENTAL—17 POINTS

206—Insurance Typist (T S Dept.)
706—Typist—Investment
403—Typist—Central File
421—I B M Operator
491—Typist and File Clerk (Mtg.)
436—Tenant Record Clerk
842—Asset Bookkeeper (Machine)
814—File Transaction Clerk (Tab.)
803—Record File Clerk
811—Typist Clerk
```

Fig. 6—4. Cross-index form.

of reviewing the values assigned to the original key jobs as well as to the supplementary key jobs. For small companies a majority of the jobs will be included in the construction of the job-comparison scale. The scale itself becomes the basis for the job classification. In large companies, a very comprehensive rating scale can be developed as jobs are evaluated and added to the scale as supplementary key jobs.

Additional methods of constructing a job-comparison scale

In *The AMA Handbook of Wage and Salary Administration*,[17] Edward N. Hay describes four methods of establishing factor scales. The first is called Benge's Plan, and has just been described in detail above. The second method is the Hay Point Plan, the third the Turner Per Cent Method, and the fourth the Hay Training Job Method. These are briefly described below.

Hay Point Plan. This plan is based on a salaried factor-comparison scale which was installed in the Pennsylvania Company in 1938 and has functioned successfully ever since. A set of scales was developed from the point values in use in the Pennsylvania Company. Levels were established on the basis of successive points on the company's factor-comparison scale. Pennsylvania Company jobs falling at each level were isolated, and level descriptions were written which applied to the jobs falling at each level. Since the jobs had been placed at the difficulty levels by means of the factor-comparison method, the specifications for these jobs furnished the material for writing the level descriptions. To illustrate, there were about 40 jobs

[17] *The AMA Handbook of Wage and Salary Administration* (American Management Association, 330 West 42nd Street, New York 18, N. Y.: 1950), pp. 56–65.

falling at 31 points for the skill factor. The average experience required was approximately 12 months, so this experience requirement, 12 months, was given 31 points on the scale for skill. The same method was followed for each of the other point levels for this factor. This is essentially a point plan derived from a factor-comparison plan. The mental requirements factor as described by Hay [18] is found in Table 6–5.

TABLE 6–5. Mental requirements point scale derived from a factor comparison scale •

Step	Points	Mental Requirements
1	5	Very simple routine manual duties, quickly learned and requiring only brief oral instructions. No reading or writing.
2	6	(Intermediate step)
3	7	Same, but must be able to read and write. May require some passive contact with employees or public. No arithmetic.
4	8	(Intermediate step)
5	10	A small number of simple, clearly defined, and well-established duties requiring some use of reading, writing, adding, and subtracting. May require contact with others.
6	11	(Intermediate step)
7	13	(a) A small number of simple, clearly defined, and well-established duties requiring the skillful use of a variety of simple verbal and numerical abilities such as reading, writing, adding, subtracting, comparing, listing, or transcribing either by hand or by machine. Work done in large volume under immediate supervision. (b) or, same as step 5 but with variety and unexpected situations requiring use of some judgment and independent action.
8	15	(Intermediate step)
9	17	Same, except more variety of duties. Close supervision and/or clear definition of duties make independent decisions infrequent.
10	20	(Intermediate step)
11	23	Same as step 9, except supervision is not close and/or duties are still more varied than step 9 and require occasional decisions within a limited number of specific situations. May involve assigning work to a small number of others, under general supervision.
12	27	(Intermediate step)
13	31	Somewhat complex routine duties, following definite rules or procedures but with some variation in application, requiring a high degree of skill in a variety of simple verbal and numerical abilities, such as reading, writing, adding, subtracting, comparing, listing, or transcribing either by hand or by machine. May involve immediate supervision of a small number of other persons doing simple work, calls for some independent decisions of a minor nature.
14	36	(Intermediate step)
15	41	Complex routine requiring varied application of general rules or procedures; and/or regular public contact on routine matters; and/or supervision of a small number of other persons (usually five to 15).
16	47	(Intermediate step)

[18] *Ibid.*, p. 60.

TABLE 6—5 (cont.).

Step	Points	
17	53	(a) Complex routine requiring the use of judgment in applying general rules or procedures in varied ways and in making or verifying decisions for subordinates; or (b) Complex procedures not routinized requiring the constant exercise of judgment in varied situations, all, however, in an area of restricted and definitely known operations with contacts but no supervision of others.
18	61	(Intermediate step)
19	70	(a) Same as 17 (a), but requiring supervision of larger numbers of persons (about 20 to 75). (b) Or same as 17 (b) but covering a wider area of operations and sometimes requiring the supervision of small numbers of persons on like work. Many contacts with others.
20	81	(Intermediate step)
21	93	Like 19 (a) or (b) but a much wider area of operations, and requiring quite a wide general knowledge.

It should be pointed out that Hay describes this method in more detail than is given here. Organizations having factor-comparison installations can convert to the Hay Point Plan without too much difficulty.

The Turner Per Cent Method.[19] This is one of the most ingenious methods of job evaluation that has appeared to date. Turner has made it possible to operate without referring to the rates for the key jobs, and has kept the advantages of the factor-comparison method. Since Turner describes the construction of his scale in considerable detail in the two articles referred to above, no attempt will be made here to duplicate this excellent presentation. The final rating scale is found in Figure 6–5. Numbers which have been written in refer to key jobs. This method should be applicable to all kinds of jobs.

The Hay Training-Job Method. Hay indicates that this is the simplest of the four methods he describes, and is also the one which can be most quickly applied. He describes the steps as follows:

1. Select about a dozen key jobs.

2. Rank the key jobs five times, and for each of the five factors.

3. Compare these jobs a factor at a time with eight of the Pennsylvania Company "training" jobs and adopt point values for the new jobs which are taken from the latter.[20]

This method requires access to the job data for the "training jobs" referred to by Hay.

[19] William D. Turner, "The Per Cent Method of Job Evaluation," *Personnel,* XXIV, No. 6 (New York: American Management Association, May 1948), pp. 476–492 and "Mathematical Basis of 'Per Cent' Job Evaluation," *Personnel,* XXV, No. 2 (September 1948), pp. 154–160.

[20] *The AMA Handbook of Wage and Salary Administration,* American Management Association (330 West 42nd Street, New York 18, N. Y., 1950), pp. 45–55.

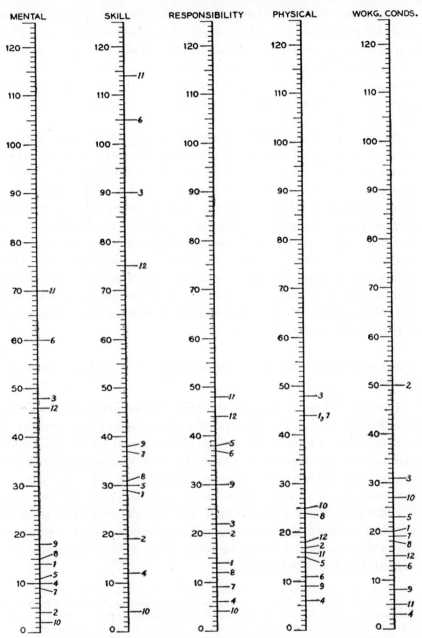

Fig. 6—5.   Graphic factor rating scales—Turner per cent method.

A combination point and factor-comparison system

Perhaps the most extensive study of job-evaluation systems and the most extensive application of job evaluation is found in the work of the Military Occupational Classification Project.[21] The need for a common job and qualification system for all military jobs, both officer and enlisted, is recognized by those who saw the problems of proper allocation of personnel during World War II. The Korean War diverted the attention of the military personnel from this project to more important and immediate considerations, so the project was not completed.

As part of this broad program it was decided that a job-analysis method, a standard job-specification format, and a job-evaluation system would be developed for common use by the services. Of interest to us is the method which was prepared for use in the development of the job-evaluation system. It must be pointed out that the method of development that was in use at the time the project was discontinued is the important aspect of this report, since the preliminary job-evaluation plan was not given a thorough test. It is believed that this method has real value in large industrial plants and in those organizations such as city and state governments which have the problem of interdepartmental classification as well as intradepartment classification.

A procedure for developing the point system based on the factor-comparison approach

The job-evaluation group of the Military Occupational Classification Project has as its objective the development of a system of job evaluation adapted to the needs of the Armed Forces. The military job universe represents a far wider area, a much greater diversity of jobs, and a wider variety of settings than industrial jobs. A characteristic of this project is that it went to the actual job data in order to find out what military jobs are like and what actually are their military characteristics. It was believed that a common job-evaluation system could be constructed so that a suitable administrative tool would result.

[21] This material is taken in part from some of the working papers of the Job Evaluation Group of the Military Occupational Classification Project and represents the work of a large number of job-evaluation and military experts. Since no final action of the Department of Defense has been taken on these findings and procedures, this material in no way represents the thinking of the Department of Defense insofar as either specific or general recommendations and conclusions are concerned. It is presented to show a methodology that is a modification of the point and factor-comparison approaches to job evaluation and that is very similar to the Hay Point Plan. However, it permits the combination of a number of factor scales into a final scale from which a point-rating plan can be constructed.

Keeping in mind the size and scope of the military establishment, it is important that the plan be one that can be applied equally well to the Departments and the numerous divisions within the Departments. This plan was carried out on a sufficient number of types of work across Departments so that it was of real value in the construction of a preliminary job-evaluation system for enlisted personnel. As the reader follows these steps, he should visualize a large number of committees at work, following the same steps for their divisions, so that comparable data will be available for the construction of the final job-evaluation plan. A company has departments and divisions, and this method can be used to construct a scale that can be used for all types of jobs for the company as a whole. It is believed that the advantages of this method of constructing a job-evaluation scale will be apparent as the various steps required are studied.

Step 1. Selection of Key Jobs.

A. Select jobs from the most heavily populated occupations. However, even though a job is not heavily populated, if it is unusually typical of that particular area under consideration and satisfies the other criteria, it should be included as a key job.

B. Select jobs from each grade level. Each pay-grade level should be represented by jobs. Select four to six jobs for each pay grade. The key jobs should be those that are typical of that pay grade. Insofar as possible, a selected job should be one that is commonly considered by experts as neither too high nor too low in rank.

C. Select jobs that are typical of the occupation areas. In those broad occupational areas in which there are a large number of specializations it may be deemed desirable to select 8 to 12 jobs for each pay-grade level.

D. Select jobs that are normally assigned to one person.

E. Select jobs on which there is written data that are adequate, clear, and concise as can be secured under the circumstances.

Step 2. Job-Evaluation Factor Pattern.

Following a series of committee meetings, a complete review of the industrial literature, and a thorough examination of the work on job evaluation, a tentative job-evaluation factor pattern can be derived for preliminary consideration. The tentative job-evaluation factor pattern for the Military Occupation Classification Project was composed of the following separate factors:

   A. Mental Skill
   B. Physical Skill
   C. Supervisory Responsibility
   D. Supervision Received
   E. Responsibility for Material
   F. Responsibility for Safety of Others
   G. Job Conditions
   H. Physical Effort
   I. Potential Combat Hazards and Hardships
   J. Command

As time went on this list was modified considerably. Definitions and a thorough discussion of each factor can be constructed on the basis of the work of the various department investigating committees. These can be submitted for further review.

Step 3. Review of Potential Key Jobs.

Review of potential key jobs as well as the preliminary ranking of jobs is done by a departmental committee. The jobs submitted as potential key jobs are submitted for review to determine whether or not these jobs are supported by adequate data in the form of descriptions, specifications, and schedules. In organizations where job analysis has preceded the construction of the job-evaluation plan, such a careful review of potential key jobs is not necessary. In those cases where reviews are made, the following things are important to keep in mind while reading the material.

   1. Do you understand the job?

   2. Can the committee reach a common understanding in regard to the job description and location in the pay range?

   3. Are the job data adequate for an interdepartmental comparison of the job in relation to other jobs in other departments?

The review should result in the selection of jobs which are clearly described and which meet the criteria mentioned in the steps above.

Step 4. Procedure for Ranking the Potential Key Jobs within Pay Grades.

The first individual operation is the ranking of potential key jobs within pay grades. The primary objectives of this operation are:

   1. To establish a ranking of all key jobs within each pay grade based on the pooled judgment of committee members.

   2. To eliminate those jobs for which common agreement as to rank cannot be obtained and, where necessary, those jobs at the extreme of the ranking; and

   3. To simplify the over-all work load during later operations.

For each pay grade, each member of the ranking committee is to study the potential key jobs and rank them according to their relative position or value in terms of over-all difficulty and responsibility. The jobs of each pay grade are to be ranked by comparing each job with the other proposed key jobs of the same pay grade.

Figure 6–6 is a data sheet for ranking key jobs within pay grades. Each member of the committee is supplied with such a data sheet and the job descriptions and specifications for each of the key jobs. From the description of the key jobs based on information collected by the job analysts, the key jobs are to be ranked by the method of paired comparison. Figure 6–6 illustrates this method. An "X" indicates that the job in the horizontal row is more difficult than the job in the vertical column in which the "X" is placed.

DATA SHEET FOR RANKING KEY JOBS WITHIN PAY GRADES					
Pay Grade 7	Columns of key job titles				
The "X" indicates that the job in the horizontal row is more difficult than the job in the vertical column in which the "X" is placed.	1	2	3	4	5
	Super Chief	Other Chief	Heavy Chief	Accessory Chief	Crew Chief
Rows of Key Job Titles					
1. Super Chief				X	X
2. Other Chief	X			X	X
3. Heavy Chief	X	X		X	X
4. Accessory Chief					
5. Crew Chief				X	
Raters Signature Total X's	2	1	0	4	3

(The "0" total under the Heavy Chief column indicates that none of the other jobs considered were found to be its equal in terms of difficulty and responsibility.)

Fig. 6—6.

The usual steps for completing the process illustrated in Figure 6–6 are as follows:

Step a.   Select the pay grade which you intend to rank first and record that pay grade number in the appropriate row at the top of the data sheet.

Step b.   List the titles and, if any, the code numbers of all the key jobs in the rows on the left side of the data sheet.

Next, list the titles of the key jobs in the same order above the columns of the data sheet.

Step c.   Compare the job in row 1 with all of the other jobs listed in the columns. In row 1 place an "X" in each column where the job in the horizontal row is considered to be more difficult than the job in the vertical column in which the "X" is placed. Perform this process for each of the rows. You will have as many rows as there are jobs being ranked for the pay grade.

Step d.   The number of times one job has been judged to be less difficult than the others is obtained by summing the crosses in the column and recording the number in the "Total X's" row. These totals can be used to determine job ranks.

Step e.   Job ranks will be discussed by the committee members to resolve discrepancies where possible. When deemed necessary, job data for any of the jobs being discussed may be re-examined by the committee.

Step f.   This paired-comparison procedure is repeated for each pay grade. In situations where committee time is limited, the ranking for pay grades may be assigned to sub-committees.

Step 5. Procedure for Ranking Key Jobs by Factors.

The second individual operation is the ranking of key jobs by factors. Step 4 results in the elimination of some of the key jobs, so this operation is usually carried out on fewer jobs than the Step 4 operation. The primary objectives of this step are:

1. To discover any additional jobs which may need to be eliminated from the list of key jobs; and

2. To establish a rank order for all key jobs in relation to each of the selected factors mentioned in Step 2.

One of the factor definitions is discussed by a person fully acquainted with the factors. When the aspects of this factor's definition are clear to each member of the committee, each one studies the key jobs and ranks them according to their relative position or value in terms of this one factor. This general process is repeated for each of the remaining factors.

Each committee member is supplied with a "Data Sheet for Ranking Key Jobs by Factors." (See Figure 6–7.) From the descriptions of the key jobs, you are to rank them in order of their relationship to the factor under consideration by the method of paired comparison. This method is similar to the one used in Step 4.

DATA SHEET FOR RANKING KEY JOBS BY FACTORS
Factor *MENTAL SKILL*

The "X" indicates that the job in the horizontal row is more difficult than the job in the vertical column in which the "X" is placed. Rows of key job titles	Columns of key job titles												
	1	2	3	4	5	6	7	8	9	10	11	12	13
	Follow Up	Heavy Chief	Runner Up	H. Maintenance	Wait Up	Stander Up	Crew Chief	Accessory Chief	Walker Up	Clean Up	Super Chief	Get Up	Other Chief
1. Follow Up			X		X	X			X	X		X	
2. Heavy Chief	X		X	X	X	X	X	X	X	X	X	X	X
3. Runner Up					X	X			X	X			
4. H. Maintenance	X		X		X	X			X	X		X	
5. Wait Up						X			X	X			
6. Stander Up													
7. Crew Chief	X		X	X	X	X			X	X		X	
8. Accessory Chief	X		X	X	X	X	X		X	X		X	
9. Walker Up						X							
10. Clean Up						X			X				
11. Super Chief	X		X	X	X	X	X	X	X	X		X	
12. Get Up			X		X	X			X	X			
13. Other Chief	X		X	X	X	X	X	X	X	X	X	X	
Total X	6	0	8	5	9	12	4	3	11	10	2	7	1

Fig. 6—7.

Since the method used is exactly the same as the method used in Step 4, only a brief review of the procedure is given. The first thing is to enter all the key jobs for all of the grades in the vertical column at the left side of the sheet. Next list the titles of the key jobs in the same order in the column at the top of the data sheet. The rater is then asked to compare the jobs in row 1 with the other jobs listed in the columns. The "X" is used to indicate a judgment when the job in the row is more difficult or involves more of the factor than the job in the column. The next step involves the addition of the crosses in each of the columns, recording the number in the "Total X's" row. These totals can be used to determine the rank of each job, but it must be kept in mind that the summation indicates the number of times that each job has been judged to be less difficult. The above is to be repeated for each of the factors. The job titles should be listed in the same order for each factor on the data sheets for ranking key jobs by factors. Step d involves a discussion of the ranks obtained by each committee member so that discrepancies can be resolved.

This step results in a committee ranking for each of the factors of the key jobs. This is quite important because it aids in the procedure for prorating points to the selected factors.

Step 6. Procedure for Prorating Points to the Selected Factors.

The final operation for individuals on the departmental committees is to prorate points to the factors. The primary objective of this step is to establish within each key job the comparative values of each of the selected factors while being careful not to disturb the over-all relationship between the key jobs which has been developed on the basis of rankings. Figure 6–8 reveals the points to be prorated for each key job according to the military pay grades. For companies or large corporations an established pay grade or a

SERVICES				Pay grade	Points to be prorated per pay grade
Army	Air Force	Marines	Navy		
M/Sgt	M/Sgt	M/Sgt	CPO	E–7	215
Sgt 1 cl	T/Sgt	T/Sgt	PO 1 cl	E–6	185
Sgt	S/Sgt	S/Sgt	PO 2 cl	E–5	155
Cpl	Sgt	Sgt	PO 3 cl	E–4	130
PFC	Cpl	Cpl	Seaman	E–3	105
Pvt	PFC	PFC	S Aprntc	E–2	90
Rct	Pvt	Pvt	S Rct	E–1	80

Fig. 6–8. Point profile.

pay grade based on community rates can be used. This step really determines whether the pay grade of each job is fair in proportion to the other key jobs. Figure 6–9 shows an actual work sheet which was used in prorating points to jobs by factors. The job titles have been disguised, but the illustration is still pertinent.

During the previous operations, the highest and lowest jobs for each of the factors were determined by the method of paired comparison. At this stage the maximum and minimum number of points to be distributed to each factor is determined through the use of individual and pooled judgments. Starting with the points presently assigned to each of the key jobs according to its pay grade, divide these points and assign them to the factors in accordance with the estimate as to the importance of each factor in relation to

DEPARTMENT_____

NAME_____

INSTRUCTIONS FOR PRORATING POINTS

Look at the first job listed. In the first column next to this job title you will see the figure 215. This is the total number of points you are to distribute across the factors for the job. Record under each factor (in POINTS column) the number of points you believe represents the importance of that factor relative to the other factors. Similarly, distribute the points for each job. The ranks given are those arrived at by the committee. In prorating points do not throw this rank out of line.

	Total points to prorate	Mental skill Rank	Mental skill Points	Physical skill Rank	Physical skill Points	Supervisory responsibility Rank	Supervisory responsibility Points	Supervision received Rank	Supervision received Points	Responsibility for material Rank	Responsibility for material Points	Responsibility for safety of others Rank	Responsibility for safety of others Points	Job conditions Rank	Job conditions Points	Physical effort Rank	Physical effort Points	Potential combat hazards and hardships Rank	Potential combat hazards and hardships Points	Command Rank	Command Points
E-7 Senior Chief	215	1		5		1		1		1		4		12		12		5			
E-7 Chief Technician (General)	215	2		9		2		2		2		6		11		11		9			
E-6 Department Technician	185	3		1		5		4		3		1		10		10		6			
E-6 Field Service Technician	185	4		6		3		3		4		2		1		2		1			
E-5 Senior Man	155	6		8		4		6		6		5		4		6		3			
E-5 Technician (General)	155	7		4		6		5		5		8		9		9		8			
E-4 Operating Technician	130	5		2		7		7		7		3		6		5		4			
E-4 Technician (General)	130	8		7		8		8		8		9		7		7		7			
E-3 Technician (Special)	105	10		10		9		9		10		7		3		3		2			
E-3 Technician	105	9		3		10		10		9		11		8		8		12			
E-2 Technician	90	12		11		12		11		11		12		5		4		11			
E-2 Apprentice	90	11		12		11		12		12		10		2		1		10			

Fig. 6–9. Data sheet for prorating points.

the key job under consideration. This process is simplified to some extent by establishing the tentative maximum and minimum number of points that can be prorated to each of the factors. No job should receive more points than are assigned to its pay grade. Some jobs may receive no points for a certain factor when that factor does not apply to the job being considered. Likewise several jobs may receive the same number of points for the same factor even though these jobs are different in pay grades. In fact, several jobs in consecutive rank order under one factor may receive the same number of points for that factor. The procedure for prorating points to the factors is illustrated in Figure 6–10. The usual steps for completing this operation are as follows:

DATA SHEET FOR PRORATING POINTS TO THE AFJES * FACTORS

KEY JOB TITLE AND CODE	Total Points for Distribution	AFJES FACTORS									
		1	2	3	4	5	6	7	8	9	10
		Mental Skill	Physical Skill	Supervisory Responsibility	Supervision Received	Responsibility for Material	Responsibility for Safety of Others	Job Conditions	Physical Effort	Potential Combat Hazards and Hardships	Command
JOB A (E–7)	215	70	0	45	30	30	20	0	0	0	20
JOB B (E–5)	155	20	45	0	55	15	0	10	10	0	0
JOB C (E–3)	105	10	15	10	5	0	5	10	30	20	0

* Armed Forces Job Evaluation System.

Fig. 6—10.

Step a.   Record the titles of the key jobs with their total number of points to be prorated onto the Data Sheet for Prorating Points to the Factors (see Figure 6–9).

Step b.   Assign points to the factors of that key job which was ranked *highest* under the Mental Skill factor during Step 5, by having the committee, through pooled judgment, tentatively establish a maximum number of points for the Mental Skill factor, as it applies to the division, department, or occupational area under consideration.

Step c.   The committee decides which of the key jobs should be the lowest-ranking one to receive points under the factor of Mental Skill. Start with the lowest-ranking job under this factor and proceed up the rank order under this factor, until a job is reached which should receive some points for the factor. In this manner assign minimum points for each factor for the jobs selected.

Step d.   During Step b, the tentative maximum number of points to be prorated to each factor for this group of jobs was determined; during Step c, the tentative minimum number of points to be prorated to each factor for these jobs was determined. Now, starting with the points presently assigned to each of the key jobs according to its pay grade, as indicated in Figure 6–8, or in the Total Points to Prorate column of the Work Sheet, Figure 6–9, divide those points and assign them to the factors in accordance with each factor's estimated importance in relation to the key job under consideration. It should be remembered that no job should receive more points than are assigned to its pay grade.

Step e.   The point distributions so obtained should be discussed by committee members to resolve discrepancies. In those instances where the proration of points destroys the job rankings under the factor, the job which cannot fit into the ranking should be eliminated as a key job.

Up to this point there is little or no difference between this method and the factor-comparison method. From this point on, however, the method is used to construct a point scale, and is an illustration of "rating-scale construction" based on the material to be used in making ratings.

Step 7. Interdepartment Study

When the procedure covered in the first six steps has been completed, either for the company as a whole, in the case of a small organization, or for the departments in a large company, the next step is to integrate the various ranks and prorated points into a scale for each factor. This is accomplished as follows:

Step a.   Select individuals who are thoroughly acquainted with the jobs in their department, and who have an understanding of the jobs in the other departments, for membership on an interdepartmental committee.

Step b.   Have this committee select, for all departments covered, those jobs which are not only representative of the department but which are also fairly familiar to the other departments. Going back to the rankings under each pay grade, make sure that each pay-grade level is represented for each department. (NOTE: Some departments may have missing pay-grade levels because of the skill level involved. These departments will probably furnish good key jobs for their skill and pay levels. This step should result in a list of key jobs which are representative of the types of work, departments, pay levels, and skill levels as found in the organization as a whole.

Step c.   Keeping in mind that each key job has had points allocated to it under each factor, the next step is to rank the selected jobs by factors, using the prorated points which were assigned under Step 6. This means that for a factor, such as Mental Skill, the job having the highest number of prorated points will have the highest rank on that factor, and the job having the lowest number or the jobs having no points will be given the lowest rank. It can be seen that this method of ranking permits a departmental combination which assumes that the pay grades are comparable for the kind of work performed, even though the work differs considerably as to type. Since most companies have been operating quite successfully, this plan tends to bring these pay policies together into a single ranking based on the factors which were selected.

Step d.   The committee is now asked to study the rank of key jobs for each factor, to attempt to determine the number of distinguishably different degree levels present in the rank of key jobs. For example, the committee is asked to determine first the number of levels of Mental Skill present in the key jobs. The usual degree number might apply, but in general from three degrees to approximately seven or eight, depending on the skill range of jobs, will result. The prorated points, as well as the nature of the jobs in the ranks, will serve as guides for this division of key jobs into distinguishably different levels or degrees of the factors.

Step e. The committee is then asked to bring together the job descriptions and job specifications for the jobs under each degree for each factor, and to isolate the material which pertains to the factor under consideration. This material consists of the job-specification statements for the factor, say Mental Skill, and also the material from the job description that shows what aspects of the job make a given mental skill level necessary. Considerable editing and integrating are required, because a fairly large number of representative key jobs are available for use. However, this material is the basis for writing the degree definition, and such degree definitions will be broad enough to cover the jobs in the organization to be evaluated. This step is really the end of a considerable amount of work, and provides the best basis for the construction of a point scale that it is possible to obtain. In those instances where a key job has specification material which is definitely out of line with the other key jobs for the degree level being studied, this job should be eliminated and be rated in the final job-evaluation study.

Step f. Since each key job at each degree level for each factor has had points prorated to it, these points can be averaged, and that average can be the point value assigned to the degree.

Step g. The committee should study the jobs at each degree level and select a representative number of jobs to be used as bench-mark jobs. In choosing bench-mark jobs, type of work, departmental representation, and familiarity to other departments should be considered.

The resulting job-evaluation scale has both degree levels and representative bench-mark jobs. In using the scale, the rating techniques for both the point systems and the factor-comparison system can be employed. The final scale is tailored for the organization; it has made possible a considerable amount of participation in its con‑ struction, and has been built upon the best practices now in exist‑ ence in the organization. It should be usable on all types of jobs in the organization, since it was constructed by studying representative jobs.

Although the illustrations below are not completely based on the method just described, enough of the method was involved so that the reader can see the type of scale which might result. Because of the tentative nature of the scale, and because the various military occupational specialties used as illustrations have not been given a final classification on the basis of this scale, they are not listed as bench-mark jobs under the degrees. However, each degree level in the scale has bench-mark jobs that further define the level and make its application in job evaluation easier.

ILLUSTRATIVE FACTORS FROM A TENTATIVE MILITARY JOB-EVALUATION SCALE BASED ON A COMBINATION POINT AND FACTOR-COMPARISON SYSTEM

1. Knowledge required

This factor measures the military and work knowledges required as a minimum to carry out assignments. Consider the kind, amount, and complexity of knowledges required, whether obtained through schools (civilian or military), informal training, self-education, and/or work experience (civilian or military). In supervisory jobs, consider knowledges required to direct others in carrying out activities. The knowledge itself is what is important, and not how it was gotten. Also, care must be taken to measure actual knowledge required by the job and not the knowledge possessed by job incumbents. Formal and informal schooling may be used as one measure of this factor but ordinarily it will not con‑ stitute the only measure. Another measure is the length of experience and the type of experience absolutely required to build up the necessary knowledge. While no indications of length of experience criteria are given in the degree levels, length of experience needed may be used in comparisons of jobs in application of this factor.

Degree 1

Knowledge sufficient to understand simple oral orders pertaining to uncomplicated work (such as that involving primarily physical effort, or pertaining to directions for following the simplest common work prac‑ tices), and sufficient to carry out without detailed instruction and train‑

ing such simple orders in any of a variety of common processes, involving such knowledge as an understanding of the types and use of tools such as shovels, picks, axes, hammers, crowbars, etc., simple lifting and stacking of bulk materials without injury to self or materials (not involving complicated sling-loading or stacking), etc.

May involve knowledge of counting to low totals and simple tallying. Also required is knowledge of defense against enemy attack, for example, use of individual weapons, unarmed defense, etc.

Bench Mark Jobs: [omitted by author]

Degree 2

Knowledge sufficient to understand and carry out simple written or somewhat less simple oral directions pertaining to slightly complex work operations without detailed instruction and training, for example, sufficient to act as a helper in a trade such as carpentry or plumbing, involving such tasks as keeping higher level workers supplied with tools and materials, unloading machines, etc., requiring some knowledge of work sequence and the uses of the tools of the trade. Or, knowledge of some clerical processes, but not necessarily of their integration in clerical occupations, such as simple adding, subtraction, multiplication and division of whole numbers; reading, writing and spelling of simple words, following alphabetical or numerical sequence for storing or pulling materials or simple filing.

Also, knowledge of defense against enemy attack, for example, use of individual weapons, unarmed defense, etc.

Bench Mark Jobs: [omitted by author]

Degree 3

Knowledge of use and operation of varied military weapons, tactics, identification of the enemy, unarmed defense, etc., sufficient to participate in offensive and defensive combat; to understand and interpret moderately difficult written or oral instructions, charts, wiring and other diagrams, and technical manuals and procedures; to perform simple arithmetic problems involving adding, subtracting, dividing and multiplying of fractions and decimals; to perform clerical techniques such as would be required in operating simple office machines (typewriter, mimeograph, key punch, and adding machines), and in filling out routine reports; to make simple explanations clearly, orally or in writing, for example, to give directions to others for carrying out uncomplicated assignments.

Bench Mark Jobs: [omitted by author]

Degree 4

Knowledge sufficient to perform the most complex and difficult individual combat assignments, or to direct others in the performance of less complex combat assignments; to understand more complicated written or oral instructions, interpret somewhat complicated drawings, diagrams, rules, procedures, maps, technical manuals, and charts; to perform moderately difficult arithmetic problems; to operate such devices as radio, radar, electronics, and sonar equipment; or to perform complex clerical activities including stenography; or to perform semi-technical laboratory assignments in a specialized field; to make slightly complex explanations clearly, orally or in writing, for example, to give directions to others for carrying out slightly complex assignments.

Bench Mark Jobs: [omitted by author]

Degree 5

Knowledge sufficient to direct others in complex and varied combat assignments; to understand complex written instructions, and to perform fairly complex assignments involving the application of shop or trade mathematics, the interpretation of technical manuals and orders, such as would be involved in maintenance and repair of complex mechanical, electrical, radar, and similar types of equipment, or to perform fairly complex administrative or related types of activities requiring the application of administrative techniques, knowledge sufficient to write comprehensive statements and instructions, for example, knowledge sufficient to write detailed operating procedures for simple equipment or assignments and work processes. Knowledge required to direct activities of others in moderately complex assignments or activities.

Bench Mark Jobs: [omitted by author]

Degree 6

Knowledge sufficient to act as enlisted commander of moderately complex military operations or to act as principal enlisted assistant to the commander of a more complex military operation involving comprehensive knowledge of a strictly military nature such as the nature of weapons used in military units including the operation, minor maintenance, limitations, capabilities, and employment of such weapons, administration, supply, and other tactical problems of the military unit to which the job is assigned, and principles and problems of military leadership; to have a sound understanding of the intricate mechanisms of machinery and equipment used by the Armed Forces in order to perform complex maintenance and repair work on such equipment involving the application of shop mathematics, interpretation of technical manuals and similar technical data; to perform very complex administrative duties; and to direct others in complex assignments and activities.

Bench Mark Jobs: [omitted by author]

Degree 7

Involves tasks demanding the highest degree of technical knowledge required in enlisted jobs in the Armed Forces. For example, thorough knowledge of military combat principles, techniques, equipment, and problems in a specialized field, and of principles of military leadership. Knowledge of a difficult and specialized technical field sufficient to perform the most complex operations, maintenance, testing and fabrication assigned to enlisted personnel, or knowledge of such a field sufficient to perform, under direction, technical research, or to render non-routine technical assistance to a higher level specialist in such research, when the research assistance required demands more knowledge than is required for any lower degree; knowledges required to direct others in carrying out the above types of activities.

Bench Mark Jobs: [omitted by author]

2. Scope of action

This factor measures the extent of the independent decisions and actions required in performance of the assignment. Consider the extent to which the nature and variety of the duties require making independent decisions or taking self-determined actions. Also consider the limitations on the decisions and actions imposed by the supervision and military command received. Consider how actions and decisions are guided and controlled by manuals or other publications, by precedent actions, or by common military or work practices. Consider how assignments are received, the character of instructions received with the assignment or during work progress and closeness with which activities and products are inspected during processing and after completion.

Degree 1

Works under explicit procedures and/or instructions with little or no responsibility for administrative or technical aspects of the work. Work is inspected in process and on completion except where other controls over work performance make such inspection unnecessary. Work is ordinarily performed within a very narrow range which provides little opportunity for individual discretion.

Bench Mark Jobs: [omitted by author]

Degree 2

Receives detailed instructions as to the results expected, and as new work situations arise; methods for attaining the results are indicated with a considerable degree of definiteness. Decisions are based on clearly applicable procedures, instructions, rules, or regulations. Review or inspection of work, made periodically during initial stages, may decrease to spot checks on repetitious aspects of the assignment. Superior usually present or readily available.

Bench Mark Jobs: [omitted by author]

Degree 3

Receives relatively short-term specific assignments of such a nature that the results desired for each major phase of the work are indicated with some definiteness, but on occasion are subject to change if unforeseen contingencies occur. Receives general instructions as to methods and procedures, and plans and performs work sequences when standard or recognized methods are available. Some interpretations or adaptations of regulations, laws, rules, and/or instructions are required on the part of the worker. Where results of work are not self-evident, work is subject to inspection on completion or at long intervals with occasional checks during progress.

Bench Mark Jobs: [omitted by author]

Degree 4

Receives broad or relatively long term assignments or has continuing responsibility for a given area of work. Results expected of the work are indicated in terms of the general kinds of results desired for major phases of the work. Plans work and performs duties where only general operation methods are available. Makes decisions on the basis of technical practices and on precedent actions which serve as unwritten guides. Assignments sometimes involve new approaches or application in new situations. Supervision received is more frequently concerned with end results than with detailed procedures during work progress.

Bench Mark Jobs: [omitted by author]

Degree 5

Receives broad or relatively long term assignments or has continuing responsibility for a given area of work. Results expected of the work are expressed in general terms of the overall objective to be accomplished. Establishes or revises work procedures and performance standards in conformance with administrative and technical policies, and completes assigned duties with infrequent reference to the superior as to details of the work. On occasion has complete discretion for determining methods or procedures when exceptional problems arise. Review or inspection from higher supervision is generally in terms of end results and the degree to which they match objectives.

Bench Mark Jobs: [omitted by author]

SUGGESTIONS FOR STUDY AND RESEARCH

1. Take any one of the quantitative systems and show why you believe it to be superior to the other systems.

2. How would you explain each system (point, factor, and modified) to the workers in a factory?

CASE PROBLEM

Select a sample of key jobs.* Check in the community and obtain an estimate of the going wage paid to workers on the sample jobs. Construct a job comparison scale, using these sample jobs as key jobs, following the directions on pages 175–188. Take ten new jobs and rate them on this job comparison scale. Rate the same ten jobs on the factory point-rating scale found on pages 159–166.

PROBLEM: What differences do you observe in the ratings when the ten jobs are rated on both the factor comparison and point scales? Which scale seems easier to use? What differences did you note when getting the committee to furnish information so that the job comparison scale could be constructed?

* The instructor may obtain one set of sample jobs from Jay L. Otis, Western Reserve University, Cleveland 6, Ohio.

Part Three

Analyzing Jobs

7

Getting Job Facts

AFTER ALL PLANS FOR THE JOB EVALUATION
have been laid, the first step in actually going to work is the collection of factual information at the source—the jobs in the company.
This collection of source data is the most time-consuming phase of all the work involved. The accumulation and recording of job information can be done poorly or it can be done well. In either case, by the time the job evaluation is completed the number of man-hours involved will be about the same, so careful attention to this phase of the work will pay dividends in the end. Pertinent facts which are missed in the original analysis of the jobs will have to be picked up later, when the descriptions and specifications are being edited or when the jobs are being rated. This takes a great deal of time, interrupts the scheduled flow of the work, and is confusing to everyone concerned.

Job analysis looks much easier than it is. Only an expert in the field can easily detect a poor job analysis without having a good one on the same job for comparison. On the other hand, the weaknesses of inadequate job information are immediately apparent to anyone trying to use these facts, especially in the rating of jobs. Thus, "regardless of the use of job information, it must be accurate, it must omit nothing judged to be essential, and it must be presented in usable form." [1]

[1] Personnel Research Institute of Western Reserve University, *Handbook of Job Evaluation for Factory Jobs*, American Institute of Bolt, Nut and Rivet Manufacturers. now Industrial Fasteners Institute (Cleveland, 1946), p. 8.

In this chapter we shall explore the various uses of job analysis, and examine discussions of analysis techniques by other writers who have had experience with them. We may attempt in this way to arrive at some principles which will guide those adventuring into this field, as well as those who have been dissatisfied with the results they have achieved in attempting to handle job analysis.

IMPORTANCE OF JOB FACTS

The fact that there is more to job analysis than meets the eye cannot alone justify this detailed exploration in a work devoted to job evaluation and wage and salary administration. Those who have handled successfully the pricing of jobs by analytical methods have invariably stressed the importance of accurate and sufficient job information. Introducing a discussion of "Collecting Facts," Knowles [2] states flatly that "the job analysis process is really the backbone of job evaluation. . . ." Hess [3] defines a "formal job evaluation plan" as "a method of job analysis based on facts. . . ." The Research Institute of America, in a brief survey of the subject for the benefit of its members, states with emphasis: "The groundwork of a job evaluation program is a three-step job analysis— collecting facts about jobs, writing descriptions based on those facts, and preparing specifications from the descriptions in terms of job requirements." [4]

Assuming, on the basis of testimony of this type, that facts about jobs are important in job evaluation, it may be worth while to explore somewhat the reasons why accuracy and completeness in job information are so vital. It has been pointed out above that all of the various job-evaluation or job-classification systems are essentially applications or adaptations of the rating-scale technique which has been used in many forms, some difficult to recognize, in evaluating everything from the grades of olives to the consumer appeal of television programs. All of these applications have in common the objective of *measurement for the purpose of classification.*

Measurement is the key to the situation. For example, it is rather easy to *classify* lubricating oils into grades according to

---

[2] Asa S. Knowles, *Management of Manpower* (New York: The Macmillan Company, 1943), p. 112.

[3] Robert G. Hess, "Basic Principles of Job Evaluation," *Machinery* (May, 1945), p. 169.

[4] *Labor Report of Executive Membership,* No. 11 (May 23, 1945), Vol. 2. Reprinted by permission of the Research Institute of America, Inc., 292 Madison Avenue, New York.

ability to flow at a specified temperature. The Society of Auto-motive Engineers has set up a *measuring* stick based on standard viscosity which can be applied to almost any sample of oil, because the viscosity of oils can be measured objectively. The *measurement* of jobs for the purpose of *classification* into pay groups is exactly the same kind of an operation, *except* that the measuring stick, or job-rating scale, is not so precise, and the accuracy of the measurement depends so much on the accuracy of the information about that which is being measured—the individual job. Thus, even though the "Experience" factor on our job-measuring stick is rather specific in terms of months or years required, it is quite a trick to apply that measure to any particular job and arrive at an answer which we feel fairly certain is correct. On the other hand, the more we know about the details of that job, the more nearly correct our judgment will be.

In the final analysis, the application of any job-rating scale to any job is not a *measurement* in the usual sense of the word, but is the best judgment which can be arrived at under the circumstances. The circumstances here should be the most specific and precise job-rating scale which can be constructed, to be applied against the most accurate and complete pertinent job information which can be accumulated under practical conditions. Thus the completeness and accuracy of pertinent job facts will in a large measure determine the validity of the judgments we make in applying a job-rating scale to evaluate jobs.

METHOD OF OBTAINING FACTS—JOB ANALYSIS

As indicated at the beginning of this chapter, the accumulation of accurate job facts and the recording of this information in clear, concise, complete job descriptions and specifications is not a simple process. The reason this point is emphasized here is that a great many persons who have done job-evaluation work have not stressed the methods and techniques of collecting the data on which the job ratings are based. In contrast, those who have had considerable experience with the study of jobs for various purposes have not failed to write in some detail in describing the forms which may be used, the sources of information, methods and techniques found to be successful, and the difficulties likely to be encountered.

As early as 1921, H. D. Kitson [5] recognized and pointed out that

5 H. D. Kitson, "Scientific Method in Job Analysis," *Journal of Political Economy,* Vol. 29 (1921), pp. 508–514.

accuracy in job analysis required the application of scientific method. In 1923, Scott and Clothier [6] described in full a detailed form for use in obtaining and recording job information.

A most striking illustration of the technical nature of job analysis is to be found in the experience of the Occupational Analysis Section of the United States Employment Service. In the introduction to its excellent *Training and Reference Manual for Job Analysis* [7] this organization states:

This manual has been prepared ten years after the first job analysis study was conducted under the Occupational Research Program. . . . It may be considered as one in the long series of instructional manuals developed over that period to meet changes in techniques and to incorporate the fruits of experience. . . . However, while the methods and procedures presented have proved their effectiveness, it is felt that there is still room for considerable improvement .

The extent of this experience is described in full by Stead and Masincup. [8]

Job analysis defined

The term *job analysis* as it has been used in this discussion refers to the technique of obtaining job information to be used in various operations in the field of personnel management. While this was the early connotation of the term, apparently originated during the first World War by the Committee on the Classification of Personnel, this term subsequently has been utilized in varying shades of meaning which have resulted in some confusion as to just what it includes.

The analysis of jobs in industry today falls into two general classifications: (1) job analysis to develop information for personnel operations, and (2) time and motion study and methods analysis for engineering purposes. These two types of analysis are compared and contrasted in Figure 7–1. It will be noted here that the approach in each case is different, the principal techniques employed are quite dissimilar, the subject matter in each method falls into distinctly different groupings, and the purposes and uses are quite

---

[6] W. D. Scott and R. C. Clothier, *Personnel Management* (Chicago: A. W. Shaw Company, 1923), pp. 141–144.

[7] *Training and Reference Manual for Job Analysis*, War Manpower Commission, Division of Occupational Analysis (Washington: United States Government Printing Office, 1944), p. iv.

[8] William H. Stead and W. Earl Masincup, *The Occupational Research Program of the United States Employment Service*, Public Administration Service (Chicago, 1941).

distinct. It is evident, therefore, that the training, experience, and qualifications of the job analyst must be significantly different from those of the time-motion-methods analyst. This difference can be illustrated in a very general way by pointing out that the job analyst must be a personnel man with an understanding of jobs from the engineering standpoint, and the time-motion-methods analyst must be an engineer with an appreciation of jobs from the point of view of the worker.

PERSONNEL—ANALYSIS OF THE JOB AS A WHOLE	ENGINEERING—TIME AND MOTION STUDY, METHODS ANALYSIS
Approach	
From the point of view of the worker	From the point of view of the job operations
Principal Techniques	
1. Questionnaire	1. Observation
2. Interview with worker	2. Motion and still photography
3. Interview with supervisors	3. Timing (stop watch)
4. Observation	
Subject Matter	
The workers':	Duties, tasks, movements:
1. Duties	1. Sequence
2. Skills	2. Time involved
3. Knowledges	3. Motions involved
4. Responsibilities	4. Methods, machines and equipment
5. Effort	
6. Working Conditions	
Purposes and Uses	
1. Personnel selection, placement, transfer, promotion	1. Improvement of sequence
2. Job Evaluation—wage and salary administration	2. Establishment of standards
3. Training	3. Work simplification
4. Changes in organization structure	4. Incentive payment
5. Changes in job content	5. Motion, time, and effort economy
6. Improvement in safety and working conditions	6. Improvement of machinery and equipment
7. Standardization of job titles and duties for all personnel operations	
8. Basis for employee evaluation	
9. Personnel inventory and budgeting	

Fig. 7—1. Analysis of jobs in industry.

Since job evaluation is one of the important applications or uses of job analysis from the point of view of the worker, the term *job analysis* as used in this discussion is defined as follows: "The process of determining, by observation and study, and reporting pertinent information relating to the nature of a specific job. It is the determination of the tasks which comprise the job and of the skills, knowledges, abilities, and responsibilities required of the worker for successful performance." [9]

It is important also to distinguish clearly job analysis as a technique from the applications or uses of job analysis. Job analysis and job evaluation are not synonymous. A job breakdown for training purposes, which may be developed by the job-analysis technique, is not a job analysis; likewise a hiring specification for use in selection is a product of job analysis. Job analysis, then, is not the end result but is the technique or procedure by which specified job facts are discovered and recorded. Thus, the items of information which are obtained, and the manner in which this information is presented, will be determined by the uses that will be made of the end product developed by the technique of job analysis.

In job analysis for the purpose of establishing training procedures, certain predetermined items of information are necessary. These facts are obtained by the job-analysis technique and are recorded in a job breakdown or training outline form, which has been determined to be the most useful method of organizing this information for training purposes for the particular job in question. This training outline has very little usefulness for any other purpose.

Another application of the job-analysis technique is one which has been developed by the Occupational Research Program of the United States Employment Service. In this case the items of information that are covered in the job analysis are quite extensive, since the purpose of this job information is to provide a rather detailed picture of the job or the occupation covered, and to provide information which will be useful for as many different purposes as possible.

Finally, the job description and job specification, which are the end products of job analysis in job evaluation, determine the kinds of information that must be obtained in job-analysis for the purpose of job evaluation.

The job-analysis technique employed in these three examples is identical: the differences are entirely in the types of information to be obtained, the extent of detail, and the form of presentation of the

[9] *Training and Reference Manual for Job Analysis*, War Manpower Commission, Division of Occupational Analysis (Washington: United States Government Printing Office, 1944), p. 1.

facts. It is important then, in preparing to analyze jobs for evaluation, to determine clearly (1) what the job-analysis technique is, (2) what items of information will be covered, and in how much detail, and (3) how the information collected by job analysis should be organized and recorded.

The job-analysis technique

A skillful job analysis—one which results in accurate information, complete in all pertinent details, presented in usable form—requires the application of a standardized procedure.

Basically, there are but three parts to the analysis of any job: (1) The job must be completely and accurately identified; (2) the tasks of the job must be completely and accurately described; (3) the requirements the job makes upon the worker for successful performance must be indicated . . . the second of these three parts is outstandingly important—the complete and accurate describing of the job tasks. Without this the rest of the analysis lacks meaning.[10]

Job Identification. The proper identification of a job requires that the information given must distinguish the job in question from all other jobs in the company, and must also indicate clearly the scope of tasks which are encompassed by this job. For example, a number of workers performing -identical tasks on identical machines, using the same materials and utilizing the same skills and abilities, may be grouped under a single job title which may be identified very specifically. On the other hand, another group of workers may be performing tasks which are essentially similar but in which there are some significant variations. These workers also may be grouped under a single job title for purposes of analysis and description, but in this case the significant variations from one worker to another must be included in the identification, so that the scope of variations in tasks which are considered to be included under the job title in question is clearly designated.

The Job-Analysis Formula. The technique for discovering the facts that are necessary to describe the tasks of the job, and to indicate the worker qualifications necessary for successful performance, has been outlined in the *Guide for Analyzing Jobs* of the War Manpower Commission.[11]

[10] *Ibid.,* p. 1.

[11] *Guide for Analyzing Jobs, Analyst's Workbook,* War Manpower Commission, Division of Occupational Analysis (Washington: United States Government Printing Office, 1944).

This *job-analysis formula* is:

> WHAT the worker does
> HOW he does it
> WHY he does it
> SKILL INVOLVED:
> Responsibility
> Job Knowledge
> Mental Application
> Dexterity and Accuracy

WHAT the worker does involves physical activity in which he may cut, grind, put together, set up, regulate, clean, and so forth; it also includes mental activity in which he may plan, compute, direct and so on. The physical and mental activities of each task of the job must be considered. HOW the worker accomplishes his task involves such physical factors as machinery, tools, measuring devices, procedures, and routines as well as mental activities such as calculation, use of formulas, and application of judgment or decision. The WHY of the job-analysis formula is particularly important for a thorough orientation of the analyst with respect to the job, since it covers the purpose or the reason why each task is performed in relation to other tasks in the same job and other jobs in the department or the company. An example of how job information can be constructed by the WHAT-HOW-WHY technique is given in the *Guide for Analyzing Jobs* [12] as follows:

Engine Lathe Operator First-Class

Work Performed. Sets up and operates an Engine Lathe (What, How) to turn small airplane fittings from brass or steel bar stock or from unfinished aluminum or magnesium alloy castings (Why), finishing the fittings down to specified close tolerances (What, How).

1. ....

2. Sets up Lathe (What): Carefully examines blueprints (What) to determine the dimensions of the part to be machined (Why), using shop mathematics (How) to calculate any dimensions (What) not given directly on the prints (Why) or to calculate machine settings (Why).

   (a) Sets up lathe to turn stock held in a chuck (What): Attaches to lathe the accessories, such as chuck and tool holder (What), necessary to perform the machining (Why), threading and locking the chuck on the headstock spindle (How) and setting. . . .

The skill involved supplements the what, how, and why by expressing the degree of difficulty of the various tasks involved in the job. The four basic factors listed under this part of the for-

[12] *Ibid.*

mula are those which must be considered in determining the degree of difficulty of any job. What a job demands of any individual in terms of responsibility, job knowledge, mental application, and dexterity and accuracy is the key to the qualifications required of a worker for successful performance on the job.

An additional area of information about jobs is essential to job evaluation and to some personnel selection problems. This information has to do with the physical effort required by the job, the surroundings or conditions under which the work must be done, and the hazards of injury or disease to which the worker may be subjected on this job. This area of information may be outlined as follows:

PHYSICAL DEMANDS
Physical activities
Working conditions
Hazards

The PHYSICAL DEMANDS information is not integrated with the basic job-analysis formula but is outlined separately, because these facts generally have rather specialized uses, such as the placement of handicapped workers or the evaluation of jobs. Therefore these facts are not basically essential to a *general* understanding of the job. It should be emphasized, however, that information in this category, while not essential for some uses of job analysis, is critical in those operations in which it is used. Information developed according to this job-analysis formula can be arranged and recorded to serve the three principal uses of job analysis: selection of workers, training of workers, and evaluation of jobs for pay purposes.

It is particularly important to note that, in general, only the factual information is contained in and results from the analysis of the job. The information used in selecting workers and the data required for the evaluation of jobs are composed not only of job facts but also of judgments or estimates or appraisals which are based upon the facts developed in the job analysis. For example, the experience which may be demanded of an applicant before he is deemed to be qualified for a given job is a judgment as to the type of experience required and the length of this experience. There is no factual information which can be obtained about a job to indicate, without the application of judgment, how much experience is required to perform successfully the job in question. Likewise, on the evaluation factor of Physical Effort the job analyst describes the activities of the worker which require physical effort, but these facts must be used as the basis for a judgment as to the physical effort required on this job in relation to (1) jobs in general, (2) jobs in the establishment, and (3) the scale set up in the job-evaluation manual to estimate the relative Physical Effort requirements of the jobs covered in the particular evaluation.

The procedure of obtaining job facts, therefore, according to the method outlined in the *job-analysis formula,* will result in factual information about the job in terms of WHAT the worker does, HOW he does it, WHY he does it, and what SKILL is INVOLVED, plus the PHYSICAL DEMANDS made on the worker. The resulting job information will be useful, providing the job analyst knows how to apply the formula.

SKILLS OF THE JOB ANALYST

What, then, are the skills and techniques which the job analyst must employ to produce accurate, complete job-analysis information? In general, there are three primary parts to his job: (1) Obtaining information; (2) analyzing this information; and (3) organizing and recording facts. There may be a fourth part, but this task will be in addition to his job-analysis functions. As a fourth task, he may make judgments, on the basis of his job-analysis facts, to construct a tool for a particular use: the selection or training of workers or the evaluation of jobs. It should be emphasized again, however, that this fourth task is not essentially a job-analysis task —a fact-finding function—but rather one of arriving at estimates on the basis of the facts which have been gathered by job analysis.

Obtaining information

There are three methods by which information about jobs in a company can be obtained—by observation, by interview, and by questionnaire. The most common method, and apparently the most successful one, combines observation of the job and interviews with personnel who can supply reliable information about the job. A combination of the interview and questionnaire methods has also been used.

The Questionnaire Method. The questionnaire method has given consistently undesirable results. Those who have had experience with attempts to accumulate usable job information by this method have found that the principal objections are as follows:

1. It is almost impossible to design a questionnaire which will bring forth the essential information.

2. The average employee will not take the time necessary to make out the questionnaire correctly.

3. If the worker does this while he is on the job, production is held up.

4. Shop workers particularly are rarely skilled at reducing to writing WHAT they do, let alone HOW they do it, WHY they do it, and what SKILL is INVOLVED.

Davis [13] points out that "the questionnaire method has been used successfully in connection with selling jobs in department stores, clerical jobs in offices, and executive positions, but even here the responses should be followed by personal interviews." Such a questionnaire, apparently designed for use with office jobs, is shown in Figure 7–2. Scott, Clothier, and Spriegel [14] state that

Although the questionnaire seems at first to offer the simplest and least expensive method of procuring the facts, it usually yields data that are misleading and that involve such careful reanalysis and study that the expense saved in procuring them is more than lost in interpreting them.

One company experimented with a rather elaborate printed questionnaire before launching it in a job evaluation program, and used the Engineering Department for sampling the method. The resulting information was entirely unsatisfactory for preparing job descriptions. The sections designed to collect facts which might be used in preparing specifications on the basis of which the jobs could be evaluated were not only inadequate but misleading. For example, a Production Engineer in charge of a small section of the Engineering Department stated that he spent three hours of his day in "Checking and analyzing of working drawings for dimensions and the methods of manufacturing, as well as tool drawing for same, or any other necessary departmental work involved to complete job." This unquestionably intelligent and qualified Production Engineer knew what he meant when he wrote that sentence, but he certainly did not convey his meaning to any reader who is not intimately familiar with this particular job.

The danger in job information of this type is that by reading and rereading this sentence and using your imagination, it is ultimately possible to convince yourself that you know what the author meant,

---

[13] Ralph C. Davis, *Industrial Organization and Management* (New York: Harper & Brothers, 1940), p. 570.

[14] By permission from *Personnel Management*, 5th ed., by Walter Dill Scott, Robert C. Clothier, and William R. Spriegel, p. 148. Copyright, 1954. McGraw-Hill Book Company, Inc.

A JOB QUESTIONNAIRE

DEPT........................ NAME .... DATE......................

JOB TITLE ....

Note: Please use additional sheets to describe important features of your job not covered by these questions or to supplement your answers to questions where added space is needed.

1. What type of formal education do you consider to be the minimum requirement for satisfactory performance of your job?
2. What special training or experience is necessary prior to being assigned to the job you are performing? Please indicate the number of days, weeks, months, years, of such training needed.
3. Please name any machines or equipment that you use in performing your job. (*Example:* Addressograph, typewriter, slide rule, computing machine, etc.) and the percentage of your time spent in this manner. If you are responsible for the care of any machine or equipment, please describe your responsibility.
4. What, in your opinion, is the most complex or difficult part of your work? What percentage of your time is spent in this manner?
5. Is your work checked by another person? YES................ NO...............? If the answer is yes, please describe briefly the nature of this check. Please indicate also the degree to which you check other persons' work or review over-all results.
6. What contacts with personnel in our office or outside are necessary in performing your job? (*Example:* Dictation, telephone calls, outside visits, library reference, etc.) What percentage of your time is spent in such contacts?
7. If you have any special responsibility that applies *only* to your job please describe this responsibility.
8. Please describe in detail your job duties that are performed on a daily basis. If the nature of your work varies from day to day or week to week please describe this variation and the approximate percentage of time spent on the various types of work.
9. Please describe in detail your job duties that are performed at periodic intervals. State whether weekly, monthly, quarterly, etc. Also describe any occasional duties that occur at irregular intervals.
10. Please describe any undesirable working conditions or hazards involved in your job. (*Example:* Noise, office layout, light, ventilation, etc.) Also, state any unusual physical requirements of your job.
11. How much "on-the-job" training (days, weeks or months of special attention from your supervisor) is necessary after the assignment to your job to help you attain satisfactory performance. Please describe the nature of this training, if any.

Reprinted by permission of the National Industrial Conference Board, Inc., from *Management Record*, October 1945, Vol. VII, No. 10, page 277.

Fig. 7—2.   Sample job questionnaire.

while in all probability you are supplying details yourself by interpreting the very general terminology in terms of particular engineering jobs with which you might be familiar. To discover how absolutely meaningless this sentence is, it is only necessary to parse it with the job-analysis formula. In other words, if you tried to discover WHAT the worker does, HOW he does it, WHY he does it,

and what SKILL is INVOLVED, you will find that you know exactly
nothing about this job.

This particular excerpt was picked at random from a large number of such questionnaires and is not an unusual case. As another
example, when the Production Engineer and his assistant stated
the educational requirements of their jobs, the engineer indicated
that his job required four years of high school, plus three years of
special night training and college courses, while the assistant stated
that his job unqualifiedly required a Mechanical Engineering degree. Incidentally, both of these men stated in good faith that they
supervised the same seven draftsmen.

Such questionnaires might be useful to the job analyst in identifying the individual with a tentative job title, and in getting a very
general idea of the duties of the job as a starting point for collecting
his information. However, considering the amount of time required of the employees to fill out such questionnaires, their usefulness would hardly seem to justify the bother.

Observation and Interview. The most direct, the most practical,
and by far the most common method of obtaining job information
is through analysis by a trained job analyst. The techniques available to the job analyst—observation and interview—are almost always combined and are used to check and supplement each other. It
appears that the general practice, wherever possible, is to identify
by title the job to be analyzed, and then obtain as much information
as possible by observation. With this background information the
analyst can later fill in additional facts in detail by interviewing the
workers on the job, the supervisors in the department, and others
who may have reliable information. If this general procedure is to
be followed, the analyst should first obtain from the foreman of the
department an over-all picture of the operations carried on in that
department, and ask the foreman to suggest work stations where
the various jobs can be observed most profitably. His observation
then begins with careful study of the worker performing his job,
through a complete work cycle if possible, and with a thorough attempt to determine WHAT the worker does, HOW he does it, WHY he
does it, what SKILL is INVOLVED, and what PHYSICAL DEMANDS the
job may put upon the worker.

It is probable that this observation of the worker at his job will
provide information principally on the WHAT, HOW, and WHY of
the job, as well as the PHYSICAL DEMANDS; with respect to SKILL
INVOLVED it will serve mainly to highlight those operations which

should be investigated more closely to determine, by other means, just what skill is demanded of the worker. Most important of all at this point, however, is the opportunity for the analyst to determine the general nature of the job, its scope and limitations, and the essential purpose of this job in relation to other jobs in the production process. In other words, the analyst begins at this point to orient himself rather clearly with respect to the job that he is beginning to analyze. This orientation to the purpose of the job is particularly important, because "an understanding of the purpose of the job will give meaning to all subsequent operations. Once the purpose of the job is fully understood, the analyst should attempt to organize a pattern of the cycle of work; i.e., the processing of a unit of work or the basic work pattern which characterizes the job." [15]

The observation of the job will, of course, be most successful in those jobs which involve relatively little skill and where the work cycle is relatively short, thus permitting the analyst to observe the entire job in a short time. In other words, those jobs which are made up primarily of tangible factors or observable actions can be almost completely analyzed by observation, while those jobs which are made up primarily of intangible factors such as judgment, calculation, decision, comparison, evaluation, and so on, will yield almost no information to the observer.

In those cases where the work cycle of the job is somewhat irregular or extends over a period of time, even several days, the observation of the job will be somewhat difficult. Sometimes it is possible for the analyst to observe the complete cycle of a job at piecemeal intervals, observing other jobs or performing other duties in the meantime. If this is not possible, the information which ordinarily might be obtained by observation must be secured by interview. In those jobs where very little can actually be learned by observation, the primary source of information again must be the interview. In any event, however, experience has shown that it is essential that each job being analyzed actually be observed, in order to determine at first hand those facts which can be observed, such as those falling into the category of PHYSICAL DEMANDS, and also to provide the analyst with some background to assist him in obtaining the necessary information by interview.

---

[15] *Training and Reference Manual for Job Analysis*, War Manpower Commission, Division of Occupational Analysis (Washington: United States Government Printing Office, 1944), p. 56.

The mechanics of observation are quite simple but are neverthe-less important. It may be advisable, as some authors suggest, to take notes unobtrusively while observing the worker, and to avoid distracting the worker or interfering with his work routine so far as is possible. On the other hand, in describing the procedure used in one plant, Benge [16] says: "The employee saw the notes the analyst made, had opportunity to amend them, and to call attention to anything he considered important about his job." In general the analyst should watch the job to discover facts which he can later organize into statements which will tell the WHAT, HOW, WHY, SKILL INVOLVED, and PHYSICAL DEMANDS of the job. He should be alert, also, for indications of important elements of the job which he cannot see so that these points may be used later as a basis for questions in the interview. For example, if the worker stops what he is doing, apparently to listen or to observe some part of the machine closely, or if he pushes some lever or discards some material for no reason apparent to the analyst, these are indications that something important may be going on which may be a clue to an important "intangible" of the job. These details make the difference between a skillful job analysis and one which is inaccurate and incomplete.

When the analyst has completed his observation of the job, he should look over his notes immediately to fill in and expand addi-tional facts and questions which have been brought out by the ob-servation. The notes need not be organized at this time, but should contain full details so that no point may be left to memory and thus omitted in the later organization and recording of the information.

The interview technique used in the analysis of jobs has two main purposes: (1) To get information which cannot be obtained by observation of the job, and (2) to verify and augment those facts which have been collected by observation. When the permission of the foreman has been obtained, the analyst may interview work-ers on the job to fill in additional facts. He may also need to get some information about the job by interviewing workers on other jobs in the department, particularly to get an understanding of the purpose of the job being analyzed and its position in the function of the department as a whole. Usually the most reliable—that is, the most complete and accurate—information is to be obtained by questioning the worker himself and the immediate supervisor of

[16] Eugene J. Benge, "Job Evaluation in a Paper Plant," *Personnel Journal*, Vol. 19, No. 2 (June 1940), p. 43.

the worker on the job being studied. Sometimes it may be advisable to question other supervisors up or down the line, and in some cases it may be necessary to obtain facts from other departments, such as cost accounting, personnel, methods, standards, and laboratory, although such cases should be rather rare. When the analyst is an employee of the company in which he is analyzing the job, however, there is considerably more freedom in this respect than when the analyst is an outsider.

This process of analyzing jobs by asking questions of people who should be able to give the correct information is termed *interview* not only because that is a convenient term, but because the technique used in getting job facts is similar to that used in all other types of interviewing. Thus, the customary fundamental rules of interviewing apply to this part of the analyst's job. For example, in interviewing various personnel in the company, he should make sure that they understand what information he is trying to get, why he has a right to it, and why they should give it to him. He should conduct himself in such a way that information is given willingly, completely, and as accurately as these people can give it to him. Those skills which are peculiar to the job analyst as an interviewer are concerned with (1) the facts he is trying to obtain and the way in which these facts will be recorded, and (2) his pre-occupation with factual information as against judgment, interpretation, impression, and evaluation by the person he is interviewing.

The items of information which the analyst is to obtain are basic not only to the interview but to the observation as well. All the information which the analyst picks up is retained or discarded on the basis of whether it is required by the outline which he is following in analyzing the job. There is a difference, however, between knowing what information you want and getting that information by questioning someone who can give you the answers. The job analyst, for example, may have a sincere desire to find out just what kinds of mathematical skills the Toolmaker must have and must use in successfully performing his job, but he may have difficulty getting this information out of the worker himself, his foreman, his departmental superintendent, or even the engineering department. This is not due to a lack of intelligence on the part of the individuals involved or to their lack of understanding of the job itself, but may be due to a lack of the perspective and detached analytical point of view which the analyst must have in order to successfully analyze the job. To cite another example: it is almost impossible for anyone who is not a Tool Hardener to discover what actual skills and knowledges are required in successfully hardening such a simple tool as a screw driver. He just "knows by experience." And yet, the analyst must find out by interview what those skills and knowledges are so that he may properly state them in such a way that they may be taken into account in evaluating the job or in training fledgling Tool Hardeners. Here again, we get a clue to the difference between a good job analyst and a poor one.

With respect to the problem of confusing facts with interpretations, it is only necessary to refer here again to the point that the analyst may evaluate facts as well as secure them, but he will be a successful analyst only if he is able to tell the difference between a fact and a judgment, or interpretation, or evaluation of fact. It is also conceivable that the person supplying the information to the job analyst may unwittingly give the wrong information, or make statements which he thinks he ought to make for one reason or another. Again it is the analyst's task to distinguish between a verifiable observation or fact, and an inference or interpretation based on fact. In other words, the job analyst must follow scientific methodology if he is to do a precise job analysis. In discussing the scientific accumulation of fact, Dockeray and Lane point out that "The chief characteristic of the scientific method is the requirement that the observer be trained to distinguish what he observes from what he would like to infer." [17]

In order to appreciate more fully the techniques required of the analyst in observing and interviewing to analyze jobs, we should consider not only the skills of the job analyst, but other *intangibles*, particularly his knowledge of jobs, of business and industry, and of the operations in which the results of his analysis will be used. In order to understand and appreciate what he sees or is told about a job, he should know how jobs generally are constituted. For example, he must know that some jobs are made up of only one or two simple tasks, while others have a large number of somewhat unrelated tasks which vary considerably in many important features, including the skill involved. He should have a rather wide acquaintance with jobs in general so that he may better understand the job he is analyzing by comparing or contrasting it with other jobs with which he is familiar.

A knowledge of business and industry in general, or even a rather

[17] Floyd C. Dockeray and G. Gorham Lane, *Psychology*, 2nd ed. (Prentice-Hall, Inc., 1950), p. 12.

thorough knowledge of the company in which he is operating, very definitely contributes to the analyst's ability to understand what he sees and hears. Through this knowledge of the structure of jobs and of industrial processes, he achieves a perspective or frame of reference into which he can fit the facts of the job he is analyzing, and which helps him understand more clearly the meaning and the purpose of the individual job. Specifically, he will comprehend more readily the facts which are presented to him if he understands technical terminology and jargon, as well as the basic processes of various businesses and industries, such as metal-cutting, selling, molding, record-keeping, heat-treating, and others.

Aids to Securing Job Facts. The job analyst will be able to work more quickly, and his information will be more complete and accurate, if he is provided with an outline or guide to follow in analyzing jobs. The *Training and Reference Manual for Job Analysis* of the Occupational Analysis Section of the United States Employment Service is an example of material of this kind. The manual goes into a great amount of detail in explaining and interpreting for the job analyst the exact scope and meaning of each item to be included in the Job Analysis Schedule, which in itself is an excellent outline to follow in analyzing a job. This job-analysis form, and the Physical Demands Form which is used in conjunction with it, are shown in Figures 7–3 and 7–4.

The general procedure suggested for the use of these forms is for the analyst to obtain his information by observation and interview, taking notes as he goes along, and then complete the Job Analysis Schedule in first-draft form immediately from his notes. This provides for a rather complete report of the job analysis, giving all source data. These data may be rearranged later and adapted to prepare job information in various forms, such as the job description, a hiring specification, a training outline, or any similar device which may depend for its usefulness upon certain basic facts about the jobs in the company.

Another example of an aid to collecting and recording job facts is the Job Analysis Sheet recommended by the Industrial Management Society for use in connection with its Occupational Rating Plan.[18] This form, Figure 7–5, is designed specifically and solely for job evaluation, in that it provides space for recording information on each of the job factors which are subsequently to be rated.

[18] *Occupational Rating Plan,* Industrial Management Society (205 West Wacker Drive, Chicago: 1943), pp. 28 and 29.

Form USES-546
(2-44)

U. S. DEPARTMENT OF LABOR
BUREAU OF EMPLOYMENT SECURITY
UNITED STATES EMPLOYMENT SERVICE

Budget Bureau No. 44-R577.2.

JOB ANALYSIS SCHEDULE

1. Job title ....

2. Number ....

3. Number employed M .... F ....

4. Establishment No. ....

6. Alternate titles ....

5. Date ....

Number of sheets ....

8. Industry ....

9. Branch ....

7. Dictionary title and code ....

10. Department ....

11. WORK PERFORMED:

(CONTINUE ON SUPPLEMENTARY SHEETS)

Analyst ....   Reviewer ....

Fig. 7—3.

This form includes, as an aid to the recording of information, the Analysis Guide, which outlines the various degrees of each attribute found in the rating scale. This helps the analyst in phrasing his statements about each of the attributes to be rated, but it is also very dangerous. It is all too easy to use such apparently quantitative terms as *minor, severe, seldom, occasional, frequent, some,*

SOURCES OF WORKERS

12. Experience: None .... Acceptable ....

....

13. Training data: Minimum training time—(a) Inexperienced workers.
(b) Experienced workers.

TRAINING	SPECIFIC JOB SKILLS ACQUIRED THROUGH TRAINING
In-plant (on job) training	
Vocational training	
Technical training	
SRW Eng. General education	
Activities and hobbies	

14. Apprenticeship: Formal .... Informal .... Length required ....
15. Relation to other jobs:
   (a) Promotions from and to, transfers, etc.: ....

....

   (b) Supervision received: General .... Close .... By ....
                                                                                                            (Title)

   (c) Supervision given: None .... Number supervised .... Titles ....

The following items must be covered on supplementary sheets.

PERFORMANCE REQUIREMENTS

16. Responsibility (consider material or product, safety of others, equipment or process, cooperation with others, instruction of others, public contacts, and the like).
17. Job knowledge (consider pre-employment and on-the-job knowledge of equipment, materials, working procedures, techniques, and processes).
18. Mental application (consider initiative, adaptability, independent judgment, and mental alertness).
19. Dexterity and accuracy (consider speed and degree of precision, dexterity, accuracy, coordination, expertness, care, and deftness of manipulation, operation, or processing of materials, tools, instruments, or gages used).

COMMENTS

20. Equipment, materials, and supplies.
21. Definition of terms.
22. General comments.

GPO 83-55451

Fig. 7—3 (cont.).

considerable, great, in the statements, without actually stating the facts about the job which would justify the application of one of these terms to the attributes being covered. For example, it is much easier for the analyst to state that a "working knowledge" of methods is required than it is to state specifically what the worker must know about methods, which would necessitate a judgment as to whether this knowledge comes in the "casual" category or should be considered as "working" or "expert" knowledge.

This same difficulty is likely to arise even where the job-evaluation manual, with the detailed definitions of degrees under each attribute, is available to the analyst as a guide in collecting and recording information. This is very clearly illustrated in the experience of a company which did its job-analysis work for job evalu-

Form USES-130

DEPARTMENT OF LABOR
BUREAU OF EMPLOYMENT SECURITY
UNITED STATES EMPLOYMENT SERVICE

Budget Bureau No. 44-R571.2.

PHYSICAL DEMANDS FORM

Job Title ....   Occupational Code ....

PHYSICAL ACTIVITIES		WORKING CONDITIONS	
1 .... Walking	16 .... Throwing	51 .... Inside	66 .... Mechanical hazards
2 .... Jumping	17 .... Pushing	52 .... Outside	67 .... Moving objects
3 .... Running	18 .... Pulling	53 .... Hot	68 .... Cramped quarters
4 .... Balancing	19 .... Handling	54 .... Cold	69 .... High places
5 .... Climbing	20 .... Fingering	55 .... Sudden temperature changes	70 .... Exposure to burns
6 .... Crawling	21 .... Feeling	56 .... Humid	71 .... Electrical hazards
7 .... Standing	22 .... Talking	57 .... Dry	72 .... Explosives
8 .... Turning	23 .... Hearing	58 .... Wet	73 .... Radiant energy
9 .... Stooping	24 .... Seeing	59 .... Dusty	74 .... Toxic conditions
10 .... Crouching	25 .... Color vision	60 .... Dirty	75 .... Working with others
11 .... Kneeling	26 .... Depth perception	61 .... Odors	76 .... Working around others
12 .... Sitting	27 .... Working speed	62 .... Noisy	77 .... Working alone
13 .... Reaching	28	63 .... Adequate lighting	78 ....
14 .... Lifting	29	64 .... Adequate ventilation	79 ....
15 .... Carrying	30	65 .... Vibration	80 ....

DETAILS OF PHYSICAL ACTIVITIES:

16—62316-1   U. S. GOVERNMENT PRINTING OFFICE

Fig. 7—4.

ation at the time when the union was just being organized, and consequently was unable to consult and clear information with worker representatives while this information was being collected. When the analysts had completed the job information and the consultants had evaluated the jobs on this basis, all of the material was made available to union officers for review and acceptance. It was immediately discovered that many of the statements on the job specification given as a basis for and justification of the ratings assigned were phrased exactly like the definitions of degrees of attributes in the job-evaluation manual. Since the original job analysis had been done by management representatives trained for this purpose, the question arose whether the consultants responsible for the work had rated the jobs on the basis of facts or whether the company employees operating as analysts had not actually pre-designated this rating by phrasing their statements in such a way

FORM 1 I. M. S.	JOB ANALYSIS SHEET		
PLANT JOB TITLE	*Elevator Operator Job #7*	PLANT NO. *6*	
OCCUPATIONAL DICTIONARY TITLE	*Elevator Operator*	CODE NO. *2-95.20*	
DEPT.	*Building Service*	DEPT. NO. *431*	

ATTRIBUTE	ANALYSIS — RATE THE JOB NOT THE MAN	ANALYSIS GUIDE	
1. PHYSICAL EFFORT	*Operator stands during busy periods which consist of approximately 60% of the time. Seat is available when operator is not operating elevator. Doors require force less than 5 pounds to open.*	Endurance	Strength
		Exertion Not Sustained	Up to 5 lbs.
		Ordinary	5 to 30 lbs.
		Constant	30 to 100 lbs.
2. HAZARDS	*There is a possibility of elevator dropping. Elevators are state inspected and licensed. Definite instructions to be followed lessen hazard. May catch fingers or hand in door. Must be careful to keep feet away from door.*	Accident	Health
		Minor Cuts Severe Burns Brok'n Bones Fatality	None
			Minor
			Major Temp.
		Seldom Occasional Frequent	Major Perm.
3. JOB CONDITIONS	*Fans are provided to secure current of air. Doors are of grill type permitting free passage of air. Building well heated in winter.*	Discomfort	Clothing Spoilage
		None	Comp. Furn.
		Some	Ordinary Shop Wear
		Considerable	Considerable Wear
		Great	Excessive Wear or Damage
4. SUPERVISION	*Supervisor is located about 60 feet away. He may be called by phone, but elevator does not have phone in it. Phone available nearly (75 ft away). Operator has written instructions governing usual problems.*	Received	Assign Work
		Always Avail	None
		Usually Avail	Has Helper
		Self Supervisory	Assigns Work
5. RESPONSIBILITY FOR THE SAFETY OF OTHERS	*Operator must use care to assure that employees are completely in elevator before closing door. If elevator is not at floor level operator cautions employees and passengers. Must count passengers to prevent overload. Gates must be closed before elevator is set in motion and not opened before stopping. Must be sure floor doors are locked before leaving floor. Passengers must face door.*	No Possibility of Causing Injury	
		Considerable Care to Prevent Injury	
		Great Care to Prevent Injury	
		Resp. for Equip., Methods, Etc., Involving Severe Health or Acc. Hazards	
6. RESPONSIBILITY FOR EQUIP. AND MATERIAL	*Elevator is equipped with automatic safety stops at top and bottom. Operator cannot cause appreciable damage to equipment. May damage freight loads if elevator is not stopped at floor level or is not properly placed in car.*	Equipment	Material
		Single Loss May Amount $0 to $100	Weekly Loss
		$100 to $500	$0 to $50
		$500 to $5000	$50 to $100
		$5000 to $20,000	$100 to $1000
		$20,000 and Over	$1000 to $5000

Fig. 7—5.

JOB ANALYSIS SHEET		PAGE 2	
ATTRIBUTE	**ANALYSIS — RATE THE JOB NOT THE MAN**	**ANALYSIS GUIDE**	
7. **KNOWLEDGE** **EQUIP.** **AND TOOLS**	*Casual knowledge of equipment not extending beyond operation of controls*	Common Hand Tools	Casual
		Simple Mach.	
		Average to Complex Tl's	Working
		Very Com- plex Tools	Expert
METHODS	*must be able to operate elevator smoothly and elevators at floor level. This is simple and quickly learned within a few days.*	Simple Work Quickly Learned	Casual
		Aver. Meth.	Working
		Complicated Methods	Expert
MATERIALS	*No knowledge of materials required*	Common Mat. Not Difficult	
		Wide Variety of Common Material	Casual
		Dangerous Explosive Critical	Working Expert
8. **SCHOOLING**	*Must be able to read instructions, read load limits posted on elevator and speak acceptable English*	Not Have to Speak, Read, or Write English Able to Speak Eng. Read, and Write Simply Read with Ease and Do Simple Arithmetic Read Blue Prints Write Reports & Letters Element. Tech. Training 2 yr. College - 4 yr. College	
9. **JUDGEMENT** **AND** **INITIATIVE**	*Must meet people and use judgment in handling them. This may involve keeping people out of loaded elevators to prevent overload. Must use judgment as to whether to mix freight and passenger loads. Use judgment to prevent overload.*	**Judgment**	**Initiative**
		None or Easy Decisions	Little or None
		Average Na- ture with Precedent	Definite In- itiative
		Difficult - No Std or Pre- cedent	Much Initi- ative
10. **MENTAL** **CAPABILITY**	*No ingenuity required. No versability as only routine work is involved.*	**Ingenuity**	**Versatility**
		None Req'd	Routine Wk. Simple
		Helpful	Lim't'd Types Average
		Required	Several Types Average
		High Degree Required	Several Types Complex
11. **PHYSICAL** **SKILL**	*Requires ability to stop elevators at floor level smoothly.*	**Dexterity**	**Precision**
		None to Little	Easy Limits
		Average	Av. Limits
		Above Aver.	Diff. Limits
		Exceptional	Extremely Exact

Fig. 7—5 (cont.).

that only one possible rating on the basis of the job-evaluation manual could be assigned. This one factor resulted in a time-consuming bipartisan review of job facts as well as job ratings in order to discover the true facts which had led the job analyst to record a *judgment* instead of the *facts* as they existed in the job.

In the discussion of adapting or constructing a manual (Chapters 4, 5, and 6), it was pointed out that best results will be achieved in any company if the job-evaluation manual is tailor-made for that company, and takes into account the significant factors which make that company or that industry different from others. The same reasoning can be applied to a form or outline for collecting job facts, since the items of information covered and the way in which the information is organized and presented will depend to a great extent on the characteristics of the job-evaluation system being used, as reflected in the job-evaluation manual. It is possible, however, to list some general characteristics which any form for gathering information should have.

1. Identification facts. All facts about the job which serve to identify it and differentiate it from other jobs in the company are a prime requisite of any form for collecting and recording job facts. This not only greatly assists in the analysis, but will help in avoiding any mistakes or confusion in handling a large number of job-analysis reports while the work is going on and after it has been completed.

2. Completeness of coverage. All major subjects or types of information should be given on the form, and each major heading should be broken down by subheadings in sufficient detail to insure complete coverage.

3. Space for writing in information. It is well to arrange the form so that it is suitable both for taking notes and for actually writing in the information under the various headings and subheadings included in the form. Thus, a single form or booklet will contain all of the basic data accumulated about the job, including the analyst's original notes and his first draft of the report on his analysis of the job.

4. Check lists. Wherever this method of recording information is usable it is usually found to be a convenience and a time-saver. The check list on the Physical Demands Form is an example (see Figure 7–4). It should be noted that detailed narrative explanations are required to amplify the information checked on the list. Closely akin to the check list is the box arrangement as found under "Sources of Workers" on the Job Analysis Schedule (Figure 7–3). An adaptation of this technique is also used in the Job Analysis Sheet (Figure 7–5). Here the information is grouped by job-evaluation attributes, and the Analysis Guide is arranged in checklist form. However, the Analysis Guide is not actually used as a check list, but only as an aid to preparing the statements under each attribute. Caution is required in constructing such aids for recording information in order to guard against the possibility of making the facts fit the form, rather than considering the form as an aid in collecting complete and accurate information.

5. *Order of items.* The order in which the items of information are listed on the form can be of great assistance, as a guide in the analysis of the job and also as an outline in writing the job descriptions and job specifications. For example, the first information obtained in analyzing a job has to do with identification of the job, so items referring to identification should be grouped at the beginning of the form. Next, the analyst observes the job and attempts to determine its purpose, and obtains information on the WHAT, HOW, and WHY of the job; therefore, after identification, the next space may be allotted to an over-all statement of duties, which not only further identifies the job but may also establish the purpose. Following such statement of duties, space for notes and also for writing in detail the WHAT, HOW, and WHY, i.e., the work performed on the job, should be provided. Finally, on the basis of work performed, the analyst discovers the SKILL INVOLVED and the PHYSICAL DEMANDS through both observation and interview. These items should then logically follow the description of work performed to complete the analysis.

It will be observed that this same arrangement of information is suitable for organization into job descriptions and job specifications. The identification information will necessarily appear on the job description, to be followed by a job summary or general statement of duties and then a more detailed breakdown of the duties and responsibilities, describing the WHAT, HOW, and WHY of the job. The items bearing upon SKILL INVOLVED and PHYSICAL DEMANDS are the basis for the job specification, and therefore should be arranged on the form in the same order in which they will be presented in the job specification to facilitate the preparation of this part of the final job-evaluation material.

6. *Suitability for permanent filing.* If the job-analysis report or record is to be a permanent one, which may be used from time to time to obtain source data about jobs or to prepare materials of various types based on job information, the job-analysis form must be suitable for permanent filing. Important in this consideration is the bulk of the paper which may be required for each job as well

as the binding of the various sheets in the form into a booklet. Paper clips or staples on the margin or corner will cause difficulty in vertical filing of these forms. A four-page, letter-size, folded form is quite convenient for filing since it is a single sheet and does not require fasteners of any kind. Furthermore, such a form can be used as a folder to hold additional sheets if such are required. If eight pages are necessary in the booklet, a double form of this type stapled on the fold is also quite easy to file and is permanent enough.

Job Analysis Forms. Where a simpler form is desired and will adequately meet the requirements for job evaluation, the forms on which the final job descriptions and job specifications are to be written can be used rather successfully as note sheets. Thus, all identifying information and description of work performed can be recorded on the job-description form, and all notes and statements regarding skill and physical demands can be recorded on the job-specification form in the spaces allotted to each of the attributes to be evaluated. Examples of these two forms—Job Description and Job Specification—prepared by the Personnel Research Institute of Western Reserve University and The National Screw & Manufacturing Company [19] are shown in Figures 7–6 and 7–7. Since these forms are designed for final recording of the job description and job specification, the identifying information is somewhat less complete than is necessary in a form designed primarily for the collection of job facts. A job-description form developed for collecting job facts, with the identifying information considerably expanded, is shown in Figure 7–8—Job Information Sheet.

If the original job-analysis report is not to be retained as a permanent record, another possibility is to prepare an outline of the items of information to be covered in the analysis [20] which can be used by the analyst in obtaining facts and making his notes. Subsequently these notes can be used to prepare the first draft of the final job description and job specification. It should be brought out here that neither of these two latter methods will yield as complete and accurate job information as will the more careful approach to this task, based on a comprehensive form constructed with the characteristics outlined above.

[19] Courtesy of The National Screw & Manufacturing Company, Cleveland, Ohio.

[20] For a comprehensive listing of items which might be considered for inclusion in the job-analysis outline see Carroll L. Shartle, *Occupational Information,* 2nd ed. (New York: Prentice-Hall, Inc., 1952), pp. 34–38.

JOB TITLE―――――――――――――――――――――――――――

DEPARTMENT――――――――――――――― JOB CODE NO. ―――――――

NO. OF EMPLOYEES ON JOB――――――― SEX-M ☐ F ☐ DATE―――――

STATEMENT OF THE JOB

DUTIES OF THE JOB

(*Actual size 8½ x 11*)

Fig. 7―6.   Job Description―The National Screw & Manufacturing Company
―job evaluation of hourly paid employees.

JOB TITLE_____CODE NO._____

DICTIONARY TITLE_____CODE NO._____

DEPARTMENT _____ TOTAL POINTS ____ CLASS ____

EXPERIENCE   POINTS

SCHOOLING   POINTS

RESPONSIBILITY FOR PRODUCT OR MATERIALS   POINTS

RESPONSIBILITY FOR MACHINERY AND EQUIPMENT POINTS

RESPONSIBILITY FOR WORK OF OTHERS   POINTS

RESPONSIBILITY FOR SAFETY OF OTHERS   POINTS

(Actual size 8½ x 11)

Fig. 7—7.   Job Specifications—The National Screw & Manufacturing Company
—job evaluation of hourly paid employees.

RESOURCEFULNESS   POINTS

MONOTONY AND COMFORT   POINTS

VISUAL EFFORT   POINTS

PHYSICAL EFFORT   POINTS

SURROUNDINGS   POINTS

HAZARDS   POINTS

Fig. 7—7 (cont.).

Date .... Written by... Job No. ....

Department Name............................ Department No. .... Sex .... Grade ....

Department Job Title.............. .... No. on Job............... Points ....

Suggested Job Title...

Dictionary Title ....

Present at Interview .... Checked by...............................

General Description of Duties:

Detailed duties:

Remarks:

Fig. 7—8.   Job Information Sheet.

A more complete form for the collection of job information, adapted from similiar forms used successfully in several different companies by the Personnel Research Institute of Western Reserve University,[21] is shown in Figure 7–9, pp. 242–245. This form has proved its usefulness as a combination job-analysis outline and report form to be retained as an original record. In one company, this form was completed by job analysts and then used by the editors to write the job descriptions and job specifications.

[21] Courtesy of the Personnel Research Institute, Western Reserve University, Cleveland, Ohio.

Analyzing information

It is only on the basis of his background information (see pages 28–30) that the job analyst can be expected to understand the facts with which he is presented, to analyze each item properly, and to fit all of these facts together into a meaningful analysis of the job. The inexperienced job analyst, for example, may omit entirely some important task from the job, simply because he did not realize that he had failed to get all the facts. Likewise he may continue to search for additional facts, without realizing that he already has all the pertinent information about the job.

The matter of determining the importance of various tasks in relation to each other and to the job as a whole is a function of perspective, but in addition it depends upon the extent to which intangibles, or the SKILL INVOLVED in the job, have been clearly discovered and analyzed. The inexperienced analyst might consider the ability of a salesman to sell a large amount of his products to be very important, for example, whereas in a particular selling job, the skill in gauging accurately the customer's immediate need may be vital to obtaining repeat business and keeping the good will of the customer. The typical amateur job description gives as much importance to "puts on rubber gloves" as it does to the task "removes product from tank when plating is finished," whereas the skill involved in putting on protective gloves is not to be compared with the skill involved in determining the exact moment when the plating job is completed according to specifications. The job analyst "should be able to sift the facts of each occupation, setting aside those which are unimportant and unessential and retaining those which are pertinent to the description of the occupation. . . ." [22] Again, these trifling details make the difference between a skillful job analysis and one which is practically useless.

The analysis and organization of the information obtained by observation and interview is very important when the analyst segregates from the total job information those facts which bear upon one particular aspect of the job. The *Training and Reference Manual for Job Analysis*, in discussing this subject, states that "It is at this point that what the analyst saw or found out about a job . . . must be supplemented by a detailed *analysis* of the report it-

[22] By permission from *Personnel Management*, 5th ed., by Walter Dill Scott, Robert C. Clothier, and William R. Spriegel, p. 148. Copyright, 1954. McGraw-Hill Book Company. Inc.

Job Title.. Code ....

Other Titles..

Suggested Title...

Department.. Dept. No............................ Dept. Head ....

No. on Job...................... Range...................... Supervised by..

Persons Interviewed ....

Analyst .... Date..........................

Location of Job ....

Other Identification...

JOB SUMMARY (key phrases that cover job) :

RELATION TO OTHER JOBS:
   Promotion From :

   Promotion To :

   Transfer To and From :

Fig. 7—9.   Job Analysis Data Sheet from Personnel Research
Institute of Western Reserve University.

Work Performed: What—How—Why (Use additional sheets if necessary)

Major Duties:

Other Tasks:

Equipment, Machines:

Fig. 7—9 (cont.).

SKILL INVOLVED—PHYSICAL DEMANDS
Experience (type and amount):

Education and Training (specific skills required):

Responsibility for Product and Material:

Responsibility for Machinery and Equipment:

Responsibility for Work of Others:
Supervision given (number, titles and type):

Other jobs directly affected:

Responsibility for Safety of Others:

Fig. 7—9 (cont.).

RESOURCEFULNESS:

MONOTONY:

Visual Effort:

Physical Effort:

Surroundings:

Hazards:

Fig. 7—9 (cont.).

self." [23]   As an example, in recording information which signifies the responsibility of the worker for material or product, it is necessary to reanalyze very carefully those tasks in which the worker can affect the form or condition of the material or product. The analyst must determine what worker skills are involved in meeting responsibility in this connection; he must describe this responsibility in such a way that it is clear which of the worker's actions may affect material or product, and to what extent each of these is important in this respect.

In recording the information on each subject of this type— Responsibility for Product and Material, for instance—the analyst must in effect reanalyze the entire job by studying his basic factual information and weighing each fact which bears upon the particular subject. He must then organize this information into a statement that clearly describes all the features of the job that are significant to an evaluation of the responsibility of the worker for material or product and that shows the relative importance of the facts covered in the statement.

Organizing and recording information

The third essential skill of the job analyst is that of organizing the information which he has obtained and analyzed, and of recording this information. The record of the job analysis must be clear, concise, and complete. It must tell the reader those facts about the job that the analyst intended to report and must place proper emphasis on those features of the job that the analyst discovered to be most important.

In a sense, this literary ability of the job analyst is his most crucial skill. Even if he has the knack of getting all the information and understanding the relative importance of the facts he has obtained, if he cannot organize these facts and report them in such a way that they convey his true meaning to the reader, his skills of observation and analysis lose their full effect. Thus the job analyst, in reporting his analysis of the job, is the key link between the facts as they exist in the job and subsequent work based on these facts, as given in the job-analysis report. Where a verification of the facts in the job-analysis report would be extremely difficult or consume a great amount of time, the skill as well as the integrity of the job

---

[23] *Training and Reference Manual for Job Analysis,* War Manpower Commission, Division of Occupational Analysis (Washington: United States Government Printing Office, 1944), p. 24.

analyst in organizing and presenting job information in writing a report is of primary importance.

Since in job evaluation the skill of organizing and recording job information is used primarly in writing the job descriptions and job specifications, the techniques are discussed more specifically in Chapters 8 and 9.

TRAINING AND SUPERVISION OF JOB ANALYSTS

The training of the persons selected to do the job analysis is well worth the time and effort spent in getting this phase of the job evaluation off to a good start. The discussions up to this point in this chapter indicate rather clearly the technical phases of this job and the signficant skills which the analyst must develop in order to do his job successfully. The experience of the authors bears out Shartle's statement: [24]

One learns job analysis by doing it rather than by reading about it. Although study is helpful and intensive training on the purpose of the analysis and the procedures to follow should be given before an analyst starts work, his basic training is in analyzing jobs and in going over the analyses with his supervisor or instructor.

The intensive training should include development of a thorough understanding of what job evaluation is all about—the principles as well as the mechanics—and emphatic explanation of the skills of the job analyst in obtaining information, analyzing it, and organizing and recording it, as well as of the necessity for accuracy, completeness, and integrity. The *Training and Reference Manual for Job Analysis* [25] and the *Guide for Analyzing Jobs* [26] are both good training devices for job analysts, no matter what form is being used or what is the primary purpose of the job analysis.

Included in such intensive training should be supervised practice in actually analyzing jobs. Experience has shown that a week of basic training along these lines is none too long to give an inexperienced person a good grounding in job-analysis techniques. However, where the analysts are to work under the close supervision of a competent technician, and a definite plan for very close super-

---

[24] Carroll L. Shartle, *Occupational Information,* 2nd ed. (New York: Prentice-Hall, Inc., 1952), p. 43.

[25] *Training and Reference Manual for Job Analysis,* War Manpower Commission, Division of Occupational Analysis (Washington: United States Government Printing Office, 1944).

[26] *Guide for Analyzing Jobs, Analyst's Workbook,* War Manpower Commission (Washington: United States Government Printing Office, 1944).

vision and training on the job is provided for when the analyst actually begins to work, this training time could be reduced considerably.

Since much of the skill of the job analyst will be developed after he actually starts to analyze jobs, it is well to give particular attention to very detailed and intensive analysis and editing of all material collected and recorded by the job analyst on the first few jobs that he undertakes. Here again, the job-analysis formula is quite useful as a standard to measure the adequacy of the job analysis report, if it is applied with a vengeance to discover the weaknesses in the reports prepared by the analysts.

MECHANICS OF JOB ANALYSIS

The step-by-step procedure followed in analyzing jobs will vary from one company to another, depending upon the specific conditions and the extent of general preparation which has preceded the analyst's entry into a department. In general these steps are as follows:

1. Obtain all pertinent information available regarding the department, including the processes, machines, and names of key personnel, and all of the information which can be obtained by a study of the Job Evaluation Control for the department. (See Figure 2-2, page 43.)

2. Contact the supervisor of the department, following whatever formalities are necessary, including clearance with this foreman's superiors.

3. Discuss with the foreman of the department the general plan to be followed and what the analyst must do in the department in order to analyze the jobs—observe, interview workers and supervisors, discuss job information with worker representatives, etc.

4. With the assistance of the foreman, contact other key personnel in the department to give them the necessary explanations and arrange for any assistance which they will be asked to supply.

5. Proceed with the analysis of the jobs after an inspection of the entire department has been made, if necessary, to become familiar with all of the processes. Analyze the key jobs in the department first, to discover in more detail the processes carried on in the department, and to establish a framework against which to compare information on other jobs that depend on or are supplementary to these key jobs.

6. Verify and get approval of all job-analysis reports from the supervisors and other personnel in the department, depending on the over-all plan for conducting the job evaluation.

Many variations of detailed steps within each of these major sections will be necessary in each individual company. In general, this outline applies to the methods which have been followed by many companies in carrying out job analysis. Following is an outline quoted from a job-analysis instruction manual which illustrates how a large electrical manufacturing company detailed the procedure for its job analysts.[27]

, THE OVER-ALL PROCEDURE

I. Visit General Foreman
   A. Explain purposes and objectives;
   B. Discuss desired method for obtaining factual data;
   C. Secure cooperation;
   D. Obtain list of all jobs in the department by titles and the number of workers in each.

II. Visit Foreman and Assistant Foreman with the approval of the General Foreman
   A. Explain purposes and objectives;
   B. Obtain necessary routine data;
   C. Discuss the nature of work and details of jobs;
   D. Obtain recommendations of the most desirable employees to observe during the course of the study on the basis of efficiency and willingness to cooperate with the Analyst.

III. Observe Employees at Work
   A. Note carefully each operation performed;
   B. Make certain all observable operations have been noted;
   C. Check for specific items to be included in the JOB ANALYSIS SCHEDULE;
   D. Record factual data of working conditions, and tools, equipment and materials used;
   E. Question worker about those operations which are not observable and obtain from the worker an estimate of the percentage of time such operations are performed;
   F. Review the notes concerning the job elements with the worker and ask for suggestions, and obtain from him an estimate of the percentage of time each operation is performed.

IV. Review Observations and Notes with Assistant Foreman
   A. Determine if the job has been thoroughly covered;
   B. Obtain estimates of percentage of time for each operation;

[27] E. S. Horning, "Job Descriptions," *Management Record*, Vol. VII, No. 10 (October 1945), p. 277. Published by the National Industrial Conference Board, Inc., New York.

    C. Ascertain what specific tools are furnished by the worker and by the company;

    D. Obtain information for RELATION TO OTHER JOBS section.

V. Write the First Draft of Analysis on Approved Form according to Instructions

VI. Have Department Foreman Review and Approve the Original Draft

    A. Allow all supervisors concerned the opportunity to review and edit the original draft;

    B. Revise draft on basis of comments, changes and criticisms suggested by the reviewers and obtain written approval of contents before final typing;

    C. Arrange for typing the completed analyses (5 copies) . . . one copy to be retained in the Analyst's files, and one copy to be forwarded to the Personnel Director, Department Foreman and two copies to be forwarded to Personnel Planning and Research.

When the analyst goes into a department he is confronted with a large number of positions, which he must organize and allocate to a number of jobs to be analyzed and recorded in a job-analysis report. He may attempt to group these positions into jobs as he proceeds with his analyses, or he may analyze almost every position as a job and subsequently combine these analyses into more inclusive jobs on the basis of his job-analysis information. In either case he will lose some time if he postpones the separating or combining of jobs. The authors have found that by far the most economical and orderly method is to attempt to determine from the Job Evaluation Control sheet exactly how all of the positions in the department are to be grouped by job titles, and then to proceed to analyze the jobs represented by the titles. Although this will minimize the amount of combining and separating of positions into jobs later on, it will not eliminate all such changes, since more detailed study during the analysis will usually indicate changes which should be made in the line-up of jobs in the department.

This determination of the jobs to be analyzed usually can be done quite successfully by a skilled analyst on the basis of information supplied by the supervisor, in addition to a brief inspection of the jobs in the department with the Job Evaluation Control sheet as a guide. However, a number of points must be considered in deciding how fine or how broad will be the grouping of positions into jobs. In other words, for evaluation purposes the positions may be grouped into very broad classifications, or jobs, in which a large number of somewhat dissimilar positions will all bear the same job title. On the other hand, the interpretation of the phrase "substantially the same" in the definition of a job (page 13) may be construed very narrowly, so that a large number of job titles, with relatively few positions in each, will result. If a very broad grouping is used, it amounts to a classification or rating of the jobs before they are analyzed, with the result that the descriptions and specifications must necessarily be written in rather general terms in order to cover all of the variations within the classification or *job*. This in turn makes it almost impossible to arrive at a very precise rating or evaluation of the individual positions in the company, since, before rating, they are already lumped into broad classifications. In contrast, when the positions are grouped into jobs in such a way that all of the positions under each title can be rated equally on each of the attributes, the analyst is certain that he has delineated jobs so that they can be rated and classified precisely. If, then, in the process of analyzing these jobs he finds that the breakdown is too fine and that the ratings on two jobs of similar content would undoubtedly be the same, he can merely combine these two groups of positions under a single job title and cover them in the same description and specification. Furthermore, at any later time jobs can easily be combined if the facts indicate that this should be done.

The most accurate and defensible evaluation, then, can be achieved by doing a thorough job analysis of the jobs of workers who are performing duties which are substantially identical, requiring the same level of skill, knowledge, responsibility, and effort, and by avoiding combinations of positions which will result in obscuring significant differences between the various positions grouped under a single job title.

JOB ANALYSIS IN JOB EVALUATION

In preparing for the collection of facts through job analysis as the basis for the evaluation of jobs, it is necessary to determine how the job-analysis technique will be employed. If we understand clearly that *job analysis* is a method or technique, we are then in a position to decide what information is going to be obtained by this method and just how the whole procedure will operate. The analyst who thoroughly understands job-analysis procedure, and who is well grounded in the techniques of obtaining, analyzing, organizing, and recording job facts, can adapt his methods to get what facts are necessary for a particular end use and apply these methods to develop a particular end product that has been designed for the purpose at hand. Thus, it is not sufficient to train workers in the techniques of job analysis. It is also necessary to determine pretty clearly at the outset what facts are to be obtained and in what detail, and also how this information is to be arranged and reported in the end product.

The *end product* in job evaluation is usually a *Job Description* and a *Job Specification,* or *Job-Rating Sheet.* Thus the information obtained by job analysis must be adequate to prepare a job description in sufficient detail to meet the specified standards, and a job specification adequate to arrive at an evaluation of the job and substantiate the ratings assigned.

The principal function of the job description will be to identify and describe the job so that it will carry the information obtained by the application of the WHAT, HOW and WHY of the job-analysis formula. The purpose of the job specification is to establish the position of each job in relation to other jobs for the purpose of determining the rate of pay. Therefore, the job specification will carry primarily the information regarding SKILL INVOLVED as well as PHYSICAL DEMANDS made upon the worker. Thus, the broad outline of what facts to secure by job analysis in order to evaluate jobs is as follows:

1. Identification of the job: Title, department, code
2. Description of the job: Duties and responsibilities
3. Specifications of the job: Worker qualifications and job requirements

Whatever outline, form, work sheet, or data sheet may be used by the job analyst as a guide in analyzing jobs and organizing the information he obtains, it should be developed on the basis of this broad outline.

Identification

Ordinarily, the information included in *Identification of the Job* will consist of all of the titles presently used to signify this job; the department name and possibly the department code; a job code number, classification title, or other classification device which may be in use in the company; a code number assigned to each job for the purpose of controlling the collection of job information; a statement regarding the location of the job such as section of the department, cost center, machine number, or a descriptive phrase; the names and titles of supervisors or group leaders; the names of other jobs in the group of which this job may be a part; or other devices which may be peculiar to the individual company for precisely locating the job.

Job description

The facts which are to be secured under the heading of *Description of the Job* are those which tell the WHAT, HOW, and WHY of the job. The extent of detail to be covered is the principal variable under this heading. In some companies, the information included on duties and responsibilities of the job is limited to a brief statement which merely defines the title by which the job is known so that the reader will get a general idea of the duties performed under this title. In such cases, the description of the job adds little to the identification. In other cases the job description is an integral part of the job-evaluation material on the job and gives a rather extensive description of duties and responsibilities. Consequently the analyst must obtain considerably more detail about the WHAT, HOW, and WHY of the job than is the case where the description is to be very brief.

Detailed information on job duties and responsibilities has two major advantages over the briefer job definition. First, a rather complete description of the job contributes to an understanding of the job as a whole when the evaluation is being considered or challenged, in that it facilitates organizing the facts on the job specification and often substantiates and reinforces the statements and conclusions given in the job specification. Second, more complete job descriptions have many by-product uses, in selection, training, and departmental and process organization. Where the company plans to adapt its basic job information to a number of different uses, a very thorough and complete description of the work performed on the job should be a part of the basic record, although it may be abbreviated and condensed in constructing the job description for pay purposes.

Job specification

Information required under the heading of *Specifications of the Job* will be determined primarily by the manual to be used in evaluating the job. All information relating to specifications of the job covering the SKILL INVOLVED and PHYSICAL DEMANDS usually will be organized under a number of headings, each of which is a factor that will be evaluated to determine the total rating of the job. Under a point-rating plan, for example, all items of information relating to worker qualifications and job requirements may be organized under seven headings, as in the example in Table 7–1. This listing of factors is the result of a survey of 17 companies by

TABLE 7—1.   Major and subfactors used. Jobs compensated for on hourly basis ●

Basic Factors	Subfactors Included		Times Reported
I. Responsibility	For equipment For materials For safety of others Supervision (given and received) Initiative—honesty Discretion—integrity Leadership—count		17
II. Skill	Dexterity—precision Versatility—accuracy Variation—sense of time and space Sense of weight—steady nerves		14
	Accuracy of {	Calculation Measurement Reading Record Selection Weight	
III. Mental Effort	Talent—blueprints Ingenuity—pace Complexity of operations Management ability Memory—observation Originality—planning Analysis—adaptability Setups		14
IV. Physical Effort	Acuteness—strength Endurance—difficult pace		14
V. Equivalent Education Required	Knowledge—judgment Ability—mental development		13
VI. Working Conditions	Hazards—accident, health Clothes spoilage—disease Internal injury—fumes Heat {	air contact radiation	13
VII. Experience Required	Time required to break in Service—age Previous experience Length training period		12

Knowles and Means [28] which indicates the basic factors that were covered in the job-evaluation plans of these companies and also shows the number of different companies that used each of the seven factors. Thus, if a company has established a job-evaluation manual, as described in Chapters 5 and 6, which includes these seven factors, the outline for obtaining information logically would also be organized along these same lines. The analyst would group his facts regarding SKILL INVOLVED and PHYSICAL DEMANDS under these seven headings, and would use this outline as a guide in observing jobs and obtaining information by interview.

PLANNING FOR MAXIMUM USEFULNESS OF JOB INFORMATION

Mention has been made above of "by-product" uses of job information obtained in the process of job evaluation. Often these additional uses of job information originally collected for the purpose of evaluating jobs have been after-thoughts and, consequently, attempts to use this job-evaluation information for other purposes have not always been too successful. Where job information is being collected for job evaluation only, the job-analysis procedure should be designed specifically to obtain the desired end product. Likewise, where information secured by job analysis is to be used for other purposes, it must, if it is to be maximally useful, be collected with these end uses in mind. Where circumstances permit—in other words where the time and money are available to do a thorough job analysis—serious consideration should be given at the beginning, rather than at the end, of the process to possible other uses of this job information. In discussing occupational information in general, Shartle [29] says:

> In far too many instances where a job evaluation program has been put into operation, it has been discovered six months or a year later that the scope of the analysis was incomplete for certain uses. The analyses are then made over again to secure information that could have been secured easily in the first instance if a careful plan had been drawn up. In one situation a plant initiated a job analysis program which did not cover any items pertaining to the physical requirements for the jobs. This plant had to go over its jobs again to discover these facts in order to aid in the employment of disabled persons.

It should be pointed out, however, that more complete and de-

---

[28] Asa S. Knowles, and F. W. Means, "A Survey of Job Evaluation to Determine Base Rates," *N.A.C.A. Bulletin*, XX, No. 7 (December 1938).

[29] Carroll L. Shartle, *Occupational Information*, 2nd ed. (New York: Prentice-Hall, Inc., 1952), p. 30.

tailed analyses than are actually required for job evaluation do demand additional time in analysis as well as in recording the information. On the other hand, when the statements regarding the importance of complete and accurate job facts in arriving at an accurate job evaluation are recalled, there is some question as to whether such detailed information is actually excessive as far as the job-evaluation program is concerned, or whether, in the final analysis, it does not contribute materially to the success of the evaluation of the jobs.

SUGGESTIONS FOR STUDY AND RESEARCH

1. How can a company make sure that job facts obtained in a job analysis are accurate?

2. Under what circumstances would the questionnaire method of getting job facts be most useful?

3. Ask a friend to tell you in complete detail what he does, how and why he does it, the skills involved, and the physical demands of his job. Ask no questions, just listen. Note all facts he gives in 5 columns: *What, How, Why, Skill Involved,* and *Physical Demands.* Now list all questions you would have to ask him to complete an analysis of his job.

4. Observe your employed friend on his job and make a list of new facts and new questions to ask which did not come out in the procedure of 3, above.

CASE PROBLEM

PREPARING TO ANALYZE JOBS: A midwestern manufacturing company in a city of 350,000 population manufactures parts for aircraft and automobile engines. From a small start in 1943, it has grown to the point of employing over 650 people in its ten factory departments. Prospects for continued expansion make it imperative, in the opinion of the executive committee, that the company install job evaluation. Accordingly, a consultant has been engaged, the Assistant Personnel Director has been designated as the key man in the company to carry through the program, and the stage has been set to begin job analysis.

PROBLEM: Assuming you are the consultant, design the forms necessary and outline the method of analyzing factory jobs. Include selection, training, and supervision of job analysts, information to executives and employees, scope and uses of job information, editing and approving job analyses, scheduling of the work, and any other points that should be included in this part of the plan.

8

Job Descriptions

THE PURPOSE OF WRITING JOB DESCRIPTIONS and job specifications is to record the information obtained on each job in a standard fashion preparatory to rating or evaluation. In preparing these end products of the job analysis for the evaluation, the analyst organizes the job facts obtained and analyzed in the process of job analysis.

The analyst at this point also does some appraising and evaluating of these facts, particularly in preparing the statements on the various attributes to be evaluated in the job specifications. In preparing the job description and the job specification, then, the writer takes the facts on each job from the report of the job analysis, presents this information in a precise description of the job, and sorts out and records on the job specification the facts bearing on each of the attributes to be evaluated. In this process he accomplishes two things: (1) He presents all information in the most accurate, meaningful, and readable fashion. (2) He standardizes the organization of information on every job so that all the information is comparable.

The descriptions and specifications on all jobs constitute the basic data of the job evaluation, and also of the salary and wage administration based on the evaluation. Therefore, this information should be set up in finished form, and should be as accurate and as complete as is necessary to evaluate the jobs and carry out the operation of salary and wage administration.

To meet these two needs—job evaluation and pay administration

—the record of the job information must (1) identify the job by defining it and by standardizing the job "tags" such as title, department, code number, and the like; (2) establish the content and the scope of the job by describing it; and (3) establish the level of difficulty of the job by specifying the job requirements and the worker qualifications under each of the attributes to be rated.

The definition and the description are customarily contained in the job description portion of the job write-up. The specifications of the job are usually recorded in a job specification section of the job information. If the description and specification are two separate sheets, the job "tags" will be included on both in order to identify the material.

JOB TITLES

A well-considered plan for titling jobs in a company can be of great assistance in systematizing all job nomenclature and can aid in the classification of jobs for various purposes. Therefore at this point the standard title to be used for each job is ordinarily established.

In those companies which have not given particular attention to setting up an organized method for titling jobs, the job titles usually are inaccurate and misleading, are not descriptive, do not indicate uniformly the skills of jobs, and are not used uniformly. Thus, at one time the very general title of Clerk may be applied to a group of jobs while at another time a more specific title is used. This reflects the fact that jobs have not been differentiated clearly in the company; at one time a group of positions may be considered as a job, while at another time these same positions may be grouped into five smaller groups of positions, each of which constitutes a job.

It is important that job nomenclature be standardized and that each job have one title and only one title, because this job title or "tag" is the basic unit with which the personnel department and to some extent the payroll and accounting departments deal constantly. For example, if a worker hired at one time is given the title of Helper, while a worker hired at another time to perform identical duties is given the title of Operator, it is quite possible that they will be assigned to two different rate ranges, and thus will be paid at different rates for performing identical duties. This is most likely to happen where the two workers are employed in different departments under different supervisors. It could not happen, of course, where such titles are accompanied by precise definitions, since the definition rather than the title would be referred to in distinguishing the two jobs.

Thus the standardization of titles goes right along with the precise definition of jobs in the company. It is logical, therefore, that the first step in this sequence should be to establish the scope and content of the job, the second, to define the job within its established limits, and the third step, to select an appropriate title to be used in conversation and records regarding the job. The job descriptions, then, become the company dictionary of job terminology, just as the *Dictionary of Occupational Titles* of the United States Employment Service is the dictionary of occupational terminology for most public agencies dealing with jobs.

Although a standard titling system in a company, if used properly, can speed up and make more accurate all matters regarding jobs, it is important to recognize that the job title itself does not define the job. For example, the title of Tool and Die Crib Man may be applied to the workers in the tool cribs in a great many departments in a company, but this does not mean that all of these jobs are identical with respect to duties, responsibilities, and skills. More frequently, in fact, each of these jobs will be different in some respects; in some cases the level of skill and difficulty from one job to another may vary greatly. It is all too easy, however, to consider all of these jobs as one group merely because they bear the same title.

The important factor is that the jobs are what they are. Titles are attached to them only to serve as convenient tags, and this process must never be reversed by inferring job duties and specifications from the job title. While this difficulty will arise largely in a titling system where the job titles are not defined, it is also possible that defined titles may be misused in this way. In order to avoid difficulties of this sort, it would seem to be necessary to (1) standardize the job terminology, (2) define the standardized titles, and (3) see that all references to jobs by title follow this standardized, defined terminology.

Requirements of a standard title

In establishing standard titles for a company in connection with the definition and description of these titles, there are a number of principles which have been found to be helpful. A few of these are as follows:

1. The standard title should be similar or identical to one of the

titles which has been applied to the job in the past, so that it will not be necessary for workers and supervisors to learn an entirely new vocabulary.

2. Titles should be set up in a natural form rather than in an inverted form; for example, Assembler-Bench is not nearly as good as Bench Assembler.

3. They should be as brief as possible while conforming to the other characteristics listed.

4. Within the limits of brevity, they should be as descriptive of all phases of the job as possible.

5. If they are brief, descriptive, and in natural form, they will tend to be conversational, so that it will be easy to use the job title in referring to the job; this is particularly important if workers and supervisors are expected to use these titles rather than abbreviations or nicknames of the titles.

6. The title should indicate wherever possible the skill level and the supervisory level of the job.

7. Standard terms indicating skill level, supervisory level, content, or other common characteristics of jobs must be used consistently in assigning titles.

In establishing its standard titles, The National Screw & Manufacturing Company has used the following outline as a guide in assigning consistent titles to jobs according to their common characteristics:

1. Setup Man—a part of the title of all jobs in which the worker spends the major part of his time setting up machines to be turned over to another worker to actually operate in producing the work.

2. Setup Operator—a part of the title of all jobs in which the worker sets up the machine for operation and operates the machine by loading it with material, removing the finished product, checking the product, and adjusting the machine in operation when necessary.

3. Operator—applied to all jobs in which the worker is assigned to a machine already set up, to load material and check work and to make minor adjustments; or who feeds a non-automatic machine piece by piece and operates the machine each time a piece is inserted, such as Punch Press Operator.

4. Feeder—a part of the title of all jobs involving loading of machines with material and removing the finished product without checking it (primarily hopper-fed machines).

5. Hand Feeder—applied to those jobs which involve feeding an automatic machine, piece by piece, by hand.[1]

[1] Courtesy of The National Screw & Manufacturing Company, Cleveland, Ohio.

Examples of the uses of these titles are as follows: Countersink Setup Man, Automatic Screw Machine Setup Man, Boltmaker Setup Operator, Turret Lathe Setup Operator, Countersink Operator, Automatic Tapper Operator, Waterbury Slotter Feeder (hopper-fed), Automatic Spoke Machine Feeder, Roll Thread Hand Feeder, Drum Slotter Hand Feeder.

Some consideration should be given also to the titles of those jobs which are definitely established as learning jobs so that these titles clearly distinguish such jobs from all others. One convenient way to do this is to insert the word "Junior" in the title of the learning job: for example, Punch Press Junior Setup Man is the learning job for Punch Press Setup Man. In some cases, more than one learning job may be necessary where the objective job requires a rather long learning time, as for example, Boltmaker Learner and Boltmaker Junior Setup Operator. If the term "Helper" is used as a part of the title of some jobs similar in skill level and general content, the use of this term should be confined to these jobs and should not be applied to any jobs that are primarily learning jobs. Thus, the Boltmaker Helper involves only unskilled duties performed in assisting in the operation of the machines and does not include any training in the setup and operation of these machines. For those jobs in which the learning time is relatively short, it will not be necessary to establish these learning jobs, as for example in the job of Punch Press Operator. In other cases, learning jobs may be provided in a series of progressively more difficult jobs, each of which has a well defined scope of duties and responsibilities. An example of this type of job progression is found in the series Automatic Screw Machine Helper, Automatic Screw Machine Operator, Automatic Screw Machine Setup Operator, and Automatic Screw Machine Setup Man.

In many cases, these learning jobs may have to be added to the job structure after the existing jobs are rated. The reason for this is that the classification levels of the jobs in a series may show wide gaps which would not provide for a steady and even progression in terms of wage rate from the lowest classification in the series to the highest. For example, the job of Toolmaker may fall in Class 8 in a classification structure of eight grades or groups of jobs, whereas the jobs of simple machine tool operators in the Tool Room may fall in Class 3 or Class 4. In order to provide for training and promotion within the Tool Room, it would be necessary to establish learning jobs in at least some of the classification levels between

Class 4 and Class 8 so that an individual could progress from one Class to the next higher Class over a period of time while learning the duties and skills of a Toolmaker. If such provision for the training and promotion of workers within the company is not a part of company policy these arrangements for training jobs would not be necessary, of course. Also, these intermediate classifications do not have to be established until they are actually needed for job assignment of employees in training.

Finally, in some job series it may be necessary to distinguish between the more difficult jobs and the less difficult jobs of similar content by indicating the classification in the title. This is usually done by using the same base title for the jobs but adding to the title such designations as First Class and Second Class; or 1, 2, and 3; or A, B, and C. For example, Packer A would be assigned the most difficult and complicated orders to pack for shipment while Packer B might be assigned only less difficult products to pack. The important point here is to distinguish very clearly and specifically between these various levels of jobs having quite similar content so that the differences in skills and responsibilities may be evaluated accurately; then the workers may be placed accurately on these jobs according to the skills and qualifications required by the work assigned to them.

PREPARING JOB DESCRIPTIONS

The purpose of the job description in the evaluation of jobs is to identify, define, and describe clearly the job to be rated, and thus to give a fairly detailed picture of the duties and responsibilities of the job. The job description is of assistance in providing a full understanding of the statements regarding each of the factors to be evaluated, as detailed in the job specification. In the rating of jobs, the rater will study carefully the identification information on the job, and then the job description, before attempting to interpret the job specification statements on each of the items that will be rated. In order to fulfill these functions, therefore, the job description must be accurate, concise, and sufficiently complete in detail to describe all of the duties which involve any phases of the factors on which the job will be evaluated.

Sources of job-description data

The information on the basis of which the job description is written will come from the job-analysis report in whatever form it may have been prepared. If the Job Analysis Data Sheet (Figure 7–9), has been used in analyzing jobs, the writing of the job description will be a process of putting into final form the information from this record. If the data sheet has been used merely for notes about the job, then the analyst, in writing the job description, must phrase all of this information which is in note form and incorporate it into the Job Summary, or statement of the job, and the Work Performed, or duties of the job.

The identifying information and the statements under the SKILL INVOLVED—PHYSICAL DEMANDS section of the data sheet also will be helpful in writing the job description. On the other hand, if the Job Analysis Data Sheet has been prepared carefully and completely, writing the job description will be primarily a matter of copying the necessary identifying information, improving and rephrasing the Job Summary, and editing in final form the Work Performed section.

Regardless of the character of the job-analysis report from which the job description is written, it may be necessary, and in many cases advisable, for the analyst, while writing the description, to check and verify those items of the job that may not be entirely clear. He should do this by discussing them again with the supervisors and by comparing the job he is writing about to other jobs in the department or to similar jobs in the company.

Extent of job descriptions

In preparing to write job descriptions for its jobs, each company must decide how much detail is going to be included in the job description itself. Generally speaking, there are three levels of detail which conceivably might be used in the job descriptions for job evaluation. These are:

1. Job Identification: All information necessary to identify the job without describing the duties in any detail.

2. Job Identification plus Job Summary: Detailed identification plus a definition of the job describing the scope, purpose, and content very briefly.

3. Job Identification plus Job Summary plus Work Performed: The same as 2 with the addition of a detailed description of the Work Performed covering the WHAT-HOW-WHY of the job.

Each of these types of job descriptions would of course necessarily have to be supplemented by the job specification, the primary source of direct information leading to the rating of the job. The Job Identification alone is not adequate for any purpose. The identifying factors such as job title, code, and so on must be defined in some manner; the best method of defining them is by reducing the definitions to writing rather than depending on general practice or memory. It appears, therefore, that level 2 gives the minimum amount of information which would serve the purposes of job evaluation. Provided the job summaries are adequately written, it is possible that this amount of detail would serve as a minimum for job-evaluation purposes.

If the time spent in analyzing jobs for the purpose of preparing specifications and adequate job summaries is not to be lost, however, it is essential that a description of the Work Performed as well as Job Identification and Job Summary be a part of the job description. While the Work Performed may not be vital to the job evaluation, it certainly contributes considerably to an understanding of the job by the rater as he begins to evaluate the job. Also, it will undoubtedly facilitate the wage and salary administration system based on job evaluation. These considerations alone justify inclusion of the Work Performed; but in addition, one may take into consideration the many valuable by-products and additional uses which the company may profit from if the job analysis information is organized into complete job descriptions. In this way, the company may make full use of the time spent and of the information collected in the process of job analysis. It should be noted that the amount of detail which may be included in the Work Performed may also be varied considerably. It seems advisable to limit or expand the amount of detail included in the Work Performed in relation to the anticipated uses (in addition to job evaluation) to be made of this material.

OUTLINE AND CONTENT OF JOB DESCRIPTIONS

The outline of the job description is comprised of three principal parts: (1) Job Identification, (2) Job Summary, and (3) Work Performed. The Job Identification will include the various identifying facts which are considered necessary for this purpose. The Job Summary will state briefly all of the significant facts regarding the duties of the job. The Work Performed section will describe in necessary detail the WHAT, HOW, and WHY of the job.

Identifying facts

The minimum identifying facts necessary on the job-description sheet are the job title, the department, and the last date on which the information contained in the description was verified as correct. This date may be the date of the analysis of the job, or it may be the date of the writing of the job description if the facts were reverified at that time. In addition to the job title there may be in the identification one or more codes that have been established to assist in identifying jobs or to be used in other ways, e.g., in classifying or sorting jobs. Such code numbers should also appear in the identifying information in the heading of the job specification.

In addition to the name of the department, its number or other code identification might well be included. If there are any other subdivisions of the department, provision should be made to include this information also.

Other data which may be included in the heading to serve some useful purpose are the number of employees on the job, the number of employees in the department, and the corresponding title and code from the *Dictionary of Occupational Titles*.[2] Depending on the individual circumstances, it may be helpful to include in the heading the name of the department head, the name of the immediate supervisor, the former title or alternate titles for the job, and possibly even the name of the analyst. It is not necessary in most cases to include any lengthy descriptive material in the heading for identification purposes, since the Job Summary and Work Performed also assist in identifying the job. Also, the standardized title itself should be much more helpful in this respect than the previous title terminology used in the company.

Job summary

If the Job Summary is prepared skillfully, it can serve many useful purposes. "Its function is to give the reader an over-all concept of the purpose, nature, and extent of the tasks performed and how the job differs generally from other jobs."[3] Thus the Job Summary can be used as a definition of the job for quick reference, when something more than the identification is required and when it is not necessary to have all of the detailed information included in the Work Performed. This definition of the job not only may be useful in rapidly referring to the job-description volume, but it may

---

[2] *Dictionary of Occupational Titles, Part I—Definitions of Titles, Part II—Titles and Codes,* United States Employment Service (Washington: United States Government Printing Office, 1939).

[3] War Manpower Commission, Division of Occupational Analysis, *Training and Reference Manual for Job Analysis* (Washington: United States Government Printing Office, 1944), p. 13.

be typed or printed separately in booklets or manuals for other uses where less complete or more complete information is not desired.

The Job Summary performs a very important function in connection with an understanding of the job description as a whole. As indicated above, the identifying information in the heading identifies the job and orients the reader to some extent with respect to the information which follows. The Job Summary carries this orientation one step further by giving a brief of the entire job—supplying information as to the scope and purpose of the job as well as an over-all statement of the duties. This method of organizing job descriptions—from identification to definition to detailed description—has been found to be very convenient in use. It is effective in very quickly putting across to a reader unfamiliar with the job a great deal of pertinent information about that job.

If the Job Summary is to perform adequately the functions given above, it is clear that it must be written very carefully according to specified standards. The following points will assist in the writing of effective Job Summaries:

1. The statement should be as brief as possible and still accomplish its purpose.

2. Words should be selected carefully to carry the maximum amount of specific meaning.

3. General or vague terms should be avoided except where they are absolutely essential as a substitute for a long, detailed explanation.

4. The statement should differentiate the job from all other jobs accurately enough to be used in classifying workers on the job.

5. The purpose of the job must be clearly stated.

6. ᐧThe most important features of the job should be brought out with only enough detail to make them clear.

7. The Job Summary must conform to the WHAT-HOW-WHY job-analysis formula.

One of the most difficult features of the writing of the Job Summary is to avoid using generalized terms such as "responsible for," "handles," and the like. In many cases it will be found that in order to avoid using rather general terms a long string of more specific verbs may be necessary as a substitute. For example, the assistant editor of a monthly company publication "assembles copy." The general task of "assembling copy" involves a great many detailed operations too numerous to include in the Job Summary, yet the use of this term "assembles" actually carries very little meaning.

In cases of this kind, where it may be necessary to use such general terms, they may be repeated in the Work Performed in such a way that the additional detail adequately explains and describes the operations covered by this general verb. While the use of such terms does impair somewhat the ability of the Job Summary to carry a maximum amount of specific meaning, these terms do not generally detract from the function of the Job Summary in identifying and differentiating the job from other jobs.

Many examples of job summaries of the type which serve quite well in the job description for job-evaluation purposes may be found in the job-description volumes for various industries published by the United States Department of Labor—*Job Machine Shops*,[4] for instance. The *Dictionary of Occupational Titles* [5] also can be helpful in establishing a pattern for job summaries, since the definitions of titles found in this volume correspond generally to the standards for the Job Summary given above.

There is one important difference however, between the job summaries used in general occupation descriptions and those which are used in specific job descriptions as discussed here. A Job Summary for a specific job in a specific company can be written in much more direct and precise fashion than a job summary written as an industry-wide description of a given occupation. Also, it is important to bear in mind that the readers and users of the job descriptions prepared as a part of a job-evaluation program usually are familiar in a general way with the jobs being described. They are also familiar with the terminology of their company and of industry in general which can be used in describing these specific jobs.

It may be advisable to write the Job Summary after all other parts of the job description are completed. In this way the Job Summary can be written as an abstract of the Work Performed after all aspects of the job have been described in detail and their relative importance in the job as a whole has been studied and taken into account. On the other hand, if the principal points to be covered are outlined in the Job Summary as the first step in recording information on the job, this outline can be used as a guide in organizing the remainder of the job information. The *Handbook of Job Evalu-*

---

[4] *Job Descriptions for Job Machine Shops*, United States Employment Service (Washington: United States Government Printing Office, April, 1938). For a comprehensive listing of these publications see Carroll L. Shartle, *Occupational Information*, Chapter 3, Selected List of Occupational Information Publications (New York: Prentice-Hall, Inc., 1946, revised 1952).

[5] *Op. cit., Part I—Definitions of Titles.*

ation for Factory Jobs of the Industrial Fasteners Institute (formerly American Institute of Bolt, Nut and Rivet Manufacturers) [6] has the following to say on this subject:

> The first thing the analyst should do in obtaining information from either a worker or a supervisor is to secure a statement of the job which is in concise form and gives an over-all identification in as few words as possible . . . The statement of the job, or job definition, serves as a useful tool in getting the interviewee to think of the scope of his job, and also to think of its purpose, nature, tasks performed, and how his job differs from other jobs. . . . The analyst should be able to use the recorded statement of the job as the outline for the recording of job duties.

In addition to the Job Summary covering the WHAT, HOW, and WHY of the job, it may also be advisable to include a reference to the supervision given and received by the workers on this job. This is usually particularly important in office jobs although it is sometimes helpful in many factory or other operative jobs as well. Thus the Job Summary for Senior Cost Accountant may start with

> Under the direction of the Chief Cost Accountant, develops and carries out cost control procedures, . . .

In some cases it may be helpful to standardize the designations of types of supervision given and received. An example of this is given by Scott, Clothier, and Spriegel as follows: [7]

> *Immediate Supervision.* The degree of supervision that an apprentice, a clerk learning office routine, or a copyist draftsman receives. It is not expected that the employee will use much initiative. Immediate supervision involves close watch over all the specific details in the work— what duties are performed, how they are performed, step by step.
>
> *Supervision.* The degree of supervision that a new clerk would receive after the first uncertainty is over and the supervisor feels that the clerk is "catching on." Supervision does not involve so close a watch over specific details, but general phases of the work are controlled by constant reference to the supervisor for advice and decision.
>
> *General Supervision.* The degree of supervision flowing from foreman to journeyman. The worker here begins to assume his share of responsibility. He is supposed to know the mechanics of his job and use that knowledge without advice or spur. The detailed method of performing a given task is usually left entirely to the worker so long as he operates within established general practice.

[6] Personnel Research Institute of Western Reserve University, *Handbook of Job Evaluation for Factory Jobs,* American Institute of Bolt, Nut and Rivet Manufacturers (Cleveland: 1946), p. 11.

[7] By permission from *Personnel Management,* 5th ed., by Walter Dill Scott, Robert C. Clothier, and William R. Spriegel, p. 168–9. Copyright, 1954. McGraw-Hill Book Company, Inc.

Direction. The degree of supervision exercised over a trained worker by his administrative chief or section head. A definite objective is set, and the worker is left to go ahead, in conformity with policies with which he has no recommendatory connection. It is expected that there will be need for frequent conference as to both the general phases of the work and the specific details.

General Direction. The degree of supervision exercised over a section head by his administrative chief. The latter expects a finished product without appreciable reference even as to general plans of the work and with practically no reference as to the specific details of how the work is to be accomplished.

General Administrative Direction. The degree of supervision exercised over a trained technical man by his administrative head. In general administrative direction the technical features of the work are practically all in the hands of the worker. An example is the direction the president of a manufacturing corporation might exercise over the chief engineer.

Work performed or duties of the job

In writing the Work Performed portion of the job description, the most important feature is the organization of all the facts about the job for an orderly presentation of this information in the description of the duties. This organization or outline of the facts to be presented is important in two respects: (1) if the facts are organized before the Work Performed section is written, it is much easier to write the detail and compose this description of the duties of the job; (2) a well-organized description of the Work Performed on the job will be much easier to read, more meaningful, and more precise than a haphazard detailing of duties.

The balance of the Work Performed should expand upon the introduction and explain the important details of the job so logically, concisely, and specifically that a totally uninformed reader can visualize the tasks and understand the job with a minimum of reorganization of the data. It must, therefore, consist of an orderly presentation of the tasks of the job. . . . It is here that the organizational ability of the analyst is called into full play for he must organize his material so that the clearest job picture is presented.[8]

The first step in the organization of the Work Performed section is to determine what are the major tasks, steps, or parts of the job. This requires a thorough study of all the available information about the job. An analysis of this information to group the facts which have been obtained into some logical organization generally

[8] War Manpower Commission, Division of Occupational Analysis, *Training and Reference Manual for Job Analysis* (Washington: Government Printing Office, 1944), p. 14.

will result in three to eight tasks or sections to be described. Generally speaking, each job described will require a somewhat different organization of the information. The tasks or sections of one job may be of an entirely different nature from the tasks of another job. It is for this reason that a task can be defined only as one of the sections used in describing the job. For example, one job of machine operator may involve the following tasks: (1) Set up the machine, (2) Operate the machine, (3) Gauge the work, and (4) Periodically oil and adjust the machine.

A setup man on this same type of machine may perform only the one task of setting up the machine, so that for purposes of description the job of setup man might be broken down into the following tasks: (1) Prepares to set up machine, (2) Inserts dies, (3) Adjusts cams and feed mechanisms, (4) Tries out operation of machine, (5) Turns machine over to OPERATOR. In addition to such regular tasks, another section may be added to describe those duties which are performed only occasionally or which may be performed only by some of the workers on the job.

Because jobs vary considerably in the way they are constructed, the organization of the description of the Work Performed will vary considerably from one job to another. In general, however, the breakdown of the Work Performed into sections for purposes of description will be organized chronologically or in some other logical fashion. For example, the section describing the setting up of the machine will come before the section describing the operation of the machine. Likewise, the duties performed regularly and by all workers on the job will comprise the principal sections of the Work Performed; those sections that describe duties performed only occasionally or by only some of the workers on the job will appear in one or two sections at the end of the Work Performed. In any event, all the information about one phase of the job will appear in one section.

The organization of office jobs or administrative jobs, which are not primarily cyclical in nature, usually will be different and somewhat more difficult than that of simpler types of jobs. In such cases the steps or sections under which the job is described will not necessarily have any chronological organization. Office jobs may be organized in many other types of logical outline—on the basis of subject matter, level of difficulty, administrative versus operative work, etc.

The development of this organized presentation of information is one of the key skills of the job analyst. It will be developed successfully only after considerable experience with various types of jobs, accompanied by criticism and suggestions from those readers who use the job descriptions. Here again it should be emphasized that the reason for the importance of the organization of this material is that it should be presented by the writer so that the reader will not be required to reorganize the material as he reads in order to understand the job clearly.

As pointed out above, the general practice in describing Work Performed is to break down the job into approximately three to eight sections for purposes of describing it. Experience has shown that most jobs can be organized clearly and successfully by such a breakdown. If more than eight separate sections are included the presentation tends to become quite confusing. As a matter of fact, factory jobs or other less complicated jobs usually can be described successfully in not more than five sections. Only a few of the more complicated administrative, executive, technical, and professional jobs will require a breakdown into more than five sections. Following are some examples of the lead statements from the Work Performed sections of several job descriptions of the Division of Occupational Analysis published in pamphlet form for the use of the local offices of the United States Employment Service: [9]

Job Description for PLATER I
1. Prepares articles for electroplating:
2. Plates articles:
3. Washes plating solution from articles and dries them:

Job Description for OFFICE MACHINE SERVICE MAN
1. Prepares to service machine:
2. Makes minor machine repairs on premises:
3. Makes major machine repairs in shop:
4. May assemble and test new machines before delivery to buyers:
5. May perform related work:

Job Description for PRECISION-LENS GRINDER
1. Prepares to grind and polish glass stock into prisms and lenses:
2. Rough-grinds prisms to approximate shape and dimensions:
3. Blocks (mounts) several prisms together preparatory to fine grinding and polishing:
4. Fine-grinds and polishes blocked prisms:
5. Grinds and polishes lenses:
6. Centers and edges lenses:
7. May form and inspect lens and prism optical systems:

[9] War Manpower Commission, Division of Occupational Analysis (Washington: Government Printing Office, 1944).

Job Description for AUTOMOBILE MECHANIC

1. Keeps automobile in good running order by making periodic inspections and adjustments of parts:

2. Restores mechanically defective vehicles to service by overhauling faulty parts:

(a) Overhauls major operating units such as motor, transmission, and differential:

(b) Repairs automobile electrical systems:

(c) Performs other repair work:

Job Description for ASBESTOS WORKER, GENERAL

1. Prepares to cover objects with insulating material:

2. Applies insulating material to surfaces by one of the following methods:

(a) Applies plastic insulating material such as asbestos, cement to such equipment as boilers, ducts, pipe lines, and tanks:

(b) Applies magnesia, cork, or asbestos blocks and sections to heating and air-conditioning equipment, pipe lines, tanks, and stills:

(c) Applies felt insulation to brine, ammonia, and ice water piping:

(d) Secures prefabricated sections of mineral wool insulating material (hollow cylinders split longitudinally) to heating pipes:

(e) May blow adhesive sound-absorbing material upon ceilings or other surfaces:

The descriptions for ASBESTOS WORKER, GENERAL, and AUTOMOBILE MECHANIC illustrate another type of organization which is sometimes very useful. The organization into two or three major sections, with subheadings under one or more, often clarifies the description of the Work Performed.

With respect to the discussion regarding the number of tasks or sections into which the Work Performed might be divided, it should be noted that the Work Performed section on PRECISION-LENS GRINDER given above is prefaced by the following:

Note—The all-around PRECISION-LENS GRINDER is comparatively rare. Precision optical grinding is usually performed by workers who specialize in such phases of the work as rough-grinding, fine-grinding, polishing and edging.

This further emphasizes the point that only in very rare cases is a large number of sections necessary or advisable in organizing and constructing the Work Performed; in this case the work described usually is performed by more than one worker and only rarely does a single worker perform all of the seven tasks described. The *Training and Reference Manual for Job Analysis* re-emphasizes this point: "The primary consideration is to organize the statements so that the uninformed reader can obtain a clear concept of the work performed on the job." [10]

STYLE

Just as a standard organization of information in the job descriptions will make for uniformity, so will the adoption of some standard rules for writing style. A few standards for style will improve greatly the usefulness of the job description, and will make it easier to read and easier to write. Careful attention to style points also will increase the accuracy of the description and will tend to make it more precise. It should be understood clearly that the adoption of a standard style or technique is not based on any desire to improve the literary excellence of the job description. It is solely for the purpose of improving the description as an instrument for recording and conveying accurately and completely the necessary job facts.

In the above examples of section headings from job descriptions of the United States Employment Service, we find one element of style which has been followed uniformly in the writing of these descriptions. Each of the section headings listed in these examples is a lead or "flag" statement introducing the detailed description of the WHAT, HOW, and WHY of that phase of the job. This flag statement technique clarifies the organization of the job description and summarizes very briefly the major tasks or sections in the job. Thus the job description can be read by looking first at the Job Summary and then skimming through the flag statements on each of the tasks in the Work Performed. Also, in a detailed reading of the job description itself, the flag statement serves to introduce each of the tasks and to orient the reader with respect to the detail which follows in the description of each task. Examples of these job descriptions are shown in Figures 8–1 and 8–2.

Another item which should receive careful attention in the writing of job descriptions has been referred to above in the discussion of the Job Summary. It is essential that the verbs particularly be selected with great care. They should convey the maximum amount of specific meaning. They must not be of such a general nature that they fail to convey any particular meaning or that they carry several possible connotations. The verbs used in the job

[10] War Manpower Commission, Division of Occupational Analysis, *Training and Reference Manual for Job Analysis* (Washington: Government Printing Office, 1944).

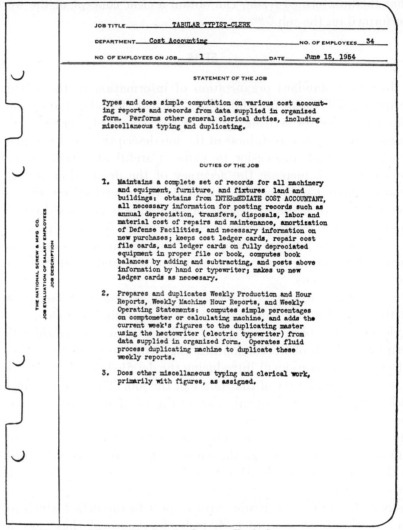

Fig. 8—1. Job Description—Tabular Typist-Clerk.

description should be of an "operational" nature, referring to a specific action, so that there is no doubt as to what is taking place in the job when the particular verb is used.

The following standards have been used as a guide in writing job descriptions:

1. The style generally should be terse and direct, with a minimum of complicated sentence structure.

2. All words and phrases or other embellishments which do not include necessary information should be omitted.

3. Each sentence should begin with a functional verb, the worker on the job being the implied subject. Passive verbs should be avoided.

4. The present tense should be used throughout the description.

5. Description of duties should be specific with emphasis on the

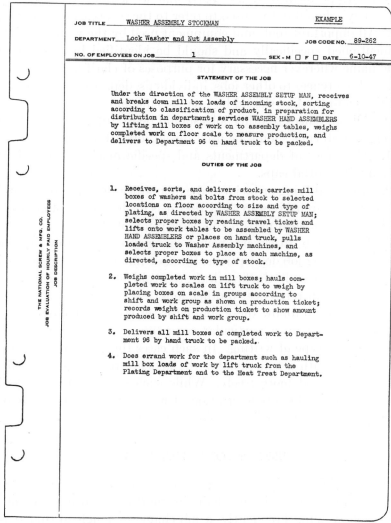

Courtesy of The National Screw & Manufacturing Company, Cleveland.

Fig. 8—2. Job Description—Washer Assembly Stockman.

skills and purposes involved, and should not be allowed to develop into a detailed motion study.

6. The term "may" should be used to introduce descriptions of tasks which only some of the workers on a job perform. For purposes of consistency, this term should never be used in any other connection.

7. The term "occasionally" should be used to introduce statements describing task performed once in a while and tasks not customarily performed by any particular workers on the job. The term "may" should not be used to refer to these "occasional" duties.

8. All important tools and equipment used by the worker should be mentioned specifically and should be identified by number or trade name wherever necessary for purposes of clarity.

9. All references to other jobs, individuals, departments, sections, machines and the like should be very specific and definite.

10. All references to other jobs should be by full title written in full caps. Full caps should be used for all job titles throughout.

11. All names of departments and specific machines should be written with initial caps.

12. Any qualifying or incidental explanatory information should be written in parentheses to show that it is in the nature of an aside and is not an integral part of the description of the task.

13. Where job titles are being changed considerably in the process of writing job descriptions, the code numbers should be used throughout, at least in the first draft, to avoid any confusion or misunderstanding in reference to other jobs.

It is possible to follow these standards for style, or modifications of them adopted by a particular company, and still introduce a more personal type of writing. In such cases the sentence may not always begin with a functional verb; articles, pronouns, and subjects may be used more freely. While such a personal style will tend to lengthen the job description, it may have the advantage of being more acceptable to the employees who are to use this material.

USES OF JOB DESCRIPTIONS

While the job description has important uses in the rating of the jobs, it is also to be used continually in the maintenance of the job-evaluation system. Frequently, a job changes enough so that it is judged to be different from what it was before, perhaps sufficiently different to place it in another wage bracket. It is essential to know not only the details of the job as it is at present but, equally important, what the details of the job were before it changed. A comparison and analysis of the change then may be made. Also, where there is some question as to whether the job actually has changed, it is essential that the job description be complete enough to serve as a measuring stick for such a determination. This is a vital feature of the entire wage and salary administration based on the job evaluation, for it is a well-known fact that jobs do change to a greater or lesser degree over a period of time. What is more important and more difficult to handle, they tend to change gradually, by small degrees. The difficult point, then, is to decide when the job has changed sufficiently in content, skill, and responsibility to justify a revision of the job description and a re-evaluation of the job.

Another factor of primary importance in this respect is the use of the job description in defining the job title and describing the job as a basis for the identification of workers by job title. Since the job title assigned to the worker will determine his pay rate or rate range, this identification of workers by job titles is a key feature of the wage and salary administration.

The third primary use of the job description has to do with operations other than pay administration. The uses of job-analysis information in employee training and in employment procedures are particularly important. There are many other uses of accurate, complete job information, because the defined job title is the basic operating unit of the personnel department. The job description as a detailed identification and explanation of the job title has many uses in labor relations, safety, placement, personnel statistics, and other personnel operations of the foremen and supervisors, as well as of the personnel department. Since job titles are used in connection with many other company operations, including those of accounting and payroll, the importance of job descriptions as a company "dictionary of job titles" cannot be overemphasized.

It is important to note that job descriptions and specifications have other uses in wage and salary administration than just the evaluation of the jobs. Such uses of the job-evaluation materials must be taken into account in determining their form and content. This is illustrated by the following excerpt from a statement of the

Research Institute of America under the heading "Job Descriptions Cut Labor Costs":

You can keep a better grip on wage costs, if you have your foremen and supervisors use job descriptions. To prevent increases in labor costs resulting from the unauthorized development of new jobs or substantial changes in existing ones, foremen should be required to abide by job descriptions in assigning work. Establishing new jobs is purely a management decision, to be reached after investigation, and upon consultation with department heads and foremen. Haphazard development of jobs in the shop can throw wage relationships out of line; cause wastage of skills; result in duplication of work; give rise to grievances and pay inequalities; and raise accident rates through inexperienced workers doing jobs requiring greater skill.

Job descriptions help the foreman to remain within his manpower budget. When he makes it a practice to keep workers' duties in line with their classifications, he has a basis for estimating how many employees he needs. He has a perpetual inventory of manpower. He can make quicker adjustments to work-load peaks because he knows exactly who can fit where. There is also less variance in workers' output and the foreman can more easily plan to meet the production quotas set for him.

When it is necessary to cut down direct labor costs, accurate job descriptions provide a basis for determining which jobs can be eliminated and what operations combined.

High labor costs due to turnover, absenteeism, diminished output—all reflecting employee discontent—can be kept down if the foreman uses job descriptions in day-to-day management. By keeping workers' duties in line with wages, numerous grievances are eliminated. Otherwise a worker either "grows" into work of a higher skill or is casually assigned to it by a busy foreman, thus acquiring valuable experience without receiving the appropriate pay and frequently lacking the seniority justifying upgrading.

When he recognizes that he should be receiving a higher wage, he becomes resentful. At the same time, other qualified employees with greater seniority rights for upgrading have reason for grievance, too. In some instances, inadvertent breach of union contract seniority provisions may result, with consequent labor difficulties.

In the case of those borderline workers who are so often the subject of conflicting claims by rival unions, job descriptions make useful testimony. In one such case before NLRB, the description of the fringe employees' duties played a large part in the Board's decision that the claimant union did not have the right to represent them. . . .

Here are the factors in the job description which the Board took into account: site of work, actual job duties, tools used, amount of supervision, wage scale, training necessary and line of promotion.[11]

[11] Labor Report of Executive Membership, Vol. 2, No. 21 (October 10, 1945). Reprinted by permission of the Research Institute of America, Inc., 292 Madison Avenue, New York.

If job descriptions are to be useful in the situations suggested above, it is obvious that they must contain considerable pertinent detail in order to be conclusive.

In deciding how much detail is going to be included in the job information collected by job analysis, and how comprehensive the record of this job analysis will be, it is necessary to weigh the cost, the time, and the technical difficulties involved in accumulating complete job-analysis information against the long-term advantages of having this information at hand for use in meeting the many problems of management where these facts will be of assistance. The National Industrial Conference Board has the following to say in regard to the uses of job information: "There is often a tendency to forget many of the important uses of job descriptions because of the emphasis placed on the function they serve in connection with wage and salary administration. Many of the important uses of a detailed system of job descriptions are given in the following summary:

1. JOB EVALUATION. Establishes a foundation upon which to build a formal job evaluation plan in which basic wage and salary differentials are based upon a sound conception of relative differences in job requirements.

2. PLACEMENT. Provides an effective and objective guide for intelligent interviewing and placement in a modern hiring program. Appropriate trade tests may be developed on the basis of major job tasks on which job applicants claim specific experience.

3. COUNSELING. Gives the vocational counselor accurate job information upon which to base his advice to inexperienced and physically handicapped workers.

4. TRAINING. Gives the training director the type of information he needs in planning a training curriculum that will utilize the maximum potential skills and abilities of all employees, and stimulates employee self-advancement. It should aid in getting the maximum amount of effective training for every dollar spent on the training program.

5. SAFETY. Aids the safety director in reducing number of accidents by giving him a manual of job characteristics that can be used in a program of detailed analysis of possible job hazards and dangerous working conditions.

6. EMPLOYEE EVALUATION. Assists in defining the dividing line between job requirements and actual employee performance on the job, an effective aid in performance or merit rating.

7. WOMEN IN INDUSTRY. In applying the "equal-pay-for-equal-work" principle, particularly in cases where women are wholly or partially performing jobs that are normally considered men's jobs, the existence of detailed job descriptions makes possible an objective determination of correct rate of pay for the job.

8. LABOR RELATIONS. By providing a means of common understanding between management and employees on the duties of each job, one source of employee grievance is likely to be eliminated and basic pay differentials based on job definitions are likely to eliminate suspicion of favoritism.

9. WAGE AND SALARY SURVEY. Provides a method of comparing rates of pay on key jobs in other companies in the community with confidence that the jobs under survey are actually comparable jobs. This aids the company in meeting its obligation of paying rates on a par with those paid by other companies on comparable jobs.

10. METHODS IMPROVEMENT. Discloses possible changes in manufacturing methods as a result of the detailed job analysis involved in the program. The purchase of automatic machinery may be based upon a study of skill requirements in view of the fact that large potential reductions in manufacturing costs lie in the jobs requiring a high degree of skill. Job analysis provides a basis for re-engineering of jobs.

11. MORALE. The procedure of writing job descriptions, particularly where employees are interviewed for job data, serves effectively in demonstrating that the employer is interested in knowing exactly what each employee is doing and in this way is a morale booster.[12]

SUGGESTIONS FOR STUDY AND RESEARCH

1. Write a description of your friend's job from the information obtained in your studies of items 3 and 4, Suggestions for Study and Research, at the end of Chapter 7.

2. Make a list of facts which are omitted or unclear, resulting in an incomplete job description.

3. Analyze your job description according to the Job Analysis Formula. (See pp. 218–219.) Mark those places where you omitted HOW and WHY information, as well as facts on important SKILL INVOLVED and PHYSICAL DEMANDS which should be mentioned in the job description.

CASE PROBLEM

ANALYZING A JOB: Using the Job Analysis Data Sheet you have designed for the engine parts manufacturing company (Chapter 7, p. 256), analyze one of the jobs to be found in such a company by observing a worker on the job and interviewing his foreman. Collect the information required to satisfy the Job Analysis Formula, including SKILL INVOLVED and PHYSICAL DEMANDS, and write the job description following a set style of organizing and writing the description. Retain all your job analysis notes for use in later writing the job specification.

PROBLEM: Exchange a copy of your job description with another job analyst and analyze his job description according to the Job Analysis Formula. (See pp. 218–219.) Underline each WHAT statement with a straight line, each HOW statement with a wavy line, and encircle each WHY statement. Indicate where the HOW and WHY statements have been omitted from the description.

[12] E. S. Horning, "Job Descriptions," *Management Record*, Vol. VII, No. 10 (October 1945), p. 275.

9

Job Specifications

Job SPECIFICATIONS ARE PRIMARILY WRITten descriptions of the SKILL INVOLVED and the PHYSICAL DEMANDS of the job. They are essentially the basis and the justification of values that will be assigned to each job factor used in the evaluation of the job. Job specification statements on each factor used in the job evaluation must describe the extent to which that factor is present in the job and the degree of difficulty of that factor as it is found in that job. This illustrates the need for very specific job information in the specification with emphasis on quantitative facts and judgments which will aid in establishing the level of difficulty on each factor.

The job facts and judgments recorded in the job specifications subsequently are compared to the standard degree-of-difficulty definitions on each factor in the job evaluation manual being used. As a result of these comparisons, the degree of difficulty of each factor in a given job is determined in relation to the standard scale represented by the evaluation manual.

SOURCES OF DATA

The SKILL INVOLVED—PHYSICAL DEMANDS section of the Job Analysis Data Sheet is the primary source of information on the basis of which the job-specification statements are to be phrased. This section of the data sheet may be in the form of rough notes on each factor, or there may be rather complete statements on each factor, developed at the time the job-analysis report was written.

Where the Job Analysis Data Sheet has been prepared quite thoroughly at the time of the job analysis, the writing of the job specification will be primarily a matter of rephrasing, editing, and improving the statements of fact which already have been recorded in the space allotted to each of the job-evaluation factors on the data sheet. (See Figure 7–9.)

In addition to the sections on each of the job-evaluation factors in the data sheet, there are other important sources of data for the job specification. The section titled Relation to Other Jobs, showing transfer and promotion possibilities into this job and from this job into other jobs, assists in obtaining a general understanding of the over-all level of difficulty of this job as it is placed in the organizational structure of the company. Also, after the job description has been completed in final form, each task should be studied carefully to determine which of the factors of the job specification may be involved in that task. Reference to the notes on the job specification then will tell whether each phase of this task has been covered adequately by statements regarding the skills, knowledges, and responsibilities involved in each task. In this way complete coverage by the job specification can be verified.

For each task covered in the job description usually there will be some corresponding statements in the job specification indicating the skills involved in those tasks. It may be important in many cases to include statements regarding the absence of skills as well as their presence. If this is done there will be no misunderstanding or suspicion of omission after the job specification has been completed. For example, it may be important to state on the job specification that a knowledge of calculus is not necessary in this job, especially if the occupation commonly requires the use of calculus.

The job description and specification also can be cross-checked in the opposite direction by taking one factor on the job specification and rereading each of the tasks in the Work Performed to be certain that all aspects of that factor occurring in any of the tasks are fully covered by the specification statement on the factor.

Many other clues to SKILL INVOLVED and PHYSICAL DEMANDS may be gleaned from the job description. For example, the materials used by the worker and the way in which he processes them may require a knowledge of the characteristics and working properties of these materials. The mere mention of the materials thus implies a knowledge that must be detailed in the job specification. Similarly, any indication in the job description of measuring devices may be a clue to specifications as to the required extent of knowledge of the measuring instruments and the techniques involved in using them in the job. In addition to equipment and tools, other items such as the industrial processes involved in the job, the condition or state of the material as it is received by the worker, and any previous processes or work on the material, may be clues to knowledge or skills which the worker must have in order to handle these materials and items of equipment in the successful performance of the duties on his job.

It also may be necessary sometimes to recheck the facts on the job by additional observation and discussion with the workers and supervisors. For example, the original notes may state that lifting weight is required without specifying the amount of weight to be lifted or the frequency or per cent of time involved. While the details on this factor of lifting of weight are not so likely to be omitted in the original job analysis, there are many less obvious factors in which such omissions may be quite common. In all cases of doubt, of course, the person writing the job specification should check the accuracy of the facts with some reliable source of information.

The job-evaluation manual also may be used to assist in checking the completeness of information on the job specification. The person writing the job specification may compare the specification on a particular factor to the description of levels of that factor in the job-evaluation manual to determine whether the facts as given in the specification statement are complete and sufficiently specific to place this job on one of the levels described under that factor. If this cannot be done accurately, the specification statement on the job may have omitted some significant detail, or the descriptions of the levels given in the job-evaluation manual may not be sufficiently detailed and complete. This suggests the possibility of improving the job-evaluation manual at this point. When specification items not covered in the descriptions of levels in the manual are discovered in a job, the manual statements may be improved and expanded by including additional details. This is a job for the person who is responsible for the job-evaluation program and for the manual used in the rating of jobs.

It has been pointed out above that extreme caution must be used in referring to the job-evaluation manual while writing the specification for a given job. In no case must there be any possibility of phrasing the specification statements in such a way that the level or degree assigned to the factor on that job is predetermined merely because language identical with that of the job-evaluation manual has been used in the job-specification statement. In some few cases it is necessary to do this, as in the item Experience, where the amount of time should be given in the specification. However, in this case the reason for specifying the particular length of experience, that is, the facts about the job which justify this length of experience, also must be included in the specification statement on that factor.

OUTLINE AND CONTENT

The outline of the job specification is composed of two main parts: (1) identifying facts, (2) job-evaluation factors to be rated. The job-identification information on the job specification will be similar to that carried in the heading of the job description except that it may be less complete. For example, for identification purposes, only the title, code, and department are essential in the heading of the job specification, since this is sufficient to tie together the job specification and job description for a single job. Thus additional identifying information carried on the job description will not have to be repeated in the heading of the job specification. In addition to this minimum identification information, the job specification heading also should provide space for the total points assigned to the job, the classification or labor grade into which the rating places this job, and other classification information which might be used in an individual company. For example, in addition to the organization title for the job, classification titles may be assigned after the rating is completed. In such instances, the classification title should appear in the heading of the job specification along with the organizational title.

It may be advisable also to include provisions for a date in the heading of the job specification, since in some cases the job specification may be improved or revised without any change in the job description, or vice versa. Having dates on both the job description and job specification takes care of such cases.

The major portion of the job specification will be organized by suitable headings to include a space for a specification statement on each of the factors on which the job is to be rated in the job evaluation. In addition to the heading for each factor, there should be a corresponding space to enter the job-evaluation rating on that factor. This may be a letter, a classification title, points, or other designation, depending on the particular job-evaluation system being used. As pointed out earlier, the headings of the job specification will be the same as those on the Job Analysis Data Sheet, and also the same as those contained in the job-evaluation manual.

Regardless of what particular factors are to be evaluated on each job, however, the information contained in the job specification under the general term of SKILL INVOLVED will cover responsibility of the worker, job requirements, mental application, and dexterity and accuracy. Under the general term PHYSICAL DEMANDS, the job specification will give specific data on the physical activities of the job, the surroundings, and the hazards involved in the work.

ORGANIZATION AND STYLE

The job specification does not require individual organization in the same manner as the job description, since it is already organized on the basis of the job factors to be evaluated. Also, the style of writing the job specification will tend to be less rigid and formal, since its purpose is to provide specific and detailed reference data rather than an over-all picture of the job. In general, the standards for style in writing a job specification may be listed somewhat as follows:

1. The statement should be definite, direct, and to the point.

2. Any unnecessary embellishments or complicated sentences should be avoided except where they add materially to an understanding of details of the statement.

3. Where the worker on the job is the subject, the sentence should be written with this subject implied.

4. The present tense should be employed in the same fashion as in the job description.

5. The statement must be positive and specific, but should not include any unnecessary detail and should not be allowed to develop into a motion analysis of the job with respect to that factor; however, terms indicating quantity, degree, duration, and so on should be used wherever applicable to specify as clearly as possible the level or degree of the factor present in the particular task of the job.

6. Those specifications which apply only to occasional duties should be indicated accordingly so that the per cent of time or frequency with which these specifications apply will not be overestimated. Specifications relating to the "may" items, on the other hand, will be rated and therefore should be specified as though all the workers on the job might perform these tasks. Where these "may" items are of such a character that they are on a relatively

high level with respect to SKILL INVOLVED or PHYSICAL DEMANDS, it may be an indication that the workers performing these "may" items should be under a different job title from those workers who do not perform such tasks, and should be written up and rated under a separate job.

7. Tools, machines, equipment, measuring devices, and the like must be identified specifically and the particular uses to which they are put must be described clearly. For example, the use of a slide rule may vary anywhere from simple multiplication to very complicated engineering calculations which employ its full scope.

8. References to job titles, other departments and sections, and so on, must always employ the exact title, and should follow the same capitalization procedure as in the job description; i.e., full caps for job titles and initial caps for machine and department names.

9. Any conclusion or judgment derived from job facts must be followed up with a justification or a detailing of the facts on which the statement is based.

10. Arbitrary statements such as requirements of company policy, established hiring requirements, safety regulations, and so on, should be specifically identified as such, so that they do not appear to be judgments of the job-specification writer without basis of fact given in the specification statement. Reasons for such arbitrary requirements might well be stated in the specification.

It was stated earlier that the job analyst, while analyzing jobs, is concerned only with factual information about the job. Within that limitation, the job analyst also may be the individual who writes the job description. If the job analyst also is to prepare in final form the job specification, it should be clearly understood that some skills and requirements in addition to those which he exercises in job analysis are necessary in writing the job specification. While the job specification has to do largely with factual information about the job, some analysis and evaluation must necessarily be used in arriving at judgments which are to be included in the specification statements. For example, with respect to Experience, it may be necessary for the analyst to determine the amount of experience he judges to be required as a minimum for this job. This judgment, however, will be based on facts about the job and, furthermore, these facts will be included in the specification as a substantiation of his judgment regarding the length of experience. Many other items of the job specification also will require that the person writing the information must include some of his own judgments, arrived at from a study of the facts of the job which bear on the factor for which he is writing the specification. It should be recognized that in preparing the job specification, the writer is actually performing the first stages of the evaluation of the job. It is possible, of course, to confine the job-specification writer to statements of fact only, so that in the rating process which follows it will be necessary to make all of the judgments which are involved in the job evaluation. This seems to be drawing a rather fine line, however. For all practical purposes it would appear far better for the person writing the specification, being thoroughly familiar with all the details of the job, to make his own judgments backed up by a listing of the facts which lead to those judgments; thus, both the judgments of the job-specification writer and the facts on which he based his judgments may be taken into account and reviewed in the process of rating the job.

In order to obtain a general idea of the kinds of information that may be required on the various job-evaluation factors and of the kinds of problems which may be encountered in specifying for various factors, the following comments should be taken into consideration:

Specifications for experience

As in the case of all other factors, the manual definition of just exactly what is to be included under Experience must be studied carefully and digested thoroughly by the analyst before he is in a position to write the specification for this item. In general, the Experience factor is specified in terms of the months or years required for the average worker to attain a satisfactory level of proficiency in this job. This statement, however, must be justified in the specification by listing either the length of experience required on the related jobs from which workers are promoted to this job, or the particular job skills it is necessary to learn by experience. Thus, the amount and type of experience and the reason for these requirements must be stated clearly and definitely in the job specification.

Specifications for education

The definition of this item generally includes both ordinary, formal, school education and specific training in special courses or by some other method of special study. Here the job must be analyzed in terms of those worker skills that he ordinarily acquires through his general education or must seek specifically through special training courses. The specifications for Education should take into account also such specific skills or knowledges as he may in some companies learn on the job; examples are the use of blueprints and measuring instruments, and shop mathematics. By approaching the specifications for the Education factor in this way, any judgment or statement regarding the years of schooling required, or the amount of time to be spent in particular technical training courses, can be substantiated very easily by reference to the requirement for the use of these skills on the job by the worker. As in the case of Experience, the recording of the statements of fact about the job—that is, skills that must be obtained by experience and skills that must be obtained by education—is much more important than any interpretation or judgment which the analyst may arrive at on the basis of these facts. If both the facts and the judgments which they substantiate are included in the specification, the raters may then judge the analyst's interpretations on the basis of the substantiating facts which he has also included in the specification statement.

Specifications for responsibility for machinery, tools, equipment, product, materials

Ordinarily the levels on items of this type are defined in terms of dollar value of potential loss where the worker fails to exercise the necessary responsibility. The dollar value of these items, however, is not the only factor. The worker may be responsible for the operation of an extremely expensive piece of machinery or equipment but any act or failure to act on the part of the worker may have absolutely no possibility of damaging the equipment. His responsibility in this case would be very little. Therefore, both the value of the material and the equipment and the actual possibility of the worker causing a loss under ordinary circumstances must be weighed in specifying for these items.

Specifications for responsibility for work of others

This item ordinarily covers a consideration of supervision given and received and also the responsibility of the worker for maintaining the necessary production on his job to avoid holding up other workers. Furthermore, responsibility for training workers is usually included in this item by definition. With respect to supervision of others, the amount of supervision required as well as the complexity of the work being supervised is an important feature.

Specifications for responsibility for safety of others

This item often includes the responsibility for teaching safe practices to workers supervised as well as direct responsibility of the worker to avoid injuring other workers. Specifications for this item should be cross-checked against those for the factor of Hazards involved in jobs of related workers, in jobs of workers who might be injured by this worker, and in the jobs of workers supervised by this worker.

Specifications for resourcefulness

This item is often quite difficult to specify because of the fact that resourcefulness may be exhibited or may be required in many different phases of a single job. For example, ingenuity may be required in one job in developing methods of meeting new situations, while in the same job the worker may be required also to plan very carefully his method of procedure so as to get the best results on the job. While these are two rather difficult types of skill which are both covered under the item Resourcefulness, they may occur in the same job, and both must be taken into account in arriving at the specifications on this factor.

Specifications for mental, visual, and physical effort

These items are relatively easy to specify in that they generally depend on rather readily verifiable facts; it is only necessary to pay particular attention to the amount and degree as well as the frequency of the effort required on the job.

Specifications for surroundings and hazards

These factors also are relatively simple to specify because the determination of the degree or level of these factors depends on facts which can be determined and verified objectively. In both cases the seriousness or the extent of the exposure must be taken into account along with the per cent or amount of time which the worker is exposed to these conditions. In addition, with respect to Hazards, the possibility of injury through ordinary carelessness of the worker, as well as the possible seriousness of the injury, must be considered.

Examples of job specifications are shown in Figures 9–1 and 9–2.

REVISION OF JOB SPECIFICATIONS

In evaluating a job it sometimes happens that the raters discover or take into account some additional facts that were not included in the job specification as originally written. Where this is done, the rater should make note of such instances so that the specifications may be revised and amplified as necessary. Even though the factual information in the specification may be complete, there may be some suggestions from the raters regarding emphasis or method of stating and explaining the specification items.

JOB TITLE_____ TABULAR TYPIST-CLERK

DICTIONARY TITLE_____ CODE NO._____

DEPARTMENT   Cost Accounting   TOTAL POINTS   CLASSIFICATION

EDUCATION   POINTS

Two to four years of high school, preferably including training in commercial subjects. Must be able to add and subtract accurately and handle figures readily.

EXPERIENCE AND TRAINING   POINTS

Two weeks required to teach the employee the details of the various duties to be performed. About six weeks to reach full proficiency. No previous experience is necessary but employee must be trained in the use of comptometer or calculator, must have previous training in typing, and should have some training in book-keeping.

RESOURCEFULNESS   POINTS

There are a number of detailed operations involved in this job which must be performed according to standard procedure. Some planning is called for in organizing work on a limited scale, although the balance between different aspects of the job is the responsibility of the INTERMEDIATE COST ACCOUNTANT or the ASSIST-ANT TO THE MANAGER OF COST ACCOUNTING.

ABILITY TO DO ROUTINE WORK   POINTS

This job is essentially routine and detailed in character, although the many tasks permit considerable variety.

THE NATIONAL SCREW & MFG. CO.
JOB EVALUATION OF SALARY EMPLOYEES
JOB SPECIFICATIONS

Courtesy of The National Screw & Manufacturing Company, Cleveland.

Fig. 9—1.   Job Specification—Tabular Typist-Clerk.

It is possible that the raters will not agree with some of the judgments and evaluations which the job-specification writer has included in his statements on the various factors, and they may wish to revise them.

In all such cases, the job specification should be reviewed after the rating is completed and the statements should be rephrased in such a way that they substantiate exactly and agree with the evalu-

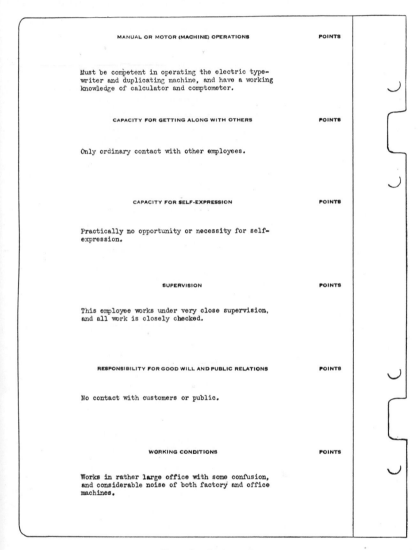

MANUAL OR MOTOR (MACHINE) OPERATIONS   POINTS

Must be competent in operating the electric type-writer and duplicating machine, and have a working knowledge of calculator and comptometer.

CAPACITY FOR GETTING ALONG WITH OTHERS   POINTS

Only ordinary contact with other employees.

CAPACITY FOR SELF-EXPRESSION   POINTS

Practically no opportunity or necessity for self-expression.

SUPERVISION   POINTS

This employee works under very close supervision, and all work is closely checked.

RESPONSIBILITY FOR GOOD WILL AND PUBLIC RELATIONS   POINTS

No contact with customers or public.

WORKING CONDITIONS   POINTS

Works in rather large office with some confusion, and considerable noise of both factory and office machines.

Fig. 9—1 (cont.).

ation degree assigned. Also, any points of view, interpretations, additional judgments, or other sidelights taken into account or developed by discussion among the raters should be added to the job-specification statement; this statement then will be a complete record of all of the items which have been taken into account in arriving at the rating assigned to that factor.

VERIFICATION OF JOB DESCRIPTIONS AND SPECIFICATIONS

Inasmuch as the job description and the job specification are the

JOB TITLE	WASHER ASSEMBLY STOCKMAN	CODE NO. 89-262
DICTIONARY TITLE		CODE NO.
DEPARTMENT	Lock Washer & Nut Assembly TOTAL POINTS	CLASS

EXPERIENCE   POINTS

Two to three months' experience required to learn which work goes to automatic assembly and which to hand assembly, and to become familiar with travel tickets to determine size and be able to recognize kinds of plating in order to properly sort material and service the WASHER HAND ASSEMBLERS.

SCHOOLING   POINTS

Must be able to read travel tickets and sort material accordingly. Equivalent of eighth grade education.

RESPONSIBILITY FOR PRODUCT OR MATERIALS   POINTS

Small losses might occur through misplacing product, mixing travel tickets, or incorrect pairing of washers and bolts in servicing WASHER HAND ASSEMBLERS.

RESPONSIBILITY FOR MACHINERY AND EQUIPMENT   POINTS

Only equipment involved is lift truck and scales. Little responsibility for even small loss.

RESPONSIBILITY FOR WORK OF OTHERS   POINTS

No supervision of others. Negligence in servicing WASHER HAND ASSEMBLERS or distributing and weighing up work would not seriously affect work of others.

RESPONSIBILITY FOR SAFETY OF OTHERS   POINTS

Reasonable care in handling mill boxes and hand lift trucks around other workers in the department will prevent endangering safety of others.

THE NATIONAL SCREW & MFG. CO.
JOB EVALUATION OF HOURLY PAID EMPLOYEES
JOB SPECIFICATIONS

Courtesy of The National Screw & Manufacturing Company, Cleveland.

Fig. 9—2.   Job Specification—Washer Assembly Stockman.

end products of the first major section of the job-evaluation undertaking, and are the basis for all of the steps to follow, it is absolutely essential that this information be accurate. Therefore, it is necessary to make a specific effort to be absolutely certain that the facts up to this point are correct and have been reported and recorded with their proper emphasis. This verification of the job descriptions and job specifications, and clearance with those concerned

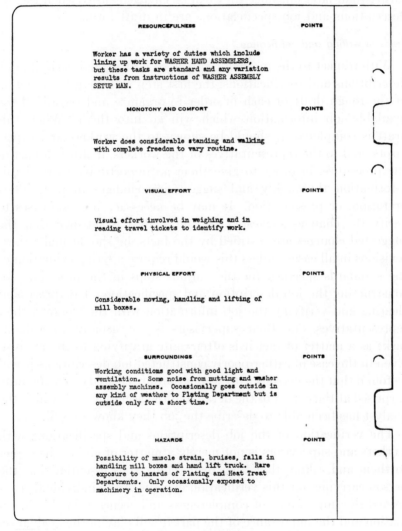

RESOURCEFULNESS   POINTS

Worker has a variety of duties which include
lining up work for WASHER HAND ASSEMBLERS,
but these tasks are standard and any variation
results from instructions of WASHER ASSEMBLY
SETUP MAN.

MONOTONY AND COMFORT   POINTS

Worker does considerable standing and walking
with complete freedom to vary routine.

VISUAL EFFORT   POINTS

Visual effort involved in weighing and in
reading travel tickets to identify work.

PHYSICAL EFFORT   POINTS

Considerable moving, handling and lifting of
mill boxes.

SURROUNDINGS   POINTS

Working conditions good with good light and
ventilation. Some noise from nutting and washer
assembly machines. Occasionally goes outside in
any kind of weather to Plating Department but is
outside only for a short time.

HAZARDS   POINTS

Possibility of muscle strain, bruises, falls in
handling mill boxes and hand lift truck. Rare
exposure to hazards of Plating and Heat Treat
Departments. Only occasionally exposed to
machinery in operation.

Fig. 9—2 (cont.).

with them, should be carried out by having the drafts of the descriptions and specifications read and agreed to by the workers and supervisors, and possibly by representatives of the workers. In addition to insuring complete accuracy, this step does much to con-

vince everyone concerned of the factual accuracy and straightfor-
wardness of the job that is being done and thus assists greatly in
securing their continued cooperation. Any facts or interpretations
subject to challenge certainly should be challenged at this point
rather than later on, since they can be changed easily when the job
descriptions and job specifications are in draft form.

Steps in writing and verification

With respect to the mechanics, then, of writing and verifying job
descriptions and specifications, the first step will be the completion
of the rough draft of each in order to organize and record all the
available job information which will go into them. When this
draft is completed, it should be shown to the workers and supervisors, and to the representatives of the workers, if this is a part of
the procedure, in order to give them an opportunity to read this
information thoroughly and suggest any changes in fact, interpretation, or presentation. It may be necessary in some cases to
verify the changes suggested. If the analyst is satisfied that the
suggested changes are justified by the facts, he should make these
revisions in all cases, unless this would require a serious violation of
the standards specified for the various steps in the procedure for
constructing the job description and specification. This process of
clearing and verifying the job information with the workers, their
representatives, and their supervisors is not usually an arduous
task; as a matter of fact it is often quite gratifying to the analyst.
Even in the case of rather poorly constructed job descriptions it will
be found that the persons with whom they are cleared often are quite
surprised at the extent of the detail and the accuracy with which the
analyst has been able to describe the job they know so well.

The verification of the job descriptions and specifications with
workers and supervisors is not merely a matter of giving the copies
to them and asking that they read them. It is essential that the
person carrying out this verification explain to the individuals concerned the importance of completeness and accuracy in this information and the importance of the part it will play in the evaluation
of jobs leading to a determination of the actual rate to be paid on
those jobs. It will be necessary also to use a different approach
with different individuals in this respect. Some may be quite familiar with the importance of this information and consequently
give this review all the careful attention which is desired. On the
other hand, some individuals may be inclined to look at this process

of verification rather lightly, and fail to read the material with the critical attention desirable at this point. Therefore, it is important that the person handling this task determine how much encouragement a particular individual needs to induce him to study the drafts carefully; the analyst will then approach this individual accordingly.

In some cases, it actually may be necessary to read the job descriptions and specifications aloud with the individual to be certain that all details are covered. Also, in this process, if the analyst finds any statements he believes may be unclear or which might possibly have an erroneous interpretation, he may discuss these with the person who is verifying them and question him in detail about their accuracy.

Another way the job descriptions and specifications may be verified is by comparing the written material on related jobs with each other. In this way, the analyst may discover discrepancies or duplications between jobs, great differences in the extent of detail from one job to another, or differences in the way the specifications are written for factors on which the levels on two different jobs are approximately equal. This cross-comparison of the written material for various jobs, especially when it is performed on jobs rather closely related with respect to skill level or content, will greatly improve the job description and specification detail and will insure uniformity and consistency from one job to another.

Editing job information

Finally, a procedure which is closely related to this comparison of job write-ups to each other is the process of thoroughly editing the individual job descriptions and specifications for internal consistency, completeness, accuracy, and conciseness. This editing process should give particular attention to a thorough analysis of the job description and specification to determine whether they conform to the standards specified for these materials. In other words, the editing process, in addition to merely grammatical editing and proofreading, should include a thorough editing of the adequacy and quality of the job information, judged in terms of the standards by which they were supposed to have been prepared.

One of the most important features to check in the editing process is the accuracy of the mechanical details such as the identification, i.e., code numbers, job title form, and so on, and particularly the reference techniques. It is important here to see that all job titles have been written in full caps and that all other types of references

have been made very definitively so that in the case of every reference there is absolutely no doubt as to what the statement means. It
is quite probable that at least some of the reference statements will
be in rather general terms. For example, the statement "Supervises
one Helper" is not adequate. If the actual job title is used, then the
reader is able to determine whether this Helper is an unskilled
laborer or an assistant foreman in charge of one section of the department. All such general references should be eliminated from
the job description and specification except where there is absolutely no doubt as to the job, or individual, or department, or section, or machine to which reference is made.

This editorial process, it should be emphasized again, is not for
the purpose of developing the literary excellence of the material, but
for the sole purpose of developing a clear, concise, and complete
statement of the job facts which it is necessary to include in the job
description and specification. Even very brief experience in writing
job information according to standards of this type will demonstrate
the value of such techniques in terms of improved clarity and accuracy.

The final step in the preparation of the job descriptions and
specifications is to have them typed in draft form in as many copies
as are required for the rating process. It will be necessary to determine at this point the number of copies needed on the basis of the
procedure to be followed in rating the jobs.

SUGGESTIONS FOR STUDY AND RESEARCH

1. Write a job specification of your friend's job, based on the information you have from the "Suggestions for Study and Research" on this job
at the end of Chapters 7 and 8.

2. List the problems you encountered in trying to state briefly and
concisely the facts pertinent to each of the specification categories. What
aids, shortcuts, rules, or suggestions have you discovered which would be
helpful in training job analysts to write job specifications?

CASE PROBLEM

WRITING A JOB SPECIFICATION: Using the job analysis notes developed in
the Case Problem of Chapter 8, write the job specification for the job
you analyzed. Compare the draft you have written with the job description to determine whether the duties which encompass the requirements

shown on the job specification are included in the job description; similarly, check over the job specification to see that all tasks included in the job description are covered by all necessary statements of requirements in the appropriate sections of the job specification. In other words, see that the job specification and job description are consistent with one another.

PROBLEM: With a fellow student, exchange copies of your job analysis data sheet, job description, and job specification. Ask him to edit all of your materials on this job analysis, indicating needed corrections or improvements in statements, omissions or lack of clarity and preciseness with regard to job facts, inconsistencies or contradictions of statements in the job materials, and other weaknesses. He should indicate all corrections necessary to make your job description and specification "a clear, concise, and complete statement of the job facts which it is necessary to include in the job description and specification." (See p. 296.)

Part Four

Evaluating Jobs

10

The Use of Job-Rating Scales

THE PREPARATION AND VERIFICATION OF the job description and the job specification represent the completion of the first major step in the evaluation of the jobs. These end products of the job analysis establish the facts and interpretations that form the basis for the rating process.

REASONS FOR RATING

After the rating scales have been set up in the job-evaluation manual and the necessary job information has been obtained, the next step is the rating of each job. This rating is essentially a comparison of the information on each job against the rating scales which have been established, to determine at what level on the scale each job is to fall. The purpose of the rating, then, is to establish the position of each individual job with respect to all other jobs in the group being evaluated through the use of some rating technique.

In most job-evaluation systems the assignment of ratings is all that is accomplished at this step. The principal exception to this is in the original factor-comparison method, in which the rating scales are set up in terms of dollars per month or cents per hour. By this method, when the rating is completed and the money value assigned to each of the five factors in the job, the total of these five money values is the monthly salary or the base hourly rate. Although this was a basic feature of the original factor-comparison system, the rating of jobs in terms of money value apparently has been abandoned by most users of the factor-comparison method.

For example, Hay,[1] in discussing the factor-comparison system of evaluation, states: "When the job has been evaluated in 'difficulty points' the experienced consultant can advise on the design of a suitable number of salary grades and the assignment of each job to the proper grade."

After a point value or some other indication of the relative value of each job, with respect to all other jobs and with respect to the scale being employed, has been decided on through the rating process, the job evaluation as such has been completed. The step of establishing the pay on each job in terms of the results of the rating or evaluation then follows.

RATING UNDER THE FOUR EVALUATION METHODS

The full scope of the job descriptions and specifications as described in Chapters 8 and 9 will be employed chiefly in those evaluation systems which classify jobs by the analytical method of breaking down each job into a number of component factors, evaluating each factor, and arriving at a total evaluation by adding up the ratings on each of the factors. The two principal types of job-evaluation systems which operate in this way are the factor-comparison method and the point-rating method. Those evaluation systems which rate the job as a whole without breaking it into component factors are the ranking method and the classification method. These whole-job methods of evaluation employ the same basic principles of evaluation or rating, however, as are used in the job-components methods.

Whole-job rating versus job-components rating

The similarities in all these job-evaluation systems can be described generally under two categories. First, any job-evaluation system is an application of one of the rating scale techniques which have been put to many different uses in business, industry, science and other fields. For example, the ranking of jobs in the ranking system of job evaluation is no different in principle from the ranking of entrants in a beauty contest. Judgments, facts, and opinions enter into the final result in both cases. Similarly, the evaluation of jobs by the classification method is no different in principle from the classification of students in a history class into final grade groups

---

[1] Edward N. Hay, "Job Evaluation for Trust Companies," *Trusts and Estates Magazine,* No. 81 (July 1945), p. 37.

of A, B, C, D, and E, or the classification of companies according to credit ratings.

The principles of rating employed in the factor-comparison method and the point-rating method also are widely used in many other fields and with many other types of subject matter. Thus, these methods follow rather well-established techniques. For example, the factor-comparison method is identical in many respects to the man-to-man rating scale employed during World War I in the evaluation of army officers; similarly, the point-rating method uses the same techniques as the graphic rating scale and descriptive rating scale in such common use in industry today in the merit rating of employees.[2]

The second category in which these two general types of job-evaluation systems are comparable is with respect to the data employed as the basis for the evaluation or rating. Just as all rating-scale techniques depend upon some type of evaluation scale against which each person or object being rated is compared, it is also essential that the rater have some specified facts as a basis for his judgment. Thus these job-evaluation systems are all similar, in that it is essential that there be some type of job information to serve the rater as a basis of comparison between the individual job and the scale he is using in the rating. The extent of detail and the method of organizing this information will depend upon the particular system being used.

In the ranking system, for example, the rater must have some information about all jobs he is ranking so that he can decide which job of those already ranked is equal to, slightly above, or slightly below the job he is ranking at the moment. He then can fit this job into the rank order at the proper place. In the classification system, the rater must compare certain characteristics of the job against some generalized characteristics given in the description of each classification in the structure he is using in order to decide into which classification category the job he is rating should fall. In the factor-comparison system, the rater likewise must have information about all jobs with respect to the factors on which he is rating these jobs so that he can decide, on each factor, which of the key jobs on the scale is equal to the job he is rating.

Finally, it is evident that in a point-rating system information about each job with respect to each of the factors to be rated is

[2] See Harold A. Burtt, *Principles of Employment Psychology,* Chapter 12, "Rating Scales" (New York: Harper & Brothers, 1942), p. 347.

essential in order to determine the level to which that job should be assigned on each factor. This is done by comparing the information on each factor against the descriptions of the various levels of that factor contained in the rating scale—that is, the job-evaluation manual.

Job-to-job rating versus job-to-category rating

It has already been noted that these four general methods of evaluating jobs may be classified also into job-to-job comparison methods and job-to-category comparison methods. Thus the factor-comparison method is a job-to-job comparison technique, just like the ranking system, except that it is further refined. Instead of comparing whole jobs to each other, the factor-comparison method breaks down the jobs to be compared into factors. One factor on a single job is compared against a scale composed of other jobs ranked with respect to that factor on the basis of the best judgment available in the company.

Likewise, the point-rating systems are a refinement of the job-classification system. In the classification system, the whole job is placed in a particular classification whose description most closely corresponds to the facts regarding the individual job. In the point-rating system, the same procedure is followed for each of a number of factors by placing each factor in that category whose description most closely corresponds to the facts regarding that factor in the job being evaluated.

RATING PRINCIPLES

In the light of these differences and similarities among the various job-evaluation methods, the following discussion of the use of job-rating scales is based on two principal considerations:

1. The principles of scientific rating scales as employed in the evaluation of jobs.

2. The application of these rating techniques in relation to the following:

    a. The type of rating scale being used;

    b. The organization of job information on which the rating judgments are based.

Without adequate rating instruments and accurate basic facts, the most careful and skilled rater is greatly handicapped, if not completely frustrated. However, assuming that the rating instruments and the job facts are adequate, the technique of rating must also come in for some careful consideration. Just as the rating scales and the job facts cannot always be in as objective and factual terms as we should like, so we cannot expect the rating itself to be an absolute measurement. In any consideration of rating, it must be clearly understood and appreciated that rating is merely a technique for assisting an individual in arriving at the most reliable and the most valid judgment possible. The reliability and validity of judgments depend upon:

1. Proper understanding and appreciation of all the facts and their relative importance.

2. A systematic method of studying the facts.

3. A thorough acquaintance with the comparison scale against which the judgment is to be made.

4. Sufficient time for careful consideration.

5. A knowledge of the systematic error and bias so common in such judgments.

6. Recognition of the importance of conscientious consideration if the judgments are to be worth anything at all.

7. Several independent judgments by the same or different individuals, or both, and a subsequent reconciliation of any differences.

8. A great deal of experience in making judgments.

9. Thorough training in the particular procedure being followed.

10. Much experience in making the particular kinds of judgments involved.

This list of "principles" which are important in the type of human judgment involved in evaluating jobs might be expanded considerably by going into many of the detailed aspects of rating. The few items listed here suggest that the process of job-rating be approached with considerable care, if not trepidation, and with the full knowledge that an effective rating is not a guess but a carefully considered decision which can be thrown off base in a good many different ways. If the job evaluation is to reflect accurately differentials in pay worth between jobs, the rating by which these differentials are established must be correct. Since there are many pitfalls and opportunities for inaccuracy in rating as a method, it must be approached very carefully in order to avoid the errors which are so easy to make.

If we are to expect the rater to evaluate jobs accurately, then we cannot just give him a manual—that is, a set of rating scales— a job description and specification, along with some perfunctory directions, and tell him to go ahead and start rating. The good rater must know *what* he is to do, *how* he is to do it, *why* he is to do it, and have a considerable amount of information about the details involved. The mechanics of rating are by far the easiest aspect to explain——"Here is a set of eight rating scales, each of which has several different levels described under it. Take this job description and specification and decide for each factor, one at a time, which level this job falls into. Write down the number of points assigned to each of the levels you have selected and add up the points to get the total value."

That's all there is to rating. When you begin to explore how this is done, however, and go into questions of why you do what, and why you do it that way, and then consider all of the details that are involved, it becomes evident immediately that a standard technique of rating must be followed if the resulting judgments are to be at all useful.

TRAINING OF RATERS

As in the case of any other job where a standard technique is to be followed, it is necessary to select, train, and supervise the workers. The selection of personnel to analyze and rate jobs has been discussed to some extent in Chapter 2. This is an appropriate place to examine more closely some of the features involved in the training and supervision of raters. The standard principles for training workers in any kind of job should be followed in the training of job raters. They should be told first what they are expected to do and how to do this job step by step; and in order that they may understand what they are doing and appreciate that it must be done according to instructions, they must be told "why" at every step in the process.

After the raters have been given the basic information on the details of evaluating jobs, the most important feature of the training will follow. There should be ample opportunity in this training period for practice in rating jobs; raters should have an opportunity to compare all their ratings on the same jobs to note the variations in judgment and to discuss these differences thoroughly. This practice in rating should be abbreviated only where very thorough supervision and inspection can be provided when these raters actually begin to rate jobs. This close supervision and checking then constitutes training on the job.

The following is a suggested outline for points to be covered in the training of raters:

1. The construction of the job-rating scale.

2. Job-analysis procedures and the content of job descriptions and specifications resulting from job analysis, as basic evaluation data.

3. Comparison of the job-rating scales and the job information as the basis for job rating.

4. The matching of job information against levels of the job-rating scales to arrive at the most appropriate level for the single job.

5. The importance of accuracy in rating as the basis for pricing jobs and for wage administration, subject to negotiation with worker representatives; the consequences of inaccuracies and inconsistencies.

6. How to achieve accuracy in rating:

    a. A thorough knowledge of how to rate.

    b. Practice in rating.

    c. Appreciation by the rater of the need for accuracy.

    d. Insistence upon factual information wherever possible.

    e. Adequate time for deliberation.

    f. Verification of own ratings; rechecking of own ratings.

    g. Consultation with other raters and with supervisors of raters.

    h. Awareness of the pitfalls in rating and of the deficiencies of human beings as raters.

RATING TECHNIQUES

Sound rating scales, reasonably complete and accurate job information, and trained and experienced raters are essentials of accurate evaluation. In addition to these three factors a standard technique of procedure, and an effective system of checking and rechecking all ratings, will assist in obtaining accurate judgments. In general this technique consists of:

1. Assigning a tentative rating to each factor of each job.

2. Verifying this rating independently, making necessary changes.

3. Reverifying all ratings after they are completed by comparing ratings on various jobs to each other.

Only the first two steps are to be discussed in this chapter. The third step, checking ratings by comparisons between jobs, is described in detail in Chapter 11.

Rating procedures

There are three general methods of organizing the rating of jobs:

1. An individual rates the jobs and records his ratings. These original ratings are then reviewed by another individual or by a committee of two or more. All cases of disagreement with the original ratings are discussed by the committee, and possibly with the rater, until agreement is reached. It may be necessary to have

the job restudied before the committee is satisfied that its judgments are correct.

2. The original rating of all jobs is done independently by two or more raters. These ratings are then compared and reviewed by a reviewing committee, which may be composed of the raters themselves. All disagreements are resolved as in 1 above.

3. The original evaluation is assigned by a committee of raters pooling their judgments and discussing all details necessary to arrive at agreement. Here again it may be necessary to obtain additional job facts by restudying the job.

The verification or checking of the ratings at this point as described above is not necessarily essential if a thorough checking procedure by cross-comparison of jobs is included in the plan. For example, Mattoon [3] describes the rating procedure in three steps, the first being the assignment of points by an individual, the second the cross-comparison process, and the third the establishment of agreement, by the department head concerned, on the evaluation assigned to each job in his department.

While it may be feasible in many individual cases to combine the review of the original rating with the cross-comparison process, it has been the experience of the authors that more accurate judgments will be achieved by making two separate verification steps. One verification is concerned only with the single job, and the other with comparisons between jobs. If the evaluation is being carried out on the so-called "bi-lateral" basis—that is, with active participation of worker representatives—the review committee discussed above may include selected union members.

The technique followed in arriving at the original ratings of the jobs will be essentially the same whether these ratings are by individuals or by a group or committee. The rater will have before him the job description, the job specification, and the job-evaluation rating scales. Taking one job at a time, he will read the job description thoroughly, and possibly the descriptions and specifications of some or all of the other jobs in the department. If he rates all of the jobs in a department before going on to other jobs, he may visit the department to review quickly all the jobs and obtain an over-all picture of the industrial processes or other activities carried on in that department. In studying the job description he may refer particularly to the information on other jobs mentioned

[3] Charles S. Mattoon, *The Technique of Job Analysis and Evaluation* (Cleveland: Printed for the Weatherhead Co., 1946), pp. 13–16.

in this description. For example, if the job he is rating is very closely related to another job in that department, there may be frequent reference to that other job. The rater will want to study this relationship carefully. If there is another job in the department in which the workers are under the direction of the man on this job, he will also study that job rather carefully.

The next step will be to study the job specification as a whole to augment the information he has obtained about the job from a study of the description and other sources of information mentioned above. He is then ready to begin actually assigning ratings to the several factors on the job. He will read the definition of the factor (usually included on the rating scale), and will then read the statement regarding that factor on the job specification. The facts in this specification statement will be compared to the description of the various levels of that factor as contained in the rating scale. Where the rating scale consists not of definitions but of the titles of key jobs, as in the factor-comparison system, he will, of course, compare the specification statement to the statements regarding the key jobs assigned to the various levels of that factor.

By comparing the job-specification statement to the levels of that factor described in the rating scale, the rater will arrive at a judgment as to which of these levels should be assigned to the job he is rating. In some cases the decision as to which level should be assigned to the job is not difficult. In many cases, however, the decision will come down to a choice between two levels on the rating scale. At this point the rater must take into account all the facts about the job bearing on that factor; also, he must study very carefully the descriptions of the two levels in question, to decide which will give the more accurate evaluation of this job. If the policy of the company is to select the higher level for each factor in such cases, this will assist the rater in arriving at a decision. Such a policy, however, must be applied very carefully, and only in those cases where the job clearly falls between the two levels in question.

In some job-evaluation systems, a range of points is provided for each level of the factor described. In this case the rater not only must decide on the level in which the job falls, but must also select the particular point value, within the range assigned to that level, which in his judgment most accurately places this job. Such a method of assigning point values calls for an extremely fine judgment if such splitting of levels is to be at all accurate. Because of the complicated nature of a job, it is almost impossible to justify the selection of 22 points, for example, as against 23 points where the range for that factor may be from 0 to 80 points. Such a judgment boils down to a matter of feeling or an unsubstantiated decision. Such an arrangement may be of considerable personal satisfaction to the rater where he is in real doubt as to which of two levels should be assigned to a job; he can select a point value which is close to the borderline between these two levels. This convenience to the rater, however, is certainly far outweighed by the difficulties which are introduced by such a system. Each rating on each factor of each job then becomes a possible source of dispute and disagreement which cannot be resolved on the basis of any objective facts. Usually such disputes must be settled on a negotiation or bargaining basis.

Recording ratings

The recording of ratings necessarily will be set up in the manner most convenient for the particular method of evaluation being used in the company. For example, where only one individual is making the original ratings these can be written down on the rough draft of the job specifications. Where several independent ratings are being used in the original instance, each rater may record his rating on his copy of the job-specification sheet or on a separate rating sheet set up for the purpose. A rating card of the type shown in Figure 10-1, developed by Mattoon,[4] would be quite satisfactory for this purpose. Various techniques for recording point values for cross-comparison purposes are discussed in more detail in the following chapter.

SOURCES OF DATA FOR EVALUATING JOBS

It has been pointed out repeatedly that the accuracy of job rating depends on the accuracy and completeness of the information about the jobs to be rated, as well as on the accuracy of the rating scale established for the purpose of evaluating the jobs. The development of effective rating scales or job-evaluation systems has been discussed fully in Chapters 4, 5, and 6. The techniques and methods of developing accurate job information have been discussed in detail in Chapters 7, 8, and 9. These two instruments, then—the job-rating scales and the job description and specification for a given job—are the basis for the rating of the job.

[4] Charles S. Mattoon, *op. cit.,* p. 17.

The rating scale in use will remain constant for the evaluation of all jobs in a particular group being evaluated. Thus, one set of scales may be used for factory jobs, another for clerical jobs, still another for supervisory, administrative, and professional jobs, and possibly another for sales jobs. The job descriptions and specifica-

---

FACTOR COMPARISON CARD

Job Title _____

Code No._____ Department_____

FINAL RATING (Labor Grade _____)

Factors	1	2	3	4	5	6	7	8	9	10
Point Rating										

INTERMEDIATE RATING (Labor Grade____)

Factors	1	2	3	4	5	6	7	8	9	10
Point Rating										

PRELIMINARY RATING (Labor Grade____)

Factors	1	2	3	4	5	6	7	8	9	10
Point Rating										

This card to be filed with the Job Analysis Report.

Fig. 10—1.

---

tions, which are the source of job information on the basis of which each individual job is rated by comparison to the rating scale, are all organized in the same fashion; thus all jobs can be rated by the same method.

Ranking

In the ranking system of job evaluation there is no rating scale except that which is developed in the process of ranking the jobs. Thus, in the ranking of a number of jobs in a department, the development of this ranking scale may be started by selecting the job judged to be worth more than all others. This job is set down at the top of the list. Next, that job which is judged to rate lowest of all jobs in the group is placed at the bottom of the list. Then, a job which rates about halfway between these two may be set down at the middle of the rank. Subsequently, as each job is added to this rank it is placed between two other jobs which have already been set up within the rank order; or, it may be set opposite a job to which it is judged to be exactly equal. In this way the comparison scale is gradually developed and further refined as each job is added to the rank order.

The other source of data—information about the jobs being ranked—will, of course, be found in the jobs themselves. Since the ranking system is a very simple method of job evaluation which can be carried out quickly, the job information used in this system usually is not developed in great detail. As a matter of fact, information about the jobs to be ranked may not even be in written form. In such cases, several executives of the company, along with several representatives from the department whose jobs are to be ranked, may sit down together in front of a blackboard and decide among themselves upon the rank order of jobs in that department. A refinement of this procedure often is introduced by recording at least some general information on each job in brief job-description form to assist in such considerations. Seldom, however, is the source of data on jobs developed as completely and accurately as in the case of other job-evaluation systems. Whenever detailed job information is collected and recorded, it becomes obvious that it is easy to adopt a more refined method of rating than the ranking system. This is because the expenditure of time and effort comes about in the collection and recording of the job information and not in the rating itself. Rating by one method is just about as quick and easy as by any other method after the necessary basic data in the form of rating scales and job information have been set up. However, those rating methods which require extensive job information will tend to be more accurate.

Classification

In this method, there is a rating scale in the form of descriptions of classification groupings. These descriptions usually are prepared in some detail and are made as specific as the circumstances permit. Where the classification system is used, there is ordinarily a rather finer or more homogeneous grouping of jobs employed than is the case in the other systems. For example, the clerical, administrative, and fiscal jobs of the federal government are rated according to one such rating scale while the professional jobs are rated according to a different scale. Still other scales are established for sub-professional jobs and custodial, protective, and crafts jobs. Each of these scales has a different number of grades or levels, varying from eight in the sub-professional series to sixteen in the clerical, administrative, and fiscal scale. Each of these grades or levels then is described in such a way that an individual job can be compared to this grade scale in order to determine in which grade the job under consideration should fall.

Since the descriptions of the grades are in some detail and are specific with respect to certain duties, responsibilities, and qualifications, the job information to be compared against these grade descriptions must be similar with respect to detail and specificity. As a matter of fact, by development over a number of years, the description of certain grades in the Federal Civil Service system has become organized into factors or attributes or areas of skill somewhat similar to the breakdown found in the job-components methods of point-rating and factor-comparison. However, in actually comparing job information to the description of various grades into which this job may be classified, the comparison is on a whole-job basis. Nevertheless, in arriving at a judgment with respect to the grade in which a job should be placed, individual factors or attributes regarding that grade and the job in question necessarily come up for consideration because of the nature of the descriptions of the grades themselves. The job information, then, under the classification system, will be patterned after the descriptions of the grades.

Factor comparison

The rating scale used in the factor-comparison system consists of a number of levels for each factor, each level being represented or defined by the title of a key job which has been judged to represent that level of that factor. For example, on a nine-point scale for the factor Skill, the job of Typist may be taken to be representative of level 9, File Clerk may represent level 4, and Bookkeeper may represent level 1, with several other jobs representing the levels in between. The source of data with respect to the rating scale under the factor-comparison system, then, is actually the detailed job information about the key jobs which have been established to form the framework of the job-comparison scale for each of the factors to be evaluated.

The source of information about a job to be rated by comparison to those jobs which constitute the scale is a job description, or job

definition, and a job specification. As in the case of the classification system, the job information—specifically the job specification
—will be organized on the basis of the scale against which the job
is to be evaluated. In other words, information about the job on the
job specification will be organized according to the factors to be
considered in rating each job. Customarily, the factor-comparison
system employs five such factors—Mental Requirements, Skill,
Physical Requirements, Responsibilities, and Working Conditions.
The job specification will carry a statement under each of these five
factors indicating the significant facts on that job with respect to
each of these factors. Thus the job is rated by comparing each of
the five factors individually to the job-comparison scale for each of
those five factors; the rater decides in each case which of the jobs
in the factor scale most closely corresponds to the job in question
with respect to that factor.

Point rating

As in the case of the factor-comparison system, several rating
scales are used in the evaluation of jobs by the point-rating method.
There is a rating scale for each factor on which the jobs are to be
evaluated. Each factor in turn is divided into levels or grades in
the same fashion as in the classification system; each of these grades
is described in some detail. Thus, in order to evaluate a job, the
job information with respect to that factor is compared to the descriptions of the various levels of that factor which constitute the
rating scale; the rating is assigned by deciding upon the level which
most nearly describes the degree of that factor present in the job
being rated.

The job-information data employed in the point-rating system
usually consist of complete information on job descriptions and job
specifications as described in Chapters 8 and 9. The information is
similar to that used in the factor-comparison system, since the information on the job specification is organized under those factors
by which the job is to be evaluated. The job specification in Figure
7–7 illustrates this point. The facts under each factor on the job
specification then are the source of data providing a basis for a
judgment as to the level to which the job should be assigned on each
of the factors to be rated. The total rating of the job is the sum
total of the ratings assigned to each of the individual factors.

Accuracy of data

Since in the final analysis the evaluation of jobs must depend primarily on judgments by individuals rather than upon objective measurement, it is extremely important that the data on which these judgments are based be as accurate as possible. The rating scales used as the common basis for the evaluation of all jobs must be accurate; they must be set up so that they can be used consistently from one time to another and by several different individuals. Similarly, the information about the jobs to be rated must be accurate, must be consistent from one job to another; this job information then will mean the same thing to a single individual from time to time and will mean the same thing to several individuals who may be rating the same job.

In the factor-comparison system, and also in the ranking system, the success of the evaluation depends to a great degree on the selection of proper key jobs as the basis for the rating scales, the proper rating of these key jobs to form the framework, and a very complete and accurate specification of these key jobs. It is important that all significant facts about the key jobs and the jobs to be rated be taken into consideration in each individual judgment that is made in evaluating the jobs.

In the classification and the point-rating systems, the accuracy of the results depends to a great degree upon accurate and complete definitions of classes and of levels of various factors being rated, the proper spacing of the various degrees under each factor, and the weighting of the factors to be evaluated in relation to their relative importance in the job as a whole with respect to the amount that job should be paid.

COMMON ERRORS IN RATING

In the training and supervision of job raters it is important to give particular attention to the common types of errors which occur in rating procedures. Such instruction can be most helpful to individuals who have not had experience with systematic rating if it is presented to them properly, with adequate examples and illustrations. Since this item represents a negative approach to the problem of securing accurate judgments, it should be brought up only after all the positive principles to be followed in rating have been thoroughly explained and are thoroughly understood.

Most of these deficiencies in rating systems in general have been discovered and investigated experimentally by psychologists in connection with the merit rating of employees and other types of rating where the objective is to arrive at a judgment about a number of individuals. Inasmuch as the rating technique applied in job evaluation is not essentially different in principle from the rating techniques applied in the evaluation of persons, the same difficulties and sources of error are present. Consequently, any standard book which discusses the principles of merit rating, not just the mechanics, can give information regarding the pitfalls to be guarded against in job evaluation.[5]

The halo effect

The so-called "halo" effect [6] has been the subject of many investigations, principally by psychologists, since it was pointed out by Thorndike in 1920.[7] The halo effect is the tendency of a rater to rate a job (or an individual) either high or low on all factors because of a high, or low, rating on one important factor. It is probable that this tendency also results from the rater's judging a job on each factor in terms of his total impression of the job as high or low. For example, there is a tendency for a rater to evaluate the job of Machinist high on all factors and the job of Punch Press Operator low on all factors because the Machinist job is commonly paid considerably more than the job of Punch Press Operator. It is difficult to say in such a case whether this halo effect is the result of the rater's general impression of the relative standing of the two jobs or whether it arises principally from the fact that the job of Machinist is usually considered to require considerably more experience than that of Punch Press Operator, Experience being a rather important and usually a heavily weighted factor in any job-evaluation system.

Although the reason for or cause of the halo effect may not be clearly determined, it can be discovered often in the work of inexperienced raters. This halo effect should be explained clearly to the rater; also, the supervisor of the rating process should be on the lookout constantly for such tendencies in the job evaluation in order to detect and remove this source of error.

Constant errors

While the halo effect may show up from time to time in the results of most raters, there are some types of rating errors which some

---

[5] See Harold A. Burtt, *Principles of Employment Psychology* (New York: Harper & Brothers, 1942), pp. 378–403, and Dale Yoder, *Personnel Management and Industrial Relations*, 3d ed. (New York: Prentice-Hall, Inc., 1948), pp. 345–353.

[6] See Joseph Tiffin, *Industrial Psychology*, 3d ed. (New York: Prentice-Hall, Inc., 1952), pp. 330 ff., for a detailed discussion of the halo effect in relation to merit rating.

[7] E. L. Thorndike, "A Constant Error in Psychological Rating," *Journal of Applied Psychology*, Vol. 4 (1920), pp. 25–29.

individuals may exhibit consistently. One general category of such constant errors may be described as a tendency toward leniency. For one reason or another, a rater may consistently rate jobs higher than other raters evaluating these same jobs. This may result from the mistaken impression that, by rating all jobs as high as possible, he is avoiding any possibility of displeasing the workers in any jobs. By following such a practice, the rater is seldom in the position of seeming to underestimate or disparage the importance of any job or the importance of any factor in a job. This tendency toward leniency may show up particularly in individual factors as well as in the total evaluation of jobs. For example, with respect to the factor Education, the rater may hesitate to decide that any job in the company requires less than high school education, whereas there may be a number of jobs which require only the ability to speak and understand English, so far as education is concerned.

In passing it may be noted that the tendency toward leniency may be adopted by the company as a policy of evaluation and in such cases, of course, would not be considered as a constant error. The reason for the adoption of such a policy is that, if the job is given the benefit of the doubt in every case in the assignment of ratings, the ratings on the individual factors in these jobs are not so likely to be questioned at a later time. There is, of course, a tendency for workers to want their jobs to be rated as high as possible. In attempting to increase their earnings, they may try to demonstrate that the evaluation of the job is too low and should be raised, thereby raising the pay worth of the job. If in the original evaluation cases of doubt were resolved generally, or even a sizable proportion of the time, by selecting the lower of two possible levels, the evaluation then contains a number of points for attack or dispute when any worker attempts to increase the pay worth of his job. If, on the other hand, all ratings have been made as high as they logically could be while remaining consistent with the levels described in the rating scale, these points of dispute are largely eliminated, unless the jobs themselves actually change.

Another type of error along this same line has been called the error of "central tendency." [8] In any situation where the rater is in doubt regarding the facts of the job, or his interpretation of these facts in assigning a rating, he may have a tendency to assign an average or middle-level rating to the job. When he assigns an

[8] Dale Yoder, *Personnel Management and Industrial Relations,* 3d ed. (New York: Prentice-Hall, Inc., 1948), p. 345.

average rating, the rater avoids "sticking his neck out" by rating the factor too low or too high. While this tendency to assign average ratings is sometimes found in job evaluation, it is not so common as in merit rating. The fact that persons are evaluated in merit rating may be partly responsible for this; moreover, facts or evidence to back up such ratings are easier to obtain in the rating of jobs than they are in the rating of individuals. Nevertheless, this type of error should be described to raters and those who are supervising them so that they may be constantly on the lookout for it.

It may be found that some raters systematically rate all jobs too high or too low, or assign ratings which are too high or too low on certain factors. These systematic errors are not necessarily the result of leniency or other types of bias on the part of the rater. They are often due to a lack of understanding of the exact meanings of the rating factors and of the exact meanings of the descriptions of the various levels within each factor. It is possible that such systematic errors may be introduced into the ratings through inadequacies of the rating scales themselves. If the definitions of the various factors or definitions of some levels of the factors are not concise and complete enough, the raters themselves may be forced to make their own interpretations of meanings which should have been written in. These interpretations may be erroneous; in any event they probably will not be consistent from one rater to another.

For example, if specific job training is given on the job, there may be a misunderstanding as to whether such training should be credited under the item Education or the item Experience. As another example, it may not be understood that the amount of physical effort credited to a job should be judged not only in terms of the degree of exertion but also in terms of the frequency or consistency with which this physical effort is required on the job. Likewise, the item Experience may be particularly difficult for inexperienced raters to understand and to judge consistently. One rater may be judging experience on the assumption that there are ideal training conditions in the company, while another rater may judge experience on the basis that there is no organized training and the worker has to learn as he can and thus spend a considerably longer time in the learning.

This tendency to systematic types of errors based on a lack of clear understanding of the rating scales themselves illustrates the importance of the basic training of the raters as well as a close follow-up and inspection of their work, especially in the beginning. It is important in the beginning to establish the proper understanding of each factor and to develop a common understanding among all the raters who are to rate the jobs.

Attitudes of raters

If we are to accept the principle that the evaluation of jobs is a matter of making a series of judgments on a systematic basis, it follows that the raters themselves must be systematic, impartial, and objective in their use of this system. It is particularly important to watch out for bias or prejudice on the part of the rater where these raters are employees of the company. Usually, where employees are selected and trained for the purpose of rating jobs in a company, these persons have a number of years experience with the company and may be selected from several different departments. Because of some considerable acquaintance with a particular department or group of departments in a company, it is to be expected that such employees would develop special loyalties to some phases of the business and possibly be prejudiced to some extent against other phases of the business. While these tendencies to prejudice may be very slight and possibly would not even be admitted by the rater to himself, nevertheless they are sometimes sufficient to influence the ratings.

Where several different raters are rating the same job, these tendencies to prejudice may be discovered and corrected easily. The correction of such errors should not be left entirely to this checking procedure, however. In anything as complicated as a job it is always easy for a skilled advocate to make out a very good case for his prejudiced judgment by rounding up a large body of facts which support his judgment and omitting some more significant facts which do not support his stand. It should be recognized also that there is the possibility that there may be company-wide prejudices or biases in favor of certain sections or departments or against certain departments. This is a manifestation of the halo effect in a slightly different sense from that discussed above.

It should be understood also that the change in attitudes of a single rater from day to day will affect the job-evaluation results. It is a well known fact that an individual's attitude will change from day to day and will even be different at different times during a single day. These changes in attitude apparently are the result of many minor details such as temperature and humidity, emotions and feelings resulting from recent experiencies, and such physical factors as fatigue, worry, tension, digestion, and the like. These attitudes or moods may affect the judgments of the individual. If the judgments made in a condition which deviates considerably from the normal are reviewed a day or so later when the attitude of the rater is quite different, he may wonder how he could ever have arrived at the judgments which are indicated by his ratings on that job.

Errors in job information

It has been pointed out repeatedly that accuracy in job information is essential to the accurate evaluation of jobs. In the process of the evaluation, the raters must be constantly on the lookout for incompleteness in this information if they are to avoid errors in judgment. Obviously, if some significant fact is lacking in the job information, this is likely to result in too low a rating on that job. It is especially important also that the amount of information and the extent of detail on each of the jobs to be evaluated be approximately the same. If there is a great amount of detail on one job and only a very general description on another job which should have about the same rating, it is probable that the first job will be rated somewhat higher because of the greater amount of evidence to support the ratings.

This positive relationship between the amount of information about the job and the rating on the job is not necessarily confined to the written job description and specification. Each of the raters will have some knowledge about certain departments or certain jobs in the company and will also have some general knowledge about some jobs or some types of work which he may have picked up from sources outside the company. It must be recognized that the rater evaluates the job not only on the basis of what is written about the job, but also on the basis of his personal knowledge of that particular job and his knowledge of similar jobs and that general kind of work. Thus the rater will tend to overrate those jobs he knows best, and possibly to underrate those jobs about which he knows very little, and on which the written information may not be adequate.

This was clearly illustrated in the experience of a company in which a committee was reviewing the ratings on all jobs. One member of the committee was particularly well informed on, and somewhat partial to, one aspect of the work performed by the company.

In discussions of the committee he succeeded in increasing the ratings on a large percentage of the jobs in this particular phase of the business by explaining additional job details not included in the written information. The other members of the committee who agreed to these upward revisions are not sure whether these revisions in the ratings are correct or whether these judgments resulted from an overpowering weight of detailed factual information presented to the committee on these particular jobs.

Another source of difficulty and error in rating having to do with facts about the job arises from the fact that some jobs may be described as they are supposed to be and not as they actually are. If the job analyst is not highly skilled, he may describe a job as the supervisor thinks it is, or as he knows it should be. Likewise, the analyst sometimes may describe what a particular worker is qualified to do rather than what he is actually required to do by the job on which he is working at the time. While this is primarily a point to catch in the job-analysis process, nevertheless the raters should be alert for such discrepancies when they are reviewing the jobs in evaluating them. For example, a worker who happens to be called a Toolmaker may be entirely confined to what amounts to routine work on one particular kind of tool. On the other hand he may be a fully qualified Toolmaker capable of doing a wide range of different types of tool work. The analyst must be certain in such cases that he obtains facts on what the worker is actually required to do on his job and not about what the worker is qualified to do in that line of work, or that occupation.

It is sometimes found, too, that a supervisor describes a job as he originally established it and instructed the worker to do it, while the worker actually has changed the job to a considerable extent without the foreman's knowledge. If the job analyst records what the foreman tells him about the job and does not verify this carefully by observation, he may have an entirely erroneous set of facts regarding that job. This tendency is not at all uncommon, for it is recognized that workers very often change their jobs to suit their own interests and skills, just as jobs are sometimes established by supervisors to fit the particular skills and interests of an individual worker.

Along this same line, the rater should be alert in picking out any jobs which are written up as they are expected to be performed somewhat later, rather than as they actually are at the present time. Such planned changes have a way of being delayed or forgotten;

as a result the description as well as the evaluation is inaccurate. If the jobs are written and rated as they exist, any subsequent changes can be followed by reanalysis and re-evaluation.

AVOIDING ERRORS IN RATING

In the previous discussion of the halo effect, it was pointed out that the rater might be influenced in his judgments on each factor by his impression of the job as a whole, or by his ratings on one or two of the more important factors on the job. In merit rating, in order to compensate for this halo effect, the rater is advised to rate all individuals in a group on one factor before going on to the next factor, and so on through all the factors on which the rating is to be done. This same arrangement will help to eliminate the halo effect from job-evaluation rating as well.

There are some difficulties, however, in applying this system to job evaluation. For one thing, in merit rating the number of people to be rated by a given supervisor is usually relatively small; also, the factors on which the judgments of the individuals are based are not usually as objective or as easily substantiated as the factors on which a job evaluation is based. Therefore the halo effect would seem to be less prevalent in job evaluation than in merit rating. Also, because of the great number of jobs to be rated, in comparison to the smaller number of individuals usually considered in merit ratings, the mere mechanics of evaluating in this manner become somewhat complicated. Secondly, after the original rating is completed, it is absolutely essential in job evaluation that these ratings be verified by comparing the ratings of all jobs on each factor individually. Therefore, since it is not usually necessary to make this cross-comparison twice, the rating of each job at a time on all factors usually works out quite satisfactorily. Any halo effect introduced by this method is rather easily detected and ruled out in the subsequent checking of these ratings by cross-comparison.

It will be necessary for the rater and the supervisor of raters to keep in mind at all times the possibility of introducing constant errors. The constant errors described above—leniency, central tendency, and systematic errors—are usually discovered by comparing the independent ratings of several raters or by rechecking the ratings of an individual.

The technique of developing the original ratings by independent evaluations by several raters is designed primarily to discover and eliminate these constant sources of error. For example, if one rater consistently assigns higher levels on one factor than any other raters rating the same jobs, the supervisor should attempt to discover why this is happening.

A rather simple statistical technique for discovering such errors is described by Yoder.[9] Where the job-evaluation program is quite large and inexperienced raters are being used, it is well worth while to subject their ratings to such an analysis, especially in the early stages, so that any tendencies toward systematic errors can be discovered and corrected.

After the error has been discovered, however, it is necessary further to determine the cause. In order to correct errors of leniency, it may even be necessary to relieve the rater of his duties. Where the error is of the central tendency type it may be necessary only to point out to the rater that, wherever he feels an average or middle rating is not fully justified by the facts, he should attempt to obtain additional facts. Probably the most frequent cause of this constant error is a misinterpretation or misunderstanding of the definition of a factor or the definitions of the levels of one of the factors. It is very important to correct these misunderstandings, of course, and it may be necessary to clarify and expand the definitions in order to establish a common understanding among all the raters.

Errors resulting from prejudice or bias of the raters will usually also be discovered in the review of the ratings by committees. Again it is the cause of these errors that is important; and, depending upon the cause, they may or may not be easy to correct.

In order to detect and eliminate the effect of any day-to-day variations in the attitude of the rater, and to develop consistency in the judgments of the individual raters, the original rating may be rechecked by the rater himself before it goes to any reviewing committee or other checking process. Thus the rater may evaluate a group of jobs on one day and the next day review all the ratings which he has made the day before. In this way he may discover some of his own inconsistencies. There is another advantage of this self-checking process. The rater, in checking his rating, may not be able to discover in the specifications the facts on which he apparently based his original rating. This means either that some additional information must be recorded on the job specification to justify his rating, or that his original rating was incorrect. In either case he has an opportunity to correct his own rating.

[9] Dale Yoder, *Personnel Management and Industrial Relations,* 3d ed. (New York: Prentice-Hall, Inc., 1948), pp. 350–351.

Wrong or incomplete job information is likely to be a most troublesome source of error because it is very difficult to detect. The other types of errors discussed above are errors of human judgment which usually can be ruled out quite successfully through the device of the reviewing committee. Although this committee arrangement cannot be depended upon to detect all errors due to lack or inaccuracy of job information, nevertheless, if the several members are familiar with a number of aspects of the business they may be expected to have some detailed information about a group of jobs, and can spot inaccuracies or omissions in job facts.

This is one of the reasons why it is important to have company employees participate in the details of job evaluation. Job analysts and raters not previously familiar with the details of the company would have to depend on their own skill as job analysts to discover all the significant facts regarding the jobs, since in making their ratings they must depend almost entirely on the written job information. Careful editing of the job descriptions and specifications and careful selection of employees of the company to serve on the reviewing committee and as raters usually will eliminate most errors of this type. The verification of the job analysis report with supervisors will provide another opportunity for picking up any additional facts which should be included in it. As part of the checking of the job evaluation, the ratings themselves also may be verified with the supervisors concerned so that another opportunity is provided to pick up any omissions.

Finally, participation by the union in the establishment of the relative values of jobs is an excellent safeguard against the omission of any significant job facts that might affect the rating. The bilateral evaluation thus not only has the advantage of satisfying the workers that the job evaluation is being done fairly and accurately, but also actually assists in arriving at a fair and accurate evaluation.

IMPROVING THE RATING SCALES WITH USE

It may be discovered in the process of using the rating scales in the evaluation of jobs that the definitions of factors are not as complete as they could be, or that the definitions of levels should be improved by adding more detail and by making them more specific. As the raters evaluate a number of different jobs they may discover that they are using some specific criterion of their own making to decide upon the level of a certain factor where this information is not included in the definition of the factor. For example, the raters may evaluate all jobs in the third level of the item Hazards where the job requires that the worker continuously work in and around any moving machinery, whereas if the worker's contact with operating machinery is very infrequent, the job may be assigned level 2; if he never comes in contact with moving machinery, and there are no other hazardous factors in his job, the job may be assigned level 1. Such specific items may be added to the definitions of the levels in the job-evaluation manual, and thus assist in developing consistency in the evaluation of Hazards on all jobs.

This is only one example of the type of detail which may be added to the rating scales after they have been put in use. The rating scales should be developed continuously throughout the process of rating the jobs. In addition to establishing consistency in the ratings, such expansion and further detailing of the rating scales themselves will assist greatly in forming a basis for substantiating the ratings whenever these judgments are questioned in the future.

As a further refinement of the rating scales, a job-comparison scale may be built up as the rating progresses. For example, after a number of jobs have been rated and reviewed, they may be written in on the various levels on the rating scales to serve as examples of these levels. Thus, the rating scale, in addition to the description of the level, has specific examples of jobs in the company which have been judged to correspond to the various levels of each of the factors. In this way, the advantages of the factor-comparison system of comparing jobs to each other can be added to advantages of the descriptive category type of scale.

Another technique along this same line may be used to incorporate the advantages of the factor-comparison system into the point-rating plan. The rater may select key jobs in each department to evaluate first and check through carefully before going on to other jobs in the department. These important jobs may then be used for comparison purposes in the rating of all other jobs in the department, and may assist in establishing consistency within the department. The subsequent cross-comparison of all jobs will pick up any interdepartmental inconsistency which might possibly develop by this method.

SUGGESTIONS FOR STUDY AND RESEARCH

1. How would you explain the rating of jobs to members of the union committee, emphasizing its objectivity but making it clear it is not a foolproof measuring device?

2. Write an article for your company magazine explaining that the

analysis of the office jobs has been completed, the job descriptions and specifications have been written and approved, and the rating of jobs is now commencing. Explain who will do the rating, how it will be checked and reviewed, and why it will establish the relative pay value of the jobs. Use charts, cartoons, drawings, tables, or photos to add interest and to clarify your explanations.

CASE PROBLEM

RATING JOBS: At this point, everyone in your group has undoubtedly analyzed at least one job and written the job description and specification. Have these duplicated so that everyone in the group can have a complete set; consider these jobs as being representative of the jobs in a given company and rate them accordingly by each of the four methods: ranking, classification, factor comparison, and point rating. Use the manuals you have constructed previously or select rating manuals from the library. The entire group should use the same manuals.

PROBLEM: Assign a role to each member of the group: foreman, consultant, job analyst, rating committee (or several rating committees), review committee, and any other roles needed for your plan of rating. Carry through the rating of these jobs and set aside a class hour to discuss the procedure and the results.

11

Verification of Job-Evaluation Ratings

THE ASSIGNMENT OF RATINGS TO ALL JOBS, as described up to this point, usually will be only the first step in the evaluation of jobs. The establishment of ratings by any one of the four general methods, plus a review of these ratings, will undoubtedly contain some percentage of error. It is essential in gaining the supervisors' and workers' respect and confidence in the job evaluation that this percentage of error be as small as possible. In order to accomplish this, suitable methods of verification of the original ratings must be developed.

The principle followed in checking or proving the original rating judgments is similar to that sometimes used in verifying mathematical computations, i.e. the use of an alternate method for arriving at the same answer. In job evaluation, each of the four systems employs a different method of arriving at job ratings. Thus, when one system has been used to arrive at the original ratings, the methods of the other systems can be used (in abbreviated form) to determine whether they would yield the same ratings.

GENERAL PRINCIPLES OF VERIFICATION

The logical method of planning the verification procedure in any job-evaluation program will take into account the characteristics and shortcomings of the rating method used and the types of errors that are likely to occur. Ranking methods ordinarily give consistent results within departments, or within other groups by which the rankings are established. This consistency is limited, however, by the fact that jobs are compared to each other as whole jobs, and

327

are not analyzed into their components. As a result, it is very difficult to justify the ranking assigned to a job. These shortcomings are inherent in the system itself, and cannot be compensated for except by actually changing the system. Also, the ranking system is not complete unless some provision is made for correlating the rankings of jobs in one department with the rankings of jobs in all other departments; a comparison of rankings across departmental lines is essential.

The classification, factor-comparison, and point-rating methods essentially do not provide for comparison of the rating of each job with that of every other job in the group. Consequently, such comparisons should be provided for in the checking procedure established under these systems. As ordinarily used, the classification system, like the ranking system, provides for judgment on the basis of whole jobs, not on the basis of job components. In order to compensate for this, again it is necessary to augment the system in some fundamental respects. The factor-comparison method does provide for comparisons of jobs across departmental lines, but this occurs in the original rating of the jobs and therefore is not an independent verification procedure. The first ratings in the point-rating method are essentially comparisons of individual factors within jobs against a standard scale, and do not provide for any job comparisons at all. Provisions for such job comparisons, therefore, should be included in the checking procedure under this method.

The various types of errors in rating which should be discovered in any checking procedure are to a large extent common to all four of the general methods of evaluation. In the more detailed rating methods—factor-comparison and point-rating—these various types of errors are more readily recognizable and consequently easier to detect and correct. For example, errors resulting from incomplete job information might enter into the ranking method but would almost never be recognized, because in this method the job facts usually are not written down in any detail. On the other hand, errors resulting from inadequate facts in the point-rating system would almost always be discovered, since written job information is essential to this method.

Each of the four general methods of job evaluation has some advantages or features which are not a basic part of any of the other methods. For example, the comparison of jobs within a department to each other is an essential feature of the ranking method. In the classification method, all jobs in a single class meet the specifications described in the description of the class. The rating of jobs by comparison to other jobs is a basic feature of the factor-comparison system. In the point-rating method, the ratings on each factor of a job are defensible by comparison to a specific description of the degree of the factor assigned to the job. None of these methods individually provides for maximum consistency in the rating of all jobs. Such consistency has been obtained only if the comparison of any job to any other job in the group results in the conclusion that all differences in rating are justifiable. If any job evaluation is to meet this test of consistency it follows that, in the final analysis, the ratings must be tested by such a method. The comparison of all jobs to all other jobs, then, is the essence of any adequate checking or verification of job evaluation ratings.

The verification procedure for any system can be built up by arranging for the comparison of all jobs with all other jobs in several different ways. All jobs may be arranged into groups by departments, and by similarity of job content, and all jobs may be taken as a single group. Within each group established in this way, the jobs may be compared to each other on the basis of the total job-evaluation rating, by preliminary labor grades or classifications, and, if the factor-comparison or point-rating method has been used, on the basis of the ratings on individual job factors. With this pattern as a foundation (see Table 11–1), the original rating, which is not essentially based on job comparison except in the ranking and factor-comparison methods, can be supplemented and verified by this job-comparison technique. A pattern of this sort allows for checking the ratings on all jobs in almost all possible combinations. If the point-rating method is employed and the ratings are checked by a job comparison along the lines of this pattern, the resulting job-evaluation system, in effect, incorporates all of the tech-

TABLE 11—1.   Verification of ratings by job comparison •

Group Jobs:	Compare Jobs Within Each Group by:
By similarity of content	Rating on each factor Total rating Labor grade or classification
By department	Rating on each factor Total rating Labor grade or classification
As a whole	Rating on each factor Total rating Labor grade or classification

niques that are used in any of the other three job-evaluation methods. It is for this reason that the point-rating method as a general procedure can be the most comprehensive, and therefore probably the most accurate, system in general usage.

The general principles of verifying the job-evaluation ratings have been discussed here as applying to a process entirely separate and distinct from the original assignment of ratings. In actual practice, however, some of the techniques of job comparison are often used in connection with the original rating. When the jobs in a given department are rated, it is only natural that the factor ratings as well as the total ratings on these jobs are compared to each other. Also, as a rater comes upon a job very similar in content to one he has rated previously, he may assign his ratings and then compare them to the ratings he has made on similar jobs in the company. This job comparison may be developed progressively as the rating of the jobs proceeds so that, as more and more jobs are rated, there are more jobs to which to compare the evaluation on each subsequent job. As was pointed out on page 325, the factor-comparison method actually may be incorporated into the point-rating method by writing in job titles on each degree of each factor to serve as examples in subsequently rating other jobs. Such practice, however, should not be considered as a substitute for a thorough systematic verification of all ratings.

IMPORTANCE OF ACCURACY IN RATINGS

It is obvious that accuracy in job rating is essential. After all, the job evaluation is undertaken for the purpose of developing more accurate relationships between all jobs in the company with respect to rate of pay. Any job evaluation which does not satisfactorily eliminate these errors in differential rates of pay does not accomplish its purpose. The mere fact that a standard job evaluation is carried out in a company does not necessarily guarantee that the relative value of jobs thus established will be an improvement over the former system. Results will be accurate only if all the necessary safeguards and checks are incorporated into the job-evaluation method. The reason for this is that, in the final analysis, the rating of jobs depends upon human judgment, which is subject to error.

By following a well-organized verification procedure, the individuals responsible for the job evaluation are given the opportunity of making the same judgments several different times in several different ways. Thus the rater may make a judgment regarding the working conditions on a number of different jobs in a department where these working conditions are practically identical. Subsequently, when all jobs in the department are compared to each other on the factor Working Conditions, the original judgment is repeated; this time, however, the emphasis is on this individual factor with respect to all jobs, rather than on this job with respect to the factor, Working Conditions. Since these two judgments are relatively independent of each other and there is ordinarily a considerable lapse of time between them, the second judgment may be considered as a good verification of the first. When four or five such checks are carried out by experienced personnel working independently or as a committee, the accuracy of the evaluation can be increased considerably.

ESTIMATING ACCURACY OF RATINGS

It is extremely difficult to determine by ordinary methods what degree of accuracy in job evaluation is satisfactory. If 90 per cent of all ratings are found to be accurate as judged by the number of changes made through the checking procedure, is this good or bad? The answer lies in comparison of data from a number of different job-evaluation programs. Unfortunately, such information is not yet readily available.

The reliability and the validity of job evaluations can be tested, however, in much the same way as the reliability and validity of any other measuring device. "Reliability" is defined as the *consistency* and *accuracy* with which a measuring device measures whatever it *does* measure. "Validity" is defined as the *extent* to which a measuring device measures what it *purports* to measure.[1]

Reliability

In one job-evaluation program, the checking procedure was carried out on 556 jobs. Since each of these jobs was evaluated on 12 different factors, this made a total of 6672 judgments. As a result of this verification of the ratings, 435 of the original judgments were changed. This represents 6½ per cent of the total number of judgments included in the entire job evaluation. However, in the process of verifying these ratings, one of the factors—Hazards—had been somewhat redefined and recast. As a result, the rating on Hazards

---

[1] cf. Albert K. Kurtz and Harold A. Edgerton, "Statistical Dictionary of Terms and Symbols" (New York: John Wiley and Sons, Inc., 1939), pp. 146, 185.

had been changed on 196 out of the 556 jobs. There remained 239 point-rating changes that were due to "incorrect" original ratings. This amounts to a 3½ per cent "error."

Rating changes resulting from the verification might also be appraised by the correlation technique. However, the correlation between the original ratings and the revised ratings will be very high in almost all cases, because for one thing the verification is not an independent rerating; also, this measure is not sensitive enough to reflect the extent of these changes accurately. The correlation technique might be used effectively in comparing the results of independent raters in making the original ratings. These measures reflect the reliability of the rating system as well as the consistency of the various raters. Correlations may be computed on the factor ratings as well as on the total evaluation of each job.

A somewhat simpler method of appraising these original ratings, when there are more than two raters, is given by Yoder.[2] The "total" error is computed according to the following formula:

$$\text{T.E.} = \frac{\Sigma|R - M|}{N}$$

M is the average rating for all raters, R is the individual rater's rating, and N is the number of jobs rated; the differences $R - M$ are added without regard to sign.

A similar formula for measuring "systematic" error is:

$$\text{S.E.} = \frac{\Sigma(R - M)}{N}$$

where the differences $R - M$ are added algebraically.

Regardless of what statistical techniques may be used as measures of the accuracy of the ratings of jobs, they will be measures only of the consistency or reliability of the job-evaluation system or of the raters. In no case will these measures indicate the statistical validity of the ratings. In the above example, when the ratings of all jobs were, in effect, done over again by several different cross-comparison techniques, the result was a change in 6½ per cent of the original judgments. Assuming that the results of this verification may be taken as a measure of the reliability of the job-evaluation system, we note that the coefficient of correlation between the original ratings and the "corrected" ratings is .984. This

[2] Dale Yoder, *Personnel Management and Industrial Relations,* 3d ed. (New York: Prentice-Hall, Inc., 1948), pp. 350–351.

correlation coefficient results from grouping the evaluation ratings into 15 classes. When the same data are correlated by grouping them into nine classes which correspond to the actual, final, labor grades, the correlation coefficient becomes .972. These reliability coefficients are well above the minimum of .800 widely used in appraising the reliability of psychological tests; the figures are also well above the minimum of .750 recommended by Yoder [3] in estimating the value of merit ratings.

While these correlation coefficients between the original ratings and the revised ratings are quite high according to ordinary standards of reliability, they are not satisfactory measures for judging the reliability of this particular set of data. As the result of the verification and consequent changes in these ratings, 51 of the 556 jobs were raised into the next higher labor grade; on the other hand, six jobs were reduced in rating sufficiently to place them in the next lower labor grade. Since 57 out of the total of 556 jobs were placed in a different labor grade as a result of the verification, this measure of the reliability of the ratings indicates a 10 per cent "error" in the original evaluation. Thus, although the labor grades were not known to reviewers at the time of this verification, a change in 6½ per cent of the original judgments resulted in a change in the classification of 10 per cent of these jobs.

Such measures of reliability as have been discussed cannot be used as the sole judge of any system of rating jobs. As a practical matter, a truly reliable job-evaluation system means one on which general agreement can be reached among all who use it, including the workers and their union representatives. In the example cited above, while 10 per cent of the original classifications were subsequently judged to be in error by as much as one labor grade, all of these changes were agreed to by a committee made up of both management and union representatives. Consequently, so far as job evaluation is concerned in this particular company, its practical reliability has been determined.

Validity

Although the job-evaluation system is sufficiently reliable to furnish a basis for management-labor agreement on job differentials, it does not necessarily follow that the ratings thus agreed upon are valid. The pay differentials established by job evaluation must

[3] *Ibid.*, p. 353.

be tested against some criterion to determine to what extent they are valid. There is no absolute criterion of validity of pay differentials between jobs. Existing differentials in business and industry have developed through accepted usage over many years as the result of the interaction of many factors. The factors which help to determine differentials of pay between jobs have been discussed in Chapter 1. Furthermore, these pay differentials are subject to continually changing factors, so that they are not at any time static.

One measure of the validity of the pay differentials within the plant might be found by analyzing the personnel turnover or the grievances primarily attributable to dissatisfaction with pay. These difficulties arise because of differentials within the company or as a result of comparison with the rates paid for similar jobs in the community. If the employees are presenting complaints or leaving the company because of low wage rates, an analysis might show that these difficulties are centered largely in a few jobs. It is entirely possible that the rates established for certain jobs are not valid.

Lack of validity may be discovered by comparisons to other jobs in the company or comparisons to similar jobs in the community. In the first case, it may be that the job is not properly evaluated. In the second case, if the evaluation is correct in relation to other jobs in the company, then there are probably some supply-and-demand factors in the labor market which result in different differentials within the community than have been established through job evaluation by the company. For example, the job of Toolmaker may be evaluated in Class 11 of a classification structure with 12 classes. It is agreed that this job is rated properly in relation to other jobs in the company. A wage structure is then established for all of the 12 classes and the rate for Toolmaker turns out to be $2.10 an hour. However, through some unusual circumstances affecting the rates of Toolmakers, the community rate may be $2.35 an hour. The rate for Toolmaker within the company, therefore, is not valid with respect to the differentials which exist in the community at that particular time. While this is an exaggerated and an isolated example, factors of this kind may operate to cause dissatisfactions and discontent among workers.

Where such wage grievances are not confined to individual occupations but are distributed throughout the entire pay range of the company, the cause of these dissatisfactions is likely to be quite different. One possibility is that a large number of jobs within the company are evaluated incorrectly. A more common explanation, however, is that the entire wage-classification structure may be below or in some other way out of line with the general community wage structure. Thus, for example, even though all differentials in the company may correspond to the differentials on the same jobs in the community, if the wage structure generally is lower than that found in the community, there may be a cause for dissatisfaction.

This discussion of the relationship of pay differentials within the company to pay differentials within the community suggests another measure of validity of the job evaluation. If the community wage structure on the jobs which exist in the company is obtainable, then the validity of the company's job structure can be estimated by correlating it with the pay structure in the community. Unfortunately, complete, accurate data of this sort in any community are almost impossible to obtain. The collection and maintenance of such information on a correct basis for any suitable number of jobs is a tremendous task. Even if it were possible, the jobs in other companies in the community are almost never directly comparable to those in any one plant. Therefore, any comparisons between company rates and community rates, from whatever source obtained, must be used with considerable caution.

The data obtained by wage surveys by some industry associations on an industry-wide basis, however, are somewhat more reliable for such comparison purposes. If some reliable information is available, even on only a few key jobs within the community or within the industry, it is possible to compare these differentials. For example, if the job differentials as established in the company through job evaluation are the same as those existing in the community, then the wage curves based on these two sets of data should have approximately the same slope. In Figure 11–1, the wage curve of Company X is superimposed on a wage curve developed from a survey of a few representative jobs in one industry ranging from the lowest paid to the highest paid. This figure illustrates that, in general, Company X pays a higher rate for the more highly skilled jobs than other companies in the same industry and about the same rate for the lowest-rated jobs. There is thus a greater difference in hourly rate between the low-paid jobs and the high-paid jobs in Company X than in the industry generally.

A similar comparison is shown in Figure 11–2, where the wage curve of Company X is superimposed on a wage curve developed

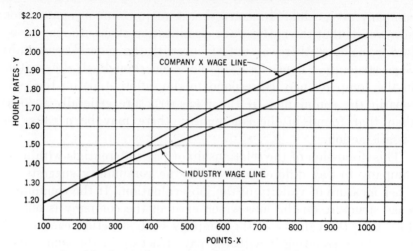

Fig. 11—1.   Industry rates plotted against Company X
job-evaluation points.

from the wage rates of representative comparable companies in the community in which Company X is located. Here the picture is somewhat different. The slope of the curve of Company X is flatter than the community curve; the company pays higher rates for lesser-skill jobs and approximately the same rates on the higher-skill jobs as are paid generally in the community according to this community wage line. It should be pointed out again that comparisons of this type should be undertaken with considerable caution. It is extremely difficult to determine whether the information on rates

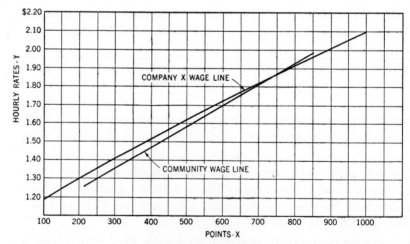

Fig. 11—2.   Community wage rates plotted against Company X
job-evaluation points.

in other companies in the industry or in the community are directly comparable to those in the company in question. Also, if information on community or industry rates is quite limited, it should be recognized that wage curves established in this way may not give a true picture of the differentials generally existing.

Although the various techniques of evaluating the accuracy of the job evaluation established in the particular company may be helpful, in the final analysis statistics are never a suitable measure of the adequacy of a job-evaluation *program*. Such analysis may point to weak spots in the job evaluation and may lead to its improvement. However, the misclassification of even one job is a serious matter, if not for the system, certainly for the individuals who are working on that job. Wherever the job classification is not internally consistent within the company, such errors directly affect the pay of individuals on those jobs in relation to the pay of other individuals in the company.

This suggests a practical method of determining the validity of the job differentials. The validity of a job evaluation can be defined in terms of "differentials between and among all jobs within the company, established by the job-evaluation system and agreed upon by management, workers, and their representatives." Such a definition of the validity of a job-evaluation structure, if accepted by all concerned, provides a definite framework for adjusting any errors in job differentials that may be discovered; thus a satisfactory *practical* validity may be maintained at all times. Any disparity between differentials in the company and differentials in the community or the industry do not enter into the pay structure within the company. Consequently, the number of pay grievances per year based upon inequities in relation to other jobs within the company becomes a measure of the validity of the job evaluation. Furthermore, a system for correcting such errors as they are discovered assures validity in the job-evaluation structure until more such errors are discovered. When these are corrected by agreement among all concerned, the validity is restored.

VERIFICATION PROCEDURE

Recording ratings for verification

Evaluation of jobs by the point-rating or factor-comparison methods will result in a large mass of data on each job. In addition to the title, department number, and job code number, there will be a rating in some form for each of the factors on which the jobs are rated, as well as a total evaluation rating. All of this information is especially complex to handle where the number of jobs in the group is large.

If all judgments recorded in the process of evaluating the jobs are to be compared in several different combinations, it is essential that these data be in such form that they can be sorted and grouped readily. There are three general methods of recording job-evaluation data so that this information can be handled readily in the verification process.

1. A small vertical file card, one for each job, on which can be recorded by hand or typewriter all of the job-evaluation details which are required for this step. An example of this kind of record is shown in Figure 10–1, page 311.

2. Hand punched cards of the Speed Sort or Keysort type, on which all of the information can be written or typed, with provision for punching all numerical information by hand around the edge for needle sorting. An example of this type of card is shown in Figure 11–3.

3. Electrical Accounting Machine Cards, such as the International Business Machines or Remington Rand systems, in which all numerical and alphabetical information may be punched and also may be printed at the top of the card. The principal advantage of these punched cards is that they may be read and sorted by hand, sorted by machine, and used to print the information in any desired arrangement for analysis. An example of this card is shown in Figure 11–4.

It will be helpful also to have various arrangements of the job-evaluation data in tabular form from time to time. For example, a book listing all jobs by labor grade and also by department will often be useful in reviewing the job structure as a whole and for reference in adding new jobs. A listing of jobs by department also will be necessary for indexes of the volumes of job descriptions and specifications. Such listings of this information can be obtained very easily from the printing tabulator of the punched-card systems if all the job-evaluation data are contained on the punched cards. Inasmuch as the punched-card system of recording is the most flexible and comprehensive, the following discussion of the mechanics of arranging job-evaluation data for verification is based primarily on this method. Most of these operations can be accomplished, although not quite so easily, with some other record sys-

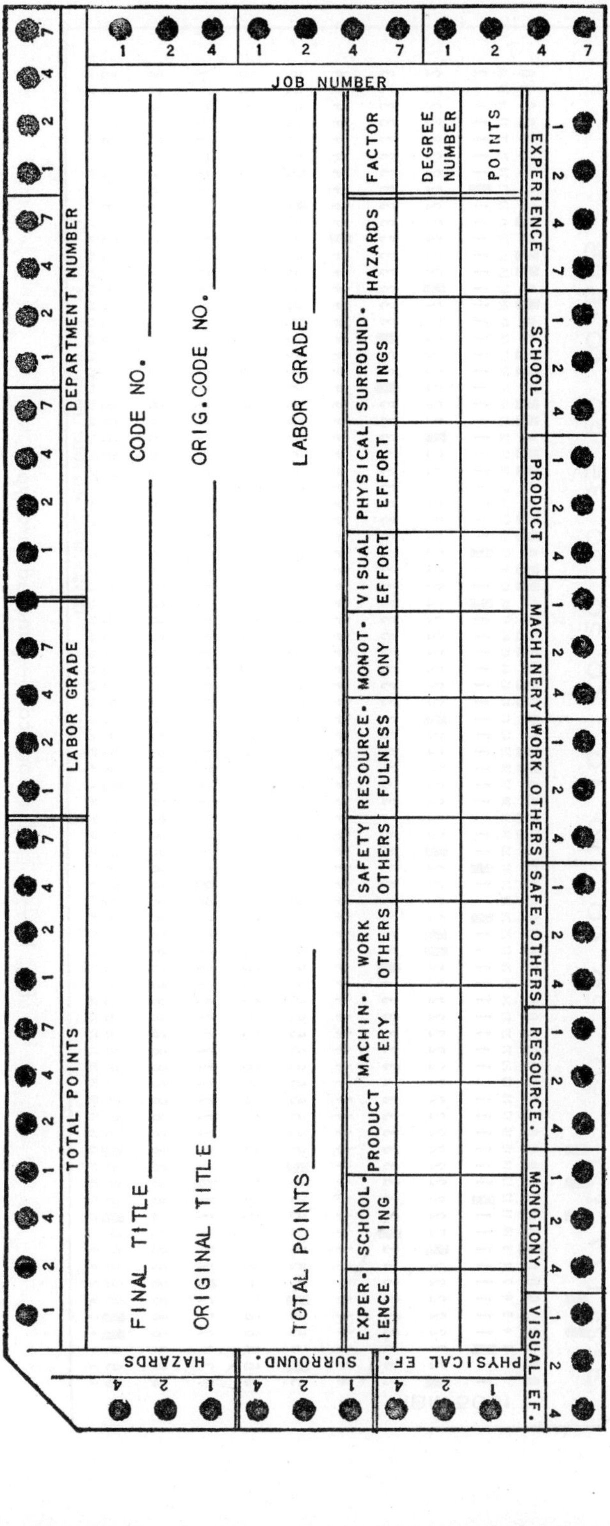

Fig. 11—3. Job record card—needle sort type.

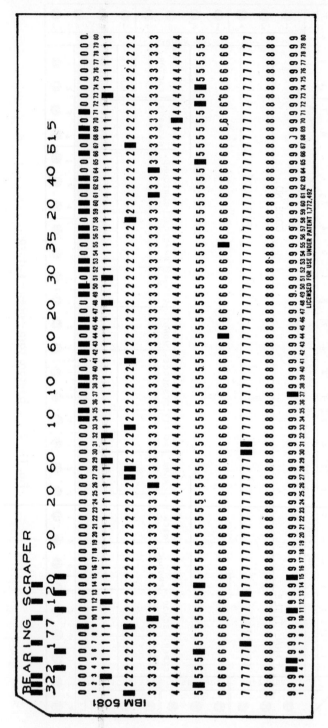

Fig. 11—4. Job record card—punched card type.

tems. An example is the use of the "Factor-Comparison Card" in Figure 10–1, described by Mattoon.[4]

Preparing the Record Card. The type of information to be recorded on the record card is illustrated in Figures 11–3 and 11–4. The Keysort type of card record is made up by writing on the face of the card the information indicated by the headings. The final title and code number are the primary identification of the record. The original title and original code number may be included as additional reference data. The points on each of the factors covered in the evaluation can be written in under the heading of each factor on the line Points.

Above each point value may be recorded the number of the degree of the factor corresponding to the point value assigned. For this purpose, the degrees on each factor can be numbered in sequence. It is necessary, for cross-comparison by this method, to assign arbitrary numbers to these degrees of each factor since the capacity of the punching on a card of this size is not sufficient to record the actual point values themselves. For cross-comparison purposes, however, these degree numbers are quite sufficient. The purpose of this cross-comparison is to determine whether all jobs assigned to a given degree on each factor are actually judged to be equal with respect to that rating. The actual point value is not essential for this purpose. The total point value of the job is entered in the space provided.

Where a sorting by labor grade or some other grouping of jobs on the basis of total points is desirable, the designation of these classification groups also can be entered on the face of the card. Although the actual point values may not be used as such in the cross-comparison procedure, they should be entered on the card so that any changes in judgments as a result of this verification can be made by crossing out the original point value and entering the revised value. Similarly, the resulting total point value also can be entered. This record card can then be made the final record of all point ratings as revised.

The degree number for each factor may be punched into the margin of the card for each job. The total points and the labor grade or other grouping designation should be punched in the same manner. The department number and the job number also may be punched in the margin for sorting on this basis. These cards

[4] Charles S. Mattoon, *The Technique of Job Analysis and Evaluation* (Cleveland: Printed for The Weatherhead Co., 1946), pp. 13–16.

then may be sorted by rating degrees on any of the factors, may be arranged by total points and by labor grades, and may be grouped by department and by occupational classification from the department number and the job number.

The first step in putting this record into punched cards for machine tabulation is to prepare a key card of the type shown in Figure 11-5. Just as the needle-sort card of Figure 11-3 limits the amount of numerical information, so the machine-sort card is limited in the amount of alphabetic information. In the example, Figure 11-5, 25 columns have been allotted to the job title. This restriction on space will require the abbreviation of many job titles. The department number and job code may be included in this card as indicated. The actual point value on each of the job-evaluation factors, followed by the total points assigned to the job, may be punched into the card. The remaining space may be allocated to labor grade or other types of codes, as this information may be found useful in arranging the jobs for various types of comparisons.

When a card of this type is punched and interpreted by printing the punched information across the top of the card, it appears as shown in Figure 11-4. These cards then may be sorted by machine on any of the job-evaluation factors, the total points, the department number, the job code, and even alphabetically by job title. An extra deck of these cards can be reproduced mechanically and interpreted as above for use in hand sorting.

Verifying the Record Cards. The Keysort type of card may be verified by proofreading the written information against the original record from which these cards were prepared. The punched information in the margin of the card may be verified by sorting on each of the job evaluation factors and inspecting each card in the resulting groups to determine that all cards in each group have the same degree number and point value. This method also may be used to verify the punching against the information recorded on the card.

The machine-punched cards may be verified in a verifying machine in the customary manner; they also may be listed on an alphabetic printing tabulator so that the job titles may be proofread and the department numbers and job numbers verified. The job-evaluation rating may be checked in several ways. First, the cards may be sorted on each factor to determine if there are any impossible values punched into the cards. For example, if the five possible ratings on one factor are 5, 10, 20, 35, and 50 points, any values

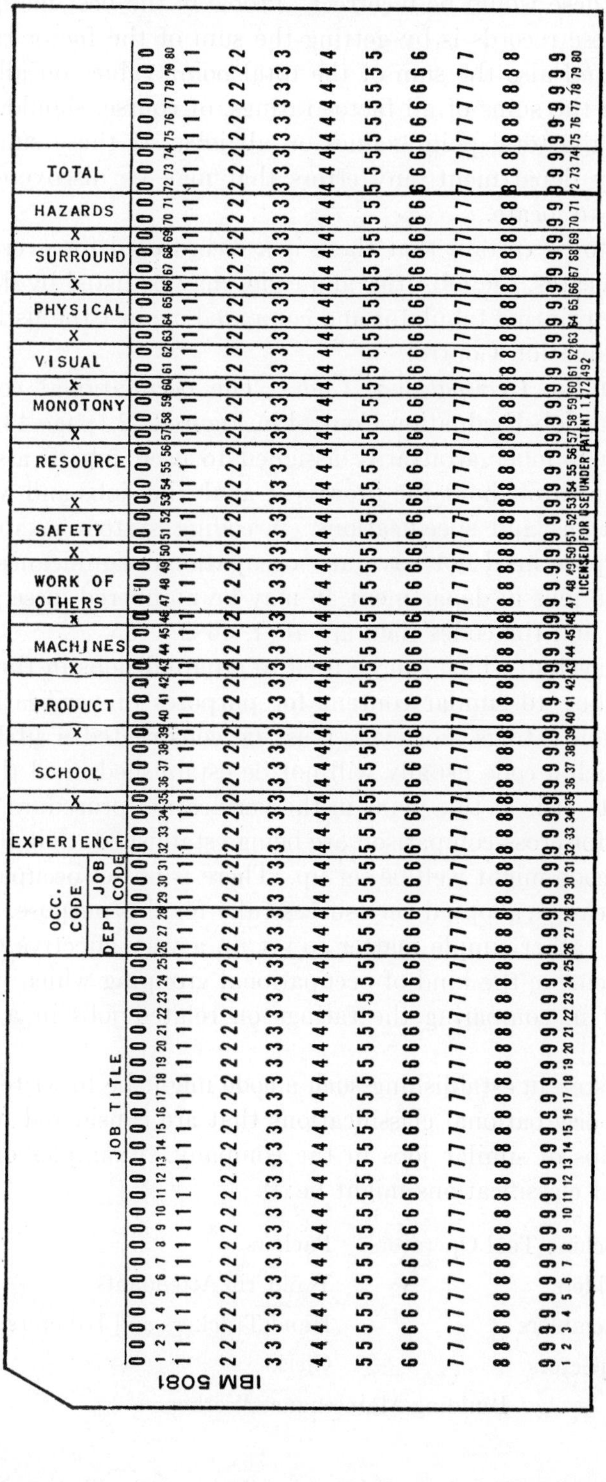

Fig. 11—5. Key card for punched record card.

other than these would be incorrect. Probably the best method of verifying these records is by getting the sum of the factor ratings on all jobs and also the sum of the total point values on all jobs. The total of the sums of all factor ratings, of course, should equal the sum of the total point values on all jobs. If these sums are tabulated by department, any errors that may be discovered are not difficult to locate.

In order to be certain that there is a record card for every job, and no duplicates, the job titles and codes may be listed by department on the printing tabulator and compared against the listing on the Job-Evaluation Control.

Preparing the Occupational Code. The occupational code as shown on the Job-Evaluation Control in Figure 2–2 (page 43) may be simply a number arbitrarily assigned to each job to assist in identification throughout the process of analyzing jobs and writing the descriptions and specifications. A coding system established for this purpose need not have any occupational significance. For example, the jobs in department 46 may be numbered in sequence from 1 to 9 and the codes then are 46–1, 46–2, etc.

A coding system which can be used to group all jobs in the company according to similar content for purposes of verification of job-evaluation ratings, however, must be constructed a little differently. Such a code usually will not be established until there is a need for it. It is at this point in the verification procedure, when the records for cross-comparison are being established, that this occupational code might well be set up. There is no set occupational code which can be adopted very successfully for this purpose. However, it is a rather simple matter to set up a very effective coding system to achieve the kind of occupational grouping which will be most useful in comparing the ratings on related jobs in a given company.

The first step in establishing such a code might be to write down the various occupational classifications that are considered to constitute groups of similar jobs in the company. Examples of such occupational classifications might be:

Machine Tool Operators	Packers
Welders	Tool Crib Attendants
Assemblers	Hand Truckers and Laborers
Inspectors	Clerks
Building Maintenance Workers	

All the jobs in the company may then be grouped experimentally under these various classifications. All jobs which do not fall into such classifications may be put aside for the present. If the record card described above is complete except for the job code number, the extra deck set up for hand sorting may be used in the process of developing this occupational code.

After all the jobs have been grouped tentatively under such classifications and additional classifications have been set up to take care of those jobs that are left over, the jobs in each tentative classification can be re-examined to determine whether any additional breakdowns are advisable. By this simple process, it is usually not too difficult to establish a rather satisfactory occupational code. A breakdown of this type in somewhat greater detail than the example just cited is shown in Figure 11–6. This is a classification structure for a plant in the bolt and nut industry.

After the occupational classifications or groups of similar jobs have been established, the next step is to set up the numerical designations for each of these classifications. The numerical code for each of these classes can be arranged in such a way that each job in each department has a distinct code number which is an absolute identification, yet also indicates the occupational classification into which this job falls. In Figure 11–6, all jobs of Setup Man have a code number from 30 to 39 and all Machine Operator jobs in the company are coded in the 50's. Since only 10 numbers are allowed for Setup Man jobs, it is evident that there are no more than 10 such jobs in any one department. However, in the case of Maintenance of Equipment, n.e.c., 20 numbers are allocated, from 170 to 189 inclusive, because in some departments there are more than 10 jobs which might fall under this category.

In order to be able to assign a distinctive number to each job in the company in a system like this, it is necessary to make the department number a part of the occupational code. A machine operating job in Department 47 may be coded 47–51, while a machine operating job in Department 49 may be coded 49–51. The first part of this occupational code indicates the department in which the job is located, while the tens digit of the second part of the code designates the occupational classification, and the units digit specifies the particular job. Thus, if there are several Machine Operator jobs in Department 47, one may be coded 47–52 and another 47–53.

Other types of occupational codes adapted to the needs of a par-

Job Code numbers below are to be prefixed by the Department number. If the job is not supervisory, use units digits *0* to *8* inclusive. Use last digit of *9* if the job clearly involves direction of a number of other workers.

PRODUCTION AND MAINTENANCE OF EQUIPMENT JOBS

Code
Number

10	Floormen, Floorladies
20	Floormen and Setup Men
30	Setup Men
40	Setup Operators
50	Machine Operators
60	Junior Setup Operators, Junior Setup Men, Junior Operators and Learners
70	Helpers on Machine Operations
80	Feeders
90	Rattlermen and Helpers
100	Product Washing and Cleaning Operators and Helpers
110	Production Machine Jobs, n.e.c.
120	Machinists
130–140	Tool and Die Makers
150–160	Tool and Die Manufacturing and Maintenance, n.e.c.
170–180	Maintenance of Equipment, n.e.c.
190	Equipment Operators and Helpers

PRODUCTION DEPARTMENT SERVICE AND PRODUCT HANDLING

200–210	Production Inspectors and Assorters
220–230	Inspection Jobs, n.e.c.
240	Tool and Die Stockmen
250	Weighup Men, Helpers
260–270	Stockmen, Service Men and Service Men's Helpers
280	Laborers and Sweepers
290	Transportation of Product
300	Production Dept. Service and Box Handling, n.e.c.
310	Packers
320	Packing Dept. Service, n.e.c.
330	Schedule Men and Expediters
340	Bonus and Weigh Clerks
350	General Clerks

BUILDING SERVICE AND MAINTENANCE

400	Electricians
410	Painters and Steeplejacks
420	Millwrights and Carpenters
430	Plumbers and Pipefitters
440	Masons
450	Boiler House
460	Porters and Charwomen
470	Plant Protection
480	Building Service and Maintenance, n.e.c.

Fig. 11—6. Occupational code—factory jobs.

ticular company might be developed on a substantially different basis. Where the above type of system has been used, however, it has worked quite successfully, and has not proved unduly cumbersome. The essential requirement of an occupational code is that it indicate the occupational classification into which a job falls; then all jobs in the company can be grouped according to similarity in content or in skill level, or with respect to other features built into the classification system. The particular system shown in Figure 11–6 accomplishes this purpose, and in addition serves as positive identification, numerically, of each job in the company when the job portion of the code number is combined with the department number.

Reviewing the ratings

When the original job-evaluation ratings and the identification data on each job are set up in records which can be sorted, grouped, and arranged in any possible combination, the reviewing or verification of the ratings is greatly facilitated. Any type of comparison which may be desired can be made without much difficulty.

If all the different techniques which have been employed in various job-evaluation systems are to be used in the verification process, this means that there are four general categories of method to consider: (1) Ranking jobs, (2) Grouping jobs into defined classifications, (3) Comparing jobs on each factor, (4) Rating jobs on a multiple-factor plan by comparison to defined degrees on each factor.

If we are to use the point-rating method as an example, technique 4 is eliminated, since that is the one which is used in establishing the original ratings. This leaves the ranking, classification, and job-comparison techniques to be employed in the verification.

The advantages of the ranking method may be incorporated into the verification of evaluations that were made by a point-rating method by sorting the record cards. All jobs in the group may be ranked with respect to total evaluation by laying these cards out on a large table, one at a time, in the rank order as determined by the judgment of the person doing the ranking. If this is done without reference to the total points already assigned to the job, or if it is done with a set of record cards which contain only the title and code, this may then constitute an independent evaluation of the jobs by a different method. The rankings assigned to the jobs in this way may then be compared to the total point evaluation assigned in the original rating of the jobs. Any discrepancies between the rankings arrived at in this way and the total point values previously assigned may be considered in detail by another rater or by a committee. This same ranking technique may be used also to verify the point ratings on each of the factors on which the jobs were evaluated. In any case, this procedure is advantageous only if the original ratings assigned are not referred to in the ranking process.

The second technique—classification into defined grades—may be carried out in a somewhat similar manner. A series of suitable classifications, ranging from the lowest paid to the highest paid jobs in the group, may be written up for this purpose. When these classifications are established and defined a rater may then sort all of the record cards into these classifications according to his judgment. Here, again, if this is to be fully effective, the rater must not refer to the original point rating. As in the case of the ranking system, any jobs which are found to be rated differently by this process than by the original may be considered in more detail by a reviewing committee. If it is considered unnecessary to write down in detail the definitions of each class before this verification begins, the rater may decide arbitrarily to sort the jobs into seven to nine different classes and only begin to define these classes after a number of the jobs have been grouped in this way. The definitions of each class then can be established somewhat on the basis of the characteristics of the jobs which have already been placed in these classes.

The job-comparison technique then can be carried out on these jobs in a fashion similar to that described above for the ranking and classification methods. The rater can select a number of jobs which he feels are typical examples of each degree of each of the evaluation factors. These can be set up into a rating scale such as that used in the factor-comparison system, and all other jobs can be rerated by this method. Again, any differences between the original ratings and the verification ratings established by this method can be studied in detail.

The methods of verification suggested above are essentially of the same pattern. In each case the jobs are re-evaluated by a different system and the results are then compared to the original judgments. An adequate substitute for this type of verification can be developed by re-examining the original ratings rather than making entirely new independent judgments. The jobs can be arranged into various types of groupings so that the ratings on all jobs in each of these groups may be compared directly to each other to determine whether the ratings seem valid when viewed in this way.

Departmental job comparison. All of the jobs in the group being evaluated can be arranged by department so that the jobs within each department can be compared to each other, factor by factor. The punched card records can be sorted on the department numbers punched into the cards and can then be listed on the alphabetic printing tabulator for this comparison. The job title, department number, job number, and point values on all factors may be printed on tabulation sheets to be used for this purpose. An example of a tabulation of this type is shown in Figure 11–7.

These tabulations can be inspected by one or several persons thoroughly familiar with the job descriptions and specifications and with the job-evaluation manual, in order to determine whether in their judgment all of the jobs in this department given equal ratings on a given factor are actually equal with respect to that factor. One or more representatives from the department may be brought in on this review to add their judgment to that of the reviewer or the committee. If, in making this tabulation, the jobs are listed in order of their total point values, the comparison will be a little bit easier, since jobs with equal ratings on the individual factors will also tend to be grouped together somewhat.

These departmental comparisons are especially valuable on those factors which are approximately equal on all jobs because of standard conditions in the department. For example, the surroundings on most jobs in a department are generally about the same, except for a few jobs which have surroundings peculiar to them. In a machine shop, the conditions of noise, light, ventilation, heat, and so on, are generally the same, except that the worker who cleans the grease from dismantled machines before they are repaired may have a higher rating, and the Tool Crib Attendant may have more favorable surroundings than most workers in the department. This same type of analysis might be applied to the item Hazards, where all workers on machine tools might have the same rating, with certain exceptions, while the Bearing Scraper working entirely with hand tools would have a lower rating, and the Tool Crib Attendant a still lower rating. By printing all of this information for a department on a single page, all types of cross-comparisons of all the jobs in the department may be made very readily.

Comparison by Degrees of Each Factor. For this verification the punched cards are sorted by the point value on one factor and,

Fig. 11—7. Tabulation of all jobs arranged by departments.

Job	DEPT. NO.	JOB NO.	EXPERIENCE	SCHOOLING	RESP. FOR PRODUCT	RESP. FOR MACHINES	WORK OF OTHERS	SAFETY	RESOURCE-FULNESS	MONOTONY	VISUAL EFFORT	PHYSICAL EFFORT	SURROUND	HAZARDS
SWEEPER	121	210	40	0	0	5	0	5	10	35	50	5	10	5
HAND FEEDER	121	102	20	10	10	15	10	40	10	50	5	60	40	20
HAND SCR MACH OP	121	52	60	10	20	15	10	0	30	50	30	15	40	40
HAND SCREW MACH S U MAN	121	33	144	60	45	35	0	10	60	35	50	35	20	40
TOOLMAKER	121	131	224	90	45	60	60	10	155	35	70	35	20	40
LABORER	206	288	20	10	10	5	0	0	10	50	5	60	40	20
FURNACE TENDER	206	196	60	30	45	15	10	20	30	50	15	60	40	40
CYANIDE FURNACE OP	206	193	112	90	75	15	30	5	30	20	30	15	20	10
TOOL HARDENER	206	390	128	60	45	60	0	10	60	50	30	35	40	20
TOOL CRIB ATTENDANT	322	242	60	60	45	15	0	5	10	20	30	15	10	5
MACHINIST HELPER	322	184	88	60	20	35	0	0	30	20	30	15	20	40
BEARING SCRAPER	322	177	120	90	20	60	0	0	60	20	30	35	20	40
MACHINIST B	322	123	160	90	75	60	30	0	155	20	50	35	10	40
MACHINIST A	322	121	192	90	110	85	60	20	155	35	70	35	20	40
LABORER	408	281	40	30	10	15	0	0	10	35	15	35	20	20
WASHER	408	102	40	10	20	15	0	5	30	50	15	60	40	20
PICKLING OPERATOR	408	101	112	30	20	15	0	0	60	35	50	15	20	20
BARREL PLATER A	408	191	128	60	20	15	60	10	100	50	15	35	40	20
PARCEL POST MAN	502	301	20	30	10	5	0	20	10	50	10	60	20	40
FREIGHT TRUCKER	502	292	20	10	10	5	10	40	10	50	5	60	60	20
STEEL STOCKMAN	502	261	60	60	20	5	30	0	30	20	15	60	40	40
FREIGHT CHECKER	502	309	80	90	45	5	60	10	30	35	30	35	20	20

within this sorting, are arranged by department. The resulting tabulation lists together all jobs which are rated in the lowest degree on the factor Physical Effort, for example. Furthermore, the jobs are arranged by department. Thus all jobs assigned the lowest rating on Physical Effort in Department 1 appear first, then jobs with the same rating on Physical Effort in Department 2, and so on through the entire list of jobs. In the next grouping will be listed, again by department, all jobs evaluated on the next to the lowest degree on Physical Effort.

In reviewing this tabulation, the rater first carefully restudies the definition of the factor, then re-examines the definition of the first degree of this factor. He then reads down the list of jobs to determine whether they are all approximately equal with respect to this factor. Any job which appears to be out of place in this list he notes for more detailed examination. He then goes on to the next degree of the factor and repeats the process until he has reviewed all jobs in the group with respect to their ratings on this first factor. He repeats this examination for each of the other factors on which the jobs have been evaluated.

This type of verification is particularly successful with a committee, for the definitions of factors and degrees can be read over and discussed by the committee, and then some member can read aloud the titles of the jobs which fall under a particular degree. Thus any member of the committee who has a question regarding the placement of any job on that degree of that factor can request clarification or discussion of that job. Samples of this type of tabulation for six different degrees of one factor are shown in Figure 11–8.

Comparison of Similar Jobs. For this type of comparison the record cards again may be rearranged and tabulated, this time by occupational code number. If a code of the type shown in Figure 11–6 has been used, all punched cards may be sorted on the tens and hundreds digits of this code. Within each code group they may be arranged by total evaluation points; the list of similar jobs then will read from low to high, or high to low, in total evaluation as determined by the original rating. In the list of Machine Operator jobs, for example, all those with the lowest rating will appear together, then the next higher jobs, and so on to the jobs rated highest in this occupational code group.

In the example in Figure 11–9, only the first digit of the total point value of each job is printed in addition to the title, department

Job Title	Dept. No.	Job No.	Visual Effort
HAND FEEDER	121	102	5
LABORER	206	288	5
FREIGHT TRUCKER	502	292	5
PARCEL POST MAN	502	301	10
FURNACE TENDER	206	196	15
LABORER	408	281	15
WASHER	408	102	15
BARREL PLATER A	408	191	15
STEEL STOCKMAN	502	261	15
HAND SCR MACH OP	121	52	30
CYANIDE FURNACE OP	206	193	30
TOOL HARDENER	206	390	30
TOOL CRIB ATTENDANT	322	242	30
MACHINIST HELPER	322	184	30
BEARING SCRAPER	322	177	30
FREIGHT CHECKER	502	309	30
SWEEPER	121	210	50
HAND SCREW MACH S U MAN	121	33	50
MACHINIST B	322	123	50
PICKLING OPERATOR	408	101	50
TOOLMAKER	121	131	70
MACHINIST A	322	121	70

Fig. 11—8.   Comparison by degrees on one factor.

Job Title	Dept. No.	Job No.	100 Point Level
HAND SCREW MACH S U MAN	121	33	5
HAND SCR MACH OP	121	52	3
HAND FEEDER	121	102	3
PICKLING OPERATOR	408	101	3
WASHER	408	102	3
MACHINIST B	322	123	7
MACHINIST A	322	121	9
TOOLMAKER	121	131	8
BEARING SCRAPER	322	177	5
MACHINIST HELPER	322	184	3
CYANIDE FURNACE OP	206	193	4
FURNACE TENDER	206	196	4
BARREL PLATER A	408	191	5
SWEEPER	121	210	1
TOOL CRIB ATTENDANT	322	242	2
STEEL STOCKMAN	502	261	3
LABORER	206	288	2
LABORER	408	281	2
FREIGHT TRUCKER	502	292	3
PARCEL POST MAN	502	301	2
FREIGHT CHECKER	502	309	4
TOOL HARDENER	206	390	5

Fig. 11—9.   Comparison of similar jobs.

number, and job number. In this particular example, the point values range from about 150 to 900, so that the first digit of the total points indicates the 100-point level in which each of these jobs fall.

In reviewing any group of jobs on such a tabulation, it should be remembered that all jobs grouped together by code number are more or less similar in content. Any major differences in skill level as shown by the first digit of the total point value then can be appraised in reviewing these tabulations. Any job that appears to be out of line can be investigated in detail to determine whether the original ratings have been assigned accurately.

Comparison by Total Point Groupings. For this comparison, all job cards are sorted by the total point value assigned on the original rating. This information then may be tabulated by printing the title, department number, and code number to identify the job, and the total point value for each job. These tabulations may be made on the printing tabulator by printing the jobs arranged in 100-point groupings as in the example in Figure 11–10. Thus all jobs with a total point value of 100 to 199 may be printed in the first group and in the next group all jobs rated in the 200's, then the 300's, etc. In reviewing these tabulations, the rater may consider all jobs in each group with respect to their similarity in total rating to determine whether in his judgment they belong in a single group. Secondly, he may consider the order in which these jobs appear in the group and thus determine whether in his judgment the rank order of these jobs is correct.

Noting Changes in Ratings on Tabulation Sheets. As changes are made in the ratings on individual factors in the first two comparisons—by department and by degrees on each factor—they may be entered on the tabulation sheets. After these first two verifications are completed, these changes also might be made on the record card itself, and the total point ratings on each job might be changed accordingly. Then, if the next two tabulations—by similar jobs and by total point groupings—are set up after the changes resulting from the first two comparisons have been made, the total points will be up to date for these second two comparisons. As a matter of technique, in punching the original cards the total points may be left off until all changes in factor values have been made. Then the revised total point ratings may be punched into these cards and the second two tabulations made for the second pair of verifications.

Throughout the verification procedure, it is necessary to keep a

Job Title	Dept. No.	Job. No.	Total Point Value
SWEEPER	121	210	95
LABORER	206	288	250
LABORER	408	281	250
TOOL CRIB ATTENDANT	322	242	285
PARCEL POST MAN	502	301	285
HAND FEEDER	121	102	300
FREIGHT TRUCKER	502	292	300
WASHER	408	102	320
MACHINIST HELPER	322	184	378
HAND SCR MACH OP	121	52	380
STEEL STOCKMAN	502	261	390
PICKLING OPERATOR	408	101	392
FURNACE TENDER	206	196	415
CYANIDE FURNACE OP	206	193	452
FREIGHT CHECKER	502	309	460
BEARING SCRAPER	322	177	515
TOOL HARDENER	206	390	548
BARREL PLATER A	408	191	553
HAND SCREW MACH S U MAN	121	33	574
MACHINIST B	322	123	735
TOOLMAKER	121	131	844
MACHINIST A	322	121	912

Fig. 11—10. Comparison by total point groupings.

careful record of all changes in point ratings. To avoid confusion, it has been found best to make all changes in point ratings as corrections on the tabulation of all jobs by departments (see Figure 11–7). Thus, when the verification is completed, all changes noted on this tabulation can be carried out on all other records of the job evaluation.

Correcting job descriptions and specifications

In addition to changes in factor point values and total point values, changes in specification statements and possibly changes in some statements on the job descriptions will be necessary as a result of the verification. It is quite probable that many changes in factor ratings will result from the discovery of new facts about the job or from revisions of judgments regarding the importance of certain evaluation factors. In either case, the specification statement for the factor on that job undoubtedly will require some change to correspond to the change in point rating. Therefore, in recording changes in factor ratings it is important also to note the reasons for these changes and to draft revisions of the specification statements.

Changes in point ratings may be accompanied by changes in the job descriptions themselves, if some significant fact not included in the job description has come to light in the verification. Here again, at the time a point change is made there should be some notation regarding any required changes or additions to statements in the job description.

OTHER USES OF JOB-COMPARISON DATA

The job records used for checking the original job-evaluation ratings, as described in this chapter, may be maintained permanently. As the final point ratings are determined through the verification procedure, all changes can be made on the punched card record as well as on the tabulation sheets, job descriptions and job specifications. When these changes are made on the cards, new tabulation sheets can be run off very easily. These tabulations then provide an excellent permanent record, in summary form, of all the details of all the ratings on the jobs. In addition, of course, these tabulations provide a record of all standard titles, the allocation of jobs by department, and records of the job codes.

Tabulations used in verification—by department, by factor, by occupational classification, and by total point grouping or labor grade—can be of great assistance in making changes in the job-evaluation structure after it is put into effect. Whenever a job is changed or a new job is created, it is necessary to repeat the entire process followed when the jobs were evaluated originally. Thus, the job is first analyzed, described, and specified; ratings then are assigned to each of the factors to determine the total evaluation. If the rating of such a new job is to be verified or checked in the same manner as the original ratings were checked, then the tabulations become very useful in verifying the evaluation of this new job. The rating on each factor, as well as the total evaluation, can be inspected in relation to all other jobs in the company by reference to the various tabulations. In this way it is possible to place all new or changed jobs in their proper place in the classification structure, and to maintain the consistency of this structure over a period of time. As in the case of the original installation of job evaluation, it is not necessary to depend entirely on the single method of rating against rating scales represented by the job-evaluation manual. All the checking and job-comparison techniques can be applied to a single new job, just as they were applied in the verification of the ratings of all jobs when the system was first installed.

Just as these tabulations are useful in the verification of original ratings, they are extremely helpful in examining the position of any job when it may be challenged, as for example in the grievance procedure. The evaluation of such a challenged job can be re-checked readily by examining its position in the whole structure with respect to all the other jobs in the job arrangements as represented by the various tabulations. This is a very important use, because, when the classification of a job is challenged, the tendency is to focus all of the attention on that one job, without due consideration to its relationship to all other jobs in the structure.

When the job evaluation is completed, it will usually be necessary to make up a volume of job descriptions and specifications for each supervisor, incorporating all the jobs under his supervision, with an index listing the title, code number, total points, and labor-grade classification of each job in the volume. Making up and subsequently revising indexes for these volumes may become a laborious task; when a job is changed or a new job is added, it is often necessary to remake the entire index. The index to be inserted in each volume can be made up by tabulating from the punched cards, and then can be used as a guide in assembling the job-evaluation volume for each supervisor. When a change in the index is necessary, it is a very simple matter to prepare a new punched card and run off on the tabulator a new index for that department.

A most important use of the punched record card is in the preparation of job-evaluation reference books. In many of the operations involved in wage and salary administration, it is necessary only to refer to the point values and identification data of the job, not to the job description and specification information. The volumes of job descriptions and specifications may be cumbersome to use when only the point values and identification information are required for reference. Record booklets containing this information can be made up easily, from the punched cards, for reference use by clerical personnel handling the routine of wage administration and other aspects of personnel records and procedures which depend on the titles, department numbers, code numbers, total points, and labor grades of the jobs in the company. As in the case of the job-description volumes, the information must be kept current for the use of employees in the payroll, cost accounting, and other departments, as well as in the personnel department. Information can be kept up to date easily, and in multiple copies, if there is electric accounting machine equipment available to run off revised tabulations.

SUGGESTIONS FOR STUDY AND RESEARCH

1. How far should the verification process be carried? How can you determine when you have reached the point of diminishing returns? What steps can be eliminated in some kinds of companies; in certain kinds of circumstances? Under what conditions should certain types of verification be given additional emphasis?

2. Outline instructions to a group to be responsible for the verification of a set of ratings of factory jobs; prepare the outline in sufficient detail so that it could be given to them to be used as a guide in doing this work.

3. Write a letter to all office supervisors, outlining the verification procedure to be used and especially their part in the process.

4. Outline how you would explain verification of ratings to a group of eight key office (nonsupervisory) employees, each of whom has been selected to represent his department in the verification of the ratings assigned to all office nonexempt jobs in the company.

5. Construct a job code for your group jobs.

CASE PROBLEM

VERIFICATION OF RATINGS: Using the ratings assigned in the Case Problem at the end of Chapter 10, assign new roles to all members of the group and plan and carry out as a group project the verification of the ratings assigned.

PROBLEM: Assess the results of the verification. What do your measures of error show? What conclusions do the results indicate as to the accuracy of the original assignment of ratings? What would have been the effect on the employees working on these jobs if the verification had not been done to insure as much accuracy as possible? What steps in the process were of most value and most revealing of weaknesses in the original ratings? What steps in the verification do you consider a waste of time in this particular case? How would you change the verification procedure the next time?

Part Five

Establishing the Pay System

12

Identifying Employees By Standard Job Titles

THE PROCESS OF "IDENTIFYING" EMPLOYEES in terms of the new job structure resulting from job evaluation is merely a matter of deciding with respect to each employee which of the job descriptions represents the work he is doing. The standard title of that job description is then assigned to him. When this is completed, we know the number of employees on each job and each employee is identified by the standard title of the job he performs.

Job-identification of employees according to their standard job titles at this point has two primary purposes: (1) to bring together information necessary for determining the wage curve and establishing the job classification structure; (2) to be sure that all jobs and all employees encompassed in the program have been included. Therefore, this step must be completed before the wage curve can be computed and before the job classification and pay structure can be set up.

The final assignment of standard job title, job code, job classification or labor grade code, and wage rate based on the new rate structure is also performed later, as of the effective date of installation of the results of the job-evaluation program. This launches the wage and salary administration on the basis of the new standardized pay structures. Accordingly, the assignment of standard job titles to employees for purposes of computing the wage curve may be kept current while the intermediate steps are being performed; thus, when the new standardized pay structures are put into effect, it is necessary only to verify the employee job-identification and enter this information on the permanent personnel records of the company. This latter step is referred to at the beginning of Chapter 15, "Establishing the Wage and Salary Administration System." Assignment of the standard job titles to employees is discussed in detail in this current chapter, however, because this job must be done at this point in the program and then either repeated or verified when the standardized pay structures are ready to be put into operation.

IMPORTANCE OF PROPER EMPLOYEE JOB-IDENTIFICATION

Accuracy in the identification of workers by the jobs titled and described in the process of developing the job evaluation is essential at this point in order to provide accurate data for subsequent steps. If some of the workers on a job of a certain point value are erroneously assigned to a job with a different point value, this will directly affect the statistical computations that are necessary in arriving at the wage curve. The importance of such an error would be in proportion to the number of workers involved in the mistake. Such errors would likewise affect the job-classification structure, since this structure is established on the same basic data.

If the job-identification of workers carried out at this time is kept up to date and used as the basis for putting job evaluation into effect when the time comes, any errors in assignment of individuals to jobs will then have an even more far-reaching effect. Incorrect job-identification of a worker, when this job-identification actually determines his pay rate, creates a problem in which the individual worker is very much concerned. Each error in employee assignment is then not just a statistical error, but results in a grievance, a dissatisfied worker, a quit, and a "black eye" for the job-evaluation system, leading to suspicion and loss of confidence in the job evaluation itself. It is theoretically true that incorrect job-identification of a worker is not a fault in the job evaluation itself, but an error in the personnel operation; nevertheless, any such mistakes in wage administration made in connection with putting the job evaluation into effect are likely to be blamed on the system. Since the wage administration based on job evaluation is not too well understood by the workers in the company at this point, and therefore may be subject to suspicion, such errors can be very costly; they may even result in complete lack of employee confidence in the whole system.

PROCEDURE FOR ASSIGNING JOB TITLES TO EMPLOYEES

Employee job-identification records

Since the revised wage structure based on job evaluation is not yet ready to be put into effect, the employee job-identification information usually cannot be recorded on the basic operating records of the personnel department. Therefore it is necessary to make a temporary set of employee job-identification records for the purpose of computing the wage curve and determining the wage structure. These temporary job-identification records can be kept current by making all changes in job titles as they occur from this point on and then can be used to put the new wage structure into effect by posting to the permanent personnel record systems.

This auxiliary record system ordinarily can be quite simple. For each employee in the group covered by the job evaluation the following information is necessary:

1. Name.
2. Badge or clock number, and possibly Social Security Number for additional identification.
3. Department in which the employee works.
4. Department number, if there is one.
5. Title of employee's present job.
6. Employee's present base rate.
7. New job title.
8. New job code.
9. Total job-evaluation points or other indication of result of evaluation.
10. Space for entering the labor grade and possibly the employee's new base rate, and the single rate or rate range after these have been determined.

The form on which this record is carried can be very simple. A card of the type shown in Figure 12–1 has been used quite successfully. It is essential that this record be on individual cards, because it will be necessary to rearrange these cards in several ways in the computation of the wage curve and other analyses of this information. Where there is punched-card tabulating equipment in the company, its use for this record can facilitate greatly the statistical computations of the wage curve. This is not recommended, however, unless there is someone in the company who is capable of carrying out product moment statistics by punched-card tabulation.

The first step in setting up the Employee Job-Identification

EMPLOYEE JOB-IDENTIFICATION RECORD

clock no.	name
department	dept. no.
new title	total pts.
job code	labor grade
present title	rate

Fig. 12—1.

Record is to enter on the card for each individual his name and other identification, the name and number of the department in which he works, and his present job title and rate. These cards should be sorted by departments or in groups according to the supervisors who are going to designate which job title should be applied to each worker. These records are then ready for the actual identification of workers by standard job titles.

Method of assigning standard job titles

The obvious method of deciding what job title should be given to each individual is to have every supervisor, on the basis of his knowledge of the work performed by the employees in his department, designate the standard job title that should be applied to each employee under his supervision. If this is to be done correctly by the supervisor, he must know exactly what each worker does, be thoroughly familiar with descriptions and definitions of each title he will assign to his workers, and understand and appreciate the importance of doing this job correctly.

These requirements suggest several points of procedure. First, it is necessary to select supervisors who are well acquainted with the details of the work of each individual under their supervision. Obviously, then, this could not be done by the general superintendent or the vice president or some other individual far removed from the workers themselves. Usually this job is done by the first line of supervision. If these first-line supervisors do not have the authority and responsibility desirable in this step, it may be necessary to go to the next higher level of supervision. If some supervisors at this level supervise a great number of workers, it may be advisable to have one or more of their assistants work with them, in order to be certain that at least one person in the group will be thoroughly acquainted with the details of the work of any individual employee.

The second point of procedure has to do with knowledge of the definitions and descriptions of the jobs on which the employees are to be placed. This means that those supervisors who are going to assign job titles to the workers must be acquainted with the job descriptions developed in the course of the job-evaluation program. Wherever possible, then, the supervisors should be given copies of the job descriptions and job specifications for all the jobs under their supervision, so that they may study them and will know them thoroughly when the time comes to allocate their workers to these jobs.

Knowledge of the duties of these individuals and knowledge of the duties included under each job title, the two points mentioned just above, are the necessary prerequisites for commencing this job.

Finally, in order to be certain that the job-identification of employees is done carefully and accurately by the supervisors selected, it has been found advisable to call the supervisors into the office to work on this task with one of the technicians thoroughly familiar with the job information. The supervisor should have with him any records or other information of his own that will assist him; the job descriptions and specifications for the jobs to be considered should be readily available.

In addition to the fact that the supervisor working alone might not be as careful and accurate as is necessary in assigning job titles, there are many other reasons why it is important that someone from the job-evaluation staff work with him. Although the process of assigning titles to workers may appear to be a simple and straightforward one, this is seldom the case. In the final analysis, the definition of a job must be in terms of the individual job descriptions of the company. In other words, any standard definition of what constitutes a job can be only a general rule or policy followed in the job evaluation. Thus, if a company decides that a relatively small number of job descriptions will be written, each job will be very broad, cover a large number of workers, and include groups of duties that are not identical for all workers assigned to this job title. For practical purposes jobs are never broken down so finely in job evaluation that all workers on each job are performing identical duties; this means that there will be some variation in duties from one worker to another on the same job. It is necessary for the foreman to recognize and to understand this when he begins identifying his workers by the standard job titles that have been established. This point illustrates clearly why it is necessary for the supervisor to be thoroughly familiar with the job descriptions as well as with the duties of the workers under his supervision.

The supervisor must assign to a single job description a number of workers who are performing slightly different duties; this job description, in some cases, may fail to describe exactly the duties of any one individual placed under that title. For example, there may be a title in the Toolroom of General Machine Hand which covers a group of workers who work on one or more of several machines. Thus a worker who spends all his time on a turret lathe may be designated as a General Machine Hand, while another worker who spends full time on a turret lathe may have the title of Turret Lathe Operator, the difference being that the General Machine Hand does only rough and routine work while the Turret Lathe Operator does certain classes of highly skilled work on particular kinds of tools. This is but one example of the kinds of distinctions which might have to be made by the supervisor in assigning his workers to the standard job-evaluation titles.

Grouping workers under more or less broad, all-inclusive job titles may be further complicated where there are two rather closely similar jobs in the department. This makes it difficult to distinguish whether an individual worker should be assigned to the one job or the other. As in the example of the Toolroom employees just mentioned, job-identification of workers cannot be done on the basis of the machine, but must take into account several other factors. It is characteristic of job evaluation, and of job analysis in general, that the delineation of jobs in the company is not based on one factor, such as type of machine, type of operation, or kind of material worked on, but usually is based on a combination of these factors, plus many others. In the case of Assembler A, B, and C, for example, the principal basis for distinction may be the skill involved in the job.

It is quite common in industry today to have two or more gradations of jobs within the same occupation. These gradations are usually indicated by A, B, and C, or Class 1, 2, 3, or some similar distinction. Thus Coremaker A is a different job from Coremaker B, and Welder B is a different job from Welder C. The differences in these jobs are almost entirely differences in skill required by the job. Another difference that is usually found is in the type or class of work assigned by the supervisor to these different jobs. The workers in the A classification of any job will be assigned those types of work requiring the greatest amount and variety of skills usually found in the occupation. On the other hand, workers in the B classification will be assigned fewer varieties of work and will be given jobs which do not require such a high degree of expertness in the occupation.

These points suggest a means by which it is possible to differentiate clearly between two jobs that are essentially two levels of the same occupation. If the distinctions between these two jobs are primarily in the types of work assigned to each, and in the corresponding amount and variety of skills involved in each type of work, then these details must be specified in the job description in order that this distinction may be clear. If the distinctions between such jobs are not clear and concise, and if such distinctions are not observed by the supervisor in assigning work to various classes of workers in the same occupation, a potent source of trouble has been created. The Class A worker will seldom protest when he is given a job that does not require his full skill and knowledge, but a Class B worker will expect to be paid Class A wages when he is assigned to Class A work. If it is found at any point that such distinctions between levels in the same occupation cannot be maintained in the assignment of work and cannot be clearly designated in the job descriptions, it is probable that distinctions in levels do not actually exist to the extent that would justify two different jobs. If the job-identification of employees is done carefully and conscientiously, such situations will be discovered easily.

The assignment of workers to various levels of the same occupation, then, represents at best a somewhat difficult problem. The distinctions between the various levels must be very specifically stated in the job descriptions, and these distinctions must be realistic—that is, they actually must exist in the jobs themselves. A further complicating factor in the job-identification of employees shows up most clearly in jobs with several levels. It is not at all unusual to find that many workers are working beneath their skill. It will often be found that the job on which a worker is properly assigned does not require him to use all of the skills he possesses.

Thus a Planer Operator in a machine shop may also know how to set up and operate a number of other machine tools used in the company, although he is not required to use these machines in his particular job.

In such an obvious example, this distinction between skill possessed by the worker and the skills required by the job does not often constitute a problem in the assignment of the worker to a job title. However, where the Molder B is capable of performing the duties of Molder A, there is an excellent opportunity to run into difficulty. Even though the worker may have all of the skills, knowledges, and other qualifications necessary for him to be a Molder A, still he may be assigned only work defined to fall into the Molder B job. Thus he does not have an opportunity to use all of his skills. There is a tendency for the foreman to take this into account in assigning titles to the workers under his supervision and he may want to designate this man as a Molder A.

There is an even stronger tendency on the part of the worker himself to want to be identified as a Molder A since that job is usually paid at a higher rate than the Molder B. The worker may argue his case on two counts: (1) he can demonstrate that he is capable of doing the same work as the men designated as Molder A; (2) he maintains that he is doing essentially the same work because the distinctions in the types of work assigned to Molder A and Molder B are fine distinctions in degree rather than in substance. Here again it is obvious that clear and specific job descriptions and specifications are of inestimable value in maintaining the accuracy and integrity of the wage administration based on job evaluation. Where the differences between the A and B classes of a job are clear and distinct, and where these distinctions are carried out in actual practice in the assignment of work, such difficulties can be straightened out very easily.

If such differences are not clearly specified in the job description, however, or if they are not followed out in the assignment of work, the only alternative is to eliminate the two classes of the job and have only the one job of Molder A, whose title now becomes Molder, and whose evaluation and wage rate are those of Molder A rather than of Molder B. The net result is that the company is paying Molder A wages to a man who may be doing A work as little as 30 per cent of the time and B work the other 70 per cent of the time. This is necessary because the job must be rated on the basis of the highest level of each of the factors as found in any of the duties of the worker. In many cases, flexibility in the assignment of work among a group of employees in the department by the supervisor is essential, so that a very fine breakdown of jobs into levels would not be workable. Where this is the case, it should be recognized as such, and the company must be prepared to pay for this freedom or flexibility by maintaining higher wage rates than would be necessary if two or more classes could be established and maintained.

In almost all cases where a hierarchy of jobs is found in a department, it is common practice for workers on one job to perform occasionally some or all of the duties of the job on the next higher level. For example, when the Buyer is ill, the Assistant Buyer takes her place, possibly for several weeks. When the Foreman is out of the department, the Assistant Foreman is in charge, and must perform some of the duties of the Foreman. When the Setup Man is too busy or is absent from work, the Assistant Foreman may do part of his work and may assist the Operators in doing some of the less complicated duties of the Setup Man. This is a common informal application of the Three-Position Promotion Plan of the Gilbreths,[1] in which any worker is at all times doing his own job, learning the job to which he will be promoted, and teaching the worker who will replace him when he is promoted.

If this plan is used, it may be necessary to establish in the beginning a policy with respect to this point in rating the jobs. Again, consistency is the important feature, although the most common approach is to consider such variations in duties as an opportunity rather than a requirement to be rated in the job evaluation. However, there are some exceptions, as in the case of supervisors' jobs, where teaching is a requirement of the job, and in "learner" jobs, where learning higher-skilled duties is the important feature of the job. Here again the supervisor, in assigning workers to standard titles, must understand the company policy with respect to this situation so that he may assign proper job titles to the workers under his jurisdiction. Also, there should be a clear understanding on this point between the management of the company and the workers on the jobs covered by the evaluation.

Verifying the employee job-identifications

The above discussion of problems in assigning standard job titles

---

[1] Frank B. Gilbreth and Lillian Gilbreth, "The Three-Position Plan of Promotion," *Personnel and Employment Problems in Industrial Management,* Vol. 65 (May 1916), p. 289 (Philadelphia: Annals of the American Academy of Political and Social Sciences).

to workers illustrates not only the difficulties that may be encountered but also the importance of accuracy. In order to insure correct decisions at this point, every effort should be made to verify the assignment of workers to the new standard job titles. The more obvious methods of verification do not work too well in this case. In some situations, it might be feasible to have two different supervisors assign titles to the employees independently and then compare the results to discover any discrepancies. However, where more than one supervisor has the information necessary to designate the job titles of workers, it is usually best to have both of them participate in the original work to avoid possibilities of conflict. Another possibility is to verify the assignment of titles by having someone from the job-evaluation unit actually observe or talk briefly with each worker to determine whether in his opinion the title assigned is correct. This would consume a tremendous amount of time, however, and usually is not necessary in view of the fact that there are automatic checks on the job titling of workers as the wage administration on the basis of job evaluation is put into effect.

Where a card similar to the Employee Job-Identification Record (Figure 12–1) has been maintained on a current basis from the beginning of the job-evaluation program, as suggested in Chapter 2, page 45, the assignment of workers to standard job titles at this point will be entirely a matter of verification. The Employee Job-Identification Record already will have been established, so that at this time it is only necessary to verify all the information contained on the record in preparation for the computation of the wage curve. The same techniques and the same precautions should be observed in this verification as are discussed above with reference to the original assignment of workers to the new job titles. It is particularly important here to watch out for any changes in duties, through transfer or job changes, that may not have been reported to the personnel office and which therefore were not made in the Employee Job-Identification Record.

The Job-Evaluation Control form (Chapter 2, Figure 2–2) also may be very helpful in verifying the job titling of employees. If this control form is carried through to the point of recording the new job titles corresponding to each of the original job titles, this conversion from old titles to new titles is an excellent guide in the designation of employees according to the new titles.

The new job title assigned to any employee should be one which corresponds to his old job title as shown on the Job-Evaluation Control. For example, the old job titles of Salem Furnace Feeder and Homo Furnace Operator may be combined to correspond with the new job title Furnace Tender. If a worker with the present title of Cyanide Furnace Operator is placed by the foreman under the new job title of Furnace Tender, this designation should be questioned. Since the present job titles will appear on the Employee Job-Identification Record, these cards can be sorted by new job title and checked to determine whether any present job titles occurring in this group do not correspond to the conversion shown on the Job-Evaluation Control. The supervisor who made the original designation according to the new titles should be questioned regarding these apparent discrepancies. Ordinarily such apparent mistakes will result either from an error by the supervisor in assigning the new standard title or from an error in the present job titles. The errors in present job titles ordinarily will be caused by transferring the employee to another job without notifying the personnel department to provide for recording the transfer.

The record of the number employed, male, female, and total in the Job-Evaluation Control, may also be helpful in verifying employee assignment to job titles. If there has been no great change in the organization of the department, or in the total number of people employed in the department since the control was originally set up, any variation in numbers of workers employed in each job may be significant. This check can be made easily by sorting all of the Employee Job-Identification Record cards for a department by present job title and comparing the number on each, by sex, to the figures shown on the Job-Evaluation Control. Even better, perhaps, the number employed by present job title may be converted on the Job-Evaluation Control to the number employed by new job title; these totals then can be compared to the totals as shown by sorting and arranging the Employee Job-Identification Record cards. Any major discrepancies in number employed by job then may be discussed with the supervisor of the department to determine whether any of these differences are due to errors in employee job-identification.

The present rates of pay also may help to indicate any mistakes in assigning job titles. Again the Employee Job-Identification Record cards may be sorted by new job title and, within each title, arranged by hourly rate. Any rates considerably out of line, either high or low, may indicate that the employee is not assigned to the proper title. For example, if the hourly rates for Machinists generally range between $2.00 and $2.15, but one worker under this title has an hourly rate of $1.85, it is possible that this individual should not be titled as a Machinist, but as a Lathe Operator or in some other job that is rated lower than Machinist.

These various techniques of verifying the assignment of workers to the new job titles may seem somewhat laborious. The Employee Job-Identification Record and the Job-Evaluation Control form, however, actually make this process quite simple because of the convenient arrangement of information on these records. Furthermore, any job titling errors which can be caught and corrected at this point are well worth the small additional effort that may be involved. Any incorrect designation of an employee as to job title may be quite expensive and cause considerably more difficulty than is involved in doing the job correctly in the first place and verifying the results carefully. A grievance or complaint from the employee, when he discovers he has been given the wrong job title, requires special handling by the supervisor and others in the company. Any large number of such grievances certainly would reflect on the personnel operations of the company and tend to damage the status of the job evaluation and wage administration in general. Possibly even more damage could result if, when an employee discovered the mistake, he merely complained about it rather than taking direct action to rectify the error.

Verification by the Employees on the Job. As indicated above, the most painful process by which the assignment of job titles to employees can be verified is by the employees themselves. Errors are most likely to be uncovered in this manner where the job descriptions and specifications are available to the employees or to the union officers or stewards. Errors in job titles discovered by this method are damaging to the employee relations within the company, particularly in the early stages of the operation of wage administration based on job evaluation, when it is still not thoroughly understood by the employees. Any such error resulting in a lower rate of pay than the employee is entitled to leads to suspicion that the entire operation is being used to discriminate against individual employees or to engage in petty miserliness. Once an orderly wage structure is adopted and accepted by the management of the company, it must be followed as accurately as possible. If it is used by the company as a device for reducing wages rather than as an orderly technique of wage administration, the many advantages of control and information on labor costs may be lost.

This entire discussion of job-identification of employees on standard job titles emphasizes the importance of this step in the process of putting the job evaluation to work in a wage or salary administration system. However, the points covered in this discussion apply to any system where pay is based on job titles or job classifications. It should be brought out again that, since job evaluation results in a more detailed and accurate method of pricing jobs, it is therefore easier to recognize errors under this system. For example, in a wage system based on undefined titles, workers under the title Machinist all may be subject to the same rate range although they may work in different departments and their jobs may be substantially different. Under such circumstances, it is almost impossible for the employee to substantiate any charge of inequity or discrimination because the title of Machinist is undefined and therefore becomes a "blanket" for any workers the company desires to classify under it. However, where each of these jobs of Machinist is defined in some detail, it is a simple matter for the worker to demonstrate that his own duties do or do not correspond generally to those incorporated in the job description for the title under which he is designated. In other words, when additional refinement and clarity are introduced into the system of titles on which the wage rates are based, the necessity of performing this function of wage administration more accurately than would be necessary under a less well-defined system is also introduced.

While this may appear to be a disadvantage, it should be recognized that where inequities in pay exist they are actually causing trouble, whether this trouble comes to the surface or not. Undoubtedly, dissatisfactions arising from pay inequities often are not recognized as such by the employee but they may nevertheless be reflected in his discontent on the job. In such cases he may simply be disgruntled without stating the reason why, or he may pick on some other condition of his work as a focus for his dissatisfactions. Wage difficulties are certainly a potent source of discontent among any group of employees. If these wage difficulties can be largely ruled out, by eliminating all pay inequities within the company through job evaluation and establishing a wage structure that is in line with the general community level of wages on corresponding jobs, important sources of discontent can be eliminated. As a result, the supervisor and the personnel department can concentrate on other sources of employee dissatisfaction and can continuously improve employee relations in the company.

Check on coverage of the job evaluation

As all workers in the group are identified in terms of the standard job titles, any omissions of jobs in the job evaluation will be discovered. However, if it is apparently impossible to find a description that corresponds to the duties of a particular employee, this does not necessarily mean that a new job description and specification must be prepared for him. When it appears that no job description has been prepared for an employee, the first step might well be to review the descriptions for closely similar jobs within the department to determine whether this employee should be placed on one of those which is already written up. Even where there may not have been an omission of this sort, it may be decided that the employee in question should be placed under a job title and description already in existence, and that this description should be modified or augmented to include the pertinent detail of particular duties of this worker. This situation is not unusual. It will be found many times that an individual will perform most or all of the functions described in a job description, yet may have some few additional duties which are peculiar to his particular position or to the job as it exists in that department as differentiated from the same job in another department. The question then comes up as to whether this job is actually a new job or a variation which is not significant enough to justify a separate description and title. Such decisions must be made on the basis of the original policy established for the job-evaluation program. This decision will be arrived at in the same manner as similar decisions that it was necessary to make during the process of getting the job facts.

In many cases, however, where there is apparently no job on which to place a certain worker, this job will actually represent an addition to the job structure. In such a case, of course, it is necessary to follow the procedure established for all other jobs—that is, analyze the job, write the description and specification of the job, and evaluate it. These new jobs will be discovered continuously through the initiative of the foremen in bringing them to the attention of the personnel office. Also, if the Employee Job-Identification Record for all workers is maintained from the beginning of the job-evaluation program, all new jobs will be discovered immediately in this way.

Whenever a new job has been created, it is quite possible that at the same time other jobs closely related to it have been changed in some significant respect. This is usually the case also when a single job has been changed in some of its important characteristics. Therefore, whenever a new job is created or a job is changed in some important respect, it is necessary to review those jobs closely related to the new or changed job to be sure that all job changes involved in this rearrangement have been taken into account. For example, when it is pointed out that the Accounting Clerk has been given the additional duty of reconciling the bank statement with the payroll account, it is obvious that some other job has been changed also. Whichever job previously included this reconciling of bank statements now no longer includes that function, and therefore is changed to that extent. Such seemingly minor changes in job duties or minor reorganizations of procedure within a department may make some major changes in the job structure of that department. In order to maintain an accurate wage structure for that department, it is necessary that the jobs be restudied and re-evaluated on the basis of the current information.

MAINTAINING THE EMPLOYEE JOB-IDENTIFICATION RECORD

The auxiliary record system, which ordinarily must be set up for the job-identification of employees on the standard job titles, may be required over a rather long period of time. If this Employee Job-Identification Record is established at the same time as the Job-Evaluation Control and carried through the entire process of job analysis and job evaluation, it may be required for a period of months. Even when it is established after the job evaluation has been completed, it may be necessary to make some provision for keeping it currently accurate at all times. If it is to be used only for the purpose of computing the wage curve and checking on the completeness of the study, the current maintenance will not be required. The principal use of the Employee Job-Identification Record, collecting data for the computation of the wage curve, can be served by obtaining information as of a given date and using the data obtained in this manner for all subsequent computations. It is then necessary to decide whether, having completed the job at this time, it is better to keep the information up to date in this form or to do the entire job over again when it comes time actually to put the job evaluation into effect.

The decision must be based on the difficulty of compiling the Employee Job-Identification Record as against the difficulty of maintaining this record currently over a period of time. If a long time will elapse between the collection of employee job-identification data and the establishment of the new wage administration system, this means that there will be a long period during which the auxiliary record system must be maintained on a current basis. The work involved in doing the job-identification all over again actually may be less than that involved in maintaining it on a current basis over a period of months.

If the Employee Job-Identification Record is to be maintained currently through this period, it is only necessary to establish some simple means for making current changes in this auxiliary record system as they occur. The necessary changes will be primarily the result of:

1. Separations
2. New employees
3. Transfers, promotions, job title changes of all types
4. Changes in base rates, total evaluation points, labor grades
5. All other changes that may result from a change in the employee's job assignment, including: department name and number, present title, new title, and clock number if this is not a permanent number.

Some consideration also might be given to the method by which this auxiliary record is maintained. Since the basic data for all computations should remain standard during the period between the completion of the evaluation and the effective date, it may be well to leave undisturbed the Employee Job-Identification Records that are the basis of the data used in the computations. This means that all changes subsequent to the cut-off date on which the employees' standard job titles are established should be kept separate from the cards bearing the original data. Thus, an Employee Job-Identification Record card would be made up for all new employees, but would not be filed with the original records. The same would apply to all other changes as outlined above. The reason for this is that it may be necessary from time to time to recheck parts of the original, basic data by going back to the Employee Job-Identification Record. If the record of the changes during this period is kept separately, they can be incorporated into the basic record data very easily at any time this is required.

There are several factors that will affect the amount of time that elapses between the assignment of standard job titles to employees and the putting of the job evaluation into effect. After the employee job-identification data are collected, the following steps are necessary:

1. Computation of the wage curve
2. Establishment of the job classification structure
3. Verification of the employee job-identification
4. Analysis and evaluation of additional and changed jobs
5. Establishment of wage structure, or its negotiation with the union.

Depending on the individual circumstances, these steps may consume a very long time. Negotiation of the wage structure with the union frequently may involve further clarification and some revision of the job-evaluation program. It is too much to expect that any job-evaluation program is completely accurate when it is set up the first time; errors and inconsistencies, although minor, will probably be discovered from time to time. During this period between the completion of the evaluation and the establishment of the wage administration based on the job evaluation, there is ample opportunity for many of these errors to be discovered. This means additional time in making corrections and leads to quite a bit of delay all along the line. It seems only reasonable to anticipate, therefore, that there will be a considerable lapse of time between the employee job-identification and the effective date of the job-evaluation wage structure.

Converting permanent records

When the time comes to put into effect the new job titles, code numbers, labor grades, job-evaluation points, and rate ranges, this information must be incorporated into all of the permanent personnel operations. Furthermore, from this time on, all personnel transactions will be in terms of this new system. At this time, therefore, the supervisor must have his copy of the job descriptions and specifications, along with the job-evaluation classification of labor grades, so that he may refer continually to them in all personnel actions. Here again the advantages of maintaining the Employee Job-Identification Record in card form are evident. These cards can be arranged or grouped in any manner most convenient for posting this information on the permanent personnel records. Ordinarily, the principal personnel records affected will be the permanent personnel card or folder, the seniority system, and possibly supplementary indexes such as alphabetical, and numerical by clock or badge number.

Keeping permanent records current

From the effective date of the new wage scale based on job evaluation, it is necessary that all subsequent personnel actions be in terms
of the new job titles, codes, and classifications. Each personnel
action will carry the standard title for the job involved in the action,
the name and number of the department, and ordinarily the labor
grades as well as base rates of the job involved. It is the responsibility of the immediate supervisor of the worker to certify that he
is performing the duties of the job indicated by the title used in
the action. The verification of the wage rate then becomes a relatively simple matter. If the wage structure includes rate ranges, the
principal concern of the personnel office is that the recommended
base rate is within that range. Where single rates are used, the rate
is automatically determined by the job title assigned to the individual, along with the indication of the labor grade in which that job
falls. These personnel operations involved in wage and salary administration are discussed in more detail in Chapter 16, Wage and
Salary Administration as a Management Control.

SUGGESTIONS FOR STUDY AND RESEARCH

1. Write a memorandum to the supervisor of personnel records in a
company with 900 factory employees and 200 office employees, explaining
how to set up the Employee Job-Identification Record, including current
information on present employees. Instruct him regarding the procedures
for keeping these records currently active, adding new employees, pulling
separations, recording transfers and other changes, etc. Point out that
these records will be used to put the new job evaluation into effect after
the wage structure is set up so that he can prepare for this step.

2. What variations in the chronological order of the steps necessary to
carry out a job evaluation program might be worthy of consideration at
this point? How can we decide whether the Employee Job-Identification
Record should be maintained currently or used only for the wage curve
and then discarded?

CASE PROBLEM

Using several of your group job descriptions and specifications, designate a committee of three to interview supervisors in a local company who
supervise workers performing jobs similar to those you have evaluated.
(As an alternative, the superintendent of a local plant may be willing to
come to your class or meet your class in his plant.) In this interview,
record the clock number and other identifying data of employees who

could be identified by the titles of your jobs and set up the Employee Job-Identification Record for each.

PROBLEM: What duties included in each job evaluation are not performed by the employees assigned to the job title? What duties do the employees perform which are not included in the job description? If these job descriptions were actually to be adapted for use in the company, would they need to be made more general and cover larger groups of duties to apply to the situation in this company? How many of the jobs would have to be divided into levels of skill, such as A, B, C? How do the standard titles of your group jobs compare to those actually in use in the company?

13

The Wage Curve

JOB EVALUATION STUDIES ARE DIRECTED toward the determination of a fair monetary value for each job. However, since a wage structure which has a different rate for each job would be quite unwieldy, the jobs are usually classified so that those of equal or approximately equal difficulty can receive the same rate. The two nonquantitative methods of job evaluation require a job-classification structure before the jobs can be priced, but the quantitative methods do not. In fact, it is somewhat easier to establish a job classification on the basis of the quantitative methods if the relationship between the job values (point values or evaluated rates) and either the present wage rates for the employees on the jobs or community wage rates is first determined.

The results of the job-evaluation study, whether it be made by the ranking, grading, factor-comparison, or point method, must ultimately be converted from ranks, grades, or points into money. The rates or money values are obtained either by securing the rates paid in the community or industry which constitutes the labor market from which employees are secured and deriving a wage curve based upon point values and community rates, or by securing a wage curve based upon the company's own rates and later comparing this curve with community rates. The first method sets up an *outside* wage standard to be used to determine plant rates, and the second sets up an *inside* or company standard as the basis of determining plant rates.

WHAT IS A WAGE CURVE?

A wage curve or "wage line" is a device to show the relationship between the point values of the point system or evaluated rates of the factor-comparison method, and some wage standard such as the present wage rates paid the employees on the evaluated jobs, community rates for certain key jobs, or rates established by collective bargaining. Some standard or criterion such as present rates or community rates must be selected to serve as the basis for determining the absolute or money value of each job.

In cases where the job-evaluation system was carefully constructed and accurately applied, the total point values obtained for the jobs are perhaps the best measures of the relative job difficulty that can be obtained. This should make it possible to price these point values and thereby establish a wage plan that takes job difficulties and values into proper consideration.

COLLECTIVE BARGAINING AND THE WAGE CURVE

Collective bargaining can destroy the relative values of jobs as established by job evaluation. This may occur in those situations where one group of employees enjoys a stronger bargaining position than other groups in the same company. This uneven wage standard, when compared with job values or point values, makes it difficult to derive a wage curve which is fair to all employees. On the other hand, when all the employees are represented by a single union, or a group of cooperating unions, this uneven bargaining position disappears and a consistent standard or criterion can be established.

It should be kept in mind that both unions and management bring such standards as community wage rates, industry wage rates, and rates for key jobs to the collective bargaining conference. Both groups should collect appropriate wage data because the economic stability of the industrial enterprise as well as employee security can be undermined by incorrect wage information. Collective bargaining deals with the absolute value of jobs, and both the company and the union should use some method of job evaluation to determine the relative value of jobs. This chapter deals with the determination of wages on the basis of present and community wage structures, and is not concerned with methods of collective bargaining which are directed toward absolute amounts. This aspect of wage determination is outside the scope of job evaluation.

SURVEYING THE WAGES

Comparable community and industry rates

It is sometimes considered desirable for an individual employer to be able to say that the rates in his plant are in line with community rates. This statement helps to prove that his plant is a good place in which to work. It helps to attract good workers by encouraging individuals to apply. It helps to maintain good employment relations. To be known as a plant with substandard or below-average wages is not desirable because it reduces the chances of obtaining satisfactory employees, lowers morale, and in the long run endangers the success of the enterprise.

It is not easy to tell whether the wages in a particular plant are in line with community rates for comparable jobs. In the first place, it is difficult in most communities to obtain accurate community rates. In the second place, it is quite difficult to determine comparable jobs. Such questions as "Are my assembly workers performing the same duties at the same job level as those used in the community wage survey?" and "Is my file clerk a File Clerk A or File Clerk B?" must be answered correctly before wage comparisons using the more common types of wage surveys can be made.

Nevertheless, it is important to know how the wage structure of the company compares with the wages in the community. Sometimes it is not possible to take community rates into consideration when pricing jobs, but it is possible to check the wage structure periodically to make sure that substandard wages are not being paid. Surveys of job rates made by chambers of commerce and trade associations may or may not have value in setting up a wage structure, depending upon whether the surveys were based upon job titles or job content. Community surveys, to be useful in establishing a wage structure, must be based not only on job content, but also on job difficulty.

The growth of large unions and the development of industry-wide collective bargaining has made it essential to study wage rates for entire industries. In those industries where industry-wide bargaining is the method for setting "minimum wage rates," wage reporting has attained a fairly high degree of accuracy. In some industries the member companies are preparing for the day when industry-wide collective bargaining will be the rule, by collecting wage data for key jobs.

Unions, of course, keep wage data for many key jobs. In fact, some union headquarters are as well informed, if not more so, about industry rates as are representative companies in the industry. Not very long ago wages were confidential, and it was considered unwise to reveal wage and salary data. The trend toward disclosure of wage information is a result of both union information and a management attempt to correct misinformation. Now that unions have a knowledge of the wage structures in most industries, and trade associations are active in collecting and reporting wage data, it is easier to secure sound wage information for specific industries to use in pricing the jobs of a single company.

One company has made it a practice to report its wage standing on a clerical community survey to its clerical employees, and a similar report based upon other surveys is made to factory employees. The evaluated jobs of this company are adjusted to the community and industry rates by setting all the rates in the upper third of the community and industry rates. This frank approach to wage-setting tends to promote a feeling of employee confidence in the company.

What are comparable community and industry rates? The answer is quite important. No company can stay in business if its rates are either abnormally high or low. On the one hand it would be handicapped by being in an unfavorable price position in relation to its competitors, and on the other it would have poor access to the labor market, except in a depression period. Observers of wage levels in any community find they vary considerably from industry to industry, and sometimes from city area to city area. Observers are also aware of the geographical differences in wage levels. Each company must determine its own wage community and must determine for itself the wage comparisons to be made. It can make itself look very bad if the comparison is with industry rates in general rather than the rates paid by its own industry. Certain of the service industries pay lower rates than do the more basic industries. Some companies manufacture products where the labor costs are the major consideration; in others, the labor costs are but a small fraction of the cost of the product. A slight change in wage level in one would have a tremendous influence on selling price of the product; in the other it might have no influence whatever. A sharp increase in wages for one industry—the laundry industry, for example— might result in its customers performing the service they formerly purchased. It cannot be over-emphasized that there is danger in an uncritical use of wage-survey information. Any user must be fully aware of the characteristics of the firms and organizations used to determine "community rates."

Matching point values and present rates

The most common method of establishing a wage curve is to base it upon the evaluated point values and the present company rates. This approach to wage administration assumes that the present wages are, for the most part, sound, and that the major fault is in the presence of inequities which should be corrected. The cost to the company involves the correction of inequities, and workers are usually assured that no wage will be reduced even though employees fall above the maximum.

No matter what method of pricing jobs is employed, it is worth while to obtain the relationship between point values and present wage rates. Before we determine what we want in a wage structure, it is important to see what we now have. Not only is it important to obtain a general wage curve; it is also important to obtain a curve for each type of job, clerical, factory, and supervisory, for which an evaluation study was made. It must be kept in mind that the point values are the best measure of relative differences among jobs that can be obtained. They represent a great deal of careful study and are specifically designed to measure the worth of jobs as compared to each other. It is of interest to note that their accuracy is usually judged by comparing them with such doubtful measures as present wages, traditional classification, and community and industrial rates. It should, of course, be the other way around. We should determine—and we shall, when job-evaluation methods are completely understood—the accuracy of plant, industry, and community wages by means of job evaluation.

The method for deriving wage curves is described below. Before the method is described, it is desirable to study ways and means of obtaining basic wage information, so that the wage curve will be based on sound data.

METHODS FOR CONDUCTING THE WAGE SURVEY

The methods of determining the monetary value for the job values obtained by job evaluation present certain problems. A new company coming in to an industrial area must key its rates into the community rates. An older company in a community wishing to add a new production unit has the problem of setting rates for the new jobs which are in line with both the community rates and the rates within the organization. Assuming that both types of organizations have completed a job-evaluation study, what procedures should they follow in establishing rates for each job? Discovery of wage rates paid in the community or industry calls for either the collection of material by an individual company or the utilization of wage data which have been collected by a civic or trade association. If an individual company makes a wage survey, it will probably not be very thorough or exhaustive. On the other hand, the more complete type of survey is usually out-of-date, and does not always reflect the present community or industry rates. The use of both sets of data is desirable.

At the present time many different methods are used to conduct wage surveys. Not only are different methods being used, but they are also being employed by a wide variety of organizations and individuals. Local companies, consultants, trade associations, professional organizations, governmental agencies, and non-profit institutions such as universities, community organizations, and associations of industries are making wage and salary surveys. Since these surveys are used by many companies, it is desirable to look at the advantages and disadvantages of the methods now in use. After a discussion of methods, illustrations of actual surveys and steps used in conducting them are given below. In general there are three methods of conducting a wage survey: job title, job description, and job evaluation.

Job-title survey

The most common and the simplest method is the telephone call or letter from one firm to another asking for wage information about specific jobs. An executive of Firm A might call one at a comparable level in Firm B, to ask what Firm B pays for keypunch operators, or laborers, or purchasing agents. With the increase in the number of personnel associations, and such associations as purchasing, traffic, engineering, management, and office, much wage comparison is carried out on a job title basis. Such wage comparisons are usually undertaken when a clerk or a laborer threatens to leave because he or she can get more money somewhere else. The method is quite informal, but because it has such a wide use it is necessary to examine it critically for possible inaccuracies.

Some possible inaccuracies are listed in a pamphlet, "How to

Make a Wage Survey," by Belcher and Heneman,[1] who point out that different duties may be performed by individuals on the jobs being surveyed in both organizations, so the wages are not directly comparable. In addition, a wage rate may be reported including or excluding overtime, shift differentials, and the like. Non-monetary factors, such as lunch and rest periods, free goods and services, or employee discounts may not be reported. The authors say that it is obvious that wage information resulting from this type of survey may not be adequate. It was because of the general inadequacy of this method that surveys based upon more complete descriptions of the job were undertaken. To develop this point further, the Research and Technical Report 4 of the Industrial Relations Center, University of Minnesota, reports on "Planning a Wage Survey" [2] as follows:

> Job titles alone are often meaningless. A bookkeeper in one organization may be doing work belonging to a recording clerk in another. One firm may have what is called a messenger doing the work which another firm assigns to the office boy. It is equally possible that two firms may have the same job titles attached to jobs having widely different duties. For instance, a bookkeeper in one organization may spend her days posting accounts payable, while a bookkeeper in another may check billing and send out "past due" notices. If wage information is asked for by job title under any of these circumstances, inaccuracies are bound to occur. It can be seen from this that proper comparison cannot be made unless the duties of the jobs being compared are definitely determined from well-constructed job descriptions.

Job-description survey

A common type of wage survey is to mail job descriptions or job definitions for selected jobs to cooperating companies and organizations. These firms are asked the wage rates for the jobs in their organizations which can be matched with the job descriptions. The rates requested may be the rates now paid to each employee, the average rates, the established base rates, the minimum and maximum rates, or base rates plus bonus. Rarely is an attempt made to verify the accuracy of "matching" company jobs with the job descriptions.

[1] David W. Belcher and Herbert G. Heneman, Jr. "How to Make a Wage Survey," Technical Report Series No. 2, Industrial Relations Center, University of Minnesota (Dubuque, Iowa: Wm. C. Brown Company, July 1948), p. 10.

[2] David W. Belcher, "Planning a Wage Survey," *Conducting Wage Surveys*, Research and Technical Report 4, Industrial Relations Center, University of Minnesota (Dubuque, Iowa: Wm. C. Brown Company, 1949), p. 10.

The job-description survey may be conducted by mail, or inter-viewers may contact each cooperating organization and work with each one in recording the data. The latter approach is perhaps the more accurate. In "How to Make a Wage Survey" [3] we find the following comments:

> The results obtained may depend on (1) the respondent's knowledge and understanding of job analysis, (2) the importance the respondent attaches to the survey, and (3) the general press of business. If question-naires are turned over to a payroll clerk for completion, he may fill in information by job title, thus subjecting the study to many of the inac-curies described above. Even where this is not done, the respondent's lack of understanding of job analysis coupled with the brevity of the enclosed job description may reduce the worth of the data.

Since the job-description approach is such an improvement over the job title approach, two illustrations are given below. It must be kept in mind that the use of carefully selected "key jobs" will make matching fairly accurate. However, for increased accuracy the methods discussed below are recommended. The possibility of ob-taining inaccurate wage information is sufficiently great through the use of both the job-title and job-description approaches that it might be desirable to show some of the risks involved. The Re-search and Technical Report 4 of the University of Minnesota In-dustrial Relations Center lists these risks as follows: [4]

> (1) all or part of an organization's work force may be lost because a reported job rate is used which refers to widely different duties; (2) con-sistent wage rate structures may be disrupted (with consequent employee dissatisfaction) as a result of acceptance of an incorrectly reported rate; (3) labor costs may be above competitive levels where rates reported are inaccurate; (4) negotiations may break down where one party to a dis-pute regards incorrect wage data as unalterable facts and refuses to com-promise; (5) expenditures for job evaluation plans may be wasted when such systems are installed in conformance with an inaccurate wage survey; (6) workers may be underpaid for the duties which they are performing.

As will be outlined below, care taken in the selection of key jobs, in the preparation of good job descriptions, in making sure that all ranges of skill are represented, and in matching jobs so that all col-lected wage data can be safely referred to job descriptions without distorting the final figures reduces the danger of securing incor-rect information.

---

[3] Belcher and Heneman, *op. cit.,* p. 4.
[4] Belcher, *op. cit.,* p. 11.

Job-evaluation survey

In certain instances several companies use the same job-evaluation manual. It is possible for these companies to survey on the basis of job-evaluation points. For example, the manual now in use by the National Metal Trades Association has been used by a large number of companies. Since the point values are the same, the companies have merely to call and ask what an organization is paying employees on jobs at a given point level. This puts an accuracy in wage surveys that is far superior to the job-description method mentioned above. Companies should be interested in how their wage structure compares with the structure of other companies. Since this method is quite similar to the job-evaluation wage-survey approach using key jobs, the discussion and illustrations below are designed to apply to both methods.

Job-evaluation wage survey using key jobs

In spite of the fact that some companies use the same job-evaluation manuals, the majority of companies having job evaluation use different job-evaluation manuals. In addition, it must be kept in mind that most companies do not have a formalized job-evaluation plan, and these companies must also be surveyed if the wage-survey data are to be truly representative. The usual method, for an organization conducting a wage survey that uses job evaluation as the way of determining comparability of jobs, is to select a number of key jobs ranging from those in the lowest labor grade to those in the highest labor grade. In one survey approach illustrated below, the key jobs were selected as those which would result in the same wage curve as was obtained by the entire number of jobs for the company from which the key job selection was made. In other words, the sample of key jobs should result in the same wage curve as the entire population of jobs.

Once the key jobs are selected, trained job analysts visit the cooperating companies, and meet with the wage administrators and other persons who are acquainted with the jobs. They select those jobs in the company which match the key jobs most closely on the basis of the job descriptions. The job analysts then proceed to rate the selected company jobs, and to make sure that all skill levels are represented. Point values are obtained for the company jobs. Wages are obtained for the employees on those jobs. The analysts then return to their office and construct a wage curve for the company.

This is in fact the wage structure of the company. The "wage structures" for all the cooperating companies are then combined into a single community wage structure.

The major disadvantage of this method is the cost. Its major advantage is its accuracy. A complete illustration of two approaches to this method of conducting a wage survey is given below. For the reader who is not fully acquainted with the derivation of a wage curve, it would be helpful to review that part of the chapter before studying the illustrations of the job-evaluation approach to making wage surveys.

ILLUSTRATIVE WAGE SURVEYS

The job-evaluation study should precede the collection of wage data. The jobs in the organization should each have a grade or point value and each one should be clearly identified, described, and specified, as discussed in Chapters 8 and 9. The exact knowledge of what wage data are necessary to price the company jobs makes it easier to collect the essential community wage data. We can now see the value of appropriate job titles, complete job descriptions, and accurate and meaningful job specifications. With these in hand, the comparison of jobs in two plants is relatively easy.

Illustrative job-description surveys

One of the oldest and best job-description surveys is the one carried out by the Ohio Bell Telephone Company. Many firms rely on these periodically reported figures, and become very skillful in using the material.

The collection of wage data involves considerable research. Useful data for approximately 76 jobs are periodically collected and distributed to cooperating firms by the Ohio Bell Telephone Company. These enable a company to study its wage rates for clerical jobs in comparison with the Ohio Bell Telephone Company sample. This survey was of value to the community in the establishment of fair rates during World War II, and it has been extremely valuable since that time to all companies interested in maintaining an acceptable wage level.

Figure 13-1 is a sample of the table and the instructions which are sent to participating companies. The form provides for reporting the number of employees at each wage and length-of-service level. Both a job title and a brief job description are included to help

JOB NO. 31 SECRETARY - DESCRIPTION #1 - FEMALE

PERFORMS SECRETARIAL WORK FOR AN ADMINISTRATIVE OR EXECUTIVE OFFICER, SUCH AS VICE PRESIDENT OR MANAGER OF MAJOR FUNCTIONAL OR GEOGRAPHIC BRANCH OF A COMPANY. GENERALLY RECORDS DICTATION AND PREPARES TYPED MATERIAL RELATING TO IMPORTANT OR CONFIDENTIAL MATTERS. WORK REQUIRES INITIATIVE, JUDGMENT, KNOWLEDGE AND ABILITY TO RELIEVE PRINCIPAL OF DESIGNATED ADMINISTRATIVE DETAILS AND TO ASSIST IN THE ORGANIZATION AND ADMINISTRATION OF OFFICE PROCEDURES BY THE PERFORMANCE OF SUCH DUTIES AS (1) DETERMINING PROPER DISPOSITION OF OR COMPOSING REPLIES TO INCOMING MAIL AND OTHER MATERIAL NOT REQUIRING THE ATTENTION OF THE PRINCIPAL AND ASSOCIATING REQUIRED INFORMATION WITH MATERIAL TO BE RE-FERRED TO THE PRINCIPAL, (2) RECEIVING VISITORS, ANSWERING TELEPHONES, SUPPLYING REQUESTED INFORMATION AND SCHEDULING APPOINTMENTS, (3) LOCATING AND OBTAINING INFORMATION FROM VARIOUS SOURCES WITHIN OR OUTSIDE THE COMPANY, (4) PREPARING SPECIAL REPORTS, SUMMARIES AND DIGESTS, AND (5) SETTING UP AND MAINTAINING SPECIAL FILES AND RECORDS. MAY SUPERVISE OR DIRECT THE WORK OF A SMALL GROUP OF STENOGRAPHIC OR CLERICAL EMPLOYEES.

EFFECTIVE MAXIMUM RATE $450.00

DOLLARS PER WEEK	DOLLARS PER MONTH								YEAR OF SERVICE										
		1	2	3	4	5	6	7	8	9	10	11	12	13-15	16-20	21-25	26 & OVER
107	476																1
	460															1	
104	451 - 454																
103	446 - 450																
102	442 - 445																
101	438 - 441																
100	433 - 437																
99	429 - 432																
98	425 - 428																
97	420 - 424																
96	416 - 419																
95	412 - 415																
94	407 - 411																
41	172 - 176																
40	172 - 176																
39	168 - 171																
38	164 - 167																
37	159 - 163							3									
36	155 - 158																
35	151 - 154																
34	146 - 150																
33	142 - 145																
32	138 - 141																
31	133 - 137																
30-29	129 - 132	1															

392

Ohio Bell Telephone Company.

"Effective maximum rate" is the wage which the usual employee can expect to attain when fully experienced in the work operations required in the occupation. If you adhere strictly to a formal wage schedule or a formal rate range, the top rate of the wage schedule or rate range should be shown. If you do not adhere to a formal schedule or range, show the rate which you consider as the normal "top" for the usual employee. Show your maximum rate for each of the occupations under which you report employees as indicated in the above sample.

To plot data on the grid, make one mark (/) for each employee in the vertical column showing the total length of service with your company and in the horizontal space corresponding to the basic wage rate. If you have more than one employee to be entered in any one space, show the total number, e.g. 3 and not ///. Note that the space for the first year of service is divided into quarters. The first column is for service up to and including three months, the second for service over three months to and including six months, etc.

The wage scale is shown in weekly and monthly rates. The weekly rates should be reported to the nearest dollar on the grids scaled by $1.00 intervals, e.g., rates ranging from $30.50 to $31.49 are reported opposite "31". On the grids scaled by $2.00 weekly intervals (male jobs only), the rate shown and the next higher dollar rate are included on the same line. For example, rates for "34" and "35" are reported opposite "34", covering rates from $33.50 to $35.49 per week. If you report on a monthly basis, the rates to be included on each line are shown in the monthly column.

The entries in the sample above illustrate the plotting of the data for seven employees with wage rates and service as follows:

1. A Secretary receiving $29.25 per week with 2 months of service would be entered in the first vertical column; since this rate is not within the grid scale, the $30 rate is crossed out and $29 entered with the employee shown opposite this rate.

2. Three Secretaries receiving $35.25 per week with 6 years and 4 months, 6 years and 6 months, and 6 years and 10 months of service would be entered in the vertical column "7" opposite the weekly rate of "35".

3. A Secretary receiving $460.00 per month with 20 years and 3 months of service would be entered in the vertical column "21-25" opposite the rate "460" written in on one of the blank spaces at the top of the grid.

4. A Secretary receiving $106.60 per week with 24 years and 8 months of service would be entered in the vertical column "21-25" opposite the rate "107" written in on one of the blank spaces at the top of the grid.

5. A Secretary receiving $475.50 per month with 25 years and 6 months service would be entered in the vertical column "26 & over" opposite the rate "476" written in one of the blank spaces at the top of the grid.

Three blank rows are provided at the top of the grid for entering each rate which is over or under the scale of rates shown. If more extra spaces are needed, cross out any rates which have not been used and enter the rate in the appropriate weekly or monthly column.

Fig. 13—1 (cont.).

participating firms identify the jobs. General instructions for recording wage-rate data are as follows:

1. Do not report by titles. Before entering your own wage rates and service records, read carefully the description for each occupation and determine which of your non-supervisory employees are in jobs that fit those described. Report the wage rates and service of only these employees. Your jobs which do not fit the descriptions in this report should be omitted. Usually not all clerical employees will be reported.

2. There are a variety of practices in effect that cause variations in salary rates and hours worked per week for clerical employees. In order to provide data that will be comparable and useful to the fullest extent, it is necessary to have all reports on a uniform basis. The rates reported should be the rates for the basic week or month *including any cost of living supplementary payments* but should *not include overtime.* Service should be reported according to "in year of service" and not completed years of service.

3. The method to be followed in reporting data is illustrated on the following page [Figure 13-1]. Note item immediately below each female job description—"Effective Maximum Rate"—for which instructions are given on the next page. If for any reason this space is not used, please write "none" in the proper space for each job under which employees have been reported.[5]

Two clerical jobs were selected, one female and one male, to illustrate the results of the Ohio Bell Telephone Company Survey made in the fall of 1952. In Figure 13–2 Job No. 13, *Payroll Clerk,* illustrates the wage results obtained for that position in the fall of 1952. Figure 13–3 shows Job No. 73, *Draftsman,* chosen to show the wage data for a male position. It is of interest to note the wide spread of wages in each of these two positions.

The National Office Management Association has conducted salary surveys which are reported both nationally and locally. In their collection of salary data, job descriptions are used to identify positions. These job descriptions are illustrated in Figure 13–4.[6] It can be seen that these definitions are quite brief; however, they are carefully written and serve to identify the jobs. Local committees are formed and report data to a national committee. There were 3,426 companies in 79 cities in the United States and 307 companies in eight Canadian cities in the 1952 survey. Both the median wage and the average wage are reported. The survey also reports the

---

[5] *Survey of Basic Salary Rates, Clerical Employees,* Cleveland Industrial Area, Ohio Bell Telephone Company (October 1952). The authors are indebted for permission to quote extensively.

[6] "Office Salaries," Survey Summary Number 14 of National Office Management Association (1952), p. 5.

number of companies participating and the total employees reported. Figure 13–5 [7] illustrates data reported for some of the eastern cities.

Such broad surveys are impossible for a single company to make. It is necessary, therefore, for a company making its own survey to select a limited number of jobs, usually referred to as bench-mark jobs, and to obtain wage data for them from a small sample of representative companies.

Job analysts have found that for some plants the ratio of employees to jobs is approximately 4 to 1, and some studies have shown a ratio as low as 3 employees to each job. In a plant employing 400 employees there might be as many as 135 jobs. It is necessary to secure wage data for a sufficient number of bench-mark jobs in order to obtain a fair comparison.

Illustrative job-evaluation wage surveys

With the exception of industry-wide surveys using the same job-evaluation manuals, there are no illustrations of job-evaluation wage surveys where data are gathered by making complete job evaluations using a uniform job-rating plan. There is no doubt that the best wage comparisons can be made in any community by having representative companies use the same job-evaluation manual and compare entire wage systems rather than the wages for a relatively few isolated key jobs.

A modification of the method of using the same manual for all jobs was suggested by Bass,[8] who recommends that a number of key jobs be evaluated by a uniform point system. He suggests that after a wage line is drawn for each plant (based on the point value for the key jobs and wages paid to the employees on those jobs), an average wage line be constructed. This would, if the company and jobs were truly representative, be a community wage curve. It is believed that in time this method will be the one most commonly used in making community wage surveys. One large eastern corporation has conducted a series of community wage surveys using the job-evaluation method (factor comparison) on selected key jobs, and expresses confidence in the results. The two illustrative surveys given below are taken from surveys conducted in the Cleveland area, one for office positions and one for factory positions.

---

[7] *Ibid,* p. 8.

[8] A. W. Bass, Jr., "How Do Your Wage Rates Compare with Those of Your Community?" *Iron Age,* 140, No. 25 (December 16, 1937), pp. 36–39.

JOB NO. 13 PAYROLL CLERK - DESCRIPTION #2 - FEMALE
ASSISTS IN THE PREPARATION OF PAYROLLS AND MAY COMPLETE SIMPLE PAYROLLS; WORK GENERALLY INVOLVES SIMPLE CALCULATIONS OR THE DETERMINATION OF SUCH ITEMS AS SIMPLE TAX OR AUTHORIZED DEDUCTIONS FROM PREPARED TABLES. GENERALLY PERFORMS SUCH DETAILED AND REPETITIVE OPERATIONS AS POSTING RECORD OF TIME WORKED FROM CLOCK CARDS OR OTHER RECORDS, POSTING DATA TO INDIVIDUAL EMPLOYEE OR MASTER RECORDS, COMPUTING EARNINGS BY MEANS OF CALCULATOR CHARTS OR CALCULATING MACHINE WHERE THE DATA TO BE USED ARE READILY IDENTIFIABLE AND OF A RECURRING NATURE, SUMMARIZING TIME TICKETS, ASSISTING IN PREPARATION OF PAY CHECKS OR PAY ENVELOPES, AND COMPUTING TOTALS. MAY USE TYPEWRITER OR OFFICE MACHINES FOR SIMPLE STANDARDIZED OPERATIONS IN PORTIONS OF THE WORK.

	NUMBER OF COMPANIES	MAXIMUM RATE	AVERAGE WEEKLY WAGE	AVERAGE MONTHLY WAGE	AVG. YRS. OF SERVICE
MAXIMUM RATE	49		$67.91	$295	
GOING RATE	66		$58.33	$254	3.5

DOLLARS PER WEEK	DOLLARS PER MONTH	1	2	3	4	5	6	7	8	9	10	11	12	13-15	16-20	21-25	26 & OVER	TOTAL
104	451 - 454																	
103	446 - 450																	
102	442 - 445																	
101	438 - 441																	
100	433 - 437																	
99	429 - 432																	
98	425 - 428																	
97	420 - 424																	
96	416 - 419																	
95	412 - 415																	
94	407 - 411																	
93	403 - 406																	
92	399 - 402																	
91	394 - 398																	
90	390 - 393																	
89	385 - 389																	
88	381 - 384																	
87	377 - 380																	
86	372 - 376																	
85	368 - 371																	
84	364 - 367																	
83	359 - 363																	
82	355 - 358																	
81	351 - 354																	
80	346 - 350																	
79	342 - 345																	
78	338 - 341																	
77	333 - 337																	

YEAR OF SERVICE

No.	Range
75	325 - 328
74	320 - 324
73	315 - 319
72	312 - 315
71	307 - 311
70	303 - 306
69	298 - 302
68	294 - 297
67	290 - 293
66	285 - 289
65	281 - 284
64	277 - 280
63	272 - 276
62	268 - 271
61	264 - 267
60	259 - 263
59	255 - 258
58	251 - 254
57	246 - 250
56	242 - 245
55	238 - 241
54	233 - 237
53	229 - 232
52	225 - 228
51	220 - 224
50	216 - 219
49	211 - 215
48	207 - 210
47	203 - 206
46	198 - 202
45	194 - 197
44	190 - 193
43	185 - 189
42	181 - 184
41	177 - 180
40	172 - 176
39	168 - 171
38	164 - 167
37	159 - 163
36	155 - 158
35	151 - 154
34	146 - 150
33	142 - 145
32	138 - 141
31	133 - 137
30	129 - 132
TOTAL	25 20 10 19 30 30 9 7 2 3 2 2 5 3 7 3 2 142

JOB NO. 73 DRAFTSMAN – MALE

PREPARES DRAWINGS OF MACHINERY, EQUIPMENT, WIRINGS, INSTRUMENTS, TOOLS, JIGS, FIXTURES AND ACCESSORIES FOLLOWING DESIGNS, SKETCHES OR REVISED PRINTS. RESPONSIBLE FOR COMPLETENESS AND CORRECTNESS OF VIEWS AND DIMENSIONS. PREPARES BILLS OF MATERIAL AND LISTS OF PARTS AS REQUIRED. MAY OCCASIONALLY DESIGN SIMPLE MECHANISMS, TOOLS, JIGS, FIXTURES, ETC.

		NUMBER OF COMPANIES	AVERAGE WEEKLY WAGE	AVERAGE MONTHLY WAGE	AVG. YRS. OF SERVICE
MAXIMUM RATE		XXX	XXX	XXX	
GOING RATE		72	$88.88	$387	5.1

Fig. 13—3. Community wage data—male draftsman.

Community Salary Survey—Federal Reserve Bank of Cleveland.
This survey was sponsored by the Federal Reserve Bank of Cleveland, and was carried out by the Personnel Research Institute of Western Reserve University. Since 1948 the Federal Reserve Bank

of Cleveland has been keeping this survey up-to-date, so it is relatively easy for organizations using the survey to compare their jobs or wage structure with the obtained community rates. The 1948 method has been modified so that it is now a combination of the job description and job evaluation methods. The material below is taken from the report made to the Federal Reserve Bank of Cleveland for its 1948 survey.[9]

Introduction—These salary surveys are based on the comparison of difficulty levels of jobs with the salaries paid to employees on those jobs. Cooperating firms covered in this study include industries, utilities, and banks, of which 17 organizations are in Cleveland, 10 in Pittsburgh, and 9 in Cincinnati.

Method Used—The same method used in making the 1947 Salary Survey was used in the 1948 study. Fifty-six representative jobs were selected from the jobs found in the Federal Reserve Bank of Cleveland. Analysts thoroughly familiar with these jobs were sent to cooperating firms where they reviewed the 56 key jobs with a company representative and selected company jobs which matched the Federal Reserve Bank jobs. Each analyst tried not only to match the 56 key jobs, but also tried to select additional jobs so that an adequate number of jobs at the low, intermediate, and high levels of difficulty would be obtained from each cooperating organization.

After the analyst and company representative had selected the company jobs to be used in the study, the analyst wrote a complete job specification for each job in terms of the factors found in the job evaluation manual. Then, using the Federal Reserve job evaluation manual, a point value, or difficulty value, was determined for each job in each cooperating organization. The job specifications and point ratings made it possible to match jobs on the basis of difficulty rather than on the basis of job description or job title. Regardless of the job title, jobs rated at the same total point value are approximately equal in difficulty and the salaries of employees on these jobs can be compared. In addition to determining the difficulty level for each job included in the list of representative jobs, the analyst also recorded the number of employees on each job, the actual salary paid to each employee, the minimum and maximum salaries of each job, and other pertinent data.

The salary curve derived for each organization shows the relationship between the difficulty of the jobs and the salaries paid to the employees on the jobs. Because representative jobs were selected and a fairly large sample of employees was secured for each organization, the salary curve can be considered a relatively accurate representation of the present salary structure of each cooperating company. Insofar as the industries, utilities, and banks are representative of their groups, the combined salary curves are representative of each of the three groups.

[9] The authors are indebted to the Federal Reserve Bank of Cleveland for permission to use the material from the Cleveland Community Salary Survey.

Using the difficulty or point values of the company jobs, these jobs were placed into the classification structure of the Federal Reserve Bank of Cleveland. This made it possible to compare the salaries paid by the Federal Reserve Bank with the salaries paid by cooperating organizations. These comparisons can be made for each job class according to the mini-

JOB TITLES & DESCRIPTIONS

1   ACCOUNTING CLERK - A (SENIOR BOOKKEEPER)

Keeps a complete and systematic set of accounting records. Examines and records the transactions in proper record books, journalizing transactions where judgment must be used as to accounts affected. Balances books and compiles reports at regular intervals.

2   ACCOUNTING CLERK - B (JUNIOR BOOKKEEPER)

Keeps a record of and works with less than a complete set of accounting records. May perform the more routine calculating and posting duties necessary in accounting; verifying the company bank account; keeping files of records; preparing invoices or monthly customer's statements; posting to and balancing accounts receivable or accounts payable sections; taking trial balances.

3   BOOKKEEPING MACHINE OPERATOR

Operates bookkeeping machine, with or without typewriter keyboard, and performs related clerical duties.

4   CLERK, GENERAL - A (SENIOR)

Performs routine clerical duties under supervision such as compiling or posting data on records or performing similar work of average difficulty. Requires some experience and the ability to complete assignments with a minimum of difficulty.

5   CLERK, GENERAL - B (JUNIOR)

Performs duties of simple or repetitive nature such as sorting, posting, checking, copying and addressing envelopes. Duties performed require little previous experience and a minimum of judgment.

6   MAIL CLERK

Processes incoming and outgoing mail. May operate related machines and equipment and perform other minor office duties.

7   MESSENGER

Delivers letters, messages, packages and other items within an establishment or to other concerns. May keep simple records and perform other minor office duties.

8   PAYROLL CLERK

Computes wages of company employees and writes the proper data on payroll sheets; calculates each worker's earnings based on timekeeper's report, individual time cards, and work or production tickets; posts calculated data on payroll sheet (such as name of worker, working days, time rate, deductions and total wages due). May make out pay checks and assist paymaster in making up and distributing pay envelopes.

9   TABULATING MACHINE OPERATOR

Operates a machine that automatically analyzes, makes calculations and translates or divides information represented by holes punched in groups of tabulating cards, and prints the translated data on form sheets, reports, special cards or accounting records. Sets or adjusts machine to add, subtract, multiply and make other calculations. May operate auxiliary machines.

10   KEY PUNCH MACHINE OPERATOR

Records accounting and statistical data in tabulating cards by punching a series of holes in specified sequence, using a key punch machine. May operate a verifying machine.

11   ADDRESSING MACHINE OPERATOR

Operates machine which uses stencils or plates for mechanical addressing of any type. May prepare original stencil or plate and is responsible for accuracy of processing.

Courtesy of the National Office Management Association.

Fig. 13—4.

12 CALCULATING MACHINE OPERATOR

Primarily occupied in operation of a machine that performs the arithmetic computations of adding, subtracting, multiplying, and dividing.

13 DUPLICATING MACHINE OPERATOR

Operates stencil, fluid (spirit), or simple offset type office duplicator. Responsible for mechanical operation, quality, and accuracy of work. May prepare stencils or masters.

14 FILE CLERK

Systematically classifies, indexes and files correspondence, cards, invoices, receipts and other records; locates and removes material from file on request. May keep a record of material removed.

15 RECEPTIONIST

Receives and routes visitors. Keeps related records and may perform incidental clerical duties.

16 SECRETARY, PRIVATE

Fully qualified stenographer to senior executive(s). Performs work of a confidential and technical nature. Takes dictation by shorthand and/or transcribing machine. Schedules appointments. Handles telephone calls. Has thorough knowledge required of routines, personnel, functions, and policies to relieve executive(s) of minor duties.

17 SECRETARY - STENOGRAPHER

Performs secretarial duties for one or more executives. Takes dictation by shorthand and/or transcribing machine. May be required to be versed in the technical language of a particular business. Relieves executives served of minor office details and duties.

18 STENOGRAPHER - A (SENIOR)

Records and transcribes dictation of more than average difficulty by use of shorthand and/or transcribing machine. Requires knowledge of proper letter forms and complicated set-ups. Must be familiar with company organization and routines. May perform related clerical duties. Works under general supervision, but must use judgment. May work in a stenographic pool.

19 STENOGRAPHER - B (JUNIOR)

Takes and transcribes from shorthand notes or from dictating machine, routine dictation involving generally used business terms and expressions. Must have general knowledge of company routines and set-ups. May type requisitions, orders, schedules, checks. May work in a stenographic pool under direct supervision.

20 TRANSCRIBING MACHINE OPERATOR

Transcribes the message, reproduced in sound, from a recording device on a transcribing machine. May type other supplementary information not recorded.

21 TYPIST - A (SENIOR)

Does general typing requiring the exercise of judgment and assumption of responsibility in carrying out assignments, involving statistical, rough draft material, copying of technical or unusual business correspondence of other materials. May cut stencils. Must be accurate, with ability to lay out and arrange work. Dictation not required.

22 TYPIST - B (JUNIOR)

Does typing of simple, routine nature, copying from plain printed or written material, corrected copy, simple form letters, reports, charts; may cut stencils and address envelopes. Able to type accurately, with fair speed. Dictation not required.

23 TELEPHONE OPERATOR

Operates switchboard handling incoming, outgoing and intra-company calls. Keeps a record of long distance calls; is responsible for checking telephone calls. May have incidental duties. Requires a good knowledge of personnel of establishment; works communication system. May work paging and public address system and/or plant music player.

Fig. 13—4 (cont.).

mum, maximum, and present salaries paid. Tables were constructed for each of the Federal Reserve Bank's job classes.

A sample table showing level IV jobs is found in Figure 13–6. A company knowing the point range for level IV jobs can compare its level IV jobs with the community minimums, maximums, and going rates. It can also see the kind of jobs which tend to fall at level IV, although this information is given more to illustrate the type of work rather than the exact job.

#	Job Class
1	ACCOUNTING CLERK A
2	ACCOUNTING CLERK B
3	BOOKKEEPING MACH. OP.
4	CLERK, GENERAL-A
5	CLERK, GENERAL-B
6	MAIL CLERK
7	MESSENGER
8	PAYROLL CLERK
9	TABULATING MACH. OP.
10	KEY PUNCH OP.
11	ADDRESSING MACH. OP.
12	CALCULATING MACH. OP.
13	DUPLICATING MACH. OP.
14	FILE CLERK
15	RECEPTIONIST
16	SECRETARY - PRIVATE
17	SECRETARY - STENO.
18	STENOGRAPHER A
19	STENOGRAPHER B
20	TRANSCRIBING MACH. OP.
21	TYPIST A
22	TYPIST B
23	TELEPHONE OPERATOR

NEW YORK — Joseph Burton, Chairman, Van Raalte Company

SUMMARY DATA	1	2	3	4	5	6	7	8	9	10	11	12	13	14	15	16	17	18	19	20	21	22	23
MEDIAN WEEKLY RATE (A)	75	58	55	61	47	45	40	69	62	53	50	56	50	43	55	75	65	59	50	57	51	45	58
TOTAL COMPANIES REPORTED (B)	81	82	59	100	91	78	69	59	43	47	40	44	49	108	65	103	105	90	66	50	96	81	111
AVERAGE WEEKLY RATE (C)	76	59	57	62	48	45	42	67	63	53	51	58	51	45	56	78	66	60	52	59	52	47	58
TOTAL EMPLOYEES REPORTED (D)	377	418	393	144	185	289	679	260	333	641	128	348	119	1116	165	1202	1733	1503	749	278	1232	1039	307

NEWARK — Jacob J. Bessler, Chairman, Socony Paint Products

SUMMARY DATA	1	2	3	4	5	6	7	8	9	10	11	12	13	14	15	16	17	18	19	20	21	22	23
MEDIAN WEEKLY RATE (A)	80	57	55	50	47	45	41	56	52	50	50	55	50	46	59	76	66	55	50	53	52	46	55
TOTAL COMPANIES REPORTED (B)	60	65	53	87	77	60	39	70	37	37	26	33	29	66	37	70	75	56	42	26	60	51	91
AVERAGE WEEKLY RATE (C)	81	62	59	59	48	46	42	62	60	52	52	58	53	47	61	78	66	60	52	59	52	47	58
TOTAL EMPLOYEES REPORTED (D)	200	339	173	1946	1743	253	257	235	450	372	87	368	65	660	51	545	865	644	407	132	609	773	186

PHILADELPHIA — John R. Jones, Chairman, Rohm & Haas

SUMMARY DATA	1	2	3	4	5	6	7	8	9	10	11	12	13	14	15	16	17	18	19	20	21	22	23
MEDIAN WEEKLY RATE (A)	82	60	46	57	42	44	37	56	62	51	44	55	48	40	53	72	63	57	48	51	49	44	53
TOTAL COMPANIES REPORTED (B)	66	77	69	98	80	53	55	61	47	45	43	43	33	68	28	84	85	80	64	46	72	68	99
AVERAGE WEEKLY RATE (C)	80	58	51	59	45	45	40	58	61	52	46	55	49	43	52	73	63	57	48	51	52	44	53
TOTAL EMPLOYEES REPORTED (D)	930	820	458	2045	2139	217	328	259	289	416	167	430	103	572	41	793	784	948	505	249	783	762	253

PITTSBURGH — Paul R. Fry, Chairman, The Manufacturer's Light and Heat Co.

SUMMARY DATA	1	2	3	4	5	6	7	8	9	10	11	12	13	14	15	16	17	18	19	20	21	22	23
MEDIAN WEEKLY RATE (A)	84	66	51	59	46	42	40	63	61	50	47	51	51	40	52	77	66	55	50	48	47	45	55
TOTAL COMPANIES REPORTED (B)	40	38	29	46	42	32	28	37	27	30	18	28	20	31	23	47	42	40	38	16	35	37	46
AVERAGE WEEKLY RATE (C)	83	66	52	60	47	46	41	62	64	50	48	53	51	44	53	77	66	55	50	48	47	45	55
TOTAL EMPLOYEES REPORTED (D)	172	194	182	904	1079	69	236	101	126	206	41	124	53	249	49	266	450	569	468	52	349	281	141

PORTLAND, ME. — Walter C. Christensen, Chairman, The Thos. Laughlin Co.

SUMMARY DATA	1	2	3	4	5	6	7	8	9	10	11	12	13	14	15	16	17	18	19	20	21	22	23
MEDIAN WEEKLY RATE (A)	72	50	40	49	50	53	33	50	55	46	39	51	47	36	54	54	48	52	49	31	46	48	54
TOTAL COMPANIES REPORTED (B)	12	11	8	15	12	5	8	12	5	5	3	5	4	8	4	8	5	5	2	7	5	12	
AVERAGE WEEKLY RATE (C)	68	51	43	50	49	49	35	51	53	46	42	50	55	38	49	55	50	50	48	38	45	48	49
TOTAL EMPLOYEES REPORTED (D)	18	26	32	147	122	5	14	43	16	21	10	11	7	18	4	38	39	41	26	5	16	67	18

PROVIDENCE — Wilfred W. Carter, Chairman, Nicholson File Co.

SUMMARY DATA	1	2	3	4	5	6	7	8	9	10	11	12	13	14	15	16	17	18	19	20	21	22	23
MEDIAN WEEKLY RATE (A)	65	56	48	45	40	42	35	52	55	46	41	49	42	38	50	60	50	48	40	45	43	38	47
TOTAL COMPANIES REPORTED (B)	30	33	22	44	37	13	17	37	15	16	8	17	12	26	13	32	42	35	20	8	30	24	44
AVERAGE WEEKLY RATE (C)	68	54	46	49	43	43	38	51	55	46	42	50	47		62	52	48	43	45	44	39	47	
TOTAL EMPLOYEES REPORTED (D)	101	83	67	525	339	25	25	140	51	99	11	108	16	132	13	128	189	362	98	24	268	229	105

Courtesy of the National Office Management Association.

Fig. 13—5. Wage data for bench-mark jobs.

Table I

DISTRIBUTION OF JOBS BY MINIMUM AND MAXIMUM WAGES

WAGE RATE	95–104	105–114	115–124	125–134	135–144	145–154	155–164	165–174	175–184	185–194	195–204	
NO. OF JOBS MINIMUM	1		4	15	11	4	15	4	5	1	1	

WAGE RATE	LESS THAN 155	155–164	165–174	175–184	185–194	195–204	205–214	215–224	225–234	235–244	245–254	MORE THAN 255
NO. OF JOBS MAXIMUM	1	2	12	8	8	9	4	5	3	3	2	4

List of Jobs in Level IV

Invoice Typist
Clerk—Typist
Key Punch Operator
Clerk (A)
Clerk (B)
Typist—Clerk
Clerk—Stenographer
Incentive and Time Clerk II
Tabulating Machine Operator
Addressing Machine Clerk
Messenger "A"
Teletype Operator
Medium Clerk—Mail Clerk—Typist
Medium Clerk—Key Punch
Elevator Starter
Blue Print Machine Operator and Clerk
Payroll Clerk
Bookkeeping Machine Operator
Telephone Operator
File Clerk
Building Office Stenographer
Clerk, General (Cost Dept.)
Senior Typist
Detailer
Routing Typist
Steno-Clerk
Check Collection Stenographer
Proof Machine Operator

Comptometer Operator II
Clerk—Typist or Statistical Typist
Stenographer
Junior Draftsman
Personnel Clerk
Typist—Stenographic Pool
Addressograph Operator
Repair Clerk
Payroll Control Clerk
Addressing and Printing Machine
    Operator
Statistical Typist "A"
Senior Clerk
Typist
Account Records Clerk
Stationery Supply Clerk
General Clerk, Junior
Machine Bookkeeper
Stock Clerk
Analysis Clerk
Stockkeeper and Receiving Clerk
Junior Checking Clerk
Senior Key Punch Operator
Stock Records Clerk
Disbursement Clerk
Secretary to Senior Night Personnel
    Supervisor
Junior Stenographer

Table II

DISTRIBUTION OF INDIVIDUALS BY WAGES

GOING RATE	LESS THAN 135	135–144	145–154	155–164	165–174	175–184	185–194	195–204	205–214	215–224	225–234	MORE THAN 235
NO. OF INDIVIDUALS	9	26	47	62	47	72	34	47	12	60	6	9

Conducted for the Federal Reserve Bank of Cleveland by the Personnel
Research Institute of Western Reserve University, February, 1948.

Fig. 13—6. Cleveland Community Salary Survey—Level IV jobs.

In addition to reporting the findings by means of tables, charts showing the relationship between actual wages paid and point values were also constructed. This method of presenting wage data is quite useful in making wage comparisons. Figure 13–7, All Participants, shows the wage curves of all the industries, utilities, and banks surveyed in the Cleveland area. This figure illustrates the great variability in wage payment for jobs at the same difficulty level

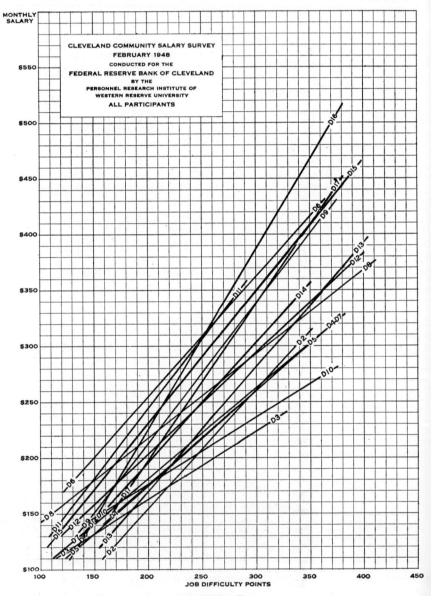

Fig. 13—7.

in a single community. For example, organization D–10 pays about
$268 for jobs falling at the 350-point level and D–16 pays approximately $470. This illustrates the caution necessary in making wage
comparisons. Figure 13–8 All Participants—1947 & 1948, shows the
change in salary level by job-difficulty level which occurred between
1947 and 1948. Errors in sampling and in rating jobs must be kept in
mind when interpreting this change.

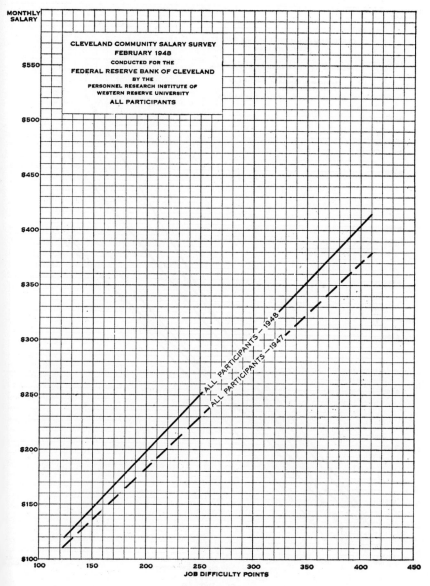

Fig. 13—8.

Figure 13–9, Reporting Industrial Companies, shows a more homogeneous picture. Even here we find considerable company difference. The salary range at the 350-point difficulty level is from $340 for company D–12 to $470 for D–16. The companies included in this survey represent the most progressive in the Cleveland area. The comparison of 1947 and 1948 wage curves for the industrial companies is shown in Figure 13–10. The greatest wage or salary

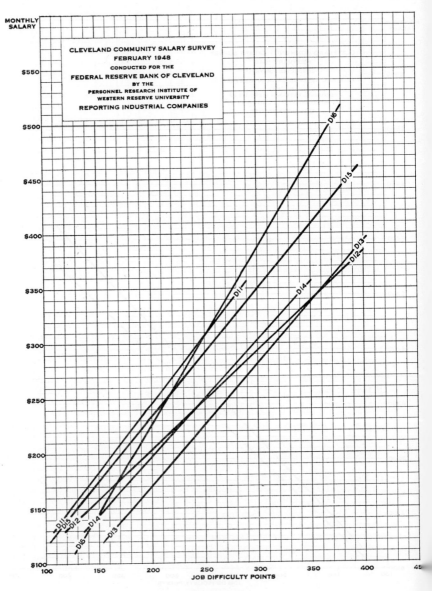

Fig. 13—9.

change was in those jobs at the high skill level. The reporting banks are more homogeneous in salary structure than the industrial participants. Figure 13–11 shows very little salary spread at any difficulty level. Figure 13–12 shows practically no salary change from 1947 to 1948. It is of interest to note the difference in salaries for the local utilities. Figure 13–13, Reporting Utility Companies— 1947 & 1948, indicates a real wage change which is fairly constant

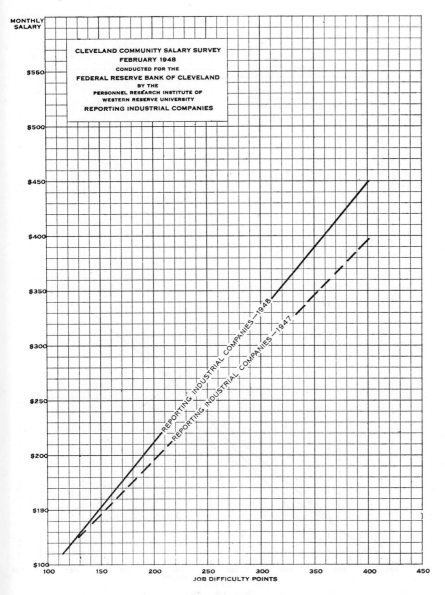

Fig. 13—10.

along the entire difficulty range. A careful study of all of the figures just described shows how complex the administration of wages in a single community can be. It also shows the necessity for a careful examination of the figures used to make wage comparisons.

This survey has been repeated annually and, although the method of reporting data has changed, the basic job-evaluation approach has been retained. These data are of real value for any company willing

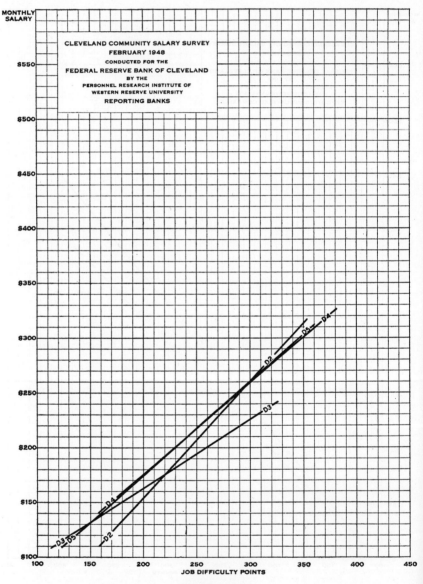

Fig. 13—11.

to evaluate its jobs using the Federal Reserve Bank manual. It is an application of the job-evaluation method to the collection of salary data for clerical and middle supervisory jobs. The next illustration is one conducted by the Associated Industries of Cleveland and shows how this same approach can be used to collect wage data for factory positions.

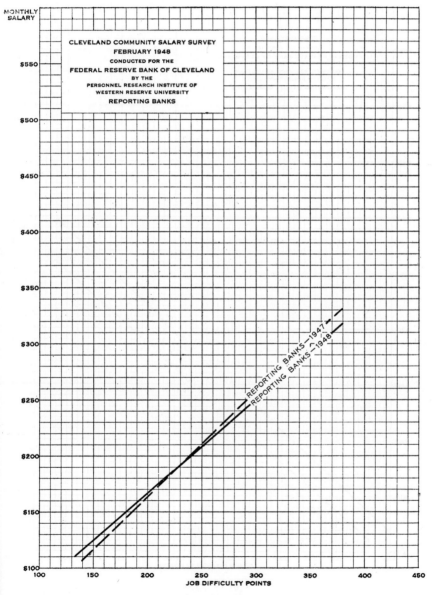

Fig. 13—12.

Community Wage Survey—Associated Industries of Cleveland.
Using the method of job-evaluation wage survey by means of bench-
mark jobs, the Associated Industries of Cleveland have been making
factory wage surveys since 1951. The resulting data are extremely
useful and approach an accuracy level which is worthy of notice.
Sixty-two key or bench-mark jobs most frequently found in every

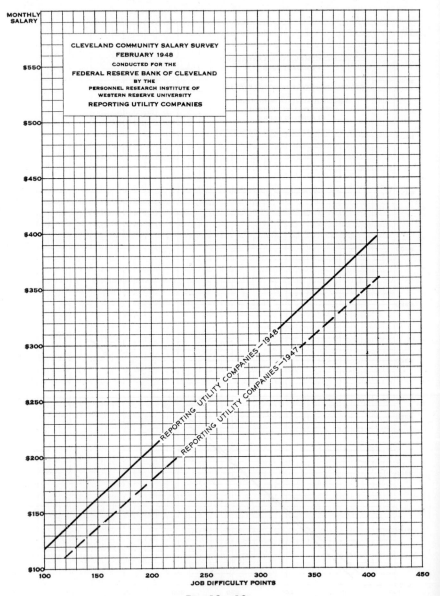

Fig. 13—13.

JOB DATA SHEET

Company Code No. ....

JOB DESCRIPTION*

Your Job Title: (If different). . . . . . . .Package Packer. . . . .

Packs a variety of products in standard containers according to pre-scribed practices. Work is repetitive. May perform simple visual inspections and do some wrapping.

INSTRUCTIONS (Please use red pencil for markings)

Non-Incentive Job:—(Lines 1 & 2 Below)

A non-incentive job is one wherein the individual's rate **does not** include any extra hourly premium, such as, piecework, bonuses, or similar incentives.

Report each regular hourly rate, exclusive of shift allowances and overtime, in Line 2, and also the number of persons at each rate in Line 1.

Incentive Jobs:—(Lines 3 & 4 Below)

An incentive job is one wherein the individual's rate **does** include extra hourly premiums **based on output**, such as, piecework, bonuses, or similar incentives.

Report each different average hourly earning, exclusive of shift allowances and overtime, in Line 4, and also the number of persons earning each average in Line 3.

Important!

Do not report under both headings unless you have both non-incentive and incentive workers on this job.

Minimum Guarantee:—(Lines 5 & 6 on Reverse Side)

Hourly rate which is guaranteed to the individual **normally** engaged on incentive jobs for performing work where no standard or piece rate is available and for other occurrences, such as, waiting for materials, tools, or repairs.

Report in Line 6 each different hourly minimum guaranteed rate, exclusive of shift allowance and overtime, and the number of persons at each rate in Line 5.

0—Non-Incentive:

Line 1															Number of Persons
Line 2															Hourly Rate

1—Incentive:

Number of Persons

Line 3	1	2	3	3	1	2	3	3	1	3	2	1	1	1
Line 4	1.05	1.06	1.15	1.18	1.20	1.23	1.25	1.28	1.30	1.33	1.38	1.40	1.48	1.50

Average Hourly Earnings

1—Incentive: (Continued).

Line 3															Number of Persons
Line 4															Average Hourly Earnings

If established minimum and maximum hourly rates are available report here: { Minimum. . . . . . .1.03. . . . . / Maximum. . . . . . .1.13. . . . .

(6)

2—Minimum Guarantee:

Number of Persons

Line 5	1	2	1	18	1	4						-
Line 6	1.03	1.05	1.06	1.07	1.12	1.13						

Hourly Minimum Guarantee Rate

Associated Industries of Cleveland Wage Survey.

Fig. 13—14. Sample job data sheet—package packer.

type of industry were selected. The questionnaire method is used to collect data. The illustrative material is taken from the first survey of this type conducted by this organization.

The questionnaire consists of a number of sections, all designed to make it possible for the participants to be consistent in submitting data. The section on instructions is followed by sections on definition of terms, code of typical key words, a general data sheet, sample copy of a questionnaire filled out for the job of Package Packer, and job-rating or job-specification sheets for the factors of Skill Requirements, Physical Effort, and Working Conditions. A job-data sheet is included for each of the key jobs which the respondent is to fill out. The instructions to the companies furnishing wage information are as follows: [10]

INSTRUCTIONS
STATISTICS ARE VALUABLE ONLY TO THE EXTENT THAT THEY ARE TRUE, ACCURATE, AND COMPLETE

In order to insure the greatest value of this Survey to you, to all participants, and to the Associated Industries of Cleveland, we ask that you *carefully read and follow the instructions below.*
To facilitate the task of submitting these data a step-by-step outline has been prepared illustrating the procedure to be followed in completing this wage survey.

STEP I   Read the DEFINITION OF TERMS USED and CODE OF TYPICAL KEY WORDS. This is merely an attempt to acquaint the reader with the connotation given certain key terms used in the job description so that a more accurate relationship between company jobs and survey jobs can be established.

STEP II   Fill out GENERAL DATA SHEET. Note items followed by arrow which are to be entered in margin; all other entries are to be made in main body of form. This sheet is to be detached and returned with all Job Data Sheets.

STEP III   Turn to Sample Job Data Sheet. Study this page briefly noting its layout arrangement generally. References will be made to this page in the balance of the Instruction. [See Figure 13-14.]

STEP IV   Turn to first job, ELEVATOR OPERATOR. This is the first Job Data Sheet. If you do not have the job of ELEVATOR OPERATOR turn to the first job following that

[10] Mr. Ben F. McClancy, general manager of the Associated Industries of Cleveland, has given permission to quote at length from the survey.

exists in your plant. (Detach all unused Job Data Sheets and place to one side.)

STEP V   Study the job description carefully, noting any differences that may exist between the description and your Company job, keeping in mind the DEFINITION OF TERMS USED and CODE OF TYPICAL KEY WORDS.

In reviewing jobs listed, and in leafing through the Job Data Sheets, you will have noticed that some jobs have more than one description. *These jobs are identified by the asterisks (*) before the job titles.* In these cases select the description that best applies to your job.

On the reverse side of each Job Data Sheet there is a space provided to comment on the accuracy or adequacy of any description, if you feel so inclined.

STEP VI   Turn to SKILL REQUIREMENTS and read the instructions carefully. [See Figure 13-15.] This is one of three factors designed to rate the value of your job in relation to all other jobs reported. Circle proper number in Column I. [See Sample—Figure 13-14.]

STEP VII   Turn to PHYSICAL EFFORT and read the instructions carefully. Check the appropriate spaces in Column II opposite the Weight of Material and Continuity of Effort scales. In the Sample Job Data Sheet the Weight of Material was estimated to be between 5 pounds and 10 pounds and the Continuity of Effort was estimated to be between 90 and 95 percent. Levels at which objects are handled were found to be waist high, the compactness of loads small, and no material handling equipment was used.

STEP VIII   Turn to JOB CONDITIONS and read the instructions carefully and check the appropriate spaces in Column III. On the Sample Job Data Sheet it was found that JOB CONDITIONS were *light* in respect to *moderate* 90 to 95 percent of the time.

STEP IX   Return to Job Data Sheet and read the Instructions regarding rates to be reported. In the Sample Job Data Sheet all persons whose rates were reported were on an incentive plan, therefore, Incentive Average Hourly Earnings (Line 3 and Line 4) and Minimum Guarantee Hourly Rates (Line 5 and Line 6) were filled in leaving Non-Incentive Hourly Rates (Line 1 and 2) blank. However, if your job involved non-incentive workers only, *or* if your job included both incentive and non-incentive workers you would fill in all six columns.

If minimum and maximum hourly rates have been established on this particular job, make entries in MINIMUM and MAXIMUM spaces provided at bottom of Job Data Sheet.

STEP X   After all entries have been made on Job Data Sheet, detach page. Turn to next reporting job. In cases where jobs do not exist or are not comparable detach and place with other Job Data Sheets.

STEP XI   You will note that after Job Data Sheet, Page No. 71, several blank Job Data Sheets have been added for your convenience. If you have a job in any classification and wish to report it, but feel that the Job Descriptions furnished are *totally* inadequate, you may use one of these sheets to submit your own description and statistics. However, *minor* inadequacies should be noted on the back of the specific Job Data Sheet. After all Job Data Sheets have been completed, assemble and return to the Associated Industries together with unused Job Data Sheets and General Data Sheet in envelope provided.

The collection of wage data using this Survey method results in very useful wage and job information. For example, each participant fills in a job-specification form for Skill Requirements, Physical Effort Required, and Job Conditions. These specifications make it possible for the Associated Industries to point rate each job reported, so that for all jobs reported a point value or difficulty value is established. The wage information for both incentive and non-incentive jobs is reported, as well as the Minimum Guarantee for individuals on incentive jobs.

This survey makes available the kind of information which permits the construction of three wage curves. These are illustrated in Figure 13–16. One curve shows the relationship between the minimum guarantee and the job-rating points. This curve refers to all of the job data reported for the incentive jobs with a minimum guarantee. A second curve obtained from these data illustrates the relationship between job difficulty and the wages paid to employees on non-incentive jobs. This is the heavy line curve in Figure 13–16. The incentive wage curve shows the relationship between incentive earnings and job difficulty. The job of Bandsaw Operator is the one illustrated in Figure 13–16, and we see according to the Legend that for those jobs reported on incentive rates the average rate paid is above the community incentive wage curve. It is exactly on the line for those employees on non-incentive wages, and the minimum guarantee is close to the minimum guarantee wage line. These are indeed helpful data; they show not only what the "general relationship between wages and difficulty" is but also the degree to which a particular key job approximates the community level.

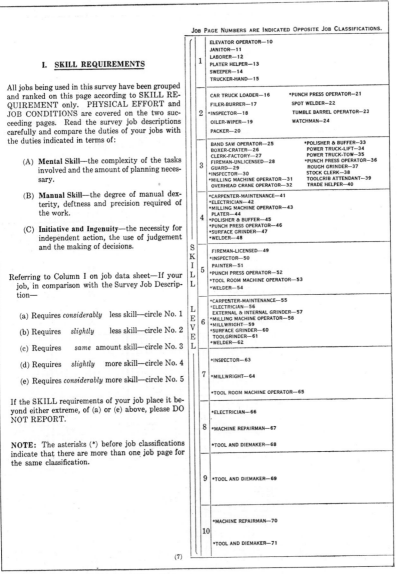

JOB PAGE NUMBERS ARE INDICATED OPPOSITE JOB CLASSIFICATIONS.

I. SKILL REQUIREMENTS

All jobs being used in this survey have been grouped and ranked on this page according to SKILL RE-QUIREMENT only. PHYSICAL EFFORT and JOB CONDITIONS are covered on the two succeeding pages. Read the survey job descriptions carefully and compare the duties of your jobs with the duties indicated in terms of:

(A) **Mental Skill**—the complexity of the tasks involved and the amount of planning necessary.

(B) **Manual Skill**—the degree of manual dexterity, deftness and precision required of the work.

(C) **Initiative and Ingenuity**—the necessity for independent action, the use of judgement and the making of decisions.

Referring to Column I on job data sheet—If your job, in comparison with the Survey Job Description—

(a) Requires *considerably* less skill—circle No. 1

(b) Requires *slightly* less skill—circle No. 2

(c) Requires *same* amount skill—circle No. 3

(d) Requires *slightly* more skill—circle No. 4

(e) Requires *considerably* more skill—circle No. 5

If the SKILL requirements of your job place it beyond either extreme, of (a) or (e) above, please DO NOT REPORT.

NOTE: The asterisks (*) before job classifications indicate that there are more than one job page for the same classification.

SKILL LEVEL

1
ELEVATOR OPERATOR—10
JANITOR—11
LABORER—12
PLATER HELPER—13
SWEEPER—14
TRUCKER-HAND—15

2
CAR TRUCK LOADER—16
FILER-BURRER—17
*INSPECTOR—18
OILER-WIPER—19
PACKER—20
*PUNCH PRESS OPERATOR—21
SPOT WELDER—22
TUMBLE BARREL OPERATOR—23
WATCHMAN—24

3
BAND SAW OPERATOR—25
BOXER-CRATER—26
CLERK-FACTORY—27
FIREMAN-UNLICENSED—28
GUARD—29
*INSPECTOR—30
*MILLING MACHINE OPERATOR—31
OVERHEAD CRANE OPERATOR—32
*POLISHER & BUFFER—33
POWER TRUCK-LIFT—34
POWER TRUCK-TOW—35
*PUNCH PRESS OPERATOR—36
ROUGH GRINDER—37
STOCK CLERK—38
TOOLCRIB ATTENDANT—39
TRADE HELPER—40

4
*CARPENTER-MAINTENANCE—41
*ELECTRICIAN—42
*MILLING MACHINE OPERATOR—43
PLATER—44
*POLISHER & BUFFER—45
*PUNCH PRESS OPERATOR—46
*SURFACE GRINDER—47
*WELDER—48

5
FIREMAN-LICENSED—49
*INSPECTOR—50
PAINTER—51
*PUNCH PRESS OPERATOR—52
*TOOL ROOM MACHINE OPERATOR—53
*WELDER—54

6
*CARPENTER-MAINTENANCE—55
*ELECTRICIAN—56
EXTERNAL & INTERNAL GRINDER—57
*MILLING MACHINE OPERATOR—58
*MILLWRIGHT—59
*SURFACE GRINDER—60
TOOLGRINDER—61
*WELDER—62

7
*INSPECTOR—63
*MILLWRIGHT—64
*TOOL ROOM MACHINE OPERATOR—65

8
*ELECTRICIAN—66
*MACHINE REPAIRMAN—67
*TOOL AND DIEMAKER—68

9
*TOOL AND DIEMAKER—69

10
*MACHINE REPAIRMAN—70
*TOOL AND DIEMAKER—71

(7)

Associated Industries of Cleveland Wage Survey.

Fig. 13—15. Skill requirements specification sheet.

Preparing wage data for use

As soon as enough companies have reported prevailing rates, the data for each key job must be tabulated. Figures 13–2 and 13–3 illustrate the method used in the Ohio Bell Telephone Survey. The average—that is, the wages paid to all workers divided by the num-

JOB TITLE: BANDSAW OPERATOR

JOB DESCRIPTION:

Adjusts and operates bandsaw to cut stock to size and shape, or to remove excess material. Selects and changes blades, sets speeds, and applies proper lubricants. Occasionally saws to close dimensions. May use standard jigs or fixtures. May direct work of a helper.

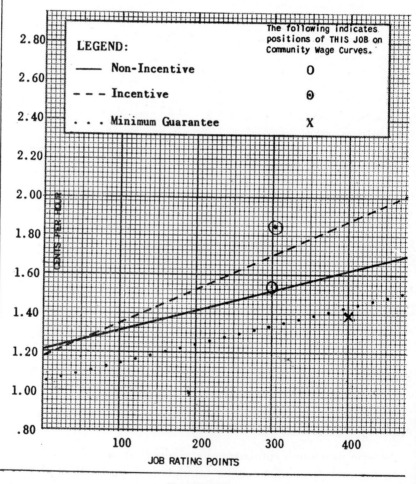

LEGEND:

——— Non-Incentive   O

– – – Incentive   ⊖

. . . Minimum Guarantee   X

The following indicates positions of THIS JOB on Community Wage Curves.

Fig. 13—16.

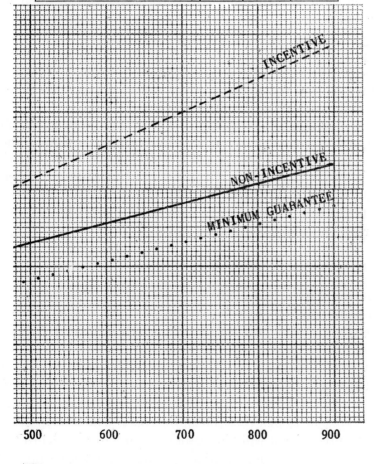

ASSOCIATED INDUSTRIES OF CLEVELAND
COMMUNITY WAGE CURVE

THIS JOB BY AVERAGE RATES AND POINTS			
TABLE (see over)	NON. INC.	INC	MIN.-GUAR.
HOURLY RATE (Average)	1.54	1. 85	1.39
JOB RATING POINTS (Average)	300	302	400
YOUR COMPANY HOURLY RATE (Average)			
YOUR COMPANY JOB RATING POINTS (Average)			

Fig. 13—16 (cont.).

ber of workers—or the median rate should be calculated. If there are extreme rates, the median is preferable because it is not influenced by the extreme rates as much as the average. It is necessary to obtain a single rate for each bench-mark job. The selection can be made from the average or the median, the minimum or the maximum reported rate, or a rate somewhere else along the distribution. It is desirable to be consistent from job to job in selecting a rate to represent the community or industry level for each key job.

Riegel [11] uses the term *standard salary* to mean the weekly or monthly rate which an employer, in the light of market conditions, pays for the services of any employee who fills a position satisfactorily but who does not exceed its requirements. Those employees who do not meet job requirements receive less than the standard rate, and those who exceed the requirements of a position receive salaries greater than the standard rate. Figure 13–17 is an example of the prevailing wage range, standard salary, and salary of individual employees for a group of key positions.[12] In this illustration the market value of the key positions is indicated by a wage range and this range is used to establish the standard salary.

The determination of a single rate or a rate range for each key job is a matter for company decision. Most companies obtain the average community or industry rate for each key job and either adopt this rate or use it as an aid to set a "standard rate." When the results of the wage survey have been collected and analyzed and a rate has been determined for each bench-mark job, the company is ready to compute the wage curve.

Setting rates on the basis of job ratings

Two sets of data are available for each job: (1) job ratings in terms of point values if the point system was used, evaluated rates if the factor-comparison method was used, grade levels if the grade-description method was employed, or ranks if the jobs were evaluated by means of ranking; and (2) the community or industry rate obtained through the wage survey. If the job ratings are located on the base of a chart and the wage rates are listed vertically on the chart, it is possible to plot each job on the chart. The result will be a series of plottings that will fall reasonably close to a straight line. Figure 13–18 is a scatter diagram showing the relationship be-

---

[11] John W. Riegel, *Salary Determination*, Report No. 2, Bureau of Industrial Relations (Ann Arbor: University of Michigan Press, 1940), pp. 34–35.

[12] *Ibid.*, p. 47.

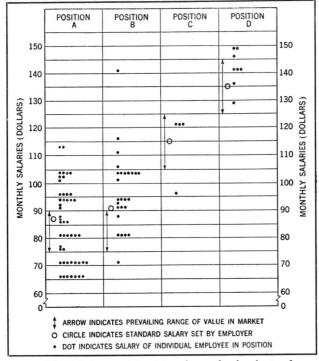

Fig. 13—17.   Determination of standard salaries for selected key positions filled by men in division X.

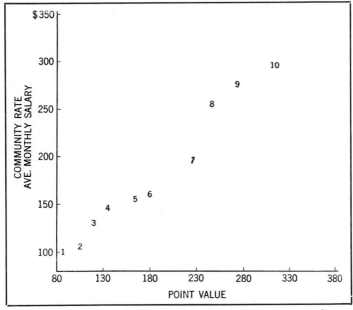

Fig. 13—18.   Relationship between point ratings and community rates for ten key jobs.

tween point ratings and community rates for ten key, or bench-mark, jobs. A freehand line can be drawn through these plottings, or a statistical procedure can be used to determine the line that best fits the plotted points. Since the statistical procedure is relatively simple, it is usually used to obtain the straight-line relationship between the point values and community rates. Those who wish to determine the relationship statistically may use the following technique.

The Method of Least Squares. The statistical details are here outlined and applied to the ten jobs in Figure 13–18, which were evaluated in a company and compared with the wage rates for the same ten jobs in other companies.

1. The ten jobs had the following point values, and their average monthly rates as obtained by a wage survey of other companies were:

Job No.	Point value	Average monthly rates
1	82	$100.00
2	115	105.00
3	120	130.00
4	135	148.00
5	164	155.00
6	180	160.00
7	225	195.00
8	248	255.00
9	275	278.00
10	318	288.00

Compute the sum of:

2. point values

82
115
120
135
164
180
225
248
275
318

Sum 1,862

3. monthly rates

$ 100.00
105.00
130.00
148.00
155.00
160.00
195.00
255.00
278.00
288.00

Sum $1,814.00

4. cross-products of point values and average rates

$82 \times \$100.00 = \quad 8,200.00$
$115 \times \quad 105.00 = \quad 12,075.00$

5. the squares of the point value

$82^2 = \quad 6,724$
$115^2 = \quad 13,225$

4. (*cont.*)

120 × 130.00 =	15,600.00
135 × 148.00 =	19,980.00
164 × 155.00 =	25,420.00
180 × 160.00 =	28,800.00
225 × 195.00 =	43,875.00
248 × 255.00 =	63,240.00
275 × 278.00 =	76,450.00
318 × 288.00 =	91,584.00

Sum 385,224.00

5. (*cont.*)

$120^2 =$	14,400
$135^2 =$	18,225
$164^2 =$	26,896
$180^2 =$	32,400
$225^2 =$	50,625
$248^2 =$	61,504
$275^2 =$	75,625
$318^2 =$	101,124

Sum   400,748

6. The equation for the straight line curve which most closely represents the trend of the data in step 1 above is

$$y = a + bx$$

where y represents the wage rate, x represents the point value, and a and b represent constant values. The values of a and b are obtained by solving the simultaneous equations,

$$\Sigma y = Na + b\Sigma x$$
$$\Sigma xy = a\Sigma x + b\Sigma x^2$$

where

Σx is the sum of the point values (step 2 above),

Σy is the sum of the average monthly rates (step 3 above),

Σxy is the sum of the cross-products of the point values and average monthly rates (step 4 above),

Σx^2 is the sum of the squares of the point values (step 5 above), and N is the number of jobs evaluated.

7. Substitute the proper values in the simultaneous equations,

$$1814 = 10a + 1862b$$
$$385,224 = 1862a + 400,748b$$

and solve for a and b. (The method of solving simultaneous equations can be found in any good high school algebra textbook.) The values for a and b are thus found to be 17.892 and .87813 respectively.

8. Substituting the values of a and b in the straight line equation $y = a + bx$ gives us

$$y^1 = 17.8921 + .87813x$$

where y^1 represents the computed monthly rate for each point value. The computed monthly rates for the ten jobs are obtained as follows:

Job No.	Point value (x)	.87813x	Computed monthly rate (17.8921 + .8713x)
1	82	72.0067	$ 89.90
2	115	100.9850	118.88
3	120	105.3756	123.27
4	135	118.5476	136.44
5	164	144.0133	161.91
6	180	158.0634	175.96
7	225	197.5793	215.47
8	248	217.7762	235.67
9	275	241.4858	259.38
10	318	279.2453	297.14

9. The actual average monthly rates compare with the computed rates as follows:

Job No.	Average monthly rate	Computed rate
1	$100.00	$ 89.90
2	105.00	118.88
3	130.00	123.27
4	148.00	136.44
5	155.00	161.91
6	160.00	175.96
7	195.00	215.47
8	255.00	235.67
9	278.00	259.38
10	288.00	297.14

10. It would appear, therefore, that on the basis of their relative point values jobs 2, 5, 6, 7, and 10 are underpaid by $13.88, $6.91, $15.96, $20.47, and $9.14, respectively; jobs 1, 3, 4, 8, and 9 are overpaid by $10.10, $6.73, $11.56, $14.33, and $18.62, respectively.

The example above is an illustration of a procedure for determining the wage slope. If observation of the scatterplot shows that a freehand line drawn through the points seems to follow a *curved line,* then a second degree curve should be computed. A thorough discussion of this statistical method can be found in most advanced statistical texts.[13]

Use of Company Wage Rates. If a company is willing to assume or has evidence that its present rates are, for the most part, in line with community rates, then it is not necessary to make a wage survey. A wage curve based upon the relationship between present company rates and the difficulty values of the jobs is an excellent device for discovering inequities in wage payments. The curve can also be used to compare the company wage structure with com-

[13] Frederick E. Croxton and Dudley J. Cowden, *Applied General Statistics* (New York: Prentice-Hall, Inc., 1939), pp. 721–727.

munity rates by checking the minimum, average, and maximum rates with the "community going rates" for jobs on similar levels. Wages are related, or should be related, to community or industry

TABLE 13—1. Wages and point values for fifty workers ●

Worker	Y Wage	X Points	Worker	Y Wage	X Points	Worker	Y Wage	X Points
1	$1.88	282	18	$1.38	230	35	$ .95	125
2	1.85	305	19	1.38	218	36	.95	125
3	1.85	280	20	1.35	215	37	.88	120
4	1.75	290	21	1.30	220	38	.88	115
5	1.75	295	22	1.25	185	39	.88	110
6	1.70	240	23	1.10	180	40	.88	105
7	1.67	253	24	1.10	165	41	.85	95
8	1.67	305	25	1.10	140	42	.85	90
9	1.65	268	26	1.10	140	43	.80	80
10	1.60	218	27	1.10	120	44	.75	110
11	1.55	235	28	1.05	135	45	.75	105
12	1.50	240	29	1.05	145	46	.75	100
13	1.50	240	30	1.05	198	47	.75	95
14	1.48	254	31	.95	140	48	.70	90
15	1.45	208	32	.95	110	49	.70	90
16	1.40	235	33	.95	110	50	.70	80
17	1.38	235	34	.95	125			

Wage Range   = $1.18   Point Value Range = 225
Class Interval = .10   Class Interval   = 20

TABLE 13—2. Frequency distribution of wages and point values ●

Wages		Point values	
Class Interval	f	Class Interval	f
1.80–1.89	3	300–319	2
1.70–1.79	3	280–299	4
1.60–1.69	4	260–279	1
1.50–1.59	3	240–259	5
1.40–1.49	3	220–239	5
1.30–1.39	5	200–219	4
1.20–1.29	1	180–199	3
1.10–1.19	5	160–179	1
1.00–1.09	3	140–159	4
.90– .99	6	120–139	6
.80– .89	7	100–119	8
.70– .79	7	80– 99	7
	N = 50		N = 50

rates because most companies attempt to keep their rates in line with those of their neighbors and competitors. Since a community wage survey is a costly and lengthy procedure, it is advisable first to establish a wage curve on the basis of the present company rate structure.

A complete description [14] for determining a wage curve based upon wages paid to workers on evaluated jobs is given below. Evaluated jobs are ones which have a difficulty value in terms of points, job ratings, or factor-comparison evaluated rates. In the description point values were used as a measure of job difficulty.

1. Set up a table of the data, listing the present wage of each worker and the obtained point value for his job starting with the worker with the highest wage. [See Table 13-1.]

2. Subtract the lowest wage from the highest wage to determine the wage range.

3. Choose a convenient class interval that will divide the range into at least 12 classes but not more than 18 classes.

4. Repeat Steps 2 and 3 for point values.

5. Tabulate the wages into a frequency distribution. [See Table 13–2.]

6. Tabulate the point values into a frequency distribution. [See Table 13-2.]

7. Set up a chart, labeling the rows with the class intervals for wages and the columns with the class intervals for points. The lowest wage class should be the bottom row and the lowest point value class should be the extreme left hand column. [See Figure 13–19.]

8. Starting with the individuals who fall in the lowest wage class, put a tally in the bottom row of the chart and in the column corresponding to the point value for each individual.

9. Plot the data for each worker in the row corresponding to the wage, and the column corresponding to the points.

10. Record the number of tallies in each row in the fy column at the right of the chart. This distribution should check with the frequency distribution of wages obtained in Step 5.

11. Record the number of tallies in each column in the fx row at the bottom of the chart. This distribution should check with the frequency distribution of point values obtained in Step 6.

12. Record the sum of each of these two distributions in the box labeled N. Each sum must equal the number of workers.

13. Starting with the lowest wage class as 0, list consecutive numbers in each row in column y'.

14. Starting with the lowest point value class as 0, list consecutive numbers in each column in row x'.

15. To obtain the figures in the fy' column, multiply each figure in the fy column by the adjacent figure in the y' column. The sum of this column equals $\Sigma fy'$.

[14] *Handbook of Job Evaluation for Factory Jobs,* Personnel Research Institute of Western Reserve University (Cleveland: Industrial Fasteners Institute [formerly American Institute of Bolt, Nut and Rivet Manufacturers], 1946), pp. 68–72.

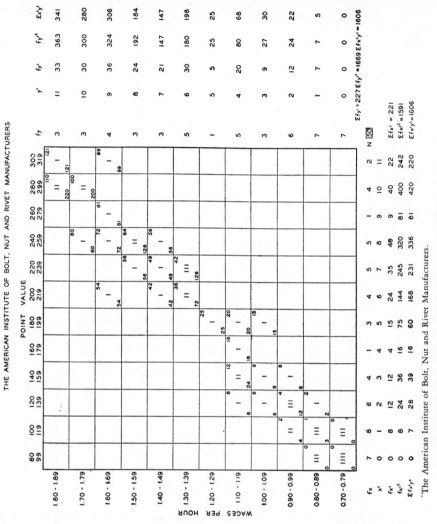

Fig. 13—19. Computational chart for the determination of a wage curve.

*The American Institute of Bolt, Nut and Rivet Manufacturers.

16. To obtain the figures in the fx' row, multiply each figure in the fx row by the adjacent figure in the x' row. The sum of this row equals Σfx'.

17. To obtain the figures in the fy'² column, multiply each figure in the y' column by the adjacent figure in the fy' column. The sum of this column equals Σfy'².

18. To obtain the figures in the fx'² row, multiply each figure in the x' row by the adjacent figure in the fx' row. The sum of this row equals Σfx'².

19. Considering each box in the chart individually, multiply the corresponding figure in the y' column by the corresponding figure in the x' column. Write the result in the upper right hand corner of each box.

20. Multiply each figure obtained in Step 19 by the total number of

tallies in each box, and record the resulting figure in the lower left hand corner of each box.

21. To obtain the figures in the $\Sigma x'y'$ column, add all the figures in the lower left hand corners of the boxes in each row. The sum of this column is $\Sigma fx'y'$.

22. To obtain the figures in the $\Sigma x'y'$ row, add all the figures in the lower left hand corner of the boxes in each column. The sum of this row is $\Sigma fx'y'$ and must equal the $\Sigma fx'y'$ obtained in Step 21.

When these 22 steps have been completed, all the data have been obtained that are necessary for the derivation of the wage curve equation. The equation for any straight line is

$$y = a + bx \tag{1}$$

where

$$a = \frac{\Sigma fx'^2 \times \Sigma fy' - \Sigma fx' \times \Sigma fx'y'}{N\Sigma fx'^2 - (\Sigma fx')^2} \tag{2}$$

$$b = \frac{N\Sigma fx'y' - \Sigma fx' \times \Sigma fy'}{N\Sigma fx'^2 - (\Sigma fx')^2} \tag{3}$$

In order to fit a straight line curve to any set of data the values of the constants "a" and "b" must first be obtained. These values can then be substituted in equation (1) and the result is the equation of the desired wage curve in deviation form.

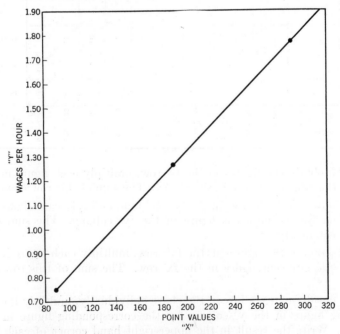

Fig. 13—20.   Wage curve plotted from data in Table 13

23. Substitute the appropriate figures into equation (2) to obtain the value of "a."

24. Substitute the appropriate figures into equation (3) to obtain the value of "b."

25. Substitute the obtained values of "a" and "b" in equation (1) to obtain the equation of the wage curve in deviation form.

26. Set up a table for determining plotting points. [See Table 13-3.] Substitute any arbitrary values of x′ into equation (1) to obtain the corresponding value of y′, and record under y′ in the table.

27. Record the midpoints of the class intervals corresponding to the selected values of x′ in the X column.

28. Obtain the values in the Y column by using the following equation:

$$Y = y'i + MP_L$$

where

y′ is obtained from [Table 13–3],

  i is the size of the class intervals for wages,

MP_L is the midpoint of the lowest class interval in the distribution of wages.

The figures in columns X and Y in Table 13-3 are the actual figures to be plotted on a graph. See Figure 13-20.

Computation of the Wage Curve Equation Using Data Obtained from Figure 13-19:

$$a = \frac{\Sigma fx'^2 \times \Sigma fy' - \Sigma fx' \times \Sigma fx'y'}{N\Sigma fx'^2 - (\Sigma fx')^2}$$

$$= \frac{1591 \times 227 - 221 \times 1606}{50 \times 1591 - (221)^2}$$

$$= .203$$

$$b = \frac{N\Sigma fx'y' - \Sigma fx' \times \Sigma fy'}{N\Sigma fx'^2 - (\Sigma fx')^2}$$

$$= \frac{50 \times 1606 - 221 \times 227}{50 \times 1591 - (221)^2}$$

$$= .98$$

Substituting in equation (1):

$$y' = a + bx'$$
$$y' = .203 + .98x'$$

TABLE 13—3. Values of X and Y for plotting wage curve ●

SCORES IN DEVIATION FORM		CONVERTED SCORES	
x′	y′	X	Y
0	.203	89.5	.765
5	5.103	189.5	1.255
10	10.003	289.5	1.745

$$y' = \quad .203 + .98x'$$
$$y' = \quad .203 + .98 \times \quad 0 = \quad .203$$
$$y' = \quad .203 + .98 \times \quad 5 = \quad 5.103$$
$$y' = \quad .203 + .98 \times 10 = 10.003$$
$$Y = y'i + MP_L$$
$$Y = \quad .203 \times .10 + .745 = \quad .765$$
$$Y = \quad 5.103 \times .10 + .745 = 1.255$$
$$Y = 10.003 \times .10 + .745 = 1.745$$

SLOPE OF WAGE CURVE

The slope of the wage curve as it rises from a low point on the left to a higher point on the right is determined by several factors. It can be seen that whenever the jobs are evaluated by means of the factor-comparison method the slope of the curve is approximately a 45° angle. This is caused by the fact that the jobs are measured by means of the job-comparison scale, which in turn receives its values from the present wage scale. A job is measured in terms of the present wage structure, so a comparison of evaluated "money points" and wages for each job should result in approximately the same value and when it is plotted on a twofold table a curve approximating a 45° angle should result.

Whenever point values are used the slope of the wage curve is determined in part by the minimum wage rates and point values and the maximum wage rates and point values, and in part by the way in which the wages of employees are weighted by the number of employees at each wage and point-value level. Any undue weighting anywhere along the wage line will alter the slope and shape the curve might have. The slope of the curve is usually determined statistically, although, as pointed out above, it can be determined by merely drawing a line between the place where the minimum points and minimum wage coincide and the place where the maximum points and maximum wage coincide on the scatter chart.

If factors are operating which affect the curve in an undesirable manner, it is better to change the slope or shape of the curve than to use a curve which might be statistically sound but impossible to install and administer. The wage curves as derived are aids to job classification and job-pricing, but are not necessarily the only basis for the determination of labor grades and wage rates.

MINIMUM AND MAXIMUM WAGES

It seems to be true that employers overpay jobs at the lowest level of difficulty when the rates for these positions are compared with the rates at the highest difficulty levels. This is in part caused by the fact that employees on the lower level jobs are closer to the bare existence level and employers tend to pay on the basis of worker need. This is not necessary for the higher rated jobs.

The problem of a minimum wage has been solved in part by government regulation. The last few years have seen drastic changes in the minimum rate, and it is entirely possible that the legal minimum will again be increased. All companies have a starting rate no lower than the legal minimum, and many companies have a rate somewhat above that level. In any event, it is a simple matter for a company to determine its minimum starting rate.

The maximum rate varies somewhat from company to company, but the tendency is for companies with the same job difficulty levels

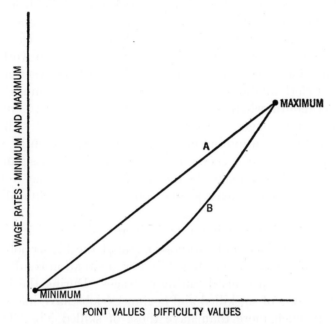

Fig. 13—21. Wage curves based upon minimum and maximum wage rates and point values. Arithmetic and geometric assignment of point values to degrees.

to have similar maximums. It is relatively easy for any organization to determine a standard rate for the most difficult job in the group which has been evaluated.

By plotting the minimum and maximum point values against the minimum and maximum wages, a line can be drawn between the two to give a rough approximation of a wage curve. If the degrees are assigned point values on the basis of a geometric progression, a straight-line wage relationship is usually obtained. The assignment of points to degrees on the basis of an arithmetic progression usually results in a positively accelerated wage curve. This is illustrated in Figure 13–21. It is very difficult to forecast what the shape or exact slope of the curve will be on so small an amount of data, but such a chart is helpful if wage data are needed in a hurry. It should be noted that under the two systems of assigning points, a job could very well fall at A on Figure 13–21 when evaluated on a plan using a geometric distribution, and at B if points were assigned to the same plan on an arithmetic distribution.

There is a tendency for wages to increase as jobs become more difficult. The rate of increase is more marked for difficult jobs than for the simple jobs. Whenever an arithmetic job-rating scale is used the points tend to increase in size, as we go from the easy to the difficult jobs, at a slower rate than the money paid to workers on these jobs. For example, the difference in points between a junior and senior clerk might be 25 and the difference in minimum salaries $50.00 per month, whereas at the higher level jobs, such as manager and assistant manager, the difference in points might still be 25 and the difference in minimum salaries $200.00 per month. On the other hand, the use of a geometric progression in the assignment of point values tends to make the increase in points similar to the increase in salaries or wages as the jobs increase in difficulty and worth.

If the minimum starting rate is increased, inequities will be created unless adjustments are also made at the higher job levels. Whenever minimums are changed by law, a situation results which ultimately causes a general raising of wages. During the last few years, the wages of unskilled and beginners' jobs have increased in proportion much more than have those of skilled jobs. There is now a gradual readjustment of wages taking place to bring the wage rates in line with the difficulty of the job.

The establishment of wage curves through job evaluation will enable individual plants to anticipate necessary wage changes by noting the current wage changes at each difficulty level.

SUGGESTIONS FOR STUDY AND RESEARCH

1. How would you determine the "community rates" for the police and firemen in your city?

2. Why is it important for a company to know how its wage rates compare with other companies in the community?

3. How can it be proved that a given company's wages are in the upper quarter of the community rates?

CASE PROBLEM

The jobs listed below have been analyzed and the rates for the employees on the jobs have been obtained. In addition, community rates for the jobs have been secured from a local trade association. Compute the company wage curve and the community wage curve. Plot them both on the same graph and make recommendations to the company for wage changes.

Job title	Point value	Employee wages*	Community wage
Accounting Clerk A	370	$75; 81; 64; 70; 65	$80
Accounting Clerk B	350	$62; 56; 48	$73
General Clerk A	275	$50; 48; 58	$59
General Clerk B	204	$42; 67; 50	$52
Mail Clerk	204	$43	$52
Messenger	151	$43; 45	$47
Payroll Clerk	310	$55; 63	$68
Tabulating Machine Operator	330	$57	$67
Key Punch Operator	221	$53; 45	$53
Addressing Machine Operator	151	$44	$47
Calculating Machine Operator	256	$50	$55
File Clerk	171	$41	$49
Private Secretary	410	$73; 60	$78
Stenographer A	318	$55; 58	$65
Stenographer B	293	$54; 47	$62
Typist A	258	$49; 49	$54
Typist B	172	$45; 45; 48	$48
Secretary-Stenographer	367	$66; 68	$70

* Each wage represents one employee.

PROBLEM: How much would it cost the company per week to adjust the wages of all employees below the community wage curve, bringing them to the community level?

14

Establishing the Classification and Pay Structure

THE PURPOSE OF A COMPLETE JOB-EVALUA-
tion study is to classify jobs so that they may be given rates in line
with their difficulty or worth. The establishment of the relative
difficulty of each job is the first step in the determination of the pay
structure. The assignment of a money value to each job, in such
a manner that the relative value as determined by job evaluation
is not destroyed, is the next step. Although it is possible through
job evaluation to assign rates to each job, it is usually the practice
to assign rates to job classes or labor grades.

Once the number of classes desired has been determined and the
task of assigning jobs to their proper classes has been completed,
wage rates should be assigned to the classes. The use of an individual rate for each job, a single rate for each job class, or the use of
a wage range for each job or job class, depends upon the history of
wage administration in the organization installing the wage structure as well as the present needs of the organization.

THREE METHODS OF WAGE PAYMENT

Individual job rate

It is possible to have a different pay rate for each job. This
method of wage payment is usually used in situations where the rate
for each position is determined without using a job classification. In
this situation each job is priced individually and there might be as

many rates or rate ranges as there are individual jobs. It can be seen that such a procedure would result in a very complicated wage structure which would be difficult to administer. It would also be true that this method would tend to promote wage inequities, because each job would be subject either to individual or collective bargaining, and equality of bargaining strength would be difficult to maintain. Supervisors and executives would tend to favor one job over another, so that inequities would result through wage administration practices.

However, if job-evaluation methods have been used to determine the relative difficulty of each job, the difficulty values can be used to determine a suitable individual rate. The wage curve or wage line, as determined by a comparison of difficulty values with either company rates or appropriate community rates, is of value in this situation. Figure 14–1 is an illustration of a conversion scale involving a wage curve and appropriate wage rates, which has been prepared by the Industrial Management Society.[1] A figure of this type is of use in setting the rates for an individual job when the job-evaluation scale used to obtain the evaluated points is applied to the job in question. Suppose, for example, a job is evaluated at 80 points. Figure 14–1 shows that this job, when compared with the difficulty values and wage rates of other jobs, should receive a minimum rate of approximately $1.10 per hour and a maximum of $1.35 per hour. The mean rate for the job should be approximately $1.22½ per hour. If the evaluation study is accepted as being approximately correct, this method of setting individual job rates is very helpful, and at the same time the wage system can be kept free of wage inequities.

Single rate

In most instances, jobs will not be priced individually but will be assigned to a number of classes, and all the jobs falling in a particular class will be given the same wage. Once the number of classes has been determined and the task of assigning jobs to their proper classes has been completed, the next step is to assign wage rates to the classes. Two types of wage rates, single rates and wage ranges, have been used successfully, and these can apply either to individual jobs or to job classes. The single rate has been in use for some time and has recently been advocated by some unions and

---

[1] *Occupational Rating Plan,* Industrial Management Society (205 West Wacker Drive, Chicago: 1943), p. 94.

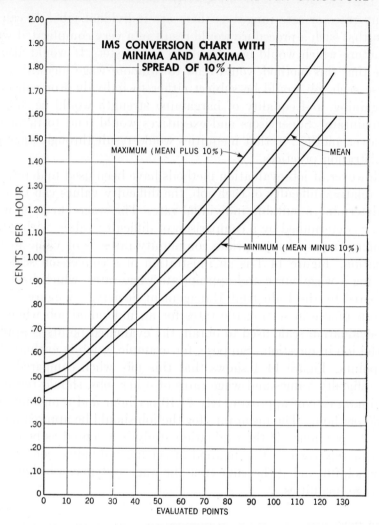

Fig. 14—1.

some managements as being the most desirable method of pricing jobs and job classes. This type of wage rate allows no range in salary for either a job or a job class, and requires the payment of the same wage to each individual employee on the job or in the job class. For example, all individuals on jobs in Class I would receive the same wage, and all individual differences in production or any type of merit consideration would be disregarded.

The single rate does do away with the problem of assigning wages on the basis of merit, and, in certain companies where the employees do not trust the management, wage grievances can be reduced. At the same time it must be remembered that where two workers of unequal proficiency are assigned to the same job and receive the same rate of pay, the more proficient worker feels that an injustice occurs when his rate is the same as that of the less proficient worker. The single rate makes it impossible to correct this situation. There is no doubt that the acceptance of the single rate by management and employees should depend upon the attitude of both toward rewarding individual merit as well as the ease of administering the payroll.

The use of a single rate for each individual job is illustrated in

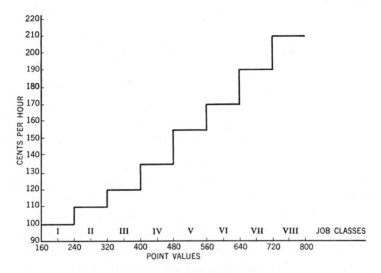

Fig. 14—2.   Single rates for job classes.

Figure 14–1, if one of the wage curves is selected—the maximum curve, for example—and each job is assigned the rate which corresponds to its point value. Figure 14–2 shows the method of setting single rates for labor grades or classes. In this illustration all jobs have been classified in 8 grades, each with a range of 80 points and a single rate assigned to each grade. For example, all of the jobs with point values from 160 to 240 fall in Class I and receive a rate of $1.00 per hour. All individuals filling these jobs would receive this rate until they were promoted to a higher class. For those who have attempted to install an objective and fair merit plan for granting wage increases, the simplicity of the single rate is perhaps attractive. An administratively simple plan is not always the most desirable, however.

Wage range

Most companies today use a wage range in pricing jobs and job classes. The wage range usually consists of a minimum or starting rate and a maximum rate, and enough money spread between the two to make it possible to grant several wage increases. Many pay structures incorporating rate ranges have been further defined by establishing definite steps within each rate range. In the range of 80 to 90 cents per hour, the only pay levels used might be 80, 85, and 90 cents per hour. This system is of some assistance in bringing additional order into the pay structure. These steps are used primarily in connection with positioning the employee within the range with respect to his individual estimated worth on the job. They generally are employed in two ways:

1. Most or all employees are started at the minimum of the range and are advanced up through the range from one step to the next.

2. Wherever an employee is being placed into the rate range, his individual rate is set at that step which most accurately compensates the worker for his ability on that job.

The first method implies that, whenever an employee is granted a merit increase in pay within the range, he is increased one or more steps. Thus, any single step increase within the 80–90 cents range would represent something less than a 5 per cent increase in pay. Under the second procedure, any employee at any time might be placed at one of the steps within the range, depending on the estimate at that time of his efficiency on the job. This would imply that, upon being placed on the job, he might be set at any one of the levels within the range; also, a worker within the range, at any time when his efficiency on the job is reviewed, might be changed within the range—that is, moved up or down—in order to be placed at the level which most nearly reflects the estimate of his individual worth on the job. Theoretically, he might be moved up or down within the range at any time, depending on his particular performance on the job.

The number and size of steps within each range can be decided in terms of the wage practices of the company. Generally, there are from three to five steps within each range. The size of these steps will vary with the size of the range, and, consequently, the size of the steps within the range in the lower classifications will be less than in the higher classifications, since ordinarily the size of the range is less at the lower end of the wage scale. Thus there might be a 10-cent range with two intermediate steps in Class I. Such steps might be 70, 73, 76, and 80 cents per hour. At the other end of the scale, with a range of $1.40 to $1.70 an hour, there might be three intermediate steps, so that the steps would be $1.40, $1.45, $1.50, $1.60, and $1.70. If the range were $1.40 to $1.60, the steps probably would be $1.40, $1.45, $1.50, $1.55, and $1.60.

The size of the rate range for clerical and salary jobs is determined on the basis of a somewhat different philosophy from that for factory jobs. The assignment of specific job tasks to a clerical position is difficult, because the type of work performed in an office does not lend itself to the assignment of standard, uniform, unchanging duties to a single worker. The clerical, supervisory, and professional employee is called upon to help out during rush periods, to substitute for absent workers, to learn to perform additional tasks which are not strictly a part of the job, and is expected to accept this variety as a job function. In describing clerical jobs, the functional job description, that is, the description of the various functions performed by the worker, is found more often than the sequential type of job description, where the duties are described in the exact sequence of performance.

The nebulous nature of clerical, supervisory, and professional functions makes it necessary to assign a fairly wide rate range to positions of this type. In most wage scales in the office field, a range based upon a percentage of the minimum, the midpoint, or the maximum is employed. According to Smyth and Murphy,[2] "The monetary spread of the rate range of each labor grade will depend on the range considered desirable for the purpose of rewarding meritorious employees. It is generally recognized that any range of much less than 20 per cent will not provide sufficient incentive." Salary ranges are often above this figure, and percentage spreads as great as 50 per cent have been used successfully. Recently, when a group of employers was polled to determine the wage spread desired for clerical and office supervisory positions, the percentage spread desired varied between 30 and 40 per cent.

It is considered a mistake by some to use a constant money spread for each labor grade. A rate range of 20 cents per hour for jobs in the lowest labor grade might be a 20 per cent spread, but at the top labor grade it might be 5 per cent. A constant per cent spread between minimum and maximum for both factory and office jobs is,

[2] By permission from *Job Evaluation and Employee Rating*, p. 129, by Richard C. Smyth and Matthew J. Murphy. Copyright, 1946. McGraw-Hill Book Company, Inc.

in general, a more equitable procedure than a constant money spread. However, the past history of wage administration, the present desires of employees and employers, and collective bargaining in organized plants will govern the extent and type of the rate range. The range should be sufficiently wide to include as many wage levels as are needed to reflect the difference between the best and poorest workers on the job.

METHODS OF GRANTING WAGE INCREASES

Automatic progression

While steps within the ranges are used frequently in rate ranges with merit progression, they are an integral part of rate ranges where progression is based automatically on length of service. Thus, in a wage range of 70 to 85 cents, the employee may be hired at 70 cents, raised to 75 cents at the end of six months, to 80 cents at the end of another year, and to 85 cents at the end of two and a half years on the job. A full automatic progression plan of this type is, in effect, a variation of the single-rate system; it provides for a period of time during which the pay rate is increased periodically before the worker attains the single rate established for the job. In this case, the single rate is the maximum of the so-called rate range.

The problem of placing workers at various points within these automatic-progression rate ranges is somewhat complicated. It is necessary to establish a few additional ground rules to cover the variations that arise. In some automatic progression systems, the factor of merit is also introduced by the condition that the automatic increase is granted at the expiration of the specified periods of time only if the employee merits this increase. If it is the opinion of those concerned that the employee has not improved sufficiently to merit this increase, provision usually is made for discharging the employee or transferring him to a different job for another chance.

Merit increases

The straight merit rate range ordinarily provides the most complete flexibility, within the limits of the rate range, with regard to compensating the various workers on the job for their individual proficiency. Theoretically, the worker can be placed at any point within the rate range in relation to his effectiveness on that job as compared to other workers on the job. Actually, however, the merit system usually operates by providing for an increase in wage rate when the employee exhibits sufficient proficiency or improvement to merit the increase in pay under the rules by which the merit system is operated. When the employee does not continue to show improvement, or his proficiency actually decreases, the usual practice is to deny any merit increase without decreasing the rate. It would be possible, with complete freedom within the rate range, to distribute workers within each rate range on the basis of their relative proficiency on the job on which they are working. The most efficient workers will be at the top of their respective rate ranges, while those who are least efficient will be at or near the bottom of the range, with the others distributed in between.

Complete freedom to place employees within the rate range according to their proficiency on the job is a condition which can only be approached. It is almost impossible to reduce an employee's hourly rate if he happens to be higher in the range than he should be in relation to his proficiency. Therefore, rate increases based on merit must be granted with extreme caution. In a merit-progression system, the eligibility of each individual suggested for an increase must be tested very carefully. The proficiency of such an employee must be gauged against the proficiency demanded at various levels within the range, and, as a check, against the proficiency of other employees now paid at the various levels within the range. It is essential to resist the temptation to gauge the proficiency of the individual by his own proficiency at some time in the past—that is, in terms of his own improvement. It is particularly dangerous to grant merit increases solely on the basis of long service or amount of experience on the job.

In order to administer merit progression it is necessary that (1) the rate range be defined in terms that will make it possible to set the rate of the employee in relation to his proficiency on that job; and (2) data measuring the proficiency of all workers be available so that the proficiency of one employee can be compared to that of all others on the same job to assist in properly setting his individual wage rate within the range.

To illustrate the first point, rate ranges in a company may be defined as follows:

MINIMUM: Able to do the job, or learning.

MIDPOINT: Knows all angles of the job satisfactorily, little supervision required, good worker.

MAXIMUM: Outstanding worker, able to do the most difficult work required on this job, quality and quantity exceptionally high, a leader.

An employee who requires little supervision and knows all angles of the job should not be kept at the minimum rate; a good worker who is not outstanding probably should not be put at the maximum of the range, if merit is to be the governing rule.

As a check on the qualifications of any employee, his proficiency should be compared to that of all other workers on the job. If his performance on the job is similar to that of those employees who are at the minimum of the range, he should be left there. This comparison to other workers on the job, coupled with the comparison to the standard scale set up in the definition of the rate range, should result in fairly accurate and equitable pay for all employees on each job in relation to the range and to each other. This approach combines the technique of man-to-man rating with that of the graphic or linear type of rating. Many standard merit-rating systems are based on one or both of these techniques. The principal difference among all merit-rating scales lies in the factors or characteristics used in determining the proficiency of the workers. For example, quantity and quality of work are standard factors in most systems; knowledge of the job is a common factor; other factors vary to a great extent.

The proficiency of the employee on his particular job is not the sole factor in determining the rate he will be assigned within the rate range. As pointed out above, all changes in rates within the range are upward—they are merit *increases*. The total of these merit adjustments (i.e., increases), therefore, increases the labor cost per employee to the extent of the increases. Usually, the only factors which tend to offset this increase are (1) the separation of employees paid rates high in the range, and (2) the replacement of these employees by promotion or by new employees hired at the minimum of the range. On the other hand, selection, placement, and training costs, along with a higher labor cost per unit of production, might easily wipe out these gains. In any event, the cost of merit increases must be taken into account. When the financial position of the company does not permit increased costs, merit increases which might otherwise be granted must be limited or eliminated entirely for a time. In such cases, the merit increases which can be given are given to those employees who deserve them the most. When business conditions permit, necessary adjustments should be made as soon as feasible.

Under a merit-progression system, it is usually wise to avoid using the system to increase the pay of workers without regard to merit, that is, to grant a general increase in pay. This situation usually comes about when a company that is willing and financially able to increase its labor cost per employee relaxes its standards to permit merit increases where they do not meet the criteria established. When the time comes to return to the criteria established for the operation of merit progression, many employees are higher in the range than they should be, and individual pay reductions are extremely difficult, if not impossible to make.

The control of wages and salaries through the administration of merit rate ranges of this type is discussed in more detail on pages 502-507, Personnel Accounting.

Combination automatic and merit-progression systems

There may be a combination of both automatic progression and merit progression within ranges in the same pay structure. There are two general plans of this type in use:

1. Full automatic progression in the job classes in the lower half of the pay scale and full merit progression in the job classes in the upper half of the scale;

2. Full automatic progression up to the midpoint of each rate range, with merit progression above the midpoint of the range of each job class or labor grade.

The reasoning behind the establishment of the first type of combined automatic and merit-progression arrangement is that, in the lower-rated jobs, it is very difficult to distinguish between the proficiency of one worker and another; as a matter of fact, on these jobs there is often very little difference between one employee and another. In the upper half of the rate range, however, where the jobs are more difficult, individuals vary to a considerable extent in their effectiveness and proficiency on the job, and these differences can be measured or estimated with some consistency and accuracy.

With respect to the second type of combination pay scale, the automatic progression up to the midpoint is provided as insurance against the possibility of any individual worker's being discriminated against by being held at the minimum of the range. This arrangement assures at least the midpoint of the range for every employee after a period of time. Furthermore, it is significant that the general labor-cost level of this second type of combination scale is likely to be somewhat higher than the first. In labor grades with full automatic progression, the average hourly rate of all workers in that grade at any one time would be just a little less than the maximum of the range. In a full merit-progression labor grade, the average of the rates of all workers in the grade probably would be somewhere between the midpoint and two thirds of the way up in the range, although this would vary considerably from one company to another and from one labor grade to another. In the labor grades with automatic progression to the midpoint with merit progression from that point on, the average rate of all workers in the grade probably would be 75 to 80 per cent of the way up in the range. As in the case of the full merit-progression range, there would be some variation here between companies and between labor grades.

Each of the different types of arrangements for progression within ranges has somewhat different characteristics and raises somewhat different types of administrative problems. The automatic progression is undoubtedly the simplest, as far as day-to-day administration is concerned, since it is a purely mechanical system. As this automatic-progression system is tempered in various ways by the introduction of the factor of merit the administrative problems increase proportionately. Offset against the difficulty, however, is the value of flexibility achieved through the merit-progression systems of various types.

Whether to use individual rates, single rates, or rate ranges is a matter which can be decided before or after the assignment of jobs to labor grades or job classes. If rate ranges are employed, the decision concerning automatic progression or merit progression can be made at the time the new wage structure is installed. In most cases, jobs are first classified on the basis of the job evaluation, and the classes so obtained are priced in accordance with their relative difficulty.

RELATIONSHIP OF MERIT RATING TO JOB EVALUATION

We may use the phrase, "pay the job and not the man," but it is the individual employee on the job who receives the pay check. His attitude toward that pay check is of concern to all who are responsible for the welfare of the company. The worker can agree that the job is fairly paid, but he sometimes cannot see why the poor workers on his job get the same rate as the good ones. In the opinion of the workers, those who do the most work ought to get the most money. No matter how accurately we price the job, we must also price the man.

Individual differences

Occupational studies of workers have revealed that they differ not only in their abilities and aptitudes but also in the way they perform various work activities. According to Otis,[3] "In studying a group of workers, one finds a considerable range in the proficiency shown by these workers on the job. One usually finds that their production varies from unacceptable or barely acceptable work to acceptable or very superior work." Tiffin gives several illustrations of individual differences in productivity and shows that the per cent of average production varies from 60 for the poorest to 145 for the best electrical fixture assemblers, and from 60 to 135 for 33 employees engaged in burning, twisting, and soldering ends of insulated wire.[4] The available evidence that workers differ in their ability to perform jobs and that these differences are reflected in their individual worth to the company is overwhelming. Workers show their value to a company in other ways than production. Such factors as receptiveness of supervision, attendance, quality of work, ability to get along with others, and length of time on the job are examples.

There are two accepted ways of paying workers within the range: (1) on the basis of length of time on the job, usually referred to as automatic progression; and (2) on the basis of merit. The use of automatic progression is becoming more common because of union pressure. The object is to get all workers to the top of the range by a series of wage increases based upon tenure. Those who have installed this method of "paying within the range" feel that fewer wage grievances will arise because increases in pay are given on an objective basis—length of time on the job—hence there is no room for argument. For those companies and workers who prefer payment on a merit basis some type of merit-rating or employee-rating system should be installed, because the informed opinion of a single supervisor is not a sound or desirable basis for granting wage increases.

Merit-rating scales

Simple rankings, paired-comparison check lists, and the graphic type of scales have been used most frequently for merit rating. Figure 14–3 shows a typical merit-rating chart.[5] No attempt is made in this volume to deal authoritatively with the field of merit rating. This would require a companion volume, for the task of employee

---

[3] William H. Stead, Carroll L. Shartle and Associates, *Occupational Counseling Techniques* (New York: The American Book Co., 1940), p. 75.

[4] Joseph Tiffin, *Industrial Psychology,* 3d ed. (New York: Prentice-Hall, Inc., 1952), pp. 11–12.

[5] *Ibid.,* p. 320.

PROGRESS RECORD

Name————————— Dept———— Div———— Date————————

Employee's Position——————————————— Job Class————————

Note   This rating will represent in a systematic way your appraisal of the employee in terms of his ACTUAL PERFORMANCE ON HIS PRESENT JOB.   In the interests of furthering careful analysis, the following suggestions are offered regarding the use of this form

1. Consider only one factor at a time
2. Study each factor and the specifications for each grade
3. Review upon completion to see that the rating of each factor applies exclusively to the individual's ACTUAL PERFORMANCE ON HIS PRESENT JOB
4. Comment fully at bottom of page and on reverse side upon any matter which in your opinion needs explanation

PERFORMANCE FACTORS	PERFORMANCE GRADE				
	Far exceeds requirements of this job	Exceeds requirements of this job	Meets requirements of this job	Partially meets requirements of this job	Does not meet requirements of this job
Quality of work Accuracy Economy of materials Economy of time (his own and others) Neatness Thoroughness	Consistently superior ☐	Sometimes superior ☐	Consistently satisfactory ☐	Usually acceptable ☐	Consistently unsatisfactory ☐
Quantity of work Productive output	Consistently exceeds requirements ☐	Frequently exceeds requirements ☐	Meets requirements ☐	Frequently below requirements ☐	Consistently below requirements ☐
Dependability Follows instructions Judgment Punctuality and attendance Safety habits	Consistently dependable ☐	Dependable in most respects ☐	Ordinarily dependable ☐	Frequently undependable ☐	Consistently undependable ☐
Compatibility Attitude toward the company Attitude toward supervision Co-operation with fellow-employees	Inspires others to work with and assist co-workers ☐	Quick to volunteer to work with and assist others ☐	Generally works well with and assists others ☐	Seldom works well with or assists others ☐	Does not work well with or assist others ☐

COMMENT———————————————————————————

Fig. 14—3.   A typical merit rating chart used in industry.

evaluation is at least as complex as the task of job evaluation. Newer methods of employee evaluation, such as the "forced choice" method and the "critical incident" approach, have changed the field of merit rating considerably. Now that merit rating is a definite part of wage administration and subject to collective bargaining, the old bias-laden approaches are being abandoned in favor of merit-rating plans with sufficient validity to earn acceptance from those whose earnings may be affected by their application. A recent method is to key the merit-rating scale into the job-evaluation system by using as many of the job-evaluation factors as possible for the merit-rating scales to rate the worker. The installation of a merit-rating system [6] requires as much work as the installation of job evaluation. However, it is possible to use a greater number of people so the burden is not too great for any one person. Each employee is rated periodically and his merit rating is compared with those of all other employees. On the basis of this comparison the employees who receive the highest ratings can be given wage increases, and those with the lowest ratings can be isolated so that their supervisors can work with them to improve their job performance.

Since merit rating has definite limitations, a great deal of care must be exercised to install a system that will permit judgment to operate effectively. Wherever possible, objective standards must be used in judging the performance of workers. To rate a man on attendance when accurate attendance records are available is obviously silly; to rate a man on quantity or quality of work when production records are available is using a relatively inaccurate measuring device when a more accurate one is available. Insofar as possible, *objective standards of merit* should be used.

Merit-rating scales are of real value in increasing the accuracy of judgments. They are an accepted personnel procedure, and are definitely preferable to the informal judgments of supervisors and foremen. Properly constructed and properly applied, they contribute immensely to "pricing the man within the range."

[6] Those interested will find excellent discussions of merit rating in the following publications: Joseph Tiffin, *Industrial Psychology* (New York: Prentice-Hall, Inc., 1952), Ch. 11; *Employee Rating*, Studies in Personnel Policy, No. 39, National Industrial Conference Board, 247 Park Ave., N. Y.; William H. Stead, Carroll L. Shartle, and associates, *Occpational Counseling Techniques* (New York: American Book Co., 1940), Ch. 4; Harold E. Burtt, *Principles of Employment Psychology* (New York: Harper & Brothers, 1942), Ch. 12; M. Joseph Dooher and Vivienne Marquis, *Rating Employee and Supervisory Performance*, American Management Association, 330 West 42nd Street, N. Y. (1950); *Personnel Psychology*, 6 vols. (Cleveland: Western Reserve University, 1948-54).

PROBLEMS OF SOUND WAGE ADMINISTRATION

The foundation of sound wage administration depends upon the suitability of the job classification and wage structure to the organization. Some personnel procedures can be altered time and again without creating any employee unrest. Selection and training procedures can be changed and modified, but those which directly affect the individual worker, such as transfer, promotion, and grievance procedures, can be changed only with difficulty. Modifying a wage structure is one of the most difficult personnel procedures to carry out. It is essential that management or management and the union establish a system of wage payment which meets the needs of the company and the approval of the employees. The welfare of the employees and of the company depends in part upon an administrable wage structure. Some of the problems encountered in establishing a new wage structure are discussed below.

Overpaid or underpaid employees

To inform a loyal employee who is paid more than the maximum determined for his job that he is *overpaid* is not a pleasant or desirable task. The new classification structure will invariably bring to light jobs that are overpaid as well as some that are underpaid. To admit to an individual or a group that errors in the wage structure have been discovered is both difficult and dangerous to employee morale. Procedures for correcting the errors should have been carefully determined in advance of the job-evaluation installation.

Bringing workers up to the minimum when they have been very much underpaid should probably be carried out by easy stages rather than by a single correction. At first glance this seems like an injustice. If some workers can be given wage increases up to 20 or 25 cents an hour, without their fellow workers feeling that they should receive an equal increase even though their jobs were correctly classified and priced before the evaluation, it is very desirable to do so. However, each company and each union must accept the responsibility of correcting inequities as quickly as possible *without upsetting the entire employee group.*

The number of job classes or labor grades

Some classification structures contain as many as 25 labor grades; however, this number of grades is much greater than the average. It is usually possible to "upgrade" a particular employee more easily when a classification structure contains many grades, than when fewer grades are used, because the difficulty level of jobs has such a fine breakdown that even a poor worker can be upgraded as he acquires skill. This is desirable in those organizations where there is a relatively large number of jobs with few workers on each job, and where promotional opportunities occur frequently. Most of us, in recalling our various jobs, classify them in terms of whether they were promotions from a lower to a higher rank. When one is called upon to evaluate a worker's new assignment, the question asked, either directly or indirectly, is invariably "Is this a promotion?"

The use of many labor grades usually results in a very narrow wage range for each grade or a very wide overlap in wages from grade to grade. When a wide range is used, it is possible to give many merit increases. It is believed by some that increases for merit tend to promote good morale, and that much of the worker's incentive is lost when he reaches the top of his wage range. On the other hand, with wide wage ranges for each labor grade it is possible for a worker in Class 2, for example, to earn more than a worker in Class 4 or even 5. Most of the value of having a high labor grade is lost when the worker in that grade finds that his pay is less than that of a worker in a lower grade.

The presence of too many labor grades decreases distinguishable differences in difficulty level between the grades. This is probably the major criticism of a large number of grades. It must be kept in mind, however, that the number of grades chosen depends upon the number of distinguishably different grades which can be obtained. If a group of jobs with a relatively narrow range of difficulty is evaluated, few classes will result. When a wide range of jobs is studied, more classes should be used. Setting an arbitrary number of grades without knowing the range of difficulty covered in the evaluation is an unsound procedure. Today there is a tendency to classify jobs into as few grades as possible. Not only has management been in favor of this reduction, but some unions have also insisted upon it.

The advantages of few classes far outweigh the disadvantages. First, the chances of having adjacent labor grades which are not distinguishably different are reduced. With fewer classes, each grade takes on a separate identity, so that there is less disagreement about the inclusion of a job in an appropriate class. Second, a wider range can be assigned to each class without having a large overlap in wages. This permits the company considerable latitude in rewarding merit or tenure by wage increases. Third, it is far easier to administer the wage structure. This last advantage is probably the most important.

Usually 10 to 12 job classes are considered sufficient, but a smaller number is often used. If the ranking technique has been employed, it is easy to divide the ranked jobs into the desired number of labor grades. Just where the lines should be drawn between grades is a problem which can be best handled by a committee. If job difficulty were distributed according to the normal curve of distribution, statistical techniques could be employed to divide the ranked jobs into grades approximately equal in difficulty. There is no evidence, however, that jobs are distributed normally. It is necessary to depend upon judgment to make sure that each labor grade is distinguishably different from the other labor grades. If it is accepted that all the jobs in Labor Grade 1 are less difficult than the jobs in Labor Grade 2, and those in Labor Grade 2 are less difficult than those in Labor Grade 3, and so on, and that all the jobs within each labor grade are the same or approximately the same in difficulty, then the correct number of labor grades has been selected.

Use of point values to establish job classes

The factor-comparison method and point systems give a difficulty value for each job. Usually the same range of points is assigned to each class. For example, Class 1 covers points 80 to 99; Class 2, points 100 to 119; Class 3, points 120 to 139, and so on. This does not mean that minor changes should not be made when an obvious error is observed, but it does mean that juggling point ranges to arrive at a preconceived classification is to deny the basic accuracy of the job evaluation. It is also a reversion to management fiat.

Varying the range of points from a narrow range for the simple jobs to a wider range for the more complex jobs has some merit (see Figure 14–4). This procedure is based on the assumption that the classes or labor grades at the lower end of the scale can be distinguished from each other on the basis of a narrow range of point values, whereas a wider range of point values is required to distinguish differences at the higher grade levels.

The difficulty point values provide a means of determining what jobs fall into each labor grade. Suppose, for example, that the job receiving the lowest point value is given 257 points, and the most difficult job is given 994 points. It would be possible to assign the

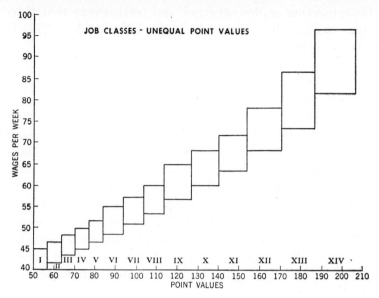

Fig. 14—4.

point values as shown in Table 14–1. This is accomplished by subtracting the minimum point value from the maximum and dividing the remaining point values among the grades. In this example the range of point values in each grade is 75.

In some situations the range for point values is determined by the minimum and maximum wage rates for all the jobs and the desired wage range for each labor grade. Suppose, for example, that the minimum rate in a factory is 75 cents per hour, and the maximum rate is $1.85 per hour. If it is desired that the first three grades have a wage range of 10 cents, the next two, a range of 15 cents,

TABLE 14—1 Grouping jobs on point value basis •		TABLE 14—2 Determining number of labor grades by wage ranges •	
Labor Grade	Point Value Range	Labor Grade	Wage Range
1	250–324	1	$ .75–$ .85
2	325–399	2	.85– .95
3	400–474	3	.95– 1.05
4	475–549	4	1.05– 1.20
5	550–624	5	1.20– 1.35
6	625–699	6	1.35– 1.55
7	700–774	7	1.55– 1.75
8	775–849	8	1.75– 1.95
9	850–924		
10	925–999		

and the remaining grades, 20 cents, and furthermore that there be no wage overlap, there would be eight labor grades. This is illustrated in Table 14–2.

Borderline jobs

One of the problems that confronts companies and unions alike is that of *borderline jobs*. These are jobs whose point values are close to the arbitrary division between two adjacent classes. One technique advanced to minimize friction is to have the classes or grades overlap in point values. For example, Class 1 jobs range in point value from 80 points to 120; Class 2, from 115 to 140; Class 3, from 135 to 180. Whenever a job falls in the point range of overlap a decision is made as to which class it more nearly resembles. This brings the point of friction to light and forces a decision before trouble occurs. When the job is priced it can be given either the rate of the higher class, or the lower class, or a rate somewhere in between the two.

Overlap in wage ranges

Wide Rate Ranges and Wide Overlap. Whenever a company wishes to have a wide rate range, it is usually necessary to have a wide overlap in the wage ranges among the labor grades. As mentioned above, this is apt to cause some worker unrest, because workers in a high grade can receive a lower wage than workers in a low grade. Figure 14–5 illustrates a wage system of this type. An individual at the minimum of Labor Grade 4, for example, would be below the maximum of Labor Grade 1. In fact the minimum of Labor Grade 5 is the same as the maximum of Labor Grade 1. This particular chart represents an interim wage structure which will ultimately be changed so that the overlap will be practically eliminated, the minimum wage for all classes will be increased, and the maximum decreased. The company using this wage chart believed that it would be better to adjust the wage structure gradually than to install a drastically new structure overnight.

A company using wide rate ranges is confronted with a dual problem. First, if the range is very wide, there will be inequities occurring within the range itself. For example, two workers of equal proficiency on different jobs in the same job classification can have a very large wage difference. This can be so wide as to cause an inequity within the wage range caused by an unfair administration of the merit system. A narrow range would have made it impossible to create a wide discrepancy in wages. It can also happen that two workers on the same job, with a small difference in job proficiency, can have a wide difference in wage payment. The wide range makes it possible to create the feeling of discrimination even though great care is exercised to pay each employee fairly. Second, if the range is very wide, there will tend to be a wide overlap in wages between the various classes. The problem is one of dealing with employees and trying to explain why a worker in Class 1 is earning the

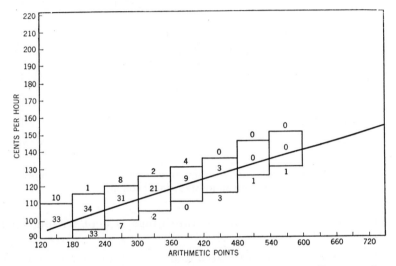

Fig. 14—5.   Maintenance and service wage curves and suggested classifications (N = 203).

same wage as a worker in Class 4 or 5. Men in higher labor grades and in higher job classes also want a higher wage.

Advantages of No Overlap. The trend in wage administration is to reduce the overlap in wage ranges as much as possible. Figure 14–6 is an example of a wage structure in which overlap has been eliminated, with the exception of an overlap between Grades 2 and 3. Whenever a company obtains a wage curve which is relatively flat, that is, one which has relatively little increase in salary or wages in proportion to the increase in point values, it is almost mandatory to have some overlap in rate ranges or to have extremely few job classes. It is also possible in an instance such as the one just cited to reduce the overlap by having very narrow rate ranges. Whenever a company has a steep wage curve, that is, one which has marked increase in salary or wages in comparison with an increase in point values, overlap can be eliminated entirely if the

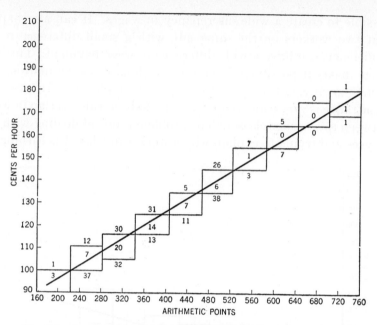

Fig. 14—6. Factory, work room, and skilled employees' wage curve and suggested classifications.

number of classes and width of rate range is kept within normal limits.

There seem to be definite advantages to having a wage structure which has acceptable wage ranges and little or no overlap between them. First, workers in a lower class will hardly ever receive a wage which is greater than workers in a higher class. In most instances an increase in rank will be accompanied by an increase in pay. The width of the wage range probably can be adjusted to the needs of the merit system without creating a wide overlap or decreasing the necessary number of classes.

Setting limits for rate ranges

Use of Money Limits for Rate Ranges. Setting rate ranges which give all employees the opportunity to receive the same amount in wage increases is sometimes desirable. Since in some plants it is difficult to promote from a lower to a higher labor grade, management must resort to "promotion through wage increases." In other plants where difference in difficulty level is not great, the use of the same "money limit" for the rate range at each difficulty level is recommended. Figure 14–7 shows how these limits are established

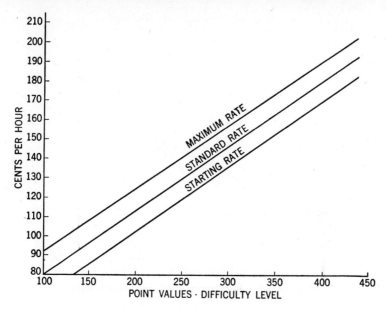

Fig. 14—7.   Rate ranges—money limits.

by using the wage curve as the base. In this example the wage curve is the standard rate and the starting rate is 10 cents below the curve. A wage structure of this kind limits all employees to a 20-cents-an-hour wage increase.

Per cent Limits. A worker earning only 80 cents an hour will definitely feel the effect of a raise of only a few cents per hour. A worker receiving $1.90 per hour will hardly notice a 5-cent-per-hour increase as it affects his standard of living. A wage range, to be noticeable, therefore, does not have to be as wide for the less skilled jobs as for the jobs at the higher difficulty levels. Where this is taken into consideration, a wage range on a percentage basis is often used. If the desire of those in charge is to make it possible for each worker to *feel* that there is the possibility of an appreciable increase in wages, then a range using a percentage basis is desirable.

Figure 14–8 illustrates a wage curve which is constructed on the basis of wages ranging from 10 per cent above the curve to 10 per cent below the wage curve. The usual practice is to have a much larger percentage than this at the higher point levels and a smaller percentage at the lower levels. Figure 14–9, which illustrates this principle, is a curve which was obtained for an evaluation involving 53 office jobs. Just as job classes should be noticeably different, so should the possible increases in salary.

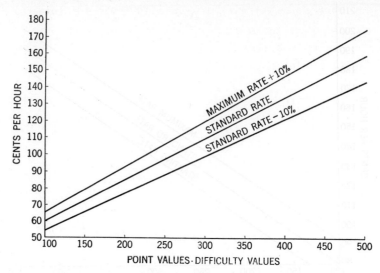

Fig. 14—8. Percentage basis for wage range.

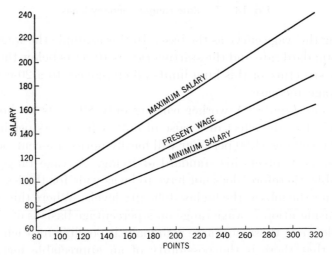

Fig. 14—9. Job evaluation of office positions. Relationship between point values and established minimum and maximum rates.

Use of Scatter Chart. The scatter chart or computational chart, Figure 13–19, page 425, can be used to determine both labor grades and wage rates. Some wage analysts attempt to "box in" as many workers as possible within an orderly wage range and point range. The tally marks in Figure 13–19 represent individual employees. Turning to this scatter chart it can be seen that if the point-value range of 80 to 119 points and the wage range of 70 cents to 89 cents per hour were selected, 13 employees would be within these ranges, 2 would be above, and none below. If this same point range (40) and wage range (20 cents an hour) were applied to the rest of the data on the scatter chart, most of the employees would fall within these ranges. Table 14–3 shows how these data taken from the scatter chart (Figure 13–19) could be "boxed" to obtain six labor grades. The number of workers falling above, within, and below the wage range is also shown. This method is designed to aid in establishing a new wage structure which is as close as possible to the old structure.

TABLE 14—3.   Results of the use of the computational chart for the determination of the wage curve in setting labor grades and wage rates •

Labor grade	Point value	Wage range	Number of workers above, within, and below wage range		
			Above	Within	Below
1	80–119	$ .70–$ .89	2	13	0
2	120–159	.90– 1.09	3	6	1
3	160–199	1.10– 1.29	1	2	1
4	200–239	1.30– 1.49	2	7	0
5	240–279	1.50– 1.69	1	4	1
6	280–319	1.70– 1.89	0	4	1

From *Handbook of Job Evaluation for Factory Jobs*, Personnel Research Institute of Western Reserve University (Cleveland: Industrial Fasteners Institute [formerly American Institute of Bolt, Nut and Rivet Manufacurers], 1946), p. 75.

CONCLUSION

Job evaluation is of the most value in determining base rates. These rates are highly important because all wage decisions and additional methods of payment must be founded upon them. The rules by which the basic wage structure is to be administered are matters for executive decision, collective bargaining, or both. The average plant has these rules established in either a formal or an informal manner. The use of a standard wage-rate system will require the installation of formal, or at least uniform, methods of wage administration.

Incentive systems, to be fair, must be based upon the difficulty values of jobs. To pay the workers on a simple assembly job an incentive which makes their total wage equal to or in excess of the wages paid at the skilled level will endanger the success of the industrial relations program. A sound basic wage structure serves as a sentinel guarding against inequities.

A great deal can be done to complicate the construction of a wage structure. There is much emotional thinking about wages, and workers are always on guard about matters affecting their pay. An army officer once explained his attitude toward psychological tests by saying, "What I'm not up on, I'm down on." This statement can be applied to the acceptance of a wage structure by people who do not understand it—they are usually "down on it." The use of complicated charts and graphs is necessary in order to be exact and accurate. However, if a freehand curve drawn through the tallies on a scatter chart is the best way of showing a group of employees how to derive a wage curve, it is better to use this technique than to confuse with exactness and accuracy.

Job-evaluation methods have been regarded with suspicion because of their complexity. "Just another way of gypping workers with something they can't understand," is a statement about the job evaluation that certainly bodes no good for the finished study. As Viteles [8] points out, ". . . to capitalize most effectively upon job evaluation, in terms of worker satisfaction, requires that they [employees] be encouraged to participate fully and *understandingly* in the preparation of the yardstick and that they be provided with a complete explanation of the principles which underlie it." This statement could be extended to include the pricing of the evaluated jobs once their difficulty level has been determined.

SUGGESTIONS FOR STUDY AND RESEARCH

1. Contrast the problems of a company having a single rate for each job class with those of a company having a 40 per cent wage spread for each job class.

2. What problems are encountered with a marked wage overlap between labor grades?

3. Set up six labor grades for the data presented for the Chapter 13 case problem.

CASE PROBLEM

One of the leading companies in a community has long been an advocate of paying employees on the basis of merit and has installed a merit rating system which is used as the basis for all wage increases. The union con-

[8] Morris S. Viteles, "A Psychologist Looks at Job Evaluation," *Personnel*, American Management Association, Vol. 17, No. 3 (February 1941), p. 175. Italics are the authors'.

tends that favoritism is present and wants to eliminate the merit rating system and have an automatic progression. Neither side is willing to change and both have agreed to arbitrate.

PROBLEM: Assume that you are the personnel director. Prepare a brief showing why the merit system should be retained and showing the advantage to the employees. Then assume you are the union president. Prepare a brief showing why the automatic progression is most advantageous to the company and to the employees.

tends that favoritism is present and wants to eliminate the merit rating system and have an automatic progression. Neither side is willing to change and both have agreed to arbitrate.

PROBLEM: Assume that you are the personnel director. Prepare a brief showing why the merit system should be retained and showing the advantage to the employees. Then assume you are the union president. Prepare a brief showing why the automatic progression is most advantageous to the company and to the employees.

Part Six

Wage and Salary Administration

15

Establishing the Wage and Salary Administration System

WHEN THE WAGE STRUCTURE HAS BEEN SET up and all jobs in the company are classified and given standard titles, each employee must then be identified by his new standard job title and code. The classification of his job will automatically determine the rate or rate range to be applied to each worker. The techniques for assigning standard job titles to employees at this point are the same as those discussed in Chapter 12. If the Employee Job-Identification Record card files described in that chapter have been kept up to date from the time they were originally set up, these records then provide the basis for putting the new job titles and their corresponding rates or rate ranges into effect at this time. Where a considerable period of time may have elapsed between the job-identification of employees for purposes of computing the wage curve and the time when the job-evaluation pay structure goes into effect, it may be necessary to do the job-identification over again. If this is the case, the above-mentioned techniques may be applied at this time just as they were in preparing the data for the wage curve. However, the job of putting the new pay structure into effect then will be a comparatively simple process.

When the new job title, code, and labor-grade classification for each individual have been determined, it is important that this information be entered on personnel records of the company. From this point on, the new standardized structure is to be used throughout all personnel operations. In order to accomplish this, it is necessary that all operating personnel have copies of the information they will need, such as the new standard titles, codes, labor-grades, rates or rate ranges, and job descriptions and specifications. As indicated in Chapter 11, the tabulations from the punched-card records of the job evaluation will be of considerable assistance in setting up reference volumes for the use of the employees concerned with the administrative details.

DETERMINING THE PAY RATE OF EACH EMPLOYEE

When each employee has been identified by the new standard job title with the corresponding rate or rate range, it is then necessary to compare his present rate with the rate established by the new pay structure. If this new structure includes rate ranges, the rate of any individual may be below the minimum, it may be within the range, or it may be above the range. If the new rate range for a given job is different from the old rate range for that job, then each employee will be in a different position in the new rate range from the one he occupied in the old range. For example, an employee who was at the maximum of his range before the new structure was established, may now be at the minimum of the new range of his job. It will be necessary to decide whether this arrangement is satisfactory or whether this individual's rate should be changed so that he will be at the maximum of the new range just as he was at the maximum of the old range.

If the wage structure calls for single rates there may be relatively few workers whose wage rates will *not* have to be changed. In such a case, should all workers' wage rates be adjusted immediately to the single rates established for each job? If ranges were used previously in the company, many workers may be above the single rate. Are the wage rates of these workers to be reduced, or are they to be left where they are until the wage scale again changes or they are promoted or retired? If the wage structure has rate ranges with progression through the ranges based on length of service, should the length-of-service progression be the same in all labor grades or should it be slower in the higher-paid labor grades? These questions and many related ones must be decided when the new wage structure is put into operation.

Overpaid employees

Regardless of the type of wage structure, the particular company, or the many individual conditions that may be encountered in putting a standardized wage structure into effect, there are some problems which are virtually universal and require certain policy decisions in almost every case. One frequently encountered problem is what to do about those employees whose wage rates are already above the maximum that will be established by the new structure. In fact, this problem is so common that in almost all cases the policy decision is made before the job evaluation is even started. Possible decisions on the problem are as follows:

1. Reduce the wage rates of all such employees to the maximum of the range, or to the single rate.

2. Do not change the wage rates on these employees.

3. Leave the rates of these employees where they are for the present, but attempt to eliminate these inequities by:

  a. Transferring or promoting such employees, where possible, into jobs where their rates will be within the range.
  b. Retiring all such employees that are of retirement age.
  c. Increasing the responsibilities on the jobs held by these overpaid employees, so that their jobs will be evaluated higher and their present rates then will fall within the range of this changed job.

4. Reduce the rate to the maximum of the range, with the understanding that the employee will be promoted at the first opportunity.

5. Continue the present rate for a specified time only, with the understanding that it will be reduced to the maximum of the range at that time.[1]

6. Reduce the wage rates of all such employees after other methods suggested above have been tried.

The decision in the individual company may incorporate all or some of the above possibilities, or variations of them, as well as individual arrangements to take care of peculiar conditions. It has been the general practice wherever possible to avoid reducing the salary or wage of any employee as a result of a new pay structure established through job evaluation to eliminate pay inequities. There are two primary reasons for this:

1. It is bad practice to reduce wages or salaries, especially if there is no specific fault on the part of the employee and if his duties and responsibilities are not changed.

2. Inequities in the wage structure are ordinarily the respon-

---

[1] Riegel states: "These periods are three months, six months, and one year in different companies." John W. Riegel, *Salary Determination*, Report No. 2, Bureau of Industrial Relations (Ann Arbor: University of Michigan Press, 1940), p. 146.

sibility of the management of the company, not of employees; therefore, any steps necessary to eliminate all or a major part of these inequities should not be at the expense of the employees.

The decision as to how to handle this problem of overpaid workers in any company will, in the final analysis, depend on the conditions in that company. One of the several possible solutions listed above, in conjunction with a policy based on these points of view with respect to the responsibility for the inequities, will be satisfactory, in most cases, to the workers involved and to the management of the company. In any case, over a period of time, these inequities due to overpayment will tend to disappear because of promotions, retirement, death, quits, or other reasons. If, in addition, any general increases in the wage or salary structure are put into effect and these overpaid workers do not receive the full amount, it is possible that they thus will be brought within the range or at least that the amount of overpayment will be reduced.

Figure 15–1 illustrates a typical distribution of wage rates plotted against the labor-grade classifications of the jobs. On this plot there is superimposed the wage structure indicating the number of workers below the minimum, above the maximum, and within the range for each classification.

Raising underpaid employees

In the example shown in Figure 15–1, it will be noted that in almost every labor grade a number of workers, prior to the installation of the new wage structure, were being paid less than the minimum wage of this new wage scale. One of the primary reasons for the installation of job evaluation—the reduction or elimination of wage inequities—centers around the "underpaid" workers. Those employees who are below the minimum of the new wage ranges simply may be raised to the minimum of the range which corresponds to their jobs when the new structure is put into effect. This step certainly is indicated where such employees have been on these jobs for a period of time, and are considered capable of at least minimum performance on their jobs.

Where the adjustment required to raise any individual to the minimum of the new range is very great, there may be some justification for making this adjustment in two or three steps rather than all at once. In discussing salaries which are below the minimum of the newly established range, Riegel [2] says "A salary deficient to a

---

[2] *Ibid.*, pp. 145–146.

greater degree (than one step) is raised the amount of one step, and, after a few months, is raised again to the minimum. If an underpaid employee's salary is corrected by a large increase, he may become resentful or may overrate the value of his services."

As a qualification of the above statement, however, Riegel [3] states further that "Ideally, all unduly low salaries should be raised to the

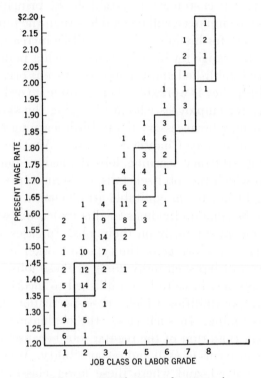

Fig. 15—1.   Distribution of ratings by labor grades against wage rates.

'minimums' before any feature of the salary scale is discussed with employees." This may be possible in the case of salaried personnel, especially if they are not organized; it would almost never be possible with employees organized in a union. Under such circumstances, it probably would be required, under the National Labor Relations Act, that such changes in wage scales be arrived at by collective bargaining. It would be necessary then, in order to raise gradually these underpaid workers to the minimum of the new salary ranges before the new structure was put into effect, to establish

[3] *Ibid.*

agreement on this point with the employee representatives in the company.

There is another factor which may well be given serious consideration in connection with coming to a decision on a policy for adjusting the pay of these underpaid workers. Where a standardized wage or salary structure replaces haphazard administration of wages in a company, it is customary to establish the principle that, from this point on, no employee will be paid less than the minimum of the range established for his job and none will be increased beyond the maximum of the range for his job. Where such a policy is adopted, the ranges are established and the job structure is organized in such a way that this policy is workable. For example, in order to establish equitable pay for employees who are learning the skills of a given occupation, it may be necessary to establish learning classifications, as discussed earlier (see Chapter 8, p. 261). Another possibility is to provide for arbitrary learning jobs defined as one labor grade below that in which the job itself falls. In some types of jobs, however, this might not be an equitable arrangement.

There may be some individuals in this underpaid group who are not performing satisfactorily on their jobs. In cases of emergency, such as an extreme shortage of the type of worker involved, where it is necessary to keep such individuals in these jobs, a lower grade of the same job may have to be established to incorporate only the duties and responsibilities which these particular employees are capable of assuming. In such cases, the evaluation of these jobs would be lower than that of the regular jobs because of the reduced requirements in terms of skill and responsibility. Where there is no emergency involved, and where these lower classifications of the occupation are not actually required in the organizational structure of the company, the obvious solution is either to place these workers in jobs which they are capable of performing or to release them from the company. This reasoning also applies to physically handicapped employees. Here again a job having requirements which these workers are capable of fulfilling may be established if such workers are to be kept on the payroll in this occupation.

While arrangements for these additional jobs may seem somewhat cumbersome and actually may tend to complicate the job structure of the company, experience has shown that under most conditions this approach is preferable to any in which the structure itself is violated in some respects. For example, it is possible to handle such deviations as these by providing, in the administration of the pay structure, for paying workers who are not fully qualified less than the minimum established for the job in which they are classified. Such deviations, however, may lead to violations of the pay structure by underpaying workers who actually are capable of fulfilling the requirements of the job. Where the same leeway is provided for overpaying workers on individual jobs, the difficulty may be even more pronounced, especially when this comes to the attention of other workers in the group covered by the structure. In either case an opportunity for introducing inequities into the pay structure is created.

Employees paid within the new ranges

The third group of workers found in any labor grade are, of course, those whose present rates are within the ranges established by the new pay structure. Depending on the circumstances in the individual company, it may or may not be necessary to make an adjustment in the rates of these workers. Where there have been no rate ranges used previously in the company or where these ranges generally have not been standardized, the simplest method (which may be as effective as any) is to make no change in the wage rates of these employees when the new structure is set up. However, where the company previously has had well established and possibly well publicized rate ranges for each job, it may be necessary to make adjustments in the individual rates.

Merit Ranges. Merit ranges provide for considerable flexibility in making adjustments when a new pay structure is installed. The range for Cost Clerk, for example, may have been changed from $215–260 a month to $240–280 a month. Those who are being paid $260 a month are within the new salary range for the job. However, whereas these Cost Clerks were previously at the top of their range, they are now at the midpoint. Therefore, although there is no change indicated, since they are within the new range, the position of these particular Cost Clerks with respect to all others who now are paid a minimum of $240 a month has been changed by making the adjustments incident to introducing the new pay structure. It may be advisable, in such a case, to place these workers in the same relative position in the new rate range as that which they occupied in the old one. Consequently, Cost Clerks earning $260 a month would be increased to $280 a month so that they would be at the maximum of the new range, just as they were at the maximum of the old range.

Such a method of adjustment might become rather expensive if the general level of the new pay structure is higher than that of the previous rate structure, as will usually be the case. Furthermore, it should be kept in mind that while some workers may be at the maximum of their ranges under the old pay structure, they may have gotten there, not because they were judged to be exceptionally well qualified for the job, but merely because it was necessary to increase their pay within the range in order to encourage them to stay with the company in times of labor shortage. Such cases are not at all uncommon where a company has failed to increase its general pay level at the same rate at which the pay level in the community has been increased over a period of years. Thus, the introduction of a new pay scale which establishes new, higher maximums for all or most jobs can be used as an opportunity for adjusting inequities *within* ranges if the pay of those workers within the new ranges is not immediately adjusted on some uniform basis. This can be accomplished by reviewing the effectiveness and merit of the work of each individual employee through a merit-rating system, and placing each employee within his rate range according to the results of this merit rating. It should be kept in mind that, even though the salaries of these workers are within the new ranges, the inequities they represent may be almost as serious as those caused by rates which are above the maximum or below the minimum.

As indicated above, the policy adopted in any company will depend on an analysis of the facts as they existed in that company under the old pay structure. These facts definitely should include figures indicating whether employees in the company are now being paid on the average near the maximum of their ranges, near the minimum of their ranges, or at some point in between. Thus, if it is found that, on the average, employees in the company are being paid at a level 90 per cent above the minimums of their ranges and thus 10 per cent below the maximums, obviously most workers are at or near the maximums of the ranges in which their jobs fall. If this situation can be justified by the fact that most workers in the company are as efficient as any that could be secured, then it may be only logical to decide that, in establishing the new structure, workers will be placed in the same position in the new ranges as they occupied in the old ranges. If, however, it is determined that this situation has come about as the result of increases within ranges without regard to merit, then the logical decision may be to make no adjustments on those workers who are within the new ranges except as subsequent merit rating may indicate their eligibility for merit increases. In this way, the salaries in the company may be stabilized in the future in such a way that the average of the salaries of all workers in each labor grade will be kept at or near the mid-point of the labor grade in which their jobs are evaluated.

Automatic Progression. In the installation of rate ranges which incorporate an automatic-progression feature, those workers who are overpaid will be handled in the same manner as under any other type of structure. However, for those workers whose wage rates are below the minimum called for by the structure or are within the ranges established for their jobs, some variation of the above procedures may be advisable. For purposes of illustration, we may assume a rate range with a 15-cent spread, from $1.40 to $1.55. The automatic progression under such a structure might call for an increase from $1.40 to $1.45 at the end of three months, from $1.45 to $1.50 after an additional six months, and from $1.50 to $1.55 after an additional year on the job. Thus, any new employee will be paid $1.40 an hour when he starts on this job, and after 21 months, through automatic increases, he will be earning $1.55 an hour.

When a structure of this type is installed, those workers whose rates are below the minimum of the range corresponding to their jobs may be handled in any one of the ways suggested above for raising underpaid workers to the minimum. In this case, however, there is another possibility. Many of these underpaid workers already may have enough service with the company on that job to qualify for the automatic-progression increases incorporated in the plan. Thus a worker earning $1.35 who has been on the job two years might be considered to be qualified now for the top of the range—that is, $1.55. This same situation would apply to individuals who are now within this $1.40–1.55 range. For example, a worker with six years of experience on this job now being paid $1.50 would, by this reasoning, be assigned a rate of $1.55 an hour when this new structure is put into operation.

The alternative to such special arrangements on automatic-progression wage structures is to institute the automatic progressions from the date at which the structure is established. Thus the worker with five years' tenure on the job earning $1.50 an hour would be increased to $1.55 an hour one year after the structure was put into effect. This approach to the problem seems much more logical and practical than the first method described above. For one thing, the installation of a new wage structure is almost always a very expensive process for the business. This is so because workers whose rates are above their corresponding new ranges are not reduced, while those below the minimum of their ranges are almost always raised at least to the minimum as soon as it is practicable.

Single Rates. A pay structure composed of single rates rather than rate ranges ordinarily will be used to put job evaluation into effect only in those companies which have had single rates or full automatic progression previously. The reason for this is that any single rate structure, in order to avoid having an extremely high percentage of workers paid above the structure on the basis of their former rates, necessarily will have to be set up at a rather high level in relation to present wages. For example, if a single rate structure were established for the hypothetical example given in Figure 15–1, these single rates would almost have to be the tops of the labor grades shown in this figure. If the single rates were established at the midpoint level of each of these labor grades, about 50 per cent of the employees in the group covered by the job evaluation then would be above the rates called for by the new structure. The installation of such a structure, therefore, would eliminate or reduce relatively few inequities in pay within this group of workers.

Since about the only practical way to install single rates is to place them at a very high level, this is practicable only in those companies which have substantially approached a single-rate system previously. As an illustration, if a company has had rate ranges over a period of time and a very high percentage of employees is already at the maximum, or close to it, the installation of single rates at the maximums of the present ranges would involve relatively little disruption of the present setup. Where a company has operated under rate ranges with merit progression, however, this situation is relatively rare, except under unusual circumstances. It will be found ordinarily only where there has been full automatic progression with rather low turnover, or where single rates have been in effect previously in the company. Under such circumstances, if the company decides to establish a pay structure based on single rates, the difficulties usually are not too great. Where a single-rate pay structure is the long-term objective of a company which now has rate ranges with merit progression or random rates, it would be logical first to establish rate ranges with merit progression, later to change to rate ranges with full automatic progression, and finally to introduce single rates.

Cost factors to be considered

As pointed out in Chapter 13, any new pay structure, based on job evaluation and instituted for the purpose of reducing or eliminating inequities in pay, almost always will have a higher general pay level than existed in the company under the old pay rates. This combination of costs to the company is usually written off as an expense resulting from management oversights or mistakes in permitting pay inequities to come about. But if we add to this the expense of a plan whereby almost all employees in the group, save those who are overpaid already, are given a pay increase at the time the new structure is installed, the cost may be prohibitive. Whenever it is considered necessary to place workers in the same relative position in the new ranges as they occupied in the old ranges, it is almost mandatory that the general level of the new ranges be equal to or somewhat lower than the pay level of the rates previously in effect, unless the company is in a position to increase its labor costs materially.

To illustrate, we may assume that the average hourly base rate of all workers in a group of jobs on which a new job-evaluation wage structure is to be established is $1.80 an hour. If only a minimum amount of rate adjustment is provided for in installing the new plan, the new structure may be set up with an average hourly base rate of $1.90. However, if, as described above, almost all workers must be given some rate increase to place them in the same position in the new ranges as they occupied in the old ones, the cost of this procedure may make it necessary to establish the new structure in such a way that the average hourly base rate will be $1.80 an hour rather than $1.90 an hour. In doing this, however, the relationship to community and industry wage rates cannot be ignored.

In addition to the actual financial problems created by this plan, we must consider the effect on all employees of increasing the hourly rate of some workers as much as 20, 25, or even 30 cents an hour when the new wage structure is installed.

This problem is somewhat different, however, where the new wage structure incorporates rate ranges with a combination of automatic progression and merit progression. Whether employees will be placed in new ranges according to their length of service on the job at the time the structure is installed will be determined by a study of the facts. These facts would include for one thing the number and type of employees who might receive large increases in hourly rates under this plan. Particularly important would be an analysis of the distribution of workers throughout the entire wage structure to determine what percentage of the employees might be involved in wage increases resulting from this method of installing a new structure. If it were necessary to grant rate increases to 90 per cent of the employees in the group under this method of installing the pay structure, the situation would be entirely different from what it would be if only 15 per cent of the workers were to be given increases.

The actual costs of several alternative methods for handling this problem can be calculated in the same manner as the cost level of the structure itself is calculated, as described in Chapter 16. As a matter of fact, in determining the cost of the pay structure, the method of installation and the policies under which wages and salaries will be administered on the basis of this structure must also be taken into account in any estimation of the future total labor costs. For example, the cost of a pay structure made up of ranges with merit progression can be calculated on the basis of the assumption that, after a period of time, the rates of all workers in each labor grade will average the midpoint of the range. If the circumstances in the individual company indicate that this average will be either higher or lower than the midpoint, the cost of the pay structure can be calculated on the basis of the estimated average.

This same pay structure with full automatic progression in all labor grades from the minimum to the maximum of each wage range will be quite different, however. In making such calculations it would be necessary to determine the average rate which might be expected in the individual labor grades. In the lowest labor grades, this would be estimated by taking into account the length of time necessary for a worker to progress from the minimum to the maximum, offsetting this by an estimate of the percentage of workers who at any one time might be below the maximum of this range based on the amount of turnover to be expected in the jobs included in this labor grade. It is necessary to do this for each labor grade individually, for the turnover of workers probably will be different in each labor grade because of the differences in types of jobs, and moreover, the automatic-progression arrangements may be more rapid in the lower labor grades than they are in the higher ones. In order to make an accurate estimate of the cost of any proposed wage structure of this type, then, it is necessary to take all of these factors into account and to estimate the effect of each factor as accurately as possible.

PUTTING THE NEW PAY RATE INTO EFFECT

The new pay rate for each individual employee covered in the job evaluation cannot be determined until a policy for the general procedure to be followed has been adopted. Then, when all workers have been identified by their new job titles and by the corresponding labor-grade classifications according to the new wage structure, the established procedure can be followed in determining what change, if any, should be made in the wage rate of each employee covered by the job evaluation.

These wage rates will be determined almost entirely by the labor-grade classifications assigned to each individual as determined by the job on which he works. Leaving out of consideration for the moment length of service on the job and any special arrangements which may be made for raising underpaid workers to the minimum, it will be seen that the assignment of workers to the new standard job titles is the key factor in determining the new wage rate. For example, in a pay structure based on ranges with merit progression, where all workers below the minimum are to be raised immediately to the minimum, all workers within the range are to retain their present rates, and all workers above the range also are to keep their present rates, the procedure is very simple. It is necessary only to determine the rate range which applies to any individual on the basis of the labor-grade classification in which his job falls. If his present rate is below the minimum, it is to be raised to the minimum; if it is at the minimum or above, no change is indicated. It only remains then to carry out the customary clerical procedures in posting the new titles, codes, labor grades, classifications, and wage rates on all personnel records which carry this information. All changes in rates resulting from this process are then put into effect through the normal payroll procedures.

A payroll authorization form [4] of the type shown in Figure 16–1 can be very useful in carrying out this process in an orderly fashion. When all required changes in wage rates are recorded on a form of this type, they can be verified very easily before they are put through officially. If copies are provided, as in the example shown, one can be retained in the files of the Personnel Department as the official record of the action; one can go to the Payroll Department as authorization to pay the new rate; a third can go to the worker's supervisor for his record, and as notification so that he can inform the employee of the change in rate.

[4] Courtesy of The National Screw & Manufacturing Company, Cleveland.

It will also be necessary to establish some system for posting changes in job titles on all records, and for recording job codes and labor-grade classifications if this information is now to be included in the record systems of the company. The payroll authorization form of Figure 16–1 will suffice for this purpose also. However, where the Employee Job-Identification Record (Figure 12–1) has been used in recording the standard job title of all workers under the new pay structure, it may be used instead. The payroll authorization form then would be used only for those employees whose wage or salary rates were being changed.

SUGGESTIONS FOR STUDY AND RESEARCH

1. On the basis of the six labor grades you have set up for the Chapter 13 case problem (see Suggestion #3 at the end of Chapter 14, page 456) what recommendations would you make to the company regarding individual wage adjustments upon the installation of the job evaluation?

2. Compute the cost to the company of raising all employees immediately to the minimum of the labor grades of your Chapter 13 case problem.

3. What are the arguments, pro and con, regarding any individual wage adjustments for employees within the wage ranges of your Chapter 13 case problem? What about those now above the maximums of their rate ranges?

CASE PROBLEM

WAGE ADJUSTMENTS UPON INSTALLATION OF THE NEW WAGE STRUCTURE: Assume that you are a consultant supervising the job evaluation program of a company in which the results are those shown in Figure 15–1. The job classes have been decided on, resulting in eight labor grades, and employees on the jobs in each labor grade have been plotted in 5¢ per hour wage intervals as shown. The company has decided it wants to establish the rate ranges shown by the boxes in Figure 15–1.

PROBLEM: Do you agree with the company's decision regarding the rate ranges to be set up? Outline your analysis of this problem, indicating why the company's decision is proper, or why your suggested changes are an improvement over the company's proposed wage structure.

Assuming that the wage structure shown in Figure 15–1 is to be installed and immediately followed by a 5¢ per hour increase in the entire wage structure—all maximums and minimums—what recommendations would you make regarding individual wage adjustments with respect to those employees now below the minimums of the present rate ranges, those above the maximums, and those now within the present rate ranges? Shall all employees' rates be increased 5¢ per hour to correspond with the increase in the wage structure? Shall some employees get more than 5¢ an hour increase? Shall some get less? Shall some get no increase now?

16

Wage and Salary Administration as a Management Control

THE PROCEDURE OF ESTABLISHING JOB evaluation has as its objective the installation of a sound wage and salary administration program in the company. This objective is the guiding principle of the entire process. Beginning with the decision by management to undertake job evaluation on through the development of the system, the analysis and rating of jobs, and the establishment of the wage structure, this objective must be the determining factor in all the decisions that are made. For example, the particular job-evaluation system that is selected is judged in terms of whether it is sound, practical, and easy to install; it must also be judged in terms of whether it will result in a wage structure that will form a sound basis for the administration of wages and salaries.

Many features of the job-evaluation system used, and particularly of the type of wage structure established on the basis of the ratings of jobs, are important factors in the administrative control procedures to be set up. The slope of the wage curve—the extent of the pay differentials between the lowest paid jobs and highest paid jobs —as well as the general level of the wage structure in relation to wage levels in the community, will affect the administrative detail established to operate on the basis of the wage structure. Such details as rate ranges versus single rates, automatic progression within ranges as against placement on the basis of merit, point range, money range, and amount of overlapping of labor grades, all must be taken into account in determining how the established wage structure is to be administered.

Actually, the types of administrative control which the management of the company wishes to establish as the result of the job evaluation will determine the detailed characteristics of the job evaluation and the resulting wage structure. For example, if it is decided that the amount of management control which can be achieved through the administration of wage ranges, where placement is determined by merit, is not worth the price in terms of the difficulties of administering such a system, the wage structure will be set up differently. In such a case, the alternatives probably are either single rates or rate ranges with predetermined progression based on length of service.

Within the scope of this book, it would be impossible to discuss in detail the administrative techniques of the innumerable types of wage structures that might be based on job evaluation. Consequently, the following discussion of techniques of administrative control necessarily must be confined to principles and illustrations of principles. Wherever individual techniques can be applied to all types of pay structures, these are discussed in some detail.

GENERAL AREAS OF CONTROL

Keeping rates in line with the structure

Once the standard pay structure based on the evaluation of all jobs is put into effect it must be followed rigidly in all assignments or changes of rates: any increases which would exceed the maximum of the established rates or ranges should not be permitted, and any worker who is capable of fulfilling the minimum requirements of the job on which he is working should not be paid less than the minimum rate established for that job. The wage policy may provide for some variations dependent upon the individual circumstances within the company. However, observance of the general principles established by the wage policy is essential in order to maintain the wage structure as an operating control.

This operating control is maintained through the accurate job-identification of all employees at all times. The importance of proper job-identification of employees lies in the fact that it serves to insure proper pay to all employees in relation to the work they are required to perform. A simple clerical record of job titles, with their corresponding labor-grade classifications and the current wage or salary rate of each employee, is the control "mechanism."

Prevention of pay inequities

The important feature of this control—its simplicity—is the fact that, when workers are properly identified by the standard job titles, their base rate ranges or single rates are established automatically. For example, the job of Furnace Tender, occupational code number 194, in job classification 3, has a corresponding rate range of $1.50 to $1.62 the same as all other jobs in Class 3. Any routine request to increase above $1.62 the wage rate of a worker whose job title is Furnace Tender, is automatically disapproved; any payroll authorization to put a Furnace Tender on the payroll at less than $1.50 likewise is not approved. Single rates operate in the same fashion except that there is no range of flexibility. With this control, only a small percentage of wage problems will require special handling— chiefly those of employees who were paid more than the job structure indicated for their jobs at the time the wage structure was installed.

Control within rate ranges

Beyond the control set up by the established maximum and minimum of each rate range, there may also be controls for adjustments within ranges—for example, the various types of automatic progression within rate ranges. Although in most cases automatic progression insures specific increases to satisfactory employees at stated intervals, it also limits the frequency with which rate increases may be given, and thus provides for little freedom of action by supervisors in making adjustments within the rate ranges. Possibilities of control within ranges, therefore, are limited largely to merit ranges, because single rates, of course, provide no flexibility in individual pay.

Control of related personnel operations

When all jobs in the company are defined, described, and identified by standard job titles, the job as the basic unit of personnel procedures in the company is clearly established. It is then possible to manipulate and classify these units, i.e., jobs, in many different ways, to establish controls in addition to those directly concerned with wage and salary administration. Some examples are selection, promotion, transfer, and training. These additional controls are the by-products of the standardization accomplished by the job evaluation. In many ways the controls in these fields of related personnel operations are just as valuable as those in the field of wage and salary administration.

IMPORTANCE OF EMPLOYEE IDENTIFICATION BY STANDARD JOB TITLES

The controls developed from the organized information obtained from job evaluation are built fundamentally on standardized job titles. The key feature of these controls is the fact that the standard job title in all cases signifies, and is the index to, a particular job in a particular department for which there is a job description and job specification. Standard job titles are thus the key to all job information in the company. Job titles can be manipulated, grouped, and classified more easily than job descriptions or other written information on jobs. For example, job titles and other identifying features of jobs can be put into punched-card tabulation records to be sorted, printed, and used in checking the original job-evaluation ratings (see Chapter 11). Punched cards containing the job title, department number, code, and other information can be made and kept current so that this information can be easily sorted, classified, and tabulated to suit a variety of purposes.

Data for a promotional chart, for example, may be obtained from the job title and information cards. Sorting and arranging record cards bearing the job title of each job in the company is, in effect, sorting and arranging all the jobs in the company. Thus, on the basis of the job information indicated by the standard job titles, a plan can be developed readily to show the normal sequences of transfer and promotion, both within and across departmental lines. While such promotional charts may be developed on the basis of any system of job titling, they are accurate only when the job titles used are based on accurate definitions and descriptions. Details of the establishment and use of promotional charts in employee development through in-plant recruitment for transfer and promotion are given in standard works on personnel and industrial management.[1]

Another important use of standard defined job titles is in connection with the seniority rights of employees on an occupational basis. In straight plant seniority, the latest date of hire representing the beginning of continuous employment is the most important fact. In departmental seniority, the important fact is the date of hire or transfer into the department. In occupational seniority, the important fact for the operation of the system is the date of hire or

---

[1] See Ralph C. Davis, *Industrial Management*, rev. ed. (New York: Harper & Brothers, 1940), p. 575; and Walter Dill Scott, Robert C. Clothier, and William R. Spriegel, *Personnel Management*, 5th ed. (New York: McGraw-Hill Book Co., Inc., 1954), pp. 227–228.

transfer into each occupation which the worker has held during his service with the company. To operate the seniority system adequately, therefore, it is essential that there be definitely established occupations in the company, that these occupations be clearly defined and indicated by standard job titles, and that all records of transfer from one occupation to another be accurate. By maintaining accurate current records of standard job titles of employees at all times, the necessary basic data for operation of an occupational seniority system are readily available.

In addition to the simple matter of maintaining the proper pay rates of all employees in relation to the jobs they are required to do, there are obviously, then, many other reasons why, in modern management practice, it is important that the personnel records reflect accurately at all times the job titles of all employees. A few of these reasons are as follows:

1. An accurate record of current job title and a record of experience in all previous jobs held in the company is essential to the operation of an occupational seniority system.

2. The results of merit rating of employees in the company can be interpreted properly only when they are recorded in relation to the job being performed by the individual at the time of the rating.

3. Any in-plant recruiting system for promotion and transfer of employees within the company requires a complete, accurate work record and current information about the jobs held by workers, as well as about the length of their experience on these jobs.

4. Many transfers within the company remove the employees from one group of workers and place them in another. For example, a promotion from an operative position to assistant foreman status makes many changes in the conditions of work of the employee, such as his seniority status, vacation privileges, type of payment, whether hourly or salary, eligibility for different types of insurance protection and other welfare programs, and many related factors.

   a. A transfer may remove an employee from a job which is included in those whose occupants are eligible for membership in the union to one which is outside the bargaining unit covered by the union. If such an employee continues his membership in the union, including payment of dues and assessments, without the knowledge that he is no longer eligible to belong to this group, he may register a justified complaint.

   b. A transfer may make the employee eligible for additional life, accident, and health insurance coverage and pension benefits to which he would not be entitled if the transfer were not made official. This is particularly important where the company pays all or a large part of the premiums or cost of such benefits.

c. Most employees promoted or transferred to different jobs require some break-in training on the new job. If the training program of the company is very closely organized and controlled, this control must be based on current accurate records of employee job-assignment and notification of any such action requiring attention of the Training Department.

d. Some transfers, promotions, or demotions may move the employee from a job which is exempt from the provisions of the Fair Labor Standards Act with respect to payment for overtime into a job in which the employer is legally required to pay for all overtime hours. If this change in status is not clear to the employee, he may lose considerable overtime payment to which he is entitled; also, if he finds out later that he has not been receiving pay to which he is entitled and that he may file a claim for this back pay, the cost of such oversights to the company is considerable. On the other hand, where the employee is transferred to a job where payment for overtime is no longer required but is continued because the change in job title is not recorded, the company will pay penalty rates for overtime work where such pay is not required.

5. Layoffs or increases in force must be planned on the basis of employees now on the payroll in relation to the reduced or increased needs by occupation. In order to plan and control these increases or decreases in number of workers, accurate information on the number of workers on each job is required.

6. Where an attempt is made to survey periodically the work force of the entire company in terms of the number or percentage of workers employed in various categories, the accurate job-identification of employees is essential. For example, an accurate comparison of the ratio of direct workers to indirect workers, of supervisory employees to total employment, of skilled workers to various groups of unskilled workers, can be made from personnel records if these records are accurate in terms of employee job titles.

7. Cost-accounting reports and cost-accounting control procedures depend in part on a record of the job performed by each individual, so that the cost of this work may be charged accurately to the proper account. If a considerable number of employees who

are actually doing work which falls in the indirect classification are classified as direct workers, the interpretation of the reports of cost distribution may be materially affected.

MAINTAINING ACCURATE EMPLOYEE JOB-IDENTIFICATION

The above list of operations in which accurate employee job-identification is essential is not complete, but it does illustrate the many phases of management control that may be affected directly by errors in the job titles of workers. In each of the examples listed, the consequences of incorrect assignment of job titles to employees can be estimated in terms of cost to the management of the company, cost to the individual employee, cost in terms of the time required to handle grievances, and the cost of lost confidence in, and respect for, the policies and management of the company.

Because of these important reasons for constantly accurate job titles for all employees, the time and effort necessary to maintain this accurate job-identification is certainly justified. Even when supervisors are well-trained and have adequate clerical assistance, it is almost too much to expect that all transfers from one job to another will be reported to the control unit responsible for keeping these records current. Explanation and training in the necessity for keeping employee job title records current is a primary requisite. Since current control record information will depend primarily on notification by the supervisors, it is important that they understand what their responsibilities are in this connection and what procedure is to be followed in filing notification of any changes.

The Payroll Authorization Form shown in Figure 16–1 illustrates the type of form customarily used for this purpose. It provides for a notification of changes in the following:

job title	code number
rate	clock number
job classification	status (exempt or nonexempt)
department number	method of payment (salary or wage)
payroll (office or factory)	

Other changes reported on this form also affect, directly or indirectly, the wage and salary administration of the company.

The amount and complexity of supervisors' duties often make it impossible to depend on the information they provide for keeping employees' job titles accurate. The many personnel functions which are now required of supervisors, added to their other duties of scheduling and supervising the work of their departments, some-

EMPLOYEE'S FIRST NAME: *Louis*   LAST NAME: *Miller*   EFFECTIVE DATE: *6-16-54*   SOCIAL SECURITY NUMBER: *299 24 0120*   CLOCK NO.: *263*   SEX: *M*   COLOR: *W*   SHIFT: *1*

NEW JOB TITLE: *Accounting Clerk*   NEW RATE: *270.00*   NEW JOB CLASS: *4*   NEW DIVISION NUMBER: *342*   NEW JOB CODE: *523*

PRESENT JOB TITLE: *Payroll Clerk*   PRESENT RATE: *270.00*   PRESENT JOB CLASS: *4*   PRESENT DIVISION NO.: *342*   PRESENT JOB CODE: *516*

HIRE	PAYROLL STATUS	RATE CHANGE	LEAVE	
☐ NEW EMPLOYEE	☒ REGULAR	☐ MERIT	☐ LEAVE OF ABSENCE	☐ FACTORY ☒ OFFICE
☐ RE-HIRE	☐ TEMPORARY	☐ RECLASSIFICATION	☐ EXTEND LEAVE	
☐ RE-CALL	☐ PART TIME	☐ PROMOTION	RETURN	APPROVED BY
	☐ VETERAN CODE	☐ UPGRADING	SENIORITY CHANGE	

SEPARATION			☐ RETURN TO FORMER CLASS	FOREMAN OR SUPERVISOR *F.A.C.*	DATE *6-8-54*
☐ QUIT	☐ EXEMPT		☐ OUT OF CLASS		
☐ DISCHARGED	☒ NON-EXEMPT	TRANSFER		FOREMAN OR SUPERVISOR	DATE
☐ RETIRED		☒ COMPANY REQUEST	RECORD CHANGE		
☐ LAY-OFF	DEDUCTION CLASS	☐ DOCTOR'S RECOMMENDATION	☐ ADDRESS PLATES	FOREMAN OR SUPERVISOR	DATE
☐ DECEASED	2 WITHHOLDING	☐ EMPLOYEE'S REQUEST	☐ MASTER CARD		
☐ MILITARY LEAVE	6 HOSPITAL SERVICE	☐ RECALL TRANSFER	☐ DEDUCTION CARDS	SUPERINTENDENT OR CONTROLLER *E.R.W.*	DATE *6/11/54*
☐ DISPLACED	3 GROUP INSURANCE	☐ LAYOFF TRANSFER	☐ B.U.C. 406	DIRECTOR INDUSTRIAL RELATIONS *RHS*	DATE *6-12-54*
	☐ MEDICAL MUTUAL	☐ DIVISION CHANGE ONLY	☐ W-2		

WORK RECORD ☒ GOOD   ☐ FAIR   ☐ POOR   WOULD YOU REHIRE? ☐ YES   ☐ NO   COMMENTS

REASON FOR ACTION: *To Fill Vacancy —*

Better Promotional Possibilities.

PAYROLL AUTHORIZATION NAT. 367   PATENTED-MOORE BUSINESS FORMS INC. NIAGARA FALLS, N.Y.

Courtesy of the International Business Machines Corporation and The National Screw & Manufacturing Company, Cleveland.

Fig. 16—1. Payroll authorization form.

times make it difficult for them to keep all necessary job records up to date. Among the most frequent causes of errors in job titles of workers are temporary transfers. In many cases a supervisor may transfer a worker or a group of workers from one job to another with the expectation that such arrangements will be only temporary. When such transfers turn out to be permanent changes, the supervisor may neglect to note the change on the personnel records. Difficulties of maintaining currently accurate job titles of all employees are further complicated in those companies which in the past have not required any continuously accurate job titling of workers on all jobs.

In order to eliminate excessive errors, it may be advisable to set up a systematic auditing procedure for employee job records. Again, punched-card tabulating equipment is extremely useful. The IBM card shown in Figure 16–2 is the basis of one such system. A master card for each employee contains the following information necessary for the audit:

Employee's name and initial	Sex
Base rate	Job classification
Department number	Occupational code
Clock number	Status (veteran, union officer)

In order to verify the job titles of all employees periodically—

for example, once a month—these cards can be sorted by department number and occupational code to arrange all workers by occupation in each department. The cards arranged in this manner then can be listed on the alphabetic tabulator so that a complete personnel list for each department, with names of workers grouped by their jobs, can be given to the supervisor regularly. He can identify the job title for each worker as shown in the record by the occupational code number which refers to one of the jobs in his department. The job description and specification for this job are contained in his volume of job-evaluation information. Any workers in his department at that time who are permanently assigned to jobs which are different from those indicated on the tabulation by the occupational code number can be checked by him. It is then a simple matter to prepare payroll authorization forms to correct the job titles of these workers. If this tabulation can be given to supervisors as frequently as once a month, this procedure alone should be sufficient to maintain a satisfactory degree of accuracy of employee job titles. An example of the tabulation which results from this procedure is shown in Figure 16–3.

Significance of job titles

It may be well to emphasize here again the fact that job titles as such are not significant; job titles become significant only as they are used as "tags" to indicate a job defined, described, specified, and classified in the occupational information of the company. Thus the job of Pickling Operator in a metal manufacturing company has no significance in and of itself, but in the job-information system in the company this "tag" denotes a job description setting forth the duties of all workers placed on this job in the company. The occupational code number 126–102 indicates that this job is in the group concerned with product washing and cleaning in the Plating Department; the job classification 5 indicates that workers on this job are paid between $1.90 and $2.00 an hour; the fact that it is included in those jobs which are on the Factory payroll indicates that the workers are paid on an hourly wage basis and, since the job is one of those included in the production incentive system, there is a bonus paid for production in excess of standard. The position of this job in the promotional charts of the department and of the company shows that workers on this job may be transferred to some other desig-

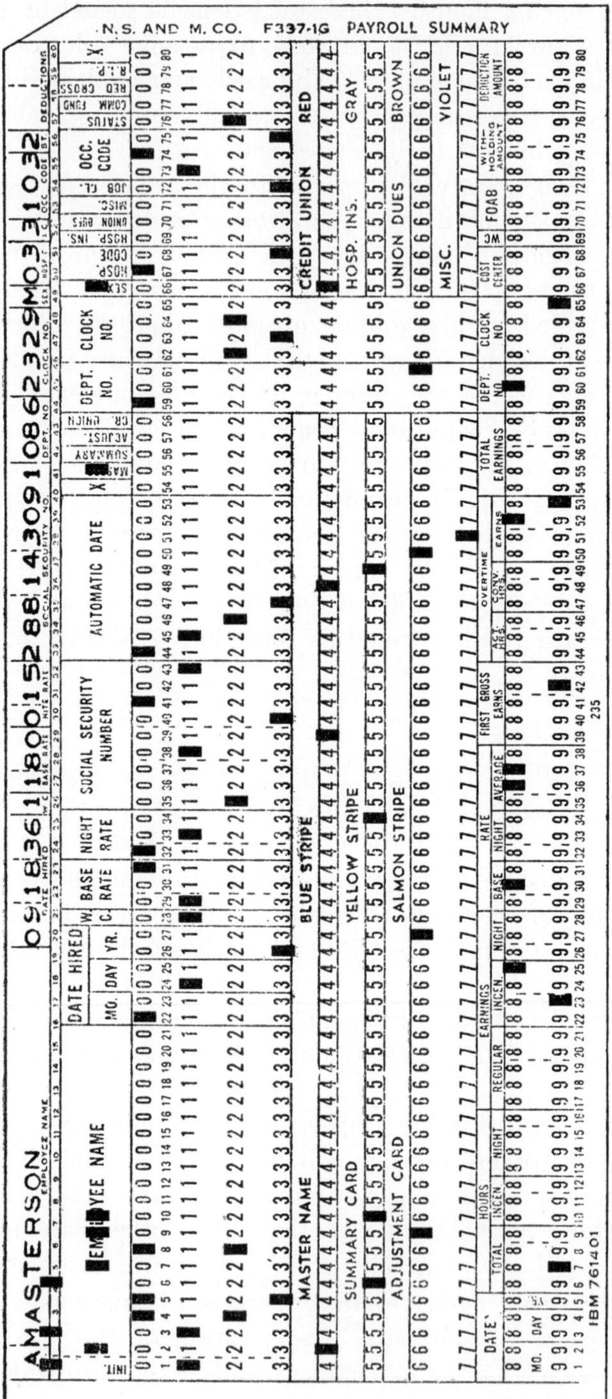

Fig. 16—2.   Sample of employee master card.

Courtesy of the International Business Machines Corporation and The National Screw & Manufacturing Company, Cleveland.

Name	Wage Rate	Sex	Clock No.	Dept. No.	Job No.	Labor Grade
I MOGRIN	150	M	473	322	194	3
F DULAK	150	M	482	322	194	3
F SINKO	155	M	596	322	194	3
T LOREN	150	F	834	322	222	3
S DIBBLE	160	F	810	322	222	3
K LENDER	165	M	142	322	111	4
S MONEY	170	M	623	322	111	4
B ODELL	165	M	251	322	111	4
K NISSLEY	180	M	22	322	193	5
T BONNER	180	M	128	322	193	5
A LIPTAK	175	M	35	322	221	5
C WALSH	185	M	162	322	192	6
A PATTERSON	180	M	437	322	192	6
V HELGER	195	M	122	322	191	7
F SLIMER	190	M	95	322	191	7
T BOXMAN	210	M	26	322	11	8

Fig. 16—3. Tabulation of employees in one department—grouped by labor grade and by job.

nated product washing and cleaning jobs in the company, particularly in the Heat Treat Department. Furthermore, within the department, workers may be promoted to the job of Barrel Plater A but, ordinarily, only after being transferred first to the job of Barrel Plater B for a period of time. The promotion chart also indicates that the worker may advance eventually to the highest-paid job in the department, General Plater, with a wage range of $2.15 to $2.35 an hour, plus a bonus. Beyond that, with the proper qualifications, the worker may be promoted to Assistant Foreman and Foreman. The occupational seniority plan of the company indicates that the job is grouped with the occupation of Scaler in the Heat Treat Department so that, at a time of layoff, the worker's length of service in the occupation will apply to both of the jobs in this occupational seniority group. The job specification indicates the reason for the job-evaluation rating on each factor as evidence for (1) determining the extent and importance of any future changes in the job, or (2) demonstrating to the foreman or worker the reasons for the classification of this job at a particular level in the classification structure of the company. The job specification also furnishes the Employment Manager with the qualifications required of new workers in this job and, along with the job description, is a guide to employment operations having to do with the job of Pickling Operator.

ADMINISTRATIVE CONTROL OF PAY RATES

The mechanics of using a standardized pay structure, developed according to the principles discussed in Chapter 14, in the administration of wages and salaries can be worked out in some detail. Because the pay structure resulting from job evaluation ordinarily is complete, consistent, symmetrical, and well defined, the control operations necessary in wage and salary administration can likewise be developed into orderly procedures and the detail work organized into systematic routine. The need for improvising, expediency, and numerous policy decisions is reduced to a minimum.

Rates of new employees

One of the most frequent uses of the pay structure will be to determine the rates of new employees. When the Employment Department and the supervisor have determined the job title to be applied to the new worker, the pay rate of this worker is determined automatically if the company uses a single rate structure. If a rate-range structure is employed, the rate of pay for this new worker will be within a relatively limited range determined by a minimum and a maximum. The fact that this range usually is relatively small limits materially the magnitude of the error which can be made at this point. Furthermore, if one of the regulations or instructions for use of this pay structure is that all new workers in any occupation are hired at the minimum of the range for that occupation, again the pay rate is automatically established.

The only time any considerable degree of judgment is required, then, is when a new worker, at the discretion of those responsible for the hiring, is hired at a rate above the minimum of the range. Rules for placement of such workers above the minimum are defined as clearly as possible. Ordinarily, the only circumstance where such action is taken is where the worker has had considerable previous experience in a similar job. Even here, however, the policy of the company may be to hire all workers at the minimum but to promote workers with previous experience up through the range rather rapidly after their qualifications have been demonstrated on the job. If the midpoint of the range is established by company policy as the "normal" or "standard" rate for the job, new workers with previous experience in the occupation may be hired at the midpoint of the range or may be increased to this point shortly after original employment.

Another factor that may justify an exception to hiring new workers at the minimum of the range may be the supply of workers available. If bookkeeping machine operators are scarce in comparison to the supply of other types of workers covered by the office pay structure of the company, a temporary policy of hiring all new operators—even those with limited experience—at the midpoint of the range may be established to compensate for the shortage. Ells [3] suggests a variation of this procedure whereby the experienced applicant is placed within the range on the basis of his years of experience in the occupation. His example is as follows:

If stenographers [within the company] with 2 years' experience are earning $125 a month, and the applicant who qualifies on all other counts has 2 years' experience, she should be offered $125. The test in cases such as this is always, "If the applicant had started in this company 2 years ago instead of with the company she did, what would she be earning today?"

[3] By permission from *Salary and Wage Administration*, by Ralph W. Ells, p. 102. Copyright, 1945. McGraw-Hill Book Company, Inc.

Many variations of the basic principles governing placement of new workers above the minimum of a range are possible in individual circumstances. The important thing to note is that there should be a policy or regulations of some kind to establish a pattern to follow in determining the beginning rate of pay for such workers.

Transfers and promotions

Transfers of employees from one job to another within the company frequently require changes in rates. Where such transfers are from a job in one pay structure to a job in another pay structure— from hourly wage to salary, for example—the question of the pay rate will be handled along much the same lines as rates for newly hired employees. Where the two jobs involved are not related to each other, the employee so transferred would be raised to the minimum of the new range, would remain at his present rate if it were within the new range, or would be reduced if his rate were above the maximum of the range. If experience on the job from which he is being transferred is closely related to the job to which he is going, then this relationship between the two jobs may be taken into account in placing the employee within the new range, on the basis that his related experience qualifies him for a rate above the minimum.

The same circumstances will exist where the transfer is from one job to another within the same pay structure. In such a case, if the minimum of the new range is higher than the present rate of the employee, he ordinarily will be raised to the minimum. Some companies provide for a probationary period for an employee who is transferred to a new job calling for a higher rate than he had been receiving. This arrangement provides the company with an opportunity to determine whether the employee will be satisfactory on the new job before adjusting his rate in line with the new range.

In a rate structure with overlapping rate ranges, however, this condition will very seldom come about. Where the policy of the company is to fill vacancies, wherever possible, by promotion or transfer of present employees, all vacancies above those in the lowest classes will be filled by such transfers or promotions, or by training workers for the occupations for which employees are needed.

Under this policy it is logical to expect, for example, that all vacancies in Class 5 jobs would be filled by transferring workers from other Class 5 jobs or promoting workers from Class 4 jobs. Where such transfers or promotions are not possible, workers in Class 3 or Class 2 may be placed in training for this Class 5 job.

If a worker in Class 4 were selected for promotion to the Class 5 job, it is quite probable that he would be at or near the top of the Class 4 range and, with overlapping, would be at or above the minimum of the Class 5 job. (See Figure 15–1.) This promotion, therefore, would not necessarily involve any increase in rate. If there is considerable overlapping in the rate ranges, it is possible that a worker in a Class 3 job at the top of his range would be paid the minimum rate for a Class 5 job. In such a case this promotion also could be made without an immediate increase in rate.

Where a worker must have considerable training in order to be able to perform the duties of a Class 5 job, it is probable that there will be a learning job one or two grades below the level at which the job in question is rated. Thus the training job for the Class 5 job might be rated at the Class 4 level; therefore, any workers in Class 3 who might be selected for the Class 4 opening very probably would be those near the top of the Class 3 range, who would, with overlap, already be paid at or above the minimum of the Class 4 training job. Here again no increase in rate would be required at the time of this promotion.

In a single-rate classification structure, such arrangements are not possible, of course, but a probationary period could be established if it were considered necessary. These examples illustrate the flexibility of a rate range structure as against the rigidity of a single rate structure.

Temporary transfers

The above considerations regarding transferred employees apply only to those transfers that are considered to be permanent. In most cases, the conditions applying to permanent transfers must be carried out within a short time after the employee's duties are changed. During World War II, for example, the War Labor Board generally permitted workers to be transferred only for a short period of time without a change in rate. This would apply either to a transfer to a higher-rated job or to a lower-rated job. In some War Labor Board Regional jurisdictions, this period of time was six days, in others two weeks. Some employers have tended to follow this general pattern in their own policies with respect to temporary transfer, aside from the problem of wage stabilization. Any transfer of longer duration than this specified time, then, would become a permanent transfer, and the policies and regulations of the company with respect to permanent transfers would apply.

Undoubtedly, this definition of temporary transfer in terms of length of time before a change in rate is required should vary according to the operating conditions peculiar to the company. In some cases, the operations of the company might be very stable in this respect, so that temporary transfers would be at a bare minimum. In other cases, however, in order to achieve efficient operation, it might be necessary frequently to use the expedient of temporary transfer in order to keep production operations in balance. In some situations of this type a separate group of workers is established as a utility group to help out where needed. In such cases the "utility" job is established and evaluated in the same way as any other job.

Demotions

Probably the most troublesome pay rate problem results when a permanent transfer requires that the rate of the employee be reduced in order to bring it within the range of the job to which he is being transferred. Such transfers, or demotions, may be brought about by the necessity of reducing the working force, or they may be required because the particular worker is not qualified to perform the job on which he has been working. There may be some justification, within the policies and practices of the company, for handling these two types of demotions differently. Generally, however, the pattern is the same. If the worker has had previous experience on the job to which he is being demoted, the general practice is to establish his rate at the maximum of the new range. This policy is followed in somewhat more liberal fashion in some companies, which place at the maximum *any* demoted workers who reasonably might be expected to be able to perform the new job satisfactorily. The intent of this practice is to make the wage reduction as small as possible without violating the pay structure, yet continuing to pay the worker in relation to the worth of the job he is doing.

Where it is necessary to demote the employee to a job in which he has not had previous experience and which is not necessarily related to the job which he has been performing, the only justification for placing this employee at the top of the new range is the desire to reduce the rate as little as possible; on the other hand, his qualifications to do that job are an unknown quantity, particularly if it is not a job in one of the lower classifications. In demotions of this type, it is the general practice to pay him a rate below the maximum of the new range, and sometimes the minimum. Even where the job requires some skill and experience, however, such employees often are placed at the midpoint of the range rather than at the minimum. The reasoning behind this practice is partly a matter of keeping the reduction in rate at a small figure; also, the fact that the employee has had some experience in the company and thus is better qualified for the job than an entirely new employee may be considered.

The danger in any demotion where the worker is placed at the maximum of the new range comes from the reaction of other employees already on that job. Unless that worker has had previous experience on the job or unless the other employees can see some definite reason why this worker should be paid as much or more than most of the workers on that job, there is quite likely to be considerable resentment. Thus, in an effort to avoid causing difficulty with one employee, the company may stir up much discontent among a number of employees. Considerable weight should be given to this factor, especially where some employees on the job have been with the company a number of years and are not at the maximum of the range.

Transferring overpaid employees

The above discussion of transfers, promotions, and demotions has been based on the assumption that the employee, before his transfer, was paid within the rate range established for the job he was performing. Where the new pay structure has been in effect only a short time, there will be some employees who are paid more than the maximum called for by the jobs on which they are working. When these employees are transferred, additional problems may be encountered. For example, if an employee on a job with a 10-cent range ($1.70–1.80) is being paid $1.85 an hour and he is transferred to a job paying $1.60 to $1.70 an hour, what shall be his rate? Or, if he is transferred to another job with a rate range of $1.70 to $1.80, shall his rate be changed?

Where the transfer is to another job in the same occupation (e.g. laborer in Dept. A to laborer in Dept. B), the general practice has been not to change the rate of the employee. In the first case, however, where there is a demotion, it is necessary to make some rate adjustment in order to maintain a reasonable consistency. The provision that is usually made, which is probably as practical as any, is that whenever an overpaid employee is transferred, his new rate *must* be within the new rate range. This is the only way to avoid violating the pay structure. As a corollary, therefore, as long as he remains on the job for which he is being overpaid, his rate will not be reduced. In order to avoid such problems, of course, those individuals who are overpaid should be transferred, if possible, to jobs having rate ranges which include their rate of pay so as to eliminate them from the overpaid group.

CONTROL WITHIN RATE RANGES

The purpose of the rate range is to establish, within rather narrow limits, the rate which should be paid for a given job. This narrow range of flexibility is provided to eliminate some of the difficulties arising from the rigidity of a single-rate structure. The flexibility provided by the rate ranges, therefore, should be used in the administration of wages and salaries to its best effect. Wherever there is any action which places an employee above the minimum of the rate range of the job on which he is working, the rate range as such is being brought into play. In the hiring and transferring of employees, for example, the entire range of possible rates is used under various circumstances. In some cases it is the maximum of the range, in other cases it may be the midpoint; and, depending on the conditions, other points within the range are also used.

The administration of automatic-progression rate ranges is primarily a clerical operation. Advancement of each employee within the range is determined by the length of time he has been within the range or on the job. Records of employee service, therefore, are the principal requirement. As an added feature, some companies require an employee to meet minimum standards of efficiency in order to qualify for automatic progression.

The administration of a merit-progression system is the antithesis of the administration of automatic progression. Each move within the range based on merit requires a decision of a rather high order, in terms of the proficiency of the individual employee as well as the financial position of the company and general economic conditions at the time. The proficiency of the employee must be gauged in relation to the performance standards required for the job, and in regard to the proficiency of the other employees on similar jobs. This subject has been discussed in some detail in Chapter 14, pages 438–445. The administration of rate ranges in relation to cost factors is discussed further on pages 505–507, Personnel Accounting.

Systems employing a combination of automatic and merit progression as described in Chapter 14 are administered by a combination of the techniques employed in the full automatic-progression and full merit-progression systems.

The important factor in administering any type of rate range is that it be operated consistently and accurately according to the established system. Like any other operation—the seniority system, for example—the system may benefit some workers and not benefit others. Consistency, a highly desirable objective in wage and salary administration, is one of the principal benefits of the careful administration of rate ranges.

VARIATIONS FROM PAY STRUCTURE AND RATE RANGES

Depending on the type of pay structure established in the company, it may be necessary to provide for some variations from the structure as established. There may be conditions under which some individual workers should be paid less than the minimum of the rate range. For example, if there are no arrangements made for including in the job structure specific jobs for training workers for a higher-rated job, this may be provided for by permitting payment of less than the minimum for workers who are in training for the job. Because of the possibility of abusing this arrangement, however, it would seem preferable to provide for training jobs.

Where there is no specific training routine for a job, there may be some need for a probationary wage rate lower than the minimum of the range for the job on which the employee is working. In some labor grades, it may be felt necessary to provide for paying newly hired workers, or even those promoted from within the plant, at a rate less than the minimum during the probationary period. Such arrangements with respect to workers transferred or promoted within the plant have been discussed above (page 488). For training on rather highly skilled jobs, there is considerable evidence and experience to indicate that a policy of promotion from within the plant is highly preferable to hiring workers from outside the plant. Where this policy cannot be followed and a worker from outside the plant is hired to be trained for the occupation, a new job can be established for this individual to provide for adequate compensation during his probationary period. Here again, the possibility of abusing any arrangement whereby an individual employee is paid less than the minimum should be taken into account.

In a few cases, it may be necessary or advisable to provide adequate compensation for superannuated or physically handicapped employees who are capable of somewhat less than the standard performance required of other workers on the same job. Here again an exception in the use of the wage structure might be considered. However, if physically handicapped or older employees are not able to perform the job as well as other workers who are not so handicapped, the answer would seem to be in a more suitable placement of these workers rather than in an arrangement to pay less than the job is actually worth. Such employees do not constitute a problem unless they are required to meet performance standards that are difficult for them to attain.

There are some circumstances, especially in salaried jobs, which suggest the possibility that some individuals should be paid more than the maximum of the range. In the more complicated jobs, where initiative and exceptional ability can be exhibited, such situations are not uncommon. As a matter of fact, the pay structure sometimes is established with an extra increment above the maximum to take care of such exceptional cases, just as there may be an additional range below the minimum to provide for workers in training for the job. Ells [4] shows an example of such a salary range schedule with a "Training Period Minimum"; a "Merit Salary Range," composed of "Minimum," "Normal," and "Maximum"; and finally a "Special Merit Maximum."

A situation sometimes may arise, usually in salaried jobs, where an individual employee who is not satisfied with his pay is actually worth much more to the company than he is being paid; similarly, an employee may be capable of doing more responsible and highly skilled work, but the company may have no job on which he can be placed. Riegel,[5] in discussing this point, states,

Other exceptions to the general principle of relating the salary to the value of the position may be warranted when capable employees, particularly in technical and supervisory positions, cannot be promoted because no vacancies have developed in positions senior to their own. In such cases, a company may pay the men something more than the maximum rate for their position. At times, it is possible to add somewhat to the responsibilities of such positions and thus, establish higher ranges of pay for them.

Where the employee is so exceptional that the company is willing to go to great lengths to keep him, the best approach would seem to be to create a job which would use his full capabilities and thus permit an increase in salary. In the final analysis, however, in jobs of this nature, a violation of the maximum of the range need not be a serious matter. Such a violation could become serious only where it becomes a general practice rather than an isolated action to take care of individual exceptional circumstances. Actually, the im-

[4] *Ibid.,* p. 34.

[5] John W. Riegel, *Salary Determination,* Report No. 2, Bureau of Industrial Relations (Ann Arbor: University of Michigan Press, 1940), p. 177, footnote,

portant feature of the policy of following the salary structure is not necessarily the elimination of inequities through overpayment, but a matter primarily of bringing such cases up for critical attention. A contemplated violation of the maximum of the range is thus assured special consideration by all concerned with the payroll administration of the company. If, after such full consideration, including that of the top executives of the company, it is determined that a violation of the salary structure is the best solution, there need be no hesitation in making an exception to the general policy.

Another situation is frequently encountered when the pay established by the structure for a given job in the company is not sufficient to meet the market price for employees in that occupation because of a shortage in the worker supply. Without a standardized pay structure and controlled wage and salary administration, vacancies in such occupations are filled by bidding up the rate sufficiently to attract workers to the company. Where such exceptions are not given full consideration to determine that this is the only solution to the problem, excessive labor costs may result.

Furthermore, the haphazard creation of inequities of this type may develop unrest and dissatisfaction among workers, not only in other jobs, but in the job in question. Whenever workers employed in a job for a number of years in a company see an entirely new employee hired into the company at the same rate they are being paid, they begin to question what they have been told about the value of long and faithful service to the company.

Here again, however, violation of the structure should not be taken as the primary solution. Other factors which should be given serious consideration are the possibility of promoting and training employees now with the company, re-engineering the work to be done into different types of jobs where workers might be available or at least where it would be easier to train workers, or even increasing the pay value of the job by adding more duties and responsiblities so that the market rate can be paid without disturbing differentials within the plant.

Once the agreed-upon differentials among all jobs in the company have been disturbed by making exceptions, this may lead to demands for exceptions in other jobs where the same conditions do not exist. This fine point of balance between job differentials within the company and the relationship of company rates to community rates must be established very carefully and must be maintained wherever possible. Thus, where only one or a few jobs have a rate range too low to attract the required workers, an exception to the pay structure should be the last resort.

Where there are a number of such cases, this situation indicates that the general level of the entire pay structure may be somewhat low in relation to the general pay structure of the community. The logical solution may be to raise the whole pay structure enough to bring it in line with the pay level in the community. The alternative to this solution, as suggested above, is to change the content of the work itself in such a way that satisfactory pay rates can be established.

CHANGES IN THE PAY STRUCTURE

It will be necessary at times to make changes in the standard pay structure in order to meet general changes in economic conditions and in the company's position with respect to (a) other firms in the community and (b) in the industry as a whole. These changes in the structure will be either general wage increases or general wage decreases. In some cases a change in the structure may involve changing the slope of the wage curve itself either to increase or decrease the differentials in pay between the lower-paid jobs and the higher-paid jobs.

A change in the slope of the wage curve may be made in conjunction with an increase or decrease or may be made solely for the purpose of adjusting the slope of the wage curve to conform to changed pay differentials in the community or industry. If it were discovered that the jobs at the high end of the wage curve were being paid less than the prevailing rates in the community, for example, while the rates for the jobs at the low end of the curve were in line with community rates, the slope of the wage curve of the company then could be made steeper. By this method, the required pay increase would be given to the high-rated jobs, lower-rated jobs would receive no increase, and a small increase would be given to intermediate jobs.

To effect a general increase in wage rates, it is only necessary to change the minimum and the maximum of the rate range in each labor grade by a given amount or percentage and to work out a plan for making corresponding adjustments in the employees' rates of pay. For example, the range $1.40–1.50 will become $1.54–1.65 after a 10 per cent increase; similarly, the range $1.60–1.75 will become $1.76–1.93 after a 10 per cent increase. If these increases are expressed in terms of cents rather than per cents, then these two ranges, after a 10-cent increase, would be $1.50–1.60 and $1.70–1.85. Such changes for the rate ranges of all labor grades are shown in Table 16–1 under the heading "After Increase by Individual Labor Grade," Columns 3 and 4.

Comparison of the two new pay structures, one resulting from a percentage increase and the other from an increase in terms of cents per hour, illustrates that neither of these two structures is of the same character as the original structure in Column 2. In the 6¼ per cent increase structure in Column 3, the slope of the wage curve has been increased and the total Range in terms of cents per hour has been increased from 95 cents to $1.02. In the structure resulting from the 10-cent increase in Column 4, the slope of the wage curve and the Range (95 cents from the lowest to the highest rate) remain the same as on the Present Wage Structure. However, percentage differentials of this structure are different from those of the Present one. The workers in labor grade 2, for example, have had their pay increased, on the average, about 7 per cent, while those in labor grade 8 have had their pay increased, on the average, only about 4⅔ per cent. This illustrates that an increase in terms of cents per hour is not a satisfactory method for increasing the level of the pay structure unless reductions in the percentage differentials between the lower-paid jobs and the higher-paid jobs are desired.

TABLE 16—1.   Wage Structures Illustrating Methods of Instituting a General Wage Increase •

Labor grade	Present wage structure	After increase by individual labor grade		After increase in total pay structure			Number of employees
		6¼%	10¢	6¼%	10¢	6¼%	
Col. 1	2	3	4	5	6	7	8
1......	$1.30–1.40	$1.38–1.49	$1.40–1.50	$1.38–1.48	$1.38–1.48	$1.36–1.47	30
2......	1.40–1.50	1.49–1.59	1.50–1.60	1.47–1.59	1.48–1.60	1.46–1.58	50
3......	1.50–1.65	1.59–1.75	1.60–1.75	1.60–1.72	1.60–1.72	1.57–1.71	40
4......	1.60–1.75	1.70–1.86	1.70–1.85	1.70–1.86	1.70–1.86	1.69–1.87	35
5......	1.70–1.85	1.81–1.97	1.80–1.95	1.82–1.98	1.82–1.98	1.83–2.03	15
6......	1.80–1.95	1.91–2.08	1.90–2.05	1.93–2.13	1.91–2.11	1.95–2.17	16
7......	1.90–2.10	2.02–2.23	2.00–2.20	2.05–2.25	2.03–2.23	2.09–2.33	9
8......	2.05–2.25	2.18–2.40	2.15–2.35	2.19–2.44	2.19–2.44	2.22–2.52	5
Weighted Average Hourly Base Rate......	$1.60	$1.70	$1.70	$1.70	$1.70	$1.70	
Range......	.95	1.02	.95	1.06	1.06	1.16	

The reasons for maintaining this same percentage differential are the same as the reasons for having small rate ranges at the lower end of the scale and much larger rate ranges at the higher end of the scale. An increase of 5 cents an hour from $1.50 to $1.55 is approximately as effective as an 8-cent increase from $2.40 an hour to $2.48 an hour, since the 5-cent increase over $1.50 an hour represents the same percentage of the worker's pay as the 8-cent increase over the $2.40 an hour. The percentage differential between higher-paid jobs and lower-paid jobs is a historic characteristic of wage rates as they are developed by free operation of the labor market and other factors; it is important that any increase in rates in a particular company be carried out in such a way that the plant differentials remain the same as the rate differentials in the community and in the industry. Therefore it may be advisable to increase somewhat the slope of the wage curve in the company each time a wage increase is given. Conversely, at a time when it may be necessary to reduce the level of the pay structure in the company, careful consideration should be given to all of the circumstances surrounding this problem in order to determine whether, at the time of the decrease, the slope of the wage curve also should be decreased.

The above considerations become even more important when there is an inflationary trend. If increases in the pay structure are to be made in terms of percentages, then wages at the high end of the scale may increase somewhat faster than in the community and in the industry in general. On the other hand, under the same conditions, if the pay structure is increased in terms of cents per hour, then the lower-rated jobs may increase in pay more rapidly than comparable industry pay structures, and the higher-rated jobs may be increased less rapidly than in the community generally and in the industry. Although these trends are exaggerated and somewhat easier to see under inflationary conditions, they are present nevertheless to a lesser degree in any situation where the pay structure of a company is being raised or lowered. To insure that undesirable features are not being introduced into the pay structure of the company, it is important that all general increases and decreases be studied carefully and that all factors and conditions be given full consideration.

It is probable that the most logical method of putting into effect a general increase in pay will be a compromise between the percentage method and the cents-per-hour method. In this way the slope of the resulting wage curve can be controlled and kept in line with the pay differentials as they change in the community and in the industry to which the company belongs. New pay structures computed on this basis, are illustrated in Table 16–1 under the heading "After Increase in Total Pay Structure," Columns 5, 6, and 7. In Column 5 is a new pay structure which provides a $6\frac{1}{4}$-percent *increase in labor costs* over the Present Structure (Column 2) and has a slightly steeper slope. The "Weighted Average Hourly Base Rate" in these examples is computed on the assumption that the average pay in each labor grade is the mid-point of the range.

A new pay structure which incorporates a stated amount of increase in overall labor costs can be constructed on the basis of the estimated average base rate which is desired, rather than by increasing the minimums and maximums of each labor grade by the amount or the per cent of the desired increase as in Columns 3 and 4.

The structures in Columns 5, 6, and 7 are set up on the basis of a desired weighted average hourly base rate. The weighted average hourly base rate of the Present Structure (Column 2) is $1.60 an hour; a $6\frac{1}{4}$ per cent increase in this figure, which represents the present labor costs of the company in terms of average base rate per hour, would make the resulting desired weighted average hourly base rate $1.70. This is the amount which applies to the structure in Column 5 of Table 16–1. This amount is the same as the estimated weighted average hourly base rate for the structure in Column 3, since both involve a $6\frac{1}{4}$ per cent increase in labor costs. The difference between these two wage structures is that the one in Column 3 is based on a straight percentage increase in each labor grade while the structure in Column 5, representing the same increase in labor costs, has a varying amount of increase in each labor grade and has a somewhat greater slope than the Present Structure in Column 2 but not as much slope as the structure in Column 3. At the same time, the percentage differentials between the lower-paid jobs and the higher-paid jobs of the structure in Column 5 are greater than those for the wage structure based on a cents-per-hour increase shown in Column 4.

The new pay structure shown in Column 6, incorporating a 10-cent-an-hour increase in wage costs, is constructed by the same method as the structure in Column 5. This illustrates that a per cent increase and the equivalent cents-per-hour increase in labor costs can result in the same wage structure if the new structure is established on the basis of the desired average increase in labor costs.

The important factor in adjusting the level of a pay structure on the basis of the weighted average salary or hourly base rate is that the adjustment is made not in terms of salary, hourly rates, or labor grades of jobs, but in terms of the increase in labor costs which will result from the installation of the new pay structure.

A new pay structure incorporating an increase in labor costs as reflected by the estimated weighted average base rate is not difficult to construct. It is necessary only to determine what the weighted average base rate for the new pay structure should be and to construct each labor grade in terms of the minimum and maximum of the rate ranges so that the resulting structure will have the desired weighted average base rate. The desired weighted average base rate of any pay structure is computed as follows:

1. Estimate the average base rate for each labor grade. If full merit progression is provided, this average can be estimated at the midpoint of the range or at any other point within the range where the management of the company feels that the average within each range will be maintained.

2. Multiply the estimated average for each labor grade by the number of workers in each labor grade and get the total of all of these multiplications for all labor grades.

3. Divide this figure by the total number of employees in the group to get the desired weighted average base rate.

In the examples in Table 16–1 the weighted average base rates have been computed by assuming the average rate for each labor grade to be at the midpoint of the range.

If the weighted average hourly base rate of the present structure is $1.60 an hour, as in the example in Table 16–1, and a 6¼ per cent increase in this pay structure is to be made, then the weighted average hourly base rate of the new structure will be $1.70 an hour. In order to construct a new pay structure which averages $1.70 an hour, it is necessary to find out what the average rate in each labor grade should be (taking into account the number of employees in each labor grade) so that the computed weighted average hourly base rate of the new structure will come out to $1.70 an hour. These average rates of the labor grades are arrived at by a "cut and try" method. The weighted average hourly base rate of the "guessed" averages can be computed; then the "guessed" averages can be adjusted as necessary to arrive at the desired weighted average hourly rate. After these averages for each labor grade have been determined, the ranges can be set up in each labor grade around these averages in order to build the structure itself.

In determining what the averages of the new labor grades will be in order to arriv. at the desired weighted average base rate, these averages should be selected in such a way that they fall approximately on a straight line, and so that the slope of this line will be the slope which will result in the desired percentage differentials between the higher-paid jobs and the lower-paid jobs. In Table 16–1, the wage structure in Column 7 incorporates a 6¼ per cent increase, the same as the one in Column 5, but the slope of the wage line in this case is somewhat different; consequently the actual minimum and maximum of each labor grade is different. This illustrates the fact that several pay structures which differ in detail actually may have the same estimated weighted average base rate.

A general decrease in the level of the pay structure in a company can be put into effect in the same manner as described above with reference to increases in the pay level.

After the changed pay structure is established, it remains to be determined how adjustments in the wage rates of individuals are to be made. One possibility is to determine for each labor grade how much increase in terms of either per cent or cents per hour has been made in the minimum and maximum of the range and then to adjust the rates of each worker in the labor grade by that amount. If all rate ranges have been increased by a standard percentage or standard amount per hour, it is only necessary to increase the rates of all individuals by this same amount. At the time of any pay increase, it is highly desirable, of course, to eliminate any wage inequities which still remain. Under the present pay structure, there may still be some individuals who are paid more than the maximum of the range provided for the jobs on which they are employed. If it is at all possible, the wage increase should be taken as an opportunity to eliminate these remaining inequities by granting a lesser pay increase to those workers who are already overpaid. Ideally, after a wage increase is put into effect in this way, there will no longer be any overpaid or underpaid workers. In general, the plan for making individual adjustments in rates after the level of a pay structure has been increased will be the same as that for adjusting individual rates when a standardized pay structure is first put into effect (see Chapter 15).

In this discussion of general pay increases and decreases, all of the examples have been given in terms of hourly rates. However, the same techniques are applicable to pay structures for salaried workers in terms of salary per week, per month, or per year.

PERSONNEL ACCOUNTING

In any business the largest, or one of the largest, single items of cost is labor. Thus, any company which seeks to control its various cost items in order to maintain or to improve its competitive position must give considerable attention to this factor of labor costs. It is not uncommon to find, particularly in manufacturing industries, that 40, 50, or even 60 per cent of the cost of the finished product must be charged to labor. For example, in a company with 5,000 employees, an increase in labor cost of 1 cent an hour for each employee would total approximately $104,000 increase a year on the base rate for a 40-hour week. If, in addition to the base rate, there is an incentive system, or overtime work, this would raise the figure even higher. If the gross annual business of this company is $30,000,000 a year, this represents 1/3 of 1 per cent of the gross sales of the company. If the net profit of the company is 3 per cent, this insignificant item, which started out as 1 cent an hour, amounts to something more than 10 per cent of the net profit of the company.

This situation is further aggravated by the fact that in some ways labor costs are more difficult to control than other cost items. For example, if there are no current records of merit increases granted to individual employees, or if this information is not used in keeping track of labor costs, the payroll costs of the company may increase markedly without anyone's being aware of that fact. This is illustrated in the case of a company in which, over a six-month period, the average base hourly rate of all employees increased by almost 2 cents an hour. During this period of six months, there had been no change in the basic wage structure of the company nor in any of the established rate ranges. There had been some changes in the occupational composition, however, which apparently were responsible for a part of the increase. There was an increase in the number of employees on higher-paid jobs and a decrease in the number of employees on lower-paid jobs. The remainder of this increase was due to increases in wage rates of individuals within the wage ranges applicable to their jobs. The portion of labor cost which is represented by the spread of rates within the rate ranges can be a very important factor in increasing or maintaining the labor cost level of the company. If the average rate range in the pay structure has a spread of 12 cents an hour, then the labor costs of the company *could* average 12 cents more an hour for each employee if all employees were at the maximum of their ranges than if they were at the minimum of their ranges. Therefore, the factor of control of wage rate within the ranges is in many ways just as important as the control established by setting up the pay structure with minimum and maximum limits on the rates for each individual job.

Another important factor in the control of labor costs is the occupational pattern or distribution of workers on jobs in the company. If all workers are classified in the highest grade of the occupation in which they are employed, regardless of whether their full time is spent in doing the most highly skilled work involved in the occupation, the labor costs of the company will be higher than if these workers were properly classified according to the skill level of the work which they actually perform.

There are many factors and operations that enter into the control and reduction of labor costs in a company. As a matter of fact, all significant features of the organization and operation of a company affect the labor costs. Such factors as plant layout, maintenance of equipment, material handling, personnel selection, training of workers, production scheduling, and many others will influence the labor costs of the company through their effect on the productivity of workers. With respect to wage and salary administration, the two important features affecting labor costs are the job-identification of workers according to the jobs which they are actually performing and the pay of individual workers within the ranges which apply to the jobs on which they are employed.

The personnel budget

When all of the jobs in the company have been analyzed and described and have been designated by standard titles, these titles can be grouped and arranged easily in order to represent clearly the entire structure of the company in terms of jobs. A listing of the job titles by department, for example, shows the occupational structure of that department. A further study of the details of the jobs designated by the standard titles indicates their relationship to each other with respect to type of function, duties, rate of pay, number of employees, and other factors which may be desired. This type of information is referred to as a "manning table." The customary operations of wage and salary administration do not enter into all of the techniques of personnel budgeting.[6] However, the

---

[6] See A. Maxwell Clark, "How to Set Up a Personnel Budget," *American Business*, Vol. 15 (November 1945), p. 10.

standardization of the basic information required for personnel budgeting, including the duties shown in the job descriptions, is extremely helpful.

The importance of budgeting the various grades of workers according to the skill level of the work that must be done in the company is illustrated by the A, B, and C classifications which may be used in some occupations. For example, a great many varieties of work may be performed in the Tool Room of the company, but only a small portion require all the skills of a fully qualified Toolmaker. Thus it may be determined that there are, in general, three different grades of difficulty of tool work in the department. The jobs in the Tool Room then may be established in such a way that the Toolmaker A is required to perform the most difficult work, the Toolmaker B, work of less difficulty, and the Toolmaker C, work which is still less difficult.

As an example, 15 Toolmakers may be required by a company under ordinary circumstances. If about one third of the work of the Tool Room is difficult, one third is in the next grade, and about a third is in the lowest grade, then there should be 5 Toolmakers A, 5 Toolmakers B, and 5 Toolmakers C. If the budget for the Tool Room in terms of employees by job-title is established on this basis, then the ratio of these three grades of Toolmakers should remain the same until the nature of the work flowing through the Tool Room has changed to a significant degree. If it is discovered that there are 10 Toolmakers A, 2 Toolmakers B, and 3 Toolmakers C at any time in the Tool Room, the foreman of the Tool Room has deviated from his personnel budget. Note that his budget is established not on the basis of the qualifications of the various Toolmakers in the department, but on the basis of the skill required in the different types of work that are performed in the Tool Room. Thus, a periodic review of the number of workers on each occupation, in comparison to a standard pattern of the distribution of workers by occupation, would easily reveal those points where the budget has been exceeded and those spots where the distribution of workers is below the standard. Any variation from this standard as represented by the budget then would require investigation. In order to operate such a control, it is necessary to change the budget, or the standards of personnel distribution, whenever there is a significant change in the production pattern of the department.

This standard pattern for distribution of personnel by jobs need not be confined to those occupations in which there are several levels or degrees. The same reasoning applies to an operator with several helpers, a setup man with several operators, and similar combinations. A monthly tabulation of workers by department by job from the punched-card system as illustrated in Figure 16–3 can be used for this control as well as for a regular verification of the designation of employees by jobs.

Control of salaries and wages

When the standard wage or salary structure based on job evaluation has been put into effect, the company has established an equitable relationship between jobs at various levels within the company, and between pay for work in the company and pay for comparable work in other plants in the community and industry. In order to maintain this equitable relationship within a pay structure which includes rate ranges with full merit progression, it is necessary that all changes in pay rates within the ranges be recorded and controlled.

In order to maintain accurate information on the activity within pay ranges, several authors [7] have suggested variations of a technique based on a "normal" or "standard" wage for each rate range. Ells [8] states that "Wages and salaries can be controlled successfully by one method only, *viz.*,

1. By establishing a normal salary or wage for each job classification.
2. By periodically comparing
   a. The total of the normal salaries and wages of all employees with
   b. The total of the actual salaries and wages of the same employees (exclusive of overtime and bonuses).
3. By maintaining a desired relationship between normal and actual salaries and wages, by either
   a. Periodically granting adjustments or
   b. Periodically withholding adjustments.

The essence of these various techniques for maintaining control information on wages and salaries is the comparison of the average wages or salaries actually paid to a standard pay figure. Thus, in the rate range $1.40–$1.50, the standard pay established might be $1.45. If the average of the rates of all employees in this labor grade

---

[7] See John W. Riegel, *Salary Determination*, Report No. 2 Bureau of Industrial Relations (Ann Arbor: University of Michigan Press, 1940), pp. 34–35; Ralph W. Ells, *Salary and Wage Administration*, Ch. 3, "Controlling Salaries and Wages" (New York: McGraw-Hill Book Co., Inc., 1945); and Eugene J. Benge, Samuel L. H. Burk, and Edward N. Hay, *Manual of Job Evaluation, Appendix*, "The Compra-Ratio" (New York: Harper & Brothers, 1941).

[8] By permission from *Salary and Wage Administration*, by Ralph W. Ells, p. 19. Copyright, 1945. McGraw-Hill Book Company, Inc.

is $1.45, then the pay of workers in this labor grade is in line with the "normal." If, however, this average is $1.42, then it indicates that increases can be given to individual workers in this labor grade if the average is to be brought up to the "normal." Conversely, when the average is higher than the standard, then increases can be withheld for a period until, through turnover within that labor grade, the average rate of all employees is gradually reduced to the "normal." The relationship between the "normal" wage for a group of workers and the actual average of their wage rates can be expressed very simply as a percentage or as a ratio. Thus, by dividing the actual average by the "normal" for the labor grade, an index of this relationship can be obtained. If the actual average of all workers is $1.47 and the "normal" for the labor grade is $1.45, the index or ratio is 1.014.

A ratio or index of this type can be computed at convenient intervals for any grouping of workers on which this information is desired. For example, the index can be computed for all employees covered by the pay structure by dividing the weighted average hourly rate by the weighted "normal" for all jobs in the group. This same figure can be obtained in a similar fashion for each labor grade in the pay structure. Other groupings in which this information might be useful are by department, by groups of similar occupations as designated by the occupational code, and possibly even by each occupation within each department.

The index or ratio of the comparison of the actual to the "normal" wages for all employees covered by a pay structure will indicate the extent to which all rates under this structure are either above or below the "normal." This index can be used as a continuous guide to the pattern of over-all wage administration in the company, but it will not indicate those particular jobs where the index may be either above or below the "normal." The index for each labor grade will indicate to some extent the location of those workers whose rates are above or below the "normal," and may assist in locating the types of jobs in which it is necessary to reduce the frequency of merit increases in order to bring the index back to standard.

The computation of the index by departments will flag those departments in which the foreman or supervisor has granted too many or not enough merit increases to his workers. This information can be used to establish a very effective control which will indicate which departments need to be studied further with regard to this problem. Also, any merit increases proposed in the future for workers in that department must be scrutinized carefully in order to determine whether they should be granted or whether the workers are in occupations where the index is already too high. In those departments where the index is considerably below standard, the reverse type of action is indicated. Here it is necessary to determine why workers in this department are, on the average, paid less than workers in other departments. If it is a matter of lack of attention to this phase of his job by the foreman or supervisor, then steps should be taken to grant merit increases to those employees who deserve them in order to bring the index in line with the standard. For those departments which are particularly out of line, either too high or too low, the more detailed analysis by computing additional indexes for labor grades or individual jobs within the department is indicated. Thus actual trouble within a department can be located.

In operating a control of this type it is not necessary that the "normal" wage be an absolute standard which must be followed rigidly. In unusual circumstances, where the employees in a job are particularly well qualified or where their performance is conspicuously below standard, a variation of the index from the "normal" should not be considered out of line. As a general practice, it is best to maintain the index department-wide and company-wide as close to the "normal" as practicable.

SUMMARY

The establishment of a standardized pay structure or a series of standardized pay structures for the various groups of jobs within a company opens up unlimited opportunities for keeping track of and controlling the wages and salaries paid to employees of the company. By establishing a well-defined job structure in the company through job descriptions and standardized job titles, and by incorporating this standardized information into a symmetrical pay structure, many techniques of control of job content and personnel distribution, as well as of wages and salaries, will suggest themselves. After a standardized pay structure has been developed and put into use in a company, the day-to-day problems which arise and the various operating conditions peculiar to that individual company will determine the policies and procedures which will be adopted in establishing wage and salary administration. The several techniques of maintaining control over wages and salaries suggested in this chapter are by no means exhaustive, but they do represent the basic approach to the problem. Variations of the techniques suggested here, following the basic principles incorporated in these techniques, should lead to a practical procedure for administrative control of wages and salaries adapted to the conditions in the company.

The techniques of control have as their primary requisite a standard pay structure, regardless of how it is developed. In other words, it is not essential that a standardized pay structure of one of the types discussed in Chapter 14 be based on a thorough-going job evaluation. However, as in the case of many other operations of this type, it is dangerous to build a careful system of control upon basic data that may not be as sound as it is practicable to make them. Therefore, the most successful control of wages and salaries will be based on a sound pay structure, developed on the basis of a sound system of job evaluation. Also, it should be understood that job evaluation as such does not provide for sound wage and salary administration; it only forms the basis for the construction of a sound pay structure, which in turn permits the development of accurate control procedures.

Finally, it must be emphasized that the purpose of wage and salary administration is to control the wages and salaries in the company and to maintain the equitable relationships (among jobs in the company, and between the company structure and the industry and community pay levels) that have been built into the standardized pay structure set up for the company. Wage and salary administration must not be maintained for the purpose of reducing wages and salaries, but for the purpose of controlling the distribution of the wage dollar by paying the worker a fair wage for the job he is doing.

SUGGESTIONS FOR STUDY AND RESEARCH

1. In promoting an employee two labor grades, what problems do you encounter with regard to his own pay adjustment and his new pay in relation to that of employees on the job to which he is being promoted?

2. What wage problems with individual employees do you encounter when, due to seniority rights in a layoff, some employees are laid off, some are transferred to jobs in other departments in the same labor grade, and some are demoted one or two labor grades to displace employees with less seniority?

3. Assuming you are the personnel director of one of the companies used in previous case problems, how would you decide what to do in the individual problems arising under items 1 and 2 above?

CASE PROBLEM

WAGE AND SALARY ADMINISTRATION POLICY: Select one of the companies used in your case problems and obtain or assume any additional facts about the company you would need to operate its wage and salary administration programs.

PROBLEM: If you were the personnel director of that company, what policy decisions would you need from top management to establish a complete policy of wage and salary administration? Now assume you are the president of the company and determine the policy, answering specifically the policy questions outlined above. Write a statement of hourly wage administration policy to be distributed to all foremen. Write the salary administration policy to be followed by all office supervisors.

Bibliography

For those interested in works published before 1943, the bibliography by J. E. Zerga, "Job Analysis: a Résumé and Bibliography," in the *Journal of Applied Psychology*, Vol. 27 (1943), pages 249–267, covers 401 titles for the years 1911 to 1941 inclusive.

A bibliography by M. H. Jones, S. F. Hulbert, and R. H. Haase entitled "A Survey of the Literature on Job Analysis of Technical Positions" is found in *Personnel Psychology*, Vol. 6 (1953), Summer Issue. This article contains 307 references covering job analysis, job evaluation, and related fields, and is not completely restricted to technical positions.

The following bibliography is representative of the articles and books which were written during the years 1943–1953. It was prepared by the Psychological Research Services of Western Reserve University, under the supervision of Richard S. Barrett.

ANDERSON, D., and HANSEN, A. H., "Common Sense in Job Evaluation," *Iron Age*, Jan. 10, 1946, 157:50-3; Jan. 17, 1946, 157:64-8; Jan. 24, 1946, 157:42-9+.

ASH, P., "The Reliability of Job Evaluation Rankings," *Journal of Applied Psychology*, 1948, 32:313-320.

———, "A Statistical Analysis of the Navy's Method of Positive Evaluation," *Public Personnel Review*, 1950, 11:130-138.

BAKER, HELEN, and TRUE, J. M., *The Operation of Job Evaluation Plans: A Survey of Experience*. Princeton University Department of Economic and Social Institutions, Research Report Ser. No. 74. Industrial Relations Section, Princeton, 1947, 111 p.

BALDERSTON, C. C., "Balance in Wage Setting," *Harvard Business Review*, Oct. 1945, Vol. 24, No. 1:51-6.

———, "Wage Setting Based on Job Analysis and Evaluation," *Industrial Relations Monograph* No. 4, 1943, 68 p. Industrial Relations Counselors, Inc., New York.

BASS, B. M., "Application of Addends to Sales and Clerical Occupational Classification," *Journal of Applied Psychology*, 1948, 32:490-502.

BELCHER, D. L., "Supervisory Acceptance of Job Evaluation," *Personnel Journal*, 1950, 28:406-410.

511

BELLOWS, R. M., *Psychology of Personnel in Business and Industry*, 2nd Ed. New York: Prentice-Hall, Inc., 1954.

BELLOWS, R. M., and ESTEP, M. F., "Job Evaluation Simplified: the Utility of the Occupational Characteristics Check List," *Journal of Applied Psychology*, 1948, 32:354-359.

BENGE, E. J., "By-Products of Job Evaluation," *Personnel Journal*, 1950, 29:94-99.

———, "How Much is the Job Worth?" *Foundry*, Oct. 1944, 72:131.

———, "Job Evaluation for Salaried Employees," *Paper Industry*, June 1944, 26:306-7.

———, "Statistical Study of a Job Evaluation Point System," *Modern Management*, 1947, 7:17-23.

———, BURK, S. L. H., and HAY, E. N., *Manual of Job Evaluation*. New York: Harper & Brothers, 1941, pp. x + 198.

BIREN, R. I., "Developing Adequate Class Specifications," *Publishers' Personnel Review*, 1944, 5:27-31.

BOSTWICK, S. E., "Principle of Basic Element Standards Applied to Job Evaluation," *Advanced Management*, April 1944, 9:82-7.

BOYD, H. E., "Negotiating Rate Grievances with Job Evaluation," *Personnel Journal*, 1950, 29:8-12.

BRASH, J. A., "Time-Study Methods Applied to Job Evaluation," *Journal of Consulting Psychology*, 1945, 9:152-60.

BRISCO, N. B., "Job Evaluation," *Journal of Retailing*, Oct. 1945, 21:97-8.

BUTLER, J. J. and others, "Job Evaluation," *Paper Industries*, 34:1228, January 1953 (et seq.).

CADY, E. L., "Job Rating for Square Dealing," *Scientific American*, Mar. 1947, 176:108-11.

CARDELL, A. J., "Occupational Classification," *Personnel Journal*, 1943, 22:54-7.

CHANDLER, A. T., "Job Evaluation," Bulletin of Industrial Psychology and Personnel Practices, Melbourne, 1952, 8:13-21.

CHESLER, D. J., "Abbreviated Job Evaluation Scales Developed on the Basis of 'Internal' and 'External' Criteria," *Journal of Applied Psychology*, 1949, 33:151-157.

———, "Reliability of Abbreviated Job Evaluation Scales," *Journal of Applied Psychology*, 1948, 32:622-628.

———, "Reliability and Comparability of Different Job Evaluation Systems," *Journal of Applied Psychology*, 1948, 32:465-475.

CHILDS, D. C., "Salary Grade for Each Point Value," *Personnel Journal*, October 1952, 31:173-175.

CHRISTMAN, F. L., "Determination of Wage Rates for Mechanical and Laboring Positions in the Federal Service," *Monthly Labor Review*, Nov. 1944, 59:1063-9.

COHEN, L., "Management and Job Evaluation," *Personnel Journal*, 1948, 27:55-61.

———, "More Reliable Job Evaluation," *Personnel Psychology*, 1948, 4:457-64.

———, "Wage Curves," *Personnel Journal*, April 1946, 24:384-6.

COLLINS, P. J., "How We Classified Jobs; General Aircraft Corporation, New York," *Factory Management*, June 1944, 102:103-7.

COOL, O. C., "Analyzing the Foreman's Job," *Iron Age*, Dec. 21, 1944, 154:46-7.

COOMBS, C. H., "A Factor Analytical Approach to Job Families," *Psychological Bulletin*, 1942, 39:452.

———, and SATTER, G. A., "A Factorial Approach to Job Families," *Psychometrika*, 1949, 14:33-42.

COOPER, R. C., "Basic Policy for Time and Motion Studies," *Advanced Management*, 1950, 15: (4) 2-4.

CURRY, L. K., "How to Classify Bank Jobs," *Banking*, Oct. 1943, 36:31-2.

———, "Job Evaluation, Salary Standardization, and Merit Rating," *Bankers Monthly*, October 1946, 63:487-9+.

DAVIS, A. R., "Job Classification in Municipal Water Works," *American Water Works Association Journal*, Nov. 1943, 35:1440-5.

DAVIS, E. W., *A Functional Pattern Technique for Classification of Jobs*. Teachers College, Columbia University, Contributions to Education, 1942, No. 844, pp. x + 128.

DAVIS, M. K., and TIFFEN, J., "Cross Validation of an Abbreviated Point Job Evaluation System," *Journal of Applied Psychology*, 1950, 34:225-228.

DENNIS, W., et al., *Current Trends in Industrial Psychology*, Pittsburgh, Pa. Pittsburgh Press, 1949, v, 198 p.

DOLD, A. W., "Salary Job Evaluation and Administration," *Controller*, Sept. 1945, 13:439-40.

DONNELL, W., "Job Evaluation Grows Up," *American Machinist*, July 18, 1946, 90:101-4.

DUNN, K. A., "Job Analysis and Evaluation in Personnel Management," *Iron and Steel Engineering*, January 1950, 27:81-87, 87-89.

EDWARDS, P. M., "Statistical Methods in Job Evaluation," *Advanced Management*, 1948, 13:158-163.

EITINGTON, J. E., "Cutting the Cost of the Job Evaluation Program," *Personnel*, 1949, 25:291-294.

———, "The Supervisor's Role in the Job Evaluation Program," *Personnel*, 1948, 24:360-366.

ELLS, R. W., "Controlling Wages and Salaries," *American Business*, Oct. 1944, 14:18-19; Nov. 1944, 14:18-20; Dec. 1944, 14:23-34.

———, "Helping Employees to Understand Salary Schedules," *American Business*, Oct. 1945, 15:14-15+.

———, "How Much is a Job Worth?" *American Business*, May 1947, 17:22-23+.

———, "How to Find Better Employees; Job Classifications and Specifications Needed," *American Business*, Sept. 1945, 15:8-10+.

———, "Job Evaluation for Office Employees," *American Business*, Sept. 1944, 14:13-15.

———, *Salary and Wage Administration*. New York: McGraw-Hill Book Company, Inc., 1945.

———, "Simple System for Job Classification," *American Business*, May 1946, 16:11+.

———, "Simplified Job Evaluation," *American Management Association Personnel Service*, 1951, No. 140, 9-21.

———, *The Basic Abilities System of Job Evaluation*. Madison, Wis.: University of Wisconsin, 1951, 91 p.

FANNING, W. M., "Job Evaluation, A Science," *Paper Industry and Paper World*, June 1945, 27:343.

FARWELL, S. P., "How is Your Salary Determined?" *Chemical Engineering Progress*, May 1951, 47:219-222.

FERGUSON, L. W., (Ed.) *Clerical Salary Administration*. New York: Life Office Management Association, 1948, xv, 220 p.

FITZPATRICK, B. H., "An Objective Test of Job Evaluation Validity," *Personnel Journal*, 1949, 281:128-132.

FLANAGAN, J. C., "Critical Requirements: A New Approach to Employee Evaluation," *Personnel Psychology*, 1949, 2:419-425.

FRICK, T. C., and RUSSELL, S. W., "Job Evaluation as Applied to the Petroleum Industry," *Oil and Gas Journal*, Dec. 2, 1943, 42:39, 41-2, 45+.

FRYER, D. H., and HENRY, E. R., *Handbook of Applied Psychology*. New York: Rinehart, 1950, 2 vols.

GATSCH, E. R., "Psychology in Job Evaluation," *Modern Management*, 1948, 8(4), 19.

GILLETT, ALBERT N., *How to Evaluate Supervisory Jobs*, National Foremen's Institute, Deep River, Conn., 1945.

GOMBERG, W., "A Trade Unionist Looks at Job Evaluation," *Journal of Applied Psychology*, 1951, 35:1-7.

———, "Joint Union-Management Evaluation: A Trade Unionist's Views," *Management Review*, August 1951, 40:474-475.

GOODFELLOW, N. J., "Job Evaluation, A Good Way to Fix Fair Wage Scales," *Engineering and Mining Journal*, April 1951, 152:86-88.

GRANT, D. L., "An Analysis of a Point Rating Job Evaluation Plan," *Journal of Applied Psychology*, 1951, 35:236-240.

GRAY, J. S., "Adjusting Base Weights in Job Evaluation," *Journal of Applied Psychology*, 1951, 35:8-10.

———, "Custom Made Systems of Job Evaluation," *Journal of Applied Psychology*, 1950, 34:378-380.

———, and JONES, M. C., "Ready Made Versus Custom Made Systems of Job Evaluation," *Journal of Applied Psychology*, 1951, 35:11-14.

GRAY, R. D., *Classification of Jobs in Small Companies*. Bulletin No. 5, 1944, 43 p. California Institute of Technology, Industrial Relations Section, Pasadena.

HALLIDAY, R. W., "Problems Involved in Classification of Professional Occupations," *Occupations*, 1949, 27:530-534.

HAMILTON, B. P., "Job Evaluation Scales," *Iron Age*, Oct. 10, 1946, 158:64-66.

HANMAN, B., "Matching the Physical Characteristics of Workers and Jobs," *Industrial Medicine*, May 1945, 14:405-426.

HAY, E. N., "Characteristics of Factor Comparison Job Evaluation," *Personnel*, May 1946, 22:370-5.

———, "Creating Factor Comparison Key Scales by the Per Cent Method," *Journal of Applied Psychology*, 1948, 32:456-464.

———, "Job Evaluation—A Discussion," *Personnel Journal*, 1949, 28:262-266.

———, "Job Evaluation for Trust Companies," *Trusts and Estates*, July 1945, 81:37-40.

———, "Successful Job Evaluation Plan," *Burroughs Clearing House*, Aug. 1944, 28:20-2.

———, "Techniques of Securing Agreement in Job Evaluation Committees," *Personnel*, 1950, 26:307-312.

———, "The Application of Weber's Law to Job Evaluation Estimates," *Journal of Applied Psychology*, 1950, 34:102-104.

———, "The Attitude of the American Federation of Labor on Job Evaluation," *Personnel Journal*, 1947, 26:163-169.

———, and PURVES, D., "Analysis and Description of High Level Jobs," *Personnel*, January 1953, 29:344-354.

———, and PURVES, D., "The Profile Method of High Level Job Evaluation," *Personnel*, 1951, 28:162-170.

HERRMANN, I. A., *Office Methods, Systems and Procedures*. New York: Ronald Press, 1950, 539 p.

HERSEY, R., "Foreman as Job Analyst," *Mill and Factory*, May 1950, 46:105-109.

HESS, R. G., "Basic Principles of Job Evaluation," *Machinery*, May 1945, 51:169-175.

HORSMAN, Q. L., "Salary Payment Plan; Bliley Electric Company, Erie, Pennsylvania," *N.A.C.A. Bulletin*, March 15, 1944, 25:751-63.

HOWARD, R. L., "Job Analysis: To Buy or Not to Buy," *Personnel Journal*, May 1946, 25:31-35.

HUSSEY, C. V., "Utility Job Analysis and Job Evaluation," *Gas Age*, Aug. 23, 1945, 96:27-30.

JENKINS, I. D., "Harrison Radiator Company Plan; Job Analysis for Facilitating Handicapped Veteran Placement," *Industrial Medicine*, Jan. 1945, 14:41-3.

JOHNSON, F. H., and others, *Job Evaluation*. New York: John Wiley & Sons, Inc., 1946, 228 p.

JOLLEY, C. C., et al., "Does He Fit the Job? Job Classification Methods," *American Gas Association Monthly*, April 1945, 27:153-4.

JONES, A. M., "Job Evaluation of Nonacademic Work at the University of Illinois," *Journal of Applied Psychology*, 1948, 32:15-19.

JUCIUS, M. J., MAYNARD, H. H., and SHARTLE, C. L., *Job Analysis for Retail Stores*, Research Monograph No. 37, 1945, 65 p. Bureau of Business Research, Ohio State University, Columbus.

JURAN, J. M., "Ten Years' Progress in Management; Wage Plan," *A.S.M.E. Transactions*, April 1943, 65:236-8.

KAISER, B. S., "Nonacademic University Positions; Classification and Compensation at the University of California," *Journal of Higher Education*, Oct. 1943, 14:365-369.

KAUFFMAN, L. J., "Job Appraisal Plan of the Detroit Edison Company," *Edison Electrical Institute Bulletin*, March 1944, 12:77-8.

KERR, C., and FISHER, L. H., "Effect of Environment on Job Evaluation," *Harvard Business Review*, 1950, 28 (3), 77-96.

KIMMEL, W. W., "Evaluate Jobs and Pay Accordingly; Case of R. G. LeTourneau, Inc.," *Factory Management*, Aug. 1945, 103:144-51.

KIRBY, W. J., and WESTBURGH, E. M., "A Job Evaluation Plan That Works," *Personnel*, May 1944, 20:344-356.

KNEISS, G. H., "Making the Salary Fit the Job," *Railway Age*, November 25, 1950, 129:28-31.

KNIGHT, F. J., "Fallacies in Job Evaluation," *Advanced Management*, 1950, 15 (6) 21-22.

KNOWLES, A. S., "Ten Years' Progress in Management; Job Evaluation and Merit Rating," *A.S.M.E. Transactions*, April 1943, 65:233-5.

KOERPER, E. C., "Matching the Job and the Man," *Production Engineering*, May 1952, 23:198-201.

KOVARSKY, M., "A Job Analysis of an Agency Executive's Task," *Jewish Social Service Quarterly*, 1949, 26:153-157.

KRESS, A. L., "Job Evaluation and Compensation Problems," *Office Management*, 1944, No. 102, p. 14-19. American Management Association, 330 W. 42nd St., New York.

KROEGER, L. J., "Job Classification and Evaluation: Planning and Administration," *Social Work Journal*, 1948, 29:70-75.

LANGLIE, T. A., "Job Description: Device to Eliminate Conflicts, Gaps, Duplicated Function," *Credit and Finance Management*, December 1952, 54:16.

LANGSTROTH, L., "Job Evaluation Discussion," *Personnel Journal*, 1950, 29:180-182.

LAWSHE, C. H., JR., "Studies in Job Evaluation: II. The Adequacy of Abbreviated Point Ratings for Hourly-Paid Jobs in Three Industrial Plants," *Journal of Applied Psychology*, June 1945, Vol. 29, 177-184.

——, and ALESSI, S. L., "Studies in Job Evaluation: IV. Analysis of Another Point Rating Scale for Hourly-Paid Jobs and the Adequacy of an Abbreviated Scale," *Journal of Applied Psychology*, Aug. 1946, Vol. 30, 310-319.

——, DUDEK, E. E., and WILSON, R. F., "Studies of Job Evaluation: VII. A Factor Analysis of Two Point Rating Methods of Job Evaluation," *Journal of Applied Psychology*, 1948, 32:118-129.

——, and FARBO, P., "Studies in Job Evaluation: VIII. The Reliability of an Abbreviated Job Evaluation System," *Journal of Applied Psychology*, 1949, 33:158-166.

——, and McCORMICK, E. J., "What Do You Buy With Your Salary Dollar?" *Personnel*, 1947, 24:102-106.

——, and MOLESKI, A. A., "Studies in Job Evaluation: III. An Analysis of Point Ratings for Salary-Paid Jobs in an Industrial Plant," *Journal of Applied Psychology*, April 1946, 30:117-128.

——, and SATTER, G. A., "Studies in Job Evaluation: I. Factor Analyses of Point Ratings for Hourly-Paid Jobs in Three Industrial Plants," *Journal of Applied Psychology*, June 1944, 28:189-198.

——, and WILSON, R. F., "Studies in Job Evaluation: V. An Analysis of the Factor Comparison System as It Functions in a Paper Mill," *Journal of Applied Psychology*, Oct. 1946, 30:426-434.

——, and WILSON, R. F., "Studies in Job Evaluation: VI. The Reliability of Two Point Rating Systems," *Journal of Applied Psychology*, 1947, 31:355-365.

LAWSON, W. F., "Installing a Job Analysis System," *Burroughs Clearing House*, April 1944, 28:280-2+.

LENDER, E., "Rating Maintenance Jobs; Star Electric Motor Company," *Factory Management*, May 1945, 103:137-141.

LITTLETON, A. C., "Occupational Levels in Public Accounting," *Journal of Accountancy*, Dec. 1944, 78:470-6.

LOCK, N., "Few Factors or Many?—An Analysis of a Point System of Classification," *Personnel*, 1949, 25:442-448.

LOONEY, C. C., "Job Analysis; Experience of Harris Trust and Savings Bank, Chicago," *Burroughs Clearing House*, Jan. 1947, 31:17-19+.

LYTLE, C. W., "An Audit for Wage and Salary Administration," *Personnel*, Jan. 1947, 23:273-277.

——, *Job Evaluation Methods*. New York: The Ronald Press, 1954, 1946, xiv, 329 p.

MAGOR, D. M., "Job Evaluation," *Power Plant Engineering*, Aug. 1943, 47:116-118+.

MATTOON, C. S., "Evaluating White-Collar Jobs," *Factory Management*, April 1946, 104:80-83.

——, *Technique of Job Analysis and Evaluation*. Cleveland: Weatherhead Co., 300 E. 131st St., 1946, 122 p.

McCANN, J. J., "Job Yardstick; Merit Rating Form of Mercantile-Commerce Bank and Trust Company, St. Louis," *Banking*, Jan. 1944, 36:63.

McDERMOTT, K. C., "Job Evaluation Maintenance," *Personnel Journal*, 1947, 26:222-226.

McDONALD, W. T., "The Navy's Method of Position Evaluation," *Public Personnel Review*, 1947, 8:89-95.

McGRATH, R. M., "New Aspects of Job Evaluation," *American Machinist*, Jan. 2, 1947, 91-98.

METZ, G. H., "Launching a Job Evaluation Program: RCA Victor Division, Radio Corporation of America," *Factory Management*, Nov. 1946, 104:95-97.

———, "Objective Methods Produce Tailor-made Job Evaluation Plan; RCA Victor Plan," *Factory Management*, May 1949, 107:78-80.

MILES, M. C., "Studies in Job Evaluation: IX. Validity of a Check List for Evaluating Office Jobs," *Journal of Applied Psychology*, 1952, 36:97-101.

MOORE, FRANKLIN G., "Job Evaluation," *Mill and Factory*, July 1946.

MOORE, H., "Problems and Methods in Job Evaluation," *Journal of Consulting Psychology*, 1944, 8:90-99.

MURPHY, M. J., and SMYTH, R. C., "Job Evaluation by the Point Plan," *Factory Management*, June 1946, 104:137-148.

NILES, P. B., "Standard Wage and Salary Administration Plan; Standard Job Classification and Job Descriptions," *American Water Works Association Journal*, April 1944, 36:405-14.

OGBURN, R. F., "Job Measurement Aids Costing," *American Gas Association Monthly*, April 1953, 35:21-22.

OLIVER, J. A., and WINN, A., "An Abbreviated Job Evaluation Plan for Salaried Personnel," *Personnel*, 1951, 28:225-229.

OTIS, J. L., "What Can Industrial Psychology Do for Small Business (A Symposium) 1. Job Analysis," *Personnel Psychology*, 1952, 5:25-29.

PAQUETTE, N. O., and FRASER, C., "Labor-Management, Joint Development and Joint Application of Job Evaluation in a Single Unit Motor Bodies Plant," *Advanced Management*, July 1943, 8:92-96.

PATTON, J. A., and SMITH, R. S., Jr., *Job Evaluation*. Chicago: Richard D. Irwin, 1949, xv, 316 p.

PERCIVAL, A. J., and GROSS, G. B., "Job Evaluation—A Case History," *Harvard Business Review*, Summer 1946, 24:466-497.

PIGAGE, L. C., and TUCKER, J. L., "Job Evaluation," *University of Illinois Bulletin*, 1952, 49 (36) 44 p.

POLLARD, D., "Man and Job Evaluation," *Personnel Journal*, April 1943, 21:344-348.

POSEGATE, J. M., "Time to Rethink Minimum Requirements," *Public Personnel Review*, 1949, Vol. 10, p. 101.

RADOS, W., "Define Your Salesman's Job or Your Training Plan Will Flop," *Sales Management*, Feb. 15, 1944, 53:36-38.

REDMON, E. J., "Wage Administration," *Personnel Journal*, April 1946, 24:380-383.

REISINGER, E. J., "Job Evaluating in the Maintenance Department," *Mill and Factory*, 1946, Vol. 38, No. 1, p. 98-104.

RISBERG, C. W., "Job Evaluation May Help to Minimize Stoppages," *Food Industries*, April 1946, 18:489-491.

ROGERS, R. C., "Analysis of Two Point-Rating Job Evaluation Plans," *Journal of Applied Psychology*, 1946, 30:579-585.

RUSH, C. H., JR., and BELLOWS, R. M., "Job Evaluation for the Small Business," *Personnel Psychology*, 1949, 2:301-310.

SAMMOND, C. J., "J-E, What It Is and How It Is Installed," *Food Industries*, May 1947, 19:614-616.

SATTER, G. A., "Method of Paired Comparisons and a Specification Scoring Key in the Evaluation of Jobs," *Journal of Applied Psychology*, 1949, 33:212-221.

SCHEUBLE, P. A., JR., "Retrospect on Job Evaluation Practices," *N.A.C.A. Bulletin*, December 1950, 32:403-407.

SCHLEH, E. C., "How Do You Use Wage Surveys?" *Personnel*, 1949, 26:88-93.

———, "Logical Approach to Office Job Evaluation," *Management Review*, April 1950, 39:189-191.

SHARP, H. M., "Tentative Job Valuation Plan," *Edison Electrical Institute Bulletin*, April 1944, 12:106-108.

SHARTLE, C. L., *Occupational Information, Its Development and Application.* New York: Prentice-Hall, Inc., 1946, xiv, 339 p.

———, "Vocational Guidance and Job Families," *Occupations*, 1942, 20:506-508.

———, and others, "Ten Years of Occupational Research," *Occupations*, 1944, 22:387-446.

SHISKIN, B., "Job Evaluation, What It Is and How It Works," *American Federationist*, 1947, 54:8-9, 30-31.

SMITH, R. A., "Job Evaluation Procedure," *N.A.C.A. Bulletin*, October 1952, 34:220-229.

SMYTH, R. C., "How to Rank and Price Management Jobs," *Factory Management*, 1950, 108 (11) 116-117.

———, "Job Evalaution Plans," *Factory Management and Maintenance*, 1952, 110 (1) 118-121.

———, and MURPHY, M. J., *Job Evaluation and Employee Rating.* New York: McGraw-Hill Book Co., Inc., 1946.

SPRIEGEL, W. R., "Job Evaluation in Banks," *Banking*, May 1952, 44:130.

———, and LANHAM, E., *Job Evaluation in Automobile and Automotive Parts Industries.* Personnel Study No. 5, University of Texas, Austin (12), 1953.

STANWAY, H. G., *Applied Job Evaluation; A Manual of Installation and Operating Methods.* New York: Ronald Press, 1947, viii, 81 p.

STEINER, M. E., *The Psychologist in Industry.* Springfield, Ill.: Charles C. Thomas, 1949, vii, 107 p.

STEVENS, R. D., "Job Evaluation," *Manufacturers Record*, July 1953, 122:33.

STEWART, D. A., "Improving Job Evaluation Results," *Personnel*, 1949, 25:356-365.

STIGERS, M. F., and REED, E. G., *The Theory and Practice of Job Rating*, 2nd Ed. New York: McGraw-Hill Book Co., Inc., 1944, xiii, 168 p.

STUMP, N. F., "Job Analysis as Related to Visual Skills," *Sight Saving Review*, 1948, 18:190-202.

THOMASMA, L. T., "Job Descriptions, An Aid in Sales Management; Todd Company, Inc.," *Management Review*, Oct. 1944, 33:366.

THOMPSON, J. W., "Functional Job Descriptions," *Personnel Journal*, 1952, 30:380-388.

THUESEN, H. G., and LOHMANN, M. R., "Job Design as Applied to the Pumpers Daily Routine," *Oil and Gas Journal*, Jan. 7, 1943, 41:115-118; Jan. 14, 1943, 42:36-38.

TIFFIN, J., "The Joint Committee in Job Evaluation," in Kornhauser, A., *Psychology of Labor Management Relations*, Champaign, Ill.: Industrial Relations Research Assoc., 1949, (Publ. No. 3) vi, 122 p.

TURNER, W. D., "Some Precautions in the Use of the Per Cent Method of Job Evaluation," *Journal of Applied Psychology*, 1949, 33:547-552.

VAN MILL, A. N., "Job Classification in the Netherlands," *International Labour Review*, Feb. 1949, 59:154-172.

VEYSEY, V. V., *Describing the Supervisor's Job.* Pasadena: California Institute of Technology, Industrial Relations Section, Bulletin No. 8, 1943, 69 p.

———, *Using Descriptions of Supervisory Jobs.* Pasadena: California Institute of Technology, Industrial Relations Section, Bulletin No. 9, 1943, 26 p.

VITELES, M. S., "A Psychologist Looks at Job Evaluation," *Personnel*, 1941, 17:165-176.

———, and SMITH, K. R., *Job Analysis Procedure.* (O.S.R.D., 1943) Publ. Bd. No. 4030. Washington, D. C., U. S. Dept. of Commerce, 1946.

VON PECHMAN, W., "Program Including Complete Job Analyses and Descriptions Is Good Insurance," *Industrial and Engineering Chemistry,* January 1951, 43: sup. 75A-76A.

WALLACE, R. F., "Job Analysis, Description and Classification," *Personnel Journal,* May 1946, 25:18-30.

WARREN, B. B., "Evaluation of Managerial Position," *American Management Association Personnel Service,* 1947, 107:3-21.

WATSON, M. H., *How to Prepare and Use Job Manuals; a Handbook for Supervisors.* New York: William Frederick Press, 1952, iii, 38 p.

WHAREN, H. S., "Job Evaluation Principles," *American Machinist,* August 1, 1946, 90:109-120.

WHELPLEY, J. A., "Job Classification and Evaluation," *American Gas Journal,* May 1947, 166:16-17.

WHITTON, R. M., "Missouri's Method of Job Evaluation," *Proceedings Highway Research Board,* 1948, 28:514-521.

WILLY, W. M., "How a Salary Plan Operates," *Banking,* October 1952, 43:52-54.

WILSON, D. C., and SICHELSTEIL, G. T., "Joint Union-Management Job Evaluation," *Personnel Journal,* 1949, 25:420-425.

WOLFF, J. J., "Job Analysis and Evaluation in the Classification of Jobs," *Sewage and Industrial Wastes,* January 1953, 25:88-92.

WOODHEAD, E. A., "Job Break-Down Under Group Study Plan; Turbo-Generator Overhaul Planned by Whole Group on Blackboard and on Paper; Idaho Power Company," *Electrical World,* Dec. 11, 1943, 120:2031-5.

ZERGA, J. E., "Personnel and Job Analysis Data," *Personnel Journal,* Sept. 1945, 24:114-118.

MISCELLANEOUS ARTICLES

"Clerical Position Evaluation Plan," Revere Copper and Brass Inc., Rome, New York. *Management Review,* Nov. 1944, Vol. 33, No. 11:391-3.

Industrial Job Evaluation Systems with an Annotated Bibliography, U. S. Employment Service, Washington, D. C., U. S. Government Printing Office, 1947, vi, 69 p.

Job Analysis as a Basis for Effective Personnel Management. Illinois University. Division of University Extension. Urbana, Ill. Institute of Labor and Industrial Relations, 1948, 33 p.

Job Classification and Job Evaluation: Their Value as a Tool of Management in Wage Negotiations. Douglas T. Sterling Co., Stamford, Conn., 1944, 28 p.

Job Evaluation, U. S. Navy Department, Administrative Office, Washington, D. C., 1948, 28 p.

"Job Evaluation Fundamentals," *Factory Management,* April 1947, 105:92+.

"Job Evaluation Solves Many Rate Problems," *Chemical Industries,* May 1947, 60:782-785.

"Jobs Evaluated; Six Aircraft Firms Simplify Their Wage Schedules," *Business Week,* Dec. 11, 1943, p. 94+.

"Keeping Wages in Line; Administration Policy," Alexander Smith, Inc., *Modern Industry,* June 1951, 21:50-52.

"Rate Jobs and Establish Wage Brackets; Case of Air Associates Inc.," *Factory Management,* Aug. 1944, 102:97-104.

"The Development of Job Analysis Procedures," *American Institute for Research, Research Note No. 4,* American Institute for Research, 1951, 4 p.

Wage Payment Systems, Bibliography Series No. 74, 1944, 25 p., Princeton University, Industrial Relations Section, Princeton.

Index